A Biographical
Encyclopedia of Scientists

Volume 1   A to K

A Biographical Encyclopedia of Scientists

John Daintith

Sarah Mitchell

Elizabeth Tootill

Volume 1   A to K

Facts On File, Inc.
460 Park Avenue South, New York, N.Y. 10016

Published by Facts On File, Inc.,
460 Park Avenue South, New York, N.Y. 10016

Compiled and prepared for typesetting by
Laurence Urdang Associates Ltd., Aylesbury, England

Library of Congress Cataloging in Publication Data

Urdang Associates.
    Biographical encyclopedia of scientists.

    Bibliography: p.
    Includes index.
    1. Scientists-Biography. I. Title.
Q141.U72 1981   509′.2′2 [B] 80-23529
ISBN 0-87196-396-5

Printed in the United States of America

Preface

This reference book presents biographical entries on important scientists — or on people who have made important contributions to science — from the earliest times to the present day.

In compiling such a book there are several difficult decisions to make on the selection of material. The most general one is that of the scope of the book — what areas of knowledge it should cover. This work concentrates on what might be called the 'traditional' pure sciences — physics, chemistry, biology, astronomy, and the earth sciences. It also covers medicine and mathematics, and includes a selection of people who have made important contributions to engineering and technology. A few of the entries cover workers in such fields as anthropology and psychology, and a small number of philosophers have also been allowed in.

Our intention has been to produce a book as much about science itself as about scientists, and this has governed our approach to selecting information. The entries contain basic biographical data — place and date of birth, posts held, etc. — but do not give exhaustive personal details about the subject's family, prizes, honorary degrees, etc. Most of the space has been given to their main scientific achievements and the nature and importance of these achievements. This has not always been easy; in particular, it has not always been possible to explain in relatively simple terms work in the higher reaches of abstract mathematics or modern theoretical physics.

Perhaps the most difficult problem was compiling the entry list. We have attempted to include people who have produced major advances in theory or have made influential or well-known discoveries. A particular difficulty has been the selection of contemporary scientists, in view of the fact that of all scientists who have ever lived, the vast majority are still alive. In this we have been guided by lists of prizes and awards made by scientific societies. We realize that there are dangers in this — the method would not, for instance, catch an unknown physicist working out a revolutionary new system of mechanics in the seclusion of the Bern patent office. It does, however, have the advantage that it is based on the judgments of other scientists.

It should also be said that the compilers and editors have used their own judgment in choosing what is important or useful. In some cases entries have been added simply because we found them interesting. We hope that the reader will find all the entries useful and share our interest in them.

We would like to thank all the organizations and individuals who have given help, advice, and encouragement during the writing of this book, in particular Alan Isaacs of Laurence Urdang Associates and Eleanora Schoenebaum of Facts on File.

The Editors
Aylesbury, England, June 1981

Guide To The Book

The book has five different sections as follows:

Biographical Section   The main part of the book containing some 2000 entries on scientists with descriptions of their lives and work. The headwords are arranged in strict alphabetical order according to surname. The entry for a scientist is given under the name by which he or she is most commonly known. Thus, the American astrophysicist James Van Allen is generally known as Van Allen (not Allen) and is entered under V. The German chemist Justus von Liebig is commonly referred to as Liebig, and is entered under L. A system of cross references is used to direct the reader to headwords at which the entry appears.

Cross references are also used in the text to indicate other headwords at which additional information can be found. These are usually denoted (q.v.). They have been used sparingly — often they are given in cases in which two or more people have collaborated on a piece of research. In such cases the work is described fully in only one entry, with cross references from the others. This has been done to avoid duplication and save space — it does not imply that the scientist with the longer entry was necessarily the senior partner in the work.

Chronology   A list of scientific discoveries and publications arranged under year and subject. It is intended to be used for tracing the development of a subject or for relating advances in one branch of science to those in another branch. Additional information can be obtained by referring to the biography section of the book.

Book List   A short list of scientific books and papers particularly influential in the development of science. Brief descriptions of the content and importance of the work are given; further information can be obtained under the author in the biography section. In almost all cases the books in the list are described under their published title, with cross references from translations of the title. The titles are listed in strict alphabetical order including the definite or indefinite article.

Index of Names   An index to the biography section listing the names of scientists who are mentioned in the text but do not themselves have entries.

Index of Subjects   An index to the biography section listing important scientific topics.

Contents

Biography Section

A

ABANO, Pietro d' *See* D'ABANO, Pietro.

ABBE, Cleveland (b. Dec. 3, 1838; New York City; d. Oct. 28, 1916; Chevy Chase, Maryland) American meteorologist.

Abbe was educated at City College, New York, and taught at the University of Michigan. He then spent two years (1864–66) in Russia at the Pulkovo Observatory under Otto Struve. On his return to America he worked as director of the Cincinnati Observatory (1868–70).

Abbe was the first official weather forecaster in America. He was appointed, in 1871, chief meteorologist with the weather service, which was later formed into the US Weather Bureau (1891), and remained in this organization for the rest of his life. He was one of the first scientists to see the revolutionary role the telegraph had to play in weather forecasting and used reports conveyed to him from all over the country.

Abbe published over 300 papers on meteorology and from 1893 he was in charge of the journals published by the US Weather Bureau. He was also responsible for the division of America into time zones in 1883.

ABBE, Ernst (b. Jan. 23, 1840; Eisenach, now in East Germany; d. Jan. 14, 1905; Jena, now in East Germany) German physicist.

Abbe came from poor parents but managed to become a lecturer at the University of Jena, where in 1886 he collaborated with Carl Zeiss, a supplier of optical instruments to the university, to improve the quality of microscope production. Up till then, this had been an empirical art without rigorous theory to aid design. Abbe's contribution was his knowledge of optical theory. He is known for the *Abbe sine condition* — a necessary condition for the elimination of spherical aberration in an optical system; such a system he described as aplanatic. He also invented the apochromatic lens system (1886), which eliminated both primary and secondary color distortions and the *Abbe condenser* (1872) — a combination of lenses for converging light onto the specimen in microscopes.

The partnership between Abbe and Zeiss was a productive combination of Zeiss's practical knowledge and Abbe's mathematical and theoretical ability. After Zeiss's death, Abbe became the sole owner of the Zeiss company.

ABEGG, Richard (b. Jan. 9, 1869; Danzig, now Gdansk, Poland; d. Apr. 4, 1910; Köslin, now Koszalin, Poland) German physical chemist.

Abegg studied chemistry at Kiel, Tübingen, and Berlin. He graduated in 1891 as a pupil of Wilhelm Hofmann. Initially an organic chemist, he was attracted by the advances being made in physical chemistry, and in 1894 moved to Göttingen as an assistant to Hermann Nernst. Here, he worked on electrochemical and related problems and with G. Bodländer produced an important paper on valence, *Die Elektronaffinität* (1869; Electron Affinity). He is remembered for *Abegg's rule* (partially anticipated by Dmitri Mendeleev), which states that each element has two valences: a normal valence and a contravalence, the sum of which is eight. In 1899 be became a professor at Breslau and was about to become the director of the Physico-Chemical Institute there when he was killed in a ballooning accident.

ABEL, Sir Frederick Augustus (b. July 17, 1827; London; d. Sept. 6, 1902; London) British chemist.

Abel's father was a well-known musician and his grandfather was court painter to the grand duke of Mecklenberg-Schwerin. Despite this artistic background Abel developed an early interest in science after visiting his uncle A.J. Abel, a mineralogist and pupil of Berzelius. In 1845 he was one of the first of the pupils to study at the Royal College of Chemistry under August von Hofmann, remaining there until 1851. After a brief appointment as chemical demonstrator at St. Bartholomew's Hospital, London, he succeeded Michael Faraday in 1852 as a lecturer in chemistry at the Royal Military Academy at Woolwich. In 1854 he became ordnance chemist and chemist to the war department.

Abel's career was thus devoted exclusively to the chemistry of explosives. New and powerful explosives, including guncotton and nitroglycerin, had recently been invented but were quite unsafe to use. Abel's first achievement was to show how guncotton could be rendered stable and safe. His method was to remove all traces of the sulfuric and nitric acids used in its manufacture by mincing, washing in soda until all the acid had been removed, and drying. In 1888 Abel was appointed president of a government committee to find new high explosives. The two existing propellants, Poudre B and ballistite, had various defects, most important of which was a tendency to deteriorate during storage. Together with Sir James Dewar, Abel introduced the new explosive, cordite, in 1889. This was a mixture of guncotton and nitroglycerin with camphor and petroleum added as stablizers and preservatives.

Abel was knighted in 1891 and created a baronet in 1893.

ABEL, John Jacob (b. May 19, 1857; Cleveland, Ohio; d. May 26, 1938; Baltimore, Maryland) American biochemist.

Abel, a farmer's son, was educated at the University of Michigan and Johns Hopkins University. He spent the years 1884–90 in Europe where he studied at Leipzig, Heidelberg, Würzburg, Vienna, Bern, and Strasbourg where he gained an MD in 1888. On his return to America he worked briefly at the University of Michigan before being appointed in 1893 to the first chair of pharmacology at Johns Hopkins, a post he retained until his retirement in 1932.

Abel approached biology with a first-rate training in chemistry and with the conviction that the study of molecules and atoms was as important as the observation of multicellular tissues under the microscope. He thus began by working on the chemical composition of various bodily tissues and fluids and, in 1897, succeeded in isolating a physiologically active substance from the adrenal glands, named by him epinephrine, also known as adrenalin. This extract was actually the monobenzoyl derivative of the hormone. It was left to Jokichi Takamine to purify it in 1900.

As early as 1912 Abel clearly formulated the idea of an artificial kidney and in 1914 isolated for the first time amino acids from the blood. He was less successful with his search (1917–24) for the pituitary hormone, being unaware that he was dealing with not one but several hormones. His announcement in 1926, that he had crystallized insulin met with considerable skepticism, especially regarding its protein nature. This work was not generally accepted until the mid 1930s.

After his retirement Abel devoted himself to a study of the tetanus toxin.

ABEL, Niels Henrik (b. Aug. 5, 1802; Finnø y, Norway; d. Apr. 6, 1829; Froland, Norway) Norwegian mathematician.

Abel, the son of a poor pastor, studied at the University of Christiana (Oslo). After the death of his father, Abel had to support a large family; he earned what he could by private teaching and was also helped out by his teacher. He was eventually given a grant by the Norwegian government to make a trip to France and Germany to visit mathematicians. In Germany he met the engineer and mathematician August Crelle, who was to be of great assistance to him. Crelle published Abel's work and exerted what influence he could to obtain him a post in Germany. Tragically Abel died just when Crelle had succeeded in getting him the chair in mathematics at Berlin.

With Evariste Galois (whom he never met), Abel founded the theory of groups (commutative groups are known as *Abelian groups* in his honor), and his early death ranks as one of the great tragedies of 19th-century mathematics. One of Abel's first achievements was to solve the long-standing problem of whether the general quintic (of the fifth degree) equation was solvable by algebraic methods. He showed that the general quintic is not solvable algebraically and sent this proof to Karl Gauss, but unfortunately Gauss threw it away unread, having assumed that it was yet another unsuccessful attempt to solve the quintic.

Abel's greatest work was in the theory of elliptic and transcendental functions. Mathematicians had previously focused their attention on problems associated with elliptic integrals. Abel showed that these problems could be immensely simplified by considering the inverse functions of these integrals — the so-called 'elliptic functions'. He also proved a fundamental theorem, *Abel's theorem*, on transcendental functions, which he submitted to Augustin Cauchy (and unfortunately fared no better than with Gauss). The study of elliptic functions inaugurated by Abel was to occupy many of the best mathemati-

cians for the remainder of the 19th century. He also made very important contributions to the theory of infinite series.

ABELSON, Philip Hauge (b. Apr. 27, 1913; Tacoma, Washington) American physical chemist.

Abelson was educated at Washington State College and at the University of California at Berkeley, where he obtained his PhD in 1939. Apart from the war years at the Naval Research Laboratory in Wshington, he has spent his entire career at the Carnegie Institution, Washington. He served as the director of the geophysics laboratory from 1953, and became president of the institute in 1971. In 1940 he assisted Edwin McMillan in creating the first transuranic element, neptunium, by bombardment of uranium with neutrons in the Berkeley cyclotron.

Abelson next worked on separating the isotopes of uranium. It was clear that a nuclear explosion was possible only if sufficient quantities of the rare isotope uranium–235 (only 7 out of every 1000 uranium atoms) could be obtained. The method Abelson chose was that of thermal diffusion. This involved circulating uranium hexafluoride vapor in a narrow space between a hot and a cold pipe; the lighter isotope tended to accumulate nearer the hot surface. Collecting sufficient uranium–235 involved Abelson in one of those massive research and engineering projects only possible in war time. In the Philadelphia Navy Yard, he constructed a hundred or so 48-foot (15-m) precision-engineered pipes through which steam was pumped. From this Abelson was able to obtain uranium enriched to 14 U–235 atoms per 1000.

Although this was still too weak a mixture for a bomb, it was sufficiently enriched to use in other separation processes. Consequently a bigger plant, consisting of over 2000 towers, was constructed at Oak Ridge, Tennessee, and provided enriched material for the separation process from which came the fuel for the first atom bomb.

After the war Abelson extended the important work of Stanley Miller on the origin of vital biological molecules. He found that amino acids could be produced from a variety of gases if carbon, nitrogen, hydrogen, and oxygen were present. He was also able to show the great stability of amino acids by identifying them in 300-million-year-old fossils.

ADAMS, John Couch (b. June 5, 1819; near Launceston, England; d. Jan. 21, 1892; Cambridge, England) British astronomer.

Adams was the son of a tenant farmer. He developed an early interest in astronomy, constructing his own sundial and observing solar altitudes, and pursuing his astronomical studies in the local Mechanics Institute. He graduated brilliantly from Cambridge University in 1843, and became Lowndean Professor of Astronomy and Geometry in 1858, and director of the Cambridge Observatory in 1860.

His fame rests largely on the dramatic events surrounding the discovery of the planet Neptune in 1846. Astronomers had detected a discrepancy between the observed and predicted positions of Uranus and thus it appeared that either Newton's theory of gravitation was not as universal as had been supposed or there was an as yet undetected body exerting a significant gravitational influence over the orbit of Uranus. There is evidence that Adams had decided to work on this problem as early as 1841. He had a general solution to the problem by 1843 and a complete solution by September, 1845. It was then that he payed a visit to George Airy, the Astronomer Royal, with the exact position of the new planet. Airy payed little attention to it and was moved to action only when, in June 1846, the French astronomer, Urbain Leverrier, also announced the position of a new planet. It was within one degree of the position predicted by Adams the previous year. Airy asked James Challis, director of the Cambridge Observatory, to start looking for the new planet with his large 25-inch (63.5-cm) refractor. Unfortunately Challis decided to cover a much wider area of the sky than was necessary and also lacked up-to-date and complete charts of the area. His start was soon lost and Johann Galle in Berlin had no difficulty in discovering the planet on his first night of observation. All the fame, prizes, and honors initially went to Leverrier. When it was publicly pointed out, by Challis and John Herschel, that Adams's work had priority over Leverrier's, the shy Adams wanted no part of the controversy that followed. In fact he seemed genuinely uninterested in honors. He declined both a knighthood and the post of Astronomer Royal, which was offered him after Airy's retirement in 1881. He later worked on the Leonids, calculating their effect on planetary perturbations (1866), and on the secular variation of the mean motion of the Moon (1852), both difficult questions of mathematical astronomy. His scientific papers were published by his brother in two volumes, in 1876 and 1901.

ADAMS, Roger (b. Jan. 2, 1889; Boston, Massachusetts; d. July 6, 1971; Urbana, Illinois) American organic chemist.

Adams studied chemistry at Harvard, where he obtained his PhD in 1912, and at the University of Berlin. After working briefly at Harvard he joined the staff of the University of Illinois in 1916 and later served as professor of organic chemistry from 1919 until his retirement in 1957.

Adams was one of the most important chemists in America in the interwar period and under him the University of Illinois became one of the leading centers of American chemistry. He developed a simple but effective method for catalyzing the hydrogenation of unsaturated organic compounds using finely divided platinum or palladium dioxides, which were reduced to the metal. He also worked out the structure of a number of naturally occurring physiologically active compounds such as chaulmoogra oil (which was used to treat leprosy) and gossypol (a poisonous constituent of animal feedstuffs derived from cotton). In the late 1930s Adams was asked by the Narcotics Bureau to examine the chemistry of marijuana alkaloids and he succeeded in isolating the active ingredient, tetrahydrocannabinol.

ADAMS, Walter Sydney (b. Dec. 20, 1876; Antioch, now in Turkey; d. May 11, 1956; Pasadena, California) American astronomer.

Adams was the son of missionaries working in Syria, then part of the Ottoman Empire, who returned to America in 1885. Adams graduated from Dartmouth College in 1898 and obtained his AM from the University of Chicago in 1900. After a year in Munich he began his career in astronomy as assistant to George Hale in 1901 at the Yerkes Observatory He moved with Hale to the newly established Mount Wilson Observatory in 1904 where he served as assistant director, 1913–23, and then as director from 1923 until his retirement in 1946.

At Mount Wilson Adams was able to use first the 60-inch (1.5-m) and from 1917 the 100-inch (2.5-m) reflecting telescopes in whose design and construction he had been closely associated. His early work was mainly concerned with solar spectroscopy, when he studied sunspots and solar rotation, but he gradually turned to stellar spectroscopy. In 1914 he showed how it was possible to distinguish between a dwarf and a giant star merely from their spectra. He also demonstrated that it was possible to determine the luminosity, i.e. intrinsic brightness, of a star from its spectrum. This led to Adams introducing the method of spectroscopic parallax whereby the luminosity deduced from a star's spectrum could be used to estimate its distance. The distance of many thousands of stars have been calculated by this method.

He is however better known for his work on the orbiting companion of Sirius, named Sirius B. Friedrich Bessel had first shown in 1844 that Sirius must have a com-

panion and had worked out its mass as about the same as our Sun. The faint star was first observed telescopically by Alvan Clark in 1862. Adams succeeded in obtaining the spectrum of Sirius B in 1915 and found the star to be considerably hotter than the Sun. Adams realized that such a hot body, just eight light-years distant, could only remain invisible to the naked eye if it was very much smaller than the Sun, no bigger in fact than the Earth. In that case it must have an extremely high density, exceeding 100 000 times the density of water. Adams had thus discovered the first 'white dwarf' — a star that has collapsed into a highly compressed object after its nuclear fuel is exhausted.

If such an interpretation was correct then Sirius B should possess a very strong gravitational field. According to Einstein's general theory of relativity, this strong field should shift the wavelength of light waves emitted by it toward the red end of the spectrum. In 1924 Adams succeeded in making the difficult spectroscopic observations and did in fact detect the predicted red shift, which confirmed his own account of Sirius B and provided strong evidence for general relativity.

ADDISON, Thomas (b. Apr. 1793; Longbenton, England; d. June 29, 1860; Brighton, England) British physician.

Addison graduated in medicine from Edinburgh University in 1815 and soon afterwards moved to practice in London. He entered Guy's Hospital in 1817, was appointed assistant physician in 1824 and later became physician and joint lecturer with Richard Bright, an eminent contemporary.

Addison was the first to describe, in 1849, the disease caused by pathological changes in the adrenal (suprarenal) glands, which is now known as *Addison's disease*. He described the characteristic anemia, bronzed skin, and other symptoms in his famous paper, *On the Constitutional and Local Effects of Disease of the Supra-Renal Capsules* (1855), and distinguished it from another form of anemia, now called pernicious anemia, which results from other causes entirely. This is sometimes called *Addisonian anemia*.

Addison also wrote papers concerning tuberculosis, skin diseases, the anatomy of the lung, and other topics, which were published in a collected edition in 1868. He collaborated with Bright in writing *Elements of the Practice of Medicine* (1839) of which only the first volume was completed.

An eloquent if rather aloof lecturer, Addison's fame as a physician came largely after his death.

ADHEMAR, Alphonse Joseph (b. February 1797; Paris; d. 1862; Paris) French mathematician.

Adhemar was a private mathematics tutor who also produced a number of popular mathematical textbooks.

His most important scientific work was his *Les Revolutions de la mer* (1842) in which he was the first to propose a plausible mechanism by which astronomical events could produce ice ages on Earth. It had been known for some time that while the Earth moved in an elliptical orbit around the Sun it also rotated about an axis that was tilted to its orbital plane. Because the orbit is elliptical and the Sun is at one focus, the Earth is closer to the Sun at certain times of year. As a result the southern hemisphere has a slightly longer winter than its northern counterpart. Adhemar saw this as a possible cause of the great Antarctic icesheet for, as this received about 170 hours less solar radiation per year that the Arctic, this could just be sufficient to keep temperatures cold enough to permit the ice to build up.

Adhemar was also aware that the Earth's axis does not always point in the same direction but itself moves around a small circular orbit every 26 000 years. Thus he postulated a 26 000-year cycle developing in the occurrence of glacial periods, but his views received little support.

ADLER, Alfred (b. Feb. 7, 1870; Penzing, Austria; d. May 28, 1937; Aberdeen, Scotland) Austrian psychologist.

Adler, the son of a corn merchant, was educated at the University of Vienna, where he obtained his MD in 1895. After two years at the Vienna General Hospital he set up in private practice in 1898.

In about 1900 Adler began investigating psychopathology and in 1902 he became an original member of Sigmund Freud's circle, which met to discuss psychoanalytical matters. His disagreements with Freud began as early as 1907 — he dismissed Freud's view that sexual conflicts in early childhood cause mental illness — and he finally broke away from the psychoanalytic movement in 1911 to form his own school of individual psychology. Adler tended to minimize the role of the unconscious and sexual repression and instead to see that neurotic as overcompensating for his or her 'inferiority complex', a term he himself introduced. His system was fully expounded in his *Practice and Theory of Individual Psychology* (1927). In 1921 Adler founded his first child-guidance clinic in Vienna, which was to be followed by over 30 more before the Nazi regime in Vienna forced their closure in 1932. From 1926 onward he began to spend more and more time in America, finally settling there permanently in 1932 and taking a professorship of psychiatry at the Long Island College of Medicine, New York, a post he retained until his death from a heart attack while lecturing in Scotland.

ADRIAN, Edgar Douglas, Baron Adrian of Cambridge (b. Nov. 30, 1889; London; d. Aug. 4, 1977; London) British neurophysiologist.

Adrian, a lawyer's son, studied at Cambridge University and St. Bartholomew's Hospital, London, where he obtained his MD in 1915. He returned to Cambridge in 1919, was appointed professor of physiology in 1937, and became the master of Trinity College, Cambridge, in 1951, an office he retained until his retirement in 1965. He was made a peer in 1955.

Adrian's greatest contribution to neurophysiology was his work on the nerve impulse. When he began it was known that nerves transmit nerve impulses as signals, but knowledge of the frequency and control of such impulses was minimal. The first insight into this process came from Adrian's colleague Keith Lucas, who demonstrated in 1905 that the impulse obeyed the 'all-or-none' law. This asserted that below a certain threshold of stimulation a nerve does not respond. However once the threshold is reached the nerve continues to respond by a fixed amount however much the stimulation increases. Thus increased stimulation, although it stimulates more fibers, does not affect the magnitude of the signal itself.

It was not until 1925 that Adrian advanced beyond this position. By painstaking surgical techniques he succeeded in separating individual nerve fibers and amplifying and recording the small action potentials in these fibers. By studying the effect of stretching the sternocutaneous muscle of the frog, Adrian demonstrated how the nerve, even though it transmits an impulse of fixed strength, can still convey a complex message. He found that as the extension increased so did the frequency of the nerve impulse, rising from 10 to 50 impulses per second. Thus, he concluded that the message is conveyed by changes in the frequency of the discharge. For this work Adrian shared the 1932 Nobel Prize for physiology or medicine with Charles Sherrington.

AGASSIZ, Jean Louis Rodolphe (b. May 28, 1807; Motier-en-Vuly, Switzerland; d. Dec. 14, 1873; Cambridge, Massachusetts) Swiss–American biologist.

Generally considered the foremost naturalist of 19th-century America, Agassiz was educated at the universities of Zurich, Heidelberg, and Munich, where he studied under the embryologist Ignaz Döllinger. At the instigation of Georges Cuvier, he cataloged and described the fishes brought back from Brazil by C.F.P. von Martius and J.B. von Spix (*Fishes of Brazil*, 1829), following this with his *History of the Freshwater Fishes of Central Europe* (1839–42) and an extensive pioneering work on fossil fishes, which eventually ran to five volumes: *Recherches sur les poissons fossiles* (1833–43; Researches on Fossil Fishes). These works, completed while Agassiz was professor of natural history at Neuchâtel (1832–46), established his reputation as the greatest ichthyologist of his day. Agassiz's best-known discovery, however, was that of the Ice Ages. Extensive field studies in the Swiss Alps, and later in America and Britain, led him to postulate glacier movements and the former advance and retreat of ice sheets; his findings were published in *Etudes sur les glaciers* (1840; Studies on Glaciers).

A successful series of lectures given at Boston, Massachusetts, in 1846 led to his permanent settlement in America. In 1847 he was appointed professor of zoology and geology at Harvard, where he also established the Museum of Comparative Zoology (1859). Agassiz's subsequent teachings inculcated a departure from established practice in emphasizing the importance of first-hand investigation of natural phenomena, thus helping to transform academic study in America. His embryological studies led to a recognition of the similarity between the developing stages of living animals and complete but more primitive species in the fossil record. Agassiz did not, however, share Darwin's view of a gradual evolution of species, but, like Cuvier, considered that there had been repeated separate creations and extinctions of species — thus explaining changes and the appearance of new forms. Unfortunately, one of Agassiz's most influential pronouncements was that there were several species, as distinct from races, of man: an argument used by slavers to justify their subjugation of the negroes as an inferior species. His ambitious *Contributions to the Natural History of the*

United States (4 vols. 1857–62) remained uncompleted at his death.

AGRICOLA, Georgius (b. Mar. 24, 1494; Glauchau, now in East Germany; d. Nov. 21, 1555; Chemnitz, now Karl Marx Stadt in East Germany) German metallurgist.

Agricola's true name was Georg Bauer but, as was the custom of the day, he latinized it (Agricola and Bauer both mean 'farmer'). Little is known about him until his entry to the University of Leipzig in 1514. He later pursued his studies of philosophy and medicine in Italy at Bologna, Padua, and Venice (1523–27). In 1527 he was engaged as physician to the Bohemian city of Joachimsthal — the center of a rich mining area — moving in 1534 to another celebrated mining town, Chemnitz. Here he became burgomaster in 1545. He wrote seven books on geological subjects but these were also so illuminating of other subjects that he was known in his lifetime as the Saxon Pliny.

His most famous work, *De re metallica* (1556), concentrates on mining and metallurgy with a wealth of information on the conditions of the time, such as management of the mines, the machinery used (e.g. pumps, windmills, and water power), and the processes employed. The book is still in print having the unique distinction of being translated and edited (1912) by a president of the United States, Herbert Hoover, with Lou Henry Hoover (his wife).

Agricola is often regarded as the father of modern mineralogy. In the Middle Ages, the subject was based on accumulated lore from the Orient, the Arabs, and antiquity. Stones were believed to come in male and female form, to have digestive organs, and to possess medicinal and supernatural powers. Agricola began to reject these theories and to provide the basis for a new discipline. Thus in his *De ortu et causis subterraneorum* (1546; On the Origin and Cause of Subterranean Things) he introduced the idea of a lapidifying juice (or *succus lapidescens*) from which stones condensed as a result of heat. This fluid was supposedly subterranean water mixed with rain, which collects earthy material when percolating through the ground.

Agricola also, in *De natura fossilium* (1546), introduced a new basis for the classification of minerals (called 'fossils' at the time). Although far from modern, it was an enormous improvement on earlier works. Agricola based his system on the physical properties of minerals, which he listed as color, weight, transparency, taste, odor, texture, solubility, combustibility, and so on. In this way he tried to distinguish between earths, stones, gems, marbles, metals, building stone, and mineral solutions, carefully describing his terms, which should not be assumed to be synonymous with today's terms, in each case.

AILLY, Pierre d' *See* D'AILLY, Pierre.

AIRY, Sir George Biddell (b. July 27, 1801; Alnwick, England; d. Jan. 2, 1892; Greenwich, near London) British astronomer.

Airy was the son of a tax collector. He attended school in Colchester before going to Cambridge University in 1819. He met with early success, producing a mathematical textbook in 1826 and numerous papers on optics. He became Lucasian Professor of Mathematics at Cambridge in 1826 and two years later was made Plumian Professor of Astronomy and director of the Cambridge Observatory. In 1835 he was appointed Astronomer Royal, a post he held for 46 years.

Airy was a very energetic, innovative, and successful Astronomer Royal. He reequipped the observatory, installing an altazimuth for lunar observation in 1847, a new transit circle and zenith tube in 1851, and a 13-inch (33-cm) equatorial telescope in 1859. He created a magnetic and meteorological department in 1838, began spectroscopic investigations in 1868, and started keeping a daily record of sunspots with the Kew Observatory heliograph in 1873. In optics he investigated the use of cylindrical lenses to correct astigmatism

(Airy was astigmatic) and examined the disklike image in the diffraction pattern of a point source of light (in an optical device with a central aperture) now called the *Airy disk*. Also named for him is his hypothesis of isostacy: the theory that mountain ranges must have root structures of lower density, proportional to their height, in order to maintain isostatic equilibrium.

Despite his many successes he is now mainly, and unfairly, remembered for his lapses. When John Adams came to him in September, 1845, with news of the position of a new planet, Airy unwisely ignored him, leaving it to others to win fame as the discoverers of Neptune. He also dismissed Michael Faraday's new field theory.

AITKEN, Robert Grant (b. Dec. 31, 1864; Jackson, California; d. Oct. 29, 1951; Berkeley, California) American astronomer.

Aitken obtained his AB in 1887 and his AM in 1892 from Williams College, Masssachusetts. He began his career at the University of the Pacific, then in San Jose, as professor of mathematics from 1891 until 1895 when he joined the staff of Lick Observatory, Mount Hamilton, California. He remained at Lick for his entire career serving as its director from 1930 until his retirement in 1935.

Aitken did much to advance knowledge of binary stars, i.e. pairs of stars orbiting about the same point under their mutual gravitational attraction. He described over 3000 binary systems and published in 1932 the comprehensive work *New General Catalogue of Double Stars Within 120° of the North Pole*. He also produced the standard work *The Binary Stars* (1918).

AKERS, Sir Wallace Allen (b. Sept. 9, 1888; London; d. Nov. 1, 1954; Alton, England) British industrial chemist.

Akers, the son of an accountant, was educated at Oxford University. He first worked for the chemical company Brunner Mond from 1911 to 1924 and, after four years in Borneo with an oil company, returned in 1928. By then Brunner Mond had become part of ICI. From 1931 he was in charge of the Billingham Research Laboratory and from 1944 was the company director responsible for all ICI research.

In World War II Akers worked under Sir John Anderson, the government minister responsible for work on the atom bomb. He was put in charge of Tube Alloys, the Ministry of Supply's front for secret nuclear work. It was Akers who led the mission of British scientists in 1943 to America to work out details of collaboration, although he proved unacceptable to the Americans and was replaced by James Chadwick. Akers returned to head Tube Alloys in the UK.

After the war one of his main tasks was the setting up of the Central Research Laboratory for ICI at Welwyn near London, later named the Akers Research Laboratory. He was knighted in 1946.

AL-BATTANI or ALBATEGNIUS (b. *c.* 858; Harran, now in Turkey; d. 929; Sammara, now in Iraq) Arab astronomer.

Al-Battani was the son of a maker of astronomical instruments. He worked mainly in Raqqah on the Euphrates (now ar-Raqqah in Syria) and was basically a follower of Ptolemy, devoting himself to refining and perfecting the work of his master. He improved Ptolemy's measurement of the obliquity of the ecliptic (the angle between the Earth's orbital and equatorial planes), the determination of the equinoxes, and the length of the year. He also corrected Ptolemy in various matters, in particular in his discovery of the movement of the solar perigee (the Sun's nearest point to the Earth) relative to the equinoxes. His work was widely known in the medieval period, having been translated by Plato of Tivoli in about 1120 as *De motu stellarum* (On Stellar Motion), which was finally published in Nuremberg in 1537.

ALBERTUS MAGNUS, St. (b. *c.* 1200; Lauingen, now in West Germany; d. Nov. 15, 1280; Cologne, now in West Germany) German scholastic philosopher.

Albertus Magnus was the son of a German lord, his real name being Count von Bollstädt. He studied at the University of Padua and then became, in 1223, a member of the Dominican order against his family's wishes. He continued his studies throughout Europe and then taught theology. From about 1245 he lectured in Paris, where the philosopher and theologian Thomas Aquinas became one of his pupils, and in 1248 he was sent to Cologne to establish a Dominican study center, returning to Paris in 1254.

Albertus Magnus's voluminous writings, including treatises on theology, physics, and natural history, were generally Aristotelian in spirit, though he stressed the importance of direct observation of nature rather than strict adherence to textual authority. He also conducted alchemical experiments and in his book, *De mineralibus* (1569; On Minerals) he claimed to have tested alchemical gold "and found after six or seven ignitions that it was converted to powder."

He retired, in 1270, to his convent at Cologne. He was made a doctor of the Church and canonized in 1931.

ALBINUS, Bernhard Siegfried (b. Feb. 22, 1697; Frankfurt an der Oder, now in East Germany; d. Sept. 9, 1770; Leiden, Netherlands) German anatomist.

Albinus was educated at the University of Leiden, where he subsequently held professorships, in anatomy and surgery and later medicine. A popular lecturer on his subject, Albinus also carried out his own studies of human anatomy, and is chiefly known for his detailed classification of contemporary and traditional knowledge in this field. He published, with his former teacher Hermann Boerhaave, the complete works of Andreas Vesalius, and also edited a new edition of the works of Hieronymus Fabricius. His own work, in which he emphasized the importance of illustrating the 'anatomical norm', was published in 1747 in *Tabulae sceleti et musculorum corporis humani* (Plates of the Skeleton and Muscles of the Human Body), which contains numerous excellent drawings.

ALBRIGHT, Arthur (b. Mar. 3, 1811; Charlbury, England; d. July 3, 1900; London) British chemist and industrialist.

Albright came from a Quaker family. He was first apprenticed as an apothecary in Bristol and became a partner in the Birmingham firm of John and Edward Sturge, manufacturing chemists. In 1844 the partners established a new works at Selly Oak to produce white phosphorus for the match industry. This was manufactured from calcium phosphate, derived from imported bones, and sulfuric acid.

White phosphorus was a difficult material to handle, being toxic and spontaneously flammable. Another allotropic form — red phosphorus — was discovered in 1845 by Anton Schrötter. Albright bought the patents and improved the process for producing red phosphorus. A larger factory was opened at Oldbury. J.E. Lundström of Sweden showed, in 1855, how Albright's phosphorus could be used in the production of safety matches. In this system the chlorate was confined to the tip of the match and the phosphorus was used only on the box.

In 1855 Albright's partnership with the Sturges was dissolved and he joined with J.W. Wilson in the following year, eventually forming the chemical company Albright and Wilson.

ALCMAEON (*fl.* 450 BC; Croton, now Crotone in Italy) Greek philosopher and physician.

Details of Alcmaeon's work come from the surviving fragments of his book and through references by later authors, including Aristotle. He was probably influenced by the school of thought founded by Pythagoras in Croton and originated the notion that health was dependent on maintaining a balance between all the pairs of opposite qualities in the body, i.e. wet and dry, hot and cold, etc. Imbalance of these qualities resulted in illness. This theory was later developed by Hippocrates and his followers.

Alcmaeon performed dissections of animals and possibly of human cadavers also. He demonstrated various anatomical features of the eye and ear, including their connections with the brain, and correctly asserted that the brain was the control center of bodily functions and the seat of intelligence.

ALDER, Kurt (b. July 10, 1902; Konigshütte, now Chorzów in Poland; d. June 20, 1958; Cologne, West Germany) German organic chemist.

Alder studied chemistry in Berlin and Kiel, receiving his doctorate in 1926 under Otto Diels (q.v.). In 1928 Diels and Alder discovered the chemical reaction that bears their name. Alder was professor of chemistry at Kiel (1934), chemist with I. G. Farben at Leverkusen (1936), and director of the Chemical Institute at the University of Cologne (1940). In 1950 Diels and Alder jointly received the Nobel Prize for chemistry for their discovery.

ALDROVANDI, Ulisse (b. Sept. 11, 1522; Bologna, Italy; d. May 4, 1604; Bologna) Italian naturalist.

Aldrovandi was educated at Bologna and Padua, where he obtained a medical degree in 1553. He was professor of botany and natural history at Bologna and in 1567 founded the Bologna Botanic Gardens. Under the patronage of popes Gregory XIII and Sixtus V, Aldrovandi traveled over a great part of Europe observing natural phenomena and collecting specimens, which he used as material for his descriptive accounts of animals, plants,

minerals, etc., many of which remained unpublished until long after his death. His collections of specimens enabled him to found a museum, and his classifications provided a basis for the subsequent development of animal taxonomy. Celebrated for his careful and accurate descriptions, Aldrovandi also wrote an official pharmacopoeia, which detailed the constituents and properties of drugs and provided a model for later such works.

ALEMBERT, Jean Le Rond d' See D'ALEMBERT, Jean Le Rond.

ALFVÉN, Hannes Olof Gösta (b. May 30, 1908; Norrkoeping, Sweden) Swedish physicist.

Alfvén was educated at the University of Uppsala where he received his PhD in 1934. He has since worked at the Royal Institute of Technology, Stockholm, where he served as professor of electronics from 1945 until 1963 when a special chair of plasma physics was created for him. He became a professor at the University of California at San Diego in 1967.

Alfvén is noted for his pioneering theoretical research in the field of magnetohydrodynamics — the study of conducting fluids and their interaction with magnetic fields. This work, for which he shared the 1970 Nobel Prize for physics with Louis Néel, has mainly been concerned with plasmas; i.e. ionized gases containing positive and negative particles. He has investigated the interactions of electrical and magnetic fields and shown theoretically that the magnetic field, under certain circumstances, can move with the plasma. In 1942 he postulated the existence of waves in plasmas; these *Alfvén waves* were later observed in both liquid metals and ionized plasmas.

Alfvén has applied his theories to the motion of particles in the Earth's magnetic field and to the properties of plasmas in stars. In 1942, and later in the 1950s, he developed a theory of the origin of the solar system. This he assumed to have formed from a magnetic plasma, which condensed into small particles that clustered together into larger bodies. His work is also applicable to the properties of plasmas in experimental nuclear fusion reactors. Alfvén's books include *Cosmical Electrodynamics* (1950), which collects his early work, and *Structure and Evolutionary History of the Solar System* (1975), written with G. Arrhenius.

ALHAZEN, (Abu Ali al-Hassan ibn al Haytham) (b. *c.* 965; Basra, now in Iraq; d. 1038; Cairo, Egypt) Arabian scientist.

Alhazen was one of the most original scientists of his time. About a hundred works are attributed to him; the main one was translated into Latin in the 12th century and finally published in 1572 as *Opticae thesaurus* (The Treasury of Optics). This was widely studied and extremely influential. It was the first authoritative work to reject the curious Greek view that the eye sends out rays to the object looked at. Alhazen also made detailed measurements of angles of incidence and refraction. He studied spherical and parabolic mirrors, the camera obscura, and the role of the lens in vision. While the Greeks had had a good understanding of the formation of an image in a plane mirror, Alhazen tackled the much more difficult problem of the formation of images in spherical and parabolic mirrors and offered geometrical solutions. It is difficult to think of any other writer who had surpassed the Greeks in any branch of the exact sciences by the 14th let alone the 11th century. He was, however, unfortunate in his relationship with the deranged caliph al-Hakim. Having rashly claimed that he could regulate the flooding of the Nile, he was forced to simulate madness to escape execution until the caliph died in 1021.

AL-KHWARIZMI, Abu Ja'far Muhammad Ibn Musa (b. *c.* 800; Khwarizm, now Khiva in the Soviet Union; d. *c.* 847) Arab mathematician, astronomer, and geographer.

Al-Khwarizmi's importance lies chiefly in the knowledge he transmitted to others. Very little is known about his life except that he was a member of the academy of sciences in Baghdad, which flourished during the rule (813–33) of caliph al-Ma'mun. Al-Khwarizmi's main astronomical treatise and his chief mathematical work, the *Algebra*, are dedicated to the caliph. The *Algebra* enlarged upon the work of Diophantus and is largely concerned with methods for solving practical computational problems rather than algebra as the term is now understood. Insofar as he did discuss algebra, al-Khwarizmi confined his discussion to equations of the first and second degrees.

His astronomical work, *Zij al-sindhind*, is also based largely on the work of other scientists. As with the *Algebra*, its chief interest is as the earliest Arab work on the subject still in existence.

Al-Khwarizmi's other main surviving works are a treatise on the Hindu system of numerals and a treatise on geography. The Hindu number system, with its epoch-making innovations, for example the incorporation of a symbol for zero, was introduced to Europe via a Latin translation (*De numero indorum*; On the Hindu Art of Reckoning) of al-Khwarizmi's work. Only the Latin translation remains but it seems certain that al-Khwarizmi was the first Arab mathematician to expound the new number system systematically. The term 'algorithm' (a rule of calculation) is a corrupted form of his name. His geographical treatise marked a considerable improvement over earlier work, notably in correcting some of the influential errors and misconceptions that had gained currency owing to Ptolemy's *Geography*.

ALLBUTT, Sir Thomas Clifford (b. July 20, 1836; Dewsbury, England; d. Feb. 22, 1925; Cambridge, England) British physician and medical historian.

Allbutt studied natural sciences at Cambridge University, graduating in 1860. He then studied medicine at St. George's Hospital, London, gaining his MB in 1861. He was appointed physician to Leeds General Infirmary in 1864 where, in 1866, he invented the short clinical thermometer, which was a great advance on previous highly cumbersome instruments. His major interest was cardiology and he was the first to describe the effects of syphilis on the cerebral arteries. His *System of Medicine* (8 vols. 1896–99) became an important medical text. In 1892 he was appointed professor of medicine at Cambridge, where he lectured and wrote several notable works on the history of medicine, including *Greek Medicine in Rome* (1921).

ALLEN, Edgar (b. 1892; Canon City, Colorado; d. Feb. 3, 1943; New Haven, Connecticut) American endocrinologist.

Allen, the son of a physician, was educated at Brown University. After war service he worked at Washington University, St. Louis, before being appointed (1923) to the chair of anatomy at the University of Missouri. In 1933 he moved to a similar post at Yale and remained there until his death.

In 1923 Allen, working with Edward Doisy, began the modern study of the sex hormones. It was widely thought that the female reproductive cycle was under the control of some substance found in the corpus luteum, the body formed in the ovary after ovulation. Allen thought rather that the active ingredient was probably in the follicles surrounding the ovum. To test this he made an extract of the follicular fluid and found that on injection it induced the physiological changes normally found only in the estrous cycle. Allen had in fact discovered estrogen although it was only identified some six years later by Adolf Butenandt.

ALLEN, James Alfred Van *See* VAN ALLEN, James Alfred.

ALPHER, Ralph Asher (b. Feb. 3, 1921; Washington DC) American physicist.

Alpher studied at George Washington University, Washington, where he obtained his BS in 1943 and his PhD in 1948. He spent the war as a physicist with the US Navy's Naval Ordnance Laboratory in Washington followed by a period (1944–55) with the applied physics laboratory of Johns Hopkins University, Baltimore. In 1955 Alpher joined the staff of the General Electric Research and Development Center, Schenectady, New York.

At George Washington, Alpher came under the influence of the physicist George Gamow with whom he collaborated in a number of papers. They produced, with Hans Bethe, a major paper on the origin of the chemical elements, sometimes called the *Alpher–Bethe–Gamow theory*, which was incorporated into Gamow's modern form of the big-bang theory of the origin of the universe, published in 1948. It was supposed that the universe was initially very hot and dense and was composed entirely of neutrons. The neutrons decayed to protons (hydrogen nuclei), which could then capture neutrons to form deuterium nuclei. A further series of reactions produced helium. It was also proposed that a further succession of reactions, mainly the capture of neutrons, could produce other elements. Calculations on the abundance of the elements as predicted by the theory were performed by Alpher and Robert C. Herman. Although it is accepted that hydrogen and helium were indeed formed in the primitive universe by such a process, heavier elements are now known to be synthesized in the stars.

The same year, 1948, saw the publication of a remarkable paper by Alpher and Herman in which they predicted that the big bang should have produced intense radiation that gradually lost energy as the universe expanded and by now would be characteristic of a temperature of about

5 K (–268°C). Unlike its later and independent formulation by Robert Dicke in 1964, the 1948 paper had surprisingly little impact. Alpher did approach a number of radar experts but was informed that it was then impossible to detect such radiation. When it was discovered by Arno Penzias and Robert Wilson in 1964–65 its effect was to initiate a major revolution in cosmology and astrophysics.

ALPINI, Prospero (b. Nov. 23, 1553; Venice, Italy; d. Feb. 6, 1617; Padua, Italy) Italian botanist and physician.

Alpini studied medicine at Padua University, receiving his MD in 1578. He became physician to Giorgio Emo, the Venetian consul in Egypt, and between 1580 and 1583 traveled widely in Egypt and the Greek Islands. This enabled him to make an extensive study of the Egyptian and Mediterranean floras, and he was the first European to describe the coffee and banana plants and a genus of the ginger family, later named *Alpinia*. He also studied the date palm and was the first to fertilize dates artificially, having realized that this palm has separate male and female trees. In 1593 Alpini was appointed professor of botany at Padua and he also became director of the Botanic Gardens there, introducing many Egyptian plants.

In 1591 Alpini published an account of current Egyptian medical practice (*De medicina Aegyptorum*) and later produced a book dealing with the prognosis of diseases (*De praesagienda vita et morte aegrotontium*, 1601; The Presages of Life and Death in Diseases, 1746). The books contained useful observations on the diseases of the Middle East.

ALTER, David (b. Dec. 3, 1807; Westmoreland County, Pennsylvania; d. Sept. 18, 1881; Freeport, Pennsylvania) American inventor and physicist.

Largely self-taught, Alter graduated from the Reformed Medical College in New York in 1831. During his lifetime he experimented at home using a variety of apparatus constructed by himself. He worked on a wide range of subjects but was little recognized for his achievements. His best work was on spectrum analysis, suggesting that each element had its own characteristic spectrum thus enabling qualitative analysis to be carried out. This was later proved correct by Gustav Kirchhoff and Robert Bunsen. Alter's inventions included a new method for purifying bromine, a process for obtaining oil from coal, an electric clock, and an electric telegraph that would spell out words with the aid of a pointer.

ALVAREZ, Luis Walter (b. June 13, 1911; San Francisco, California) American physicist.

Alvarez, the son of a physician, studied at the University of Chicago, where he gained his bachelor's degree and doctorate. In 1936 he moved to the University of California, becoming a professor in 1945.

His first major discovery was the phenomenon of orbital electron capture. For certain elements, the nucleus can capture an electron that is in an inner orbit and this results in the transformation of the nuclide into one that has a proton number smaller by one. In 1939, with Felix Bloch, he made the first measurement of the magnetic moment of the neutron.

During World War II, Alvarez, like many prominent American physicists, was involved in both the development of radar and of the atomic bomb. From 1940 to 1943 he worked at the radiation laboratory of the Massachusetts Institute of Technology, and is credited with the development of microwave beacons, linear radar antennas, and the ground-controlled radar landing approach system for aircraft. Subsequently, at the Los Alamos Scientific Laboratory, New Mexico (1944–45), he worked on the atomic bomb, attending the first atomic explosion at Alamogordo and later flying over Hiroshima as an observer.

After the war, Alvarez turned his skills

to constructing the first linear accelerator for protons (1947) and developing the bubble-chamber technique for observing electrically charged subatomic particles. His techniques for detecting, recording, and analyzing such particles (or resonances) swelled their numbers from around 30 to well over 100. For this contribution he received the Nobel Prize for physics in 1968.

Other inventions and discoveries attributed to Alvarez are a color-television system, radioactive helium, and a method of x-ray examination of the pyramids.

AMAGAT, Emile Hilaire (b. Jan. 2, 1841; Saint-Satur, France; d. Feb. 15, 1915; Saint-Satur) French physicist.

Amagat obtained his doctorate in 1872 from Paris and became a professor of physics at the Faculté Libre des Sciences at Lyons and eventually a full member of the French Academy of Sciences.

He started work plotting isotherms of carbon dioxide at high pressures, expanding the results of Thomas Andrews (q.v.); this research was published in 1872 as his doctoral thesis. In 1877 followed a publication on the coefficient of compressibility of fluids, showing conclusively that this decreased with an increase in pressure, a result contradicting the results of other scientists.

Between 1879 and 1882 Amagat researched into a number of gases, publishing data on isotherms and reaching the limit of pressures obtainable using glass apparatus — about 400 atmospheres. To go yet further Amagat invented a hydraulic manometer that could produce and measure up to 3200 atmospheres. (This manometer was later used in firearms factories for testing purposes).

AMALDI, Edoardo (b. Sept. 5, 1908; Carpaneto, Italy) Italian physicist.

Amaldi graduated from the University of Rome in 1929, where he had studied

under Enrico Fermi. Together with Fermi and others he discovered that fast-moving neutrons are slowed down (moderated) by substances containing hydrogen, and can thus be brought to energies at which they more easily interact with nuclei. He has also contributed to the study of tau-mesons, hyperons, and antiprotons.

In 1937 he was made professor of general physics at the University of Rome, and from 1952 until 1954 he was secretary-general of the European Organization for Nuclear Research. He has also served as president of the International Union of Pure and Applied Physics (1957–60) and president of the Istituto Nazionale di Fisica Nucleare (1960–65).

AMBARTSUMIAN, Viktor Amazaspovich (b. Sept. 18, 1908; Tbilisi, now in the Soviet Union) Soviet astrophysicist.

Ambartsumian, the son of a distinguished Armenian philologist, graduated from the University of Leningrad in 1928 and did graduate work at Pulkovo Observatory, near Leningrad, from 1928 to 1931. He was professor of astrophysics from 1934 to 1946 at Leningrad and has held the same post from 1947 at the State University at Yerevan in Armenia. In 1946 he organized the construction, near Yerevan, of the Byurakan Astronomical Observatory, having been appointed its director in 1944.

Ambartsumian's work has been mainly concerned with the evolution of stellar systems, both galaxies and smaller clusters of stars, and the processes taking place during the evolution of stars. The idea of a stellar 'association' was introduced into astronomy by Ambartsumian in 1947. These are loose clusters of hot stars that lie in or near the disk-shaped plane of our Galaxy. These associations must be young, no more than a few million years old, as the gravitational field of the Galaxy will tend to disperse them. This must mean that star formation is still going on in the Galaxy.

He also argued in 1955 that the idea of colliding galaxies proposed by Rudolph

Minkowski and Walter Baade to explain such radio sources as Cygnus A would not produce the required energy. Instead, he proposed that the source of energy was gigantic explosions occurring in the dense central regions of galaxies and these would be adequate to provide the 10^{55} joules emitted by the most energetic radio sources.

AMICI, Giovanni Battista (b. Mar. 25, 1786; Modena, Italy; d. Apr. 10, 1863; Florence, Italy) Italian astronomer and instrument maker.

Amici was professor of mathematics at the University of Modena and in 1835 became the director of the observatory at the Royal Museum in Florence. He made great improvements in the design of parabolic mirrors for reflecting telescopes, and constructed and designed prismatic spectroscopes. In 1840 he made two achromatic objective lenses with diameters of 9.5 and 11 inches (24 and 28 cm), which were used by Giovanni Donati. He also made advances in microscopy, improving the compound microscope and using it to study plant reproduction.

AMONTONS, Guillaume (b. Aug. 31, 1663; Paris; d. Oct. 11, 1705; Paris) French physicist.

Amontons, who had been deaf since childhood, invented and perfected various scientific instruments. In 1687 he made a hygrometer (an instrument for measuring moisture in the air); in 1695 he produced an improved barometer; and in 1702–03 a constant-volume air thermometer. In 1699 he published the results of his studies on the effects of change in temperature on the volume and pressure of air. He noticed that equal drops in temperature resulted in equal drops in pressure and realized that at a low enough temperature the volume and pressure of the air would become zero — an early recognition of the idea of absolute zero. These results lay largely unnoticed and the relationship between temperature and pressure of gases was not reexamined until the next century (by scientists such as Jacques Charles).

Amontons also published in 1699 the results of his studies on friction, which he considered to be proportional to load.

AMPERE, André Marie (b. Jan. 22, 1775; Lyons, France; d. June 10, 1836; Marseille, France) French physicist and mathematician.

Ampère, the son of a wealthy merchant, was privately tutored, and to a large extent self-taught. His genius was evident at an early age. He was particularly proficient at mathematics and, following his marriage in 1799 he was able to make a modest living as a mathematics teacher in Lyons. In 1802 he moved first to Bourg-en-Bresse to take up an appointment, then to Paris as professor of physics and chemistry at the Ecole Centrale.

His first publication was on the statistics of games of chance *Considérations sur la théorie mathématique de jeu* (1802; Considerations on the Mathematical Theory of Games) and his work at Bourg led to his appointment as professor of mathematics at the Lyceum of Lyons, and then in 1809 as professor of analysis at the Ecole Polytechnique in Paris. His talents were recognized by Napoleon, who in 1808 appointed him inspector general of the newly formed university system — a post Ampère held until his death.

Ampère's most famous scientific work was in establishing a mathematical basis for electromagnetism. The Danish physicist Hans Christian Oersted had made the important experimental discovery that a current passing through a wire could cause the movement of a magnetic compass needle. Ampère witnessed a demonstration of electromagnetism by François Arago at the Academy of Science on 11 September, 1820. He set to work immediately on his own investigations, and within seven days was able to report the results of his experiments.

In a succession of presentations to the academy in the next four months, he developed a mathematical theory to explain the interaction between electricity and magnetism, to which he gave the name 'electrodynamics' (now more commonly: electromagnetism) to distinguish it from the study of stationary electric forces, which he christened 'electrostatics'.

Having recognized that electric currents in wires caused the motion of magnets, and that a magnet can affect another magnet, he looked for evidence that electric currents could influence other electric currents. The simplest example of this interaction is found by arranging for currents to flow through two parallel wires. Ampère discovered that if the currents passed in the same direction the wires were attracted to each other, but if they passed in opposite directions the wires were repelled. From this he went on to consider more complex configurations of closed loops, helices, and other geometrical figures, and was able to provide a mathematical analysis that allowed quantitative predictions.

In 1825 he had been able to deduce an empirical law of forces (*Ampère's law*) between two current-carrying elements, which showed an inverse-square law (the force decreases as the square of the distance between the two elements, and is proportional to the product of the two currents). By 1827 he was able to give a precise mathematical formulation of the law, and it was in this year that his most famous work *Mémoirs sur la théorie mathématique des phénomènes electrodynamiques uniquement déducte de l'expérience* (Notes on the Mathematical Theory of Electrodynamic Phenomena, Solely Deduced from Experiment) was published.

Besides explaining the macroscopic effects of electromagnetism, he attempted to construct a microscopic theory that would fit the phenomenon, and postulated an electrodynamic molecule in which electric-fluid currents circulated, giving each molecule a magnetic field.

In his honor, the unit of electric current is named for him, and in fact the ampère is defined in terms of the force between two parallel current-carrying wires.

ANAXAGORAS of Clazomenae (b. *c.* 500 BC; Clazomenae, now in Turkey; d. *c.* 428 BC; Lampsacus, now in Turkey) Greek philosopher.

Anaxagoras left Asia Minor in about 480 BC and taught in Athens during its most brilliant period under Pericles, himself one of Anaxagoras's pupils. In about 450 BC he was exiled to Lampsacus after being prosecuted for impiety by the enemies of Pericles.

Although he wrote a book, *On Nature*, only fragments of his writings survive; his work is known through later writers, notably Aristotle and Simplicius, and is open to contradictory interpretations. The difficulty consists in reconciling his principle of homoeomereity, which states that matter is infinitely divisible and retains its character on division, with his statement "there is a portion of everything in everything." His work can be seen as a criticism of the Eleatic school of Parmenides and Zeno of Elea, who had argued against plurality and even motion.

Anaxagoras's astronomy was more rational than that of his predecessors; he stated that the Sun and stars were incandescent stones, that the Moon derived its light from the Sun, and he gave the modern explanation for eclipses of the Sun and Moon.

ANAXIMANDER of Miletus (b. *c.* 611 BC; Miletus, now in Turkey; d. *c.* 547 BC; Miletus) Greek philosopher.

Anaximander belonged to the first school of natural philosophy and was the pupil of Thales. He wrote one of the earliest scientific treatises but none of his writings survive and his work in known only through later writers, notably Aristotle and Theophrastus.

Anaximander criticized Thales' idea

that water was the basic element of the universe by pointing out that no one element gains the upper hand and that "they pay penalty and retribution to each other according to the assessment of time." From this he deduced that the primal matter was what he called the *apeiron* or the indefinite. This idea was later developed by the atomists. He was the first to realize that the Earth did not have to float on water or be supported in any way; he stated that it was in equilibrium with the other bodies in the universe.

Anaximander was the first philosopher to speculate on the origin of man. He is also credited with the first determinations of the solstices and equinoxes and the production of the first map of the world as he knew it. He was the first to recognize that the Earth's surface is curved but believed it was curved only in the north–south direction and consequently represented the Earth as a cylinder.

ANAXIMENES of Miletus (*fl.* 546 BC; b. Miletus, now in Turkey) Greek philosopher.

Anaximenes was the last of the great Milesian philosophers. He was probably a pupil of Anaximander of Miletus and, like Thales before him, he identified one of the tangible elements as the primal substance. For Anaximenes this was air, which by processes of condensation and rarefaction could produce every other kind of matter. He used the rather mystical argument that since air is the breath of life for man it must also be the main principle of the universe.

ANDERSON, Carl David (b. Sept. 3, 1905; New York City) American physicist.

Anderson, the son of Swedish immigrants, was educated at the California Institute of Technology where he obtained his PhD in 1930 and where he remained for his entire career, serving as professor of physics from 1939 until his retirement in 1978.

Anderson was deeply involved in the discovery of two new elementary particles. In 1930 he began to study cosmic rays by photographing their tracks in a cloud chamber and noted that particles of positive charge occurred as abundantly as those of negative charge. The negative particles were clearly electrons but those of positive charge could not be protons (the only positive particles known at the time) as they did not produce sufficient ionization in the chamber. Eventually Anderson concluded that such results "could logically be interpreted only in terms of particles of a positive charge and a mass of the same order of magnitude as that normally possessed by a free negative electron." It was in fact the positron or positive electron, whose existence he announced in September 1932. In the following year his results were confirmed by Patrick Blackett and Giuseppe Occhialini and won for Anderson the 1936 Nobel Physics Prize.

In the same year Anderson noted some further unusual cosmic-ray tracks. As they appeared to be made by a particle more massive than an electron but lighter than a proton it was at first thought to be the particle predicted by Hideki Yukawa that was thought to carry the strong nuclear force and hold the nucleus together. The particle was initially named the 'mesotron' or 'yukon'. However, this identification proved to be premature, as its interaction with nucleons was found to be so infrequent that it could not possibly perform the role described by Yukawa. From 1938 the particle became known as the meson, and the confusion was partly dispelled in 1947 when Cecil Powell discovered another and more active meson, to be known as the pi-meson or pion to distinguish it from Anderson's mu-meson or muon. While the role of the pion is readily explained, that of Anderson's muon is still far from clear.

ANDERSON, Philip Warren (b. Dec. 13, 1923; Indianapolis, Indiana) American physicist.

Anderson obtained his BS (1943), MS (1947), and PhD (1949) at Harvard University, doing his doctoral thesis under John Van Vleck. The period 1943–45 was spent at the Naval Research Laboratory working on antenna engineering. Upon receiving his doctorate, Anderson joined the Bell Telephone Laboratories at Murray Hill, New Jersey, where he has worked ever since.

Anderson's main research has been in the physics of the solid state, incorporating such topics as spectral-line broadening, exchange interactions in insulators, the Josephson effect, quantum coherence, superconductors, and nuclear theory. Under Van Vleck he worked initially on elucidating the phenomenon of pressure broadening of lines in microwave, infrared, and optical spectroscopy. In 1959 he developed a theory to explain 'superexchange' — the coupling of spins of two magnetic atoms in a crystal through their interaction with a nonmagnetic atom located between them. He went on to develop the theoretical treatments of antiferromagnetics, ferroelectrics, and superconductors.

In 1961 Anderson conceived a theoretical model to describe what happens where an impurity atom is present in a metal — now widely known and used as the *Anderson model*. Also named for him is the phenomenon of *Anderson localization*, describing the migration of impurities within a crystal. In the 1960s Anderson concentrated particularly on superconductivity and superfluidity, predicting the existence of resistance in superconductors and (with Pierre Morel) pointing out the nature of the possible superfluid states of ^{3}He. In 1971 he returned to disordered media, working on low-temperature properties of glass and later studying spin glasses.

Along with his Harvard tutor Van Vleck and the British physicist Nevill Mott, Anderson shared the 1977 Nobel Prize for physics "for their fundamental theoretical investigation of the electronic structure of magnetic and disordered systems."

Besides his post at Bell Laboratories

(where he is now consulting director for physics research) Anderson has worked as a part-time visiting professor at Cambridge University, England, and since 1975 has held a professorship at Princeton University.

ANDERSON, Thomas (b. July 2, 1819; Leith, Scotland; d. Nov. 2, 1874; London) British organic chemist.

After graduating in medicine from Edinburgh University in 1841, Anderson studied with Jons Berzelius and Justus von Liebig. He taught chemistry at Edinburgh and in 1852 succeeded Thomas Thompson as professor of chemistry at Glasgow University. He is remembered for his discovery of various organic bases in bone oil, the most notable of which was pyridine.

ANDRADE, Edward Neville da Costa (b. Dec. 27, 1887; London; d. Jan. 6, 1971; London) British physicist.

Andrade was educated at University College, London, and at Heidelberg where he obtained his PhD in 1911. He then worked with Ernest Rutherford at Manchester before joining the Royal Artillery in 1914. After the war he was appointed professor of physics at the Artillery College, Woolwich, and moved to a similar chair at University College, London, in 1928. Andrade resigned in 1950 to take up the directorship of the Royal Institution, a post he held until his retirement in 1952.

Andrade worked mainly on the physics of metals and the viscosity of liquids. On the former subject he made the first serious scientific study of creep in metals while on the latter subject he investigated the effect of an electric field on viscosity. In addition to writing a number of popular works on science, Andrade was also widely known as a student of 17th-century physics. He was an expert on Robert Hooke and as first chairman in 1938 of the Royal Society Newton letters committee he played an important role in beginning the monumental task of the publication of Newton's letters, a task requiring 40 years for its completion.

ANDREWS, Roy Chapman (b. Jan. 26, 1884; Beloit, Wisconsin; d. Mar. 11, 1960; Carmel, California) American naturalist and paleontologist.

Andrews was educated at Beloit College and took up a post at the American Museum of Natural History, New York, after graduating. His early interest lay in whales and other aquatic mammals, and these he collected assiduously on a number of museum-sponsored expeditions to Alaska, North Korea, and the Dutch East Indies (Indonesia) between 1908 and 1913. It was largely through Andrews's efforts that the collection of cetaceans at the American Museum of Natural History became one of the most complete in the world.

Andrews is best known for his discovery of previously unknown Asiatic fossils. Most of his findings were made on three expeditions to Asia, which he led as chief of the Asiatic Exploration Division of the American Museum of Natural History. The first of these was to Tibet, southwestern China, and Burma (1916–17); he then visited northern China and Outer Mongolia (1919), and central Asia (1921–22 and 1925). The third Asian expedition produced major finds of fossil reptiles and mammals, including remains of the largest known land mammal, the Paraceratherium (formerly called Baluchitherium), an Oligocene relative of the modern rhinoceros, which stood some 17–18 feet (5.5 m) at the shoulder. In Mongolia, Andrews discovered the first known fossil dinosaur eggs. He was also able to trace previously unknown geological strata, and unearthed evidence of primitive human life on the central Asian plateau.

Andrews was appointed director of the American Museum of Natural History in 1935, but resigned in 1942 in order to devote himself entirely to writing about his travels and discoveries.

ANDREWS, Thomas (b. Dec. 19, 1813; Belfast, now in Northern Ireland; d. Nov. 26, 1885; Belfast) Irish physical chemist.

The son of a linen merchant, Andrews studied chemistry under Thomas Thomson at Glasgow, under Jean Dumas in Paris, and under Justus von Liebig at Giessen. He also studied medicine at Edinburgh and obtained his MD in 1835. He practiced medicine in Belfast before becoming vice-president of Queen's College, Belfast, in 1845 and professor of chemistry in 1849.

Andrews made experimental studies on the heat evolved in chemical reactions and also showed that ozone is an allotrope of oxygen. He was a brilliant experimentalist and his work on the liquefaction of gases brought order to a confused subject. Andrews performed a famous series of experiments on the variation of the volume of carbon dioxide gas with pressure. He studied the behavior of the gas at different temperatures, and showed that there was a certain temperature — the critical temperature — above which the gas could not be liquefied by pressure alone. This work, which was published as *On the Continuity of the Liquid and Gaseous States of Matter* (1869) led to the liquefaction of those gases previously held to be 'permanent' gases.

ANFINSEN, Christian Boehmer (b. Mar. 26, 1916; Monessen, Pennsylvania) American biochemist.

Anfinsen was educated at Swarthmore College, the University of Pennsylvania, and Harvard, where he obtained his PhD in 1943. He taught at Harvard Medical School from 1943 to 1950, when he moved to the National Heart Institute at Bethesda, Maryland, where from 1952 to 1962 he served as head of the laboratory of cellular physiology. In 1963 Anfinsen joined the National Institute of Arthritis and Metabolic Diseases at Bethesda, where he was appointed head of the laboratory of chemical biology.

By 1960 Stanford Moore and William Stein had fully determined the sequence of the 124 amino acids in ribonuclease, the first enzyme to be so analyzed. Anfinsen, however, was more concerned with the shape and structure of the enzyme and the forces that permit it always to adopt the same unique configuration. The molecule of ribonuclease — a globular protein — consists of one chain twisted into a ball and held together by four disulfide bridges. By chemical means, the sulfur bridges can be separated so that the enzyme becomes a simple polypeptide chain with no power to hydrolyze ribonucleic acid, i.e. it becomes denatured. Once the bridges are broken they can be reunited in any one of 105 different ways. Anfinsen found that the minimum of chemical intervention — merely putting the enzyme into a favorable environment — was sufficient to induce the ribonuclease to adopt the one configuration that restores enzymatic activity.

The important conclusion Anfinsen drew from this observation was that all the information for the assembly of the three-dimensional protein must be contained in the protein's sequence of amino acids — its primary structure. He went on to show similar behavior in other proteins. For this work Anfinsen shared the 1972 Nobel Prize for physiology or medicine with Moore and Stein.

ÅNGSTROM, Anders Jonas (b. Aug. 13, 1814; Lögdö, Sweden; d. June 21, 1874; Uppsala, Sweden) Swedish physicist and astronomer.

Ångstrom was the son of a chaplain. He studied and taught physics and astronomy at the University of Uppsala, where he obtained his doctorate (1839) and later became professor of physics (1858), a position he held up to his death.

Ångstrom was one of the pioneers of spectroscopy. His most important work was *Optiska Undersökningar* (1853; Optical Investigations), in which he published measurements on atomic spectra, particularly of electric sparks. He noted spectral lines that were characteristic of both the gas and the electrodes used. Ångstrom applied Euler's theory of resonance to his measurements and deduced that a hot gas emits light at precisely the same wavelength at which it absorbs light when it is cool. In this he anticipated the experimental proof of Gustav Kirchhoff. He was also able to show the composite nature of the spectra of alloys.

Having established the principles of spectroscopy in the laboratory, Ångstrom turned his attention to the Sun's spectrum, publishing *Recherches sur le spectre solaire* (1868; Researches on the Solar Spectrum) in which he made the inference, important to astrophysics, that hydrogen was present in the Sun. In this work he also reported the wavelengths of some 1000 Fraunhofer lines measured to six significant figures in units of 10^{-8} centimeter. Since 1905 his name has been officially honored as a unit of length used by spectroscopists and microscopists; 1 Ångstrom = 10^{-8} cm. His map of the *Normal Solar Spectrum* (1869) became a standard reference for some 20 years. Ångstrom was also the first to examine the spectrum of the aurora borealis and to measure the characteristic bright yellow–green light sometimes named for him.

ANTONIADI, Eugène Michael (b. 1870; Constantinople, now Istanbul, Turkey; d. Feb. 10, 1944; Meudon, France) Greek-French astronomer.

Antoniadi established quite early a reputation as a brilliant observer and in 1893 was invited by Camille Flammarion to work at his observatory at Juvisy near Paris. From 1909 he worked mainly with the 33-inch (84-cm) refracting telescope at the observatory at Meudon. He became a French citizen in 1928.

In his two works *La Planète Mars* (1930) and *La Planète Mercure* (1934) Antoniadi published the results of many years' observations and presented the best maps of Mars and Mercury to appear until the space probes of recent times. With regard to Mars he took the strong line: "Nobody has ever seen a genuine canal on Mars," attributing the "completely illusory canals", 'seen' by astronomers such as Percival Lowell and Flammarion, to irregular natural features of the Martian surface. Antoniadi also observed the great Martian storms of 1909, 1911, and 1924 noting after the last one, that the planet had become covered with yellow clouds and presented a color similar to Jupiter.

On Mercury his observations made between 1914 and 1929 seemed to confirm Giovanni Schiaparelli's rotation period of 88 days, identical with the planet's period of revolution around the Sun. The effect of this would be for Mercury always to turn the same face to the Sun, in the same way as the Moon always turns the same face to the Earth. Antoniadi cited nearly 300 observations of identifiable features always in the same position, as required by the 88-day rotation period.

However radar studies of Mercury in 1965 revealed a 59-day rotation period for Mercury. This time is however very close to half the synodic period of Mercury (116 days) so that when the planet returns to the same favorable viewing position in the sky, at intervals of 116 days, it does present the same face to observers.

Antoniadi also wrote on the history of astronomy, publishing *L'Astronomie Égyptienne* in 1934.

APKER, Leroy (b. June 11, 1915; Rochester, New York) American physicist.

Apker was educated at the University of Rochester where he obtained his PhD in 1941. He later joined the staff of General Electric where he has worked as a research associate.

Apker has worked on the photoelectric effect applied to semiconductors and ionic crystals. A particular aspect of his work has been photoemission from the alkali-metal halides, such as potassium iodide. Crystals of these compounds can contain a type of defect involving a missing negative ion replaced by an electron — called a 'color center' (because such defects color the crystal). Apker has studied the photoemission from such crystals, and the interaction of excitons with color centers causing the ejection of electrons.

APOLLONIUS of Perga (b. *c.* 262 BC; Perga, now in Turkey; d. *c.* 190 BC Alexandria, Egypt) Greek mathematician and geometer.

Apollonius studied in Alexandria possibly under pupils of Euclid, and later he taught there himself. One of the great Greek geometers, Apollonius's major work was in the study of conic sections and the only one of his many works to have survived is his eight-book work on this subject, the *Conics*. Apollonius's work on conics makes full use of the work of his predecessors, notable Euclid and Conon of Samos, but it is a great advance in terms of its thoroughness and systematic treatment. The *Conics* also contains a large number of important new theorems that are entirely Apollonius's creation. He was the first to define the parabola, hyperbola, and ellipse. In addition, he considered the general problem of finding normals from a given point to a given curve (i.e. lines at right angles to a tangent at a point on the curve).

Apart from the geometrical work that has survived, Apollonius is known to have contributed to optics — in particular to the study of the properties of mirrors of various shapes. This work, however, is now lost.

APPERT, Nicolas-François (b. *c.* 1750; Chalôns-sur-Marne, France; d. June 3, 1841; Massy, near Paris) French inventor.

Appert was a chef, confectioner, and distiller who invented the canning of food. In 1795 he started to experiment with sealed containers, using corked glass sealed with wax. He succeeded in preserving fruits, soups, marmalades, etc., for several years. To claim a 12 000-franc award in

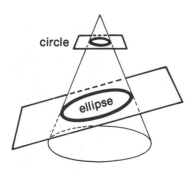 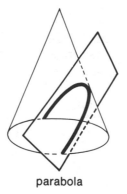 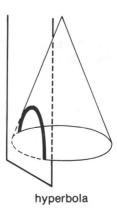

CONIC SECTIONS The curves are formed by cutting a conical surface at different angles.

1810 he published his findings in *L'art de conserver, pendant plusiers années, toutes les substances animal et végétales* (The Art of Preserving All Kinds of Animal and Vegetable Substances for Several Years). He used the money to set up the first commercial cannery in the world, the House of Appert, at Massy, which was open from 1812 to 1833.

APPLETON, Sir Edward Victor (b. Sept. 6, 1892; Bradford, England; d. Apr. 21, 1965; Edinburgh) British physicist.

Appleton studied physics at Cambridge University from 1910 to 1913. During World War I, while he was serving in the Royal Engineers, he developed the interest in radio that was to influence his later research. After the war he returned to Cambridge and worked in the Cavendish Laboratory from 1920. In 1924 he was appointed Wheatstone Professor of Experimental Physics at King's College, London.

Here, in his first year, he used a BBC transmitter to conduct a famous experiment, which established beyond doubt the presence of a layer of ionized gas in the upper atmosphere capable of reflecting radio waves. The existence of such a layer had been postulated by Oliver Heaviside and Arthur Kennelly to explain Marconi's transatlantic radio transmissions. By varying the frequency of a transmitter in Bournemouth and detecting the signal some 140 miles (225 km) away in Cambridge, he showed that interference occurred between direct (ground) waves and waves reflected off the layer (sky waves). Furthermore, the experiment measured the height of the layer, which he estimated at 60 miles (96 km). He proceeded to do theoretical work on the reflection or transmission of radio waves by an ionized layer and found, using further measurements, a second layer above the Heaviside–Kennelly layer. The *Appleton layer* undergoes daily fluctuations in ionization and he established a link between these variations and the occurrence of sunspots.

In 1936 he became the Jacksonian Professor of Natural Philosophy at Cambridge, and during the war years until 1949 he was secretary of the department of scientific and industrial research, in which period he led research into radar and the atomic bomb.

For his great achievements in ionospheric physics he was knighted in 1941 and in 1947 won the Nobel Physics Prize. From 1949 until his death he was principal of Edinburgh University.

ARAGO, Dominique François Jean (b. Feb. 26, 1786; Estagel, France; d. Oct. 2, 1853; Paris) French physicist.

Arago was educated at the Ecole Polytechnique and then spent some years in Spain, where he accompanied Jean Bap-

23

tiste Biot on a measurement of an arc of meridian. On his return to Paris in 1809 he was elected to the Académie des Sciences and received the chair of analytical geometry at the Ecole Polytechnique. In 1830 he succeeded J.B.J. Fourier as the permanent secretary of the Ecole Polytechnique. Arago worked in a number of branches of physics.

His first investigations concerned the polarization of light and in 1811 he discovered chromatic polarization. He was a vigorous defender of A.J. Fresnel's wave theory of light against the criticisms of Pierre Simon Laplace and Jean Baptiste Biot, who both supported the corpuscular theory. In 1838 he described an experiment to decide the issue by comparing the velocity of light in air and in a denser medium. Shortly before Arago's death, Léon Foucault and Armand Fizeau proved that the experiment supported the wave theory.

Arago also worked on electromagnetism, showing that a coil of wire carrying a current could act as a magnet. He also found that a rotating copper disk could deflect a magnetic needle suspended above it. (This arrangement, known as *Arago's disk*, depends on magnetic induction.)

In astronomy, Arago discovered the Sun's chromosphere. He also played a part in the discovery of Neptune by Urbain Leverrier.

Arago was a fierce republican and, from 1830 onward, he was involved in political life as deputy for the Pyrénées Orientales. In 1848 he became a government minister and, among other measures, abolished slavery in the French colonies.

ARBER, Werner (b. June 3, 1929; Gränichen, Switzerland) Swiss microbiologist.

Arber graduated from the Swiss Federal Institute of Technology in 1953 and gained his PhD from the University of Geneva in 1958. He spent a year at the University of Southern California before returning to Geneva where he became professor of molecular genetics in 1965. In 1970 Arber moved to Basel to take the chair of molecular biology.

In the early 1950s Giuseppe Bertani reported a phenomenon he described as 'host-controlled variation' in which phage (the viruses that infect bacteria) successfully growing on one host found it difficult to establish themselves on a different bacterium. In 1962 Arber proposed that bacteria possess highly specific enzymes capable of destroying invading phage by cutting up their DNA. The existence of such 'restriction enzymes' as they came to be called was later established by Hamilton Smith.

It turned out that, as Arber had proposed, the enzymes attack the invading DNA at a specific site, always cutting them at exactly the same place. It was this property that endowed restriction enzymes with such interest for if strands of DNA could be so manipulated to be cut at particular known points, it only needed the power to join such strands together in desired combinations for genetic engineering to be a reality. As restriction enzymes were found to leave DNA strands 'sticky' and ready to combine with certain other 'sticky' strands it was soon apparent to molecular biologists that genetic engineering was at last a practical proposition.

For his work on restriction enzymes Arber shared the 1978 Nobel Prize for physiology or medicine with Smith and Daniel Nathans.

ARCHIMEDES (b. 287 BC; Syracuse, now in Sicily; d. 212 BC; Syracuse) Greek mathematician.

Archimedes' father was an astronomer and he himself inherited an interest in the subject. He was educated in Alexandria and spent most of the rest of his life in Syracuse under the patronage of King Hieron. Archimedes was without question the greatest mathematician and scientist that classical Greek civilization produced and is usually considered to be one of the greatest mathematicians of all time. He was held in very high regard even by his contemporaries, and Karl Friedrich Gauss thought that only Isaac Newton was Archimedes' equal as a mathematician. Archimedes was as much an applied mathematician as a pure mathematician. He was very much interested in putting his theoretical discoveries to practical use and is known to have been skilled in making his own equipment and carrying out his own experiments. It is no exaggeration to describe Archimedes as the creator of the science of mechanics. Naturally before his time many isolated facts had been discovered, but it was only with him that mechanics became a unified body of theory capable of yielding new and unexpected practical applications.

Archimedes was able to find methods for determining the center of gravity of a variety of bodies. He also gave the first general theory of levers, and organized a practical demonstration to show how, with a suitable series of levers, a very small force is capable of moving a very large weight. He amazed his contemporaries by arranging for the king of Syracuse to move a large ship simply by pressing a small lever. In connection with his work on levers Archimedes made one of his famous statements, "Give me a place to stand on and I will move the Earth." Archimedes also had a practical interest in optics, although no writings of his on the subject have come down to us. He put all this new-found theoretical knowledge to deadly effect when Syracuse was besieged by the Romans, by designing and building a variety of war machines. Among these were enormous mirrors to focus the Sun's rays and set fire to the Roman ships, and a variety of catapults.

Archimedes also successfully applied his scientific discoveries in hydrostatics. He designed all sorts of pumps, and the *Archimedean water-screw* is still widely used. But his most famous practical success was in solving a problem presented to him by King Hieron. Hieron wished to know whether a newly made crown, which was supposed to be of pure gold was, as he suspected, partly silver. Archimedes solved the problem by grasping the concept of

relative density. If the crown was pure gold it would displace less water than if it was partly silver. So by immersing successively the crown itself and pieces of gold and silver of equal weight in full containers of water and observing the amount of water each displaced, Archimedes was able to show that the crown was indeed not made of pure gold. One of the famous stories associated with Archimedes tells how this occurred to him when he was getting into his bath and observed how the more of his body was immersed the more water overflowed from the bath. He saw instantly how to solve his problem, leaped from the bath, and rushed through the streets, stark naked, shouting "Eureka!" (I have found it).

Archimedes' work in applied mathematics and science ensured him great contemporary fame, but some of his greatest work was probably in his more esoteric researches in pure mathematics. Like all Greek mathematicians, his work was primarily concentrated on geometry. Arithmetic was greatly hampered by a very cumbersome system of notation. Although Archimedes himself invented a much improved system for notating very large numbers, algebra had yet to be invented, in Europe at least. Archimedes' most profound achievement was to perfect the 'method of exhaustion' for calculating the areas and volumes of curved figures. The method involves successively approximating the figure concerned by inscribed and circumscribed polygons. This method essentially used the concept of limit — a concept that took some time for later European mathematicians to grasp. Archimedes used this method to determine an approximate value for π, which was not to be improved on for many centuries.

Archimedes was put to death by a Roman soldier when the Romans, under general Marcellus, finally successfully besieged Syracuse. The killing was against the orders of Marcellus who respected Archimedes and wished for him to be protected. Archimedes was apparently drawing mathematical symbols in the sand when killed.

ARGELANDER, Friedrich Wilhelm August (b. Mar. 22, 1799; Memel, now Klaipeda, Soviet Union; d. Feb. 17, 1875; Bonn, now in West Germany) German astronomer.

Argelander studied at Königsberg where he was a student and later an assistant of Friedrich Bessel. In 1837 he became director of the Bonn Observatory. His major achievement took him 25 years to complete; from 1837 to 1862 he plotted all the stars from the north celestial pole to two degrees south of the celestial equator, down to the ninth magnitude — a task that involved working out the coordinates of 324 189 stars. The results were published in the four volumes of the famous *Bonner Durchmusterung* (1859–62; Bonn Survey). Stars are still identified by their number in Argelander's work, although it has been somewhat revised.

ARISTARCHUS of Samos (b. *c.* 320 BC; Samos, Greece; d. *c.* 250 BC; Alexandria, Egypt) Greek astronomer.

Little is known of the life of Aristarchus, but Archimedes reported that Aristarchus had proposed that, while the Sun and the fixed stars are motionless, the Earth moves around the Sun on the circumference of a circle. Just what led Aristarchus to this view and how firmly he held it is not known. It received no support until the late medieval period.

One short work of Aristarchus has survived — *On the Sizes and Distances of the Sun and Moon*. In this work he calculated that the Earth is about 18 times further away from the Sun than from the Moon. His method was to use the fact that when the Moon is exactly in the second quarter it will form a right-angled triangle with the Earth and the Sun, and the relative lengths of the sides of the triangle can be determined by angular measurement. Aristarchus's method is correct, but his measurement was inaccurate (the Sun is roughly 400 times further away). Despite the size of the error it was nevertheless the first attempt to come to grips with astronomical distances by something more sophisticated than revelation or guesswork.

ARISTOTLE (b. 384 BC; Stagira, Greece; d. 322 BC; Chalcis, Greece) Greek philosopher, logician, and scientist.

Aristotle, the son of Nicomachus, physician at the court of Mayntas II of Macedon, moved to Athens in 367 BC where he was a member of the academy until Plato's death in 347. For the next 12 years he worked in Assos in Asia Minor, Mytilene on Lesbos, and, from 342 until 335, in Macedon as the tutor of the young Alexander the Great. Unfortunately little is known of this legendary relationship apart from the fact that Alexander took with him on his campaigns a copy of Homer's *Iliad* annotated by Aristotle. Also, Plutarch quotes a letter from Alexander rebuking his former tutor for publishing his *Metaphysics* and revealing to all what had been privately and, he assumed, exclusively taught to him. Following Alexander's accession to the throne of Macedon in 335 Aristotle returned to Athens to found his own school, the Lyceum. When, however, Athens, with little cause to love the power of Macedon, heard of the death of Alexander (323) they turned against Aristotle and accused him, as they had Socrates earlier in the century, of impiety. To prevent Athens from "sinning twice against philosophy" he moved to Chalcis where he died the following year.

Aristotle not only developed an original and systematic philosophy but applied it in a deliberate manner to most areas of the knowledge of his day. The resulting treatises on such subjects as physics, cosmology, embryology, and mineralogy acquired a considerable authority, becoming for medieval scholars if not the last word on any subject then invariably the first. Aristotelian science was not overthrown until the great scientific revolution of the 16th and 17th centuries.

In cosmology Aristotle basically accepted the scheme in which the Earth was at the center of the universe with the planets and fixed stars moving around it with uniform speed in perfectly circular orbits. (He also believed, on empirical grounds, that the Earth was round.) But Aristotle was not content simply to construct models of the universe and faced the problem of how to account for the various forms of motion. He began by accepting that matter was composed of the four elements of Empedocles — earth, water, fire, and air. Left to themselves the elements would either fall freely, like earth and water, or rise naturally like air and fire. This for Aristotle was natural motion, self-explanatory and consisting simply of bodies freely falling or rising to their natural place in the universe. For a stone to fall to the ground no one had to push or pull it but merely to remove all constraints for it to fall in a straight line to the Earth.

But the heavenly bodies do not move up or down in straight lines. Therefore, Aristotle concluded, they must consist of a fifth element, aether (or *quinta essentia* to the medieval schoolmen) whose natural motion was circular. Thus in the Aristotelian universe different bodies obey different laws; celestial and terrestrial bodies move differently because the laws of motion are different in the heavens from those operating below the Moon. Nor was this the only distinction. For Aristotle the heavens were, with their supposed regularity, incorruptible, without change or decay; such processes were only too apparent on the Earth.

Aristotle also produced a number of volumes on biological problems. In particular his *De partibus animalium* (On the Parts of Animals) and his *De generatione animalium* (On the Generation of Animals) show a detailed knowledge of the fauna of the Mediterranean world and a concern to understand their anatomy and physiology. Over 500 species of animal are referred to by Aristotle. He was also a keen observer and had obviously made empirical investigations on the development of the chick embryo for example, noting the appearance of its heart on the fourth day. In fact some of his observations were only confirmed by zoologists in the 19th century

and had for long been thought to be as erroneous as his physics.

In embryology he was also able to refute by dissection the view that the sex of the embryo is determined by its site in the womb. He also argued against the doctrine of pangenesis, that the seed comes from the whole of the body, as he also did against the classical version of preformationism, that the embryo contains all parts already preformed. His physiology, which could not be obtained so readily from simple dissection, was less acute. Respiration was thought to cool the body, an exercise unnecessary for fish who could cool themselves merely by drawing water through their gills.

He, further, produced a rudimentary taxonomy that went to some length to show that divisions based on number of limbs turned out to be obviously arbitrary. Instead, he proposed that mode of reproduction be used. This gave him the basic division between viviparous (exclusively mammalian) and the oviparous, subdivided into birds and reptiles laying proper eggs and the fishes laying 'imperfect eggs'. He added the insects, who lay no eggs at all but simply produce larvae.

If Aristotle had produced only his *Organon* — works on logic — he would have been considered a prolific and powerful thinker. His style of logic lasted unchallenged even longer than his physics for it was not until 1847 that George Boole laid the foundations of a more modern logic and it was not until the present century that non-Aristotelian logics were systematically developed.

ARKWRIGHT, Sir Richard (b. Dec. 23, 1732; Preston, England; d. Aug. 3, 1792; Cromford, England) British inventor.

Arkwright was apprenticed to a barber at the age of 18 and became a wigmaker. Through travel and self-education he developed an interest in spinning machinery and in 1769 he patented a water-powered machine that unlike previous machines produced a cotton yarn strong enough for use as warp. This machine was used in the horse-driven mill he established at Nottingham (1768) to produce machine-spun yarn. In 1771 he set up a water-powered mill in Cromford, Derbyshire, and in the following years established a number of factories employing machinery for all processes of textile manufacture from carding to spinning. This established the cotton industry as the main industry in the north of England. He was knighted in 1786 and died a wealthy man.

ARMSTRONG, Henry Edward (b. May 6, 1848; Lewisham, near London; d. July 13, 1937; London) British chemist and teacher.

The son of a London provisions merchant, Armstrong studied under Frankland at the Royal College of Chemistry and completed his doctorate in 1870 under Adolph Kolbe at Leipzig. A man of great energy and wide interests, he was a pioneer of British technical education, a prolific researcher, and leader of a major school of chemical research. After various teaching posts in London, he was appointed (1884–1911) professor at the Central Technical College in London (forerunner of the Imperial College of Science and Technology). He served on many committees and was secretary (1883–93) and later president (1893–95) of the Chemical Society.

Armstrong's research work covered many fields, including aromatic substitution, crystallography, stereochemistry, terpenes, and enzymes. He proposed the quinone theory of color and the work carried out by his school on orientation and isomeric change in naphthalene derivatives, although little regarded in Britain, was of fundamental importance to the German dyestuffs industry.

ARNALD of Villanova (b. c. 1235; Valencia, Spain; d. 1313; at sea) Spanish alchemist.

Arnald was educated in Paris and Montpellier, and studied medicine at Naples. He became a famous physician much in demand by popes and monarchs. In 1285 he became a professor at the University at Montpellier, but came into conflict with the Church in 1299 and was charged with heresy in Paris. He was imprisoned but finally released about 1303 and died at sea between Naples and Genoa in about 1313.

Arnald was one of the first scholars to mention alcohol. In medicine he used it to extract the 'virtues of herbs', which became known as tinctures. Some of his other medical ideas were less progressive: he wrote at length on the efficacy of seals and amulets claiming to be able to provide one that would defend its wearer from witchcraft, storms, quinsy, inflammation of the brain, and financial difficulties.

He produced many works on medicine, most notably, *Medicinalium introductionum speculum*, and also works on theology and chemistry. The many alchemical works, including *Rosarius philosophorum*, that were attributed to him and that had considerable influence in the following centuries are now not thought to be his work.

ARRHENIUS, Svante August (b. Feb. 19, 1859; Wijk, near Uppsala, Sweden; d. Oct. 2, 1927; Stockholm) Swedish physical chemist.

Arrhenius originally went to Uppsala University to study chemistry, changing later to physics. Finding the standard mediocre, he transferred to Stockholm in 1881 to do research under the physicist Erik Edlund, working initially on electrical polarization and then on the conductivity of solutions (electrolytes).

At the time it was known that solutions of certain compounds conduct electricity and that chemical reactions could occur when a current was passed. It was thought that the current decomposed the substance. In 1883 Arrhenius proposed a theory that substances were partly converted into an active form when dissolved.

The active part was responsible for conductivity. In the case of acids and bases, he correlated the strength with the degree of decomposition on solution. This work was published as *Recherches sur la conductibilité galvanique des electrolytes* (1884; Researches on the Electrical Conductivity of Electrolytes) and submitted as his doctoral dissertation. The paper's great merit was not recognized by the Swedish authorities and he was awarded only a fourth-class doctorate. Arrhenius sent his work to several leading physical chemists, including Jacobus van't Hoff, Friedrich Ostwald, and Rudolf Clausius, who were immediately impressed. This led to a period of travel and work in various European laboratories in the period 1885–91.

In 1887 van't Hoff showed that although the gas law (pV = RT) could be applied to the osmotic pressure of solutions, certain solutions behaved as if there were more molecules than expected. Arrhenius immediately realized that this was due to dissociation — a conclusion confirmed by further experimental work and published in the classic paper *Über die Dissociation der in Wasser gelösten Stoffe* (1887; On the Dissociation of Substances in Water). The idea that electrolytes were dissociated even without a current being passed proved difficult for many chemists but the theory has stood the test of time.

This work won Arrhenius a high international reputation but only limited acclaim in Sweden. Despite this he returned to Stockholm in 1891 as lecturer at the Technical Institute and in 1895 became professor there. In 1903 he was awarded the Nobel Prize for chemistry and in 1905 he became the director of the Nobel Institute, a post he held until shortly before his death.

Arrhenius was a man of wide-ranging intellect and besides developing his work on solutions, in later life he worked on cosmogony and on serum therapy, being especially interested in the relation between toxins and antitoxins. He also investigated the greenhouse effect by which carbon dioxide regulates atmospheric temperature and calculated the changes that would have been necessary to have produced the Ice Ages.

ASCHOFF, Karl Albert Ludwig (b. Jan. 10, 1866; Berlin; d. June 24, 1942; Freiburg-im-Breisgau, now in West Germany) German pathologist.

Educated at Bonn, Berlin, and Strasbourg, Aschoff was later professor of pathological anatomy, firstly at Marburg (1903–06) and then at Freiburg, where he remained for the rest of his career. He carried out investigations of a number of human pathological conditions, including jaundice, appendicitis, cholecystitis, tuberculosis, and thrombosis. In 1904 he described the inflammatory nodules located in the muscle of the heart and associated with rheumatism (*Aschoff's bodies*). He recognized the bacteria-engulfing activity of the phagocytes in various tissues and named them the reticuloendothelial system. The pathological institute that Aschoff built up at Freiburg was attended by students from all over the world.

ASELLI, Gaspare (b. *c.* 1581; Cremona, Italy; d. Sept. 9, 1625; Milan, Italy) Italian anatomist.

Aselli, who came from a prosperous family, was educated at the University of Pavia where he later served as professor of anatomy and surgery.

In 1622 while dissecting a recently fed dog he noticed various white vessels spread throughout the intestines. As they exuded a milky fluid when pricked he called them the 'lacteals' or the 'albas venas'. He claimed to trace them to the liver and not unnaturally assumed them to be the vessels transporting the chyle, broken down food products, to the liver to be changed into blood — a process demanded by the current physiology of Galen. Aselli's observations were fully described in the posthumously published work, *De lactibus*

29

(1627), a work that also contained the first colored anatomical illustrations.

It was not until 1651 that Jean Pecquet showed that lacteals did not go to the liver.

ASTBURY, William Thomas (b. Feb. 25, 1889; Longton, England; d. June 4, 1961; Leeds, England) British x-ray crystallographer and molecular biologist.

William Astbury was the son of a potter. In 1916 he won a scholarship to Cambridge University, to study chemistry, physics, and mathematics, and graduated in 1921 after spending two years of the war doing x-ray work for the army. He then joined William Henry Bragg's brilliant group of crystallographers, first at University College, London, and from 1923 at the Royal Institution. In 1945 Astbury was appointed to the new chair of biomolecular structure at Leeds.

Astbury's early structural studies were carried out on tartaric acid but in 1926 Bragg asked him to prepare some x-ray photographs of fibers for his lectures. The results stimulated an interest in biological macromolecules that Astbury retained for the rest of his life. In 1928 he moved to the University of Leeds as lecturer in textile physics and by 1930 had produced an explanation of the extensibility of wool in terms of two keratin structures: α-keratin in which the polypeptides were hexagonally folded (unextended wool) and β-keratin in which the chain was drawn out in zigzag fashion. A popular account of this work was given in *Fundamentals of Fibre Structure* (1933).

The keratin structure established his reputation, and he quickly extended his studies to other fibers and proteins. He showed that the globular proteins consisted of three-dimensionally folded chains that could be denatured and drawn out into protein fibers. This work laid the foundation for the x-ray structural investigations of hemoglobin and myoglobin. The hexagonal α-keratin structure dominated British crystallographic protein studies until 1951, when it was shown to be

incorrect by Linus Pauling who demonstrated the α-helical structure of polypeptide chains.

In 1935 Astbury began to study nucleic acids by x-ray crystallography, and in 1938 he and his research student Florence Bell produced the first hypothetical structure of DNA.

ASTON, Francis William (b. Sept. 1, 1877; Harborne, England; d. Nov. 20, 1945; Cambridge, England) British chemist and physicist.

Aston was the son of a metal merchant. He was educated at Mason College, the forerunner of Birmingham University, where he studied chemistry. From 1898 until 1900 he did research under P.F. Frankland on optical rotation. He left Birmingham in 1900 to work in a Wolverhampton brewery for three years. During this time he continued with scientific research in a home laboratory, where he worked on the production of vacua for x-ray discharge tubes. This work came to the notice of J.H. Poynting of the University of Birmingham who invited Aston to work with him. He remained at Birmingham until 1910 when he moved to Cambridge as research assistant to J.J. Thomson. He became a research fellow at Cambridge in 1920 and stayed there for the rest of his life, apart from the war years spent at the Royal Aircraft Establishment, Farnborough. Aston's main work, for which he received the Nobel Prize for chemistry in 1922, was on the design and use of the mass spectrograph, which was used to clear up several outstanding problems and became one of the basic tools of the new atomic physics.

Thomson had invented an earlier form of spectrograph in which a beam of positive rays from a discharge tube passed through a magnetic and an electric field, which deflected the beam both horizontally and vertically. All particles (ions) with the same mass fell onto a fluorescent screen in a parabola. Aston improved the design by arranging the fields such that ions of the same mass were focused in a straight line rather than a parabola. Different ions were deflected by different amounts, and the spectrograph produced a photographic record of a series of lines, each corresponding to one type of ion. The deflections allowed accurate calculation of the mass of the ions.

Aston's first spectrograph was ready in 1919 and with it he was soon able to throw light on one outstanding problem about the nature of the elements. In 1816 William Prout had put forward his hypothesis that all elements are built up from the hydrogen atom and that their atomic weights are integral multiples of that of hydrogen. Although receiving considerable support it was eventually rejected when it was found that many elements have non-integral weights (e.g. chlorine: 35.453). Frederick Soddy in 1913 had introduced the idea of isotopes; that is, the same chemical element in different forms having differing weights. Aston established that isotopes are not restricted to radioactive elements but are common throughout the periodic table. He also saw that they could explain Prout's hypothesis. Thus he found that neon was made from the two isotopes ^{20}Ne and ^{22}Ne in the proportion of 10 to 1. This will give a weighted average of 20.2 for a large number of neon atoms. The value of 35.453 for chlorine can be similarly explained. The whole-number rule is his principle that atoms have a mass that is equivalent to a whole number of hydrogen atoms.

Aston then went on to determine as many atomic weights as accurately as his instruments would allow. His first spectrograph was only suitable for gases but by 1927 he had introduced a new model capable of dealing with solids. From 1927 to 1935 he resurveyed the atomic weights of the elements with his new spectrograph.

In the course of this activity he found some minor discrepancies with the whole-number rule. Thus the atomic weight of hydrogen is given not as 1 but 1.008, of oxygen–16 as 15.9949 and of oxygen–17 as 16.99913. Aston attempted to show why these values are so tantalizingly close to

the integral values of Prout — why the isotopes of oxygen are not simply 16 and 17 times as massive as the hydrogen atom. He argued that the missing mass is in fact, by the mass–energy equivalence of Einstein, not really missing but present as the binding energy of the nucleus. By dividing the missing mass by the mass number and multiplying by 10 000, Aston went on to calculate what was later called the 'packing fraction' and is a measure of the stability of the atom and the amount of energy required to break up or transform the nucleus.

Thus, contained in Aston's work were the implications of atomic energy and destruction and he believed in the possibility of using nuclear energy — he also warned of the dangers. He lived just long enough to see the dropping of the first atomic bomb in August 1945.

AUDUBON, John James (b. Apr. 26, 1785; Les Cayes, Haiti; d. Jan. 27, 1851; New York City) American ornithologist and naturalist.

Audubon was the son of a French sea captain who had fought for George Washington at Yorktown. He was brought up in Paris, where he studied art. He then went to Pennsylvania, where his father had estates, to become a planter, but turned to merchandizing and portrait painting, and to those studies of American birds that made his name. Travels through primeval forests and along rivers, such as the Ohio and Mississippi, provided material for bird paintings that eventually appeared in *The Birds of America* (1827–38) and other ornithological works. Audubon was one of the first of America's conservationists. He also made some pioneering studies of bird migration, by means of ringing. In his later years he turned to the study of mammals, producing (with John Bachman) *The Viviparous Quadrupeds of North America* (1845–49).

AUENBRUGGER VON AUENBRUGG, Joseph Leopold (b. Nov. 19, 1722; Graz, Austria; d. May 18, 1809; Vienna) Austrian physician.

Auenbrugger learned medicine at the University of Vienna and subsequently worked (1751–62) at the Spanish Hospital, Vienna, where he became chief physician. In the course of his work, he noticed how the note made by tapping the chest altered between healthy and diseased patients and described how this technique of chest percussion could be used to diagnose congestion of the lungs and other conditions. Auenbrugger published his findings in *Inventum novum* (1761) but their value was slow in gaining recognition. Only after a French translation by Jean-Nicholas Corvisart in 1808 did chest percussion achieve widespread application. It is still used today.

Auenbrugger became one of Vienna's most celebrated physicians and was ennobled by Emperor Joseph II in 1784.

AUER, Karl, Baron von Welsbach (b. Sept. 1, 1858; Vienna; d. Aug. 4, 1929; Triebach, Austria) Austrian chemist.

Auer was the son of the director of the Imperial Printing Press in Vienna. He was educated at the Vienna Polytechnic and at Heidelberg University, where he was a pupil of Robert Bunsen.

In 1885 he made a major contribution to knowledge of the lanthanoid (rare-earth) elements. In 1840, Carl Mosander had isolated a new 'element' called didymium. Auer showed (1885) that this contained, on fractionation, green and rose-red portions. He named them *praseodymia* ('green twin') and *neodymia* ('new twin').

Auer was also one of the first to find some use for the rare-earth elements. Gas had been in use as an illuminant since the beginning of the century and, although an improvement on the early oil lamps, it had many disadvantages of its own. It was expensive, hot, smoky, and smelly. Auer realized that it would be better to use the gas to heat a solid that would itself provide light, rather than use the luminosity of the flame. He used a mantle over the flame, impregnated with thorium oxide and a small amount of cerium. The *Welsbach mantle*, patented in 1885, delayed the end of gas lighting for a few years. Unfortunately for Auer, his invention was too late for, in 1879, Edison had managed to burn an electric bulb for 40 continuous hours.

Later, in 1898, Auer tried to improve the electric lamp by replacing its carbonized filament by metallic osmium, which had a melting point of 2700°C. Once more he failed, for the future lay with tungsten, which has a higher melting point of 3410°C.

He was more successful with the so-called *Auer metal* — an alloy consisting mainly of cerium with other lanthanoid elements. It is also called Mischmetal (German: mixed metal) and is widely used as flints in cigarette lighters.

AUGER, Pierre Victor (b. May 14, 1899; Paris) French physicist.

Auger was educated at the Ecole Normale Supérieure where he obtained his doctorate in 1926. He was later appointed to the staff of the University of Paris and after serving there as professor of physics from 1937 became director of higher education for France in 1945. From 1948 until 1960 he was director of the science department of UNESCO; he left UNESCO to become president of the French Space Commission but in 1964 he took the post of director-general of the European Space and Research Organization, a post he retained until his retirement in 1967.

Auger's work has mainly been on nuclear physics and cosmic rays. In 1925 he discovered the *Auger effect* in which an excited atom emits an electron (rather than a photon) in reverting to a lower energy state. In 1938 Auger made a careful study of 'air showers', a cascade of particles produced by a cosmic ray entering the atmosphere and later known as an *Auger shower*.

AVERROËS, Abu al-Walid Muhammad Ibn Ahmad Ibn Rushd (b. 1126, Cordoba, Spain; d. Dec. 10, 1198; Marrakesh, now in Morocco) Spanish-Muslim physician and philosopher.

Averroës, also known simply as The Commentator to the Latin West, or Ibn Rushd, came from a family of jurists. He himself trained in law and medicine and later served as *qadi* or judge in Seville and Cordoba. In 1182 he was appointed physician to the court of caliph Abu Ya'qub Yusuf in Marrakesh in 1182 and to his son, Abu Yusuf Ya'qub, in 1195 but was recalled shortly before his death.

In the field of medicine Averroës produced his *Kulliyat fi al tib* (General Medicine) between 1162 and 1169. He is however better known for his great commentaries on Aristotle but, above all, for his *Tahafut al-Tahafut* (The Incoherence of the Incoherence), a strong attack on the Muslim philosopher al-Ghazzali's *Tahafut al-Falasifah* (The Incoherence of the Philosophers). The work was more influential in the Latin Christian West than in the Muslim East, and its contents paved the way for the medieval separation of faith and reason.

AVERY, Oswald Theodore (b. Oct. 21, 1877; Halifax, Nova Scotia; d. Feb. 20, 1955; Nashville, Tennessee) American bacteriologist.

Educated at Colgate University, Avery received his AB in 1900 and his medical degree in 1904. After a time at the Hoagland Laboratory, New York, as a lecturer and researcher in bacteriology, he joined the Rockefeller Institute Hospital (1913–48). While investigating the pneumococcus bacteria responsible for causing lobar pneumonia, Avery found that the bacteria produced soluble substances, derived from the cell wall and identified as polysaccharides, that were specific in their chemical composition for each different type of pneumococcus. This work provided a basis for establishing the immunologic identity of a cell in biochemical terms.

In 1932 Avery started work on the phenomenon of transformation in bacteria. It had already been shown that heat-killed cells of a virulent pneumococcus strain could transform a living avirulent strain into the virulent form. In 1944 Avery and his colleagues Maclyn McCarty and Colin MacLeod extracted and purified the transforming substance and showed it to be deoxyribonucleic acid (DNA). Previously it had been thought that protein was the hereditary material and thus Avery's work was an important step toward the eventual discovery, made nine years later by James Watson and Francis Crick, of the chemical basis of heredity.

AVICENNA (Abu-'Ali al-Husayn ibn-Sina) (b. 980; Bokhara, now in the Soviet Union; d. June, 1037; Hamadan, Iran) Persian physician and philosopher.

Avicenna, whose works span the entire spectrum of arts and sciences, is one of the most famous figures of Persian culture. A child prodigy, he learned and practiced medicine in his teens and was appointed court physician to Prince Nuh ibn Mansur when still only 18. This gave Avicenna access to the library of the Samanid court, of which he took full advantage. However, the Samanid rulers were overthrown by Turkish forces and Avicenna was forced to flee. After a period spent traveling and in several short-lived posts, he became physician to Prince Shams ad-Dawlah in Hamadan. Here he started on a massive medical textbook, the *Canon* (*Al Qanun*). In this, Avicenna collated virtually all preceding medical knowledge and set down his own ideas. Comprising five books, the *Canon* deals with anatomy, physiology, etiology, diagnosis, obstetrics, drugs, and so on, and runs to over one million words. It subsequently became a standard text throughout Europe and the Middle East until the 17th century, being translated into Hebrew and Latin. During this period, he also wrote his *Book of Healing*, a comprehensive encyclopedia covering mathematics, logic, natural sciences, and metaphysics and based largely on the ideas of Aristotle and other Greek philosophers.

In 1022, the death of Prince ad-Dawlah caused Avicenna to quit Hamadan. He found refuge at the court of Prince 'Ala ad-Dawlah, where his immense output of writings continued. This included his account of the paths to spiritual enlightenment, the *Book of Directives and Remarks*. He also composed some notable works of poetry and wrote on many other topics, including astronomy, physics, and chemistry.

Avicenna was frequently involved in the political turmoil of warring Persian states and on several occasions had to escape possible capture and imprisonment. He was fond of wine, women, and, doubtless, song too and prescribed himself a glass of wine to combat fatigue. He died while accompanying the prince on a campaign, evidently of colic and exhaustion.

AVOGADRO, Lorenzo Romano Amedeo Carlo, count of Quaregna and Cerreto (b. Aug. 9, 1776; Turin, Italy; d. July 9, 1856; Turin) Italian physicist and chemist.

Avogadro came from a long line of lawyers. He too was trained in law and practiced for some years before taking up the study of mathematics and physics in 1800. His early work was carried out in the field of electricity, and in 1809 he became professor of physics at the Royal College at Vercelli. He was professor of mathematical physics at Turin from 1820 until 1822 and from 1834 to 1850.

His fame rests on his paper *Essai d'une manière de determiner les masses relatives des molecules des corps et les proportions selon lesquelles entrent dans cet combinaisons*, (1811; On a Way of Finding the Relative Masses of Molecules and the Proportions in which They Combine), published in the *Journal de Physique*. This states the famous hypothesis that equal volumes of gases at the same temperature and pressure contain equal numbers of molecules. It follows from the hypothesis that relative molecular weights can be obtained from vapor densities and that the proportion by volume in which gases combine reflects the combining ratio of the molecules. Using this theory, Avogadro showed that simple gases such as hydrogen and oxygen are diatomic (H_2, O_2) and assigned the formula H_2O to water, whereas John Dalton had arbitrarily assumed that the simplest compound of two elements would be binary, giving water the formula HO.

Avogadro's work provided the essential link between Gay Lussac's law of combining volumes and Dalton's atomic theory. This was not, however, realized at the time and as a consequence the determination of a self-consistent set of atomic weights was delayed for 50 years. The French physicist André Ampère was one of the few who accepted the theory and for many years it was taken to be Ampère's own.

Avogadro's contribution to chemistry was not appreciated in his own lifetime. The importance and truth of the theory was unrecognized until 1860 when his fellow Italian, Stanislao Cannizzaro, forcefully restated it at the Karlsruhe Conference and demonstrated that it was the key needed to unlock the problem of atomic and molecular weights. The number of particles in one mole of a substance was named *Avogadro's constant* in his honor. It is equal to $6.022\,52 \times 10^{23}$.

AXELROD, Julius (b. May 30, 1912; New York City) American neuropharmacologist.

Axelrod was educated at the City College of New York. Denied a medical career by poverty during the depression, Axelrod instead worked as a technician in a food-testing laboratory for 12 years. But still with an ambition for a career in scientific research, and after some years at the Goldwater Memorial Hospital and the National Heart Institute, he took a year off in 1955, obtained a PhD from George Washington University, and moved to the

National Institute of Mental Health as chief of the pharmacology section.

Axelrod has thrown much light on the action of the catecholamines, the neurotransmitters of the sympathetic nervous system. The most important of these is norepinephrine, first identified as a neurotransmitter by Ulf von Euler in 1946. Axelrod realized that once the molecule had interacted with its target cell some mechanism must come into action to switch it off. Later he was able to describe the role of two enzymes, catechol-o-methyltransferase (COMT) and monoamine oxidase (MAO), which degrade the catecholamines.

However, studies with radioactive norepinephrine showed its persistence in the sympathetic nerves for some hours. This led Axelrod to propose that norepinephrine is taken up into, as well as released from, sympathetic nerves. This recapture inactivates the neurotransmitter.

For work on the catecholamines Axelrod shared the 1970 Nobel Prize for physiology or medicine with von Euler and Bernard Katz.

Axelrod has also worked on the role of the pineal gland in the control of circadian rhythms, and the neuropharmacology of schizophrenia.

AYALA, Francisco José (b. Mar. 12, 1934; Madrid) Spanish–American biologist.

Ayala began his higher education at the University of Madrid, moved to America in 1961, and obtained his PhD from Columbia in 1964. He worked initially at Rockefeller before joining the Davis campus of the University of California in 1971, where he was later appointed professor of genetics in 1974.

Ayala has worked extensively in the field of molecular evolution. He has also sought to measure genetic variation in natural populations, rates of evolution, and the amount of genetic change needed to produce new species. Many of his results were published in his *Molecular Evolution* (1976) and in a work he coauthored in 1977 entitled *Evolution*.

AYRTON, William Edward (b. Sept. 14, 1847; London; d. Nov. 8, 1908; London) British physicist.

Ayrton's father was a lawyer. After attending University College, London, and Glasgow University, he worked for the Indian Telegraph Company, and in 1873 was appointed to teach natural philosophy and telegraphy at the Imperial Engineering College, Tokyo, Japan. He returned to London in 1879 and became a professor at the City and Guilds College and later at Finsbury Technical College (1881). In 1884 he became a professor at the Central College.

Ayrton's work was mainly in practical applications for electricity. He invented several new measuring devices and worked on telegraphy, railroad electrification, and high-voltage power transmission, and was the first to suggest transmission at high voltages (1879). From 1904 he worked on the electric searchlight in collaboration with his second wife, Hertha Marks (who at the time of his death was the only woman member of the Institute of Electrical Engineers). Ayrton was well known for his advanced teaching methods, letting his students gain experimental practice wherever possible.

B

BAADE, Wilhelm Heinrich Walter (b. Mar. 24, 1893; Schröttinghausen, now in West Germany; d. June 25, 1960; Göttingen, West Germany) German–American astronomer.

Baade, the son of a schoolteacher, was educated at the universities of Münster and Göttingen where he obtained his PhD in 1919. He worked at the University of Hamburg's Bergedorf Observatory from 1919 to 1931, when he moved to America. He spent the rest of his career at the Mount Wilson and Palomar Observatories, retiring in 1958.

In 1920 Baade discovered the minor planet Hidalgo, whose immense orbit extends to that of Saturn. He was also, in 1949, to detect the minor planet Icarus, whose orbit, which lies within that of Mercury, can bring it very close to Earth. In the 1930s he did important work with Fritz Zwicky on supernovae, with Edwin Hubble on galactic distances, and with his old Hamburg colleague, Rudolph Minkowski, on the optical identification of radio sources.

Baade's most significant work however began in 1942. As he was of German origin he was precluded from the general induction of scientists into military research, being allowed to spend the war observing the heavens. In early 1943 he was blessed with ideal viewing conditions. Los Angeles was blacked out because of wartime restrictions and, for a short while, the air was calm and the temperature constant. Under these near-perfect conditions Baade took some famous photographs with the 100-inch (2.5-m) reflecting telescope of the central region of the Andromeda galaxy.

To his great excitement he was able to resolve stars in the inner region where Hubble before him had found only a blur of light.

These observations allowed Baade to introduce a fundamental distinction between types of stars. The first type, Population I stars, he found in the spiral arms of the Andromeda galaxy. They were young hot blue stars as opposed to the Population II stars of the central part of the galaxy, which were older and redder with a lower metal content. This distinction, now much expanded, has played a crucial role in theories of galactic evolution.

Some of the stars that Baade observed in the Andromeda galaxy were Cepheid variables, stars that vary regularly in brightness. His realization that there were two kinds of Cepheids had an immediate impact. The relationship between period and luminosity of Cepheids, had been discovered by Henrietta Leavitt in 1912 and put into a quantified form by Harlow Shapley so that it could be used in the determination of stellar distances of great magnitude. In the 1920s Hubble had found Cepheids in the outer part of the Andromeda galaxy, and, using the period-luminosity rule, had calculated its distance as 800 000 light-years. Since then the relationship had been used by many astronomers.

Baade, by 1952, was able to show that the original period-luminosity relationship was valid only for Population II Cepheids whereas Hubble's calculation involved Population I Cepheids. Baade worked out a new period-luminosity relationship for these Cepheids and found that the Andromeda galaxy was two million light-years distant.

The distance to the Andromeda galaxy had been used by Hubble to estimate the age of the universe as two billion years. Baade's revised figure gave the age as five billion years. This result was greeted with considerable relief by astronomers as Hubble's figure conflicted with the three to four billion years that the geologists were demanding for the age of the Earth. Further, with Baade's revision of the distance of the Andromeda galaxy without any change in its luminosity, it was now clear that its size must also be increased together with the size of all the other galaxies for which it had been a yardstick. Baade was thus able to establish that while our Galaxy was somewhat bigger than normal it was not the largest, as Hubble's work had implied.

BABBAGE, Charles (b. Dec. 26, 1792; Teignmouth, England; d. Oct. 18, 1871; London) British mathematician.

Babbage, whose father was a banker, studied at Cambridge and played a major role in ending the isolationist attitudes prevalent in British mathematical circles in the early 19th century. In 1815 he helped to found the Analytical Society, which aimed to make the work of Continental mathematicians better known in Britain. Babbage's interest in stimulating British scientific activity was by no means confined to mathematics. In 1820 he was a founder of the Royal Astronomical Society and in 1834 of the Statistical Society, and he continued to attack the British public for their lack of interest in science. Among his inventions were a speedometer, and the locomotive 'cowcatcher'. Babbage also did mathematical work that contributed to the setting up of the British postal system in 1840. From 1828 to 1839 he was Lucasian Professor of Mathematics at Cambridge University.

Babbage is best known for his pioneering work in designing and building a mechanical computer. Earlier mathematicians such as Blaise Pascal and Gottfried Leibniz had designed primitive computing machines, but Babbage's 'analytical engine', as he called it, was very much more sophisticated than anything that had been thought of before. Many key ideas subsequently taken up when modern electronic computers were being developed were due to Babbage; for example, the ideas of giving the machine instructions in the form of punched cards, having the results in the form of a print-out, and the need for the computer to have a 'memory' — all originate with Babbage.

However although Babbage had these theoretical insights into computer design he was never able to complete the prototype of his analytical engine owing to the limitations of the purely mechanical technology available to him and to lack of money. Originally he had been able to get financial backing from the British government for the project, but as time went by without Babbage's completing the machine, the government refused to put any more money into the venture. Babbage then began to spend more and more of his own money on the machine. One keen supporter of the project who came to his aid was Lord Byron's daughter Ada, Countess of Lovelace, who had considerable mathematical ability. Lady Lovelace and Babbage devised a scheme aimed at winning enormous sums on horse races but unfortunately this was not a success and Babbage's financial situation continued to deteriorate. It was largely through Lady Lovelace's enthusiastic interest in Babbage's machine and her attempts to interest others in it that it is as well known as it is. Eventually Babbage used up all his own money on the computer project and the prototype remained incomplete. It still exists and can be seen in the Science Museum in London.

BABCOCK, Harold Delos (b. Jan. 24, 1882; Edgerton, Wisconsin; d. Apr. 8, 1968; Pasadena, California) American astronomer.

Babcock was educated at the University of California, Berkeley where he graduated in 1907. In 1908 he joined the staff of the Mount Wilson Observatory with whom he remained until his retirement in 1948. After his formal retirement he continued to work for many years with his son Horace Babcock.

When he first joined the observatory George Hale had just discovered the presence of strong magnetic fields in sunspots by noting the splitting of their spectral lines, the so-called 'Zeeman effect' first described by Pieter Zeeman in 1896. Babcock's first task was to supply the basic laboratory data on the effects of strong magnetic fields on various chemical elements.

Many years later, in collaboration with his son, he used their joint invention, the magnetograph, to detect the presence of weak and more generalized magnetic fields on the Sun. They also, in 1948, revealed the existence of strong magnetic fields in certain stars.

BABCOCK, Horace Welcome (b. Sept. 13, 1912; Pasadena, California) American astronomer.

Babcock was the son of Harold Delos Babcock, a distinguished American astronomer who spent a lifetime observing at the Mount Wilson Observatory. Horace Babcock graduated in 1934 from the California Institute of Technology and obtained his PhD in 1938 from the University of California. He worked initially at Lick Observatory from 1938 to 1939 and at the Yerkes and McDonald observatories from 1939 to 1941. He then engaged in war work at the radiation laboratory at the Massachusetts Institute of Technology (1941–42) and at Cal Tech (1942–45). In 1946 Babcock returned to astronomy and joined his father at Mount Wilson where they began an enormously profitable collaboration. Babcock later served from 1964 until his retirement in 1978 as director of the Mount Wilson and Palomar Observatories, which became known in 1969 as the Hale Observatories.

In 1908 George Hale had detected splitting of the spectral lines in the light from sunspots. Such an effect results from the presence of a magnetic field, an effect first described by Pieter Zeeman in 1896. The fields observed by Hale were of considerable strength, ranging up to some 4000 gauss. The field of the Earth by contrast is less than one gauss. The question then arose as to whether the Sun itself possessed a general magnetic field distinct from fields associated with sunspots. The problem facing early investigators was how to detect weak fields and was not overcome until 1948 when the Babcocks successfully developed their magnetograph, permitting them to measure and record the Zeeman effect continuously and automatically. By the late 1940s they were able to report the presence of weak magnetic fields on the Sun, about one gauss in strength and restricted to latitudes greater than 55°. Further unexpected features were changes in polarity discovered in the 1950s: when examined in 1955 the north solar pole possessed positive polarity, the south negative polarity; by 1958 the situation was completely reversed.

In 1948 the Babcocks announced the further major discovery of stellar magnetic fields. By 1958 they had established the presence of magnetic fields in some 89 stars. The fields tended to be strong, of the order of several thousand gauss, and seemed to belong mainly to stars of spectral types O and B. Attempts to explain the presence of such fields were made considerably more difficult by the realization that some stars were 'magnetic variables': the field of the brighter component of the binary star Alpha Canes Venatici was found to vary, with reversing polarity, from +5000 to –4000 gauss in 5.5 days. Such studies have done much to stimulate work on magnetohydrodynamics.

BABCOCK, Stephen Moulton (b. Oct. 22, 1843; near Bridgewater, New York; d. July

1, 1931; Madison, Wisconsin) American agricultural chemist.

A farmer's son, Babcock gained his AB degree from Tufts College, Massachusetts, in 1866 and after a period of farming became a chemistry assistant and (from 1875) instructor at Cornell University. In 1879 he gained his doctorate under Hans Hübner at Göttingen, Germany. After a further spell at Cornell on his return, he became chemist at the New York Agricultural Station in 1882, where he worked on the analysis of milk.

In 1888 Babcock became professor of agricultural chemistry at the University of Wisconsin. Here, in 1890, he devised an efficient test (the *Babcock test*), which quickly became standard, for measuring the butterfat content of milk. Studies followed on rennet, fermentation, metabolic water, and animal nutrition. In 1907 Babcock's associates began studies in which cattle were fed balanced diets derived from a single source — corn, wheat, or oats. The results obtained provided further evidence for the existence of accessory food factors and Babcock's school played an important part in the vitamin studies that followed.

BABINET, Jacques (b. Mar. 5, 1794; Lusignan, France; d. Oct. 21, 1872; Paris) French physicist.

Babinet studied at the Ecole Polytechnique and from 1820 he was a professor at the Collège Louis le Grand. He was elected to the Académie des Sciences in 1840.

His major work was devoted to the diffraction of light; he used diffraction to measure wavelengths more accurately than before, and did theoretical work on general diffraction systems. The *Babinet theorem* states that there is an approximate equivalence between the diffraction pattern of a large system and that of the complementary system, which is opaque where the original system is transparent and vice versa.

Furthermore he showed an interest in the optical properties of minerals, developing new instruments for the measurement of angles and polarizations. He also studied meteorological phenomena, especially those of an optical nature, investigating rainbows and the polarization of skylight. Babinet was the first to suggest (1829) that the wavelength of a given spectral line could be used as a fundamental standard of length.

BABO, Lambert Heinrich Clemens von (b. Nov. 25, 1818; Ladenberg, now in West Germany; d. Apr. 15, 1899; Karlsruhe, now in West Germany) German chemist.

Babo was a student at Giessen where he studied under Justus von Liebig. He was appointed as an assistant professor at Freiburg University in 1845, later being appointed professor of chemistry in 1859.

In 1847 he showed that the vapor pressure of a liquid can be lowered by dissolving substances in it. He also succeeded in demonstrating that the degree of depression of the vapor pressure is, in general, proportional to the concentration of the solution (known as *Babo's law*). François Raoult was able to use Babo's discovery in 1886 to establish some general rules and to determine molecular weights.

BACHE, Alexander Dallas (b. July 19, 1806; Philadelphia, Pennsylvania; d. Feb. 17, 1867; Newport, Rhode Island) American geophysicist.

Bache, the great-grandson of Benjamin Franklin, graduated from West Point in 1825. After two years in the army he became professor of natural science and chemistry (1828–41) at the University of Pennsylvania. He spent the period 1836–38 studying the European educational system, publishing his findings in *Education in Europe* (1839).

In 1840 Bache founded the first American magnetic observatory at Girard College. He became, in 1843, superintendent of the US Coast Survey, which he built up into a major institution. He had the entire coastline surveyed during his lifetime, his own particular research being into the Gulf Stream, an area also studied by his great-grandfather.

Dissatisfied with the American Association for the Advancement of Science he gathered around himself a group of scientists known as the 'Lazzorconi', or beggars. He was successful in persuading Congress to create, in 1863, the National Academy of Sciences "to investigate, examine, experiment, and report upon any question of science and art." Bache was made its first president.

BACON, Francis, Baron Verulam, Viscount St. Albans (b. Jan. 22, 1561; London; d. Apr. 9, 1626; London) British philosopher.

Bacon was born into the Elizabethan ruling class; his father was Sir Nicholas Bacon, lord keeper of the Seal, and his uncle was Lord Burleigh. He entered Cambridge University in 1573 to study law, qualified in 1582, and entered parliament in 1584. His political career was noted for his ability both to attach himself to the side of royal favorites (and thereby rise) and to make sure that he was on the opposing side when they fell from favor (and thereby rise further). He held many state offices including those of attorney general (1613) and lord chancellor (1618).

Bacon's first work of philosophy was the *Advancement of Learning* (1605), a review of the current state of knowledge. He planned an encyclopedia of all knowledge, the *Instauratio magna* (Great Renewal), but this was never completed, the most substantial fragment being the *Novum organum* (1620; New Organum). Bacon rejected completely deference to the authority of the ancients, in particular the deductive logic of Aristotle, in dealing with science and the investigation of the world. He asserted that nature could be understood and even controlled by man. Bacon's method to accomplish this was induction,

by which he understood a method of proceeding from the particular to the general by a process of exclusions, generalizing from particular experiments and investigations. Bacon had a great influence on the first generation of British experimental scientists. Despite his urge towards completeness Bacon's knowledge of the science of his day was inadequate. In one field, however, he was highly prescient: by induction he concluded that heat was a form of motion.

In 1621 Bacon was accused of bribery, imprisoned for a few days, fined, and banished from Parliament and the Court. He retired to his estate in Hertfordshire and in this last period of his life he wrote a revision of the *Advancement*, *De augmentis scientarum* (1623), some fragments of the *Instauratio*, and the *New Atlantis*, a utopia that foreshadowed the scientific societies founded later in the century. Bacon's death was brought on by his last scientific experiment. He had the idea that snow might preserve flesh and to test this he stuffed a chicken with snow, which he himself collected. It is said that as a result he caught a chill and died soon after.

BACON, Roger (b. *c.* 1220; Ilchester, England; d. June 11, 1292; Oxford, England) English philosopher and alchemist.

Bacon studied at Oxford and then at Paris (1234–50) under Petrus Peregrinus. In about 1257 he joined the Franciscan Order and from about 1250 until 1277 he was at Oxford, where he studied under Grosseteste. He is supposed to have been confined in Paris from 1277.

Bacon was often in disgrace with the authorities but he had a considerable reputation as a philosopher and alchemist, being called *Doctor Mirabilis* (Miraculous Doctor). From about 1247 until 1257 he concentrated on research in mathematics, optics, alchemy, and astronomy and during this developed a magnifying glass, defined reflection and refraction, and also mentioned gunpowder in his writings. Bacon distinguished two kinds of alchemy, speculative and operative, and he believed firmly in the practical benefits of science. His writings, the *Opus majus* (published in 1733), *Opus secundus*, and *Opus tertius*, include a number of predictions, of powered cars, aircraft, and ships, and of machines for extending the powers of man. He was committed to the belief that the Earth was round, and suggested that it could be circumnavigated. He stressed that experimentation was essential to the progress of science.

BAEKELAND, Leo Hendrik (b. Nov. 14, 1863; Ghent, Belgium; d. Feb. 23, 1944; New York City) Belgian-American industrial chemist.

Baekeland was educated at the University of Ghent, graduating in 1884. He was professor of physics and chemistry at Bruges in 1887 and returned to Ghent the next year as assistant professor of chemistry. But Baekeland grew impatient with academic life and in 1889 a honeymoon tour took him to America where he settled.

Baekeland worked at first as a photographic chemist and in 1891 he opened his own consulting laboratory. In 1893 he began to manufacture a photographic paper, which he called Velox, and six years later his company was bought out by the Kodak Corporation for one million dollars. Now financially independent, Baekeland returned to Europe to study at the Technical Institute at Charlottenburg.

On his return to America, Baekeland began to investigate, as a synthetic substitute for shellac, the phenol-formaldehyde resins discovered by Karl Baeyer in 1871. Since nothing remotely like shellac emerged, he began to look for other uses for this material. By choosing suitable reaction conditions he produced a hard amberlike resin, which could be cast and machined and which had excellent durability and electrical properties. Bakelite was finally unveiled in 1909 and Baekeland set up the General Bakelite Corporation to manufacture it.

In 1922 Baekeland's company merged with two rivals and in 1939 it became a subsidiary of the Union Carbide and Carbon Corporation. Baekeland continued to produce scientific papers throughout this period. He received many honors and held many professional posts, including that of president of the American Chemical Society.

BAER, Karl Ernst von (b. Feb. 29, 1792; Piep, now in the Soviet Union; d. Nov. 28, 1876; Dorpat, now Tartu in the Soviet Union) German-Estonian biologist, comparative anatomist, and embryologist.

Baer is generally considered the father of modern embryology. He was born on his family's estate in Piep, Estonia, and received private tutoring and schooling before entering Dorpat University to study medicine. He graduated in 1814 and then studied comparative anatomy at the University of Würzburg, where he was introduced to embryology by Ignaz Döllinger. In 1817 Baer became professor of zoology at Königsberg and in 1834 was appointed academician and librarian of the Academy of Sciences at St. Petersburg (now Leningrad).

It was prior to his move to St. Petersburg that Baer did most of his pioneering work in laying the foundation of comparative embryology as a separate discipline. In distinguishing the mammalian ovum within the Graafian follicle he established that all mammals, including man, develop from eggs. He also traced the development of the fertilized egg and the order in which the organs of the body appear and develop, showing that similar (homologous) organs arise from the same germ layers in different animals, thus extending the work of Kaspar Wolff and the German anatomist Christian Pander. His expounding of the 'biogenetic law', demonstrating the increasing similarity and lack of specialization in the embryos of different animals as one investigates younger and younger embryos, provided Darwin with basic arguments for his evolutionary theory. Baer was, however, opposed to the idea of there being a common ancestor for all animal life, although he conceded that some animals and some races of man might have had common ancestry. His other notable discoveries included the mammalian notochord and the neural folds as the precursors of the nervous system. Baer intended his embryological work to be, at least partly, a means of improving animal classification by demonstrating vertebrate affinities. Indeed modern zoological classification is now based partly on biogenetic principles. His great work on the mammalian egg, *De ovi mammalium et hominis genesi* (1827; On the Origin of the Mammalian and Human Ovum) was followed (1828–37) by *Über Entwickelungsgeschichte der Tiere* (On the Development of Animals), in which he surveyed all existing knowledge of vertebrate development.

A man of wide interests, Baer did much work in other scientific disciplines. He was instrumental in founding the German Anthropological Society and helped to found the Russian Geographical and Entomological Societies.

BAEYER, Johann Friedrich Adolph von (b. Oct. 31, 1835; Berlin; d. Aug. 20, 1917; Munich, now in West Germany) German organic chemist.

Baeyer's father was a member of the Prussian General Staff and his mother was the daughter of a celebrated jurist and literary historian. In 1856 Baeyer went to Heidelberg to study chemistry with Bunsen. Here he met Kekulé, who had a profound influence on his development as a chemist and gave him the theoretical foundation for his work. After obtaining his PhD (1858) Baeyer took up a teaching position in 1860 at a small technical school, the Gewerbe-Institut, in Berlin. In 1872 he was appointed professor of chemistry at Strasbourg and in 1875 succeeded Liebig as professor of chemistry at Munich, where he remained for the rest of his life.

In 1864, continuing the work of Wöhler, Liebig, and Schlieper on uric acid, Baeyer

characterized a related series of derivatives including alloxan, parabanic acid, hydantoin, and barbituric acid. In 1871 he discovered the phthalein dyes, phenolphthalein and fluorescein, by heating phenols with phthalic anhydride. In the course of this work he discovered the phenol–formaldehyde resins, which were later developed commercially by Baekeland. The centerpiece of Baeyer's prolific researches, however, was his work on indigo, which started in 1865 and lasted for 20 years.

The first step consisted of the reduction of indigo to its parent substance, indole, which Baeyer accomplished by the new method of heating with zinc dust. The first synthesis was a lengthy one, starting from phenylacetic acid. This was soon followed by shorter methods starting from *o*-nitrocinnamic acid and *o*-nitrophenylpropiolic acid. In 1883 he gave a structure of indigo that was correct except for the stereochemical arrangement of the double bond, which was later shown to be *trans* by x-ray crystallography (1928). Baeyer's syntheses proved too costly for commercial manufacture and he took no part in the industrial development of indigo, terminating his work in 1885. Commercial synthetic indigo was eventually produced in 1890. Baeyer's work also led to the production of many other new dyes.

From indigo Baeyer turned to the polyacetylenes, compounds whose explosive properties led him to consider the stability of carbon–carbon bonds in unsaturated and ring compounds. He formulated the *Baeyer strain theory*, stating that compounds are less stable the more their bond angles depart from the ideal tetrahedral arrangement. Baeyer's other researches included work on oxonium compounds; on the reduction of aromatic compounds, in which he observed a loss of aromaticity on reduction; and on terpenes, including the first synthesis of a terpene in 1888.

The strain theory was one of Baeyer's few theoretical contributions; he was a virtuoso of test-tube chemistry at a time when this could produce extraordinary results.

In 1905 he received the Nobel Chemistry Prize for his work on indigo and hydroaromatic compounds.

BAILAR, John Christian Jr. (b. May 24, 1904; Golden, Colorado) American chemist.

Bailar was educated at the universities of Colorado and Michigan where he obtained his PhD in 1928. Since 1928 he has worked at the University of Illinois, Urbana, being appointed professor of chemistry in 1943. He is known mainly for his work on the stereochemistry of the inorganic coordination compounds first described by Alfred Werner in the 1890s. Bailar edited and contributed to a major survey of the field, *Chemistry of Coordination Compounds* (1956).

BAILLIE, Matthew (b. Oct. 27, 1761; Shotts, Scotland; d. Sept. 23, 1823; Duntisbourne, England) British physician.

Baillie studied classics, mathematics, and philosophy at Glasgow University and then arts and medicine at Oxford University. He graduated MD in 1787 and was appointed physician to St. George's Hospital, London. A nephew of William and John Hunter, he inherited William Hunter's house and medical school at Windmill Street in 1783. Baillie's major work was the *Morbid Anatomy of Some of the Most Important Parts of the Human Body* (1793). This was a pioneering work, illustrated by a series of engravings, that helped establish pathology as a separate subject. From 1810 onward he was a physician to the royal family, attending George III during his final illness.

His sister was the poet and dramatist, Joanna Baillie.

BAILY, Francis (b. Apr. 28, 1774; Newbury, England; d. Aug. 30, 1844; London) British astronomer.

Baily was a prosperous stockbroker who, on retirement, devoted himself to astronomy. During the total eclipse of the Sun in 1836 he noted that immediately before and after totality a number of bright points of light, or 'beads', appear around the edge of the Moon. This effect, known as *Baily's beads*, is caused by light from the Sun shining through the lunar valleys.

BAIRD, John Logie (b. Aug. 13, 1888; Helensburgh, Scotland; d. June 14, 1946; Bexhill, England) British inventor.

Baird studied electrical engineering at the Royal Technical College in Glasgow and then went to Glasgow University. His poor health prevented him from active service during World War I and from completing various business enterprises in the years following the war.

After a breakdown in 1922 he retired to Hastings and engaged in amateur experiments on the transmission of pictures. Using primitive equipment he succeeded in transmitting an image over a distance of a couple of feet, and in 1926 he demonstrated his apparatus before a group of scientists. Recognition followed, and the next year he transmitted pictures by telephone wire between London and Glasgow. In the same year he set up the Baird Television Development Company. He continued to work on improvements and on 30 September, 1929, gave the first experimental BBC broadcast. Synchronization of sound and vision was achieved a few months later. In 1937, however, the Baird system of mechanical scanning was ousted by the all-electronic system put forward by Marconi–EMI. Baird was at the forefront of virtually all developments in television and continued research into color, stereoscopic, and big-screen television until his death.

BAIRD, Spencer Fullerton (b. Feb. 3, 1823; Reading, Pennsylvania; d. Aug. 19, 1887; Woods Hole, Massachusetts) American biologist.

Educated at Dickinson College, Pennsylvania, Baird was professor of natural sciences at the college, 1845–50. He went on several expeditions, making immense collections of North American fauna. From 1874 he was United States Commissioner of Fish and Fisheries. He was assistant secretary and then full secretary (1878–87) of the Smithsonian Institution and in 1857 was one of the founders of the Institution's National Museum. Baird was also one of the principle founders of the Woods Hole Marine Laboratory. A colleague of Louis Agassiz and John J. Audubon, Baird did much to introduce field study in botany and zoology in the United States, in ornithology in particular, stressing the importance of extreme accuracy in descriptions. From 1853 to 1884 he published several accounts of North American reptiles, birds, and mammals.

BAKEWELL, Robert (b. 1725; Dishley, England; d. Oct. 1, 1795; Dishley) British stock breeder.

Little is known about Bakewell's early life except that he helped his father on their 440-acre rented farm, which he took over in 1760 on the death of his father. Bakewell's aim was to "get beasts to weigh where you want them to weigh." His most impressive achievement was the production of his Leicester breed of sheep. Within 50 years the breed had spread throughout the world and Bakewell apparently succeeded in producing two pounds of mutton where there had only been one before. He also introduced the custom of letting out his rams for breeding. He was, however, less successful with his Leicester long horn cattle, which, though good meat-producers, did not yield much milk.

BALARD, Antoine-Jérôme (b. Sept. 30, 1802; Montpellier, France; d. Mar. 30, 1876; Paris) French chemist.

Balard studied at the School of Pharmacy in Montpellier. After graduating in 1826, he remained at Montpellier as a demonstrator in chemistry. In 1825, while investigating the salts contained in seawater, he discovered a dark red liquid, which he proved was an element with properties similar to chlorine and iodine. Balard proposed the name 'muride' but the editors of *Annales de chimie* preferred 'brome' (because of the element's strong odor, from the Greek for 'stink') and the element came to be called bromine. Balard also (1834) discovered dichlorine oxide (Cl_2O) and chloric(I) acid ($HClO$).

In 1833 he became professor at Montpellier and in 1843 succeeded Louis Thenard at the Sorbonne as professor of chemistry. In 1854 he was appointed professor of general chemistry at the Collège de France, where he remained until his death.

BALFOUR, Francis Maitland (b. Nov. 10, 1851; Edinburgh; d. July 19, 1882; Mont Blanc, Switzerland) British zoologist.

The younger brother of the statesman Earl Balfour, Francis Balfour's career was cut short when, while convalescing from typhoid fever in Switzerland, he died attempting an ascent of the Aiguille Blanche, Mont Blanc. He held the position of animal morphologist at the Naples Zoological Station and in 1882 was appointed to the specially created post of professor of animal morphology at Cambridge University. Much influenced by the work of Michael Foster, with whom he wrote *Elements of Embryology* (1883), Balfour showed the evolutionary connection between vertebrates and certain invertebrates, both of which have a notochord (a flexible rod of cells extending the length of the body) in their embryonic stages. Similar research was being conducted at that time by Aleksandr Kovalevski. Balfour proposed the term Chordata for all animals possessing a notochord at some stage in their development, the Vertebrata (backboned animals) being a subphylum of the Chordata. He was an early exponent of recapitulation — the theory that ancestral forms are repeated in successive embryonic stages undergone by modern species. Balfour also did pioneer work on the development of the kidneys and related organs, as well as the spinal nervous system. His other important publications include *On the Development of Elasmobranch Fishes* (1878) and *Comparative Embryology* (1880–81) published in two volumes (invertebrates and vertebrates), the latter forming the basis of modern embryological study.

BALMER, Johann Jakob (b. May 1, 1825; Lausanne, Switzerland; d. Mar. 12, 1898; Basel, Switzerland) Swiss mathematician.

Balmer was not a professional scientist but worked as a school teacher in Basel from 1859. In 1885 he discovered that there was a simple mathematical formula that gave the wavelengths of the spectral lines of hydrogen — the *Balmer series*. This formula proved to be of great importance in atomic spectroscopy and in developing the atomic theory. Balmer arrived at his formula purely from empirical evidence and was unable to explain why it yielded correct results. Not until the further development of the atomic theory by Niels Bohr (q.v.) and others was this possible.

BALTIMORE, David (b. Mar. 7, 1938; New York City) American molecular biologist.

Baltimore studied chemistry at Swarthmore College and continued with postgraduate work at the Massachusetts Institute of Technology, and at Rockefeller University, where he obtained his PhD in 1964. After three years at the Salk Institute in California, he returned to MIT in 1968 where, in 1972, he became professor of biology.

Francis Crick had formulated what came to be known as the Central Dogma of molecular biology, namely, that information could flow from DNA to RNA to protein but could not flow backward from protein to either DNA or RNA. Although he had not actually excluded the passage of information from RNA to DNA it became widely assumed that such a flow was equally forbidden. In June 1970 Baltimore and, quite independently, Howard Temin announced the discovery of an enzyme later to be known as reverse transcriptase, which is capable of transcribing RNA into DNA. Apparently certain viruses, like the RNA tumor viruses used by Baltimore, could produce DNA from an RNA template. For this work Baltimore shared the 1975 Nobel Prize for physiology or medicine with Temin and Renato Dulbecco.

Earlier (1968) Baltimore had done important work on the replication of the polio virus. He revealed that the RNA of the virus first constructed a 'polyprotein' (or giant protein molecule), which then split into a number of smaller protein molecules. Two of these polymerized further RNA while the remainder formed the protein coat of the new viral particles.

BAMBERGER, Eugen (b. July 19, 1857; Berlin; d. Dec. 10, 1932; Ponte Tresa, Switzerland) German chemist.

Bamberger studied at Breslau, Heidelberg, and at Berlin, where he graduated under August von Hofmann. After working as an assistant, first to Karl Rammelsberg in Berlin (1882) and then to Adolf von Baeyer in Munich (1883), he became professor of chemistry at the Federal Institute of Technology in Zurich in 1893.

Bamberger worked on a number of topics in organic chemistry, including the synthesis of nitroso compounds and quinols, the conversion of sulfonic acids into sulfanilic acids, and the production of diazonium anhydrides. He also extended Baeyer's ideas on benzene structure to naphthalene and first proposed the term 'alicyclic' to describe unsaturated organic ring compounds.

BANKS, Sir Joseph (b. Feb. 13, 1743; London; d. June 19, 1820; Isleworth, England) British botanist.

The son of William Banks of Revesby Abbey, Lincolnshire, Joseph Banks inherited a large fortune when he came of age, and later used this money to finance his scientific expeditions. He studied botany at Oxford, graduating in 1763, and three years later traveled abroad for the first time as naturalist on a fishery-protection vessel heading for Labrador and Newfoundland. On the voyage he was able to collect many new species of plants and insects and, on his return, was elected a fellow of the Royal Society.

In London Banks learned that the Royal Society was organizing a voyage to the South Pacific to observe the transit of Venus across the Sun. In 1768 James Cook set sail in the *Endeavour* and Banks, together with a team of artists and the botanist Daniel Solander, accompanied him. Cook landed in Australia, a continent with a flora and fauna different from any found elsewhere. Banks found that most of the Australian mammals were marsupials, which are more primitive, in evolutionary terms, than the placental mammals of other continents.

After three years with the *Endeavour* Banks returned, with a large collection of unique specimens, to find himself famous. George III, interested in hearing a firsthand account of Banks's travels, invited him to Windsor. This visit was the start of a long friendship with the king, which helped Banks establish many influential contacts — possibly a factor in his election as president of the Royal Society in 1778, a post that he held until his death.

Throughout his life Banks retained his interest in natural history and in the specimens collected on the many expeditions mounted during that period. As honorary director of Kew Gardens he played a major part in establishing living representatives of as many species as possible at Kew and in providing a center for advice on the practical use of plants. He initiated many successful projects, including the introduction of the tea plant to India from its native China and the transport of the breadfruit from Tahiti to the West Indies. By George III's request, he also played an active role in importing merino sheep into Britain from Spain.

The British Museum now houses Banks's library and herbarium, both regarded as major collections.

BANTING, Sir Frederick Grant (b. Nov. 14, 1891; Alliston, Ontario; d. Feb. 21, 1941; Newfoundland) Canadian physiologist.

Banting, a farmer's son, began studying to be a medical missionary at Victoria College, Toronto, in 1910. During his studies he concentrated increasingly on medicine and graduated MD in 1916, whereupon he immediately joined the Canadian Army Medical Corps. In 1918 he was awarded the Military Cross for gallantry in action and was invalided out of the army.

Banting then returned to Toronto and worked for a time studying children's diseases before setting up practice in London, Ontario, in 1920. He also began work at the London Medical School, specializing in studies on the pancreas, particularly the small patches of pancreatic cells known as the islets of Langerhans. Earlier work had shown a connection between the pancreas and diabetes and Banting wondered if a hormone was produced in the islets of Langerhans that regulated glucose metabolism. In 1921 he approached John Macleod, professor of physiology at Toronto University, who was initially skeptical. Feeling that Banting needed help in physiological and biochemical methods, Macleod suggested the assistance of a young research student, Charles Best, and eventually merely granted Banting and Best some laboratory space during the vacation, while he went abroad.

Over the next six months Banting and Best devised a series of elegant experiments. They tied off the pancreatic ducts of dogs and made extracts of the islets of Langerhans free from other pancreatic substances. These extracts, called 'isletin', were found to have some effect against diabetes in dogs. Prior to trials on humans, Macleod asked a biochemist, James Collip, to purify the extracts and the purification method for what was now known as insulin were patented by Banting, Best, and Collip in 1923. They allowed manufacturers freedom to produce the hormone but required a small royalty to be paid to finance future medical research.

The pharmaceutical firm Eli Lilley began industrial production of insulin in 1923 and in the same year Banting was awarded the chair of medical research at Toronto University and a government annuity of $7000. The Nobel Prize for physiology or medicine was awarded jointly to Banting and Macleod in 1923; Banting was furious that Best had not been included in the award and shared his part of the prize money with him. Macleod shared his portion with Collip. In 1930 the Banting Institute opened in Toronto and under Banting's guidance this was to become the home of Canadian medical research with work on cancer, coronary thrombosis, and silicosis as well as diabetes. Banting was knighted in 1934. When war broke out in 1939 he joined an army medical unit and worked on many committees linking Canadian and British wartime medical research. His bravery was much in evidence at this time, particularly his personal involvement in research into mustard gas and blackout problems experienced by airmen. In 1941 on a flight from Gander, Newfoundland, to Britain his plane crashed and he died in the snow.

BÁRÁNY, Robert (b. Apr. 22, 1876; Vienna; d. Apr. 8, 1936; Uppsala, Sweden) Austro-Hungarian physician.

Bárány was educated at the University of Vienna, graduating in medicine in 1900. After studying at various German clinics, he returned to Vienna to become an assistant at the university's ear clinic. In 1909 he was appointed lecturer in otology. Through his work at the clinic he devised a test, now called the *Bárány test*, for diagnosing disease of the semicircular canals of the inner ear by syringing the ear with either hot or cold water. For this he

was awarded the 1914 Nobel Prize in physiology or medicine. At this time he was being held as a prisoner of war in Siberia, but through the offices of the Swedish Red Cross he was released and the award presented to him.

In 1917 Bárány was appointed professor at Uppsala University, where he continued his investigations on the inner ear and the role of the cerebellum in the brain in controlling body movement. *Bárány's pointing test* is used to test for brain lesions.

BARCROFT, Sir Joseph (b. July 26, 1872; Glen Newry, now in Northern Ireland; d. Mar. 21, 1947; Cambridge, England) Irish physiologist.

Professor of physiology at Cambridge University (1926–37) and director of animal physiology for the Agricultural Research Council (1941–47), Barcroft carried out extensive research into human embryology, physiology, and histology. He investigated the oxygen-carrying role of hemoglobin, and devised (1908) an apparatus for the analysis of blood gases.

Barcroft led three high-altitude expeditions — to Tenerife (1910); Monte Rosa, Italy (1911); and the Peruvian Andes (1922) — in order to study acclimatization and the effects of rarefied atmospheres on respiration. He found that, at low oxygen pressures, the human lung is not able to secrete oxygen into the blood at a higher pressure than the pressure of the inhaled air.

During World War I, Barcroft was chief physiologist at the Experimental Station at Porton, Wiltshire, where he studied the effects of poisonous gases. Elected a fellow of the Royal Society in 1910 and knighted in 1935, Barcroft wrote the famous text *Respiratory Function of the Blood* (1914), as well as publications on the brain and its environment and on prenatal conditions.

BARDEEN, John (b. May 23, 1908; Madison, Wisconsin) American physicist.

Bardeen, the son of a professor of anatomy, studied electrical engineering at the University of Wisconsin and obtained his PhD in mathematical physics at Princeton in 1936. He began work as a geophysicist with Gulf Research and Development Corporation, Pittsburgh, in 1931 but in 1935 entered academic life as a junior fellow at Harvard, moving to the University of Minnesota in 1938. Bardeen spent the war years at the Naval Ordnance Laboratory, followed by six creative years from 1945 until 1951 at the Bell Telephone Laboratory, after which he was appointed professor of physics and electrical engineering at the University of Illinois.

Bardeen is a unique figure in science — the only recipient of two Nobel Physics Prizes. The first, awarded in 1956, he shared with Walter Brattain (q.v.) and William Shockley for their development of the point-contact transistor (1947), thus preparing the way for the development of the more efficient junction transistor by Shockley.

Bardeen's second prize was awarded in 1972 for his formulation, in collaboration with Leon Cooper and John Schrieffer, of the first satisfactory theory of superconductivity — the so-called BCS theory. In 1911 Heike Kamerlingh-Onnes had discovered that mercury lost all electrical resistance when its temperature was lowered to $4.2\,K$. Superconductivity was also shown to be a property of many other metals, yet despite much effort to understand the phenomenon, a full explanation was not given until 1957. The basic innovation of the BCS theory was that the current in a superconductor is carried not by individual electrons but by bound pairs of them, later known as *Cooper pairs*. The pairs form as a result of interactions between the electrons and vibrations of the atoms in the crystal. The scattering of one electron by a lattice atom does not change the total momentum of the pair, and the flow of electrons continues indefinitely.

The success of the BCS theory led to an enormous revival of interest in both the theory of superconductors and their practical application. Beginning in the 1970s, there began to emerge a new industry capable of exploiting superconducting materials, especially in devices based on the effects discovered by Brian Josephson.

BARGER, George (b. Apr. 4, 1878; Manchester, England; d. Jan. 5, 1939; Aeschi, Switzerland) British organic chemist.

Barger, of Anglo-Dutch parentage, went to school in Holland, and read natural sciences at Cambridge University, where he graduated with equal distinction in chemistry and botany.

While a demonstrator in botany at the University of Brussels (1901–03) Barger discovered a method of determining the molecular weight of small samples by vapor-pressure measurements. From 1903 to 1909 he was a researcher at the Wellcome Physiological Research Laboratories, where he worked mainly on ergot, isolating ergotoxine in collaboration with Francis Carr (1906).

In the course of the work on ergot Barger and Henry Dale isolated a series of related amines, derived from tyramine, which had sympathomimetic activity. This work led to a better understanding of the nervous system and to the development of new drugs. The work on active amines was collected in *The Simpler Natural Bases* (1914) and the work on ergot culminated in the definitive monograph on every facet of the subject, *Ergot and Ergotism* (1931).

From 1909 to 1919 Barger worked in London, as head of chemistry at Goldsmiths' College, professor of chemistry at Royal Holloway College, and from 1914 as chemist with the National Institute of Medical Research. In 1919 he was elected a fellow of the Royal Society and appointed to the new chair of chemistry in relation to medicine at Edinburgh. The most notable researches of this period were Charles Harington's structural elucidation and synthesis of thyroxine, in which Barger collaborated, and Barger's synthesis of methionine. His school did important work on physostigmine, cholinesterase, and vitamin B_1. In 1938 Barger became professor of chemistry at the University of Glasgow. He was a pioneer of medicinal chemistry, an excellent linguist, and a tireless ambassador for science.

BARKHAUSEN, Heinrich Georg (b. Dec. 2, 1881; Bremen, now in West Germany; d. Feb. 20, 1956; Dresden, East Germany) German physicist.

After attending the gymnasium and engineering college in Bremen, Barkhausen gained his PhD in Göttingen and in 1911 became professor of electrical engineering in Dresden. Here he formulated the basic equations governing the coefficients of the amplifier valve.

In 1919 he discovered the *Barkhausen effect*, observing that a slow continuous increase in the magnetic field applied to a ferromagnetic material gave rise to discontinuous leaps in magnetization, which could be heard as distinct clicking sounds through a loudspeaker. This effect is caused by domains of elementary magnets changing direction or size as the field increases.

In 1920, with K. Kurz he developed an ultrahighfrequency oscillator, which became the forerunner of microwave-technology developments. After World War II he returned to Dresden to aid the reconstruction of his Institute of High-Frequency Electron-Tube Technology, which had been destroyed by bombing, and remained there until his death.

BARKLA, Charles Glover (b. June 27, 1877; Widnes, England; d. Oct. 23, 1944; Edinburgh) British x-ray physicist.

After taking his master's degree in 1899 at Liverpool, Barkla went to Trinity College, Cambridge but, because of his passion for singing, he transferred to King's College to sing in the choir. At King's College he started his important research on x-rays. In 1902 he returned to Liverpool as Oliver Lodge Fellow and in 1909 became Wheatstone Professor at King's College, London. From 1913 onward he was professor of natural philosophy at Edinburgh University.

His scientific work, for which he received the 1917 Nobel Physics Prize, concerned the properties of x-rays — in particular, the way in which they are scattered by various materials. He showed in 1903 that the scattering of x-rays by gases depends on the molecular weight of the gas. In 1904 he observed the polarization of x-rays — a result that indicated that x-rays are a form of electromagnetic radiation like light. Further confirmation of this was obtained in 1907 when he performed certain experiments on the direction of scattering of a beam of x-rays as evidence to resolve a controversy with William Henry Bragg who argued, at the time, that x-rays were particles.

Barkla also demonstrated x-ray fluorescence, in which primary x-rays are absorbed and the excited atoms then emit characteristic secondary x-rays. The frequencies of the characteristic x-rays depend on the atomic number of the element, as shown by Henry Mosely, who could well have shared Barkla's Nobel Prize but for his untimely death.

From about 1916, Barkla became isolated from modern physics with an increasingly dogmatic attitude, a tendency to cite only his own papers, and a concentration on untenable theories.

BARNARD, Christiaan Neethling (b. Nov. 8, 1922; Beaufort West, South Africa) South African surgeon.

Barnard was awarded his MD from the University of Cape Town in 1953 and joined the Medical Faculty as a research fellow in surgery. After three years at the University of Minnesota (1955–58), where he studied heart surgery, he returned to Cape Town as director of surgical research. He concentrated on improving techniques for artificially sustaining bodily functions during surgery and for keeping organs alive outside the body. On 2 December, 1967, Barnard performed the first heart-transplant operation on a human patient, a 54-year-old grocer named Louis Washkansky. He received the heart of Denise Duvall, a traffic accident victim. The heart functioned but the recipient died of pneumonia 18 days after the operation. The body's immune system had broken down following the administration of drugs to suppress rejection of the new heart as a foreign protein.

Barnard subsequently performed further similar operations with improved postoperative treatment giving much greater success. His pioneering work generated worldwide publicity for heart-transplant surgery and it is now fairly widely practiced.

BARNARD, Edward Emerson (b. Dec. 16, 1857; Nashville, Tennessee; d. Feb. 6, 1923; Williams Bay, Wisconsin) American astronomer.

Although Barnard came from a poor background with little formal education he developed a great interest in astronomy and also became familiar with photographic techniques from his work in a portrait studio. He managed both to study and instruct at Vanderbilt University from 1883 to 1887. From 1888 he worked at the Lick Observatory until in 1895 he became professor of astronomy at Chicago and was thus able to work at the newly established Yerkes Observatory.

Barnard was a keen observer and had detected more than ten comets by 1887 and several more in subsequent years. In 1892 he became the first astronomer after Galileo to discover a new satellite of Jupiter, subsequently named Amalthea, which lay inside the orbits of the four Galilean satellites and was much smaller and fainter. In 1916 he discovered a nearby red star with a very pronounced proper motion of 10.3 seconds of arc per year: in 180 years it will appear to us to have moved a very considerable distance, equal to the diameter of the Moon. The star is now called *Barnard's star*.

Barnard's other discoveries included various novae, variable stars, and binary stars. He was also one of the first to appreciate that dark nebulae were not areas of the sky containing no stars at all (as William Herschel had thought) but as Barnard and Max Wolf demonstrated were enormous clouds of dust and gas that shielded the stars behind them from our view. By 1919 he had discovered nearly 200 such nebulae.

BARNARD, Joseph Edwin (b. Dec. 7, 1870; London; d. Oct. 25, 1949; Addiscombe, England) British physicist.

Whilst working in his father's business, Barnard used his spare time to study at the Lister Institute, King's College, London, where he developed an interest in microscopy, especially photomicrography, which led to his receiving a chair at the Charing Cross Medical School. He was a fellow and three times president of the Royal Microscopical Society and in 1920 became honorary director of the applied-optics department at the National Institute for Medical Research.

His research and experience in photomicrography led him to write *Practical Photomicrography* (1911), which became a standard work. Later he developed a technique for using ultraviolet radiation, which is of shorter wavelength than visible light, and therefore gives greater resolution. With W. E. Gye he used this method to identify several ultramicroscopic organisms connected with malignant growths that were too small to see using standard microscopy.

BARRINGER, Daniel Moreau (b. May 25, 1860; Raleigh, North Carolina; d. 1929) American mining engineer and geologist.

Barringer graduated from Princeton in 1879 and then studied law at Pennsylvania, geology at Harvard, and chemistry and mineralogy at the University of Virginia. In 1890 he established himself as a consulting mining engineer and geologist; he was the author of the standard work *Law of Mines and Mining in the US* (1907).

Barringer is remembered for his investigation of the massive Diabolo Crater in Arizona, which is nearly 600 feet (200 m) deep and over 4000 feet (1200 m) in diameter. The cause of such a gigantic hole was a matter of speculation, most considering it to be of volcanic origin. Barringer, finding numerous nickel–iron rocks in the area, became convinced that the remains of an enormous meteorite lay buried at the center of the crater. He began drilling in 1902 but failed to find anything of significance. He later concluded that a meteorite would have been unlikely to enter vertically; after experimenting with projectiles he established that it probably entered at an angle of 45° and would therefore be embedded to one side. In 1922 drilling began again but rapid flooding of the shafts caused Barringer to abandon the search. After his death the crater became known as the *Barringer Meteor Crater*.

BARROW, Isaac (b. 1630; London; d. May 4, 1677; London) British mathematician.

Barrow obtained his degree in 1648 but because of the unrest of the Cromwellian period was unable to take up an academic post until 1660 when he became professor of Greek at Cambridge University.

He held the Lucasian Chair in Mathematics at Cambridge University from 1664 until 1669 when he resigned the chair in favor of his brilliant pupil Isaac Newton. Barrow's own mathematical work came very close to anticipating some of the basic concepts of the differential calculus; in his *Lectiones geometriae* (1670) he describes a method of calculating tangents to curves. In addition to being a mathematician Barrow was also a noted classicist and theologian and he produced a widely used translation of Euclid's *Elements*.

BARTHOLIN, Erasmus (b. Aug. 13, 1625; Roskilde, Denmark; d. Nov. 4, 1698; Copenhagen) Danish mathematician.

Bartholin, the son of Caspar and brother of Thomas Bartholin, who were both distinguished anatomists, was educated in Leiden and Padua, where he obtained his MD in 1654. After further travel in France and England he returned to Denmark in 1656 and held chairs in mathematics and medicine at the University of Copenhagen from 1657 until his death.

Bartholin worked on the theory of equations and with Olaus Rømer made an unsuccessful attempt to calculate the orbits of the comets prominent in the late 1660s. He is however best remembered for his discovery of double refraction announced in his *Experimenta crystalli Islandici disdiaclastici* (1669). In it he described how Icelandic feldspar (calcite) produces a double image of objects observed through it. This discovery greatly puzzled scientists and was much discussed by Newton and Christiaan Huygens who tried unsuccessfully to incorporate the strange phenomenon into their respective theories of light.

Double refraction proved remarkably recalcitrant to all proposed explanations for well over a century and it was only with the work of Etienne Malus on polarized light in 1808, and that of Augustin Fresnel in 1817 that Bartholin's observations could at last be understood.

BARTLETT, Neil (b. Sept. 15, 1932; Newcastle-upon-Tyne, England) British–American chemist.

Bartlett was educated at the University of Durham, England, where he obtained his PhD in 1957. He taught at the University of British Columbia, Canada, and at Princeton before being appointed to a chemistry professorship in 1969 at the University of California, Berkeley.

Bartlett was studying metal fluorides and found that the compound platinum hexafluoride (PtF_6) is extremely active. In fact it reacted with molecular oxygen to form the novel compound $O_2^+PtF_6^-$. At the time it was an unquestioned assumption of chemistry that the noble gases — helium, neon, argon, krypton, and xenon — were completely inert, incapable of forming any compounds whatsoever. Further, there was a solid body of valence theory that provided good reasons why this should be so.

So struck was Bartlett with the ability of PtF_6 to react with other substances that he tried, in 1962, to form a compound between it and xenon. To his and other chemists' surprise xenon fluoroplatinate ($XePtF_6$) was produced — the first compound of a noble gas. Once the first compound had been detected xenon was soon shown to form other compounds, such as xenon fluoride (XeF_4) and oxyfluoride ($XeOF_4$). Krypton and radon were also found to form compounds although the lighter inert gases have so far remained inactive.

BARTLETT, Paul Doughty (b. Aug. 14, 1907; Ann Arbor, Michigan) American chemist.

Bartlett was educated at Amherst College and Harvard, where he obtained his PhD in 1931. After teaching briefly at the Rockefeller Institute and the University of Minnesota he returned to Harvard in 1934 and served there as professor of chemistry from 1948 until his retirement in 1975.

Bartlett has worked mainly on the mechanisms involved in organic reactions; for example, the behavior of free radicals and the kinetics of polymerization reactions. He has also investigated the chemistry of elemental sulfur and the terpenes (a family of hydrocarbons found in the essential oil of plants).

BARTON, Sir Derek Harold Richard (b. Sept. 8, 1918; Gravesend, England) British chemist.

Barton was educated at Imperial College, London, where he obtained his PhD in 1942. After doing some industrial research he spent a year as visiting lecturer at Harvard before being appointed reader (1950) and then professor (1953) in organic chemistry at Birkbeck College, London. Barton moved to a similar chair at Glasgow University in 1955 but returned to Imperial College in 1957 and held the chair of chemistry until 1978, when he became director of the Institute for the Chemistry of Natural Substances at Gif-sur-Yvette in France.

In 1950 Barton published a fundamental paper on conformational analysis in which he proposed that the orientations in space of functional groups affect the rates of reaction in isomers. Barton discussed six-membered organic rings, particularly, following the earlier work of Odd Hassell, the 'chair' conformation of cyclohexane and explained its distinctive stability.

This was done in terms of the distinction between equatorial conformations, in which the hydrogen atoms lie in the same plane as the carbon ring, and axial, where they are perpendicular to the ring. He confirmed these notions with further work on the stability and reactivity of steroids and terpenes.

It was for this work that he shared the 1969 Nobel Chemistry Prize with Hassell. Barton's later work on oxyradicals and his predictions about their behavior in reactions helped in the development of a simple method for synthesizing the hormone aldosterone.

BARY, Heinrich Anton de See DE BARY, Heinrich Anton.

BASOV, Nikolai Gennediyevich (b. Dec. 14, 1922; Voronezh, now in the Soviet Union) Russian physicist.

Basov served in the Soviet army in World War II, following which he graduated from the Moscow Institute of Engineering Physics (1950). He studied at the Lebedev Institute of Physics of the Soviet Academy of Sciences in Moscow, gaining his doctoral degree in 1956 and going on to become deputy directory (1958) and later head of the laboratory (1962).

Basov's major contribution was in the development of the maser (*m*icrowave *a*mplification by *s*timulated *e*mission of *r*adiation), the forerunner of the laser. From 1952 he had been researching the possibility of amplifying electromagnetic radiation using excited atoms or molecules. His colleague at the Lebedev Institute, Aleksandr Prokhorov, was involved in the microwave spectroscopy of gases, with the aim of creating a precise frequency standard, for use in very accurate clocks and navigational systems. Their work led to theories and experiments designed to produce a state of 'population inversion' in molecular beams, through which amplification of radiofrequency radiation became possible.

Together Basov and Prokhorov in 1955 developed a generator using a beam of excited ammonia molecules. This was the maser, developed simultaneously but independently in America by Charles Townes. Basov, Prokhorov, and Townes received the 1964 Nobel Prize for physics for this work.

The first masers used a method of selecting the more excited molecules from a beam, but a more efficient method was proposed by Basov and Prokhorov in 1955, the so-called 'three-level' method of producing population inversion by 'pumping' with a powerful auxilliary source of radiation. The next year the method was applied by Nicolaas Bloembergen in America in a quantum amplifier.

Basov went on to develop the laser principle, and in 1958 introduced the idea of using semiconductors to achieve laser action. In the years 1960–65 he realized many of his ideas in practical systems. He has since done considerable theoretical work on pulsed ruby and neodymium-glass lasers, which are now in common use, and on the interaction of radiation with matter. In particular, he has studied the production of short powerful pulses of coherent light.

BASSI, Agostino (b. Sept. 25, 1773; Lodi, now in Italy; d. Feb. 8, 1856; Lodi) Italian microbiologist.

Bassi, who was educated at the University of Pavia, conducted valuable research into animal diseases. Anticipating Pasteur, he suggested that certain diseases are caused by minute animal or plant parasites. Some of his most important studies were concerned with cholera and with pellagra, a deficiency disease of the skin. In 1835 he was able to show that the disease of silkworms known as *muscardine* was caused by a fungus, subsequently named *Botrytis bassiana* in his honor. He demonstrated that muscardine is contagious and formulated methods to prevent and eliminate the disease. Bassi also published accounts of work on potato cultivation, cheese-making, and vinification.

BATES, Henry Walter (b. Feb. 8, 1825; Leicester, England; d. Feb. 16, 1892; London) British naturalist and explorer.

The son of a stocking-factory owner, Bates left school at 13 and was apprenticed to a hosiery manufacturer, but still found time for indulging his hobby of beetle collecting. In 1844 he met Alfred Wallace and stimulated the latter's interest in entomology. This led, three years later, to Wallace suggesting they should travel together to the tropics to collect specimens and data that might throw light on the evolution of species.

In May 1848 they arrived at Pará, Brazil, near the mouth of the Amazon. After two years collecting together they split up, and Bates spent a further nine years in the Amazon basin. By the time he returned to England in 1859, he estimated he had collected 14712 species, 8000 of which were new to science.

While collecting Bates had noted startling similarities between certain butterfly species — a phenomenon later to be termed *Batesian mimicry*. He attributed this to natural selection, since palatable butterflies that closely resembled noxious species would be left alone by predators and thus tend to increase. His paper on this, *Contributions to an Insect Fauna of the Amazon Valley, Lepidoptera: Heliconidae* (1861) provided strong supportive evidence for the Darwin–Wallace evolutionary theory published three years earlier.

Darwin persuaded Bates to write a book on his travels, which resulted in the appearance of *The Naturalist on the River Amazon* (1863), an objective account of the animals, humans, and natural phenomena Bates encountered. Although one of the best and most popular books of its kind, Bates was to comment that he would rather spend a further 11 years on the Amazon than write another book.

Bates became assistant secretary of the Royal Geographic Society in 1864, a post he held until his death. His later work was mostly concerned with insect classification and the editing of travel books.

BATES, Leslie Fleetwood (b. Mar. 7, 1897; Bristol, England; d. Jan. 20, 1978; Nottingham, England) British physicist.

Bates was educated at Bristol University and at Cambridge University, where he obtained his PhD in 1922. After teaching first at University College, London, he moved to Nottingham where he served as professor of physics from 1936, apart from wartime duties on the degaussing of ships, until his retirement in 1964.

Most of Bates's work was on the magnetic properties of materials. He was the author of a widely used textbook, which went through many editions, *Modern Magnetism* (1938).

BATESON, William (b. Aug. 8, 1861; Whitby, England; d. Feb. 8, 1926; Merton, England) British geneticist.

Bateson graduated in natural sciences from Cambridge University in 1883, having specialized in zoology. He then traveled to America, where he studied the embryology of the wormlike marine creature *Balanog-*

lossus. He discovered that, although its larval stage resembles that of the echinoderms (e.g. starfish), it also has gill slits, the beginnings of a notochord, and a dorsal nervecord, proving it to be a primitive chordate. This was the first evidence that the chordates have affinities with the echinoderms.

Back at Cambridge Bateson began studying variation within populations and soon found instances of discontinuous variation that could not simply be related to environmental conditions. He believed this to be of evolutionary importance, and began breeding experiments to investigate the phenomenon more fully. These prepared him to accept Mendel's work when it was rediscovered in 1900, although other British scientists were largely skeptical of the work. Bateson translated Mendel's paper into English and set up a research group at Grantchester to investigate heredity in plants and animals.

Through his study of the inheritance of comb shape in poultry, Bateson demonstrated that Mendelian ratios are found in animal crosses (as well as plants). He turned up various deviations from the normal dihybrid ratio (9:3:3:1), which he rightly attributed to gene interaction. He also found that certain traits are governed by two or more genes, and in his sweet-pea crosses showed that some characters are not inherited independently. This was the first hint that genes are linked on chromosomes, but Bateson never accepted T. H. Morgan's explanation of linkage or the chromosome theory of inheritance.

In 1908 Bateson became the first professor of the subject he himself named — genetics. However he left Cambridge only a year later and in 1910 became director of the newly formed John Innes Horticultural Institution at Merton, Surrey, where he remained until his death. He was the leading proponent of Mendelian genetics in Britain and became involved in a heated controversy with supporters of biometrical genetics such as Karl Pearson. The views of both sides were later reconciled by the work of Ronald Fisher. Bateson wrote a number of books, including the controversial *Materials for the Study of Variation* (1894) and *Mendelian Heredity — A Defence* (1902); he also founded, with R. C. Punnett, the *Journal of Genetics* in 1910.

BAWDEN, Sir Frederick Charles (b. Aug. 18, 1908; North Tawton, England) British plant pathologist.

Bawden was educated at Cambridge University, receiving his MA in 1933. From 1936 to 1940 he worked in the virus physiology department at Rothamsted Experimental Station, becoming the head of the plant pathology department in 1940 and director of the station in 1958.

In 1937 Bawden discovered that the tobacco mosaic virus (TMV) contains ribonucleic acid, this being the first demonstration that nucleic acids occur in viruses. With Norman Pirie, Bawden isolated TMV in crystalline form and made important contributions to elucidating virus structure and means of multiplication. Bawden's work also helped in revealing the mechanisms of protein formation.

BAYER, Johann (b. 1572; Rhain, now in West Germany; d. Mar. 7, 1625; Augsburg, now in West Germany) German astronomer.

Bayer was an advocate (lawyer) by profession. In 1603 he published *Uranometria,* the most complete catalog of pretelescopic astronomy. To Tycho Brahe's catalog of 1602, he added nearly a thousand new stars and twelve new southern constellations. The catalog's main importance, however, rests on Bayer's innovation of naming stars by letters of the Greek alphabet. Before Bayer, prominent stars were given proper names, mainly Arabic ones such as Altair and Rigel. If not individually named, they would be referred to by their position in the constellation. Bayer introduced the scheme, which is still used, of referring to the brightest star of a constellation by 'alpha', the second brightest by 'beta', and

so on. Thus, Altair, which is the brightest star in the constellation Aquila, is systematically named Alpha Aquilae. If there were more stars than letters of the Greek alphabet, the dimmer ones could be denoted by letters of the Roman alphabet and, if necessary, numbers. Bayer's other proposed innovation — to name constellations after characters in the Bible — was less successful.

BAYLISS, Sir William Maddock (b. May 2, 1860; Wolverhampton, England; d. Aug. 27, 1924; London) British physiologist.

Bayliss was the son of a wealthy iron manufacturer. In 1881 he entered University College, London, as a medical student but when he failed his second MB exam in anatomy he gave up medicine to concentrate on physiology. He graduated from Oxford University in 1888, then returned to University College, London, where he worked for the rest of his life, holding the chair of general physiology from 1912. Bayliss was elected a fellow of the Royal Society in 1903 and was knighted in 1922. He was chiefly interested in the physiology of the nervous, digestive, and vascular systems, on which he worked in association with his brother-in-law, Ernest Starling. Their most important work, published in 1902, was the discovery of the action of a hormone (secretin) in controlling digestion. They showed that in normal digestion the acidic contents of the stomach stimulate production of the hormone secretin when they reach the duodenum. Secretin is transported in the bloodstream to initiate secretion of digestive juices by the pancreas. In 1915 Bayliss produced a standard textbook on physiology, *Principles of General Physiology,* which treated the subject from a physicochemical point of view.

BEADLE, George Wells (b. Oct. 22, 1903; Wahoo, Nebraska) American geneticist.

Beadle graduated from the University of Nebraska in 1926 and gained his PhD from Cornell University in 1931. He then spent two years doing research in genetics under T. H. Morgan at the California Institute of Technology. In 1937 Beadle went to Stanford University, where in 1940 he began working with Edward Tatum on the mold *Neurospora*. They used nutritional mutants, which were unable to synthesize certain essential dietary compounds, to determine the sequence of various metabolic pathways. Substances similar to the missing compound were added to the mutant mold cultures to find whether or not they could substitute for the lacking chemical. If the culture survived then it could be assumed that the mold could convert the supplied substance into the chemical it needed, showing that the added nutrient was likely to be a precursor of the missing chemical.

From this and similar work Beadle and Tatum concluded that the function of a gene was to control the production of a particular enzyme and that a mutation in any one gene would cause the formation of an abnormal enzyme that would be unable to catalyze a certain step in a chain of reactions. This reasoning led to the formulation of the one gene–one enzyme hypothesis, for which Beadle and Tatum received the 1958 Nobel Prize for physiology or medicine, sharing the prize with Joshua Lederberg, who had worked with Tatum on bacterial genetics.

BEAUFORT, Sir Francis (b. May 27, 1774; Navan, now in the Republic of Ireland; d. Dec. 17, 1857; Brighton, England) British hydrographer.

Beaufort's father was a cleric of Huguenot origin who took an active interest in geography and topography, publishing in 1792 one of the earliest detailed maps of Ireland. Beaufort joined the East India Company in 1789 and enlisted in the Royal Navy the following year, remaining on active service until 1812.

He proposed, in 1806, the wind scale named after him. This was an objective scale ranging from calm (0) up to storm (13) in which wind strength was correlated with the amount of sail a full-rigged ship would carry appropriate to the wind conditions. It was first used officially by Robert Fitzroy in 1831 and adopted by the British Admiralty in 1838. When sail gave way to steam the scale was modified by defining levels on it in terms of the state of the sea or, following George Simpson (q.v.), wind speed.

In 1812 Beaufort surveyed and charted the Turkish coast, later writing his account of the expedition, *Karamania* (1817). He was appointed hydrographer to the Royal Navy in 1829. In this office Beaufort commissioned voyages to survey and chart areas of the world, such as those of the *Beagle* with Charles Darwin and the *Erebus* with Joseph Hooker. The sea north of Alaska was named for him.

BEAUMONT, (Jean Baptiste Armand Léonce) Elie de (b. Sept. 25, 1798; Canon, France; d. Sept. 21, 1874; Canon) French geologist.

Beaumont was educated at the Ecole Polytechnique and the School of Mines, Paris, and taught at the School of Mines from 1827, later becoming professor of geology there (1835). He is remembered chiefly for his theory on the origin of mountains. He published his views in 1830 in his *Revolutions de la surface du globe*, in which he argued that mountain ranges came into existence suddenly and were the result of distortions produced by the cooling crust of the Earth. Such a view fitted in well with the catastrophism of such zoologists as Georges Cuvier. Beaumont summarized his theories in his *Notice sur les systèmes des montagnes* (1852; On Mountain Systems).

Beaumont served as engineer-in-chief of mines for the period 1833–47. He also collaborated with Ours Pierre Dufrénoy in compiling the great geological map of France, published in 1840.

BEAUMONT, William (b. Nov. 21, 1785; Lebanon, Connecticut; d. Apr. 25, 1853; St. Louis, Missouri) American physician.

Beaumont started out as a farmhand and then a schoolteacher before becoming a doctor's apprentice. He received his license to practice medicine in 1812 and joined the army as a surgeon's mate. While serving as post surgeon at Fort Mackinac, Michigan, he treated a Canadian trapper, Alexis St. Martin, for wounds caused by a close-range shotgun blast. His patient recovered but was left with an opening (fistula) in his stomach wall. Beaumont took this opportunity to conduct pioneering experiments on the process of digestion in the human stomach, sampling its contents through the fistula and studying the rates of digestion of various foods and the effects of emotional changes on digestion. His *Experiments and Observations on the Gastric Juice and the Physiology of Digestion* (1833) helped trigger further research in this field.

BECHE, Sir Henry Thomas De La *See* DE LA BECHE, Sir Henry Thomas.

BECHER, Johann Joachim (b. May 6, 1635; Speyer, now in West Germany; d. 1682; England) German chemist and physician.

Becher, a pastor's son, was largely self-taught. After traveling throughout Europe he gained his MD from the University of Mainz in 1661 and became professor of medicine there in 1663. Short spells as court physician in Mainz (1663–64) and physician to the elector of Bavaria (1664) were followed by a period in Vienna from 1665, where he attempted to realise several economic projects, including a Rhine–Danube canal. He fell from favor and was forced to flee via Holland to England, where he died.

Becher is a transitional figure between alchemy and modern chemistry. He claimed to have a process for producing gold from silver and sand and his chemical system was an extension of the Paracelsian *Tria prima* of sulfur, salt, and mercury. He stated that all inorganic bodies were a mixture of water and three earthy principles: vitreous earth (*terra fusilis*), combustible earth (*terra pinguis*), and mercurial earth (*terra fluida*). *Terra pinguis* was identified as the cause of combustion and this became the phlogiston of Georg Stahl's later theory. Becher's most influential work was *Physicae subterraneae* (1669; Subterranean Physics), which was republished by Stahl in 1703. This work contained his theories on the nature of minerals and experiments.

BECKMANN, Ernst Otto (b. July 4, 1853; Sölingen, now in West Germany; d. July 12, 1923; Dahlem, now in West Berlin) German organic and physical chemist.

Beckmann's father was an industrial chemist who independently discovered the pigment Paris green. Ernst served an apprenticeship as a pharmacist before studying chemistry at the University of Leipzig, where he graduated in 1878. In 1886, while *Privatdozent* at Leipzig, he discovered the *Beckmann rearrangement* whereby ketoximes are converted into amides. This reaction was soon to be used by Arthur Hantzsch to determine the stereochemistry of the oximes.

Needing an efficient method for finding molecular weights, Beckmann devised the *Beckmann thermometer*, suitable for measuring changes in temperature over a small range. It is used in finding the elevation in boiling point or depression of freezing point for a solution — which can then be used to calculate the molecular weight of the solute. His other research included work on terpenes and the chlorides of sulfur and selenium. Beckmann was professor at Giessen (1891), Erlangen (1892), and Leipzig (1897). In 1912 he became the first director of the Kaiser Wilhelm Institute at Dahlem, a post with opportunities that never materialized owing to the demands of World War I.

BECQUEREL, Antoine Henri (b. Dec. 15, 1852; Paris; d. Aug. 25, 1908; Le Croisic, France) French physicist.

Becquerel's early scientific and engineering training was at the Ecole Polytechnique and the School of Bridges and Highways, and in 1876 he started teaching at the Polytechnique. From 1875 he researched into various aspects of optics and obtained his doctorate in 1888. In 1899 he was elected to the French Academy of Sciences, continuing the family tradition as his father and grandfather, both renowned physicists, had also been members. He held chairs at the Ecole Polytechnique, the Museum of Natural History, and the National Conservatory of Arts and Crafts, and became chief engineer in the department of bridges and highways.

Becquerel is remembered as the discoverer of radioactivity in 1896. Following Wilhelm Röntgen's discovery of x-rays the previous year, Becquerel began to look for x-rays in the fluorescence observed when certain salts absorb ultraviolet radiation. His method was to take crystals of potassium uranyl sulfate and place them in sunlight next to a piece of photographic film wrapped in black paper. The reasoning was that the sunlight induced fluorescence in the crystals and any x-rays present would penetrate the black paper and darken the film.

The experiments appeared to work and his first conclusion was that x-rays were present in the fluorescence. The true explanation of the darkened plate was discovered by chance. He left a plate in black paper next to some crystals in a drawer and some time later developed the plate. He found that this too was fogged, even though the crystals were not fluorescing. Becquerel investigated further and discovered that the salt gave off a penetrating radiation independently, without ultraviolet radiation. He deduced that the radiation came from the uranium in the salt.

Becquerel went on to study the properties of this radiation; in 1899 he showed that part of it could be deflected by a magnetic field and thus consisted of charged particles. In 1903 he shared the Nobel Physics Prize with Pierre and Marie Curie.

BEDDOES, Thomas (b. Apr. 13, 1760; Shiffnal, England; d. Dec. 24, 1808; London) British chemist and physician.

Beddoes studied classics at Oxford and medicine and chemistry at Edinburgh, where he was the pupil of Joseph Black. After obtaining his MD in 1787 he returned to Oxford as reader in chemistry.

When, in 1792, Beddoes lost his Oxford post because of his sympathy for the French Revolution, he approached the Lunar Society of Birmingham, which included Josiah Wedgwood, Joseph Priestley, Matthew Boulton, and James Watt, with the idea of forming an institute to investigate the medicinal uses of the gases discovered in the previous 20 years. As a result one of the first specialized research institutes, the Pneumatic Medical Institute was opened at Clifton, Bristol, in 1799 with Humphry Davy, then 19 years old, as Beddoes's assistant. The work proved disappointing except in the case of dinitrogen oxide (nitrous oxide, N_2O), the euphoriant properties of which provided Davy with his first serious chemical paper.

Beddoes's work on gases was published as *Considerations on the Medicinal Use of Factitious Airs* (1794–96). Beddoes later moved to London where he built up a successful medical practice.

BEEBE, Charles William (b. July 29, 1887; Brooklyn, New York; d. June 4, 1962; near Arima, Trinidad) American naturalist.

Beebe graduated from Columbia University in 1898 and the following year began organizing and building up the bird collection of the New York Zoological Park. After serving as a fighter pilot in World War I he became, in 1919, director of the Department of Tropical Research of the New York Zoological Society.

Beebe is noted as one of the pioneers of deep-sea exploration. His first observation capsule was a cylinder; later collaboration with the geologist and engineer Otis Barton resulted in the design of a spherical capsule (the *bathysphere*). Various dives were made and in August 1934 Beebe and Barton were lowered to a (then) record depth of 3028 feet (923 m) near Bermuda. Beebe made many interesting observations, such as the absence of light at 2000 feet (610 m), phosphorescent organisms, and an apparently unknown animal estimated to be some 20 feet (6.1 m) long. He abandoned deep-sea exploration after making thirty dives. Descents to even greater depths were subsequently made by Auguste Piccard and others.

BEER, Sir Gavin Rylands de *See* DE BEER, Sir Gavin Rylands.

BEER, Wilhelm (b. Jan. 4, 1797; Berlin; d. Mar. 27, 1850; Berlin) German astronomer.

Beer was a banker who, like his friend Johann Heinrich von Mädler, was a very competent amateur observer of Mars and the Moon. In 1830 they published the first reasonable map of Mars. It did not show the canals that Giovanni Schiaparelli and others were later to 'observe'. In 1836 they published a large map of the Moon that was the most comprehensive of its time. Beer also measured the heights of the larger lunar mountains.

BEGUYER DE CHANCOURTOIS, Alexandre Emile (b. Jan. 20, 1820; Paris; d. Nov. 14, 1886; Paris) French mineralogist.

Béguyer de Chancourtois, who was inspector-general of mines in France, is remembered for his work on the classification of the elements. In 1862 he proposed his system, known as the 'telluric screw', in which the elements were arranged in order of atomic weight and then plotted on a line descending at an angle of 45° from the top of a cylinder. It was found that elements on the same vertical line resembled each other.

The proposal received little attention, largely because it was published without the explanatory diagram, which made the article virtually impossible to understand. As with John Newlands's system of classifying the elements, Béguyer de Chancourtois's proposal was overshadowed by that of Dmitri Mendeleev, first published in 1869.

BEHRING, Emil Adolf von (b. Mar. 15, 1854; Hansdorf, now in East Germany; d. Mar. 31, 1917; Marburg, now in West Germany) German immunologist.

Behring graduated in medicine at Berlin University and entered the Army Medical Corps before becoming (in 1888) a lecturer in the Army Medical College, Berlin. In 1889 he moved to Robert Koch's Institute of Hygiene and transferred to the Institute of Infectious Diseases in 1891, when Koch was appointed its chief.

In 1890, working with Shibasaburo Kitasato, Behring showed that injections of blood serum from an animal suffering from tetanus could confer immunity to the disease in other animals. Behring found that the same was true for diphtheria and this led to the development of a diphtheria antitoxin for human patients, in collaboration with Paul Ehrlich. This treatment was first used in 1891 and subsequently caused a dramatic fall in mortality due to diphtheria.

Behring's success brought him many prizes, including the first Nobel Prize in physiology or medicine, awarded in 1901. He was appointed professor of hygiene at Halle University in 1894 and one year later moved to a similar post at Marburg. In 1913 he introduced toxin–antitoxin mixtures to immunize against diphtheria, a refinement of the immunization technique already in use. He also devised a vaccine for the immunization of calves against tuberculosis.

BEILBY, Sir George Thomas (b. Nov. 17, 1850; Edinburgh; d. Aug. 1, 1924; London) British industrial chemist.

Beilby, the son of a clergyman, was educated at Edinburgh University. He began work with an oil-shale company as a chemist in 1869 and increased the yield of paraffin and ammonia from oil shales by improving the process of their distillation. He also worked on cyanides, patenting, in 1890, a process for the synthesis of potassium cyanide in which ammonia was passed over a heated mixture of charcoal and potassium carbonate. This had wide use in the gold-extracting industry.

From 1907 to 1923 Beilby was chairman of the Royal Technical College, Glasgow, later the University of Strathclyde. He became interested in the economic use of fuel and smoke prevention, submitting evidence to the Royal Commission on Coal Supplies in 1902. In 1917 he was appointed as the first chairman of the Fuel Research Board. He was knighted in 1916.

BEILSTEIN, Friedrich Konrad (b. Feb. 17, 1838; St. Petersburg, now Leningrad in the Soviet Union; d. Oct. 18, 1906; St. Petersburg) Russian organic chemist.

Of German parentage, Beilstein studied chemistry in Germany under Bunsen, Liebig, and Wurtz and gained his PhD under Wöhler at Göttingen (1858). He was lecturer at Göttingen (1860–66) and from 1866 professor of chemistry at the Technological Institute at St. Petersburg.

Beilstein's many researches in organic chemistry included work on isomeric benzene derivatives. He is better remembered, however, for his monumental *Handbuch der organischen Chemie* (1880–82), in which he set out to record systematically all that was known of every organic compound. He produced the second (1886) and third (1900) editions, after which the work was assigned to the Deutsch Chemische Gesellschaft, who have published it ever since.

BÉKÉSY, Georg von (b. June 3, 1899; Budapest; d. June 13, 1972; Honolulu, Hawaii) Hungarian–American physicist.

Békésy, the son of a diplomat, studied chemistry at the University of Bern and physics at Budapest University, where he obtained his PhD in 1923. He immediately joined the research staff of the Hungarian Telephone Laboratory where he remained until 1946 while simultaneously holding the chair of experimental physics at Budapest University from 1939. He left Hungary in 1947, via the Swedish Karolinska Institute, for America, where he served first as a senior fellow in psychophysics at Harvard from 1949 to 1966 and finally as professor of sensory science at the University of Hawaii from 1966 until his death.

Békésy first worked on problems of long-distance telephone communication before moving to the study of the physical mechanisms of the cochlea within the inner ear. When he began this study it was generally thought, following the work of Hermann von Helmholtz, that sound waves entering the ear selectively stimulated a particular fiber of the basilar membrane; this in turn stimulated hairs of the organ of Corti resting on it, which transferred the signal to the auditory nerve.

Using the techniques of microsurgery, Békésy was able to show that a different mechanism is involved. He found that when sound enters the cochlea, a traveling wave sweeps along the basilar membrane. The wave amplitude increases to a maximum, falling sharply thereafter; it is this maximum point to which the organ of Corti is sensitive. For this insight into the mechanism of hearing, Békésy was awarded the 1961 Nobel Prize for physiology or medicine.

BEL, Joseph Achille Le *See* LE BEL, Joseph Achille.

BELL, Alexander Graham (b. Mar. 3, 1847;

Edinburgh; d. Aug. 2, 1922; Cape Breton Island, Nova Scotia) British inventor.

Bell's family were practitioners in elocution and speech correction and he himself trained in this. As a child he was taught mainly at home. For a short time he attended Edinburgh University and University College, London, after which he taught music and elocution at a school in Elgin, Scotland. It was in Elgin that he carried out his first studies on sound.

From 1868 Bell worked in London as his father's assistant, but after the death of his two brothers from tuberculosis, the family moved to Canada, where Alexander, who had also become ill, recovered. In 1871 he went to Boston where he gave lectures on his father's method of 'visible speech' — a system of phonetic symbols for teaching the deaf to speak. A year later he opened a school for teachers of the deaf. In 1873 he became professor of vocal physiology at Boston University.

With financial help from two of his deaf students, Bell experimented with the transmission of sound by electricity, aided by Thomas Watson, his technician. His multiple telegraph was patented in 1875 and, in 1876, the patent for the telephone was also granted. Bell's wife Mabel Hubbard, whom he married in 1877, was deaf. Later she founded the Aerial Experiment Association.

In 1880 he received the Volta Prize from France and the money was used to fund the laboratories in which an improved form of the gramophone was invented by Thomas Edison. Although best known as the inventor of the telephone, Bell investigated a wide range of related technical subjects, including sonar and various equipment for the deaf. In 1885 he bought land and established laboratories and a summer home on Cape Breton Island.

BELL, Sir Charles (b. Nov. 1774; Edinburgh; d. Apr. 28, 1842; Hallow, England) British physician.

Bell studied under his elder brother John, a surgeon, and attended lectures at Edinburgh University. In 1804, Charles moved to London, where he started his own surgical practice and began his investigations into the nervous system. In *A New Idea of the Anatomy of the Brain* (1811), Bell described how nerves are not single structures but bundles of many nerve fibers. He also showed that the anterior and posterior roots of each spinal nerve carry different types of nerve fibers, which he later clarified as being respectively excitatory (motor) and sensory in function. The French physiologist François Magendie is also credited with this discovery and the functional differentiation of the spinal nerve roots is sometimes called the *Bell–Magendie law*. In *The Nervous System of the Human Body* (1830), Bell amplified his findings, establishing that a nerve fiber can carry impulses in one direction only and that each muscle must be supplied with both excitatory and sensory fibers.

Bell also contributed to knowledge of facial paralysis and to other surgical fields besides lecturing at the Great Windmill Street School of Anatomy and the Middlesex Hospital. In addition, he wrote *Essays on the Anatomy of Expression in Painting* (1806). He received the first medal awarded by the Royal Society in 1829 and was knighted two years later.

BELL, (Susan) Jocelyn (Burnell) (b. July 15, 1943; York, England) British radio astronomer.

Bell, whose married name is Burnell, studied at Glasgow University and Cambridge University, from where she obtained her PhD in 1968. She was a research fellow at the University of Southampton from 1968 to 1973 since when she has been a part-time research fellow at the Mullard Space Science Laboratory, University College, London.

It was Bell who discovered the first pulsar in 1967. She was a research student of Antony Hewish at Cambridge University and was using the 4.5-acre telescope at a radio wavelength of 3.7 meters. This produced 400 feet of recorder-chart paper a week, which it was Bell's job to analyze for what is known as 'interstellar scintillation'. This could be used to detect radio sources with tiny angular diameters, as opposed to larger radio galaxies. From early August 1967 she began to notice some strange scintillations coming from a weak source in the middle of the night when scintillation is normally low. They came and went unpredictably over the next three months and it was not until late November, when they returned once more, that high-speed recordings were made of them. They revealed a regular succession of pulses at intervals of just over a second — 1.337 301 13 seconds to be precise with an accuracy better than one part in a hundred million.

This led to intense activity by the Cambridge astronomers in which such obvious explanations as satellite signals and signals from 'Little Green Men' in extraterrestrial civilizations were eliminated before Hewish finally made the discovery public in 1968. Many theories were proposed concerning the nature of the pulsar and eventually the idea of a rapidly rotating neutron star, put forward independently in 1968 by Franco Pacini and Thomas Gold, was accepted.

In an earlier age the pulsar would no doubt have been known as 'Bell's star'; today it is simply known as CP 1919.

BELON, Pierre (b. 1517; Le Mans, France; d. April 1564; Paris) French naturalist.

Belon studied medicine in Paris, and in 1540 went to Germany to study botany. He became a leading figure in the 16th-century revival of natural history that followed the great voyages, the invention of printing, and the new artistic realism of the Renaissance.

Between 1546 and 1549 Belon traveled in the eastern Mediterranean countries, comparing the animals and plants he observed with their descriptions by classi-

cal authors. The results were published as *Les Observations des plusieurs singularitez et choses mémorables trouvées en Grèce, Asie, Judée, Egypte, Arabie et autre pays éstranges* (1553; Observations of Many Singularities and Memorable Items in Greece, Asia, Judea, Egypt, Arabia, and Other Foreign Countries). On his travels, Belon was in the habit of investigating the birds and fishes that came to market, and in England he met the Venetian, Daniel Barbaro, who had made many drawings of Adriatic fishes. From these sources Belon produced two books on fishes: *L'Histoire naturelle des éstranges poissons marins* (1551; The Natural History of Foreign Sea Fish) and *De aquatilibus* (1553). The first is notable for its dissertation on the dolphin, in which he identified the common Atlantic species with the dolphin of the ancients and distinguished it from the porpoise.

Belon's principal achievement is a history of birds, *L'Histoire de la nature des oyseaux* (1555; The Natural History of Birds). An illustrated book of the kind inspired by the drawings of Albrecht Dürer and Leonardo da Vinci, it describes about 200 birds, mostly of European origin. He drew attention to the correspondence between the skeletons of birds and man, an early hint of the discipline of comparative anatomy.

Belon was also interested in geology and botany and is reputed to have introduced the Cedar of Lebanon into western Europe. He also established two botanical gardens in France and suggested that many exotic plants might be acclimatized and grown in temperate regions. In many ways a typical figure of the Renaissance, Belon's end was all too typical of that time, for he was murdered in the Bois de Boulougne in 1564.

BELOUSOV, Vladimir Vladimirovich (b. Oct. 30, 1907; Moscow) Russian geologist and geophysicist.

Belousov became head of the department of geodynamics at the Soviet

Academy of Sciences, Moscow, in 1942 and was later (1953) made professor of geophysics at Moscow University. His main work has concentrated on the structure and development of the Earth's crust. In 1942 he put forward his theory on Earth movements, in which he proposed that the Earth's material has gradually separated according to its density and this is responsible for movements in the crust. He at first rejected theories on continental drift.

Belousov became chairman of the Soviet Joint Geophysical Committee in 1961. His works include *Principles of Geotectonics* (1975).

BENACERRAF, Baruj (b. Oct. 29, 1920; Caracas, Venezuela) American immunologist.

Benacerraf was brought up in France but moved to America in 1940, becoming naturalized in 1943. He studied at Columbia and the University of Virginia where he obtained his MD in 1945. He worked first at the Columbia Medical School before spending the period 1950–56 at the Hospital Broussais in Paris. He returned to America in 1956 to the New York Medical School where he served from 1960 to 1968 as professor of pathology. After a short period at the National Institute of Allergy and Infectious Diseases at Bethesda, Maryland, Benacerraf accepted the chair of comparative pathology at Harvard in 1970.

In the 1960s, working with guinea pigs, Benacerraf began to reveal some of the complex activity of the H-2 system, described by George Snell (q.v.). In particular he identified the Ir (immune response) genes of the H2 segment as playing a crucial role in the immune system. This was achieved by injecting simple, synthetic, and controllable 'antigens' into his experimental animals and noting that some strains responded immunologically while others were quite tolerant. Such differential responses have so far indicated there are over 30 Ir genes in the H2 complex.

Later work began to show how virtually all responses of the immune system, whether to grafts, tumor cells, bacteria, or viruses, are under the control of the H2 region. Benacerraf and his colleagues continued to explore its genetic and immunologic properties and also to extend their work to the analagous HLA system in humans. This work may well be important in the study of certain diseases, such as multiple sclerosis and ankylosing spondylitis, which have been shown to entail defective immune responses.

In 1980 Benacerraf was awarded for this work, together with Snell and Jean Dausset, the Nobel Physiology or Medicine Prize.

BENEDEN, Edouard van (b. Mar. 5, 1846; Louvain, Belgium; d. Apr. 28, 1910; Liège, Belgium) Belgian cytologist and embryologist.

Son of the zoologist Pierre-Joseph van Beneden, Edouard followed his father's footsteps, taking charge of zoology teaching at Liège University in 1870. Here he extended Walther Flemming's work on cell division. Working with the horse intestinal worm, *Ascaris megalocephala*, Beneden had demonstrated by 1887 that the chromosome number in all the body cells is constant, but that this number is halved in the germ cells. This halving is achieved because the two successive divisions preceding ova and spermatozoa formation are accompanied by only one chromosome doubling. Such a reduction division (meiosis) is necessary to prevent chromosome numbers from doubling on fertilization.

Beneden also made important contributions to embryology from his studies on the cleavage and gastrulation of the fertilized egg.

BENNET, Abraham (b. 1750; England; d. 1799; England) British physicist.

Bennet's scientific work was in electrostatics, the study of stationary electric charges and their effects, and he contributed many experiments and observations to the early development of this field. He was the inventor of the gold-leaf electrometer (an instrument for detecting and measuring electric charges) and did various experiments on electrostatic induction (the effect by which one body induces a charge on a nearby uncharged body). He also tried, though unsuccessfully, to demonstrate that light has momentum by focusing light rays on a sheet of paper hanging free in a vacuum.

BENTHAM, George (b. Sept. 22, 1800; Stoke, near Plymouth, England; d. Sept. 10, 1884; London) British botanist.

Bentham, son of the naval architect Samuel Bentham, first became interested in botany at the age of 17, while living in France with his parents. There he read Augustin Pyrame de Candolle's revision of J.B. Lamarck's *Flore Française* and was much impressed with its analytical keys for plant identification. Thus began his consuming interest in plant taxonomy, on which he consistently worked during his leisure time.

From 1826 to 1832 he was secretary to his uncle, the famous jurist and philosopher, Jeremy Bentham, and studied for the bar at Lincoln's Inn. However, in 1833 he abandoned law for his growing botanical collection and library, which he generously presented to the Royal Botanic Gardens, Kew, in 1854. He then worked at Kew for the rest of his life.

His first botanical work, *Catalogue des plantes indigènes des Pyrénées et du bas Languedoc* (Catalog of the Indigenous Plants of the Pyrenees and lower Languedoc), was published in Paris in November 1826. On his return to England he published *Outlines of a New System of Logic* (1827). Then beginning in the early 1830s, Bentham turned his attention more to botany and his first important work in this field, *Labiatarum Genera et Species*,

appeared between 1832 and 1836. While at Kew he published his popular *Handbook of the British Flora* (1858) and contributed to the Kew series of colonial floras with his *Flora Hongkongensis* (1861) and the seven-volume *Flora Australiensis* (1863–78). In collaboration with Joseph Hooker (q.v.) he produced his greatest work, the *Genera Plantarum* (1862–83), which remains a standard in plant classification.

BENZ, Karl Friedrich (b. Nov. 25, 1844; Karlsruhe, now in West Germany; d. Apr. 4, 1929; Ladenburg, now in West Germany) German engineer.

Benz, the son of a railway engineer, trained in mechanical engineering (1853–64). He opened his own machine-tools works in Mannheim and in 1877 began experimenting with a two-cycle engine. In 1885 he ran his first Benz car, a three-wheeled vehicle now preserved in Munich, which was the first practical automobile powered by an internal-combustion engine. The vehicle was not patented until January 1886. The company founded by Benz to manufacture the vehicle, Benz & Cie., produced its first four-wheeled automobile in 1893 and its first series of racing cars in 1899. Benz left the company in about 1906; it later merged to form Daimler–Benz (1926), the makers of Mercedes-Benz automobiles.

BENZER, Seymour (b. Oct. 15, 1921; New York City) American geneticist.

Benzer graduated from Brooklyn College in 1942 and gained his PhD in physics from Purdue University in 1947. He spent the years 1948–52 at various research institutes to familiarize himself with biological techniques, returning to Purdue as assistant professor in biophysics.

Benzer hoped to disprove the theory that the gene is an indivisible unit by demonstrating that recombination can occur within genes. However, such recombinations would be expected to occur so rarely that huge numbers of organisms would need to be studied to find one. In 1954 Benzer found a suitable organism to work on — the virus T4, a bacteriophage that infects the bacterium *Escherichia coli*. It multiplies approximately 100 fold in 20 minutes, giving millions of phage in a relatively short period.

Benzer found various mutants of T4, termed rII mutants, that had lost the ability to multiply on a specific strain of *E. coli*. He mixed together mutants that had mutated in different parts of the same gene and placed the mixture on a dish of *E. coli*. Any recombination within the gene that restored its function (and thus its ability to multiply in and destroy the bacteria) could be easily identified as clear areas in the *E. coli* dish. Such areas were indeed found, which proved that the gene can be split into recombining elements and verified James Watson's and Francis Crick's model of the gene as consisting of many nucleotide pairs.

Benzer went on to show that the number of distinguishable mutation sites corresponds with the estimated number of nucleotide pairs for that gene and that the sites are arranged linearly. He identified functionally independent units within the gene, naming these 'cistrons'.

Benzer has also done important work on chemical mutagens and on the degeneracy of the genetic code. More recently he has concentrated on the genetic control of behavior and the application of molecular biology to brain function. He moved from Purdue University to the California Institute of Technology in 1965, becoming professor of biology in 1967 and Boswell Professor of Neuroscience in 1975.

BERG, Paul (b. June 30, 1926; New York City) American molecular biologist.

Berg was educated at Pennsylvania State University and Western Reserve, where he obtained his PhD in 1952. He taught first at the School of Medicine at Washington University, St. Louis, moving to the University of Stanford in California in 1959, where he became professor of biochemistry in 1960.

In 1955 Francis Crick proposed his adaptor hypothesis, in which he argued that amino acids did not interact directly with the RNA template but were brought together by an adaptor molecule. Crick offered little information on the nature of such molecules, merely arguing that they were unlikely to be large protein molecules and suggesting that there might well be a specific adaptor for each of the 20 amino acids. In 1956 Berg successfully identified such an adaptor, later known as transfer RNA, even though he was then unaware of Crick's hypothesis. He found a small RNA molecule that appeared to be quite specific to the amino acid methionine.

Berg's name later became known to a much wider public with the publication in *Science* (24 July, 1974) of the 'Berg letter', written with the backing of many leading molecular biologists, in which he gave clear warning of the dangers inherent in the uncontrolled practice of recombinant DNA experiments. It had become possible, Berg stated, to excise portions of DNA from one organism, using specialized enzymes, and to insert them into the DNA of another organism. For example, the harmless microorganism *Escherichia coli*, found in all laboratories, could be implanted with active DNA from the tumor-causing virus SV 40 and perhaps allowed to spread throughout a human population with quite unpredictable results. Berg consequently proposed an absolute voluntary moratorium on certain types of experiment and strict control on a large number of others. An international conference was held in Asilomar, California, followed by the publication of strict guidelines by the National Institutes of Health in 1976. That such agreement could be reached and maintained, it has been claimed, was largely a result of the integrity and authority of Berg. Ironically Berg was awarded the Nobel Chemistry Prize in 1980 for the large part he played in developing the splicing techniques that made recombinant DNA techniques possible in the first place.

BERGER, Hans (b. May 21, 1873; Neuses, now in West Germany; d. June 1, 1941; Bad Blankenburg, now in East Germany) German psychiatrist.

Berger studied medicine at the University of Jena and then joined the university psychiatric clinic in 1897 as an assistant, eventually serving as its director and professor of psychiatry (1919–38). In his early work, he attempted to correlate physical factors in the brain, such as blood flow and temperature, with brain function. Disappointing results in this area made Berger turn to investigating the electrical activity of the brain. In 1924 he made the first human electroencephalogram by recording, as a trace, the minute changes in electrical potential measured between two electrodes placed on the surface of the head. Berger subsequently characterized the resultant wave patterns, including alpha and beta waves, and published his findings in 1929. The technique of electroencephalography is now used to diagnose such diseases as brain tumors and epilepsy. It is also used in psychiatric research and in diagnosing brain death.

BERGERON, Tor Harold Percival (b. Aug. 15, 1891; Stockholm) Swedish meteorologist.

Bergeron studied at the universities of Stockholm and Leipzig. During the period 1925–28 he worked at the famous Geophysical Institute at Bergen before taking a teaching appointment at Oslo University (1929–35). He held various appointments in the Swedish Meteorological Institute and was elected to the chair of meteorology at Uppsala in 1947.

Bergeron is best known for his work on cloud formation and in 1935 published the fundamental paper *On the Physics of Clouds and Precipitation*. Clouds consist of minute drops of water, but these drops will only fall as rain when they coalesce to form sufficiently large drops. Bergeron considered various processes, such as electric attraction and collisions caused by tur-

bulence, but dismissed these as being too slow and inefficient. He therefore proposed a mechanism in which both ice crystals and water droplets are present in clouds. The water droplets tend to evaporate and the vapor then condenses onto the crystals. These fall, melt, and produce rain. Thus all rain, according to Bergeron, begins as snow and without the presence of ice crystals in the upper reaches of clouds there can be no rain. This theory was supported by the experimental and observational work of Walter Findeisen in 1939 and became known as the *Bergeron–Findeisen theory*. It does not explain precipitation from tropical clouds where temperatures are above freezing point.

Bergeron also produced important work on weather fronts, methods of weather forecasting, and the growth of ice sheets.

BERGIUS, Friedrich Karl Rudolph (b. Oct. 11, 1884; Goldschmieden, now in Poland; d. Mar. 30, 1949; Buenos Aires, Argentina) German industrial chemist.

The son of a chemicals industrialist, Bergius gained his doctorate at Leipzig (1907) and worked with Hermann Nernst at Berlin and Fritz Haber at Karlsruhe, where he became interested in high-pressure chemical reactions. He was a professor at the Technical University at Hannover (1909–14) and then worked for the Goldschmidt Organization until 1945.

He is noted for his development of the *Bergius process* — a method of treating coal or heavy oil with hydrogen in the presence of catalysts, so as to produce lower-molecular-weight hydrocarbons. The process was important as a German source of gasoline in World War II. After the war Bergius lived in Austria and Spain before settling in Argentina as a technical adviser to the government, working on the production of sugar, alcohol, and cattle feed from wood. He shared the Nobel Prize for chemistry with Carl Bosch in 1931.

BERGMAN, Torbern Olaf (b. Mar. 20, 1735; Katrineberg, Sweden; d. July 8, 1784; Medivi, Sweden) Swedish chemist.

Bergman studied at the University of Uppsala, at first reading law and theology before turning to science and mathematics. He was a prolific scientist, working in physics, mathematics, and physical geography as well as chemistry. After graduating with a master's degree in 1758, he became professor of mathematics at Uppsala in 1761 and later professor of chemistry and pharmacy in 1767.

Bergman carried out many quantitative analyses, especially of minerals, and he extended the chemical classification of minerals devised by Axel Cronstedt. He remained an adherent of the phlogiston theory and although he firmly supported the doctrine of constant composition his analyses were not as solidly based as those of his later compatriot Jöns Berzelius. His most influential work was probably *Disquisitio de Attractionibus Electivis* (1785; A Dissertation on Elective Attractions). He compiled extensive tables listing relative chemical affinities of acids and bases. Bergman gave early encouragement to Karl Scheele, some of whose work he published.

BERGMANN, Max (b. Feb. 12, 1886; Fuerth, now in West Germany; d. Nov. 7, 1944; New York City) German organic chemist and biochemist.

Bergmann studied in Munich and Berlin and gained his PhD under Emil Fischer in 1911. He worked as Fischer's assistant in Berlin until the latter's death in 1919. From 1921 to 1934 he was director of the Kaiser Wilhelm Institute for Leather Research, Dresden, from which he resigned on Hitler's coming to power. He then emigrated to America where he worked as a member of the Rockefeller Institute for Medical Research.

Bergmann's research interests were those of his teacher, Fischer: carbohydrates and amino acids. In 1932 he dis-covered the carbobenzoxy method of peptide synthesis, the greatest advance in this field since Fischer's first peptide synthesis in 1901. In this method the amino group of amino acids is 'protected' by the carbobenzoxy group during condensation to form the peptide linkage and later freed by hydrolysis. Following Bergmann's work, many other protective groups have been used in peptide syntheses.

In America Bergmann investigated the specificity of proteinase enzymes and discovered (1937) that enzymes like papain were capable of splitting quite small peptides at precise linkages. The last three years of his life were devoted mainly to problems connected with the war.

BERGSTRÖM, Sune (b. Jan. 10, 1916; Stockholm) Swedish biochemist.

Bergström was educated at the Karolinska Institute, Stockholm, where he obtained his MD in 1943. In 1947 he was appointed to the chair of biochemistry at Lund, which he held until 1958 when he moved to a comparable position at the Karolinska Institute.

In the 1930s Ulf von Euler found an active substance in human semen capable of lowering blood pressure and causing muscle tissue to contract. He named it prostaglandin on the assumption that it came from the prostate gland. It soon became clear that there was not one such substance but a good many closely related ones with a variety of important physiological roles. Bergström has worked extensively on these compounds and in the late 1950s succeeded in purifying and crystallizing two of them.

BERINGER, Johann Bartholomaeus Adam (b. *c.* 1667; Würzburg, now in West Germany; d. Apr. 11, 1740; Würzburg) German geologist.

Beringer's father was the dean of medicine at the University of Würzburg. Beringer obtained his doctorate from Würzburg in 1693, and was appointed professor in 1694 — a position he held for the rest of his life.

He is largely remembered today for his extreme gullibility. Some colleagues, knowing him to be a keen fossil collector, decided to see if he could recognize artificial 'fossils'. They therefore prepared and scattered on the local hillside 'fossils' of an increasingly unlikely nature. Nothing seemed to alert the suspicions of Beringer and indeed, the more bizarre the figure, the more excited he became. He published an account of them in 1726 with full illustrations despite warnings that he was dealing with fakes. Finally, the story goes although there is no documentary evidence for this, he found a stone with his own name on it and spent the rest of his life trying to buy up copies of his book.

BERNAL, John Desmond (b. May 10, 1901; Nenagh, now in the Republic of Ireland; d. Sept. 15, 1971; London) British crystallographer.

Bernal's family were farmers in Ireland; his mother was an American journalist. He was educated at Cambridge University, where his first work on crystallography was done as an undergraduate on the mathematical theory of crystal symmetry. William Bragg offered him a post at the Royal Institution, which he joined in 1922.

Here Bernal worked on x-ray crystallography, studying a number of subjects including graphite, metals, vitamin D, and inorganic complexes. In 1927 he moved to Cambridge where he obtained the first x-ray photograph of a single-crystal protein (1933) and also worked on the tobacco mosaic virus. In 1937 he became professor of physics at Birkbeck College, London, and during World War II he was a government advisor working with Lord Mountbatten. After the war he continued at Birkbeck, where he concentrated on molecular biology.

Bernal was a prominent Marxist who was politically active in many committees. He was interested in the social function of science and wrote extensively on this subject including *The Social Function of Science* (1939).

BERNARD, Claude (b. July 12, 1813; St.-Julien, France; d. Feb. 10, 1878; Paris) French physiologist.

Bernard, the son of a poor wine grower, began writing plays to earn money but turned to medicine on the advice of a literary critic. His first experiences of medicine were discouraging but, following his appointment as assistant to François Magendie at the Collège de France, he began a period of extremely productive research. He drew attention to the importance of the pancreas in producing secretions for breaking down fat molecules into fatty acid and glycerine and showed that the main processes of digestion occur in the small intestine and not, as was previously thought, in the stomach. In 1856 he discovered glycogen, the starchlike substance in the liver, whose role is to build up a reserve of carbohydrate, which can be broken down to sugars as required; normally the sugar content of the blood remains steady as a result of this interaction. The digestive system, he found, is not just catabolic (breaking down complex molecules into simple ones), but anabolic, producing complex molecules (such as glycogen) from simple ones (such as sugars).

Bernard also did valuable work on the vasomotor system, demonstrating that certain nerves control the dilation and constriction of blood vessels; in hot weather blood vessels of the skin expand, releasing surplus heat, contracting during cold to conserve heat. The body is thus able to maintain a constant environment separate from outside influences. Apart from elucidating the role of the red blood corpuscles in transporting oxygen, Bernard's investigation of the action of carbon monoxide on the blood proved that the gas combines with hemoglobin, the effect being to cause oxygen starvation. He also carried out important work on the actions of drugs, such as the opium alkaloids and curare (curarine), on the sympathetic nerves.

Bernard's health deteriorated from 1860 and he spent less time in the laboratory. He thus turned to the philosophy of science and in 1865 published the famous *Introduction à la médecine expérimentale* (An Introduction to the Study of Experimental Medicine, 1927). The book discusses the importance of the constancy of the internal environment, refutes the notion of the 'vital force' to explain life, and emphasizes the need in planning experiments for a clear hypothesis to be stated, which may then be either proved or disproved. On the strength of this work he was elected to the French Academy in 1869.

BERNOULLI, Daniel (b. Jan. 29, 1700; Groningen, Netherlands; d. Mar. 17, 1782; Basel, Switzerland) Swiss mathematician.

Daniel was a son of Johann I Bernoulli. Of all the Bernoulli family he was probably the most outstanding mathematician and certainly the one with the widest scientific interests. Daniel studied at the universities of Basel, Strasbourg, and Heidelberg. His studies, which reflected his already wide interests, included logic, philosophy, and medicine in addition to mathematics.

In 1724 Daniel produced his first important piece of mathematical research. This was a work on differential equations, which sufficiently impressed the European scientific community to earn him an invitation to the St. Petersburg Academy of Sciences as a professor of mathematics. Once installed in Russia he continued to pursue his varied interests and obtained a post at the academy for his friend Leonhard Euler. In 1733 he left Russia to return to Switzerland to take up a chair in mathematics at Basel. Bernoulli's wide interests continued to occupy him and during his time at Basel he also held posts in botany, anatomy, physiology, and physics.

In Switzerland Daniel did the work for which he is best known, namely his virtual founding of the modern science of hydrodynamics using Isaac Newton's laws of force. He published these ideas in his *Hydrodynamica* (1738). Apart from his work in fluid dynamics Daniel made distinguished contributions to probability theory and differential equations in mathematics, and to electrostatics in physics. He also laid the basis for the kinetic theory of gases. Like his uncle, Jakob I Bernoulli, Daniel corresponded voluminously with many scholars throughout Europe, thus extensively disseminating his new ideas.

BERNOULLI, Jakob (or Jacques) I (b. Dec. 27, 1654; Basel, Switzerland; d. Aug. 16, 1705; Basel) Swiss mathematician.

Jakob I was the first of the Bernoulli family of scientists to achieve fame as a mathematician. As with the two other particularly outstanding Bernoullis — his brother, Johann I and nephew, Daniel — Jakob I played an important role in the development and popularization of the then recently invented integral and differential calculus of Isaac Newton and Gottfried Leibniz. His particular contribution to the calculus consisted in showing how it could be applied to a wide variety of fields of applied mathematics.

Jakob I began studying theology and in 1676 traveled through Europe where he met many of the important scientists of the day, such as Robert Boyle in England. He returned to Basel in 1682 where he began lecturing on mechanics and held a chair in mathematics at Basel University from 1687 until his death. Apart from his mathematical work he was an influential figure in the European scientific community through his voluminous correspondence.

His most important contributions to mathematics were in the fields of probability and in the calculus of variations. His work on probability is contained in his treatise the *Ars conjectandi* (1713; The Art of Conjecturing) in which he made numerous important contributions to the subject, among which was his discovery of what is now known as the law of large numbers. This work also contains Bernoulli's work on permutations and combinations. The Bernoulli family were always prone to rivalry and Jakob I and his younger brother, Johann I, became involved in a controversy over the problem of finding the shortest path between two points of a particle moving solely under the influence of gravity. The result of this vigorous dispute was the creation of the calculus of variations, a field that Leonhard Euler was later to develop. In addition to this Jakob I did important and useful work in the study of the catenary, which he applied to the design of bridges.

BERNOULLI, Johann (or Jean) I (b. Aug. 6, 1667; Basel, Switzerland; d. Jan. 1, 1748; Basel) Swiss mathematician.

Johann I was the brother of Jakob I Bernoulli (q.v.). As in the case of several of the Bernoulli family Johann I's father did not encourage him to make a career of mathematics and he graduated in medicine in 1694.

Once he had abandoned medicine for mathematics he became chiefly interested in applying the calculus to physical problems. He played an important role as a propagandist for the calculus in general and in particular as a champion of Gottfried Leibniz's priority over Isaac Newton. Johann I held a chair in mathematics at Groningen, Holland, from 1695 and returned to Switzerland to take up a chair in mathematics at Basel on the death of his brother in 1705. Johann I's interests ranged over many fields outside mathematics including physics, chemistry, and astronomy. His mathematical work also included particularly important contributions to optics, to the theory of differential equations, and to the mathematics of ship sails.

BERT, Paul (b. Oct. 17, 1833; Auxerre, France; d. Nov. 11, 1886; Hanoi, now in Vietnam) French physiologist and politician.

Bert initially studied engineering and law but turned to medicine, becoming a pupil of the eminent physiologist, Claude Bernard, at the Sorbonne, Paris. From his studies of the effects of low and high pressures on the human body, Bert showed how deep-sea divers and others working at high external pressure could avoid the condition known as the bends by returning gradually to normal pressure conditions. In this way, the nitrogen gas that dissolves in blood at high pressure is removed slowly instead of forming bubbles in the blood and causing agonizing and possibly fatal cramps. Bert wrote *La Pression barométrique* (1878), which was translated into English in 1943 for the benefit of aircrews flying at high altitudes during World War II.

Bert entered politics in 1876 as deputy for Yonne and served briefly as minister of education and welfare (1881–82). He was staunchly anti-clerical and left-wing in his views. In 1886 he was appointed governor-general to the Annan and Tonkin provinces in Indochina but died of dysentery in the same year.

BERTHELOT, Pierre Eugène Marcellin (b. Oct. 25, 1827; Paris; d. Mar. 18, 1907; Paris) French chemist.

The son of a doctor, Berthelot studied medicine at the Collège de France but became interested in chemistry, becoming assistant to Antoine-Jérôme Balard in 1851. He was professor of organic chemistry at the Ecole Supérieure de Pharmacie (1859–76) and professor of chemistry at the Collège de France (1864–1907).

Alcohols were Berthelot's early research interest and he introduced the terms mono-, di-, and polyatomic alcohols. He showed that glycerin was a triatomic alcohol and in 1854 he synthesized fats from glycerin and fatty acids. He carried out a great deal of work on sugars, which he recognized as being both polyhydric alcohols and aldehydes.

Berthelot was one of the pioneers of organic synthesis. Before his time, organic chemists had mainly been concerned with degradations of natural products but Berthelot, in keeping with his logical systematic nature, began with the simplest molecules; his syntheses included methane, methanol, formic acid, ethanol, acetylene, benzene, naphthalene, and anthracene. His favored techniques were reduction using red-hot copper and the silent electric discharge. His methods were somewhat crude and the yields were low. Berthelot's work on organic synthesis was published as *Chimie organique fondée sur la synthèse* (1860).

Arising from his interest in esterification, Berthelot studied the kinetics of reversible reactions. In 1862, working with Péan de Saint Gilles, he produced an equation for the reaction velocity. This was incorrect but it inspired Cato Guldberg and Peter Waage to enunciate the law of mass action (1864).

In 1864 Berthelot turned to thermochemistry. In his book *Mecanique chimique* (1879) he introduced the terms 'endothermic' and 'exothermic' to describe reactions that respectively absorb and release heat. He also introduced the bomb calorimeter for the determination of heats of reaction and investigated the kinetics of explosions.

Berthelot's interest in agricultural chemistry was stimulated by his discovery of nitrogen uptake by plants in the presence of an electrical discharge. In 1883 he established an agricultural station at Meudon, where fundamental work on the nitrogen cycle was carried out. He looked forward to the day when poverty and squalor would be eradicated by the application of synthetic chemistry and new sources of energy.

Berthelot was a pioneer of historical studies in chemistry. In this he was influenced by his friend, the scholar Renan. In later life he became increasingly involved in affairs of state, mostly concerned with education, and in 1895–96 he served as foreign minister.

BERTHOLLET, Comte Claude-Louis (b. Dec. 9, 1748; Talloires, France; d. Nov. 6, 1822; Arcueil, near Paris) French chemist.

Berthollet studied medicine at Turin and gained his MD in 1768. He went to Paris in 1772 where he began publishing chemical researches in 1776 and was elected a member of the Académie Française in 1780. His Italian medical degree was not recognized in France so he obtained a Parisian degree in 1778.

When Berthollet published his important paper on chlorine, *Mémoire sur l'acide marin déphlogistique* (1785), he was the first French chemist to accept Antoine Lavoisier's new system. Unfortunately, he also accepted Lavoisier's erroneous idea that chlorine contains oxygen. In 1784 Berthollet became inspector of a dyeworks and he discovered and developed the use of chlorine as a bleach. He published a standard text on dyeing *Eléments de l'art de la teinture* (1791).

Berthollet was neither a great manipulator nor a persuasive lecturer, but he did original work in many fields. He analyzed ammonia (1785), prussic acid (hydrogen cyanide, 1787), hydrogen sulfide (1798), and discovered potassium chlorate (1787). Although a convert, he remained skeptical about Lavoisier's oxygen theory of acidity: his analyses showed no oxygen in prussic acid or hydrogen sulfide, despite their undoubted acidity. Berthollet attempted to use his newly discovered potassium chlorate in gunpowder but it proved too unstable, destroying a powder mill at Essones in 1788. More productive were his analyses of iron and steel, which resulted in better quality steel.

After the French Revolution of 1789 Berthollet was a member of various commissions and in 1795 he became a director of the national mint. In 1798 he was entrusted by Napoleon with the organization of scientific work on the expedition to Egypt and he established an Institute of

Egypt. On his return to Paris in 1799 Berthollet bought a large house at Arcueil in the suburbs of Paris, where he set up a laboratory and subsequently founded the Société d'Arcueil, which included Pierre de Laplace, Alexander von Humboldt, Jean Biot, Louis Thenard, and Joseph Gay-Lussac. At Arcueil, Berthollet produced his magnum opus, the *Essai de statique chimique* (1803), in which he propounded a theory of indefinite proportions. By 1808, following the work of John Dalton, Jöns Berzelius, and Gay-Lussac, indefinite proportions was decisively rejected, but Berthollet's idea that mass influences the course of chemical reactions was eventually vindicated in the law of mass action of Cato Guldberg and Peter Waage (1864).

Berthollet was made a senator in 1804 and in his later years was regarded as the elder statesman of French science.

BERZELIUS, Jöns Jacob (b. Aug. 20, 1779; Väversunda, Sweden; d. Aug. 7, 1848; Stockholm) Swedish chemist.

Berzelius's early life was marked by a struggle to obtain a satisfactory education. In 1796 he entered the University of Uppsala but his studies were interrupted because of lack of funds. He began his chemical experiments without any official encouragement and from 1799 he worked during the summers as a physician at Medevi Springs where he analyzed the waters. He finally obtained his MD degree in 1802 with a dissertation on the medical uses of the voltaic pile.

After graduating Berzelius moved to Stockholm where he did research with Wilhelm Hisinger, a mining chemist. Their first success came in 1803 with the isolation of cerium but they were anticipated in this by Martin Klaproth. Berzelius later discovered selenium (1817), thorium (1828), and his co-workers discovered lithium (1818) and vanadium (1830). In 1807 Berzelius was appointed professor at the School of Surgery in Stockholm (later the Karolinska Institute), and he was soon able to abandon medicine and to concentrate on chemistry.

Berzelius was a meticulous experimenter and systemizer of chemistry. His early work was on electrochemistry and he formed a 'dualistic' view of compounds, in which they were composed of positive and negative parts. He was an ardent supporter of John Dalton's atomic theory, but, like Lavoisier, believed in the importance of oxygen — thus, he argued for many years that chlorine contained oxygen.

In 1810 Berzelius began a long series of studies on combining proportions that established Dalton's atomic theory on a quantitative basis. This work led to tables of atomic weights that were generally very accurate, but he never accepted Amedeo Avogadro's hypothesis and this led to some confusion. He was a prolific author with about 250 papers to his credit. His *Lärbok i kemien* (1808–1818; Textbook of Chemistry) subsequently passed through many editions and was translated into most languages except English. Pupils who came to study with him included Friedrich Wöhler, Leopold Gmelin, and Eilhard Mitscherlich. His ideas on chemical proportions and electrochemistry are set out in *Essai sur la théorie des proportions chimiques et sur l'influence chimique de l'électricité* (1819; Essay on the Theory of Chemical Proportions and on the Chemical Effects of Electricity).

Berzelius's work in organic chemistry was less fruitful than the rest of his work but he improved organic analysis by introducing a tube of calcium chloride for the collection of water and the use of copper(II) oxide as an oxidizing agent. From 1835 Berzelius's rigid adherence to the dualistic theory proved obstructive to progress in organic chemistry, although it was given a certain plausibility by Wöhler and Justus von Liebig's discovery of the benzoyl radical (1832).

Berzelius introduced much of the familiar chemical apparatus, including rubber tubing and filter paper, and the modern chemical symbols, although these were little used in his lifetime. He had a knack of coining words for phenomena and substances — 'catalysis', 'protein', and 'isomerism' were all introduced by him.

BESICOVITCH, Abram Samoilovich (b. Jan. 24, 1891; Berdjansk, now in the Soviet Union; d. Nov. 2, 1970; Cambridge, England) Soviet–British mathematician.

Besicovitch graduated in 1912 from the University of St. Petersburg (now Leningrad), having studied under A.A. Markov. In 1917 he became professor of mathematics at Perm (later Molotov University) and then taught at Leningrad Pedagogical Institute and Leningrad University. He left the Soviet Union in 1924 to work briefly with Harald Bohr in Copenhagen before moving to England. G.H. Hardy was sufficiently impressed by Besicovitch's analytical powers to secure him a lectureship at Liverpool University. After a year he became a lecturer at Cambridge and in 1950 became Rouse Ball Professor of Mathematics, a post that he held for eight years.

Besicovitch was primarily an analyst. The subject with which he is most associated is that of almost periodic functions, an interest stemming from his collaboration with Bohr. 1932 saw the publication of his book *Almost Periodic Functions*. He also did important work on the 'Karkeya problem', general real analysis, complex analysis, and various geometric problems. His other main work was on geometric measure theory.

BESSEL, Friedrich Wilhelm (b. July 22, 1784; Minden, now in West Germany; d. Mar. 17, 1846; Königsberg, now Kaliningrad, in the Soviet Union) German astronomer.

Bessel came from a poor family and started work as a clerk. His interest in and aptitude for astronomy brought him to the attention of Heinrich Olbers, who obtained a position for him in the observatory at Lilienthal. Four years later he was entrusted with the construction of the observatory at Königsberg and appointed its director.

Bessel made many advances in astronomy. He cataloged the position of 50 000 stars down to the ninth magnitude between 15°S and 45°N and, using James Bradley's results, achieved new levels of accuracy. He also made careful observations of 61 Cygni and was able to detect a parallax of 30 arc seconds and to calculate the star's distance — the first such determination — as 10.3 light years. (The distance is now known to be 11.2 light years.) Although Bessel was the first to announce the detection of parallax (1838), Thomas Henderson had in fact measured it in 1832 in his observations of Alpha Centauri.

Bessel's other great discovery came after observing a slight displacement in the proper motion of Sirius, which he explained as the effect of an orbit around an unseen star, and announced in 1844 that Sirius was a double star system having a dark companion. Sirius B was detected optically by Alvan Clark in 1862. Bessel made a similar claim for Procyon whose companion was discovered optically in 1895. He also noted irregularities in the motion of Uranus and suggested that they were caused by an unknown planet, but died just before the discovery of Neptune.

In mathematics Bessel worked on the theory of the functions, named for him, that he introduced to determine motions of bodies under mutual gravitation and planetary perturbations. They still have a wide application in modern physics.

BESSEMER, Sir Henry (b. Jan. 19, 1813; Charlton, England; d. Mar. 15, 1898; London) British inventor and engineer.

Bessemer was the son of a mechanical engineer who had fled from the French Revolution. After leaving the village school Bessemer worked as a type-caster, until the family moved to London in 1830. At the age of 17 he set up his own business to produce metal alloys and bronze powder. In 1843 he had an idea that made his fortune. On purchasing some 'gold' paint (made of brass) for his sister he was horrified at its high price. He designed an automatic plant to manufacture the paint and made sufficient money to pursue a career as a professional inventor.

During the Crimean War (1853–56) Bessemer invented a new type of gun with a rifled barrel. To manufacture the gun he needed a strong metal that could be run into a mold in a fluid state. At that time cast iron (pig iron) contained carbon and silicon impurities, which made it brittle. Wrought iron, which was relatively pure, was made by a laborious process of refining pig iron. The temperature of the furnace, while sufficient to melt the pig iron, was not sufficient to keep the purer iron molten. The refined metal was extracted in lumps after which it was 'wrought'. Bessemer proposed burning away the impurities by blowing air through the molten metal. The *Bessemer converter* that he invented is a cylindrical vessel mounted in such a way that it can be tilted to receive a charge of molten metal from the blast furnace. It is then brought upright for the 'blow' to take place. Air is blown in through a series of nozzles at the base and the carbon impurities are oxidized and carried away by the stream of air.

Bessemer announced his discovery in 1856. At first his idea was accepted enthusiastically and within weeks he obtained £27000 in license fees. However, though the process had worked for him, elsewhere it failed dismally because of excess oxygen trapped in the metal, and because of the presence of phosphorus in the ores. (By chance Bessemer's ore had been phosphorus-free.) His invention was dropped and Bessemer found himself the subject of much ridicule and criticism. Bessemer established his own steelworks in Sheffield (1859) using imported phosphorus-free iron ore.

Robert Mushet (about 1856) solved the problem of the excess oxygen by the addition of an alloy of iron, manganese, and carbon to the melt. Bessemer's process then worked provided nonphosphoric ores

were used, but it took much time and determination to convince ironworkers after the initial failure. The invention eventually reduced the price of steel to a fifth of its former cost, made it possible to produce it in large quantities, and made possible its use in a variety of new products. The problem of dealing with the phosphorus impurities was solved in 1878 by Sydney Gilchrist Thomas and Percy Carlyle Gilchrist. Bessemer retired a rich man in 1873.

BEST, Charles Herbert (b. Feb. 27, 1899; West Pembroke, Maine; d. Mar. 31, 1978; Toronto, Ontario) American–Canadian physiologist.

Best graduated in physiology and biochemistry from the University of Toronto in 1921. In the summer of that year he gave up a lucrative holiday playing professional football and baseball to begin work with Frederick Banting (q.v.). Together they isolated the hormone insulin, and showed its use in the treatment of diabetes. Banting was furious when Best was not awarded a share in the 1923 Nobel Prize for physiology or medicine for the discovery of insulin.

Best remained at the University of Toronto and gained his MB in 1925. He was made head of the physiology department in 1929 and became director of the Banting and Best Department of Medical Research when Banting was killed in 1941. He continued the work on insulin throughout these years and in an important paper published in 1936 he suggested the administration of zinc along with insulin to reduce its rate of absorption and make it more effective over a longer time. He also studied cardiovascular disease and established the clinical use of heparin as an anticoagulant for blood in the treatment of thrombosis. He discovered the vitamin choline, which prevents liver damage, and the important enzyme histaminase, which takes part in local inflammation reactions, breaking down histamine.

BETHE, Hans Albrecht (b. July 2, 1906; Strasbourg, now in France) German-American physicist.

Bethe, the son of an academic, was educated at the universities of Frankfurt and Munich, where he obtained his doctorate in 1928. He taught in Germany until 1933 when he moved first to England and, in 1935, to America. He held the chair of physics at Cornell from 1937 until his retirement in 1975, serving in the war as director of theoretical physics at Los Alamos from 1943 to 1946.

Bethe soon established a reputation for his impressive knowledge of nuclear reactions. This was, in part, based on three review articles on nuclear physics he published in 1936 and 1937, which have been described as the first presentation of this field as a branch of science.

Bethe collaborated with George Gamow (q.v.) and Ralph Alpher (q.v.) in their paper on the origin of the chemical elements. He is widely known for his paper *Energy Production in Stars* (1939) in which for the first time a plausible and precise mechanism for the production of stellar energy was proposed. The process, suggested independently by Carl von Weizsäcker, is one of striking simplicity and elegance. It begins with the interaction of a proton (hydrogen nucleus) and a carbon-12 atom, which combine to form a nitrogen-13 nucleus. In successive stages of this chain of reactions a further three protons enter into the process. The net result is that the four protons are converted into a helium nucleus with the release of fusion energy, while the carbon-12 atoms are cyclically regenerated from the nitrogen-13. The energy generated per atom is relatively small but, given the large amount of stellar matter involved, the process does give predictions that agree closely with the observed amounts of energy emitted by certain types of star. The system is called the 'carbon cycle'.

For this and for many other important contributions to the study of nuclear reactions Bethe was awarded the Nobel Physics Prize in 1967.

Bethe has also played a part in public affairs. In 1958 he served as a delegate to the first International Test Ban Conference at Geneva and has continued to advise on problems of nuclear disarmament.

BEVAN, Edward John (b. Dec. 11, 1856; Birkenhead, England; d. Oct. 17, 1921; London) British industrial chemist.

Bevan was educated privately and in 1873 began employment with the Runcorn Soap and Alkali Company. From 1877 to 1879 he studied chemistry at Owens College, Manchester, where he met Charles Cross with whom he went into partnership in 1885 as consulting chemists.

Their main interest was cellulose and in 1892 they patented the viscose process of rayon manufacture in which cellulose (woodpulp) is dissolved in carbon disulfide and alkali. The cellulose is regenerated by acid, either in the form of yarn (rayon) or film (cellophane). He wrote several books, including *Cellulose* (1895), which he coauthored with Cross.

BICHAT, Marie François Xavier (b. Nov. 14, 1771; Thoirette, France; d. July 22, 1802; Paris) French pathologist.

Bichat, the son of a physician, studied humanities at Montpellier and philosophy at Lyons. He switched to studies in surgery and anatomy and moved to Paris in 1793 where he worked for some years under the patronage of Pierre Desault, the leading French surgeon. He was appointed physician at the Hôtel-Dieu in 1800 shortly before his death from tuberculous meningitis.

Despite his short life Bichat produced two highly influential works, *Traité des membranes* (1800) and *Anatomie générale* (1801). He revealed the inadequacies of Giovanni Morgagni's claim that disease resided in the organs of the body, and instead stressed the role of the component tissues in determining health and disease.

He consequently went on to make a detailed investigation of the tissues of the body, distinguishing 21 different types. He argued that in an organ made up of a number of tissues it is often found that while one tissue type is diseased the remainder are healthy.

This work was significant in bridging the gap between the organ pathology of Morgagni and the cell pathology of Rudolf Virchow.

BIELA, Wilhelm von (b. Mar. 19, 1784; Rossia, Austria; d. Feb. 18, 1856; Venice, now in Italy) Austrian astronomer.

Biela was an Austrian army officer and an amateur astronomer. In 1826 he observed a comet with a short period of 6.6 years. When *Biela's comet* reappeared in 1845 it had split into two parts. It was last seen in 1852 when it presumably broke up, for in November 1872 what was probably its remains was seen as a fantastic meteor shower, which caused a worldwide sensation. The shower can still be seen faintly in Andromeda in late November. The meteors are sometimes called the Bielids or, alternatively, the Andromedids.

BIFFEN, Sir Rowland Harry (b. May 28, 1894; Cheltenham, England; d. July 12, 1949; Cambridge, England) British geneticist and plant breeder.

After graduating in natural sciences from Cambridge in 1896, Biffen joined a team investigating rubber production in Mexico, the West Indies, and Brazil. On his return he was appointed lecturer in botany at Cambridge and patented a method for handling rubber latex.

Biffen was inclined more toward applied than pure botany and joined the Cambridge School of Agriculture shortly after its foundation in 1899. He began conducting cereal trials in order to select improved types, and when Gregor Mendel's laws of inheritance were rediscovered in 1900, he realized immediately that they could be applied to improving plant-breeding methods. Biffen speculated that physiological as well as morphological traits would prove to be inherited in Mendelian ratios, and in 1905 demonstrated that this was true for resistance to yellow rust, a fungal disease of wheat.

Little Joss and Yeoman, two wheat varieties bred by Biffen, were unequaled for many years. In 1912 Biffen became director of the Plant Breeding Institute at Trumpington, a newly formed research center established by the government to promote Biffen's work and the application of scientific principles to plant breeding. Biffen was also professor of agricultural botany at the university from 1908 to 1931 and was instrumental in setting up the National Institute of Agricultural Botany at Cambridge. He was knighted for his services to agriculture in 1925.

BILLROTH, Christian Albert Theodor (b. Apr. 26, 1829; Bergen, now in East Germany; d. Feb. 6, 1894; Abbazia, now Opatija in Yugoslavia) Austrian surgeon.

Billroth first studied natural sciences and later medicine at the University of Göttingen and subsequently in Berlin, becoming qualified to practice in 1852. In the following year he was appointed to the surgical clinic at Berlin University and in 1860 became director of a similar clinic at the University of Zurich, where he wrote his *Allgemeine chirurgische Pathologie und Therapie* (1863; General Surgical Pathology and Therapy). However, it was as professor of surgery at the University of Vienna (1867–94) that Billroth made his greatest contributions to surgery. Here, he introduced the new antiseptic methods in abdominal surgery, thus enabling hitherto impossibly dangerous operations. Billroth was the first to perform the removal of a section of the esophagus (1872), to undertake a complete laryngectomy (1873), and to excise the lower half of the stomach, rejoining the upper half to the duodenum. This is sometimes called *Billroth's operation*.

Apart from being an eminent surgeon of international repute, Billroth was also a gifted musician and like Theodor Engelmann a friend of Johannes Brahms.

BIOT, Jean Baptiste (b. Apr. 21, 1774; Paris; d. Feb. 3, 1862; Paris) French physicist.

Biot grew up during the French Revolution and at the age of 18 he joined the army as a gunner. He left a year later to study mathematics at the Ecole Polytechnique in Paris. On leaving he taught at a school in Beauvais but soon returned to Paris to become a professor of physics at the Collège de France.

In 1804 Biot made an ascent in a balloon with Joseph Gay-Lussac. They reached a height of three miles and made many observations, including the fact that the Earth's magnetism was not measurably weaker at that height.

For the next few years Biot collaborated with François Arago in many fields of research and they traveled to Spain together to measure the length of an arc of meridian, in order to calibrate a standard unit of length. Biot later went on a number of other important expeditions.

His most famous work was on optical activity, for which, in 1840, he was awarded the Rumford medal of the Royal Society. He was the first to show that certain liquids and solutions, as well as solids, can rotate the plane of polarized light passing through them. Biot suggested that this is due to asymmetry in the molecules. From this idea grew the technique of polarimetry as a method of measuring the concentration of solutions.

BIRKELAND, Kristian Olaf Bernhard (b. Nov. 13, 1867; Christiania, now Oslo; d. June 15, 1917; Tokyo) Norwegian physicist and chemist.

Birkeland studied in Paris, Geneva, and Bonn where he was a pupil of Robert Bunsen. In 1898 he was appointed to the chair of physics in Oslo University. He is remembered today for his discovery of a means for the fixation of nitrogen (the *Birkeland–Eyde process*).

Energy crises are not monopolies of the 1970s. In 1898 William Crookes in his presidential address to the British Association had pointed out that, given the world demand for nitrogenous fertilizers, the deposits of nitrates would rapidly be exhausted. As there is a virtually unlimited supply of nitrogen in the atmosphere the obvious solution was to find some way in

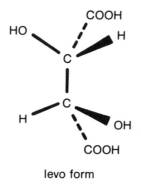

levo form

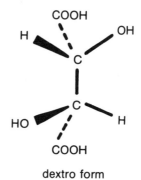

dextro form

Biot showed that compounds such as tartaric acid could rotate polarized light in solution – in other words the effect depended on the individual molecule. The explanation was later given by Le Bel and van't Hoff, who suggested that carbon molecules have a three dimensional tetrahedral structure. Tartaric acid (above) has two isomers that are mirror images of each other. One rotates the light to the left (levo); the other to the right (dextro).

OPTICAL ACTIVITY

which it could be used. Birkeland, in collaboration with Samuel Eyde, solved the problem in 1903 by passing air through an electric arc to form oxides of nitrogen, which could then be absorbed in water to give nitric acid. This was mixed with lime to give calcium nitrate. The process is particularly useful in regions (as in Scandinavia) where there is a plentiful supply of hydroelectric power, although the Haber process is now the main industrial method of fixing nitrogen.

Birkeland also spent much time studying the aurora borealis, making several expeditions and establishing a geophysical laboratory as far north as 70°. In 1896 he was the first to suggest the correct explanation that the aurora borealis could be the result of charged rays emitted by the Sun and trapped in the Earth's magnetic field near the poles. He derived this idea from the resemblance between the newly discovered cathode rays and the aurora.

BIRKHOFF, George David (b. Mar. 21, 1884; Overisel, Michigan; d. Nov. 12, 1944; Cambridge, Massachusetts) American mathematician.

Birkhoff studied at the Lewis Institute (now the Illinois Institute of Technology) from 1896 to 1902, and subsequently at the University of Chicago and at Harvard. In 1907 he obtained his PhD from Chicago and took up a teaching post at the University of Wisconsin, moving to Princeton in 1909. In 1912 he became assistant professor at Harvard and, in 1919, professor there, a post he held until 1939.

Birkhoff's mathematical interests were wide, and among the many areas to which he made notable contributions were differential equations, celestial mechanics, difference equations, and the three-body problem. His main field of research was mathematical analysis, especially applied to dynamics. In the course of his work on dynamical systems Birkhoff obtained a famous proof of a conjecture made by Henri Poincaré in topology, usually known as Poincaré's last geometric theorem. The

ergodic theorem, a result concerned with the formal mathematics of probability theory, that Birkhoff proved in 1931, is another of his outstanding achievements. Modern dynamics received an enormous impetus from Birkhoff's work, and he also worked on the foundations of relativity and quantum mechanics.

BITTNER, John Joseph (b. Feb. 25, 1904; Meadville, Pennsylvania; d. Dec. 14, 1961; Minneapolis, Minnesota) American experimental biologist.

Bittner gained his doctorate at the University of Michigan and spent the greater part of his academic life involved in cancer research. He was George Chase Christian Professor of Cancer Research at the University of Michigan and director of cancer biology of the University of Minnesota's medical school (1942–57), and latterly professor of experimental biology.

While working at Ben Harbor Research Station, Maine (1936), Bittner found that some strains of mice were highly resistant to cancer, while others were very prone to it. If the young of cancer-resistant mice were transferred to cancer-prone mothers they became cancerous, apparently via the mothers' milk, whereas cancer-resistant parents induced resistance in cancer-prone young. Bittner's discovery of viruslike organisms in the milk of cancer-prone parents suggested that these organisms are the cause of the cancer. Bittner's findings followed and may be linked with those of Francis Rous, who made the controversial finding that other viruslike organisms are, perhaps, the cause of sarcomas (tumors originating in connective tissue) in chickens. Such work does not, of course, suggest that all cancers are caused by viruses or viruslike organisms, merely that some forms may be.

BJERKNES, Jacob Aall Bonnevie (b. Nov. 2, 1897; Stockholm) Norwegian meteorologist.

Bjerknes, the son of Vilhelm Bjerknes, followed the example of his father in studying meteorology. He was educated at the University of Oslo, where he obtained his PhD in 1924, and worked at the Geophysical Institute at Bergen with his father from 1917, remaining there when Vilhelm moved to Oslo in 1926.

During World War I Bjerknes worked with his father in establishing a series of weather observation stations throughout Norway. From the data collected, and working with other notable meteorologists, including Tor Bergeron, they developed their theory of polar fronts, also known as the *Bergen theory* or the *frontal theory*. They had established that the atmosphere is composed of distinct air masses possessing different characteristics and applied the term 'front' to the boundary between two air masses. The polar front theory showed how cyclones (low-pressure centers) originated from atmospheric fronts over the Atlantic Ocean where a warm air mass met a cold air mass.

In 1939 Bjerknes moved to America and, unable to return to occupied Norway, became professor of meteorology at the University of California where he continued to study atmospheric circulation. In 1952 he became one of the first to use space techniques for meteorological research when he used photographs of cloud cover taken by research rockets for weather analysis.

BJERKNES, Vilhelm Friman Koren (b. Mar. 14, 1862; Christiania, now Oslo; d. Apr. 9, 1951; Oslo) Norwegian meteorologist.

Bjerknes's father, Carl, was professor of mathematics at the University of Christiania (now Oslo). In 1890 Vilhelm traveled to Germany and became assistant to Heinrich Hertz. He was made professor of applied mechanics and mathematical physics at the University of Stockholm in 1895. He returned to Norway in 1907 and in 1912 moved to the University of Leipzig to become professor of geophysics.

Bjerknes's important contributions to meteorology and weather forecasting include his mathematical models (1897) of atmospheric and oceanic motions, which later led to the theory of air masses. In 1904 he produced a program for weather prediction based on physical principles. He returned to Norway in 1907 and in 1912 moved to the University of Leipzig to become professor of geophysics.

During World War I he founded the famous Bergen Geophysical Institute, gathering there a group of notable meteorologists, including his son, Jacob Bjerknes, Tor Bergeron, and Carl-Gustav Rossby. In 1921 he produced an important work, *On the Dynamics of the Circular Vortex with Applications to the Atmospheric Vortex and Wave Motion.*

BJERRUM, Niels (b. Mar. 11, 1879; Copenhagen; d. Sept. 30, 1958) Danish physical chemist.

The son of a professor of ophthalmology, Bjerrum received his master's degree in 1902 and doctorate in 1908, becoming professor at the Royal Veterinary and Agricultural College (1914–49). His first notable work was an extensive study of chromium complexes by means of conductivity, equilibrium constant, and absorption spectrum measurements. In 1909 he proposed (contrary to Svante Arrhenius's original dissociation theory) that strong electrolytes are completely dissociated. In 1911, working with Hermann Nernst, he applied the quantum theory of a harmonic oscillator to the temperature dependence of the specific heats of gases. This led to work on molecular rotation and vibration and hence to pioneer work on the infrared spectra of polyatomic molecules.

BLACK, Joseph (b. Apr. 16, 1728; Bordeaux, France; d. Nov. 10, 1799; Edinburgh) British physician and chemist.

Black, the son of a wine merchant, studied languages and natural philosophy, and later, medicine and chemistry at Glasgow University (1746–50). He moved to Edinburgh in 1751, where he presented his thesis in 1754. Black published very little and the thesis, expanded and published as *Experiments upon Magnesia Alba, Quicklime, and some other Alcaline Substances* (1756), contained his most influential work. The paper in fact marked the beginning of modern chemistry. Black investigated quantitatively the cycle of reactions: limestone —> quicklime —> slaked lime —> limestone, and showed that the gas evolved ('fixed air' or carbon dioxide) is distinct from and a constituent of atmospheric air, and is the cause of the effervescence of limestone with acids. He proved that mild alkalis will become more alkaline when they lose carbon dioxide and they are converted back to mild alkalis through reabsorption of the gas.

Black's other great discovery was that of latent heat (the heat required to produce a change of state). The concept of latent heat came to him in 1757 and the experimental determination of the latent heat of fusion of ice was made in 1761. The next year he determined the latent heat of formation of steam. Black also distinguished the difference between heat and temperature and conceived the idea of specific heat.

Black was professor of medicine and lecturer in chemistry at Glasgow (1756–66) and then professor of chemistry at Edinburgh for the rest of his life. Black's lectures, which he gave for over 30 years, were immensely popular and were published in 1803.

BLACKETT, Patrick Maynard Stuart (b. Nov. 18, 1897; London; d. July 13, 1974; London) British physicist.

Blackett, the son of a stockbroker, attended the Royal Naval College at Dartmouth. After serving with the navy in World War I, during which he fought at the Battle of the Falklands and Jutland, he entered Cambridge University, resigned his commission, and decided to become a scientist. He worked in the 1920s with Ernest Rutherford at the Cavendish Laboratory and, in 1933, was appointed professor of physics at London University. In 1937 he moved to Manchester, returning to London in 1953 to take the chair at Imperial College where he remained until his retirement in 1963. During World War II he worked on numerous advisory bodies and from 1942 to 1945 was director of operational research at the admiralty.

Just as Blackett was beginning his research career Rutherford had announced his discovery of the atomic transmutation of nitrogen into oxygen by bombardment with alpha particles. Blackett, using a cloud chamber, took some 23 000 photographs containing some 400 000 alpha particle tracks in nitrogen and found in 1925 just eight branched tracks in which the ejected proton was clearly separated from the newly formed oxygen isotope.

Blackett continued with the Wilson cloud chamber and began, in collaboration with Giuseppe Occhialini, to use it to detect cosmic rays. As the appearance of cosmic rays is unpredictable it was standard practice to set up the chamber to take a photograph every 15 seconds, producing a vast amount of worthless material for analysis. To avoid this Blackett introduced in 1932 the counter-controlled chamber. Geiger counters were so arranged above and below the chamber that when a cosmic ray passed through both, it activated the expansion of the chamber and photographed the ion tracks produced by the ray. Using this device they confirmed in 1933 Carl Anderson's discovery of the positron. They also suggested that the positron was produced by the interaction of gamma rays with matter, such that a photon is converted into an electron–positron pair. The phenomenon is known as pair production.

After the war Blackett's research interests moved from cosmic rays to terrestrial magnetism. Using new sensitive magnetometers his group began a major survey of the magnetic history of the Earth. By 1960 they could report that there had been considerable change in the relative positions of the continents over the past 500 million years, thus providing further support for the doctrine of continental drift.

Blackett was also active in public affairs and a noted opponent of nuclear weapons. In 1948 he was awarded the Nobel Physics Prize for "his development of the Wilson cloud chamber and his discoveries therewith in the field of nuclear physics and cosmic radiation." He was made a life peer in 1969.

BLACKMAN, Frederick Frost (b. July 25, 1866; London; d. Jan. 30, 1947; Cambridge, England) British plant physiologist.

Blackman, the son of a doctor, studied medicine at St. Bartholomew's Hospital, London, and natural sciences at Cambridge University. He remained in Cambridge for the whole of his career where he served as head of plant physiology until his retirement in 1936.

Blackman is mainly remembered for his classic 1905 paper, *Optima and Limiting Factors*, in which he demonstrated that where a process depends on a number of independent factors, the rate at which it can take place is limited by the rate of the slowest factor. This paper was stimulated by the research of one of his students, who showed that raising the temperature only increased the rate of photosynthesis if the level of illumination was high. Increased temperatures had no effect at low light intensities.

He had earlier, in 1895, provided convincing experimental support for the long held view that gaseous exchange between the leaves and the atmosphere takes place through the stomata, the pores on the leaf's surface.

BLAEU, Willem Janszoon (b. 1571; Alkmaar, Holland; d. Oct. 21, 1638; Amsterdam) Dutch cartographer.

Blaeu began work as a carpenter. In 1595 he spent a year with Tycho Brahe at his observatory at Hven. He opened his cartographic shop in Amsterdam soon after his return to Holland and specialized in producing globes. He published his first world map in 1605 and his first atlas in 1633.

After his death the business was carried on by his sons, Jan and Cornelis. In 1648 they produced their world map, which contained much that was new including the coastline of north and west Australia and parts of New Zealand and the Antarctic. It also abandoned the great southern continent previously believed to exist.

BLAGDEN, Sir Charles (b. Apr. 17, 1748; Wotton under Edge, England; d. Mar. 26, 1820; near Paris) British physician and chemist.

Blagden studied medicine at Edinburgh, where one of his professors was Joseph Black, and graduated in 1768. He became a medical officer in the British army in the same year and theoretically remained in that post until 1814. From 1782 to 1789 Blagden was assistant to Henry Cavendish, a post that involved him in the so-called 'water controversy', a dispute between James Watt, Cavendish, and Antoine Lavoisier concerning the priority of the discovery of the synthesis of water from its elements. Blagden was friendly with the great French scientists of the day, especially Claude Berthollet, and on a visit to Paris in 1783 he told Lavoisier of Cavendish's synthesis, an experiment that Lavoisier repeated in Blagden's presence. Blagden became secretary of the Royal Society soon afterward, in which capacity he published Watt's papers on the same subject. The dispute was largely artificial because the three men drew different conclusions from their work.

Blagden's own scientific work was concerned with the freezing of mercury, the supercooling of water, and the freezing of salt solutions. He discovered, in 1788, that the lowering of the freezing point of a solution is proportional to the concentration of the solute present. This became known as *Blagden's law*. Blagden was knighted in 1792.

BLAKESLEE, Albert Francis (b. Nov. 9, 1874; Geneseo, New York; d. Nov. 16, 1954; Northampton, Massachusetts) American botanist and geneticist.

Blakeslee was educated at the Wesleyan University, Connecticut, graduating in 1896. He taught science for four years before entering Harvard to do post-graduate research, gaining his PhD in 1904. In this year he discovered that the bread molds (*Mucorales*) exhibit heterothallism (self sterility) and spent the next two years in Germany making further investigations on the fungi.

From 1907 to 1914 Blakeslee was professor of botany at Connecticut Agricultural College. In 1915 he moved to the department of genetics at the Carnegie Institution, where he remained until 1941. In 1924 he began work on the alkaloid colchicine, which is found in the autumn crocus, and 13 years later he discovered that plants soaked in this alkaloid had multiple sets of chromosomes in their cells. Such plants, termed polyploids, often exhibit gigantism and this discovery proved of immediate use in the horticultural industry in producing giant varieties of popular ornamentals. More importantly, however, colchicine often converts sterile hybrids into fertile polyploids and is therefore an invaluable tool in crop-breeding research.

Other contributions made by Blakeslee to plant genetics include his study of inheritance in the jimson weed and his research on embryo culture as a method of growing hybrid embryos that would abort if left on the parent plant.

BLANE, Sir Gilbert (b. Aug. 29, 1749; Blanefield, Scotland; d. June 26, 1834; London) British physician.

Blane studied medicine at Edinburgh and Glasgow, receiving his MD in 1778. In the following year he sailed with the fleet as personal physician to Admiral Lord Rodney and later as physician to the fleet. While in the West Indies, he made intelligent use of James Lind's (q.v.) results and introduced the provision of lime juice and other citrus fruits to combat scurvy among the seamen. He also generally improved the standards of hygiene on board ship.

He returned to London in 1783 and became a physician at St. Thomas's Hospital, London, and later attended both George IV and William IV as physician-in-ordinary. He was instrumental in enforcing his health regulations throughout the Royal Navy and helped draft the Quarantine Act of 1799. He was made a baronet in 1812.

His rather grave manner earned him the nickname of "chilblaine" among his colleagues.

BLOCH, Felix (b. Oct. 23, 1905; Zurich, Switzerland) Swiss-American physicist.

Bloch was educated at the Federal Institute of Technology, Zurich, and the University of Leipzig, where he obtained his PhD in 1928. He taught briefly in Germany and in 1933 moved to America, via various institutions in Italy, Denmark, and Holland. In 1934 he joined the Stanford staff, remaining there until his retirement in 1971 and serving from 1936 onward as professor of physics. He also served briefly as first director of the international laboratory for high-energy physics in Geneva, known as CERN (1954–55).

In 1946, Bloch and Edward Purcell independently introduced the technique of nuclear magnetic resonance (NMR). This utilizes the magnetic property of a nucleus, which will interact with an applied magnetic field such that it takes certain orientations in the field (a quantum mechanical effect known as space quantization). The different orientations have slightly different energies and a nucleus can change from one state to another by absorbing a photon of electromagnetic radiation (in the radiofrequency region of the spectrum). The technique was used initially to determine the magnetic moment (i.e. the torque felt by a magnet in a magnetic field at right angles to it) of the proton and of the neutron. It has since, however, been developed into a powerful tool for the analysis of the more complex molecules of organic chemistry. The energy states of the nucleus are affected slightly by the surrounding electrons, and the precise frequency at which a nucleus absorbs depends on its position in the molecule. In 1952 Bloch shared the Nobel Prize for physics with Purcell for this work on NMR.

Bloch has also worked extensively in the field of solid-state physics developing a detailed theory of the behavior of electrons in crystals and revealing much about the properties of ferromagnetic domains.

BLOCH, Konrad Emil (b. Jan. 21, 1912; Neisse, now Nysa in Poland) German-American biochemist.

Bloch was educated at the Technical University, Munich, and — after his emigration to America in 1936 — at Columbia University, New York, where he obtained his PhD in 1938. He then taught at Columbia until 1946, when he moved to the University of Chicago, becoming professor of biochemistry there in 1950. In 1954 Bloch accepted the position of Higgins Professor of Chemistry at Harvard, a post he retained until his retirement in 1978.

In 1940 the important radioisotope carbon-14 was discovered by Martin Kamen and Samuel Ruben. Bloch was quick to see that it could be used to determine the biosynthesis of such complex molecules as cholesterol, a basic constituent of animal tissues characterized by four rings of carbon atoms. Thus in 1942, in collaboration with David Rittenberg, Bloch was able to confirm the earlier supposition that cholesterol was partly derived from the two-carbon acetate molecule.

The actual steps through which the two-carbon acetate develops into the 27-carbon

cholesterol were numerous and took many years of detailed analysis to establish. The crucial breakthrough came in 1953, when Bloch and R. Langdon identified squalene as an intermediate in the synthesis of cholesterol. This hydrocarbon, a terpene with an open chain of 30 carbon atoms, is able to initiate the folding necessary to produce the four rings of cholesterol.

For this work Bloch shared the 1964 Nobel Prize for physiology or medicine with Feodor Lynen.

BLOEMBERGEN, Nicolaas (b. Mar. 11, 1920; Dordrecht, Netherlands) Dutch-American physicst.

Bloembergen was educated at the universities of Utrecht and Leiden, where he obtained his PhD in 1948. He moved to America soon afterward, joined the Harvard staff in 1949, and has served since 1957 as Gordon McKay Professor of Applied Physics and since 1974 also as Rumford Professor of Physics.

In the mid 1950s Bloembergen introduced a simple yet effective modification to the design of the maser. First built by Charles Townes in 1953, the early maser could only work intermittently: once the electrons in the higher energy level had been stimulated they would fall down to the lower energy level and nothing further could happen until they had been raised to the higher level once more. Bloembergen developed the three-level and multilevel masers, which were also worked on by Nikolai Basov (q.v.) and Aleksandr Prokhorov in the Soviet Union. In the three-level maser, electrons are pumped to the highest level and stimulated. They consequently emit microwave radiation and fall down to the middle level where they can once more be stimulated and emit energy of a lower frequency. At the same time more electrons are being pumped from the lowest to the highest level making the process continuous.

Bloembergen wrote *Nuclear Magnetic Relaxations* (1948) and *Nonlinear Optics* (1965).

BLUMBERG, Baruch Samuel (b. July 28, 1925; New York City) American physician.

Blumberg studied physics and mathematics at Union College, Schenectady, and at Columbia, where, after a year, he changed to medical studies. He received his MD from Columbia in 1951 and his PhD in biochemistry from Oxford University in 1957. After working at the National Institutes of Health in Bethesda from 1957 until 1964 Blumberg was appointed professor of medicine at the University of Pennsylvania.

In 1963, while examining literally thousands of blood samples in a study of the variation in serum proteins in different populations, Blumberg made the important discovery of what soon became known as the 'Australian antigen'. He found in the blood of an Australian aborigine an antigen that reacted with an antibody in the serum of an American thalassemia patient. It turned out that the antigen was found frequently in the serum of those suffering from viral hepatitis, hepatitis B, and was in fact a hepatitis B antigen.

It was hoped that from this discovery techniques for the control of the virus would develop. It certainly made it easier to screen blood for transfusion for the presence of the hepatitis virus; it also permitted the development of a vaccine, from the serum of those with the Australian antigen. Blumberg has also suggested that the virus is involved in primary liver cancer.

For his work on the Australian antigen Blumberg shared the 1976 Nobel Prize for physiology or medicine with Carleton Gajdusek.

BLUMENBACH, Johann Friedrich (b. May 11, 1752; Gotha, now in East Germany; d. Jan. 22, 1840; Göttingen, now in West Germany) German anthropologist.

Blumenbach, the son of an assistant headmaster of the local gymnasium, was educated at the universities of Jena and Göttingen where he obtained his MD in 1775. He remained at Göttingen for the whole of his career, serving as professor of medicine from 1778 onward.

In his *De generis humani variatate nativa* (1776; Concerning the Natural Diversity of the Human Race) Blumenbach took up the problem posed by Linnaeus in 1747, which challenged scientists to find a generic character that would distinguish between men and apes. Blumenbach's solution was to attribute two hands to humans and four hands to monkeys. This enabled him to form a separate order, Bimanus, for man alone while including apes, monkeys, and lemurs in the Quadrumana.

In Bimanus he included five races — Caucasian, Ethiopian, Mongolian, Malayan, and American Indian — insisting that they were "all related and only differing from each other in degree." Nonetheless he favored a monogenetic view of mankind, which led him to see the Caucasian race as primary, with the other four races existing as 'degenerate' forms. Blumenbach's version of this common 18th-century view was relatively mild. He argued that the degeneration was an acquired trait, the result of climatic and dietary influences. The rampant racism found in some of his contemporaries is on the whole absent from the works of Blumenbach. To show that 'degenerate' forms were not the same as inferior forms he produced in 1799 a paper in which he provided biographies of those African poets, philosophers, and jurists who had established themselves in European society.

BODE, Johann Elert (b. Jan. 19, 1747; Hamburg, now in West Germany; d. Nov. 23, 1826; Berlin) German astronomer.

Bode, who was the director of the Berlin Observatory, popularized a discovery made earlier in 1772 by Johann Titius of Wittenberg. This was a simple but inexplicable numerical rule governing the distance of the planets from the Sun measured in astronomical units (the mean distance of the Earth from the Sun). The rule, known as *Bode's law*, is to take the series 0, 3, 6, 12, 24 ..., add 4 to each member, and divide by 10. The result is the distance in astronomical units of the planets from the Sun. The law and its application can be tabulated and, provided that the asteroids are counted as a single planet, quite an impressive fit can be achieved. It breaks down for Neptune and is hopelessly wrong for Pluto. It played a role in the discovery of Neptune by Urbain Leverrier in 1846. It is not known whether the law is simply a pure coincidence, or whether it is a consequence of the way in which the solar system formed.

BODENSTEIN, Max Ernst August (b. July 15, 1871; Magdeburg, Germany; d. Sept. 3, 1942; Berlin) German physical chemist.

Bodenstein gained his doctorate at Heidelberg (1893) and worked with Wilhelm Ostwald at Leipzig before becoming a professor at Hannover (1908–23) and at the Institute for Physical Chemistry, Berlin (1923–36). He made a series of classic studies on the equilibria of gaseous reactions, especially that of hydrogen and iodine (1897). His technique was to mix hydrogen and iodine in a sealed tube, which he placed in a thermostat and held at a constant high temperature. The reaction eventually reached an equilibrium, at which the rate of formation of hydrogen iodide (HI) was equal to the rate of decomposition to the original reactants:

$$H_2 + I_2 = 2HI$$

The equilibrium mixture of H_2, I_2, and HI was 'frozen' by rapid cooling, and the amount of hydrogen iodide present could be analyzed. Using different amounts of initial reactants, Bodenstein could vary the amounts present at equilibrium and verify the law of chemical equilibrium proposed in 1863 by Cato Guldberg and Peter Waage.

Bodenstein also worked in photochemistry and was the first to show how the large yield per quantum for the reaction of hydrogen and chlorine could be explained by a chain reaction.

BOERHAAVE, Hermann (b. Dec. 31, 1668; Voorhout, near Leiden, Netherlands; d. Sept. 23, 1738; Leiden) Dutch physician and chemist.

Boerhaave studied philosophy at the University of Leiden, and was intended to enter the Church. However an accusation of impiety turned him from theology to medicine and he obtained his MD in 1693 at Harderwijk. Boerhaave returned to Leiden where he began to teach medicine and chemistry and practiced medicine privately. Boerhaave was a polymath, learned in medicine, botany, and chemistry. His lectures were immensely successful and he occupied the chairs of medicine and botany (1709), practical medicine (1714), and chemistry (1718). Boerhaave was celebrated during his life for his medical works, *Institutiones medicae* (1708), and *Aphorismi de cognoscendis et curandis morbis* (1709; The Book of Aphorisms) but posthumously he exerted great influence as a chemist through his excellent work *Elementia chemiae* (1723). Boerhaave made no great discoveries but he had unerring judgment in selecting that which was most valuable in the work of others. He tried to apply the mechanistic philosophy of Newton and Robert Boyle to both medicine and chemistry. His early work on calorimetry was the foundation on which Joseph Black subsequently built. He was elected a fellow of The Royal Society and during his lifetime was as famous as Newton.

BOETHIUS, Anicius Manlius Severinus (b. *c.* 475; d. 524; Pavia, Italy) Roman philosopher.

Boethius, a member of the noble Anicii family, was born in a Rome conquered and ruled by the Ostrogoths. He flourished under the Ostrogothic king Theodoric, being appointed consul in 510 and *magister officiorum*, the head of the Imperial civil administration, in about 520. For reasons that are not clear Boethius was imprisoned in Pavia, tortured, and finally put to death.

As a scholar Boethius had expressed a wish to translate "the whole work of Aristotle into the Roman idiom" but only succeeded in dealing with the logical works. He also produced works on arithmetic, geometry, astronomy, and music, later to form the basis for the teaching of the 'quadrivium' (the course of studies in medieval universities), a term he may well have introduced. Such works were based closely on earlier Greek works of Nichomacus and Euclid. Boethius is historically important for keeping the tradition of Greek thought and science alive in Europe until the works of the great Arab scholars were translated some six centuries later.

BOGOLIUBOV, Nikolai Nikolaevich (b. Aug. 5, 1909; Nizhny Novgorod, now in the Soviet Union) Soviet mathematician and physicist.

Bogoliubov was accepted for graduate work at the Academy of Sciences of the Ukranian SSR, and subsequently worked there and at the Soviet Academy of Sciences.

His main contribution has been in the application of mathematical techniques to theoretical physics. He developed a method of distribution-function for nonequilibrium processes, and has also worked on superfluidity, quantum field theory, and superconductivity. His work was partly paralleled by the work of John Bardeen, Leon Cooper, and John Robert Schrieffer.

Bogoliubov has been a prolific author, with many of his works translated into English. He has also been active in founding scientific schools in nonlinear mechanics, statistical physics, and quantum-field theory. Since 1963 he has been academician-secretary of the Soviet Academy of Sciences and was made director of the Joint Institute for Nuclear Research in Dubna in 1965. The next year he was also made a deputy to the Supreme Soviet. He has been honored by scientific societies throughout the world, and in his own country has received the State Prize twice (1947 and 1953) and the Lenin Prize (1958).

BOHN, René (b. Mar. 7, 1862; Dornach, France; d. Mar. 6, 1922; Mannheim, now in West Germany) German organic chemist.

Bohn studied chemistry at the Federal Institute of Technology at Zurich and obtained his doctorate from the University of Zurich in 1883. From 1884 he was a chemist with the Badische Anilin und Soda Fabrik at Ludwigshafen, becoming a director in 1906. He worked mainly on the synthesis of anthraquinone dyes and his most notable synthesis was that of the blue vat dye, indanthrone (1901), the first nonindigo vat dye. He also did important work on the red alizarin dyes.

BOHR, Aage Niels (b. June 19, 1922; Copenhagen) Danish physicist.

Bohr, the son of Niels Bohr, was educated at the University of Copenhagen. After postgraduate work at the University of London from 1942 to 1945 he returned to Copenhagen to the Institute of Theoretical Physics, where he has served since 1956 as professor of physics.

When Bohr began his research career the shell model of the nucleus of Maria Goeppert-Mayer and Hans Jensen had just been proposed in 1949. Almost immediately Leo James Rainwater produced experimental results at odds with the predictions derived from a spherical shell model, and proposed that some nuclei were distorted rather than perfectly spherical.

Bohr, in collaboration with Ben Mottelson, followed Rainwater's work by proposing their collective model of nuclear structure (1952), so called because it was argued that the distorted nuclear shape was produced by the participation of many nucleons. For this work Bohr shared the 1975 Nobel Physics Prize with Rainwater and Mottelson.

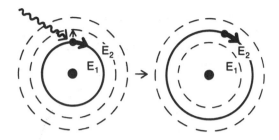

ABSORPTION: The atom initially has an electron in its inner orbit and the outside orbits are empty. In absorbing a photon the electron moves to an outer orbit. The photon energy is hv and absorption only occurs at frequency v such that $hv = E_2 - E_1$.

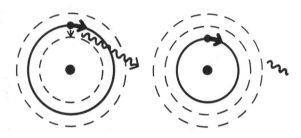

EMISSION: The atom is initially in an excited state. A photon of appropriate energy is emitted when the electron moves to a lower-energy orbit.

BOHR THEORY The emission and absorption of radiation by a hydrogen atom.

BOHR, Niels Hendrik David (b. Oct. 7, 1885; Copenhagen; d. Nov. 18, 1962; Copenhagen) Danish physicist.

Niels Bohr came from a very distinguished scientific family. His father, Christian, was professor of physiology at Copenhagen and his brother Harald was a mathematician of great distinction. (His own son, Aage, was later to win the 1975 Nobel Physics Prize.) Bohr was educated at the University of Copenhagen where he obtained his PhD in 1911. After four productive years with Ernest Rutherford in Manchester, Bohr returned to Denmark becoming in 1918 director of the newly created Institute of Theoretical Physics.

Under Bohr (who after Albert Einstein was probably the most respected theoretical physicist of the century) the institute became one of the most exciting research centers in the world. A generation of physicists from around the world were to pass through it and eventually it was to bestow on the orthodox account of quantum theory the apt description of the 'Copenhagen interpretation'.

In 1913 Bohr published a classic paper, *On the Constitution of Atoms and Molecules*, in which he used the quantum of energy, h, introduced into physics by Max Planck in 1900, to rescue Rutherford's account of atomic structure from a vital objection and also to account for the line spectrum of hydrogen. The first problem Bohr faced was to explain the stability of the atom. Rutherford's 1911 model of the atom with electrons orbiting a central nucleus (the so-called planetary model) was theoretically unstable. This was because, unlike planets orbiting the Sun, electrons are charged particles, which, according to classical physics, should radiate energy and consequently spiral in toward the nucleus.

Bohr began by assuming that there were 'stationary' orbits for the electrons in which the electron did not radiate energy. He further assumed that such orbits occurred when the electron had definite values of angular momentum, specifically values $h/2\pi$, $2h/2\pi$, $3h/2\pi$, etc., where h is Planck's constant. Using this idea he was able to calculate energies E_1, E_2, E_3, etc., for possible orbits of the electron. He further postulated that emission of light occurred when an electron moved from one orbit to a lower-energy orbit; absorption was accompanied by a change to a higher-energy orbit. In each case the energy difference produced radiation of energy hv, where v is the frequency. In 1913 he realized that, using this idea, he could obtain a theoretical formula similar to the empirical formula of Johannes Balmer for a series of lines in the hydrogen spectrum. Bohr received the Nobel Physics Prize for this work in 1922. The Bohr theory was developed further by Arnold Sommerfeld.

Bohr also made other major contributions to this early development of quantum theory. The 'correspondence principle' (1916) is his principle that the quantum-theory description of the atom corresponds to classical physics at large magnitudes.

In 1927, Bohr publicly formulated the 'complementarity principle'. This argued against continuing attempts to eliminate such supposed difficulties as the wave–particle duality of light and many other atomic phenomena. His starting point was the impossibility to distinguish satisfactorily between the actual behavior of atomic objects, and their interaction with the measuring instruments that serve to define the conditions under which the phenomena appear. Examine light with one instrument, the argument went, and it undulates like a wave; select another and it scatters like a particle. His conclusion was that evidence obtained under different experimental conditions cannot be comprehended within a single picture, but must be regarded as complementary in the sense that only the totality of the phenomenon exhausts the possible information about the objects. It was a principle Bohr remained faithful to, even representing it on his coat of arms in 1947 with the motto *Contraria sunt complementa* above the Yin/Yang symbols. Together with the indeterminancy principle of Werner Heisenberg and the probability waves of Max Born, this principle emerged from the 1930 Solvay conference (the last one Einstein attended) as the most authoritative and widely accepted theory to describe atomic phenomena.

Bohr also made major contributions to the work on radioactivity that led to the discovery and exploitation of nuclear fission. Bohr's liquid-drop model of the nucleus, which was published in 1936, provided the basis for the first theoretical account of fission worked out in collaboration with John Wheeler in 1939. It was also Bohr who, in 1939, made the crucial suggestion that fission was more likely to occur with the rarer isotope uranium–235 than the more common variety uranium–238.

In 1943 Bohr, who had a Jewish mother, felt it necessary to escape from occupied Denmark and eventually made his way to Los Alamos in America where he served as a consultant on the atomic bomb project. He was quick to appreciate the consequences of using such weapons and in 1944 made an early approach to Roosevelt and Churchill proposing that such obvious danger could perhaps be used to bring about a rapprochement between Russia and the West. Scientists were in a unique position, he argued, in having the Soviet contacts and the knowledge to make the first approach. Much of Bohr's time after the war was spent working, among scientists, for adequate controls of nuclear weapons and in 1955 he organized the first Atoms for Peace conference in Geneva.

BOK, Bart Jan (b. Apr. 28, 1906; Hoorn, Netherlands) Dutch–American astronomer.

Bok studied at the universities of Leiden (1924–27) and Groningen (1927–29) and obtained his PhD from Groningen in 1932. He had moved to America in 1929, becoming naturalized in 1938, and served at Harvard from 1929 to 1957 with the appointment of professor of astronomy from 1947 onward. Bok spent the period 1957–66 in Australia as director of the Mount Stromlo Observatory, Canberra, and professor of astronomy at the Australian National University. He returned to America in 1966 to become director of the Steward Observatory, Arizona, until 1970 and professor of astronomy (since 1974 emeritus professor) at the University of Arizona, Tucson.

Bok's major interest has been the structure of our galaxy, the Milky Way. With his wife, Priscilla, he published a survey of the subject: *The Milky Way* (1941). Although it had been long assumed that the Milky Way had a spiral structure it was not until Walter Baade identified in the 1940s the hot young O and B stars of the Andromeda galaxy as spiral markers that such a conjecture could be confirmed. The actual structure was first worked out in some detail by William Morgan. The existence of 21-centimeter radio signals from clouds of neutral hydrogen in the galaxy was predicted by Hendrik van de Hulst and their discovery in 1951 provided a second tracer. It was clear to Bok by the late 1950s that the radio data, which were expected to support the optical picture, instead contradicted it. He consequently attempted to harmonize the two structures by modifying Morgan's somewhat elliptical arms, making them much more spherical, and giving more emphasis to the Carina–Centaurus arm.

Bok's name is also associated with his discovery in 1947 of small dark circular clouds visible against a background of stars or luminous gas and since known as *Bok globules*. Since they are thought to be precursors of stars, as Bok himself conjectured, they have received considerable attention in recent years.

BOLTWOOD, Bertram Borden (b. July 27, 1870; Amherst, Massachusetts; d. Aug. 15, 1927; Hancock Point, Maine) American chemist and physicist.

Boltwood, the son of a lawyer, was educated at Yale and the University of Munich. Apart from the period 1900–06, when he served as a private consultant, and the year 1909–10, which he spent with Ernest Rutherford at the University of Manchester, England, he devoted the whole of his academic career to Yale. He occupied the chair of physics (1906–10), the chair of radioactivity (1910–18), and the chair of chemistry from 1918 until his death by suicide in 1927.

Boltwood made a number of contributions to the study of radioactivity. The radioactivity of uranium and radium had been discovered in the 1890s by Henri Becquerel and Marie Curie. Starting in 1902 Rutherford and Frederick Soddy had shown that radium, uranium, and other radioactive elements broke down in a quite complicated sequence into other elements. Boltwood worked on the breakdown of uranium into radium, a process that Soddy

had not found easy to demonstrate. Soddy had tried to obtain radium directly from uranium in 1904 and failed. Boltwood postulated that this was because uranium did not decay directly into radium but into some intermediate element, and began to search for it. After much effort Boltwood eventually found what he was looking for in 'actinium X', which, as it appeared different from anything else, he felt confident enough to claim as a new element and named it 'ionium' in 1907. This claim ran into trouble when ionium was found to behave very much like thorium and in 1908 it was shown by B. Keetman that if ionium and thorium are mixed together no chemical technique can separate them. Soddy decided the matter in 1913 when he was able to obtain a spectrograph of ionium and found it to be the same as thorium. Although he was wrong in detail, the general picture Boltwood had developed of the decay of uranium to radium was valid until superseded by Soddy's idea of the isotope.

One important byproduct of Boltwood's work was his demonstration in 1905 that lead was always found in uranium and was probably the final stable product of its decay. He argued that in minerals of the same age the lead–uranium ratio would be constant, and in minerals of different ages the ratio would be different. He calculated some estimates of the ages of several rocks based on the estimates then accepted for decay rates and came up with some good results. This was the beginning of attempts to date rocks and fossils by radiation measurements and other physical techniques, which have so revolutionized geology and archeology.

BOLTZMANN, Ludwig Edward (b. Feb. 20, 1844; Vienna; d. Sept. 5, 1906; Duino, now in Italy) Austrian theoretical physicist.

Boltzmann studied at the University of Vienna, where he received his doctorate in 1866. He held professorships in physics or mathematics at Graz (1869–73; 1876–79),

Vienna (1873–76; 1894–1900; 1902–06), Munich (1889–93), and Leipzig (1900–02).

Boltzmann made important contributions to the kinetic theory of gases. He developed the law of equipartition of energy, which states that the total energy of an atom or molecule is, on average, equally distributed over the motions (degrees of freedom). He also produced an equation showing how the energy of a gas was distributed among the molecules (called the *Maxwell–Boltzmann distribution*).

Boltzmann also worked on thermodynamics, in which he developed the idea that heat, entropy, and other thermodynamic properties were the result of the behavior of large numbers of atoms, and could be treated by mechanics and statistics. In particular, Boltzmann showed that entropy — introduced by Rudolf Clausius — was a measure of the disorder of a system. *Boltzmann's equation* (1896) relates entropy (S) to probability (p): $S = a\log/p + b$. The equation is engraved on his gravestone.

Boltzmann's work in this field was heavily criticized by opponents of atomism, particularly Wilhelm Ostwald. It did however lead to the science of statistical mechanics developed later by Josiah Willard Gibbs and others. Boltzmann also worked on electromagnetism. He is further noted for a theoretical derivation of the law of radiation discovered by Josef Stefan (q.v.).

Toward the end of his life he suffered from illness and depression, and committed suicide in 1906.

BOLYAI, Janos (b. Dec. 15, 1802; Koloszvár, now Cluj in Rumania; d. Jan. 27, 1860; Marosvásárhely, now Tîrgu-Mureş in Rumania) Hungarian mathematician.

Bolyai's father Farkas was a distinguished mathematician who had an obsession with the status of Euclid's famous parallel postulate and devoted his life to trying to prove it. Despite his father's warnings that it would ruin his health, peace of mind, and happiness,

Janos too started working on this axiom until, in about 1820, he came to the conclusion that it could not be proved. He went on to develop a consistent geometry in which the parallel postulate is not used, thus establishing the independence of this axiom from the others. Bolyai published an account of his non-Euclidean geometry in 1832. Although his discovery had been anticipated by Nikolai Lobachevsky (q.v.) and Karl Gauss he was unaware of their work.

The discovery of the possibility of non-Euclidean geometries had a tremendous impact on both mathematics and philosophy. In mathematics it opened the way for a far more general and abstract approach to geometry than had previously been pursued, and in philosophy it settled once and for all the arguments about the supposed privileged status of Euclid's geometry. Bolyai also did valuable work in the theory of complex numbers.

BOND, George Phillips (b. May 20, 1825; Dorchester, Massachusetts; d. Feb. 17, 1865; Cambridge, Massachusetts) American astronomer.

George Bond spent most of his early life assisting his father, William Bond, whom he succeeded as director of the Harvard Observatory. He therefore contributed to most of his father's observational and photographic work. Apart from the joint discovery of Hyperion with his father he is best known for showing how stellar magnitude could be calculated from photographs. In 1857 he noted that the size of the image is relative to the brightness of the star and the length of the exposure. It is this basic fact that has been used by the compilers of the Astrographic Catalog to record measurements of stellar magnitudes. He was also the first to photograph a double star, Mizar, in 1857.

BOND, William Cranch (b. Sept. 9, 1789; Portland, Maine; d. Jan. 29, 1859; Cambridge, Massachusetts) American astronomer.

Bond was probably the first American astronomer to make a European reputation for himself. He was a watchmaker whose passion for astronomy was awakened by an eclipse, witnessed in 1806. He built his own observatory, which soon became one of the best in America. In 1847 the self-educated craftsman was invited to be director of the Harvard Observatory.

Bond's achievements were mainly observational and photographic. He made the first photograph of a star (Vega) in 1850, and was also the first to photograph the Moon. In 1848 with his son George Bond he discovered the eighth satellite of Saturn, Hyperion, and in 1850 he detected the third ring of Saturn between the two brighter ones — the so-called 'crepe' ring. He was succeeded by his son as director of the observatory.

BONDI, Sir Hermann (b. Nov. 1, 1919; Vienna) British–Austrian mathematician and cosmologist.

Bondi studied at Cambridge University, where he later taught. In 1954 he moved to London to take up the chair in mathematics at King's College. Bondi has always been actively interested in the wider implications of science and the scientific outlook, as his membership of the British Humanist Association and the Science Policy Foundation testify. He has served as chief scientific adviser to the Ministry of Defence (1971–77), chief scientist at the Department of Energy (from 1977), and chairman of the Natural Environment Research Council (from 1980). He was knighted in 1973.

Bondi's most important work has been in applied mathematics and especially in cosmology. In collaboration with Thomas Gold, he propounded, in 1948, a new version of the steady-state theory of the universe. This, among other topics, forms the substance of Bondi's book *Cosmology* (1952). The idea of a steady-state theory

had first been suggested by Fred Hoyle, the purpose being to devise a model of the universe that could accommodate both the fact that the universe is the same throughout, and yet is expanding. Bondi and Gold's model was innovatory in postulating that there is continuous creation of matter in order to maintain the universe's homogeneity despite its expansion. Although it enjoyed considerable popularity, Bondi and Gold's steady-state model is now considered to have been decisively refuted by observational evidence and the big-bang theory is favored.

BONNER, James Frederick (b. Sept. 1, 1910; Ansley, Nebraska) American biologist.

Bonner graduated in chemistry from the University of Utah in 1931 but turned to biology under the influence of Theodosius Dobzhansky. He received his PhD from the California Institute of Technology in 1934, which was then becoming known as the main center for molecular biology. Here he became interested in developmental biology and the question of why only some genes of the chromosome complement of an organism are expressed in any one cell. He discovered that histone, a protein that is found associated with the chromosomes, is responsible for shutting off gene activity, and that if the histone is removed then the repressed genes become functional again. He also discovered that certain hormones act by repressing and derepressing genes.

Bonner has in addition conducted research on the artificial synthesis of ribonucleic acid and studied ribosomes and mitochondria. Since 1946 he has been professor of biology at Cal Tech, and has written many books including *The Nucleohistones* (1964) and *The Molecular Biology of Development* (1965).

BONNET, Charles (b. Mar. 13, 1720; Geneva, Switzerland; d. May 20, 1793; Genthod, Switzerland) Swiss naturalist.

Bonnet studied law, gaining his doctorate in 1743. In the same year he was elected a fellow of the Royal Society for his work on regeneration in lower animals and his demonstration of breathing pores (stigmata or spiracles) in caterpillars and butterflies. He is chiefly remembered however for discovering parthenogenesis (reproduction without fertilization) in the spindle-tree aphid and for the ideas on evolution he proposed following this observation.

Bonnet believed all organisms are preformed and that the germs of every subsequent generation are contained within the female. Such thinking implied that species remain constant, leaving Bonnet to explain how species become extinct as evidenced by fossil remains. He argued that the Earth had experienced periodic catastrophes, each destroying many life forms, but the remaining species all evolved to some degree. (Bonnet was the first to use the term 'evolution' in a biological context.) Thus after the next catastrophe apes progress to men, and men become angels. The catastrophism theory was adopted by Georges Cuvier, and strongly influenced geological thinking until the 1820s.

BOOLE, George (b. Nov. 2, 1815; Lincoln, England; d. Dec. 8, 1864; Ballintemple, now in the Republic of Ireland) British mathematician.

Boole came from a poor background and was virtually self-taught in mathematics. He discovered for himself the theory of invariants. Before he obtained an academic post Boole spent several years as a school teacher, first in Yorkshire and later at a school he opened himself. In 1849 he became professor of mathematics at Queen's College, Cork, Ireland.

Boole's main work was in showing how mathematical techniques could be applied to the study of logic. His book *The Laws of Thought* (1854) is a landmark in the study of logic. Boole laid the foundations for an axiomatic treatment of logic that proved essential for the further fundamental developments soon to be made in the subject by such workers as Gottlob Frege and Bertrand Russell.

Boole's own logical algebra is essentially an algebra of classes, being based on such concepts as complement and union of classes. His work was an important advance in considering algebraic operations abstractly — that is, studying the formal properties of operations and their combinations without reference to their interpretation or 'meaning'. Fundamental formal properties like commutativity and associativity were first studied in purely abstract terms by Boole.

Boole's work led to the recognition of a new and fundamental algebraic structure the *Boolean algebra* alongside such structures as the field, ring, and group. The study of Boolean algebras both in themselves and their application to other areas of mathematics has been an important concern of 20th-century mathematics. Boolean algebras find important applications in such diverse fields as topology, measure theory, probability and statistics, and computing.

BORDA, Jean-Charles de (b. May 4, 1733; Dax, France; d. Feb. 19, 1791; Paris) French mathematician and nautical astronomer.

Borda was educated at La Flèche and entered the army as a military engineer. He entered the navy in 1767 and participated in a number of scientific voyages. In 1782 he was captured by the English while participating in the American War of Independence.

His main scientific work was in such practical areas of science as fluid mechanics and in the design of instruments for geodesy and navigation. His work in fluid mechanics had a strongly experimental slant and he applied his discoveries to such practical military problems as the design of artillery, ships, and pumps. He is notable for having shown that the theory of fluid resistance put forward by Newton was erroneous. Borda was also involved in instituting the metric system of weights and measures and introduced the term 'meter'. He made contributions to the calculus of variations and was notable for his hostility to religion.

BORDET, Jules Jean Baptiste Vincent (b. June 13, 1870; Soignies, Belgium; d. Apr. 6, 1961; Brussels) Belgian immunologist.

Bordet graduated in medicine from Brussels University in 1892 and in 1894 joined the Pasteur Institute, Paris, where he worked under the bacteriologist Elie Metchnikoff. In collaboration with Octave Gengou, Bordet discovered that in an immunized animal the antibodies produced by the immune response work in conjunction with another component of blood (which Bordet termed 'alexin' but which is now called 'complement') to destroy foreign cells that invade the body. This component, Bordet found, was present in both immunized and nonimmunized animals and was destroyed by heating to over 55°C. This work formed the basis of the *complement-fixation test*, a particularly sensitive means of detecting the presence of any specific type of cell or its specific antibody. A notable application of this was the test to detect syphilis devised by August von Wasserman.

In 1901 Bordet left Paris to found and direct the Pasteur Institute in Brussels and in 1907 he was appointed professor of pathology and bacteriology at Brussels University. In 1906 Bordet isolated the bacterium responsible for whooping cough, which is named after him: *Bordetella* (*Haemophilus*) *pertussis*. For his discovery of complement and other contributions to medicine, he was awarded the 1919 Nobel Prize in physiology or medicine.

BORELLI, Giovanni Alfonso (b. Jan. 28, 1608; Naples, Italy; d. Dec. 31, 1679; Rome) Italian mathematician and physiologist.

Borelli's mathematical training — he was professor at Messina and Pisa — led him to apply mathematical and mechanical laws to his two main interests, astronomy and animal physiology. He rightly explained muscular action and the movements of bones in terms of levers, and also carried out detailed studies of the flight mechanism of birds. However, his extension of such principles to internal organs, such as the heart, stomach, and lungs, overlooked the essential chemical actions that take place in these organs. Borelli's *De motu animalium* (1680; On the Movement of Animals), which includes his theory of blood circulation, is thus in part erroneous.

In astronomy, he tried to explain the motion of Jupiter's planets by postulating that Jupiter, as well as the Sun, exerts a gravitational pull. He also emphasized the findings of Johannes Kepler and Jeremiah Horrocks in drawing attention to the elliptical orbits of the Sun, Moon, and the planets and was the first to suggest that comets trace a parabolic path through the solar system.

BORLAUG, Norman Ernest (b. Mar. 25, 1914; Cresco, Iowa) American agronomist and plant breeder.

Borlaug graduated in forestry from Minnesota University in 1937 and gained his doctorate in plant pathology in 1941. He then spent three years with the Du Pont Chemical Company, testing the effects of chemicals on plants and plant diseases. In 1944 he joined the newly formed International Maize and Wheat Improvement Center in Mexico and began the breeding work that was to produce the highly adaptable dwarf wheats that played so large a part in the 'Green Revolution' of the late 1960s and early 1970s.

Borlaug's high-yielding cereals increased agricultural production in the developing countries to the extent that many became self-sufficient for grain. For his major role in temporarily alleviating world famine, Borlaug was awarded the Nobel Peace Prize in 1970.

BORN, Max (b. Dec. 11, 1882; Breslau, now Wroclaw in Poland; d. Jan. 5, 1970; Göttingen, West Germany) German physicist.

Born was the son of an embryologist, a professor of anatomy at the University of Breslau. He was educated at the universities of Breslau, Heidelberg, Zurich, and Göttingen, where he obtained his PhD in 1907. From 1909 until 1933 he taught at Göttingen, being appointed professor of physics in 1921. With the rise of Hitler he moved to Britain, and from 1936 served as professor of natural philosophy at the University of Edinburgh, returning to Germany on his retirement in 1953.

Born's early work was on crystals, particularly the vibrations of atoms in crystal lattices. The *Born–Haber cycle* is a theoretical cycle of reactions and changes by which it is possible to calculate the lattice energy of ionic crystals. He is noted for his role in the development of the new quantum theory. Together with Pascual Jordan, he developed (1925) the matrix mechanics introduced by Werner Heisenberg (q.v.). He also showed how to interpret the theoretical results of Louis de Broglie and the experiments of such people as Clinton J. Davisson, which showed that particles have wavelike behavior.

At the time, it was known that in some circumstances light, electrons, etc., behaved as waves whereas in others they acted like particles. (William Bragg once suggested using the corpuscular (particle) theory on Monday, Wednesday, and Friday, and the undulatory (wave) theory on Tuesday, Thursday, and Saturday.) Mathematical treatments could be used to predict behavior, but there was a problem in finding some accepted physical picture of how electrons, for instance, could act in this way. Erwin Schrödinger, who developed wave mechanics, interpreted particles as 'wave packets', but this was unsatisfactory because such packets would dissipate in time. Born's interpretation was

that the particles exist but are 'guided' by a wave. At any point, the amplitude (actually the square of the amplitude) indicates the probability of finding a particle there.

An essential part of this idea of electrons, atoms, etc., is that it depends on probability — there is no predetermined way in which absolute predictions can be made, as in classical physics. A similar result is embodied in the uncertainty principle of Werner Heisenberg. Einstein, amongst others, could never accept this and Born corresponded with him on the subject (the *Born–Einstein letters* were published in 1971).

Born shared (with Walter Bothe) the 1954 Nobel Prize for physics. He is buried in Göttingen, where his tombstone displays his fundamental equation of matrix mechanics:

$$pq - qp = h/2\pi i$$

BOSCH, Carl (b. Aug. 27, 1874; Cologne, now in West Germany; d. Apr. 26, 1940; Heidelberg, now in West Germany) German industrial chemist.

Bosch was trained as both metallurgist and chemist and gained his doctorate under Johannes Wislicenus at Leipzig (1898). He joined the large German dyestuffs company, Badische Anilin und Soda Fabrik (BASF), in 1899. Following Fritz Haber's successful small-scale ammonia synthesis in 1909, Bosch began to develop a high-pressure ammonia plant at Oppau for BASF. The plant was opened in 1912 — a successful application of the Haber process on a large scale. Bosch also introduced the use of the water-gas shift reaction as a source of hydrogen for the process:

$$CO + H_2O = CO_2 + H_2$$

After World War I the large-scale ammonia fertilizer industry was established and the high-pressure technique was extended by BASF to the synthesis of methanol from carbon monoxide and hydrogen in 1923. Bosch was chairman of BASF's successor, IG Farben (1935–40) and concurrently director of the Kaiser Wilhelm institutes. He shared the Nobel Prize for chemistry with Friedrich Bergius in 1931.

BOSE, Sir Jagadis Chandra (b. Nov. 30, 1858; Mymensingh, now in Bangladesh; d. Nov. 23, 1937; Giridih, India) Indian plant physiologist and physicist.

Bose began his studies in London as a medical student. He then won a scholarship to Cambridge University, from where he graduated in natural sciences in 1884. He was appointed professor of physical science at Presidency College, Calcutta, in 1885 and retained this post until 1915. In 1917 he founded and became director of the Bose Research Institute, Calcutta. He was knighted in 1917 and in 1920 became the first Indian to be elected a fellow of the Royal Society.

Bose's early research was on the properties of very short radio waves — work in which he showed their similarity to light. He also designed an improved version of Oliver Lodge's coherer, then used to detect radio waves, and as a result was able to put forward a general theory of the properties of contact-sensitive materials.

His most famous work concerned his investigations into plant physiology and the similarities between the behavioral response of plant and animal tissue. By devising extremely sensitive instruments he was able to demonstrate the minute movements of plants to external stimuli and to measure their rate of growth. While his experimental skill was widely admired, this work did not at the time gain universal acceptance.

BOSE, Satyendra Nath (b. Jan. 1, 1894; Calcutta, India; d. Feb. 4, 1974, Calcutta) Indian physicist.

Bose was educated at Presidency College, Calcutta. Among his teachers was the eminent Indian physicist Jagadis Chandra Bose. Bose held the post of lecturer at the Calcutta University College of Science from 1917 until he left in 1921 to become a reader in physics at the new University of Dacca in East Bengal. His work ranged over many aspects of physics, among them statistical mechanics, the electromagnetic properties of the ionosphere, theories of x-ray crystallography, and unified field theory. However it is for his work in quantum statistics that he is best known.

Bose attracted the attention of Albert Einstein and other European physicists by publishing a paper in 1924 in which he was able to derive Max Planck's black body radiation law, but without using the classical electrodynamics as Planck himself had done. On the strength of this work Bose was able to get two years' study leave in Europe and during his visit he came into contact with many of the great physicists of the day, such as Louis de Broglie, Max Born, and Einstein. Einstein's generalization of Bose's work led to the system of statistical quantum mechanics now known as *Bose–Einstein* statistics. This system of statistics contrasts with the rival Fermi–Dirac statistics in that it applies only to particles not limited to single occupancy of the same state, i.e. particles (known as bosons) that do not obey the Pauli exclusion principle.

BOSS, Lewis (b. Oct. 26, 1846; Providence, Rhode Island; d. Oct. 5, 1912; Albany, New York) American astronomer.

Boss studied at Dartmouth College where he graduated in 1870. In 1872 he was appointed assistant astronomer to the 49th parallel survey for the American–Canadian boundary, accurately locating stations from which the surveyors could work with confidence. In 1876 Boss was appointed director of the Dudley Observatory, Albany, a post he held until his death in 1912.

While working on the parallel survey Boss became aware of the many errors made in the measurement of stellar positions, which thus caused the current catalogs to be inaccurate. He consequently made his own observations, publishing the positions of 500 stars in 1878. He then undertook the observation and reduction of a zone for the Leipzig *Astronomische Gesellschaft* and also began work on his own catalog. This was published in 1910 as the *Preliminary General Catalogue* containing the position and proper motion of 6188 of the brighter stars. His work was extended by his son, Benjamin Boss, who published in 1937 the *General Catalogue* containing comparable details of 33342 stars.

BOTHE, Walther Wilhelm Georg Franz (b. June 8, 1891; Oranienburg, now in East Germany; d. Feb. 8, 1957; Heidelberg, West Germany) German atomic physicist.

Bothe studied at the University of Berlin under Max Planck and received his PhD in 1914. For the next few years, he was a prisoner of war in Russia but, on his return to Germany in 1920, he started teaching at Berlin and worked in Hans Geiger's radioactivity laboratory.

He devised the 'coincidence method' of detecting the emission of electrons by x-rays in which electrons passing through two adjacent Geiger tubes at almost the same time are registered as a coincidental event. He used it to show that momentum and energy are conserved at the atomic level. In 1929 he applied the method to the study of cosmic rays and was able to show that they consisted of massive particles rather than photons. For this research he shared the 1954 Nobel Prize for physics with Max Born.

By 1930 his reputation was established and he was appointed professor of physics at Giessen. The same year he observed a strange radiation emitted from beryllium when it was exposed to alpha particles. This radiation was later identified by Chadwick as consisting of neutrons.

While director of the Max Planck Institute in Heidelberg, Bothe supervised the construction of Germany's first cyclotron. This work was finished in 1943 and during World War II he led German scientists in their search for atomic energy. When the war ended he was given the chair of physics at Heidelberg, which he retained until his death.

BOUCHER DE CREVECOEUR DE PERTHES, Jacques (b. Sept. 10, 1788; Rethel, France; d. Aug. 5, 1868; Abbeville, France) French archeologist.

Boucher de Perthes, the son of a customs official, followed in his father's profession and in 1825 was appointed director of the Abbeville customs, a post he occupied for his entire career.

His hobby was investigating the fossil-rich beds of the nearby Somme Valley and in *Antiquités celtiques et antédiluviennes (3 vols. 1847–64; Celtic Antediluvian Antiquities)* Boucher de Perthes first revealed the existence of a prehistoric world occupied by man. He reported finding such objects as polished stone axes, which he attributed to the people he called 'celtiques' and also older tools linked with the remains of extinct mammalian species. These he claimed must have belonged to 'homme antédiluvien'.

Inevitably such revolutionary ideas initially received little support in France where Georges Cuvier's views still dominated evolutionary thinking. British scientists were more sympathetic, and in 1859 Boucher de Perthes's views were publicly and authoritatively acknowledged before the Royal Society by two British geologists, Joseph Prestwich and Hugh Falconer. However later evidence that some of the finds at Abbeville were forgeries tended to discredit Boucher de Perthes early work, even though it was never satisfactorily established whether or not he played a part in producing the fakes.

BOUGUER, Pierre (b. Feb. 16, 1698; Le Croisic, France; d. Aug. 15, 1758; Paris) French physicist and mathematician.

Bouguer's father was a hydrographer and mathematician and Bouguer followed him into the same profession. He was a child prodigy and obtained a post as professor of hydrography at the remarkably early age of 15. The study of the problems associated with navigation and ship design was his chief interest. Bouguer took part in an extended expedition to Peru led by Charles de la Condamine to determine the length of a degree of the meridian near the equator. While on this expedition Bouguer also did a great deal of other valuable experimental work.

One of Bouguer's most successful inventions was the heliometer to measure the light of the Sun and other luminous bodies. Although it was not his chief interest the work for which Bouguer is now best remembered was on photometry. Here too he did much valuable experimental work and one of his major discoveries was of the law now named for him. This states that in a medium of uniform transparency the light remaining in a collimated beam is an exponential function of the length of its path in the medium. The law is sometimes unjustly attributed to Johann Lambert. Bouguer's work in optics can be seen as the beginning of the science of atmospheric optics.

BOULTON, Matthew (b. Sept. 3, 1728; Birmingham, England; d. Aug. 17, 1809; Birmingham) British engineer.

Boulton was the manufacturer who supported and financed James Watt's (q.v.) steam engine. He had founded a small factory at Soho near Birmingham (1762), which produced metal articles, and realized that better power sources were needed. He met James Watt in 1768 and recognized the potential of Watt's engine. They became partners in 1775. In 1786 he designed steam-powered coining machinery, which was patented in 1790, and supplied machinery to the Royal Mint and coins to the East India Company.

BOURBAKI, Nicolas French group of mathematicians.

'Bourbaki' is the collective *nom de plume* of a group of some of the most outstanding of contemporary mathematicians. The precise membership of Bourbaki, which naturally has changed over the years, is a closely guarded secret but it is known that most of the members are French.

Since 1939, Bourbaki has been publishing a monumental work, the *Eléments de mathématique* (Elements of Mathematics), of which over thirty volumes have so far appeared. In this Bourbaki attempts to expound and display the architecture of the whole mathematical edifice starting from certain carefully chosen logical and set-theoretic concepts. The emphasis throughout the *Eléments* is on the interrelationships to be found between the various structures present in mathematics, and to a certain extent this means that Bourbaki's exposition cuts across traditional boundaries, such as that between algebra and topology. Indeed for Bourbaki, pure mathematics is to be thought of as nothing other than the study of pure structure.

Since the members of Bourbaki are all working mathematicians, rather than pure logicians, in contrast to other foundational enterprises (e.g. those of Gottlob Frege, Bertrand Russell, and A. N. Whitehead) the influence of Bourbaki's writings on contemporary mathematicians and their conception of the subject has been immense.

BOUSSINGAULT, Jean Baptiste (b. Feb. 2, 1802; Paris; d. May 12, 1887; Paris) French agricultural chemist.

Boussingault began his career as a mineralogist after studying at the mining school in Paris. He spent several years in Latin America, where he is reported to have fought in the wars of independence under Bolívar. He returned to France in 1832 and shortly afterward became professor of chemistry at Lyons. In 1839 he moved to the Sorbonne in Paris. Boussingault entered politics in 1848 but returned to chemistry after the coup of 1851. Between 1860 and 1874 he published a comprehensive eight-volume work on agricultural chemistry.

His most important work was on the role of nitrogen in plants. In 1837 he began a series of experiments proving that leguminous plants (peas, clover, etc.) are capable of using atmospheric nitrogen. By growing a wide variety of plants in nitrogen-deficient soils he was able to show that grains could not support themselves but that the legumes could survive (he was not sure how the nitrogen was taken up by the plants). He further demonstrated that animals could not utilize atmospheric nitrogen when living on nitrogen-free diets.

In 1864 Boussingault made the fundamental discovery that the volume of carbon dioxide absorbed by a plant is equal to the volume of oxygen given out.

BOVERI, Theodor Heinrich (b. Oct. 12, 1862; Bamberg, now in West Germany; d. Oct. 15, 1915; Würzburg, now in West Germany) German zoologist.

Boveri graduated in medicine from Munich in 1885, remaining at Munich to do cytological research until his appointment as professor of zoology and comparative anatomy at Würzburg in 1893. In 1888, he coined the term *centrosome* for the region of the cell that contains the centriole, first discovered by Edouard van Beneden. Boveri also proved Beneden's theory that equal numbers of chromosomes are contributed by the egg and the sperm to the zygote. Boveri accurately described the formation of the polar bodies following meiosis in the egg cell, and made pioneering studies of sperm formation (spermatogenesis), introducing a diagrammatic representation of the process (1892), which is still in use today.

BOVET, Daniel (b. Mar. 23, 1907; Neuchâtel, Switzerland) Swiss–Italian pharmacologist.

In 1929 Bovet gained a DSc in zoology and comparative anatomy from the University of Geneva where his father was professor of pedagogy. He continued research work at the Pasteur Institute in Paris, where he followed up the discoveries of Gerhard Domagk on prontosil. He and his co-workers were able to show that the sulfonamide group is responsible for the antibacterial action of prontosil. The drug is only active *in vivo* as the animals metabolize the parent drug into sulfanilamide, which is the antibacterial compound.

Prontosil was a dye, protected by patents and expensive. Sulfanilamide was colorless, freely available, cheap to manufacture, and equally as effective as a bactericide. Many analogs, known as sulfadrugs, have been made and these are widely used against streptococcal infections such as pneumonia, meningitis, and scarlet fever.

These researches led Bovet to develop the earlier ideas of Paul Ehrlich, Emil Fischer, and Juda Quastel into a more refined 'antimetabolite hypothesis', which is one of the fundamental lines of approach in modern drug research. It is based on the idea that a chemical compound whose properties and molecular shape resemble those of a normal body metabolite may affect the functions of that metabolite. Just as a lock (a metabolic reaction) is opened by just one shape of key (a metabolite) so another slightly different shape of key (an antimetabolite) may jam the lock and prevent the new key from fitting. These ideas led Bovet to develop the antihistamine drug "933F" in 1937 and this gave rise to a series of drugs that are useful for asthma and hay fever.

Later, after a trip to Brazil, Bovet became interested in the Indian nerve poison curare. The structure of curare had already been worked out and in 1946 Bovet began work on analogs, which led to the use of succinylcholine as a muscle relaxant in surgical operations.

In 1947 Bovet became head of pharmacology and chemotherapeutics at the Superior Institute of Health in Rome. He became an Italian citizen and in more recent years has carried out research work on tranquilizers and anesthetics. He was awarded the Nobel Prize for physiology or medicine in 1957.

BOWEN, Edmund John (b. Apr. 29, 1898; Worcester, England) British physical chemist.

Bowen spent his entire career at Oxford University, beginning in 1915 as a student at Balliol College and continuing after graduation as a fellow of University College from 1922 until his retirement in 1965.

He worked mainly on photochemistry, investigating a large number of photochemical reactions and producing a survey of the subject, *Chemical Aspects of Light* (1942). He also produced, with F. Wokes, the more specialized *The Fluorescence of Solutions* (1953) and edited and contributed to *Luminescence in Chemistry* (1968).

BOWEN, Ira Sprague (b. Dec. 21, 1898; Seneca Falls, New York; d. Feb. 6, 1973; Los Angeles, California) American astronomer.

Bowen graduated from Oberlin College, Chicago in 1919 and gained his PhD from the California Institute of Technology, Pasadena in 1926. He taught physics at Cal Tech from 1921 to 1945, serving from 1931 as professor. In 1946 he was made director of the Mount Wilson Observatory and in 1948 of the newly opened Palomar Observatory, posts he continued to hold until his retirement in 1964.

In 1928 Bowen tackled the problem of the strange lines first observed by William Huggins in the 1860s in the spectrum of planetary nebulae and the Orion nebula.

The difficulty was, according to Bowen, that the strong lines had not been reproduced in the laboratory. Spectrographic evidence showed that such lines must be emitted by an element of low atomic weight. Talk of a new element, known as 'nebulium', that could produce the observed spectral lines was however dismissed by Bowen as nonsense.

Bowen was able to show that the lines were in fact due to radiation emitted from ionized atoms of oxygen and nitrogen as they decayed into more stable lower-energy levels. Specifically he was able to show that triply and doubly ionized oxygen as well as doubly ionized nitrogen would radiate at the wavelengths attributed to 'nebulium' but only in the highly rarified conditions of nebulae where collisions between atoms are very infrequent. It is this radiation that contributes to the green and red colors observed in emission and planetary nebulae.

BOWMAN, Sir William (b. July 20, 1816; Nantwich, England; d. Mar. 29, 1892; Dorking, England) British physician.

Bowman studied medicine at King's College, London, and in 1840 was appointed assistant surgeon at the newly founded King's College Hospital. His main interest was the investigation of the microscopic structure of tissues (histology). Although he studied voluntary (striated) muscle and liver, it is for his work on the kidney that Bowman is best known. He showed that the capsule (now called Bowman's capsule) that surrounds the bunch of blood capillaries (glomerulus) in each Malpighian corpuscle is continuous with the renal tubule, which in turn leads to the collecting ducts and ultimately to the ureter. This piece of structural evidence prompted him to propose that fluid passed from the glomerulus into the tubule. He reported his findings in his famous paper, *On the Structure and Use of the Malpighian Bodies of the Kidney* (1842).

In the following years, he increasingly devoted his attentions to eye surgery and in 1846 became assistant surgeon at the Royal London Ophthalmic Hospital (now Moorfields Eye Hospital) and full surgeon in 1851. One of the most celebrated eye surgeons of his day, he introduced the newly invented ophthalmoscope into his practice and described many anatomical features of the eye including the basement membrane of the cornea and the radial fibers of the ciliary muscle, both of which bear his name. He also advanced techniques in eye surgery.

Bowman's *The Physiological Anatomy and Physiology of Man* (5 vols. 1845–56), which he wrote with his teacher, Robert Todd, was one of the first texts in which histology assumed real significance in medicine and testifies to the valuable contribution of its author. A popular lecturer with his students, Bowman was also a methodical and kindly practitioner. In 1880 he founded the Ophthalmological Society and was its first president. He was knighted in 1884.

BOYD, William Clouser (b. Mar. 4, 1903; Dearborn, Missouri) American biochemist.

Boyd was educated at Harvard and Boston where he obtained his PhD in 1930 and later taught in the medical school, serving as professor of immunochemistry from 1948 until his retirement in 1969.

Karl Landsteiner's discovery of blood groups in 1902 and subsequent studies of their global distribution permitted a far more accurate estimate of racial types than had previously been possible. To this end Boyd began the systematic collection and analysis of blood samples from all over the world.

Eventually, in the 1950s, in such works as *Genetics and the Races of Man* (1950) he began to present evidence for the existence of 13 races — early European, northern and eastern European, Lapp, Mediterranean, African, Asian, Dravidian, Amerind, Indonesian, Melanesian, Polynesian, and Australian aborigine.

BOYER, Herbert Wayne (b. July 10, 1936; Pittsburgh, Pennsylvania) American biochemist.

Boyer was educated at St. Vincent College, Latrobe, and the University of Pittsburgh where he obtained his PhD in 1963. He joined the faculty of the University of California, San Francisco, shortly afterward in 1966 and has served since 1976 as professor of biochemistry.

Much of Boyer's work has been concerned with developing some of the basic techniques of recombinant DNA, known more popularly as genetic engineering. Thus, in 1973 he succeeded with Robert Helling,and independently of the work of Stanley Cohen and Annie Chang, in constructing functional DNA from two different sources. Such chimeras, as they became called, were initially engineered by splicing together segments from two different plasmids (extrachromosomal DNA found in some bacteria) from the *Escherichia coli* bacillus. The chimera was then inserted into *E. coli* and was found to replicate and, equally significant, to express traits derived from both plasmids.

Development after 1973 was so rapid that by 1976 it had occurred to Boyer and a number of other workers that recombinant DNA could be used to produce such important proteins as insulin, interferon, and growth hormone in commercial quantities. Consequently in 1976 he joined with financier Robert Swanson to invest $500 each to form the company Genentech, which went public in 1980.

Despite successfully developing techniques for the production of somastatin in 1977, insulin in 1978, and growth hormone in 1979, the position of Genentech was far from secure at the beginning of 1981 with the emergence of competition from a number of rival companies and legal problems concerned with the ownership of genes.

BOYLE, Robert (b. Jan. 25, 1627; Lismore Castle, now in the Republic of Ireland; d. Dec. 30, 1691; London) British chemist and physicist.

The son of the Earl of Cork, Boyle was a member of an aristocratic and wealthy family. He spent four years at Eton College and from 1638 studied at Geneva, returning to London in 1644. He then retired to his estate at Stalbridge, Dorset, where he took up the life of a scientific 'virtuoso'.

In 1654 Boyle moved to Oxford, where he worked on pneumatics. In 1658–59 he had an air pump built for him by Robert Hooke, after the type invented by Otto von Guericke in 1654. Boyle was ably assisted by Hooke in various pioneering experiments in which he showed that air was essential for the transmission of sound, and for respiration and combustion — and that the last two processes exhausted only part of the air.

In Boyle's most famous experiment he took a U-shaped tube with a shorter closed end, and a longer open end into which he poured mercury, thus isolating a given volume of air in the shorter end. When the mercury was level in both 'limbs' the air was under atmospheric pressure, and by adding more mercury to the longer limb the pressure could be increased. Boyle found that the volume was halved if the pressure was doubled, reduced to a third if the pressure was tripled, and so on — and that this process was reversible. Boyle's work on the compressibility of air was published in *New Experiments Physico-Mechanicall, Touching the Spring of the Air and its Effects* (1660) but the famous law stating that the pressure and volume of air are inversely proportional was not stated explicitly until the second edition (1662). The law, known as *Boyle's law* in America and Britain but in Europe as *Mariotte's law*, can be expressed (where C is a constant) as $p \times V = C$; that is, the product of the pressure and volume of a gas remains constant if, as Edmé Mariotte noted, the temperature remains constant. This law (together with its companion gas law, that of Jacques Charles) is true only for ideal gases, but holds for real gases at very low pressures and high temperatures.

Boyle developed a mechanical corpuscular philosophy of his own, derived from the Greek tradition and the work of Galileo

and Pierre Gassendi. In Boyle's conception all physical phenomena could be explained by corpuscles of different shapes, sizes, and motions, this corpuscular matter being capable of infinite transformations (which allowed the possibility of alchemy and excluded the existence of elements).

However, in *The Sceptical Chymist* (1661) Boyle proposed a view of matter that presaged modern views and certainly disposed effectively of the Aristotelian doctrine of the four elements. He supposed that all matter was composed of primary particles, some of which joined together to form semi-indivisible corpuscles and whose organization and motion explained all qualities of matter.

Boyle's main contribution to chemistry was his insistence on experiment, precision, and accurate observation. He devised many analytical tests including the use of vegetable dyes as acid–base indicators and of flame tests to detect metals. The chemist's concern for the purity of his materials began with Boyle. Although he prepared hydrogen by the action of acids on iron and observed the oxidation of mercury and its subsequent regeneration on further heating, the 'fixation' of gases in bodies remained unexplained in his work. Likewise, he observed the increase in weight of metals on calcination but attributed this to heat, which he sometimes regarded as material.

Boyle left Oxford for London in 1668 where, despite his scholarly nature and poor health, he was very much at the center of scientific life as a founder member of the Royal Society. He believed, like his hero Francis Bacon, that science could be put to practical use.

BRACHET, Jean Louis Auguste (b. Mar. 19, 1909; Brussels) Belgian cell biologist.

Brachet was educated at the Free University of Brussels where his father, an embryologist, was rector. After gaining his MD in 1934 he joined the faculty as an anatomy instructor and in 1943 was appointed professor of general biology.

Brachet began his career by studying the then poorly understood nucleic acids. It had been thought that plant cells contain RNA and animal cells DNA but, in 1933, Brachet demonstrated that both types of nucleic acid occur in both plant and animal cells. He proved this by developing a cytochemical technique that made it possible to localize the RNA-containing structures in the cell. Brachet also noted that cells rich in RNA tend to be those actively engaged in protein synthesis. On this basis Brachet was led in 1942 to propose the important hypothesis that ribonucleoprotein granules could be the agents of protein synthesis. Such granules, later termed ribosomes, were indeed shown to function in this way by George Palade in 1956.

Later experiments, in which Brachet removed the nucleus from the cell, showed that although protein synthesis continued for a while the amount of RNA in the cytoplasm decreased until there was none left. This indicated that the production of RNA occurs in the nucleus and that it is then transported from the nucleus to the cytoplasm.

BRACONNOT, Henri (b. May 29, 1781; Commercy, France; d. Jan. 13, 1855; Nancy, France) French naturalist and biochemist.

Educated at Strasbourg and Paris, Braconnot was professor of natural history at the Lyceum, Nancy, and director of the botanical gardens. Braconnot was interested in the chemical make-up of plants and discovered (1819) a means of obtaining glucose from various plant products lacking in starch, such as tree bark and sawdust. (Until then, glucose had been obtained by boiling starch with acid.) The non-starch material was later isolated and named cellulose by Anselme Payen. Braconnot also did work on saponification and discovered some of the acids occurring in plants.

BRADLEY, James (b. Mar. 1693; Sherborne, England; d. July 13, 1762; Chalford, England) British astronomer.

Bradley was educated at Oxford University, and was taught astronomy by his uncle, the Rev James Pound, also an astronomer. In 1721 Bradley became Savilian Professor of Astronomy at Oxford and in 1742 he succeeded Edmond Halley as Astronomer Royal. His astronomical career began with a determined effort to detect parallax — the angular displacement of a body when viewed from spatially separate positions (or, more significantly, one position on a *moving* Earth). He fixed a telescope in as vertical a position as possible to minimize the effects of atmospheric refraction and began to observe the star Gamma Draconis. He soon found that the star had apparently moved position but prolonged observation convinced him that it could not be parallax he had measured, for he found the greatest shift in position in September and March and not in December and June as it should have been if he was observing parallax. However, the change in position was so regular (every six months) that it could be due only to the observer being on a moving Earth. It took him until 1729 to find the precise cause of the change in position. He realized that as light has a finite speed it will therefore take some time, however small, to travel down the length of the telescope. While it is traveling from the top to the bottom of the telescope the bottom of the instrument will have been carried by the orbital motion of the Earth. The image of the star will therefore be slightly displaced. Bradley realized that he had at last produced hard observational evidence for the Earth's motion, for the finite speed of light, and for a new aberration that had to be taken into account if truly accurate stellar positions were to be calculated. He worked out the constant of aberration at between 20″ and 20″.5 — a very accurate figure. He also discovered another small displacement, which, because it had the same period as the regression of the nodes of the Moon, he identified as the result of the 5° inclination of the Moon's orbit to the ecliptic. This caused a slight wobble of the Earth's axis, which he called nutation. Friedrich Bessel later used Bradley's observations to construct a catalog of unprecedented accuracy.

BRAGG, Sir William Henry (b. July 2, 1862; Westwood, England; d. Mar. 12, 1942; London) British physicist.

Bragg's father was a merchant seaman turned farmer. William Henry Bragg was educated at a variety of schools before going as a scholar to Cambridge University. He graduated in 1884 and after a year's research under J.J. Thomson took the chair of mathematics and physics at the University of Adelaide, Australia, in 1886. He returned to England as professor of physics at Leeds University in 1909, moving from there to University College, London, in 1915.

In Australia, Bragg concentrated on lecturing and started original research late in life (in 1904). He first worked on alpha radiation, investigating the range of the particles. Later he turned his attention to x-rays, originally believing (in opposition to Charles Barkla) that they were neutral particles. With the observation of x-ray diffraction by Max von Laue, he accepted that the x-rays were waves and constructed (1915) the first x-ray spectrometer to measure the wavelengths of x-rays. Much of his work was on x-ray crystallography, in collaboration with his son, William Lawrence Bragg (q.v.). They shared the Nobel Physics Prize in 1915.

During the war Bragg worked on the development of hydrophones for the admiralty. In some ways his most significant work was done at the Royal Institution, London, where he was director from 1923. Under James Dewar's directorship the research functions of the Royal Institution had virtually disappeared. Bragg recruited several young and brilliant crystallographers who shared with him a commitment to applying the new technique to the analysis of organic compounds.

There was no reason to suppose there was much chance of success but as early as the 1920s Bragg was planning to investigate biological molecules with x-rays. His first attempts were made on anthracene and naphthalene in 1921.

BRAGG, Sir William Lawrence (b. Mar. 31, 1890; Adelaide, Australia; d. July 1, 1971; London) British physicist.

William Lawrence Bragg, who was the son of William Henry Bragg, was educated at Adelaide University and Cambridge University, where he became a fellow and lecturer. After the war, in 1919, he was appointed professor of physics at Manchester University. He succeeded Ernest Rutherford in 1938, after a short period in 1937 as director of the National Physical Laboratory, as head of the Cavendish Laboratory and Cavendish Professor at Cambridge. Finally, in 1953, he became director of the Royal Institution, London, a post his father had held previously and which he held until his retirement in 1961.

Success came very early to Bragg, who shared the Nobel Physics Prize with his father in 1915. Following Max von Laue's discovery of x-ray diffraction by crystals in 1912, Lawrence Bragg in the same year formulated what is now known as the *Bragg law*:

$$n\lambda = 2d\sin\theta$$

which relates the wavelength of x-rays (λ), the angle of incidence on a crystal θ, and the spacing of crystal planes d, for x-ray diffraction. n is an integer (1, 2, 3, etc.). Bragg collaborated with his father in working out the crystal structures of a number of substances. Early in this work they showed that sodium chloride does not have individual molecules in the solid, but is an array of sodium and chloride ions. In 1915 the Braggs published their book *X-rays and Crystal Structure*.

Lawrence Bragg later worked on silicates and on metallurgy. He was responsible for setting up a program for structure determinations of proteins.

BRAHE, Tycho (b. Dec. 14, 1546; Knudstrup, Denmark; d. Oct. 24, 1601; Prague, now in Czechoslovakia) Danish astronomer.

Tycho's father Otto was a nobleman, the governor of Helsingborg castle. Tycho was kidnapped by and brought up by his uncle Jörgen, an admiral in the Danish navy. He was sent to Leipzig University in 1562 to study law, but already his interest in astronomy had been kindled. He witnessed a partial solar eclipse in 1560 in Copenhagen whose predictability so impressed him that he began a serious study of Ptolemy's *Almagest*. He was allowed to continue with the formal study of astronomy and began a tour of the universities of northern Europe. It was while at Rostock in 1566 that, according to tradition, he became involved in a dispute with another young Danish nobleman over who was the better mathematician. The dispute led to a duel in which Tycho lost part of his nose. This he replaced with a mixture of gold, silver, and wax; the nose is clearly visible in contemporary engravings.

Tycho became aware that the successful solar-eclipse prediction of 1560 was not a typical index of the state of 16th-century astronomy. For instance, a conjunction of Jupiter and Saturn predicted by current tables was wrong by ten days. Tycho therefore began his long apprenticeship, traveling through northern Europe meeting the astronomers, instrument makers, and patrons who would support him later on.

His international reputation was made with the dramatic events that centered upon the nova of 1572 — ever since known as *Tycho's star*. Not since the days of Hipparchus (second century BC) had a new star visible to the naked eye appeared in the sky. In *De nova stella* (1573; On the New Star), Tycho was able to demonstrate that the new star showed no parallax and therefore truly belonged to the sphere of the fixed stars. This was important cosmologically because according to Aristotle no change could take place in the heavens, which were supposed to be eternal and incorruptible; change could take place only in the sublunary sphere. By demonstrating that the new star of 1572 and the great comet of 1577 were changes in the heavens, Tycho was providing new evidence against the traditional Aristotelian cosmology.

In order to induce him to stay in Denmark, Tycho's monarch, Frederick II, offered him the island of Hven and unlimited funds to build an observatory there at Uraniborg. Tycho moved there in 1577, building an observatory/castle stocked with the best instruments then in existence, and constructing enormous quadrants and sextants. He became the greatest observational astronomer of the pretelescopic age. Before Tycho, astronomers tended to work with observations many centuries old. Copernicus would be more likely to use the tables of Ptolemy (second century AD) than to make his own observations. When modern tables, such as the *Prutenic Tables* of Erasmus Reinhold, were constructed, although based on the Copernican system, they were scarcely more reliable. Tycho changed all this. Twenty years' careful observation using accurate instruments enabled him to determine the positions of 777 stars with unparalleled accuracy. He did not, however, accept the Copernican heliocentric system. Instead he proposed a compromise between that and the Ptolemaic, suggesting that the Earth remains at the center, immobile; the Sun and Moon move round the Earth; and all other bodies move round the Sun. His system received hardly any support.

After the death of Frederick II in 1588, Tycho quarreled with his successor, Christian IV, on his coming of age. The last recorded observation made at Hven was on 15 March, 1596. Tycho set off once more on his travels, this time encumbered by his enormous instruments. Eventually he found a new patron, one even stranger than himself, the mad Holy Roman Emperor Rudolph II. Tycho was made Imperial Mathematician in 1599, given yet another castle at Benatek outside Prague, and, more important, given the young Johannes Kepler as an assistant. Although the relationship was a stormy one, both benefited enormously. Tycho died suddenly in 1601 after a short illness leaving Kepler to publish Tycho's *Rudolphine Tables* posthumously in 1602. His last words were: "Let me not seemed to have lived in vain." That such a fear was groundless is witnessed on the title page of Kepler's great work, *Astronomia nova*:

"Founded on observations of the noble Tycho Brahe."

BRAHMAGUPTA (b. *c.* 598; d. *c.* 665) Indian mathematician and astronomer.

Brahmagupta was the director of the observatory at Ujjain, a town in central India. In 628 he wrote the *Brahma-sphuta-siddhānta* (The Opening of the Universe) half of which is about mathematics and half about astronomy. He introduced negative numbers into India, gave a satisfactory rule for the solution of quadratic equations, and attempted to apply algebra to astronomy. He discovered the formula for the area of a cyclic quadrilateral:

$$A = \sqrt{[(s-a)(s-b)(s-c)(s-d)]}$$

where s is half the perimeter and a, b, c, and d are the lengths of the sides. One innovation introduced by him was the use of oval epicycles for Mars and Venus. He rejected the view that the stars are stationary and the Earth moves, on the grounds that any such movement would cause high buildings to fall.

BRAID, James (b. 1795; Rylaw House, Scotland; d. Mar. 25, 1860; Manchester, England) British physician.

Braid was educated at Edinburgh University and became apprenticed to a doctor in Leith. On obtaining his medical diploma, he became a surgeon to colliery workers but later moved to Manchester where he established in practice as a surgeon. It was here that he began his scientific study of mesmerism — the induction of a trancelike state in a patient, first made famous by Anton Mesmer. Braid dis-

covered that by concentrating on a moving pendulum or similar object, a patient could enter into a state of what he termed 'neuro-hypnotism', which he later shortened to 'hypnosis'. In his paper, *A Practical Essay on the Curative Agency of Neuro-Hypnotism* (1842), Braid suggested several therapeutic applications for his techniques, including the alleviation of pain and anxiety and the treatment of certain nervous diseases.

Although his work encountered criticism from some quarters, Braid undoubtedly influenced his successors, notably the French school of neuropsychiatry, and introduced the word hypnotism, which is sometimes called 'braidism'.

BRAMAH, Joseph (b. Apr. 13, 1748; Stainborough, England; d. Dec. 9, 1814; London) British engineer and inventor.

A former cabinetmaker, Bramah designed and built many of the machine tools that facilitated the expansion of British manufacturing in the 19th century. In order to make a pick-proof lock, he developed very precisely engineered tools, many of which were made by Henry Maudslay, then a young blacksmith. Bramah displayed the lock in his shop window (1784) offering a prize to whoever could pick it. This was not achieved until 67 years later when a mechanic took 51 hours to open it.

Bramah also invented a hydraulic press, an improved water closet, a wood-planing machine, and a machine for numbering banknotes.

BRAMBELL, Francis William Rogers (b. Feb. 25, 1901; Sandycove, now in the Republic of Ireland; d. June 6, 1970; Bangor, Wales) British zoologist.

Brambell gained both his BA and PhD from Trinity College, Dublin and then worked successively at University College and King's College, London. In 1930 he became professor of zoology at Bangor

University, remaining there until his retirement in 1968.

Brambell's work on prenatal mortality in wild rabbits led to his discovery that protein molecules are transferred from mother to fetus not through the placenta as previously supposed but by the uterine cavity and fetal yolk sac. He further found that this process is selective; for example the gamma globulins are transferred more readily than other serum proteins. Such work is important in studies of resistance to disease in the newborn and of hemolytic diseases of infants. For this work Brambell received the Royal Medal of the Royal Society of London in 1964.

BRAND, Hennig (*fl.* 1670; Hamburg, now in West Germany) German alchemist.

Brand is remembered as the discoverer of phosphorus, probably in 1669, and as such the first known discoverer of an element. The discovery was of particular importance because few new elements had been discovered since classical times. True to the traditions of alchemy, Brand kept his method secret but samples and hints on the method were obtained by Johann Daniel Kraft and Johann Kunckel. The latter prepared phosphorus independently in 1676 by the distillation of concentrated urine with sand but still the method remained unpublished. Eventually, Robert Boyle, having obtained a sample from Kraft, repeated the isolation and published his findings in the *Aerial noctiluca* (1680).

BRANDT, Georg (b. July 21, 1694; Riddarhyta, Sweden; d. Apr. 29, 1768; Stockholm) Swedish chemist.

Brandt was the son of an ironworker and former apothecary and from an early age he helped his father with metallurgical experiments. He studied medicine and chemistry at Leiden, and gained his MD at Rheims in 1726. He was later made warden of the Stockholm mint (1730), and pro-fessor of chemistry at the University of Uppsala.

In 1733 he systematically investigated arsenic and its compounds. He invented the classification of semimetals (now called metalloids), in which he included arsenic, bismuth, antimony, mercury, and zinc.

In 1735 Brandt postulated that the blue color of the ore known as smalt was due to the presence of an unknown metal or semimetal. He named this 'cobalt rex' from the Old Teutonic 'kobold', originally meaning 'demon', later applied to the 'false ores' that did not yield metals under the traditional processes. In 1742 Brandt isolated cobalt, and found it was magnetic and alloyed readily with iron. His results were confirmed in 1780 by Torbern Bergman, who first obtained fairly pure cobalt.

Brandt also, in 1748, experimented with the dissolution of gold in hot concentrated acid, and with its precipitation from solution. These experiments clarified some of the alleged transmutations of silver into gold. Indeed, Brandt devoted his later years to exposing fraudulent transmutations of metals into gold, and it was said of him that no chemist did more to combat alchemy.

BRANS, Carl Henry (b. Dec. 13, 1935; Dallas, Texas) American mathematical physicist.

Brans graduated in 1957 from Loyola University, Louisiana, and obtained his PhD in 1961 from Princeton. He returned to Loyola in 1960 and in 1970 was appointed professor of physics.

Brans has worked mainly in the field of general relativity. He is best known for his production with Robert Dicke (q.v.) in 1961 of a variant of Einstein's theory in which the gravitational constant varies with time. A number of very accurate measurements made in the late 1970s has failed to detect this and some of the other predictions made by the *Brans–Dicke theory*.

BRATTAIN, Walter Houser (b. Dec. 10, 1902; Amoy, China) American physicist.

Brattain, brought up on a cattle ranch, was educated at Whitman College, at the University of Oregon, and at Minnesota, where he obtained his PhD in 1929. He immediately joined the Bell Telephone Company with which he worked as a research physicist until his retirement in 1967. Since leaving Bell, Brattain has taught at Whitman College and done research there on phospholipids.

Brattain's main field of work was the surface properties of semiconductors. It was known that a junction at a semiconductor would rectify an alternating current and that this effect was a surface property. Brattain was particularly interested in using semiconductors to amplify signals. Working with John Bardeen, he investigated various arrangements for achieving this — originally studying silicon in contact with electrolytes, but later using germanium in contact with gold. Their first efficient point-contact transistor (1947) consisted of a thin wafer of germanium with two close point contacts on one side and a large normal contact on the other. It had a power amplification of 18. Bardeen and Brattain shared the 1956 Nobel Prize for physics with William Shockley for their development of the transistor.

BRAUN, Karl Ferdinand (b. June 6, 1850; Fulda, now in West Germany; d. Apr. 20, 1918; New York City) German physicist.

Braun studied at Marburg and, in 1872, received a doctorate from the University of Berlin. He taught in various university posts. In 1885 he became professor of experimental physics at Tübingen and in 1895 he became professor of physics at Strasbourg.

In 1874, Braun observed that certain semiconducting crystals could be used as rectifiers to convert alternating to direct currents. At the turn of the century, he used this fact in the invention of crystal diodes, which led to the crystal radio. He also adapted the cathode-ray tube so that the electron beam was deflected by a changing voltage, thus inventing the oscilloscope and providing the basic component of a television receiver. His fame comes mainly from his improvements to Marconi's wireless communication system and, in 1909, they shared the Nobel Prize for physics. Braun's system, which used magnetically coupled resonant circuits, was the main one used in all receivers and transmitters in the first half of the 20th century.

Braun went to America to testify in litigation about radio patents but, when the United States entered World War I in 1917, he was detained as an alien and died in New York a year later.

BRAUN, Wernher von *See* VON BRAUN, Wernher Magnus Maximilian.

BREDT, Konrad Julius (b. Mar. 29, 1855; Berlin; d. Sept. 21, 1937; Aachen, now in West Germany) German organic chemist.

Bredt studied in Leipzig and Frankfurt and gained his doctorate at Strasbourg in 1880 under Rudolph Fittig. He became professor at the technical institute at Aachen in 1897. His most important research was the structural elucidation of camphor in 1893. The empirical formula had been determined by Jean Dumas in 1833 and over 30 formulae were proposed before Bredt deduced the correct structure.

BREIT, Gregory (b. July 14, 1899; Nickolaev, now in the Soviet Union) Russian-American physicist.

Although born in Russia, Breit moved to America in 1915 and became a naturalized citizen in 1918. He studied at Johns Hopkins University, gaining his PhD in 1921. From 1921 until 1924 he worked successively at the universities of Leiden, Harvard, and Minnesota, before joining the

Carnegie Institution, Washington (1924–29).

At Carnegie, Breit worked in the department of terrestrial magnetism as a mathematical physicist, and it was there that he conducted, with Merle A. Tuve, some of the earliest experiments to measure the height and density of the ionosphere. Their technique was to transmit short bursts of radio waves and analyze the reflected waves received. Their work is now seen as a significant step in the historical development of radar.

Besides his pioneering work on the ionosphere, Breit has researched quantum theory, nuclear physics, and quantum electrodynamics. In particular, he and Eugene Wigner were able to show that the experimental observations of the interactions of neutrons and protons indicated that the particles differed only in their charge and other electrical properties, and not in their nuclear forces. The *Breit–Wigner formula* is a formula for the energy dependence of the absorption cross-section of a compound nucleus in a nuclear reaction.

Between 1929 and 1973 Breit held professorial posts at the universities of New York, Wisconsin, and Yale, and the State University of New York, Buffalo.

BRENNER, Sydney (b. Jan. 13, 1927; Germiston, South Africa) South African–British molecular biologist.

Brenner, the son of a Lithuanian exile, was educated at the universities of the Witwatersrand and Oxford, where he obtained his DPhil in 1954. In 1957 he joined the staff of the Medical Research Council's molecular biology laboratory in Cambridge.

Brenner's first major success came in 1957 when he demonstrated that the triplets of nucleotide bases that form the genetic code do not overlap along the genetic material (DNA). The basic idea was that the amino-acid sequence of a protein is determined by the sequence of the four nucleotides — A, T, C, and G — in the DNA, with a specific amino acid being specified by a sequence of three nucleotides. Thus, in an *overlapping* code the sequence:

ATTAGTACGTCGA...

would yield the following triplets, ATT, TTA, TAG, AGT, GTA, etc., each of which specified a particular amino acid.

Brenner however pointed out that such a code imposed severe restrictions on the permitted order of bases. ATT, for example in an overlapping code, could be followed by the four bases TTA, TTT, TTC, and TTG only. This was relatively easy to test without in any way understanding the true nature of the code, and it was soon shown that such implied restrictions were frequently broken.

A greater triumph followed in 1961 when Brenner, in collaboration with Francis Crick and others, reported the results of careful experiments with the bacteriophage T4, which clearly showed that the code did consist of base triplets that neither overlapped nor appeared to be separated by 'punctuation marks'.

The same year also saw Brenner, this time in collaboration with François Jacob and Matthew Meselson, introducing a new form of RNA, messenger RNA (mRNA). With this came one of the central insights of molecular biology — an explanation of the mechanism of information transfer whereby the protein-synthesizing centers (ribosomes) play the role of nonspecific constituents that can synthesize different proteins, according to specific instructions, which they receive from the genes through mRNA.

Since such early successes in the pioneering days of molecular biology, Brenner has become involved in a major investigation into the development of the nervous system of nematodes.

BRETONNEAU, Pierre Fidèle (b. Apr. 3, 1778; St.-Georges-sur-Cher, France; d. Feb. 18, 1862; Passy, France) French physician.

Bretonneau, a surgeon's son, went to clinical lectures at the Ecole de Santé in Paris, graduated in 1815, and later practiced in Tours, where he served for some time as the chief physician at the Tours hospital. Bretonneau carefully studied a particular disease, which, beginning in 1818, reached epidemic proportions in Tours. In 1821 he proposed to call it diphtheria, from the Greek word for leather, as the disease was characterized by the formation of a membrane over the mucosa of the throat. He realized it was contagious despite his failure to transmit it to animals. He did however distinguish it from scarlet fever and, in 1825, performed the first successful tracheotomy (incision of the trachea through the neck muscles to prevent asphyxiation) on a diphtheria patient.

He further made an early attempt to describe typhoid and distinguished it from typhus. His theories on infectious diseases partly anticipated the germ theory of Pasteur.

BREWSTER, Sir David (b. Dec. 11, 1781; Jedburgh, Scotland; d. Feb. 10, 1868; Allerby, Scotland) British physicist.

Brewster started by studying for the ministry at Edinburgh University but, after completing the course, he abandoned the Church for science. He earned his living by editing various journals and spent much time popularizing science.

Brewster published almost 300 papers, mainly concerning optical measurements. He was an early worker in spectroscopy, obtaining (1832) spectra of gases and of colored glass. His most famous work was on the polarization of light. In 1813 he discovered *Brewster's law*, which states that if a beam of light is split into a reflected ray and a refracted ray at a glass surface, then they are polarized, and the polarization is complete when the two rays are at right angles. The angle of incidence at which this occurs is called the *Brewster angle*. He is also well known for his invention, in 1816, of the kaleidoscope.

Brewster was knighted in 1832. From 1859 he was principal of Edinburgh University.

BRIDGMAN, Percy Williams (b. Apr. 21, 1882; Cambridge, Massachusetts; d. Aug. 20, 1961; Randolph, New Hampshire) American physicist.

Bridgman, the son of a journalist, was educated at Harvard where he obtained his PhD in 1908. He immediately joined the faculty, leaving only on his retirement in 1954 after serving as professor of physics from 1919 to 1926, professor of mathematics and natural philosophy from 1926 to 1950, and as Huggins Professor from 1950 to 1954.

Most of Bridgman's research has been in the field of high-pressure physics. When he began he found it necessary to design and build virtually all his own equipment and instruments. In 1909 he introduced the self-tightening joint and with the appearance of high tensile steels he could aim for pressures well beyond the scope of earlier workers. At the beginning of the century Emile Amagat and Louis Cailletet had attained pressures of some 3000 kilograms per square centimeter; Bridgman increased this enormously, regularly attaining pressures of 100 000 kg/cm².

Bridgman used such pressures to explore the properties of numerous liquids and solids. In the course of this work he discovered two new forms of ice, freezing at temperatures above 0°C. He also, in 1955, transformed graphite into synthetic diamond. Bridgman was awarded the 1946 Nobel Physics Prize for his work on extremely high pressures.

He was also widely known as a philosopher of science and in his book *The Logic of Modern Physics* (1927) formulated his theory of 'operationalism' in which he argued that a concept is simply a set of operations. In his 70s Bridgman developed Paget's disease, which gave him considerable pain and little prospect of relief. He committed suicide in 1961.

BRIGGS, Henry (b. February 1561; Warley Wood, England; d. Jan. 26, 1630; Oxford, England) English mathematician.

Briggs became a fellow of Cambridge University in 1588 and was later made a lecturer (1592) and a professor (1596) of geometry at Gresham College, London.

He is remembered chiefly for the modifications he made to John Napier's (q.v.) logarithms, which were first published in 1614. Napier had produced these to base e (natural logarithms) but Briggs considerably improved their convenience of use by introducing the base 10 (common logarithms). He also introduced the modern method of long division. Briggs became Savilian Professor of Geometry at Oxford in 1619.

BRIGHT, Richard (b. Sept. 28, 1789; Bristol, England; d. Dec. 16, 1858; London) British physician.

Educated at Edinburgh University and Guy's Hospital, London, Bright received his MD from Edinburgh in 1813. After a period spent traveling in Europe, he was appointed assistant physician to Guy's Hospital in 1820, becoming full physician four years later. One of Bright's major interests was kidney disease. He was able to correlate symptoms in his patients with the results of postmortem examinations, and described how the presence of albumin in urine (albuminaria) and the accumulation of fluid in the body (dropsy) were caused by pathological changes in the kidneys. The term Bright's disease is now used for several renal diseases all sharing the above symptoms.

Bright also studied and wrote on subjects such as abdominal tumors, jaundice, and nervous diseases, and collaborated with his famous contemporary at Guy's, Thomas Addison, in writing *Elements of the Practice of Medicine* (vol. 1, 1839). An amiable and distinguished consultant, Bright also did much to develop teaching methods at Guy's and helped found the

Guy's Hospital Reports, in which he published much of his work.

BROCA, Pierre Paul (b. June 28, 1824; Sainte-Foy-la-Grande, France; d. July 9, 1880; Paris) French physician and anthropologist.

Broca studied at the University of Paris, received his MD in 1849, and in 1853 was appointed assistant professor in the faculty of medicine. His specialty was the brain and, through surgical work and postmortem examination, he was able to demonstrate that damage to one particular region (the left inferior frontal gyrus, now also known as Broca's convolution) of the cortex was associated with impairment or loss of speech. This was one of the first conclusive demonstrations that control of different bodily functions resides in localized regions of the cerebral cortex.

Broca applied his knowledge of the brain to anthropology. He devised techniques of accurately measuring skulls to enable comparison between the different races of modern man and skulls unearthed at prehistoric sites. Broca's findings supported the then highly contentious theory of Charles Darwin that man, like other living things, had evolved from primitive ancestors. Broca helped found several notable anthropological institutions, including the Société d'Anthropologie de Paris (1859) and the Ecole d'Anthropologie (1876), thus helping to establish anthropology as a respectable branch of science.

BRODIE, Sir Benjamin Collins (b. June 8, 1783; Winterslow, England; d. Oct. 21, 1862; Broome Parke, England) British physician.

Brodie learnt medicine in London, first as apprentice to an apothecary and then at the Windmill Street School of Anatomy. He later studied at St. George's Hospital, where he was subsequently appointed house surgeon (1805) and assistant surgeon (1808). Between 1809 and 1814 he contributed six papers to the Royal Society in which he challenged the prevailing contemporary view that body heat was caused, more or less, by simple chemical combustion. Brodie argued that it was a complex process under the influence of the brain, which controlled the functioning of vital organs, such as the heart. This brought Brodie to prominence and he was elected a fellow of the Royal Society in 1810.

Brodie soon had a large and lucrative practice. He wrote *Diseases of the Joints* (1818), which ran to several editions, and in 1819 he was appointed professor of comparative anatomy and physiology at the Royal College of Surgeons, of which he later (1844) became president. A surgeon to both George IV and William IV, Brodie was made a baronet in 1834. As one of the most prominent members of the medical establishment, he was chosen (1858) to be the first president of the newly formed General Medical Council, which administered the registration of all persons qualified to practice medicine.

BRODIE, Bernard Beryl (b. Aug. 7, 1909; Liverpool, England) American pharmacologist.

Brodie was educated at McGill University in Canada and at New York University, where he obtained his PhD in 1935. He worked at the Medical School there from 1943 to 1950 when he moved to the National Institutes of Health at Bethesda, Maryland, where he served as chief of the chemical pharmacology laboratory until 1970.

Brodie has worked in a wide variety of fields including chemotherapy, anesthesia, drug metabolism, and neuropharmacology. In 1955 Brodie and his colleagues produced some results that once more raised the possibility of a chemical basis of mental disease. Basically they showed that the tranquilizer reserpine — an alkaloid extracted from the roots of *Rauwolfia* — can produce a profound fall in the level of serotonin, a naturally occurring monoamine in the brain. The question then arose as to whether the tranquilizing effect of reserpine is due to its reduction of too high a level of serotonin.

It was further shown that some of the actions of serotonin could be neutralized by the presence of the hallucinogen LSD. As the structure of the two molecules are somewhat similar the possibility arose that LSD could monopolize the enzyme that normally breaks down serotonin and thus permit the accumulation of unusually high levels of serotonin. It is perhaps this action that causes the hallucinogenic state and which, it has been argued, mimics the schizophrenic state.

In reality the speculations arising from Brodie's work have turned out to be surprisingly difficult to confirm or reject.

BROGLIE, Prince Louis Victor de *See* DE BROGLIE, Prince Louis Victor.

BRONGNIART, Alexandre (b. Feb. 5, 1770; Paris; d. Oct. 7, 1847; Paris) French geologist and paleontologist.

Brongniart was the son of an architect. He was educated at the School of Mines and served in the army as an engineer before being appointed director of the Sèvres porcelain factory (1800–47). He also served as professor of natural history at the Ecole Centrale des Quatre Nations, Paris, from 1797. In 1822 he succeeded René Haüy to the chair of mineralogy at the Natural History Museum, Paris.

Brongniart's early work included his *Essai d'une classification naturelle des reptiles* (1800; Essay on the Classification of Reptiles) in which he divided the Reptilia into the Chelonia, Sauria, Ophidia, and Batrachia. In 1822 he published the first full-length account of trilobites, the important paleozoic arthropods.

His most significant work was done in collaboration with Georges Cuvier on the geology of the Paris region, published jointly by them in 1811 as *Essai sur la géo-*

graphie minéralogique des environs de Paris (Essay on the Mineralogical Geography of the Environs of Paris). In this monograph they were among the first geologists to identify strata within a formation by their fossil content; earlier geologists had tended to rely on the characteristics of the rocks rather than their content. They were able to show a constant order of fossil sequence, mainly of mollusks, over the whole Paris region.

They also produced evidence that counted strongly against the neptunism of Abraham Werner in their discovery of alternate strata of fresh- and saltwater mollusks. The solution to the problem of how fresh- and saltwater strata could alternate was crucial for the new science of geology and was to lead to the catastrophism of Cuvier and the evolution theory of Charles Darwin.

Outside science his major achievement was the revival of the Sèvres factory which, when he took over in 1800, was at a particularly low point in its history. He abandoned the production of soft-paste ware and developed a new range of colors, producing works as richly colored as paintings.

His son, Adolph, was a distinguished botanist who, in 1828, published a history of fossil plants.

BRONK, Detlev Wulf (b. Aug. 13, 1897; New York City; d. Nov. 19, 1975; New York City) American physiologist.

Bronk, the son of a Baptist minister, came from Dutch stock: the family name survives in the Bronx district of New York. He was educated at Swarthmore, Pennsylvania, and at Michigan, where he obtained his PhD in 1922. Bronk spent some time in England working with Edgar Adrian in Cambridge before accepting, in 1929, the post of director of the Johnson Institute, attached to the University of Pennsylvania, where he was already serving as professor of biophysics and director of the Institute of Neurology. In 1949 Bronk became president of Johns Hopkins University but left there in 1953 to take the presidency of the Rockefeller Institute (later Rockefeller University) in New York, where he remained until his retirement in 1968.

Bronk established an early reputation with his fundamental work with Edgar Adrian on nerve impulses (1928–29). They demonstrated that both motor and sensory nerves transmit their messages by varying the number of impulses sent rather than by using impulses of different intensities. By careful experiments they established that the range of the impulses is between 5 and 150 per second, with greater stimuli producing higher frequencies.

In the 1930s Bronk worked mainly on the autonomic nervous system. He is, however, mainly remembered for his crucial role in organizing the institutional structure of American science.

BRØNSTED, Johannes Nicolaus (b. Feb. 22, 1879; Varde, Denmark; d. Dec. 17, 1947; Copenhagen) Danish physical chemist.

Brønsted studied at the Polytechnic Institute, Copenhagen, from 1897, obtaining degrees in engineering (1899) and chemistry (1902), and a doctorate (1908). The same year he became professor of chemistry at Copenhagen.

Brønsted worked mainly in thermodynamics, especially in the fields of electrochemistry and reaction kinetics. In 1923 he proposed, concurrently with Thomas Lowry, a new definition of acids and bases. This, the *Lowry–Brønsted theory*, states that an acid is a substance that tends to lose a proton and a base is a substance that tends to gain a proton. In 1924, working with V. K. La Mer on the activity coefficients of dilute solutions, he confirmed the theoretical expression of Peter Debye (q.v.) and Erich Hückel for electrolytes.

BROOM, Robert (b. Nov. 30, 1866; Paisley, Scotland; d. Apr. 6, 1951; Pretoria, South

Africa) British-South African morphologist and paleontologist.

Broom graduated in medicine from Glasgow University in 1889. He traveled to Australia in 1892 and in 1897 settled in South Africa where he practiced medicine, often in remote rural communities, until 1928. He also held posts as professor of geology and zoology (1903–10) at Victoria College, now Stellenbosch University, South Africa, and curator of paleontology at the Transvaal Museum, Pretoria from 1934 until his death.

Apart from studies of the embryology of Australian marsupials and monotremes, Broom's major contributions to science have been concerned with the evolutionary origins of mammals, including man. He excavated and studied the fossils of the Karroo beds of the Cape, and in the 1940s discovered numbers of Australopithecine skeletons in Pleistocene age quarries at Sterkfontein, Transvaal. These latter have proved of considerable importance in investigations of man's ancestry and Broom's account of their discovery is given in *Finding the Missing Link* (1950).

BROUNCKER, William, Viscount (b. 1620; d. Apr. 5, 1685; London) English mathematician and experimental scientist.

Brouncker graduated from Oxford University in 1647 with a degree in medicine. He held a variety of official posts, including serving as member of Parliament and president of Gresham's College. He was a friend of the eminent mathematician John Wallis and his own most notable work was also in mathematics. He was a founder and first president of the Royal Society (1662–77) and as such carried out experimental work. Brouncker usually contented himself with solving problems arising from the work of other mathematicians rather than doing creative work himself but was the first to use continued fractions. He was a friend of Samuel Pepys and frequently figures in Pepys's *Diary*.

Apart from science Brouncker had a lively interest in music.

BROUWER, Dirk (b. Sept. 1, 1902; Rotterdam, Netherlands; d. Jan. 31, 1966; New Haven, Connecticut) Dutch-American astronomer.

Brouwer, the son of a civil servant, studied at the University of Leiden where he obtained his PhD under Willem de Sitter in 1927. He then moved to America to do postdoctoral research at the University of California at Berkeley. He joined the Yale faculty in 1928, serving from 1941 until his death as professor of astronomy and director of the Yale Observatory.

Brouwer worked mainly in celestial mechanics, particularly in the analysis of observations concerning orbiting bodies and on planetary theory, providing new methods by which the motion of a planet could be determined and by which the very long term changes in orbits could be calculated. He collaborated with Gerald Clemence (q.v.) and W.J. Eckert in the production in 1951 of the basic paper in which the accurate orbits of the outer planets were given for the years 1653–2060. Brouwer's other major contribution was to astrometry, or positional astronomy, where he introduced new techniques and initiated programs for the measurement of stellar positions, especially in the southern sky.

He was also involved in the decision to adopt a new time scale, known at Brouwer's suggestion as 'Ephemeris Time' (ET). This became necessary when the rotation rate of the Earth, on which time measurements had been based, was found to vary very slightly. Ephemeris Time is derived from the orbital motions of the Moon and the Earth and is perfectly uniform. It is only used by astronomers however; more general timekeeping now involves atomic clocks.

BROUWER, Luitzen Egbertus Jan (b. Feb. 27, 1881; Overschie, Netherlands; d. Dec.

2, 1966; Blaricum, Netherlands) Dutch mathematician and philosopher of mathematics.

Brouwer took his first degree and doctorate at the University of Amsterdam, where he became successively *Privatdozent* and professor in the mathematics department. From 1903 to 1909 he did important work in topology, presenting several fundamental results, including the fixed-point theorem. This is the result that, given a circle (or sphere) and the points inside it, then any transformation of all points to other points in the circle (or sphere) must leave at least one point unchanged. A physical example is stirring a cup of coffee — there will always be at least one particle of liquid that returns to its original position no matter how well the coffee is stirred.

Brouwer's best-known achievement was the creation of the philosophy of mathematics known as *intuitionism*. The central ideas of intuitionism are a rejection of the concept of the completed infinite (and hence of the transfinite set theory of Georg Cantor) and an insistence that acceptable mathematical proofs be constructive. That is, they must not merely show that a certain mathematical entity (e.g. a number or a function) *exists*, but must actually be able to construct it. This view leads to the rejection of large amounts of widely accepted classical mathematics and one of the three fundamental laws of logic, the law of excluded middle (either p or not-p; a proposition is either true or not true).

Brouwer was able to re-prove many classical results in an intuitionistically acceptable way, including his own fixed-point theorem.

BROWN, Alexander Crum *See* CRUM BROWN, Alexander.

BROWN, Herbert Charles (b. May 22, 1912; London) American chemist.

Brown moved from England to Chicago with his family when he was two years old. His father, originally a cabinet maker, ran a hardware store but Brown had to leave school to help support his mother and three sisters. When he finally did get to college, Crane Junior, it was forced to close in 1933 for lack of funds. He eventually made it to the University of Chicago where he obtained his doctorate in 1938. Brown then worked at Wayne University, Detroit from 1943 until 1947, when he moved to Purdue University, Indiana, where he served as professor of inorganic chemistry until his retirement in 1978.

Brown has become particularly noted for his work on compounds of boron. He discovered a method of making sodium borohydride ($NaBH_4$), a reagent used extensively in organic chemistry for reduction. He also found a simple way of preparing diborane (B_2H_6). By reacting diborane (B_2H_6) with alkenes (unsaturated hydrocarbons containing a double bond) he produced a new class of compounds, organoboranes, which are also useful in organic chemistry. Brown has also used addition compounds of amines with boron compounds to investigate the role of steric effects in organic chemistry. He received the 1979 Nobel Chemistry Prize.

BROWN, Robert (b. Dec. 21, 1773; Montrose, Scotland; d. June 10, 1858; London) British botanist.

Brown, a clergyman's son, studied medicine at Edinburgh University. He joined the Fifeshire Regiment of Fencibles in 1795 and served five years in Ireland as a medical officer. During a visit to London in 1798 he was introduced to Sir Joseph Banks. This led, two years later, to his being recommended by Banks for the post of naturalist on the *Investigator* in an expedition to survey the coast of New Holland (Australia) under the command of Matthew Flinders. Brown accepted the appointment and the *Investigator* set sail for the Cape of Good Hope and Australia in 1801. During his five years with the expedition Brown collected 4000 plant specimens, and on his return to England spent another five years classifying these. Rather than use Linnaeus's artificial classification, he followed Antoine de Jussieu's more natural system, adding his own modifications and using microscopic characters to help delimit species. By 1810 he had described 2200 species, over 1700 of which were new (including 140 new genera). He intended to produce an extensive treatise on Australian plants but the poor sales of the first volume, which appeared in 1810, led him to discontinue publication of the remainder.

In the course of his painstaking work Brown became very familiar with plant morphology, which led him to make many important observations. He found that in conifers and related plants the ovary around the ovule is missing, thus establishing the basic difference between these plants and flowering plants or between the gymnosperms and the angiosperms, as the two groups of seed-bearing plants were later named. He also observed and named the nucleus, recognizing it as an essential part of living cells.

In 1827, while examining a suspension of pollen grains in water, under a microscope, Brown observed that the grains were in continuous erratic motion. Initially he believed that this movement was caused by some life force in the pollen, but when he extended his observations to inanimate particles suspended in water he found the same effect. This phenomenon was named *Brownian motion* and remained unexplained until the kinetic theory was developed.

From 1806 to 1822 Brown was librarian of the Linnaean Society; in 1810 he also became librarian and curator at Banks's Soho Square residence. Banks stipulated in his will that on his death Brown should take charge of his house, library, and herbarium. In 1820 Brown duly inherited this responsibility and in 1827 he donated Banks's library and herbarium to the British Museum on the understanding that the trustees established an independent botany department in the museum. Thus a botanical collection became accessible to the general public for the first time in Britain.

BROWN, Robert Hanbury (b. Aug. 31, 1916) British radio astronomer.

Brown was educated at the City and Guilds College, London. From 1936 to 1942 he worked on the development of radar at the Air Ministry Research Station, Bawdsey. This was followed by three years in Washington with the British Air Commission and two years with the Ministry of Supply. By the late 1940s Brown was keen to enter academic research and persuaded Bernard Lovell to admit him as a research student at the Jodrell Bank radio observatory. Brown later served there as professor of radio astronomy from 1960 to 1963 when he was appointed to a professorship in physics at the University of Sydney.

In 1950 Brown plotted the first radio map of an external galaxy, the spiral nebula in Andromeda. This was followed by the identification of emissions from four other extragalactic nebulae. Brown further proposed radical changes in the design of standard interferometers that allowed him to measure in 1952 a radio source in Cygnus with a diameter of only 30 seconds of arc. Further work produced in 1954 a new type of interferometer — the so-called optical intensity interferometer.

BROWN-SEQUARD, Charles-Edouard (b. Apr. 8, 1817; Port Louis, Mauritius; d. Apr. 1, 1894; Paris) British-French physiologist and neurologist.

Brown-Séquard studied medicine in Paris, graduating in 1846. He was professor of physiology and pathology at Harvard (1864–68) and in 1878 succeeded Claude Bernard as professor of experimental medicine at the Collège de France. The intervening years were spent in a variety of posts in New York, London, and Paris. He is perhaps best known for his work on the adrenal gland. In his experiments on hormonal secretions, he demonstrated the connection between excision of the adrenal glands and Addison's disease.

Continuing the work of Galen on dissection of the spinal cord, he discovered the *Brown-Séquard syndrome* (crossed hemiplegia), a condition of motor nerve paralysis resulting from the lesion of one side of the spinal cord. This produces an absence of sensation on the opposite side of the body to the nerve paralysis. Brown-Séquard also investigated the possibility of prolonging human life by the use of extracts prepared from the testes of sheep. The majority of his research findings were published as papers in the *Archives de physiologie*, of which he was one of the founders.

BRUCE, Sir David (b. May 29, 1855; Melbourne, Australia; d. Nov. 27, 1931; London) British bacteriologist.

A one-time colleague of Robert Koch in Berlin, Bruce spent the greater part of his career as a military physician. Educated at Edinburgh University, he was assistant professor of pathology at the Army Medical School, Netley (1889–94), and then commandant of the Royal Army Medical College, Millbank, where he was also director of research on tetanus and trench fever (1914–18). He undertook royal commissions of enquiry into various diseases of man and domestic animals in Malta and central Africa. In Malta he was able to trace the cause of Malta fever (brucellosis or undulant fever found in the milk of goats) to a bacterium later named after him as *Brucella melitensis*. Bruce also investigated the cause of nagana, a disease of horses and cattle in central and southern Africa, and found it to be transmitted by a trypanosome parasite carried by the tsetse fly. This work was of great help in his later research on sleeping sickness (trypanosomiasis), which he also proved to be transmitted by the tsetse fly. The recipient of many honors for his humanitarian work, Bruce was chairman of the War Office's Pathological Committee during World War I. He was knighted in 1908.

BRUNHES, Jean (b. Oct 25, 1869; Toulouse, France; d. Apr. 25, 1930; Boulogne-sur-Seine, France) French geographer.

Brunhes came from an academic background with both his father and brother being professors of physics. He was educated at the Ecole Normal Supérieure, Paris, (1889–92) and taught at the University of Fribourg from 1896 until 1912, when he moved to the Collège de France, Paris, as professor of human geography.

His most important work was his three-volume *Geographie humaine* (1910), which was translated into English in 1920. Following his teacher, Vidal de la Blache, he argued against the geographical determinism implicit in the work of Friedrich Ratzel (q.v.). Instead he was more concerned to reveal the complicated interplay beween man, society, and the environment.

BRUNNER, Sir John Tomlinson (b. Feb. 8, 1842; Liverpool, England; d. July 1, 1919; Chertsey, England) British industrialist.

Brunner's father had traveled to England from Switzerland in 1832 and settled in Liverpool. Brunner began working in the office of a shipping clerk in 1857 and in 1861 joined a chemical firm in Widnes and became chief cashier. There he met Ludwig Mond, a research chemist who had acquired the rights to Ernest Solvay's new ammonia–soda process. The two entered into a partnership in 1875 and established a firm in Cheshire to produce soda. Within a few years they had converted an initial loss into a profit, which continued to grow in the succeeding years. In 1881 the partnership was converted into a limited company with capital assets of £600000. Brunner, Mond, and Company merged with other companies in 1926 to form Imperial Chemical Industries (ICI).

Brunner was made a baronet in 1895 and

served as a member of parliament (1885–1910).

BRUNO, Giordano (b. January 1548; Nola, Italy; d. Feb. 17, 1600; Rome) Italian philosopher.

The son of a soldier, Bruno entered the Dominican Order in 1565 but was forced to leave in 1576 for unspecified reasons. The following 15 years were spent traveling in France, England, and Germany before visiting Venice in 1591 where he was arrested and handed over to the Inquisition (1592). He was extradited by the Roman Inquisition in 1593. As details of the trial have been destroyed it is no longer known which eight heretical propositions he refused to recant. The results of his action are not however in any doubt: he was burned at the stake.

The exact role of Bruno in 16th-century intellectual history remains a matter of considerable controversy and he was clearly a man of many parts. He was first an expert on the art of mnemonics (memory), a renaissance 'science' long extinct, and he was also involved with a revival of the occult mystical philosophical system of hermeticism. More importantly Bruno was also a keen supporter of the heliocentric system of Nicolaus Copernicus and in his *Cena de le Ceneri* (1584; The Ash Wednesday Supper) proposed some rather implausible arguments in defence of Copernicus's claims for the infinity of the universe. His championing of the then unorthodox heliocentric theory was certainly considered heretical and his unhappy end may well have influenced Galileo's actions before the Inquisition.

BUCH, Christian Leopold von *See* VON BUCH, Christian Leopold.

BUCHNER, Eduard (b. May 20, 1860; Munich, now in West Germany; d. Aug. 13, 1917; Focsani, Rumania) German organic chemist and biochemist.

Buchner studied chemistry under Adolf von Baeyer and botany at Munich, gaining his doctorate in 1888. He was Baeyer's assistant until 1893. In 1897, whilst associate professor of analytical and pharmaceutical chemistry at Tübingen, he observed fermentation of sugar by cell-free extracts of yeast. Following Pasteur's work (1860), fermentation had been thought to require intact cells, and Buchner's discovery of zymase was the first proof that fermentation was caused by enzymes and did not require the presence of living cells. The name 'enzyme' came from the Greek *en* = in and *zyme* = yeast. Buchner also synthesized pyrazole (1889). He was professor of chemistry at the University of Berlin from 1898 and won the Nobel Prize for chemistry in 1907 for his work on fermentation. He was killed in Rumania, whilst serving as a major in World War I.

BUCHNER, Hans Ernst Angass (b. Dec. 16, 1850; Munich, now in West Germany; d. Apr. 8, 1902; Munich) German bacteriologist.

Buchner, the brother of Eduard Buchner, gained his MD from the University of Leipzig in 1874. He later worked at Munich University serving as professor of hygiene from 1894 until his death.

In 1888 George Nuttall had shown that the ability of blood to destroy invading bacteria lay in the serum. Buchner followed up this work and went on to demonstrate that the bacteriolytic power was lost when the serum was heated to 56°C. He therefore concluded that serum possessed a heat labile substance that he proposed to name alexin.

This work was soon extended by Jules Bordet and the alexins were later renamed complement by Paul Ehrlich. Buchner also did basic work on gamma globulins and developed techniques to study anaerobic bacteria.

BUCKLAND, Francis Trevelyan (b. Dec. 17, 1826; Oxford, England; d. Dec. 19,

1880; Oxford) British surgeon and naturalist.

Buckland was the son of William (Dean) Buckland (founder of the Oxford University Museum of Geology). Educated at Oxford and at St. George's Hospital, London, Buckland practiced medicine and was an army surgeon from 1852 to 1863. Buckland was an authority on pisciculture, investigating the economic aspects of artificial salmon supply, devising ladders to assist the salmon in reaching their marine spawning beds, and observing the preponderance of male as opposed to female trout. He also carried out research into the homing instinct of salmon, deducing that the fish were able to recognize rivers by chemo-tactile (taste/smell) means. A popular science writer, Buckland is perhaps best known for his many volumes of *Curiosities of Natural History* (1857–72). Buckland also did much to secure international agreement to prevent the extermination of the North Atlantic fur seal.

BUDD, William (b. Sept. 14, 1811; North Tawton, England; d. Jan. 9, 1880; Clevedon, England) British physician.

Budd, the son of a surgeon, was the fifth of nine sons, six of whom became doctors. He studied medicine at the Ecole de Médecine in Paris and at the University of Edinburgh where he obtained his MD in 1838. He then practiced in Bristol where he also served as physician at the Royal Infirmary and lectured in medicine at the medical college.

From observations on an outbreak of typhoid fever in North Tawton in 1839 Budd developed a clearly argued case against the view that such outbreaks were due to a generalized atmospheric miasma. He published a number of studies over the years, collected later in his *Typhoid Fever* (1873). He argued that the causative factor could not be atmospheric and stressed that poor sanitary conditions did not of themselves generate typhoid but were impor-

tant in spreading it. The cause was related to the movement of people, as could be demonstrated by its spread from village to village, and Budd postulated the existence of infective agents, released in the excreta of typhoid sufferers. He thus emphasized the importance of disinfection and a clean water supply. Such views however had little impact on the leading typhoid expert of the day, Charles Murchison, who in his *Treatise on the Continued Fevers* (1873) continued to insist that disease arose spontaneously from dirt and excrement.

Budd also wrote on cholera and in *Malignant Cholera* (1849) narrowly missed anticipating the claim of John Snow that the disease was waterborne.

BUFFON, Comte Georges Louis Leclerc de (b. Sept. 7, 1707; Montbard, France; d. Apr. 16, 1788; Paris) French naturalist.

Buffon, a magistrate's son, studied law at Dijon before turning to mathematics and general science. He abandoned studies at Angers in 1730 following a duel and toured Italy, returning to France in 1732 when he inherited his mother's fortune. He soon made his mark in scientific and political life with work on the tensile strength of timber for the naval minister, who later used his influence to instate Buffon as keeper of the Jardin du Roi in 1739. During the 50 years of Buffon's management the botanical gardens doubled in area and many new specimens were acquired.

For his own amusement Buffon devised elaborate experiments to satisfy himself that Archimedes' feat — setting the Roman fleet on fire with lenses — was possible. He studied widely and translated certain works of Newton and Stephen Hales. He also published much original material including *Discours sur le style* (1753) and *Histoire naturelle générale et particulière* begun in 1749 with 36 volumes published by his death.

Buffon suggested the Earth came into being through a comet colliding with the Sun 75 000 years ago, and was thus the first to extend the time scale beyond the 6000 years set by the Bible. He was also the first to suggest that coal and mineral oils are the decomposed remains of organic matter. Buffon recorded the vestigial organs of certain animals and proposed that this reduction of parts might be extended and applied to the degeneration of species; thus the donkey is a degenerate horse, the ape a degenerate man, etc. This concept contributed to evolutionary thinking by implying that certain species have common ancestors.

BULLARD, Sir Edward Crisp (b. Sept. 21, 1907; Norwich, England; d. Apr. 3, 1980; California) British geophysicist.

Bullard was educated at Cambridge University, England. After war service in naval research he returned to Cambridge as a reader in geophysics before accepting a post as head of the physics department of the University of Toronto (1948) and visiting the Scripps Institute of Oceanography, California, (1949). After a five-year spell as director of the National Physical Laboratory, he returned to Cambridge as a reader and later, in 1964, professor of geophysics and director of the department of geodesy and geophysics. Here he remained until his retirement in 1974.

Bullard made a number of contributions to the revolution in the Earth sciences that took place in the 1950s and 1960s. He carried out major work on the measurement of the heat flow from the Earth. It had been assumed that as the ocean floor was less rich in radioactive material than the continental crust, it would be measurably cooler. The technical difficulties of actually measuring the temperature of the ocean floor were not overcome until 1950, and in 1954 Bullard was able to announce that there was no significant temperature difference between the continental crust and the ocean floor. This led Bullard to reintroduce the idea of convection currents.

In 1965 Bullard studied continental drift, using a computer to analyze the fit

between the Atlantic continents. An excellent fit was found for the South Atlantic at the 500-fathom contour line. However, a reasonable fit could only be made for the North Atlantic if a number of assumptions, such as deformation and sedimentation since the continents drifted apart, were taken into account. Later, when independent evidence for these assumptions was obtained, it gave powerful support for the theory of continental drift.

Bullard was knighted in 1953.

BULLEN, Keith Edward (b. June 29, 1906; Auckland, New Zealand; d. Sept. 23, 1976; Sydney, Australia) Australian applied mathematician and geophysicist.

Bullen, the son of Anglo-Irish parents, was educated at the universities of Auckland, Melbourne, and Cambridge, England. He began his career as a teacher in Auckland then lectured in mathematics at Melbourne and Hull, England. In 1946 he became professor of applied mathematics at the University of Sydney.

Bullen made his chief contributions to science from his mathematical studies of earthquake waves and the ellipticity of the Earth. In 1936 he gave values of the density inside the Earth down to a depth of 3100 miles (5000 km). He also determined values for the pressure, gravitation intensity, compressibility, and rigidity throughout the interior of the Earth as a result of his mathematical studies. From the results on the Earth's density he inferred that the core was solid and he also applied the results to the internal structure of the planets Mars, Venus, and Mercury and to the origin of the Moon.

Bullen conducted some of his early work in collaboration with Harold Jeffreys on earthquake travel times. This resulted in the publication of the Jeffreys–Bullen (JB) tables in 1940.

BUNSEN, Robert Wilhelm (b. Mar. 31, 1811; Göttingen, now in West Germany; d.

Aug. 16, 1899; Heidelberg, now in West Germany) German chemist.

Bunsen, the son of a professor of linguistics, gained his doctorate at Göttingen (1830) with a thesis on hygrometers. After an extensive scientific tour in Europe, he became a lecturer at Göttingen in 1834. He was professor of chemistry at Kassel (1836), Marburg (1841), and Heidelberg (1852–89).

Bunsen carried out one great series of researches in organic chemistry, *Studies in the Cacodyl Series* (1837–42), after which he abandoned organic for analytical and inorganic chemistry. During his research on the highly toxic cacodyl compound he lost one eye in an explosion and twice nearly killed himself through arsenic poisoning. He prepared various derivatives of cacodyl (tetramethylarsine, $(CH_3)_2$-$As_2(CH_3)_2$), including the chloride, iodide, fluoride, and cyanide, and his work was eagerly welcomed by Jöns Berzelius as confirmation of his theory that organic chemistry mirrored inorganic, the 'radical theory'.

Bunsen was a great experimentalist, an expert in gas analysis and glass blowing, and a pioneer of photochemistry and spectroscopy. He also worked in electrochemistry, devising an improved version of the Grove cell. At Heidelberg he used his new cell to produce metals by electrodeposition. The classic paper *Chemical Analysis through Observation of the Spectrum* (1860) by Bunsen and Gustav Kirchhoff (q.v.) ushered in the era of chemical spectroscopy. The spectroscope was an extremely sensitive analytical instrument. With it Bunsen discovered two new elements: rubidium and cesium.

The famous *Bunsen burner* was introduced by him in 1855, although a similar burner, used by Michael Faraday, did exist before Bunsen and the regulating collar was a later refinement. He greatly refined gas analysis and wrote a standard treatise on the subject, *Gasometrische Methoden* (1857, Methods in Gas Measurement).

Bunsen was a great teacher and at Heidelberg he became a legend. Chemists who came to study with him included Adolph Kolbe, Edward Frankland, Victor and Lothar Meyer, Friedrich Beilstein, and Johann Baeyer.

BURBANK, Luther (b. Mar. 7, 1849; Lancaster, Massachusetts; d. Apr. 11, 1926; Santa Rosa, California) American plant breeder.

Burbank was brought up on a farm and received only an elementary education. He began breeding plants in 1870, when he bought a seven-hectare plot of land. After about a year he had developed the Burbank potato, which was introduced to Ireland to help combat the blight epidemics. By selling the rights to this potato he made $150, which he used to travel to California, where three of his brothers had already settled.

Burbank established a nursery and experimental farm in Santa Rosa, where the climate was especially conducive to fruit and flower breeding — his occupation for the next 50 years. He worked by making multiple crosses between native and introduced strains, using his remarkable skill to select commercially promising types. These were then grafted onto mature plants to hasten development, so that their value could be rapidly assessed. In this way he produced numerous new cultivated varieties of plums, lilies, and many other ornamentals and fruits.

The works of Charles Darwin, particularly *The Variation of Animals and Plants under Domestication*, greatly influenced Burbank. However his success in varying plant characters reinforced his belief in the inheritance of acquired characteristics, even though he knew of Gregor Mendel's research.

BURBIDGE, Eleanor Margaret (b. 1922; Davenport, England) British astronomer.

Born Margaret Peachey, Burbidge studied physics at the University of London. After graduation in 1948 she joined the University of London Observatory where she obtained her PhD and served as acting director (1950–51). She then went to America as a research fellow, first at the Yerkes Observatory of the University of Chicago (1951–53) and then at the California Institute of Technology (1955–57). The period 1953–55 was spent in highly productive work at the Cavendish Laboratory in Cambridge, England. She returned to Yerkes in 1957, serving as associate professor of astronomy from 1959 to 1962 and then transferred to the University of California, San Diego, where she has been professor of astronomy since 1964 and has also served since 1979 as director of the Center for Astrophysics and Space Sciences.

Burbidge returned briefly to England in 1972 on leave of absence to become director of the Royal Greenwich Observatory, now situated at Herstmonceux Castle in Sussex. She declared her aim to be to strengthen optical astronomy in Britain. But as the 98-inch (2.5-m) Isaac Newton telescope at Herstmonceux was only a few hundred feet above sea level and sited above a marsh her opportunities for observation at the Royal Observatory were somewhat limited. A little over a year later, in October 1973, Burbidge resigned amid much speculation declaring simply that she preferred "to return to her own research work rather than devote a major part of her time to administrative matters."

In 1948 she married Geoffrey Burbidge a theoretical physicist, and began a highly productive partnership. They collaborated with Fred Hoyle and William Fowler in 1957 in publishing a key paper on the synthesis of the chemical elements in stars. They also produced one of the first comprehensive works on quasars in their *Quasi-Stellar Objects* (1967). She had earlier recorded the spectra of a number of quasars with the 120-inch (3-m) Lick reflector and discovered that their spectral lines displayed different red shifts, probably indicating the ejection of matter at very high speeds.

The first accurate estimates of the masses of galaxies were based on Margaret Burbidge's careful observation of their rotation.

BURBIDGE, Geoffrey (b. Sept. 24, 1925; Chipping Norton, England) British astrophysicist.

Burbidge graduated in 1946 from the University of Bristol and obtained his PhD in 1951 from the University of London. In the period 1950–58 he held junior university positions at London, Harvard, Chicago, Cambridge (England), and the Mount Wilson and Palomar Observatories in California. He became associate professor at Chicago (1958–62) before being appointed associate professor (1962), then professor of physics (1963) at the University of California, San Diego. In 1978 Burbidge accepted the post of director of the Kitt Peak National Observatory, Arizona.

Burbidge began his research career studying particle physics but after his marriage in 1948 to Margaret Peachey (*see* Eleanor Margaret Burbidge), who was to become one of the world's leading optical astronomers, he turned to astrophysics and began a productive research partnership with his wife. The Burbidges worked on the mysterious quasars, first described by Allan Sandage in 1960, and produced in their *Quasi-Stellar Objects* (1967) one of the earliest surveys of the subject. Geoffrey Burbidge was far from convinced that quasars were 'cosmologically distant' in accordance with the orthodox interpretation of their massive red shifts. In 1965 he proposed with Hoyle that they were perhaps comparatively small objects ejected at relativistic speeds from highly active radio galaxies such as Centaurus A. The effect of this would be to place the main body of quasars only 3–30 million light years from our Galaxy and not the 3 billion light years or more demanded by the generally accepted view.

He was equally reluctant to accept without reservation that other emerging orthodoxy of the 1960s, the big-bang theory on the origin of the universe. In 1971 he published a paper in which he maintained that we still do not know whether the big-bang occurred and that much more effort must be devoted to cosmological tests. Although such views have found little favor, Burbidge has continued, like Hoyle, to be highly productive, rich in new ideas, and yet to remain outside and somewhat skeptical of prevailing cosmological and astrophysical orthodoxy.

BURIDAN, Jean (b. 1300; Béthune, France; d. 1358; Paris) French philosopher and logician.

Little is known of Buridan's life except that he studied at the University of Paris under William of Ockham and was appointed professor of philosophy there. It is likely that he remained there all his life as a secular cleric as he is reported to have served as rector of the university in 1328 and 1340.

In his physical works Buridan developed a devastating critique of Aristotle's account of motion. In its place he proposed an impetus theory in which an enforced motion such as the spinning of a millstone is explained by something being impressed into it by the original motive force. Without any external resistance, according to Buridan, the stone would continue spinning forever. The greater the mass and speed of a body the greater its impetus. With such an explanatory framework Buridan and later theorists could begin to tackle some of the basic problems of motion.

Buridan was also an acute logician with his *Sophismata* containing argument sufficiently subtle to interest contemporary logicians. The animal known as *Buridan's ass* (which was unable to choose between two equidistant bundles of hay) does not, however, appear in any of his works. A similar example does occur in Buridan's commentary on Aristotle's *De caelo* (On the Heavens) where the ass is in fact a dog.

BURNELL, Jocelyn *see* BELL, (Susan) Jocelyn.

BURNET, Sir Frank Macfarlane (b. Sept. 3, 1899; Traralgon, Australia) Australian virologist.

Burnet graduated in biology and medicine from Geelong College, Victoria, then attended the University of Melbourne, gaining his MD in 1923. From 1926 to 1927 he worked as research fellow at the Lister Institute of Preventative Medicine, London, receiving his PhD in bacteriology in 1927. On his return to Australia he became assistant director of the Walter and Eliza Hall Institute in Melbourne, assuming directorship of the institute in 1944, a position held until retirement in 1965. Burnet developed the now common laboratory method of multiplying viruses by injecting them into living chick embryos. During the course of this work he realized that embryos injected with a given virus do not produce the appropriate antibodies to combat infection by that virus. He thus speculated that an organism's ability to distinguish its own tissue from foreign tissue has not yet developed at the embryonic stage. Immunologic tolerance to a certain substance might therefore be induced artificially and retained after birth and at maturity by injecting that substance into the embryo. This theory was tested in Burnet's laboratory, but it remained for the Britsh immunologist Peter Medawar (q.v.) to demonstrate conclusively that tolerance to potential antigens can indeed be acquired by the embryo. The concept of acquired immunologic tolerance has important implications in immunity, especially in the ability of an organism to tolerate foreign transplants. For their achievements Burnet and Medawar received the 1960 Nobel Prize for physiology or medicine.

Burnet also made important contributions to an understanding of the epidemiology of several diseases, including influenza, polio, and herpes, and he isolated the causative microorganism of Q fever — the rickettsia. He was president of the Australian Academy of Sciences from 1965 to 1969 and has written many influential books on virology and immunology.

BURNET, Thomas (b. *c.* 1635; Croft, England; d. Sept. 27, 1715; London) English cleric and geologist.

Burnet was educated at Cambridge University and became a fellow of Christ's College in 1657. After a period as tutor to various noblemen he was appointed master of Charterhouse school in 1685. He was also appointed chaplain to William III in 1686 but was later forced to resign (1692) because of his controversial account of the history of the Earth.

In 1681 he published his *Telluris theoria sacra*, which was published in an English version as *The Sacred Theory of the Earth* in 1684 and revised and extended in 1691. In this he tackled the problem that was to face all geologists until this century — how to write a history of the Earth that was consistent with the account given in Genesis. His aim was to take the facts of scripture and show how they could be used to give a rational account of the development of the Earth.

His theory was that the Earth had once been entirely smooth, trapping beneath its shell a large volume of water. Owing to the action of the Sun this shell, the Earth's crust, cracked and released the flood of water; parts of the shattered crust remaining formed the mountains.

Burnet's attempt to explain the history of the Earth in natural terms met a torrent of opposition, both theological and scientific. The strongest argument against this explanation was the presence of marine fossils in mountains for, if the Earth's crust from which the mountains were formed was created before the flood, how could it have come to contain evidence of marine life?

BUTENANDT, Adolf Friedrich Johann (b. Mar. 24, 1903; Bremerhaven-Lehe, now Wesermünde in West Germany) German organic chemist and biochemist.

Butenandt took his first degree in chemistry at the University of Marburg and gained his doctorate in 1927 under Adolf Windaus at Göttingen. He remained at Göttingen as *Privatdozent* until 1933. Following the work of Windaus on cholesterol, Butenandt investigated the sex hormones and in 1929 he isolated the first pure sex hormone, estrone, from the urine of pregnant women (the compound was also discovered independently by Edward Doisy). A search for the male sex hormone resulted in the isolation in 1931 of 15 milligrams of androsterone from 3960 gallons of urine.

In 1933 he became professor of organic chemistry at the Danzig Institute of Technology and here he demonstrated the similarities between the molecular structures of androsterone and cholesterol. His proposed structure for androsterone was confirmed by Leopold Ružička's synthesis in 1934. The male hormone testosterone was synthesized by Butenandt and Ružička only months after its isolation in 1935. Butenandt and Ružička were jointly awarded the Nobel Chemistry Prize in 1939 but Butenandt was forbidden to accept it by the Nazi government. Butenandt was also the first to crystallize an insect hormone, ecdysone, and found that this too was a derivative of cholesterol. Later he led research on the isolation and synthesis of the pheromones.

From 1936 to 1945 Butenandt was director of the Max Planck Institute for Biochemistry at Tübingen and from 1945 to 1956 professor of physiological chemistry there. He retained these posts when the institute moved to Munich in 1956, and in 1960 he succeeded Otto Hahn as president of the Max Planck Society.

BUTLEROV, Aleksandr Mikhailovich (b. Sept. 6, 1828; Chistopol, now in the Soviet Union; d. Aug. 17, 1886; Biarritz, France) Russian chemist.

Butlerov studied at the University of Kazan, graduating as a master of chemistry in 1851. He received his doctorate in 1854 at Moscow and then worked at Kazan, as lecturer (1852) and professor (1857). Russian chemistry, which had been largely dominated by Germans, was backward and Butlerov spent the period 1857–58 traveling in Europe, where he met Friedrich Kekulé, Justus von Liebig, Friedrich Wöhler, and Archibald Couper, and worked in Charles Wurtz's laboratory in Paris.

Butlerov was mainly a theoretician and he extended Kekulé's concepts of organic structure. He proposed that each organic compound has a unique configuration and he invented the term 'chemical structure'. In 1864 he predicted the existence of tertiary alcohols and in 1876 first introduced the idea of isomers in chemical equilibrium (tautomerism). He wrote *An Introduction to the Full Study of Organic Compounds* (1864).

Butlerov was appointed rector of the University of Kazan in 1860 but amid student unrest and clashes between the Russian and German factions he resigned, was reinstated, and finally resigned in 1863. In 1867 he became professor of chemistry at St. Petersburg, where he became increasingly involved in other activities, such as beekeeping and spiritualism.

BUYS BALLOT, Christoph Hendrik Diederik (b. Oct. 10, 1817; Kloetinge, Netherlands; d. Feb. 3, 1890; Utrecht, Netherlands) Dutch meteorologist.

Buys Ballot was the son of a minister. He was educated at the University of Utrecht, obtaining his PhD in 1844, and became professor of mathematics in 1847 and professor of physics in 1867. He did much to organize the observation and collection of meteorological data in the Netherlands and founded, in 1854, the Netherlands Meteorological Institute.

He is best remembered for the law on wind direction he formulated in 1857. This states that an observer facing the wind in the northern hemisphere has the lower pressure on his right and the higher pressure on his left; in the southern hemisphere this is reversed. Its justification is clearer if stated in the equivalent form: in the northern hemisphere winds circulate counterclockwise around low-pressure areas and clockwise around high-pressure ones.

BYRD, Richard Evelyn (b. Oct. 25, 1888; Winchester, Virginia; d. Mar. 11, 1957; Boston, Massuchusetts) American polar explorer.

Byrd graduated from the US Naval Academy in 1912. Forced in 1916 to resign from the navy with an injured leg, he joined the air force. After the end of World War I he became interested in polar aviation. He joined the MacMillan expedition to the Arctic (1924) and, with Floydd Bennett, reputedly made the first flight over the North Pole on May 9, 1926.

Byrd then became interested in Antarctic exploration, leading his first expedition there in 1928. He established his base camp, Little America, on the Ross Ice Shelf and, in 1929, flew over the South Pole. The Antarctic was the largest remaining unmapped and unexplored area of the world and Byrd contributed greatly to opening up and mapping the continent. A more extensive expedition was undertaken in 1933–35, during which Byrd spent five months alone at an Antarctic weather station in 1934, followed by three more, the last in 1955–56.

A large section of the Antarctic was named Marie Byrd Land, after his wife.

C

CAGNIARD DE LA TOUR, Charles (b. May 31, 1777; Paris; d. July 5, 1859; Paris) French physicist.

Cagniard de la Tour was educated at the Ecole Polytechnique and then spent his time as an amateur inventor. In 1819 he invented the disk siren, in which the sound is produced by air blowing through holes in a rotating disk, the pitch being determined by the speed of rotation. Three years later he made his most famous discovery. When he heated certain liquids in sealed tubes he observed that at a particular temperature and pressure the meniscus dividing liquid from vapor disappeared. Under these conditions — known as the *critical state* — the densities of liquid and vapor become the same and the two are identical.

In the field of biology Cagniard de la Tour discovered, independently of Theodor Schwann, the role of yeast in alcoholic fermentation. He also studied the physics of the human larynx and the sounds produced by it, invented a machine for studying bird flight and, in 1847, attempted, without success, to convert carbon into diamond.

CAHOURS, August André Thomas (b. Oct. 2, 1813; Paris; d. Mar. 17, 1891; Paris) French organic chemist.

Cahours was professor at the Ecole Polytechnique in Paris (1871) and warden of the Paris mint. He made many notable discoveries, including methyl salicylate, amyl alcohol in fusel oil, anisole and phellandrene in fennel oil, and the alkyl compounds of aluminum, arsenic, and beryllium.

CAILLETET, Louis Paul (b. Sept. 21, 1832; Chatillon-sur-Seine, France; d. Jan. 5, 1913; Paris) French physicist.

Cailletet was the son of a metallurgist and, after studying in Paris, became a manager at his father's foundry.

He is most famous for his work on the liquefaction of gases. Cailletet realized that the failure of others to liquefy the permanent gases, even under enormous pressures, was explained by Thomas Andrew's (q.v.) concept of critical temperature. In 1877 he succeeded in producing liquid oxygen by allowing the cold, compressed gas to expand. This technique, depending on the effect discovered by James Joule and Lord Kelvin, cooled the gas to below its critical temperature. In later experiments he liquefied nitrogen and air. Raoul Pictet, working independently, used a similar technique. In 1884 Cailletet was elected to the Paris Academy for his work. He is also the inventor of the altimeter and the high-pressure manometer.

CALLINICUS of Heliopolis (b. *c.* 620; Heliopolis, now Baalbeck in Syria) Syrian inventor.

Callinicus was a Jewish refugee who was forced to flee to Constantinople (now Istanbul) from the Arabs. There he invented Greek fire, an incendiary liquid for use as a weapon.

In about 673 Caliph Mu'awiyah led his

victorious Arabian forces in a naval attack on Constantinople. The city's fall at that time would have opened Europe up to penetration through Greece and the Italian peninsula with no state powerful enough to resist them. Instead, the Arabian navy was destroyed by the first use of Callinicus's Greek fire in the Battle of Cyzicus off Constantinople.

The ingredients of Greek fire were kept a secret by Callinicus's family and these remain a mystery. It seems to have been a compound of naphtha, potassium nitrate, and possibly quicklime. This would spread on water, burn freely, and give out a great deal of heat. Callinicus's main innovation seems to have been the introduction of a kind of 'siphon' to propel the fire. Greek fire found its way into Europe in the 12th century being first used in 1151 in France.

CALLIPUS (b. *c.* 370 BC; Cyzicus, now in Turkey; d. *c.* 300 BC) Greek astronomer.

Callipus was a younger contemporary and possibly a pupil of Eudoxus. He is also known to have had discussions on astronomy with Aristotle in Athens. Although none of his works have survived he is known to have reformed the Eudoxan system. Callipus is also reported as suggesting improvements in the Metonic cycle, the period — of 19 years or 235 synodic (lunar) months — after which the phases of the Moon recur on the same days of the year. He proposed taking a period of 76 years (4 Metonic cycles) made from 940 lunar months, 28 of which would be intercalary (inserted). This would give a solar year of precisely 365¼ days. The Greeks never actually adopted any of these cycles but they do give some indication of how accurately their astronomers had worked out the length of the year.

CALVIN, Melvin (b. Apr. 8, 1911; St. Paul, Minnesota) American chemist and biochemist.

Calvin studied chemistry at the Michigan College of Mining and Technology and gained his BS degree in 1931. After obtaining his PhD from the University of Minnesota in 1935 he spent two years at the Victoria University of Manchester, England, working with Michael Polanyi. Here he became interested in chlorophyll and its role in the photosynthetic process in plants. Calvin began a long association with the University of California at Berkeley in 1937. From 1941 to 1945 he worked on scientific problems connected with the war, including two years on the Manhattan Project (the atomic bomb).

In 1946 Calvin became director of the Bio-organic Division of the Lawrence Radiation Laboratory at Berkeley, where he used the new analytical techniques developed during the war — ion-exchange chromatography, paper chromatography, and radioisotopes — to investigate the 'dark reactions' of photosynthesis, i.e. those reactions that do not need the presence of light. Plant cells were allowed to absorb carbon dioxide labeled with the radioisotope carbon–14, then immersed at varying intervals in boiling alcohol so that the compounds they synthesized could be identified. In this way the cycle of photosynthetic reactions (known as the *Calvin cycle*) was elucidated and shown to be related in part to the familiar cycle of cell respiration. This work, which was collected in *The Path of Carbon in Photosynthesis* (1957), earned Calvin the Nobel Chemistry Prize in 1961.

Calvin has remained at Berkeley, as director of the Laboratory of Chemical Biodynamics (1960–63), professor of molecular biology (1963–71), and professor of chemistry (1971). He has continued to work on problems of photosynthesis (especially on the role of chlorophyll in quantum conversion) and on the evolution of photosynthesis.

CAMERARIUS, Rudolph Jacob (b. Feb. 17, 1665; Tübingen, now in West Germany; d. Sept. 11, 1721; Tübingen) German botanist.

The son of a professor of medicine at Tübingen, Camerarius was himself educated there and received his doctorate in 1687. He joined the staff at Tübingen and following his father's death in 1695 was appointed professor of medicine and director of the botanic gardens, posts he occupied until his death from TB in 1721.

In 1694 in *De sexu plantarum* (On the Sex of Plants) Camerarius produced clear experimental evidence for the sexuality of plants first proposed by John Ray and Nehemiah Grew. By isolating pistillate (female) dioecious plants from staminate (male) plants (dioecious meaning plant species where the male and female flowers are borne on separate plants), he was able to show that although the pistillate plants produced fruit, they lacked seeds. With monoecious plants (those that bear separate unisexual male and female flowers on the same plant e.g. maize) he found that removing the male inflorescence also resulted in sterile fruit.

In his description of plant anatomy Camerarius identified the stamens as the male organ and the style and stigma as the female part. He also described the role of pollination.

CAMERON, Sir Gordon Roy (b. June 30, 1899; Echuca, Australia; d. Oct. 7, 1966; London) Australian pathologist.

Cameron, the son of a Methodist minister, studied medicine at Melbourne University, graduating in 1922. He worked first at the university and then at the Walter and Eliza Hall Institute before leaving for Europe in 1927 to do postgraduate work at Freiburg. Shortly afterward he was appointed to the staff of University College Hospital, London, where he served as professor of morbid anatomy from 1937 until his retirement in 1964.

Cameron worked on a wide range of problems including pulmonary edema, inflammation, and the pathology of the spleen and liver. He also produced a major

survey of all aspects of the field with his *Pathology of the Cell* (1952).

CANDOLLE, Augustin Pyrame de (b. Feb. 4, 1778; Geneva, Switzerland; d. Sept. 9, 1841; Geneva) Swiss botanist.

Candolle studied medicine for two years at the Academy of Geneva before moving to Paris in 1796 to study both medicine and natural sciences. In Paris he met many distinguished naturalists, including Georges Cuvier and Jean Baptiste Lamarck, and quickly established his own reputation through the publication of many outstanding monographs on plants. He received his MD from the University of Paris in 1804 and, at the request of the French government, made a botanical and agricultural survey of France between 1806 and 1812.

In 1813 he published his famous *Théorie élémentaire de la botanique* (Elementary Theory of Botany), in which he introduced the term 'taxonomy' to mean classification. This work was based on the natural classificatory systems of Cuvier and Antoine Jussieu, and in it Candolle maintained that relationships between plants could be established through similarities in the plan of symmetry of their sexual parts. He realized that the symmetry could be disguised by fusion, degeneration, or loss of sexual organs, making structures with a common ancestry appear different. Candolle thus formulated the idea of homologous parts — a concept that lends much weight to the theory of evolution, but surprisingly he continued to believe in the immutability of species. Candolle's classification replaced that of Linnaeus and was used widely until George Bentham and Joseph Hooker produced their improved system 50 years later.

Candolle also made important contributions to plant geography, realizing that the distribution of vegetation can be profoundly influenced by soil type. The relationships he described between plants and soil were backed up by personal observations from his travels in Brazil, East India, and North China.

From 1808 to 1816 Candolle was professor of botany at Montpelier University, after which he returned to Geneva to take the chair of natural history at the Academy. On his arrival in Geneva he completely reorganized the gardens. Between 1824 and 1839 he published the first seven volumes of his huge *Prodromus Systematis Naturalis Regni Vegetabilis* (Guide to Natural Classification for the Plant Kingdom), an encyclopedia of the plant kingdom. His son, Alphonse de Candolle, saw to the publication of the remaining ten volumes after his father's death and also carried on many of his father's other schemes.

CANNIZZARO, Stanislao (b. July 13, 1826; Palermo, Sicily; d. May 10, 1910; Rome) Italian chemist.

The son of a magistrate, Cannizzaro studied physiology at Palermo and Naples. He turned to organic chemistry after realizing the importance of chemical processes in neurophysiology, and from 1845 to 1847 worked as a laboratory assistant to R. Piria at Pisa. Cannizzaro was an ardent liberal and in 1847 he returned to Sicily to fight as an officer in the insurrection against the ruling Bourbon regime. Following the abortive revolution of 1848 he went into exile and returned to chemistry, working with Michel Eugène Chevreul in Paris (1849–51).

Cannizzaro returned to Italy in 1851 as professor of chemistry and physics at the Collegio Nazionale at Alessandria. In 1853 he discovered the reaction known as *Cannizzaro's reaction*, in which an aromatic aldehyde is simultaneously oxidized and reduced in the presence of concentrated alkali to give an acid and an alcohol.

In 1855 Cannizzaro moved to Genoa as professor of chemistry and here he produced the work for which he is chiefly remembered. His pamphlet *Sunto di un corso di filosofia chimica* (1858; Epitome of a Course of Chemical Philosophy)

finally resolved more than 50 years of confusion about atomic weights. In 1860 a conference was held at Karlsruhe, Germany, to discuss the problem. No agreement was reached but Cannizzaro's pamphlet was circulated and soon after was widely accepted. In it Cannizzaro restated the hypothesis first put forward by Amedeo Avogadro (q.v.), clearly defined atoms and molecules, and showed that molecular weights could be determined from vapor-density measurements.

Politics intervened once more in Cannizzaro's life and in the struggle to reunite Italy he returned to Palermo in 1860 to join Garibaldi. He was professor of inorganic and organic chemistry at Palermo until 1870, when he went to Rome to found the Italian Institute of Chemistry. The most notable research of this last period was that on santonin, a compound derived from species of *Artemisia* (wormwoods) that is active against intestinal worms, which Cannizzaro showed to be a derivative of naphthalene. He was widely honored and became a senator in 1871.

CANNON, Annie Jump (b. Dec. 11, 1863; Dover, Delaware; d. Apr. 13, 1941; Cambridge, Massachusetts) American astronomer.

Cannon was the daughter of a Delaware state senator. She was one of the first girls from Delaware to attend university, being a student at Wellesley College from 1880 to 1884. After a decade spent at home, where she became deaf through scarlet fever, she entered Radcliffe College in 1895 to study astronomy. In 1896 she was appointed to the staff of the Harvard College Observatory, as it was the practice of the observatory, under the directorship of Edward Pickering, to employ young well-educated women as computers. She worked there for the rest of her career, serving from 1911 to 1932 as curator of astronomical photographs. In 1938, after nearly half a century of distinguished service, she was appointed William Cranch Bond Astronomer.

One of the main programs of the observatory was the preparation of the *Henry Draper Catalogue* of a quarter of a million stellar spectra. Stars were originally to be classified into one of the 17 spectral types, A to Q, which were ordered alphabetically in terms of the intensity of the hydrogen absorption lines. Cannon saw that a more natural order could be achieved if some classes were omitted, others added, and the total reordered in terms of decreasing surface temperature. This produced the sequence O, B, A, F, G, K, M, R, N, and S. Cannon showed that the great majority of stars can be placed in one of the groups between O and M. Her classification scheme has since only been slightly altered.

Cannon developed a phenomenal skill in cataloging stars and at the height of her power it was claimed that she could classify three stars a minute. Her classification of over 225 000 stars, brighter than 9th or 10th magnitude, and the compilation of the *Catalogue* took many years. It was finally published, between 1918 and 1924, as volumes 91 to 99 of the *Annals of Harvard College Observatory*. She continued the work unabated, later publications including an additional 47 000 classifications in the *Henry Draper Extension* (*Annals*, vol. 100, 1925–36). Even as late as 1936 when she was over 70 she undertook the classification of 10 000 faint stars submitted to her by the Cape of Good Hope Observatory.

CANNON, Walter Bradford (b. Oct. 19, 1871; Prairie du Chien, Wisconsin; d. Oct. 1, 1945; Boston, Massachusetts) American physiologist.

Cannon graduated from Harvard in 1896 and was professor of physiology there from 1906 to 1942. His early work included studies of the digestive system, in particular the use of x-rays to study stomach disorders. For this he introduced the *bismuth meal*. Most of his working life, however, was spent studying the nervous system, particularly the way in which various body functions are regulated by hormones. As early as 1915 he showed the connection between secretions of the endocrine glands and the emotions. In the 1930s he worked on the role of epinephrine in helping the body to meet 'fight or flight' situations. He also studied the way hormonelike substances are involved in transmitting messages along nerves.

CANTON, John (b. July 31, 1718; Stroud, England; d. Mar. 22, 1772; London) British physicist.

Canton was a schoolmaster in London and a gifted amateur physicist. He invented a new technique for making artificial magnets in 1749 and was elected to the Royal Society which gave him a medal for this work in 1751.

He followed Benjamin Franklin's theories of electrostatics and was the first in England to repeat Franklin's experiments with lightning. He also discovered a few more properties of electrostatic induction, including the fact that both glass and clouds could become negatively charged instead of, as was usual, positively. In 1757, he made the first observations of fluctuations in the Earth's magnetic field, which, at the end of the next century, led to the discovery of charged layers in the atmosphere. In 1762 he demonstrated that — in spite of scientific opinion to the contrary — water was compressible.

CANTOR, Georg (b. Mar. 3, 1845; St. Petersburg, now Leningrad in Russia; d. Jan. 6, 1918; Halle, now in East Germany) German mathematician.

Cantor was born of (Christian) Danish parents of Jewish descent, who moved to Germany in 1856. He studied at the universities of Zurich, Berlin, and Göttingen and taught at the University of Halle. In addition to mathematics he was deeply interested in philosophy and theology. Rather surprisingly he also took astrology seriously.

Cantor began his mathematical work in the field of analysis, but his interest in the sets of points of convergence of Fourier series led him to the work for which he is remembered — the creation of the theory of transfinite sets. For centuries the concept of infinity had been a highly controversial one both mathematically and philosophically. Before Cantor a mathematician of the stature of Karl Friedrich Gauss could declare that all talk of the 'completed infinite' was a dangerous confusion that had no place in mathematics. What Cantor did was to show that the concepts of cardinal and ordinal number could be defined mathematically in such a way that it made perfectly clear sense to talk of infinite or transfinite numbers.

Cantor's mathematics of the transfinite met initially with a very hostile response from mathematicians. A prominent exception was Richard Dedekind who recognized the value of Cantor's work from the start. The mathematician Leopold Kronecker launched a particularly vitriolic attack on Cantor that may well have contributed to the decline in Cantor's mental health. He actually died in a mental hospital.

Cantor did not present his set theory in the completely rigorous way which is now customary since he took the notion of 'set' to be intuitively clear. But the discovery of set-theoretic paradoxes by Cantor himself, by Bertrand Russell, and others showed that some refinement was needed. This led to the development of axiomatic set theory by Ernst Zermelo and others.

CARDANO, Gerolamo (b. Sept. 24, 1501; Pavia, Italy; d. Sept. 21, 1576; Rome) Italian mathematician, physician, and astrologer.

The work of Cardano constitutes a landmark in the development of algebra and yet in his own time he was chiefly known as a physician. He studied medicine at the universities of Pavia and Padua, receiving his degree in 1526, and spent much of his life as a practicing physician. He became professor of medicine at Pavia in 1543 and one of his notable nonmathematical achievements was to give the first clinical description of typhus fever.

It was however in mathematics that Cardano's real talents lay. His chief work was the *Ars magna* (1545; The Great Skill) in which he gave ways of solving both the general cubic and the general quartic. This was the first important printed treatise on algebra. The solution of the general cubic equation was revealed to him by Niccolò Tartaglia in confidence and Cardano's publication aroused a bitter controversy between the two. Cardano's former servant, Lodovico Ferrari, had discovered the solution of the general quartic equation. In his later *Liber de ludo aleae* (Book on Games of Chance) Cardano did some pioneering work in the mathematical theory of probability.

Cardano's interests were not, however, limited to mathematics and medicine. He also indulged in philosophical and astrological speculation and this had the unfortunate consequence that in 1570 he was charged with heresy by the Church. He was briefly jailed but was soon released after the necessary recantation. As a result of this episode Cardano lost his post as a professor at the University of Bologna, which he had held since 1562.

CARNAP, Rudolf (b. May 18, 1891; Ronsdorf, now in West Germany; d. Sept. 14, 1970; Santa Monica, California) German-American philosopher and logician.

Carnap had a rigorous scientific and philosophical education, which was reflected in the style and content of all his later work. He studied mathematics, physics, and philosophy at the universities of Jena and Freiburg (1910–14) and obtained a doctorate from Jena with a thesis on the concept of space in 1921.

In 1926 Carnap was invited to take up a post at the university of Vienna where he became a major figure in the Vienna Circle — a group of philosophers and mathematicians founded by Moritz Schlick. This group had an empiricist outlook, i.e. that all our ideas, concepts, and beliefs about the external world derive from our immediate sensory experience. Out of this evolved the logical empiricist or logical positivist school of thought, which states that the meaningful statements we can make are just those that have logical consequences that are observably verifiable. That is, meaningful statements must be testable by experience; those that are not, like the propositions of metaphysics and religion, are, strictly, meaningless.

Throughout his life Carnap used the tools of symbolic logic to bring a greater precision to philosophical inquiry, including investigations into the philosophy of language and into probability and inductive reasoning. He produced his first major work in 1928, *Der Logische Aufban der Welt*, translated into English in 1967 as *The Logical Structure of the World*. In this he developed a version of the empiricist reducibility thesis, holding that scientific theories and theoretical sentences must be reducible to sentences that describe immediate experiences, which are observably verifiable. His other works included *Logishe Syntax der Sprache* (1934); The Logical Syntax of Language) and *Logical Foundations of Probability* (1950).

He emigrated to America in 1936 becoming professor of philosophy at Chicago until 1952 and at UCLA until 1961.

CARNOT, Nicolas Leonard Sadi (b. June 1, 1796; Paris; d. Aug. 24, 1832; Paris) French physicist.

Carnot came from a distinguished political family; his father, Lazare, was a leading politician under Napoleon Bonaparte. Sadi Carnot studied at the Ecole Polytechnique, from which he graduated in 1814. For the next few years he worked as a military engineer, but the political climate had changed with the fall of Bonaparte and, in 1819, he transferred to Paris and concentrated on scientific research.

The fruits of this work ripened in 1824 in the form of a book called *Réflexions sur la puissance motrice de feu* (On the Motive Power of Fire). The main theme of this masterpiece was an analysis of the efficiency of engines in converting heat into work. He found a simple formula depending only on the temperature differences in the engine and not on intermediate stages through which the engine passed. He also introduced the concept of reversibility in the form of the ideal *Carnot cycle*. Using these ideas he derived an early form of the second law of thermodynamics, stating that heat always flows from hot to cold. It became an inspiration, many years later, for Rudolf Clausius's formulations of thermodynamics. Carnot died of cholera at the age of 36.

CARO, Heinrich (b. Feb. 13, 1834; Posen, now Poznan in Poland; d. Sept. 11, 1910) German organic chemist.

Caro studied at the University of Berlin (1852–55) before entering the dyestuffs industry, first in Mülheim then in Manchester, England, where he worked on mauveine, the first synthetic dye. He joined the Badische Anilin und Soda Fabrik in 1866, becoming a director in 1868. In 1869 Caro, Karl Graebe, and Karl Liebermann synthesized alizarin, the first natural dye to be synthesized (also discovered simultaneously by William Perkin). Caro made many subsequent discoveries, including methylene blue (1877) and Fast Red A, the first acidic azo dye (1878). He discovered *Caro's acid*, a powerful oxidizing agent (H_2SO_5), in 1898.

CAROTHERS, Wallace Hume (b. Apr. 27, 1896; Burlington, Iowa; d. Apr. 29, 1937; Philadelphia, Pennsylvania) American industrial chemist.

Carothers, the son of a teacher, gained a BS degree from Tarkio College, Missouri (1920), after working his way through college. He gained his PhD in 1924 from the University of Illinois and was an instructor in chemistry at Illinois and Harvard before joining the Du Pont company at Wilmington, Delaware, as head of organic chemistry research in 1928.

Carother's early work was in the application of electronic theory to organic chemistry but at Du Pont he worked on polymerization. His first great success was the production of the synthetic rubber, neoprene (1931). Working with acetylenes he discovered that the action of hydrochloric acid on monovinylacetylene produced 2-chloro-buta-1,3-diene (chloroprene), which polymerized very readily to give a polymer that was superior in some respects to natural rubber.

In a systematic search for synthetic analogs of silk and cellulose he prepared many condensation polymers, especially polyesters and polyethers. In 1935 one polyamide, produced by condensation of adipic acid and hexamethylenediamine, proved outstanding in its properties and came into full-scale production in 1940 as Nylon 66. But Carothers did not live to see the results of his achievements; despite his brilliant successes he suffered from fits of depression and took his own life at the age of 41.

CARREL, Alexis (b. June 28, 1873; Lyons, France; d. Nov. 5, 1944; Paris) French surgeon.

Carrel received his medical degree from the University of Lyons in 1900. In 1902 he started to investigate techniques for joining (suturing) blood vessels end to end. He continued his work at the University of Chicago (1904) and later (1906) at the Rockefeller Institute for Medical Research, New York. Carrel's techniques, which minimized tissue damage and infection and reduced the risk of blood clots, were a major advance in vascular surgery and paved the way for the replacement and transplantation of organs. In recognition of this work, Carrel was awarded the 1912 Nobel Prize for physiology or medicine.

During World War I, Carrel served in the French army. With the chemist Henry Dakin, he formulated the Carrel–Dakin antiseptic for deep wounds. Returning to the Rockefeller Institute after the war, Carrel turned his attention to methods of keeping tissues and organs alive outside the body. He maintained chick embryo heart tissue for many years on artificial nutrient solutions and with the aviator Charles Lindbergh he devised a so-called artificial heart that could pump physiological fluids through large organs, such as the heart or kidneys.

In *Man, the Unknown* (1935), Carrel published his controversial views about the possible role of science in organizing and improving society along rather authoritarian lines. During World War II he founded and directed the Carrel Foundation for the Study of Human Problems under the Vichy government, in Paris. Following the Allied liberation, Carrel faced charges of collaboration but died before a trial was arranged.

CARRINGTON, Richard Christopher (b. May 26, 1826; London; d. Nov. 27, 1875; Churt, England) British astronomer.

Carrington was the son of a wealthy brewer. He went to Cambridge University intending to go into the Church but a lecture by James Challis awakened in him a consuming interest in astronomy. From 1848 to 1852 he worked as an observer at Durham Observatory and, in 1857, produced a catalog of 3735 stars within 9° of the celestial pole, based on his Durham work. In 1853 he established his own observatory at Redhill in Surrey.

Carrington's most important work was done on the rotation of the Sun. In between 1853 and 1861 he made 5290 observations of 954 groups of sunspots. On the basis of these he was able to establish the surprising conclusion that the Sun does not rotate as a rigid body; at the equator it has a rotational period of 25 days while at latitude 45° it takes as much as 27.5 days.

CARTAN, Elie Joseph (b. Apr. 9, 1869; Dolomieu, France; d. May 6, 1951; Paris) French mathematician.

Cartan is now recognized as one of the most powerful and original mathematicians of the 20th century, but his work only became widely known toward the end of his life. Cartan studied at the Ecole Normale Supérieure in Paris, and held teaching posts at the universities of Montpellier, Lyons, Nancy, and, from 1912 to 1940, Paris.

Cartan's most significant work was in developing the concept of analysis on differentiable manifolds, which now occupies a central place in mathematics. He began his research career with a dissertation on Lie groups — a topic that led him on to his pioneering work on differential systems. The most important innovation in his work on Lie groups was his creation of methods for studying their global properties. Similarly his work on differential systems was distinguished by its global approach. One of his most useful inventions was the 'calculus of exterior differential forms', which he applied to problems in many fields including differential geometry, Lie groups, analytical dynamics, and general relativity. Cartan's son Henri is also an eminent mathematician.

CARTWRIGHT, Edmund (b. Apr. 24, 1743; Marnham, England; d. Oct. 30, 1823; Hastings, England) British inventor.

Cartwright began his career as a clergyman. However, after visiting Richard Arkwright's cotton-spinning mills in Derbyshire in 1784, he became interested in developing machinery for the textile industry. He built a simple form of power loom, which was patented in 1785, and set up a weaving and spinning factory in Doncaster the same year. In 1789 he patented a wool-carding machine. He was not financially successful — his factory went bankrupt in 1794 — but in 1809 he was awarded £10 000 by the House of Commons in recognition of the benefit to the nation from his invention of the power loom.

CARTY, John Joseph (b. Apr. 14, 1861; Cambridge, Massachusetts; d. Dec. 27, 1932; Baltimore, Maryland) American telephone engineer.

Carty was educated at high school in Cambridge, Massachusetts, but because of eye trouble was delayed in entering college. During this delay his imagination was captured by the invention of the telephone (1875) by Alexander Graham Bell in neighboring Boston. He consequently joined the Bell System in 1879, eventually becoming chief engineer there. He served as chief engineer of the New York Telephone Company (1889–1907) and of the American Telephone and Telegraph Company (1907–19) and finally became vice president of the latter company until his retirement in 1930.

Carty was responsible for a number of technical innovations in the development of the commercial use of the telephone. These included the introduction of the 'common' battery, which, by providing current from a central source to a number of interconnected telephones, allowed the development of a complex urban network. He also directed the project to provide the first transcontinental telephone wire line, completing in 1915 the 3400-mile (5400-km) link between New York and San Francisco.

CARVER, George Washington (b. 1864; Diamond Grove, Missouri; d. Jan. 5, 1943; Tuskegee, Alabama) American agricultural chemist.

It is impossible to be more accurate about the birth of Carver for he was born a slave. He managed to acquire some elementary education and went on to study at the Iowa State Agricultural College from which he graduated in 1892. He taught at Iowa until 1896, when he returned to the South to become director of the department of agricultural research at the Tuskegee Institute, Alabama. There he stayed despite lucrative offers to work for such magnates as Henry Ford and Thomas Edison.

His main achievement was to introduce new crops into the agricultural system of the South, in particular arguing for large-scale plantings of peanuts and sweet potatoes. He saw that such new crops were vital if only to replenish the soil, which had become impoverished by the regular growth of cotton and tobacco.

But he did much more than introduce new crops for he tried to show that they could be used to develop many new products. He showed that peanuts contained several different kinds of oil. So successful was he in this that by the 1930s the South was producing 60 million dollars worth of oil a year. Peanut butter was another of his innovations. All in all he is reported to have developed over 300 new products from peanuts and over 100 from sweet potatoes.

CASIMIR, Hendrik Brugt Gerhard (b. July 15, 1909; The Hague, Netherlands) Dutch physicist.

Casimir studied at the universities of Leiden, Copenhagen, and Zurich, and held various research positions between 1933 and 1942.

He has published many papers in the fields of theoretical physics, applied mathematics, and low-temperature physics. His most notable work has been in the theory of the superconducting state. Following the work of W. Meissner, Casimir and his colleague Cornelis Gorter advanced a 'two-fluid' model of superconductivity in 1934 in which a fraction of the electrons were regarded as superconducting, while the rest remained 'normal' electrons. They were successful in explaining the high degree of interrelationship between the magnetic and thermal properties of superconductors.

From 1942, Casimir has pursued a highly successful career with the Philips company, becoming director of the Philips Research Laboratories in 1946, and a member of the board of management (1957–72).

He has supervized Philips's research activities in several countries.

CASPERSSON, Torbjörn Oskar (b. Oct. 15, 1910; Motala, Sweden) Swedish cytochemist.

Caspersson gained his MD from Stockholm University in 1936. He then joined the staff of the Nobel Institute being appointed professor of medical cellular research and genetics in 1944.

In the late 1930s Caspersson spent a few years working on DNA. In 1936 with the Swiss chemist Rudolf Signer he made fundamental measurements of the molecule that suggested a molecular weight between 500 000 and a million, so showing the nucleic acids to be larger than protein molecules.

Further important data was collected by a photoelectric spectrophotometer developed by Caspersson. This allowed the movement of RNA in the cell to be followed by its characteristic absorption peak in the ultraviolet at 2600 angstroms and to establish that protein synthesis in the cell was associated with an abundance of RNA. Despite this Caspersson remained committed to the orthodox view that genes were proteins and believed nucleic acids to be a structure-determining supporting substance.

CASSEGRAIN, N. (*fl.* 1672; Chartres, France) French telescope designer.

Little is known about Cassegrain's life. He was apparently a physician at Chartres and was credited, in 1672, as the inventor of a reflecting telescope, which is named for him. James Short was one of the first to use the design, producing his telescopes in about 1740.

CASSINI, Giovanni Domenico (b. June 8, 1625; Perinaldo, Italy; d. Sept. 11, 1712; Paris) Italian–French astronomer.

Cassini was educated in Genoa, and at the early age of 25 he became professor of astronomy at Bologna. He remained there until 1669 when he moved to France in order to take charge of Louis XIV's new Paris Observatory. He became a French citizen in 1673.

While still at Bologna he worked out, fairly accurately, the rotational periods of Jupiter and Mars. In 1668 he constructed a table of the movements of the Medici planets — the satellites of Jupiter discovered by Galileo. It was this table that allowed Ole Rømer to calculate the speed of light. In Paris, using aerial telescopes up to 150 feet (45.7 m) long, he discovered four new satellites of Saturn — Iapetus in 1671, Rhea in 1672, and Dione and Tethys in 1684. In 1675 he discovered the gap that divides Saturn's rings into two parts and has since been called *Cassini's division*.

Cassini's most important work concerned the size of the solar system. Using data collected by Jean Richer in Cayenne, together with his own observations in Paris, he was able to work out the parallax of Mars and thus calculate the astronomical unit (AU) — the mean distance between the Earth and the Sun. His figure of 87 million miles (140 million km) may have been 7% too low, but compared with earlier figures of Tycho Brahe (5 million miles) and Johannes Kepler (15 million miles) his results gave mankind a realistic picture of the size of the universe for the first time. Cassini also made fundamental measurements on the size and shape of the Earth concluding, erroneously, that it was a prolate spheroid. He became blind in 1710 and was succeeded in the directorship of his observatory by both his son, Jacques Cassini, and his grandson, César François Cassini.

CASTNER, Hamilton Young (b. Sept. 11, 1858; New York City; d. Oct. 11, 1898; Saranac Lake, New York) American chemist.

Castner studied at Brooklyn Polytechnic and at Columbia University, New York. He started as a chemical consultant in 1879 and moved to Britain in 1886 when he failed to gain any backing in America for his process for the production of sodium.

Henri Sainte-Claire Deville had developed a system in which caustic soda could be reduced to sodium with charcoal at high temperatures. However this system ran into a variety of practical difficulties, which were satisfactorily cleared up by Castner. Castner intended to use the sodium for producing aluminum by reduction of aluminum chloride — at the time aluminum was a very expensive metal. A factory was opened in 1888 at Oldbury, England, to manufacture 100 000 lbs of aluminum per annum. But it was too late for, two years earlier, Charles Hall in America and Paul Héroult in France had independently discovered a cheap way to produce aluminum by electrolysis. Castner quickly had to invent some uses for his sodium, for which there was little demand at the time. One was the manufacture of sodium peroxide (by burning sodium in air), used as a bleach. By passing ammonia over molten sodium and charcoal he produced sodium cyanide, which was used in the extraction of gold.

By the early 1890s, with the growing demand for his products, his problem was an inability to produce enough sodium. He solved this with a new method of making sodium by the electrolysis of brine using a mercury cathode. The process had been anticipated by Carl Kellner in Austria; rather than litigate the two chemists cooperated and in 1897 set up the Castner–Kellner Alkali Company in Runcorn, Cheshire, England, where there was a cheap and abundant supply of salt. In the year of his death it was already producing 20 tons of caustic soda a day with a production of 40 tons of bleaching powder daily as a byproduct.

CAUCHY, Baron Augustin Louis (b. Aug. 21, 1789; Paris; d. May 23, 1857; Sceaux, France) French mathematician.

Cauchy showed great mathematical talent at an early age and came to the attention of Joseph Lagrange and Pierre Laplace, who encouraged him in his studies. He was educated at the Ecole Polytechnique, where he later lectured and became professor of mechanics in 1816, and worked briefly as an engineer in Napoleon's army. He held extreme conservative views in religion and politics, typical of which was the strong allegiance to the Bourbon dynasty that caused him to follow Charles X (who had ennobled Cauchy) into exile in 1830. Cauchy then became professor of mathematics at Turin, but returned to France in 1838 and resumed his post at the Ecole Polytechnique.

Cauchy was an extremely prolific mathematician who made outstanding contributions to many branches of the subject, ranging from pure algebra and analysis to mathematical physics and astronomy. He was also an outstanding teacher. His greatest achievements were in the fields of real and complex analysis in which he was one of the first mathematicians to insist on the high standards of rigor now taken for granted in mathematics. He gave the first fully satisfactory definitions of the fundamentally important concepts of limit and convergence.

CAVALIERI, Francesco Bonaventura (b. 1598; Milan, Italy; d. Nov. 30, 1647; Bologna, Italy) Italian mathematician and geometer.

Cavalieri joined the Jesuits as a boy. He became interested in mathematics while studying Euclid's works and met Galileo, whose follower he became.

Cavalieri's fame rests chiefly on his work in geometry in which he paved the way for the development of the integral calculus by Isaac Newton and Gottfried Leibniz. In 1629 Cavalieri became professor of mathematics at Bologna, a post he held for the rest of his life. At Bologna he developed his 'method of indivisibles', published in his *Geometria indivisibilibus continuorum nova quadam ratione promota*

(1635; A Certain Method for the Development of a New Geometry of Continuous Indivisibles), which had much in common with the basic ideas of integral calculus.

Cavalieri also helped to popularize the use of logarithms in Italy through the publication of his *Directorium generale uranometricum* (1632; A General Directory of Uranometry).

CAVALLI-SFORZA, Luigi Luca (b. Jan. 25, 1922; Genoa, Italy) Italian geneticist.

Cavalli-Sforza was educated at the University of Pavia where he gained his MD in 1944. After working on bacterial genetics at Cambridge (1948–50) and Milan (1950–57) he has held chairs in genetics at Parma (1958–62) and Pavia (1962–70). In 1970 he was appointed professor of genetics at Stanford University, California.

Cavalli-Sforza has specialized mainly in the genetics of human populations, producing with Walter Bodmer a comprehensive survey of the subject in their *Genetics, Evolution and Man* (1976).

He has also done much to show how genetic data from present human racial groups could be used to reconstruct their past separations. This reconstruction, based on the analysis of 58 genes, yields a bifurcated evolutionary tree with Caucasian and African races in one branch and Orientals, Oceanians, and Amerinds in the other. The main division appeared, according to Cavalli-Sforza, some 35–40 000 years ago.

CAVENDISH, Henry (b. Oct. 10, 1731; Nice, France; d. Feb. 28, 1810; London) English chemist and physicist.

Cavendish was the son of Lord Charles Cavendish, himself a fellow of the Royal Society and administrator of the British Museum. Henry was educated at Cambridge University (1749–53), but left without a degree. Following this he devoted the rest of his life to science. He inherited from his uncle a vast fortune with which he built up a large library and financed his scientific interests. Throughout his life he was an eccentric recluse, appearing only rarely in public and then chiefly at scientific meetings. He communicated with his housekeeper by a system of notes and was such a misogynist that he ordered all his female domestics to keep out of his sight.

Cavendish's first published work was *Three Papers containing Experiments on Factitious Airs* (1766). In these he clearly distinguished hydrogen ('inflammable air') and carbon dioxide ('fixed air') as gases separate from common air. Some of the work on fixed air duplicated that of Joseph Black, little of which had been published, but Cavendish was the first to weigh gases accurately.

Much of Cavendish's work remained unpublished in his lifetime and he is now known to have anticipated or come very close to several major discoveries. His electrical studies, which were edited by Clerk Maxwell in 1879, following the discovery of his notebooks and manuscripts, included the clear distinction between electrical quantity and potential, the measurement of capacitance, and the anticipation of Ohm's law (1781). He had the concept of specific heat in 1765 but the work was not published. In 1778, working on the effect of water vapor on the compressibility of air, he arrived at what is essentially the law of partial pressures (*see* John Dalton). One important physical investigation that was published was the determination of the mean density of the Earth (1798) by means of the torsion balance in what became known as the *Cavendish experiment*.

In his chemical work Cavendish came close to the concepts of equivalent weights and multiple proportions but he was not a generalizer and the concepts only became explicit in the works of others. His most illustrious and controversial work was his synthesis of water. The paper *Experiments on Air* (1784) reported his researches on exploding hydrogen with oxygen and air. He concluded that air consisted of a mixture of oxygen and nitrogen in a ratio of 1:4 and that hydrogen and oxygen mixed in proportions of 2:1 yielded their own weight of water. This work was carried out in 1781, and although Cavendish's priority is quite clear a dispute ensued between James Watt, Antoine Lavoisier, and Cavendish. It was discovered from this work that water is not an element but a compound.

The reason for Cavendish's three-year delay in publishing his work on water was the persistent discovery of nitric acid (then called nitrous acid) in the water after sparking hydrogen and air. In further experiments he accomplished the conversion of nitrogen to nitric acid by sparking over alkali, which then formed potassium nitrate. This synthesis was the basis of the commercial production of nitric acid until 1789. In the course of his work on gases Cavendish refined the eudiometer and his measurements of the oxygen content of air showed it to be the same everywhere.

On his death Cavendish left over a million pounds sterling to his relatives. From this the endowment of the famous Cavendish Laboratory was made to Cambridge University in 1871.

CAVENTOU, Jean Bienaimé (b. June 30, 1795); St. Omer, France; d. May 5, 1877; Paris) French pharmacist and organic chemist.

Caventou was the son of an army apothecary and studied pharmacy in Paris, eventually becoming professor of toxicology at the Ecole de Pharmacie (1835–60); he also had a pharmacy business. He learnt the technique of solvent extraction of alkaloids from plants from Joseph Pelletier, with whom (1817–20) he isolated the alkaloids strychnine, brucine, cinchonine, quinine, veratrine, and colchicine. Caventou and Pelletier are regarded as the founders of alkaloid chemistry. Curiously, until 1823 they believed that alkaloids contained no nitrogen when in fact they are now defined as nitrogenous substances. Caventou's early success was not repeated in later life and after Pelletier's death in 1842 he published nothing.

CAYLEY, Arthur (b. Aug. 16, 1821; Richmond, England; d. Jan. 26, 1895; Cambridge, England) British mathematician.

Cayley studied mathematics at Cambridge University, but before becoming a professional mathematician he spent 14 years working as a barrister. He was forced to do this since he was unwilling to take holy orders — at that time a necessary condition of continuing his mathematical career at Cambridge. When this requirement was dropped Cayley was able to return to Cambridge and in 1863 became Sadlerian Professor there.

Cayley was an extremely prolific mathematician. His greatest work was the creation of the theory of invariants, in which he worked closely with his friend James Joseph Sylvester. Cayley developed this theory as a branch of pure mathematics but it turned out to play a crucial role in the theory of relativity, as it is important in the calculation of space–time relationships in physics. He also developed the theory of matrices and made major contributions to the study of n-dimensional geometry. He went a considerable way toward unifying the study of geometry. Cayley also did important work in the theory of elliptic functions.

One of Cayley's notable nonmathematical achievements was playing a large role in persuading the University of Cambridge to admit women as students.

CAYLEY, Sir George (b. Dec. 27, 1773; Scarborough, England; d. Dec. 15; 1857; Scarborough) British inventor.

Cayley, a man of independent means, succeeded to the family estates on the death of his father in 1797. He had been educated at schools in York and Nottingham and had learned some science from a nonconformist clergyman who was also a fellow of the Royal Society.

Cayley is recognized as the founder of the science of aerodynamics. As early as 1799, in a design engraved on a small silver disk, he made an important step in the history of aeronautics by separating for the first time the system providing power from that contributing lift. He realized that man would never fly by flapping his arms but only by building a rigid wing to which he could attach an external power source. This was followed by a series of papers produced during the period 1804–55 in which he worked out many of the details implicit in his original idea.

Cayley designed an undercarriage fitted with tension wheels (later to find use on the bicycle) in 1808, streamlining in 1809, and a glider that was capable of lifting him up for a few yards. In the same year he produced his important paper *On aerial navigation*, which introduced the cambered wing, followed by his designs for a hot-air airship in 1816 and a helicopter in 1818. In the 1840s and 1850s he designed a large number of powered gliders, culminating in his construction of the first man-carrying glider in 1853, which was reluctantly tested by his coachman on the first successful manned glider flight in the same year.

In addition to his aeronautical works Cayley produced designs for the caterpillar tractor and for artificial limbs, and was interested in land reclamation and railroad engineering. He also founded the Regent Street Polytechnic Institution, London, in 1839.

CELSIUS, Anders (b. Nov. 27, 1701; Uppsala, Sweden; d. Apr. 25, 1744; Uppsala) Swedish astronomer.

Celsius, the son of a mathematician, was professor of astronomy at Uppsala University where he opened an observatory in 1740. In 1742 he devised a temperature scale in which the temperature of melting ice was taken as 100° and the temperature of boiling water was taken to be 0°. The modern *Celsius* (or *centigrade*) scale has the opposite fixed points (ice point 0°; steam point 100°C).

CELSUS, Aulus Cornelius (b. *c.* 10 BC) Roman encyclopedist.

Celsus, a member of a noble Roman family, was the author of a comprehensive encyclopedia of knowledge covering many topics, including agriculture, military art, and philosophy. However, only the part dealing with medicine has survived, and it is for this work, *De medicina*, that he is remembered. Comprising eight sections, it covers medical history, diet, symptoms and treatments of various diseases, surgical techniques, and drugs. Celsus's work was rediscovered by Pope Nicholas V and became, in 1478, one of the first medical texts to be printed. Its lucid and elegant Latin prose made it widely acclaimed during the Renaissance period.

CESALPINO, Andrea (b. June 6, 1519; Arezzo, Italy; d. Feb. 23, 1603; Rome) Italian physician and botanist.

Cesalpino studied anatomy and medicine at the University of Pisa, where he graduated in 1551 and in 1555 became professor of medicine and director of the botanic garden. In 1592 he became physician to Pope Clement VIII and professor at the Sapienza College.

He is most famous for his plant classification based on fruit and seed characteristics, which is described in his work, *De plantis* (1583; On Plants). This work also discusses the whole of theoretical botany and had great influence on later botanists.

Cesalpino also wrote a number of anatomical books in which he partly anticipated the theory of the circulation of the blood proposed by William Harvey.

CHADWICK, Sir James (b. Oct. 20, 1891; Macclesfield, England; d. July 24, 1974; Cambridge, England) British physicist.

Chadwick was educated at the University of Manchester, England, where he graduated in 1911 and remained as a graduate student under Ernest Rutherford. In 1913 he went to Leipzig to work under Hans Geiger and found himself interned in 1914 near Spandau as an enemy alien. There he remained for the duration of the war, cold and hungry but permitted, with the help of Walther Nernst, to carry out rudimentary research.

On his return to England in 1919 he was invited by Rutherford to accompany him to Cambridge University where from 1922 until 1935 he served as assistant director of research at the Cavendish Laboratory. It was during this period that Chadwick, in 1932, made his greatest discovery — the neutron. Before this, physicists had accepted the existence of only two elementary particles: the proton (p) with a positive charge, and the electron (e) with a negative charge. It was however clear to all that these two particles could not account for all the atomic phenomena observed. The helium atom, for example, was thought to consist of four protons; that it only possessed a positive charge of two was due to the nucleus also containing two 'internal electrons' which neutralized the charge on two of the protons. The difficulty of such a view was the failure of a disintegrating nucleus to produce the electrons supposedly contained in it.

In 1920 Rutherford had provided an alternative solution by introducing the possibility of "an atom of mass 1 which has zero nuclear charge." Chadwick attempted unsuccessfully to discover such a particle in the 1920s by bombarding aluminum with alpha particles (helium nuclei). More promising, however, was the report in 1930 that the bombardment of beryllium with alpha particles yielded a very penetrating radiation. In 1932 Irène and Frédéric Joliot-Curie found that this radiation could eject protons with considerable velocities from matter containing hydrogen. They thought such radiation consisted of gamma rays — electromagnetic radiation of very short wavelength. Chadwick showed that the gamma rays would not eject protons, but that the result was explained if the particles had nearly the same mass as protons but no charge; i.e. neutrons. It was for this work that Chadwick was awarded the 1935 Nobel Physics Prize.

By 1936 a certain amount of friction had begun to appear between Chadwick, who wished to build a cyclotron at the Cavendish Laboratory, and Rutherford who initially was violently opposed to any such project. It was therefore with some relief that Chadwick decided in 1935 to accept the offer of the chair of physics at Liverpool University. There he built Britain's first cyclotron and was on hand at the outbreak of war to support the claims made by Otto Frisch and Rudolph Peierls on the feasibility of the atomic bomb. Chadwick consequently spent most of the war in America as head of the British mission to the Manhattan project.

For this service he was knighted in 1945. He returned to Cambridge in 1958 as Master of Gonville and Caius College, in which office he remained until his retirement in 1958.

CHAIN, Ernst Boris (b. June 19, 1906; Berlin; d. Aug. 14, 1979; Ireland) German–British biochemist.

Chain, the son of a chemist, graduated in 1930 from the Friedrich-Wilhelm University with a degree in chemistry. He left Germany for England in 1933 and, after two years' research at Cambridge University, joined Howard Florey (q.v.) at Oxford. Here his brilliance as a biochemist was put to good use in the difficult isolation and purification of penicillin — work that Alexander Fleming had been unable to carry out. He shared the 1945 Nobel Prize for physiology or medicine with Florey and Fleming for this work.

After 1945 he was professor of biochemistry at the Superior Institute of Health in Rome, returning to England in 1961 for the chair of biochemistry at Imperial College, London. During this time he discovered penicillinase — an enzyme that some bacteria can synthesize and so destroy the drug. He also worked on tumor metabolism and the mode of action of insulin in diabetes.

CHAMBERLAIN, Owen (b. July 10, 1920; San Francisco, California) American physicist.

The son of a prominent radiologist, Edward Chamberlain, Owen Chamberlain followed his father's interest in physics. He graduated from Dartmouth College in 1941 and gained his doctorate in physics from the University of Chicago in 1949. From 1948 until 1950 he was an instructor in physics at the University of California at Berkeley, becoming associate professor in 1954 and professor in 1958.

The onset of America's involvement in World War II interrupted his university studies, and he spent the years 1942–1946 under the leadership of Emilio Segrè working on the Manhattan atom-bomb project at Los Alamos. There he investigated spontaneous fission of the heavy elements and nuclear cross sections. Later he worked with Enrico Fermi on neutron diffraction by liquids.

At Berkeley, Chamberlain experimented with the bevatron particle accelerator of the Lawrence Radiation Laboratory, and in 1955 (together with Segrè, C. Weigand and T. Ypsilantis) discovered the antiproton — a particle with the same mass as the proton, but of opposite (negative) charge. For their discovery, Chamberlain and Segrè received the 1959 Nobel Prize for physics. The existence of antiparticles had been predicted by Paul Dirac's theory of 1926, and the first of these, the positive electron (or positron) had been found by Carl David Anderson in cosmic radiation in 1932.

Chamberlain's more recent work has been on the interaction of antiprotons with hydrogen and deuterium, the production of antineutrons from antiprotons, and the scattering of pions. He is currently at the University of California at Berkeley.

CHAMBERLIN, Thomas Chrowder (b. Sept. 25, 1843; Mattoon, Illinois; d. Nov. 15, 1928; Chicago, Illinois) American geologist.

Chamberlin came from a farming background. His discovery of fossils in a local limestone quarry aroused his interest in geology, which he pursued at the University of Michigan. He worked for the Wisconsin Geological Survey from 1873, serving as chief geologist for the period 1876–82. From 1881 until 1904 he was in charge of the glacial division of the US Geological Survey. After a period as president of the University of Wisconsin (1887–92) he became professor of geology at the University of Chicago (1892–1918).

Apart from his work on the geological surveys, Chamberlin's most significant work was in the field of glaciation. Early work on glaciation had assumed that there had been one great ice age but James Geikie, in his *The Great Ice Age* (1874–84), had begun collecting evidence that there had been several ice ages separated by nonglacial epochs. Chamberlin contributed the chapter on North America to Geikie's work. He showed that drift deposits are composed of at least three layers and went on to establish four major ice ages, which were named the Nebraskan, Kansan, Illinoian, and Wisconsin after the states in which they were most easily studied.

Together with the astronomer Forest Moulton, Chamberlin formulated, in 1906, the planetismal hypothesis on the origin of the planets in the solar system. They supposed that a star had passed close to the Sun causing matter to be pulled out of both. Within the gravitational field of the Sun this gaseous matter would condense into small planetismals, and eventually into planets. The theory was published in *The Two Solar Families* (1928) but it has little support today as it cannot account for the distribution of angular momentum in the solar system.

CHAMISSO, Adelbert von, (Louis Charles Adélaide de) (b. Jan. 30, 1781; Cham-pagne, France; d. Aug. 21, 1838; Berlin) French–German naturalist and poet.

Chamisso studied medicine and botany at Berlin, and from 1815 to 1818 accompanied Otto Kotzebue as naturalist on his Russian scientific expedition in which an attempt was made to find a sea passage through the Arctic. In 1819 he was appointed curator of the Berlin Botanic Gardens, and in the same year studies of tunicates (primitive vertebrates) and mollusks led him to observe the occurrence of both sexual and asexual forms in their life cycles.

Chamisso is however better known as a talented lyricist and wrote a number of well-known stories, ballads, and poems.

CHANCE, Alexander Macomb (b. June 28, 1844; Birmingham, England; d. 1917; Torquay, England) British chemical industrialist.

Chance was the son of a Birmingham glassmaker who had branched out into the manufacture of soda to guarantee his supply of raw materials. In 1868 he became manager of an alkali works.

During the latter half of the 19th century the Leblanc process for producing soda was facing competition from newer methods, such as the ammonia–soda process of Ernest Solvay. Chance extended the Leblanc process, making it commercially viable, by finding a way of recovering sulfur from calcium sulfide, which was one of the waste products. His method was to pump carbon dioxide through the calcium sulfide solution, freeing hydrogen sulfide, which was then partially oxidized to sulfur.

CHANCE, Britton (b. July 24, 1913; Wilkes-Barre, Pennsylvania) American biophysicist.

Chance, an engineer's son, was educated at the University of Pennsylvania where he obtained his PhD in 1940 and where, in

1949, he was appointed to the E.R. Johnson Professorship of Biophysics.

In 1943 he carried out a spectroscopic analysis that provided firm evidence for the enzyme–substrate complex whose existence had been confidently assumed by biochemists since the beginning of the century. Working with the iron-containing enzyme peroxidase, which strongly absorbs certain wavelengths of light, he found that variations in light absorption could be precisely correlated with rates of production of the enzyme–substrate complex. This was seen as confirming the important work of Leonor Michaelis.

Chance has also contributed to one of the great achievements of modern biochemistry, namely the unraveling of the complicated maze through which energy is released at the cellular level. He found that the concentration of ADP (adenosinediphosphate) as well as oxygen concentration determined the oxidation and reduction states of the proteins in the respiratory (electron-transport) chain. His studies of changes in ADP concentration led to a better understanding of how glucose is used in the body.

CHANDLER, Seth Carlo (b. Sept. 17, 1846; Boston, Massachusetts; d. Dec. 13, 1913; Wellesley Hills, Massachusetts) American astronomer.

Chandler graduated from Harvard in 1861 and then acted as assistant to Benjamin Gould, an astronomer with the US Coast Survey, from 1861 to 1864. He remained with the Survey until 1870 when he started work as an actuary, returning to scientific work with the Harvard Observatory in 1881. From 1885 he devoted himself to private research.

Chandler is best known for his discovery of the variation in the location of the geographic poles — and, hence, of the variation in latitude of points on the Earth's surface. In 1891 he announced the discovery of a 428-day cycle during which latitude varied by 0.3 seconds. This variation in the Earth's rotation became

known as the *Chandler wobble* and was soon confirmed by the International Latitude Service, established in 1900.

CHANDRASEKHAR, Subrahmanyan (b. Oct. 19, 1910; Lahore, now in Pakistan) Indian–American astrophysicist.

Chandrasekhar studied at the Presidency College, Madras, gaining his MA in 1930. He then went to Cambridge University, England, where in 1933 he both obtained his PhD and was elected to a fellowship. In 1936 he moved to America and has worked since 1937 at the University of Chicago and the Yerkes Observatory. He became an American citizen in 1953.

Chandrasekhar's major fields of study have been stellar evolution and stellar structure and the processes of energy transfer within stars. It was known that stars could end their life either dramatically and explosively as a supernova or as an extremely small dense star of low luminosity known as a white dwarf. But what decided the particular path a star took was answered by Chandrasekhar in his *Introduction to the Study of Stellar Structure* (1939). He showed that when a star has exhausted its nuclear fuel, an inward gravitational collapse will begin. This will eventually be halted in most stars by the outward pressure exerted by a degenerate gas, i.e. a gas that is completely ionized, with the electrons stripped away from the atomic nuclei, and that is very highly compressed. The star will therefore have shrunk into an object so dense that a matchbox of it would weigh many tons.

Chandrasekhar showed that such a star would have the unusual property that the larger its mass, the smaller its radius. There will therefore be a point at which the mass of a star is too great for it to evolve into a white dwarf. He calculated this mass to be 1.4 times the mass of the Sun. This has since become known as the *Chandrasekhar limit*. A star lying above this limit must either lose mass before it can become a white dwarf or take a different evolutionary path. In support of Chandrasekhar's theoretical work, it has been established that all known white dwarfs fall within the predicted limit.

CHANG, Min Chueh (b. Oct. 10, 1908; T'aiyüan, China) Chinese–American biologist.

Chang was educated at the Tsinghua University in Peking, and at Cambridge University, England, where he obtained his PhD in 1941. He emigrated to America in 1945 and joined the Worcester Foundation in Shrewsbury, Massachusetts, where he has remained while also serving since 1961 as professor of reproductive biology at Boston University.

Chang has carried out a number of major research projects from which emerged not only greater understanding of the mechanisms of mammalian fertilization, but also such practical consequences as oral contraceptives and the transplantation of human ova fertilized *in vitro* (by Robert Edwards and Patrick Steptoe in 1978). In 1951, at the same time as Colin Austin, Chang discovered that a "period of time in the female tract is required for the spermatozoa to acquire their fertilizing capacity", a phenomenon known later as capacitation. He further demonstrated, in 1957, that there is a decapacitation factor in the seminal fluid, which, although it can be removed by centrifugation, has resisted further attempts at identification.

Chang also made the important advance in 1959 of fertilizing rabbit eggs *in vitro* and transplanting them into a recipient doe. This was followed in 1964 by comparable work for the first time with rodents. It was also Chang who provided much of the experimental basis for Gregory Pincus's 1953 paper showing that injections of progesterone into rabbits could serve as a contraceptive by inhibiting ovulation.

CHANG HENG (b. AD 78; d. 142) Chinese astronomer, mathematician, and instrument maker.

Chang Heng was the Astronomer Royal at the court of the emperors of the Later Han. Although none of his works have survived there are detailed reports of his achievements, which are, by any standard, numerous and impressive. As a mathematician he is reported to have given 3.1622 or the square root of 10 as the value of π which was as good as any other attempt of that period, apart from that of Archimedes. In astronomy he gave a detailed description of the figure of the universe in which the Earth lies at the center of a large sphere like the yolk of an egg, which was an improvement on the earlier conception of a hemispherical heaven standing over the Earth like an umbrella.

His real originality however lay in the introduction and design of scientific instruments. Thus he introduced a complete armilliary sphere at about the same time as his western contemporary, Ptolemy. This was used to determine positions of celestial bodies and consisted of an interconnected set of such main circles of the celestial sphere as the equator, ecliptic, horizon, and meridian. Chang Heng went much further and constructed one that rotated by the force of flowing water in such a way that its movement coincided with the rising and setting of the stars . What is intriguing about this is whether he had devised some primitive form of clockwork — some early escapement, preparing the way for Su Sung's water clock of the 11th century — 1200 years before Giovanni de Dondi was to introduce it into Europe.

Even more impressive is his construction of the world's first seismograph. It is clearly described as consisting of a vessel on the outside of which were eight dragon heads containing a ball. When an earthquake occurred the ball was propelled out of a dragon's mouth and caught by a bronze toad waiting underneath. Inside there was, presumably, some pendulum mechanism, which would release just one ball selectively giving the direction of the shock. It is interesting to note that the first seismograph recorded in the west, depending on the spilling of an overfilled saucer of mercury, was in 1703.

CHAPMAN, Sydney (b. Jan. 29, 1888; Eccles, England; d. June 16, 1970; Boulder, Colorado) British mathematician and geophysicist.

Chapman entered Manchester University in 1904 to study engineering. After graduating in 1907, his interest was diverted into more strictly mathematical areas, and he went to Cambridge to study mathematics, graduating in 1910. His first post was as chief assistant at the Royal Observatory, Greenwich, and his work there sparked off his lasting interest in a number of fields of applied mathematics, notably geomagnetism. In 1914 Chapman returned to Cambridge as a lecturer in mathematics, and in 1919 he moved back to Manchester as professor of mathematics, remaining there for five years. From 1924 to 1946 he was professor of mathematics at Imperial College, London. After working at the War Office during World War II he moved to Oxford to take up the Sedleian Chair in natural philosophy, from which he retired in 1953. However, his retirement meant no lessening in his teaching and research activity, which continued for many years at the Geophysical Institute, Alaska, and at the High Altitude Observatory at Boulder, Colorado.

The two main topics of Chapman's mathematical work were the kinetic theory of gases and geomagnetism. In the 19th century James Clerk Maxwell and Ludwig Boltzmann had put forward ideas about the properties of gases as determined by the motion of the molecules of the gas. Chapman's work, which he began in 1911, was the next major step in the development of a full mathematical treatment of the kinetic theory. The Swedish mathematician Enskog had been working, independently of Chapman, along similar lines, and the resulting theory is now generally known as the *Chapman–Enskog theory of gases*. While working in 1917 on mixtures of gases Chapman predicted the phenomenon of gaseous thermal diffusion. His subsequent work on the upper atmosphere was a practical application of his earlier more theoretical study of gases.

Highlights of Chapman's work on geomagnetism are his work on the variations in the Earth's magnetic field in periods of a lunar day (27.3 days) and its submultiples. This he showed to be the result of a small tidal movement set up in the Earth's atmosphere by the Moon. He also developed, in 1930, in collaboration with one of his students, what has become known as the *Chapman–Ferraro theory* of magnetic storms. In collaboration with Julius Bartels, Chapman wrote *Geomagnetism* (2 vols. 1940), which soon established itself as a standard work.

CHAPPE, Claude (b. Dec. 25, 1763; Brûlon, France; d. Jan. 23, 1805; Paris) French engineer.

Chappe, a former cleric, invented the semaphore arm-signaling system that was first used during the French Revolution to signal between Lille and Paris. His brother was a member of the Legislative Assembly and put forward Claude's idea for building a series of towers equipped with telescopes and two-arm semaphores. In 1794 it took less than an hour to semaphore to Paris the news that Condé-sur-l'Escaut had been taken from the Austrians. After others challenged his claim to be the inventor of semaphore, Chappe killed himself in a fit of depression.

CHAPTAL, Jean Antoine Claude (b. June 4, 1756; Nogaret, France; d. July 30, 1832; Paris) French chemist.

Chaptal, the son of an apothecary, studied medicine at Montpellier, graduating in 1777. He later switched to chemistry, becoming professor at Montpellier in 1781. During the French Revolution he was arrested but then released to manage the saltpeter works at Grenelle. He also helped to organize the introduction of the metric system and published a textbook, *Elémens de chimie* (1790–1803).

Chaptal is mainly remembered as an industrial chemist; he was the first to produce sulfuric acid commercially in France at his factory at Montpellier. His early paper on bleaching (1787) was translated and published in England in 1790 by Robert Kerr. In 1800 he proposed a new method of bleaching using vapor from a boiling alkaline liquor, which was soon introduced into England. Chaptal also wrote one of the first books on industrial chemistry, *Chimie appliquée aux arts* (1807; Chemistry Applied to the Arts).

CHARCOT, Jean-Martin (b. Nov. 29, 1825; Paris; d. Aug. 16, 1893; Nièvre, France) French neurologist.

Charcot studied at the University Faculty of Medicine in Paris and received his MD in 1853. His interest in disease of the nervous system led to his appointment, in 1862, to the Salpêtrière Hospital for nervous and mental disorders. This marked the beginning of a long and distinguished association. Charcot described the pathological changes associated with several degenerative conditions of the nervous system, including the disintegration of ligaments and joint surfaces (known as *Charcot's disease*) that occurs in advanced stages of locomotor ataxia. His studies of brain damage in cases of speech loss (aphasia) and epilepsy supported the findings of his contemporary, Paul Broca, that is, different bodily functions are controlled by different regions of the cerebral cortex.

In 1872, Charcot was appointed professor of pathological anatomy at the faculty of medicine and later (1882) became professor of neurology at the Salpêtrière. He was increasingly concerned with the link between mind and body in cases of hysteria and trauma. With his eloquent manner and a dramatic presentation of his lectures on a small stage, he became a widely celebrated teacher. Among many famous students was Sigmund Freud, who was influenced by Charcot's use of hypnosis on patients.

Charcot's son, Jean, became a famous polar explorer.

CHARDONNET, Louis Marie Hilaire Bernigaud, Comte de (b. May 1, 1839; Besançon, France; d. Mar. 12, 1924; Paris) French chemist.

Chardonnet acted as an assistant to Louis Pasteur while he was working on silk worms. This stimulated his interest in the chemistry of fibers and led him to search for means to produce a synthetic fiber.

In 1884 Chardonnet took out a patent for a process for producing the world's first artificial fiber, which he made by dissolving nitrocellulose in alcohol and ether, and then forcing the solution through tiny holes leaving thin threads once the solvent had evaporated. Products of the fiber, called 'Chardonnet silk' or rayon, were first exhibited in the Paris Exposition of 1889. Despite the fiber's origin in nitrocellulose it was not actually explosive but was highly flammable. Modifications to the process that made rayon less flammable enabled it to be manufactured for a mass market.

CHARGAFF, Erwin (b. Aug. 11, 1905; Czernowitz, now Chernovtsy in the Soviet Union) Austrian–American biochemist.

Chargaff gained his PhD from the University of Vienna in 1928 and then spent two years at Yale University. He returned to Europe, working first in Berlin and then at the Pasteur Institute, Paris, before returning permanently to America in 1935.

Initially Chargaff's work covered a range of biochemical fields, including lipid metabolism and the process of blood coagulation. Later his attention became concentrated on the DNA molecule, following the announcement in 1944 by Oswald Avery that the factor causing the heritable transformation of bacteria is pure DNA. Chargaff reasoned that, if this were so, there must be many more different types of DNA molecules than people had believed. He examined DNA using the recently developed techniques of paper chromatography and ultraviolet spectroscopy and found the composition of

DNA to be constant within a species but to differ widely between species. This led him to conclude that there must be as many different types of DNA as there are different species. However, some interesting and very important consistencies emerged. Firstly the number of purine bases (adenine and guanine) was always equal to the number of pyrimidine bases (cytosine and thiamine), and secondly the number of adenine bases is equal to the number of thiamine bases and the number of guanine bases equals the number of cytosine bases. This information, announced by Chargaff in 1950, was of crucial importance in constructing the Watson–Crick model of DNA.

Since 1935 Chargaff has worked at Columbia University, as professor of biochemistry from 1952 and as emeritus professor from 1974.

CHARLES, Jacques Alexandre César (b. Nov. 12, 1746; Beaugency, France; d. Apr. 7, 1823; Paris) French physicist and physical chemist.

Charles was a clerk in the finance ministry who developed an interest in science, especially in the preparation of gases. Eventually he became professor of physics at the Conservatoire des Arts et Métiers in Paris. He constructed the first hydrogen balloons, making an ascent to over 3000 meters (1.9 mi) in 1783. This feat brought him popular fame and royal patronage.

His name is chiefly remembered, however, for his discovery of *Charles's law*, which states that the volume of a fixed quantity of gas at constant pressure is inversely proportional to its temperature. Hence all gases, at the same pressure, expand equally for the same rise in temperature. Strictly speaking, the law holds only for ideal gases but it is valid for real gases at low pressures and high temperatures. Charles deduced the law in about 1787, working with oxygen, nitrogen, carbon dioxide, and hydrogen, but he did not publish it. He communicated his results to Joseph Gay-Lussac, who pub-

lished his own experimental results in 1802, six months after Dalton had also deduced the law. The priority, as Gay-Lussac himself pointed out, belongs to Charles but Gay-Lussac's figures were more accurate (and thus the law is sometimes referred to as *Gay-Lussac's law*). This law and the law formulated by Robert Boyle (q.v.) comprise the gas laws.

CHARPENTIER, Jean de (b. Dec. 7, 1786; Freiberg, now in East Germany; d. Sept. 12, 1885; Bex, Switzerland) Swiss geologist and glaciologist.

Charpentier studied under Abraham Werner at the Mining Academy at Freiberg, where his father was also a professor. He worked as an engineer in the Silesian mines before being appointed director of the Bex salt mines in 1813.

He studied the problem of the widely scattered and impressively large erratic boulders and soon rejected the current theories of their origin. The theory that these boulders were meteorites was unlikely for they were identical with other Alpine rocks. The flood theory, supported by Charles Lyell, supposed that they had been distributed by boulder-laden icebergs. However, this raised the problems of where the water had come from and where it had gone to.

Charpentier concluded that the agent responsible was glaciation and first presented his glacial theory publicly in Lucerne in 1835. He gained little support but did attract the attention of Louis Agassiz. In 1841 Charpentier published his results in his *Essai sur les glaciers* (Essay on Glaciers) but was anticipated by Agassiz's earlier publication, in 1840, of his *Etudes sur les glaciers* (Studies on Glaciers).

CHATELIER, Henri Louis Le *See* LE CHATELIER, Henri Louis.

CHERENKOV, Pavel Alekseyevich (b. July

28, 1904; Voronezh, now in the Soviet Union) Russian physicist.

Cherenkov came from a peasant family. He was educated at the University of Voronezh where he graduated in 1928. Since 1930 he has been a member of the Lebedev Institute of Physics in Moscow, serving there since 1953 as professor of experimental physics.

In 1934 Cherenkov was investigating the absorption of radioactive radiation by water when he noticed that the water was emitting an unusual blue light. At first he thought it was due simply to fluorescence but was forced to reject this idea when it became apparent that the blue radiation was independent of the composition of the liquid and depended only on the presence of fast-moving electrons passing through the medium.

It was later shown by Ilya Frank and Igor Tamm in 1937 that the radiation was caused by electrons traveling through the water with a speed greater than that of light in water (though not of course greater than that of light in a vacuum). This *Cherenkov radiation* can be produced by other charged particles and can be used as a method of detecting elementary particles. Cherenkov, Frank, and Tamm shared the Nobel Physics Prize in 1958.

CHEVREUL, Michel Eugène (b. Aug. 31, 1786; Angers, France; d. Apr. 8, 1889; Paris) French organic chemist.

One of the longest-lived of all chemists, Chevreul studied at the Collège de France (1803). He was an assistant to Antoine François de Fourcroy (1809), assistant at the Musée d'Histoire Naturelle (1810), then professor of physics at the Lycée Charlemagne (1813–30).

In 1810 Chevreul began a great program of research into fats, which was published in his classic book *Recherches chimiques sur les corps gras d'origine animale* (1823; Chemical Researches on Animal Fats). By acidification of soaps derived from animal fats and subsequent crystallization from

alcohol he was able to identify for the first time various fatty acids: oleic acid, 'margaric acid' (a mixture of stearic and palmitic acids), butyric acid, capric and caproic acids, and valeric acid. He recognized that fats are esters (called 'ethers' in the nomenclature of the day) of glycerol and fatty acids and that saponification produces salts of the fatty acids (soaps) and glycerol. In 1825 Chevreul and Joseph Gay-Lussac patented a process for making candles from crude stearic acid. Other fats investigated by Chevreul were spermaceti, lanolin, and cholesterol.

In 1824 Chevreul became director of the dyeworks for the Gobelins Tapestry, where he did important work on coloring matters, discovering hematoxylin in logwood, quercitrin in yellow oak, and preparing the reduced colorless form of indigo. He also investigated the science and art of color with special application to the production of massed color by aggregations of small monochromatic 'dots', as in the threads of a tapestry.

Chevreul's later appointments were professor of chemistry at the Musée d'Histoire Naturelle (1830) and director there (1864). His other work included the discovery of creatine (1832) and studies on the history of chemistry.

CHITTENDEN, Russell Henry (b. Feb. 18, 1856; New Haven, Connecticut; d. Dec. 26, 1943; New Haven) American physiologist and biochemist.

As part of his undergraduate course at Yale, Chittenden was asked to investigate why scallops taste sweeter when reheated from a previous meal than when freshly cooked. This project led to his discovery of glycogen and glycine in the muscle tissue — the first demonstration of the free occurrence of glycine (or glycocoll as it was then known) in nature. The work attracted the attention of Willy Kühne at Heidelberg who invited Chittenden to his laboratory. Later collaboration between Chittenden (at New Haven) and Kühne (in Heidelberg) provided a strong foundation for studies in enzymology.

Chittenden also did important work in toxicology and on the protein requirements of man, showing that the so-called Voit standard, which recommended 118 grams of protein per day, was a vast overestimate, and that good health could be maintained on 50 grams a day. He played a major part in the establishment of physiological chemistry (biochemistry) as a science in its own right.

CHLADNI, Ernst Florens Friedrich (b. Nov. 30, 1756; Wittenberg, now in East Germany; d. Apr. 3, 1827; Breslau, now Wroclaw in Poland) German physicist.

Chladni was forced to study law by his father and he obtained his degree from Leipzig in 1782. When his father died, Chladni turned to science. He is noted for his work on acoustics, being the first to analyze sound in a rigorous mathematical way. For this he invented the sand-pattern technique, in which thin metal plates covered in sand are made to vibrate. The sand collects in the nodal lines producing symmetrical patterns (called *Chladni's figures*).

Chladni also had a great interest in music and designed two musical instruments: the euphonium and the clavicylinder. He also measured the speed of sound in gases other than air by filling organ pipes with the gas and measuring the change in pitch.

Chladni was one of the first scientists to believe that meteorites fell from the sky but his opinion was treated with disdain, until Jean Baptiste Biot proved him to be correct in 1803.

CHOU KUNG (*fl.* 12th century BC) Chinese mathematician.

Chou Kung, or the duke of Chou, was the brother of Wu Wang, the founder of the Chou dynasty. He served briefly as regent on his brother's death.

He is remembered for his name in the *Chou-li*, one of the earliest Chinese mathematical works, in which he supposedly takes part in a dialog with someone called Shang Kao. The dialog was thought to date back to the time of Chou Kung but scholars now think this extravagant. Although they are prepared to accept some parts as going back to the sixth century BC, the bulk of it they assign to the Hab dynasty (200 BC – AD 200). The work is important in providing hard evidence for the state of early Chinese mathematics.

The most significant feature of the work is a demonstration of the truth of Pythagoras's theorem for triangles with sides of 3, 4, and 5 units. The 'proof', described as 'piling up the rectangles', is purely diagrammatic. The work also shows knowledge of the multiplication and division of fractions, the finding of common denominators, and the extraction of square roots.

Compared with Greek works of a comparable period, such as Archimedes, the work is unimpressive and gives little indication of future achievement.

CHRISTIE, Sir William Henry Mahoney (b. Oct. 1, 1845; London; d. Jan. 22, 1922; at sea) British astronomer.

Christie was the grandson of the founder of the firm of auctioneers and the son of a mathematician. He graduated from Cambridge University in 1868 and immediately joined the staff of the Royal Greenwich Observatory. He later served from 1881–1910 as Astronomer Royal and was knighted in 1904.

During Christie's period of office the observatory saw considerable expansion and refurbishment. The Physical Observatory, later known as the South Building, was built at Greenwich from 1891–99 and equipped with new telescopes: a 28-inch (71-cm) refractor for visual use and a 26-inch (66-cm) for photographic purposes were provided in the 1890s.

The Observatory agreed to cooperate in an international project, involving 18 observatories, to produce the first photographic chart of the heavens. The ambitious project was proposed by the director of the Paris Observatory, Admiral E. Mouchez, in 1887 and the chart became known as the 'Carte du Ciel'. The Royal Observatory was made responsible for the necessary observations and measurements for the large area of the sky from the north celestial pole to 65°N declination. This work was completed and published by 1909, long after the estimated time but before the other participants had finished.

Christie's own research was spent mainly on sunspot activity in collaboration with Edward Maunder and on unsuccessful attempts to measure stellar radial velocities.

CHU SHIH-CHIEH (*fl.* 1300) Chinese mathematician.

Little seems to be known about the life of Chu Shih-Chieh other than that he traveled around China teaching mathematics and that he wrote two important works, the *Introduction to Mathematical Studies* (1299) and, one of the high-water marks of Chinese mathematics, the *Precious Mirror of the Four Elements* (1303).

The first work states clearly the rule of signs for both algebraic addition and multiplication. Its treatment of negative signs, elementary as it may now seem, contrasts markedly with the practice of the ancients and the medieval West in ignoring them.

The second work contains an advanced treatment of equations both simple and higher. It begins with a remarkably clear diagram of what came to be known as Pascal's triangle. He also produced the first formula in China for the sum of arithmetical progressions.

CLAIRAUT, Alexis-Claude (b. May 7, 1713; Paris; d. May 17, 1765; Paris) French mathematician and physicist.

Clairaut contributed to many fields of science, chief among these being mathematics, physics, and geodesy. He was a child prodigy and was elected to the Paris Academy of Sciences for promising work in geometry when he was only 18. after joining the academy Clairaut developed a lively interest in geodesy. He was an early supporter of Newton at a time when his views were not yet popular in France. Clairaut is known to have studied mathematics briefly with Johann I Bernoulli in Basel.

In 1736 Clairaut's interest in geodesy took a practical turn when he embarked on an expedition to Lapland led by Pierre Maupertuis. This was undertaken in order to measure a meridian arc of one degree inside the Arctic Circle. This expedition successfully completed (1737), Clairaut's interests reverted to more mathematical matters and in particular to what was then known as 'celestial mechanics', as pioneered by Newton. Clairaut's enthusiasm for the ideas of Newton led him to collaborate on preparing a French translation of Newton's great work, the *Principia*. Clairaut also added a considerable amount of explanatory material of his own to clarify Newton's ideas and much of his best work found its way into these often extensive explanatory additions. This translation was a great influence in popularizing Newton's ideas in France.

Clairaut's best and most important writings are devoted chiefly to mathematical astronomy and to algebra and geometry. He made valuable contributions to the development of the calculus and to the study of differential equations. He also did notable work in practical optics, which he put to good use in designing better telescopes, and was particularly interested in Newton's corpuscular theory of light. Clairaut wrote influential treatises on algebra and geometry.

CLAISEN, Ludwig (b. Jan. 14, 1851; Cologne, now in West Germany; d. Jan. 5, 1930; Godesberg, now in West Germany) German organic chemist.

Claisen gained his PhD under Friedrich Kekulé at Bonn, later becoming professor at Kiel (1897–1904) and honorary professor at Berlin.

He is best known for the condensation reactions that bear his name. The *Claisen–Schmidt condensation* is a method of synthesizing α,β-unsaturated aldehydes and ketones, by reaction of an aldehyde with another aldehyde or a ketone. This type of reaction was first discovered by J. Gustav Schmidt in Zurich (1880). The *Claisen condensation* (1890) involves condensation between similar or different esters, or esters and ketones, in the presence of sodium ethoxide to give unsaturated esters. The *Claisen flask*, used for vacuum distillation, was developed in 1893. Claisen also made an important contribution to the study of tautomerism by isolating (simultaneously with Johannes Wislicenus) the keto and enol forms of acetyldibenzoylmethane and dibenzoylacetone.

CLARK, Alvan Graham (b. July 10, 1832; Fall River, Massachusetts; d. June 9, 1897; Cambridge, Massachusetts) American astronomer and instrument maker.

Clark was the son of the instrument-maker, Alvan Clark. He started life as a portrait painter but soon joined his father's firm and became a lens grinder, preparing the mirrors and lenses for some of the best telescopes of the late 19th century. In 1861 he had made a lens for Edward Barnard at the University of Mississippi. Testing it before parting with it he looked through it at Sirius and to his surprise observed a faint image near the star. It was, in fact, Sirius B, the famous companion predicted by Friedrich Bessel in 1844. Clark made many more observations, and discovered 16 double stars.

The Clark firm provided Simon Newcomb, head of the US Naval Observatory, with a 26-inch (66-cm) refractor. It was with this that the very small satellites of Mars, Phobos, and Deimos were detected by Asaph Hall in 1877. In 1888 Clark built the 36-inch (91-cm) refractor for the Lick Observatory and his final achievement, just before his death, was to install his 40-inch (101-cm) refractor in the Yerkes Observatory. A practical limit is reached in using lenses larger than this and after Clark's death astronomers put their faith in mirrors rather than lenses. For this reason the Lick 36-inch and the Yerkes 40-inch are still the largest and the second largest refractors in the world.

CLARK, Sir Wilfrid Edward Le Gros *See* LE GROS CLARK, Sir Wilfrid Edward.

CLARKE, Sir Cyril Astley (b. Aug. 22, 1907; Leicester; England) British physician.

Clarke was educated at the University of Cambridge and Guy's Hospital, London, where he qualified in 1932. He remained at Guy's until 1936 when he engaged in life-insurance work before spending the war years in the Royal Navy. From 1946 Clarke worked as a consultant physician in Liverpool until 1958 when he joined the staff of the university. Here he later served as professor of medicine from 1965 to 1972 and also, from 1963 to 1972, as director of the Nuffield unit of medical genetics.

Although a consultant physician Clarke was also a skilled amateur lepidopterist. In 1952 he became interested in the genetics of the wing colors of swallowtail butterflies and began a collaboration with Philip Sheppard, a professional geneticist who later became a colleague at Liverpool University. In particular, they worked on the inheritance of mimicry in the wing patterns of certain swallowtails. They noted that the gene controlling the wing pattern is actually a group of closely linked genes behaving as a single unit — a supergene. They also found that even though the males also carry such supergenes, the patterns only show in the females.

At this point Clarke was struck by certain striking parallels between the inheritance of swallowtail wing patterns and human blood types. Above all it aroused his interest in Rhesus babies. This condition arises when a Rh-negative mother, that is someone whose blood lacks the Rh factor or antigen, and a Rh-positive father produce a Rh-positive child. Occasionally the fetus's blood leaks from the placenta into the mother's blood and stimulates the production of Rh antibodies. This will cause her to destroy unwittingly the red cells of any subsequent Rh-positive babies she may carry.

Clarke and Sheppard puzzled over how to prevent the mother producing the destructive Rh antibodies. The answer eventually came from Clarke's wife who in an inspired moment told him to inject the Rh-negative mothers with Rh-antibodies. As this is what destroys the blood of the fetus in the first place, the answer initially sounds absurd. However the Rh-antibodies should destroy incompatible Rh-positive cells before the mother's own antibody machinery acted, that is, before the mother could become sensitized to Rh-positive blood.

In 1964 Clarke and his colleagues were able to announce a major breakthrough in preventive medicine. Since then thousands of women have received injections of Rh-antibodies with only a few failures.

CLAUDE, Albert (b. Aug. 24, 1898; Longlier, Belgium) Belgian–American cell biologist.

Claude was educated at the University of Liège where he obtained his doctorate in 1928. He joined the staff of the Rockefeller Institute, New York, in 1929 and in 1941 adopted American citizenship. Claude returned to Belgium in 1948 to serve as director of the Jules Bordet Research Institute, a post he retained until his retirement in 1972.

In the 1930s Claude attempted to purify Peyton Rous's chicken sarcoma virus (RSV) using a centrifuge. He succeeded in producing a fraction with an enhanced sarcogenic power, noting that small granules containing nucleoprotein were present. Suspecting these granules to be the cause of the RSV, he was somewhat surprised to find similar granules present in centrifuged cells taken from uninfected chicken embryo.

Over the next 20 years, using electron microscopes as well as improved centrifuges, Claude began to chart the constitution of the protoplasm. Although the mitochondria had first been described as early as 1897, Claude was able to distinguish them from what he originally termed 'microsomes'. Among such microsomes he could make out a 'lacelike reticulum' spread throughout the cytoplasm, a structure later named the endoplasmic reticulum. Another member of Claude's laboratory, George Palade, went on to identify the ribosome.

For his work in opening up the study of cell structures Claude shared the 1974 Nobel Prize for physiology or medicine with Palade and Christian de Duve.

CLAUDE, Georges (b. Sept. 24, 1870; Paris; d. May 23, 1960; St. Cloud, France) French chemist.

Claude was educated at the Ecole de Physique et Chimie after which he worked as an engineer in various industries.

Claude made a number of important contributions to technology, including the discovery (1886) that acetylene (ethyne) could be handled with safety if dissolved in acetone, and a method of liquefying air (1902), which he used for the large-scale production of nitrogen and oxygen. In 1910 he introduced neon lighting, using neon gas at low pressure excited by an electric discharge to emit a bright red light.

The latter part of his life was, however, less successful. From 1926 onward he worked on new sources of energy. In particular, he tried to show how it could be extracted from the temperature difference between the surface and the bottom of the sea. Although his argument was sound he never overcame the formidable engineering difficulties.

Although an old man of 75 when World War II ended Claude was imprisoned as a Vichy sympathizer.

CLAUSIUS, Rudolf Julius Emmanuel (b. Jan. 2, 1822; Köslin, now Koszalin in Poland; d. Aug. 24, 1888; Bonn, now in West Germany) German physicist.

Clausius studied at the University of Berlin and obtained his doctorate from Halle in 1848. He was professor of physics at the Royal Artillery and Engineering School, Berlin (1850–55) and professor of mathematical physics at Zurich (1855–67). He then transferred to the University of Würzburg (1867) and, from there, moved to Bonn (1869).

He is noted for his formulation of what is now known as the second law of thermodynamics. Clausius arrived at this by considering the theorem of Sadi Carnot on heat engines and attempting to reconcile this with the mechanical theory of heat, which was developing at the time. In 1850 he published a famous paper *Uber die bewegende Kraft der Wärme* (On the Motive Force of Heat), in which he first introduced the principle that "it is impossible by a cyclic process to transfer heat from a colder to a warmer reservoir without net changes in other bodies." An alternative statement of this, the second law, is "heat does not flow spontaneously from a colder to a hotter body." The second law of thermodynamics was independently recognized by Lord Kelvin.

Clausius gave the law a mathematical statement in 1854 and published a number of papers on the topic over the next few years. In 1865 he introduced the term 'entropy' as a measure of the availability of heat. The change in entropy of a system is the heat absorbed or lost at a given temperature divided by the temperature. An increase in entropy corresponds to a lower availability of heat for performing work.

The second law of thermodynamics is one of the fundamental principles of physics. It describes the fact that, although the total energy in a system is conserved, the availability of energy for performing work is lost. Clausius showed that in any nonideal (irreversible) process the entropy increases. The first and second laws of thermodynamics are encapsulated in his famous statement, "The energy of the universe is a constant; the entropy of the universe always tends toward a maximum."

Clausius also followed the work of James Joule on the kinetic theory of gases, introducing the ideas of effective diameter and mean free path (the average distance between collisions). A contribution to electrochemistry was his idea that substances dissociated into ions on solution. In the field of electrodynamics he produced a theoretical expression for the force between two moving electrons — a formula later used by Hendrik Lorentz.

CLEMENCE, Gerald Maurice (b. Aug. 16, 1908; Smithfield, Rhode Island; d. Nov. 22, 1974; Providence, Rhode Island) American astronomer.

Clemence studied mathematics at Brown University, Rhode Island. After graduating he joined the staff of the US Naval Observatory in 1930 where he remained until 1963, serving as head astronomer and director of the Nautical Almanac from 1945 to 1958 and science director of the Observatory from 1958. In 1963 he was appointed senior research associate and lecturer at Yale, becoming professor of astronomy in 1966, a post he held until his death.

Clemence's work was primarily concerned with the orbital motions of the Earth, Moon, and planets. In 1951, in collaboration with Dirk Brouwer and W.J. Eckert, Clemence published the basic paper *Coordinates of the Five Outer Planets 1653–2060*. This was a considerable advance on the tables for the outer planets calculated by Simon Newcomb and George W. Hill 50 years earlier. Clemence and his colleagues calculated the precise positions of the outer planets at 40-day intervals over a period of 400 years. It was the first time that the influence of the planets on each other was calculated at each step instead of the prevailing custom of assuming that the paths of all except one were known in advance.

Such an ambitious scheme was only

made possible by the emergence of high-speed computers, one of which was made available to them by IBM from 1948. For each step some 800 multiplications and several hundred other arithmetical operations were required and would, Clemence commented, have taken a human computer 80 years if he could have completed the work without committing any errors en route.

Clemence also conceived the idea that Brouwer named 'Ephemeris Time', by which time could be determined very accurately from the orbital positions of the Moon and the Earth. This followed the discovery that the Earth's period of rotation was not constant and should not therefore be used in the measurement of time. Ephemeris Time eventually came into use in 1958, although it has been superseded for most purposes by the more convenient and even more accurate atomic time scale.

CLEVE, Per Teodor (b. Feb. 10, 1840; Stockholm; d. June 18, 1905; Uppsala, Sweden) Swedish chemist.

Cleve became assistant professor of chemistry at the University of Uppsala in 1868 and later was made professor of general and agricultural chemistry at Uppsala. He is mainly remembered for his work on the rare earth elements.

In 1874 Cleve concluded that didymium was in fact two elements; this was proved in 1885 and the two elements were named neodymium and praseodymium. In 1879 he showed that the element scandium, newly discovered by Lars Nilson, was in fact the eka-boron predicted by Dmitri Mendeleev in his periodic table. In the same year, working with a sample of erbia from which he had removed all traces of scandia and ytterbia, Cleve found two new earths, which he named holmium, after Stockholm, and thulium, after the old name for Scandinavia. Holmium in fact turned out to be a mixture for, in 1886, Lecoq de Boisbaudran discovered that it contained the new element dysprosium.

Cleve is also remembered as the teacher of Svante Arrhenius.

COBLENTZ, William Weber (b. Oct. 25, 1873; North Lima, Ohio; d. Sept. 15, 1962; Washington DC) American physicist.

Coblentz, the son of a farmer, was educated at the Case Institute of Technology and at Cornell, where he obtained his PhD in 1903. In 1904 he joined the National Bureau of Standards in Washington and in the following year founded the radiometry section of the bureau, where he remained until his retirement in 1945.

Coblentz worked mainly on studies of infrared radiation. At the Lick Observatory he began, in 1914, a series of measurements aimed at determining the heat radiated by stars. He was also one of the pioneers of absorption spectroscopy in the infrared region as a technique for identifying compounds.

COCKCROFT, Sir John Douglas (b. May 27, 1897; Todmorden, England; d. Sept. 18, 1967; Cambridge, England) British physicist.

Cockcroft entered Manchester University, England, in 1914 to study mathematics, but left the following year to join the army. After World War I he was apprenticed to the engineering firm Metropolitan Vickers, which sent him to study electrical engineering at the Manchester College of Technology. He later went to Cambridge University, graduated in mathematics, and joined Ernest Rutherford's team at the Cavendish Laboratory.

Cockcroft soon became interested in designing a device for accelerating protons and, with E. T. S. Walton, constructed a voltage multiplier. Using this Cockcroft and Walton bombarded nuclei of lithium with protons and, in 1932, brought about the first nuclear transformation by artificial means:

$$^7_3 Li + ^1_1 H \longrightarrow ^4_2 He + ^4_2 He + 17.2 \; MeV$$

For this work Cockcroft and Walton received the 1951 Nobel Prize for physics. During World War II Cockcroft played a leading part in the development of radar. In 1940 he visited America as a member of the Tizard mission to negotiate exchanges of military, scientific, and technological information. In 1944 he became director of the Anglo-Canadian Atomic Energy Commission. He returned to Britain in 1946 to direct the new Atomic Energy Research Establishment at Harwell and remained there until 1959, when he was appointed master of Churchill College, Cambridge, a new college devoted especially to science and technology. Cockcroft received a knighthood in 1948.

COCKER, Edward (b. 1631; d. 1675; London) English engraver and mathematician.

Cocker was famous for writing and engraving a very influential and popular textbook, the *Arithmetic* (1678). He was also a teacher of arithmetic and writing. Cocker produced notable textbooks on other subjects, including several writing manuals and an English dictionary but none of these rivaled in popularity his book on arithmetic, which went through over 100 editions. Cocker is mentioned by Samuel Pepys who thought his skill as an engraver sufficient to comment favorably on it in his *Diary*.

COHEN, Seymour Stanley (b. Apr. 30, 1917; New York City) American biochemist.

Cohen was educated in New York, at the City College and at Columbia, where he obtained his PhD in 1941. He joined the University of Pennsylvania in 1943, serving as professor of biochemistry from 1954 until 1971, when he moved to the University of Denver, Colorado, as professor of microbiology. Cohen returned to New York in 1976 to take the chair of pharmaceutical sciences at the State University, Stony Brook.

In 1946 Cohen began a series of studies in molecular biology using the technique of radioactive labeling. The common microorganism *Escherichia coli* could be infected in the laboratory with the bacteriophage known as T2. Within a matter of minutes the bacterial cell would burst releasing several hundred replicas of the invading T2. The problem was to understand the process. It was known that phages were nucleoproteins consisting of a protein coat surrounding a mass of nucleic acid (DNA in the case of T2). But, as Cohen realized, nucleic acid differed from protein in containing measurable amounts of phosphorus. This could in theory be traced through any biochemical reaction by labeling it with the radioactive isotope phosphorus–32.

Cohen used this technique in a number of experiments in the late 1940s that suggested rather than demonstrated the vital role of DNA in heredity. It was not until 1952, when Alfred Hershey and Martha Chase used Cohen's labeling technique, that more substantial results were available.

COHN, Ferdinand Julius (b. Jan. 24, 1828; Breslau, now Wroclaw in Poland; d. June 25, 1898; Breslau) German botanist and bacteriologist.

Cohn was an extremely intelligent child and progressed through school rapidly, being admitted to the philosophy department at Breslau University at the early age of 14. He later developed an interest in botany but was prevented from graduating at Breslau by the university's anti-Semitic regulations. He therefore moved to Berlin, where he received his doctorate in botany in 1847.

Cohn returned to Breslau, becoming professor of botany there in 1872. He had long argued that the state should be responsible for the establishment of botanical research institutes, and as a result of his campaign the world's first institute for plant physiology was set up in Breslau in 1866. Cohn was director of this institute until his death and in 1870 he founded the journal *Beiträge zur Biologie der Pflanzen*, mainly for the purpose of publishing work carried out at Breslau.

Cohn's early research concentrated on the morphology and life histories of the microscopic algae and fungi, which led to his demonstration that the protoplasm of plant and animal cells is essentially similar. Later, stimulated by the work of Louis Pasteur, he became increasingly interested in bacteria. His classic treatise *Untersuchungen über Bacterien* (Researches on Bacteria), published in his journal in 1872, laid the foundations of modern bacteriology. In it he defined bacteria, used the constancy of their external form to divide them into four groups, and described six genera under these groups. This widely accepted classification was the first systematic attempt to classify bacteria and its fundamental divisions are still used in today's nomenclature.

Although Cohn did not believe in the theory of spontaneous generation he was aware that bacteria could develop in boiled infusions kept in sealed containers. He postulated the existence of a resistant developmental stage and through careful observation was able to demonstrate the formation of heat-resistant spores by *Bacillus subtilis*.

Through his book *Die Pflanze* (1872) and the printing of many of his popular lectures, Cohn presented the study of biology to a wide and appreciative public. He was also responsible for the publication of Robert Koch's important work on the life cycle of the anthrax bacillus. Before his death Cohn published the first three volumes of his cryptogam (non-seed-bearing) flora of Silesia.

COHNHEIM, Julius (b. July 20, 1839; Demmin, now in East Germany; d. Aug. 15, 1884; Leipzig, now in East Germany) German pathologist.

Cohnheim graduated from the University of Berlin in 1861, remaining there as assistant to the pathologist Rudolf Virchow. He later held chairs of pathological anatomy at Kiel, Breslau, and, from 1878, at Leipzig, until his death from gout complications.

Cohnheim threw considerable light on the process of inflammation. He inflicted relatively minor wounds on the tongue and intestines of frogs and observed the consequences. He noted that at the site of injury large numbers of white blood cells (leukocytes) pass through the walls of the veins to produce the swelling characteristic of inflammation. This disproved Virchow's theory that pus corpuscles originate at the point of wounding and showed them instead to be disintegrated leukocytes.

Cohnheim also did important work on tuberculosis, confirming Jean Villemin's theory that the disease is contagious by injecting tuberculous material into the chamber of a rabbit's eye and watching its development through the transparent cornea.

Cohnheim's technique of freezing material before sectioning is now a standard laboratory practice.

COLOMBO, Matteo Realdo (b. *c.* 1516; Cremona, Italy; d. 1559; Rome) Italian anatomist.

A pupil of the famous anatomist Andreas Vesalius, Colombo succeeded his teacher to the chair of anatomy at Padua University. His book, *De re anatomica*, published after his death in 1559, contained descriptions of the pleura, peritoneum, and other organs that were more accurate than preceding ones. However, his most important contribution to medicine was to demonstrate that blood from the lungs returns to the heart via the pulmonary vein.

COMPTON, Arthur Holly (b. Sept. 10, 1892; Wooster, Ohio; d. Mar. 15, 1962; Berkeley, California) American physicist.

Compton came from a distinguished intellectual family. His father, Elias, was a professor of philosophy at Wooster College while his brother, Karl, also a physicist, became president of the Massachusetts Institute of Technology. He was educated at Wooster College and at Princeton, where he obtained his PhD in 1916. He began his career by teaching at the University of Minnesota and, after two years with the Westinghouse Corporation in Pittsburgh, he returned to academic life when in 1920 he was appointed professor of physics at Washington University, St. Louis, Missouri. The main part of his career however was spent at the University of Chicago where he served as professor of physics from 1923 to 1945. Compton then returned to Washington University first as chancellor and then (1953–61) as professor of natural philosophy.

Compton is best remembered for the discovery and explanation in 1923 of the effect named for him for which, in 1927, he shared the Nobel Physics Prize with Charles T. R. Wilson. Compton was investigating the scattering of x-rays by light elements such as carbon, and found that some of the scattered radiation had an increased wavelength, an increase that varied with the angle of scattering. According to classical physics there should be no such change, for it is difficult to see how the scattering of a wave can increase its wavelength, and Compton was led to seek its explanation elsewhere.

He thus assumed that the x-rays also exhibited particle-like behavior. Hence they could collide with an electron, being scattered and losing some of their energy in the process. This would lead to a lowering of the frequency with a corresponding increase in the wavelength. Compton went on to work out the formula that would predict the change of wavelength produced in the secondary x-rays and found that his precise predictions were fully confirmed by measurements made of cloud–chamber tracks by Wilson. Significantly, this was to provide the first hard experimental evidence for the dual nature of electromagnetic radiation; that is, that it could behave both as a wave and a particle. This would be developed much further in the 1920s as

one of the cornerstones of the new quantum physics.

In the 1930s Compton concentrated on a major investigation into the nature of cosmic rays. The crucial issue, following the work of Robert Millikan, was whether or not a variation in the distribution of cosmic rays with latitude could be detected. Such an effect would show that the rays were charged particles, deflected by the Earth's magnetic field, and not electromagnetic radiation. As a result of much travel and the organization of a considerable amount of the research and measurements of others Compton was by 1938 able to establish conclusively that there was a clearly marked latitude effect.

During the war Compton was an important figure in the manufacture of the atomic bomb. He was a member of the committee directing research on the Manhattan project. He also set up at Chicago the Metallurgical Laboratory, which acted as a cover for the construction of the first atomic pile under the direction of Enrico Fermi and took responsibility for the production of plutonium. Compton later wrote a full account of this work in his book *Atomic Quest* (1956).

CONANT, James Bryant (b. Mar. 26, 1893; Dorchester, Massachusetts; d. Feb. 11, 1978; Hanover, New Hampshire) American chemist.

Conant studied at Harvard, gaining his PhD in 1916, was professor of chemistry there (1919–33), and then president (1933–53). He had a multifaceted career as a research chemist, administrator, diplomat, and educationalist. In the research phase he worked on organic reaction mechanisms and he also showed that oxyhemoglobin contains ferrous iron (1923). During World War II he was head of the National Defense Research Committee and deputy head of the Office of Scientific Research and Development; he played an important role in the development of the atomic bomb. On retiring from Harvard he became commissioner and then ambassador to Germany (1953–57), and wrote many controversial books on education.

CONDAMINE, Charles Marie de La *See* LA CONDAMINE, Charles Marie de.

CONON of Samos (*fl.* 245 BC; Alexandria, Egypt) Greek mathematician and astronomer.

Conon settled in Alexandria and was employed as court astronomer to the Egyptian monarch Ptolemy III. None of Conon's own writings survive and what is known of his work is through secondhand references to him by other Greek mathematicians. For example, Conon's work on conics was made use of by Apollonius of Perga in his famous treatise on conics.

Among Conon's activities as an astronomer was the compilation of tables of the times of the rising and setting of the stars, known as the *parapegma*. He was also responsible for naming a constellation of stars. The consort of Ptolemy III, Berenice II, presented her hair as an offering at the temple of Aphrodite. This disappeared and Conon claimed that the hair now hung as a new constellation of stars, which he named Coma Berenices ('Berenice's Hair').

Conon was known to have been a friend of Archimedes and it is probable that the 'Spiral of Archimedes', a mathematical curve, was in fact Conon's discovery.

CONYBEARE, William Daniel (b. June 7, 1787; St. Botolph, England; d. Aug. 12, 1857; Itchen Stoke, England) British geologist.

Conybeare, the son of a clergyman, was educated at Oxford University. He entered the Church himself and was vicar of Axminster, Devon, before being made dean of Llandaff in Wales in 1844.

He became interested in geology and was an early member of the Geological Society, founded in 1807. His most significant work was *Outlines of the Geology of England and Wales*, which was published in collaboration with William Phillips in 1822. In this influential work fossils were used to date sedimentary strata and the stratigraphy of British rocks was outlined beginning with the 350-million-year-old Carboniferous, which they named from its abundant carbon deposits.

Conybeare also wrote on the geology of the coalfields of the Bristol area with William Buckland and was one of the first to use geological cross-sections. He participated in the dramatic discoveries of the remains of giant reptiles and was instrumental in the naming of Gideon Mantell's iguanodon from the Tilgate Forest in Sussex and of Buckland's Megalosaurus. In 1824 he succeeded in reconstructing the plesiosaur from its remains, claiming it as a link between the ichthyosaur and the crocodiles.

In theory, he largely followed his friend Buckland in attempting to explain the structure of the Earth and the disappearance of species in terms of a series of catastrophes. He thus argued strongly against Charles Lyell.

COOK, James (b. Oct. 27, 1728; Marston, England; d. Feb. 14, 1778; Kealakekua Bay, Hawaii) British navigator and explorer.

Cook was the son of a Scottish farm laborer. He was educated at the local village school and joined the Royal Navy as an able seaman in 1755. He became a ship's master in 1759, spending eight years on survey work before being appointed by the Royal Society to take command of the *Endeavour* in 1768 on its voyage to the islands of Tahiti. He made two further major voyages of discovery in 1772–75 and in 1776.

In many ways Cook's journeys were the first modern voyages. Cook's voyage in 1768 was to be the first of the great scientific expeditions that were to become so common in the following century. One of his main duties was to carry Royal Society observers to Tahiti to watch the transit of

Venus across the Sun; transits of planets across the Sun were valuable for determining the distance between the Earth and the Sun. The scientists on board included the distinguished naturalists Joseph Banks and his assistant, Daniel Solander, and the expedition also carried artists to maintain a visual record.

The voyage's second main objective was to discover the southern continent, Terra Australis, which was believed to exist. It was assumed that the northern land mass of Eurasia must be symmetrically balanced by a southern land mass. Cook found New Zealand and extensively charted this over a period of six months and then, continuing his voyage, sighted the southeast coast of Australia on 19 April, 1770. He continued up the east coast of Australia, charting this and successfully navigating the treacherous Great Barrier Reef. The *Endeavour* returned to England with a vast collection of scientific observations. Cook also won fame for preventing any of his crew members from dying of scurvy by insisting on a diet that included forms of fresh fruit and vegetables.

Cook led a second expedition (1772–75) to the South Seas in the *Resolution* and the *Adventure* in which he circumnavigated the high latitudes and traveled as far south as latitude 72°. He discovered new lands, including New Caledonia and the South Sandwich Islands, but found no trace of the 'great southern continent'. It was also on the second voyage that the chronometer was used as a standard issue after its successful testing. Before 1772 navigators determined their longitude either by guesswork or by some very complicated calculations based on the Moon. Now, merely by noting the time and making comparatively simple calculations, it was possible to determine positions east or west of Greenwich. On his return he was made a fellow of the Royal Society and, for his paper on scurvy and its prevention, was awarded the Copley Medal.

Cook's third voyage (1776), again in the *Resolution*, ended in disaster. In trying to recover one of the ship's boats, which had been stolen by Polynesian islanders, Cook was attacked and killed by the natives on the beach of Kealakekua Bay.

COOKE, Sir William Fothergill (b. May 4, 1806; London; d. June 25, 1879; Farnham, England) British physicist.

William Cooke was the son of a surgeon. After a period spent at Durham and Edinburgh Universities he joined the Indian Army and, on his return, started to study medicine at Heidelberg, but his interest was caught by the practical potential of the electric telegraph.

Returning to England in 1837, he entered into partnership with Charles Wheatstone and, together, they patented many telegraphic alarm systems for use on the railroads. Cooke received his knighthood in 1869.

COOPER, Leon Neil (b. Feb. 28, 1930; New York City) American physicist.

Cooper was educated at Columbia where he obtained his PhD in 1954. After brief spells at the Institute for Advanced Study, Princeton, the University of Illinois, and Ohio State University, he moved in 1958 to Brown University, Providence, and was later (1962) appointed to a professorship of physics.

Cooper's early work was in nuclear physics. In 1955 he began work with John Bardeen (q.v.) and John Robert Schrieffer on the theory of superconductivity. In 1956 he showed theoretically that at low temperatures electrons in a conductor could act in bound pairs (now called *Cooper pairs*). Bardeen, Cooper, and Schrieffer showed that such pairs act together with the result that there is no electrical resistance to flow of electrons through the solid. The resulting BCS theory stimulated further theoretical and experimental work on superconductivity and won its three authors the 1972 Nobel Prize for physics.

Cooper has also worked on the superfluid state at low temperatures and, in a different field, on the theory of the central nervous system.

COPE, Edward Drinker (b. July 28, 1840; Philadelphia, Pennsylvania; d. Apr. 12, 1897; Philadelphia) American vertebrate paleontologist and comparative anatomist.

Educated in his home town of Philadelphia, Cope displayed an interest in natural history from earliest youth. From 1864 to 1867 he was professor of comparative zoology and botany at Haverford College, Pennsylvania. In 1872 Cope joined the US Geological Survey, and was subsequently professor of geology and mineralogy (1889–95) and of zoology and comparative anatomy (1895–97) at the University of Pennsylvania.

Cope's early studies were mainly concerned with living fishes, reptiles, and amphibians, and in 1861 he went to Washington to study the Smithsonian Institution's herpetological collections. Having resigned from his Haverford College professorship in order to be free to study and collect North American animals, Cope's interests gradually began to turn to fossils, and it was during his long association with the US Geological Survey that he made the valuable contributions to paleontological knowledge associated with his name. During explorations of western America, from Texas to Wyoming, Cope discovered a great many new species of extinct (Tertiary) vertebrates (fishes, reptiles, mammals, etc.). Like his rival Othniel Marsh he is credited with the discovery of about 1000 species of fossils new to science. With Joseph Leidy he described those fossils collected by the Ferdinand Hayden Survey in Wyoming. He also traced the evolutionary history of the horse and other mammals, proposed a theory for the origin and evolution of mammalian teeth (since somewhat modified), and made important contributions to knowledge of the stratigraphy of North America, indicating parallels with European strata.

Cope was a leading paleontological protagonist for the revival of Jean Baptiste Lamarck's theory of the inheritance of acquired characters, based on his own experience and theory of kinetogenesis, which suggested that the limbs and other moving parts of an animal were altered and modified according to their use or disuse. Cope's Lamarckian views were elaborated in *The Origin of the Fittest* (1886) and *Primary Factors in Organic Evolution* (1896).

In 1878 Cope became editor of the *American Naturalist* but soon resigned owing to differences with Marsh, head of the US Geological Survey.

COPERNICUS, Nicolaus (b. Feb. 19, 1473; Torun, Poland; d. May 24, 1543; Frauenburg, now in Poland) Polish astronomer.

Following the death of his father, a merchant, in 1484 Copernicus was brought up by his maternal uncle Lucas, the bishop of Ermeland. In 1491 he entered the University of Cracow where he became interested in astronomy. In 1496 he went to Italy, studying law and medicine at the universities of Bologna and Padua and finally taking a doctorate in canon law at the University of Ferrara in 1503. By this time he had become, through a literal case of nepotism, a canon of Frauenburg, a post he was to hold until his death. In 1506 Copernicus returned home to serve his uncle as his doctor and secretary at Heinsberg castle. When his uncle died in 1512 Copernicus moved to Frauenburg to take up his modest duties as a canon.

Copernicus's pursuit of his interest in astronomy both brought him a distinguished reputation and led to a dissatisfaction with the prevailing system of astronomy. However his first statement of his revolutionary views, the *Commentariolus* (written between about 1510 and 1514) was circulated privately in manuscript form. The system Copernicus was rebelling against goes back to the Greece of Plato and received its fullest development in the *Almagest* of Ptolemy in the second century AD. It assumed that the Earth, unmoving, was at the center of the universe around which not only the Moon but the Sun and the other known planets revolved with perfect uniform circular motion. However, in order to fit the complicated movements of the planets into such a simple scheme, all kinds of compromises had to be made and complications brought in. Hence the introduction of such concepts as epicycles, eccentrics, and equants into the basically simple system. The second weakness was its failure to predict at all accurately the movement of the planets. Thus a conjunction of the major planets in 1503 predicted by the almanacs of the day was as much as ten days out. Copernicus, unlike Tycho Brahe, seemed unworried about the second point and, in all his writings, emphasized the urgency of a return to uniform circular motion. How, he asked himself in the *Commentariolus*, could this be achieved? It is at this point that he came up with his revolutionary hypothesis, "All the spheres revolve about the Sun as their midpoint and therefore the Sun is the center of the universe."

Copernicus then worked his system out in detail. His great work *De revolutionibus orbium coelestium* (On the Revolution of the Celestial Spheres) although finished by the early 1530s was to be published only in the month of his death in 1543. Why Copernicus withheld his masterpiece from the world is a matter for speculation. News of his system seems to have spread quite widely. The popes Leo X and Clement VII refer to it without any obvious hostility although Luther makes an abusive reference to it. The publication of *De revolutionibus* was due to a young professor of mathematics from Wittenberg, Rheticus. Having heard of Copernicus's system and wishing to study it at first hand he turned up in Frauenburg bearing the typical gifts of the humanist scholar, the first printed editions of Euclid and Ptolemy. But Copernicus was still reluctant to publish and would only agree to Rheticus writing a description of the new system, which appeared as *Narratio prima* (1539; First Narrative). Copernicus finally agreed, under strong pressure from Rheti-

cus and his friends, to Rheticus's copying and publishing his manuscript. Rheticus went to Nuremburg intending to see the work through the press, but before its completion he had to leave to take up a new appointment in Leipzig. The task of seeing the work through the press was left with Andreas Osiander, a Nuremburg theologian who added to the work a famous and unauthorized preface asserting that the heliocentric hypothesis was not intended to be a true description of the universe but was merely a useful supposition. He was presumably trying to avoid any church opposition. It was finally published in March, 1543. It is recorded by a friend of Copernicus's that "he only saw his completed book at the last moment, on the day of his death." The book did meet opposition from theologians who found that it conflicted with the Bible. The Aristotelians were opposed to it and to many it seemed simply absurd that the Earth could be flying through space. Even professional astronomers like Tycho found it unacceptable. A moving Earth ought to imply apparent movement in the fixed stars, but none could be observed. Acceptance of Copernicus's explanation — that the stars were too far away for parallax to be observed — would involve a radical change in the accepted size of the universe. Moreover, although the heliocentric theory explained the movements of the Moon and the planets in a much more elegant way than the Ptolemaic system, Copernicus's insistence on perfect circular orbits involved nearly as much complexity as was found in Ptolemy.

However, there was no real official opposition to *De revolutionibus* and the system outlined in it until it was placed on the index of those books banned by the Catholic Church in 1616 (from which it was not removed until 1835). But it did find acceptance with many humanist mathematicians and astronomers, so that by the end of the century the issue had switched from whether to accept Ptolemy or Copernicus, to how one should accept Copernicus — as a true description or a useful mathematical trick.

COREY, Elias James (b. July 12, 1928; Methuen, Massachusetts) American chemist.

Corey was educated at the Massachusetts Institute of Technology where he obtained his PhD in 1951. He immediately joined the staff of the University of Illinois and was appointed professor of chemistry there in 1955. In 1959 he moved to a similar chair at Harvard.

Corey has made a number of organic syntheses and has been particularly successful in synthesizing a variety of terpenes, a family of hydrocarbons found in natural plant oils and important precursors of several biologically active compounds.

In 1968 Corey and his colleagues announced they had synthesized five of the prostaglandin hormones. Until this work the main source of the very limited supplies of prostaglandin available was the testes of Icelandic sheep.

CORI, Carl Ferdinand (b. Dec. 5, 1896; Prague) Czechoslovakian–American biochemist.

Cori was educated at the gymnasium in Trieste, where his father was director of the Marine Biological Station, and the University of Prague Medical School. He graduated in 1920, the year he married Gerty Radnitz, a fellow student who was to become his lifelong collaborator. The Coris moved to America in 1922, taking up an appointment at the New York State Institute for the Study of Malignant Diseases in Buffalo. In 1931 they both transferred to the Washington University Medical School, where Cori was successively professor of pharmacology and of biochemistry until his retirement in 1966.

The great French physiologist Claude Bernard had shown as long ago as 1850 that glucose is converted in the body into the complex carbohydrate glycogen. This is stored in the liver and muscle, ready to be converted back into glucose as the body needs a further energy supply. Just what steps are involved in this process was the fundamental problem the Coris began to tackle in the mid 1930s.

The first clue came in 1935, when they discovered an unknown compound in minced frog muscle. This was glucose-1-phosphate, in which the phosphate molecule is joined to the glucose 6-carbon ring at the standard position (1). It was next established that when this new compound, or *Cori ester* as it was soon called, was added to a frog or rabbit muscle extract, it was converted rapidly to glucose-6-phosphate by an enzyme that was named phosphoglucomutase, a process that was reversible. As only glucose itself can enter the cells of the body, glucose-6-phosphate must be converted to glucose by the enzyme phosphatase.

Although the actual pathway of glycolysis is much more detailed and took several years to elucidate, the value of the Coris' work is undeniable. Above all they pointed the way to the crucial role of phosphates in the provision of cellular energy, the details of which were soon to be worked out by Fritz Lipmann.

For their work the Coris shared the 1947 Nobel Prize for physiology or medicine with Bernardo Houssay.

CORI, Gerty Theresa Radnitz (b. Aug. 15, 1896; Prague; d. Oct. 26, 1957; St. Louis, Missouri) Czech–American biochemist.

Gerty Radnitz graduated from the Medical School of Prague University in 1920, the year in which she married her lifelong collaborator Carl Cori (q.v.). She moved with him to America, taking a post in 1922 at the New York State Institute for the Study of Malignant Diseases in Buffalo. In 1931 she went with her husband to the Washington University Medical School, where she became professor of biochemistry in 1947.

In 1947 the Coris and Bernardo Houssay shared the Nobel Prize for physiology or medicine for their discovery of how glycogen is broken down and resynthesized in the body.

CORIOLIS, Gustave-Gaspard (b. May 21, 1792; Paris; d. Sept. 19, 1843; Paris) French physicist.

Coriolis studied and taught at the Ecole Polytechnique becoming assistant professor of analysis and mechanics in 1816. He was the first to give precise definitions of work and kinetic energy in his work *Du calcul de l'effet des machines* (1829; On the Calculation of Mechanical Action) and he particularly studied the apparent effect of a change in the coordinate system on these quantities.

From this latter research grew his most famous discovery. In 1835, while studying rotating coordinate systems, he arrived at the idea of the *Coriolis force*. This is an inertial force which acts on a rotating surface at right angles to its direction of motion causing a body to follow a curved path instead of a straight line. This force is of particular significance to astrophysics, ballistics, and to earth sciences, particularly meteorology and oceanography. It affects terrestrial air and sea currents; currents moving away from the equator will have a greater eastward velocity than the ground underneath them, and so will appear to be deflected. The idea was developed independently by William Ferrel in America.

In 1838 Coriolis stopped teaching and became director of studies at the Polytechnique, but his poor health grew worse and he died five years later.

CORMACK, Allan Macleod (b. 1924; Johannesburg, South Africa) South African physicist.

Cormack was educated at the University of Cape Town and he became interested in x-ray imaging at the Groote Schuur Hospital in Johannesburg, where he worked as a physicist in the radioisotopes department. In 1956 he moved to America where he became professor at Tufts University, Massachusetts.

Cormack was the first to analyze theoretically the possibilities of developing a radiological cross-section of a biological system. Independently of the British engineer Godfrey Hounsfield, he developed the mathematical basis for the technique of computer-assisted x-ray tomography (CAT), describing this in two papers in 1963 and 1964, and provided the first practical demonstration. X-ray tomography is a process by which a picture of an imaginary slice through an object (or the human body) is built up from information from detectors rotating around the body. The application of this technique to medical x-ray imaging was to lead to diagnostic machines that could provide very accurate pictures of tissue distribution in the human brain and body. Hounsfield was unaware of the work of Cormack when he developed the first commercially successful CAT scanners for EMI in England.

Cormack also pointed out that the reconstruction technique might equally be applied to proton tomography, or to gamma radiation from positron annihilations within a patient, and he is investigating these as possible imaging techniques.

Cormack shared the 1979 Nobel Prize for physiology or medicine with Hounsfield for the development of CAT.

CORNER, Edred John Henry (b. Jan. 12, 1906; London) British botanist.

Corner graduated from Cambridge University in 1929. He then spent 20 years overseas, first as assistant director of the Gardens Department of the Straits Settlements (Singapore) and from 1947 to 1948 as a field officer for UNESCO in Latin America. Corner returned to Cambridge in 1949 and later, from 1966 until his retirement in 1973, served as professor of tropical botany.

Although Corner originally began as a mycologist such was the general level of knowledge of tropical plants that he felt compelled to work in a less specialized field. He produced a large number of books on the subject of which his *Life of Plants*

(1964) and *Natural History of Palms* (1966) have become widely known.

CORNFORTH, Sir John Warcup (b. Sept. 7, 1917; Sydney, Australia) Australian chemist.

Cornforth was educated at the universities of Sydney and Oxford, England, where he obtained his D Phil in 1941. He spent the war in Oxford working on the structure of penicillin before joining the staff of the Medical Research Council in 1946. In 1962 Cornforth moved to the Shell research center at Sittingbourne in Kent to serve as director of the Milstead Laboratory of Chemical Enzymology. In 1975 he accepted the post of Royal Society Research Professor at Sussex University.

In 1951 the American chemist Robert Woodward had succeeded in synthesizing the important steroid, cholesterol; Cornforth was interested in how the molecule is actually synthesized in the living cell. Using labeled isotopes of hydrogen, he traced out in considerable detail the chemical steps adopted by the cell to form the $C_{27}H_{45}OH$ molecule of cholesterol from the initial CH_3COOH of acetic acid. It was for this work that he shared the 1975 Nobel Chemistry Prize with Vladimir Prelog. Cornforth has also synthesized alkenes, oxazoles, and the plant hormone abscisic acid.

CORRENS, Karl Erich (b. Sept. 19, 1864; Munich, now in West Germany; d. Feb. 14, 1933; Berlin) German botanist and geneticist.

Correns was the only child of the painter Erich Correns. He studied at Tübingen University, where he began his research on the effect of foreign pollen in changing the visible characters of the endosperm (nutritive tissue surrounding the plant embryo). In some of his crossing experiments Correns used varieties of pea plants, following the ratios of certain characters in the progeny of these. After four genera-

tions he had gathered sufficient evidence to formulate the basic laws of inheritance. Not until he searched for relevant literature did he find that Gregor Mendel had reached the same conclusion a generation earlier. Correns' own work, published in 1900, thus only provided further proof for Mendel's theories. His later research concentrated on establishing how widely Mendel's laws could be applied. Using variegated plants he obtained, in 1909, the first conclusive evidence for cytoplasmic, or non-Mendelian, inheritance, in which certain features of the offspring are determined by the cytoplasm of the egg cell. Other contributions to plant genetics include his proposal that genes must be physically linked to explain why some characters are always inherited together. Correns was also the first to relate Mendelian segregation (the separation of paired genes, or alleles) to meiosis and the first to obtain evidence for differential fertilization between gametes. From 1914 until his death he was director of the Kaiser Wilhelm Institute for Biology in Berlin.

CORT, Henry (b. 1740; Lancaster, England; d. 1800; London) British metallurgist and inventor.

Cort, after working as a navy agent in London, took over an ironworks near Gosport (1775). He experimented with ways of improving wrought iron and in 1783 he patented a method of piling and rolling iron into bars using grooved rollers. The following year he patented his dry-puddling process for converting pig iron into wrought iron. Although his techniques of ironworking were an important contribution to the Industrial Revolution, Cort was financially ruined by the debts of a partnership and lost his patents.

CORVISART, Jean-Nicolas (b. Feb. 15, 1755; Dricourt, France; d. Sept. 18, 1821; Paris) French physician.

Corvisart, the son of an attorney, entered medicine against strong opposition from his family who wished him to pursue a legal career. He nevertheless graduated in medicine in 1785 and later held posts at the Charité and the Collège de France. He was then appointed personal physician to Napoleon.

Corvisart, who emphasized the importance of thorough clinical examinations, did much to introduce the new technique of percussion, first described by Leopold Auenbrugger. He not only practiced it himself but also, in 1808, produced a French translation of Auenbrugger's classic work. He was less receptive though to the introduction by his pupil René Laennec of the stethoscope, an instrument he seems not to have used.

He also produced *Essais sur les maladies organiques du coeur et des gros vaisseaux* (1806) one of the earliest works devoted to diseases of the heart.

COSTER, Dirk (b. Oct. 5, 1889; Amsterdam, Netherlands; d. Feb. 12, 1950; Groningen, Netherlands) Dutch physicist.

Coster was educated at the University of Leiden where he obtained his doctorate in 1922. From 1924 to 1949 he was professor of physics at the University of Groningen. In 1923, in collaboration with Georg von Hevesy, he discovered the element hafnium. The element was named for Hafnia, an old Roman name for Copenhagen. Copenhagen was the home of Niels Bohr, who had suggested to them that the new element would most likely be found in zirconium ores.

COTTRELL, Sir Alan Howard (b. July 17, 1919; Birmingham, England) British physicist and metallurgist.

Cottrell studied at the University of Birmingham, gaining his BSc in 1939 and PhD in 1949. After leaving Birmingham in 1955, he took the post of deputy head of the metallurgy division of the Atomic Energy Research Establishment at Harwell until 1958, when he became Goldsmiths Professor of Metallurgy at Cambridge University. From 1965 he held a number of posts as a scientific adviser to the British government. In 1974 he became master of Jesus College, Cambridge, and subsequently vice-chancellor of the University of Cambridge (1977–79).

Cottrell's most notable research has been in the study of dislocations in crystals. In experiments on the yield points of carbon steels he discovered that, because of the interactions of the carbon atoms with dislocations in the steel, a region enriched with carbon atoms develops around the dislocations (the *Cottrell atmosphere*). This leads to an increase in yield stress compared to the value in the pure material.

Cottrell's analysis of the forces between impurity atoms is basic to dislocation theories of yield point and strain aging. In 1949 Cottrell and B. A. Bilby correctly predicted the time law of strain aging from the rate of diffusion of impurity atoms to dislocations. Cottrell has also worked on the effect of radiation on crystal structure — work that was important in design changes to the fuel rods in early nuclear reactors.

COULOMB, Charles Augustin de (b. June 14, 1736; Angoulême, France; d. Aug. 23, 1806; Paris) French physicist.

Coulomb was educated in Paris and then joined the army, serving as an engineer. He spent nine years in Martinique designing and building fortifications, returning to France because of ill health. On his return he accepted several public offices but with the coming of the revolution he withdrew from Paris, spending his time quietly and safely at Blois and devoting himself to science. He returned to public life under Napoleon, serving as an inspector of public instruction from 1802.

He made an early reputation for himself by publishing work on problems of statics and friction. Some of the concepts that he introduced and analyzed are still used in engineering theory, for example, the notion of a *thrust line*. This describes how a building must be constructed if it is to control the oblique force arising from such items as roof members. Coulomb gave a general solution to the problem.

He is however most widely remembered for his statement of the inverse square laws of electrical and magnetic attraction and repulsion published in 1785. The secret of his work was the invention of a simple but successful torsion balance, which he used with great experimental skill. It was so sensitive that a force equivalent to about 1/100 000 of a gram could be detected. The balance consisted of a silken thread carrying a carefully balanced straw covered with wax. The straw, to which a charged sphere could be fixed, was free to rotate in a large glass tube that was marked in degrees around its circumference. He could now bring another charged ball within various distances of the rotatable straw and measure the amount of twist produced. By varying the distances involved and the nature and amount of the charge, Coulomb was able to deduce a number of laws. He stated his 'fundamental law of electricity' as "the repulsive forces between two small spheres charged with the same sort of electricity is in the inverse ratio of the squares of the distances between the centers of the two spheres." That is, two like charged bodies will repel each other and the force of that repulsion will fall off with the square of the distance separating them: if a body moves twice as far away the repulsive force will be four times weaker, if the body moves thrice as far away the repulsive force will be nine times weaker, and so on for any distance between them. Coulomb went on to show that the same form of law applies to magnetic as well as electrical attraction and repulsion. What is surprising about Coulomb (and his generation) was an inability to see any relationship between electricity and magnetism. Despite having demonstrated that the two phenomena obey basically the same laws he insisted that they consisted of two distinct fluids.

Coulomb was immortalized by having the unit of electric charge named in his honor: the quantity of electricity carried by a current of one ampere in one second is a coulomb.

COULSON, Charles Alfred (b. Dec. 13, 1910; Dudley, England; d. Jan. 8, 1974; Oxford, England) British theoretical chemist, physicist, and mathematician.

Coulson's father was principal of a local technical college. He was educated at Cambridge University, where he obtained his PhD in 1935 and afterward taught mathematics at the universities of Dundee and Oxford. Coulson then successively held appointments as professor of theoretical physics at King's College, London (1947–52), Rouse Ball Professor of Mathematics at Oxford (1952–72), and, still at Oxford, professor of theoretical chemistry from 1972 until his death in 1974.

As a physicist Coulson wrote the widely read *Waves* (1941) and *Electricity* (1948). His most creative work however was as a theoretical chemist. In 1933 he did early work on calculating the energy levels in polyatomic molecules and in 1937 he provided a theory of partial bond order (e.g. chemical bonding intermediate between double and single bonding). He also worked on aromatic molecules (benzene, naphthalene, etc.) with Christopher Longuet-Higgins. His book *Valence* (1952) covers the application of quantum mechanics to chemical bonding. Later Coulson turned to theoretical studies of carcinogens, drugs, and other topics of biological interest.

Coulson was also one of the leading Methodists of his generation and, from 1965 to 1971, chairman of Oxfam, the third-world charity. He produced a number of works on the relationship between Christianity and science of which *Science and Christian Belief* (1955) is a typical example.

COUPER, Archibald Scott (b. Mar. 31, 1831; Kirkintilloch, Scotland; d. Mar. 11, 1892; Kirkintilloch) British organic chemist.

The son of a mill owner, Couper was educated at Glasgow and Edinburgh universities, reading humanities, classics, and philosophy. He traveled extensively in Europe and in about 1854 began to study chemistry, working with Charles Wurtz in Paris (1854–56).

In 1858 he produced an important paper, *On a New Chemical Theory*, in which he anticipated August Kekulé's theory of the formation of carbon compounds. The publication of Couper's paper, which he had entrusted to Wurtz, was delayed and Kekulé thus had priority. Couper returned to Edinburgh in 1858 as assistant to Lyon Playfair but suffered a nervous breakdown soon after.

Couper did no more work and he was largely forgotten until Richard Anschütz, who was Kekulé's successor at Bonn, discovered some work on salicylic acid in which Couper had used an early form of graphic formulae based on dotted lines for the valence bonds. The paper on chemical theory was also rediscovered and Couper's work achieved full recognition.

COURNAND, André Frederic (b. Sept. 24, 1895; Paris) French–American physician.

Cournand, the son of a physician, was educated at the Sorbonne and, after serving in World War I, at the University of Paris where he finally obtained his MD in 1930. He then went to America for postgraduate work at Bellevue Hospital, New York, and began working in collaboration with Dickinson Richards. Cournand remained in America, became naturalized in 1941, and continued at Bellevue where he served as professor of medicine from 1951 until his retirement in 1964.

In 1941 Cournand, in collaboration with H. Ranges, continued the earlier work of Werner Forssmann and developed cardiac catheterization as a tool of physiological research. He found, contrary to expectation, that the technique did not lead to blood clotting and involved virtually no discomfort.

Cournand spent much time in attempting to determine the pressure drop across the pulmonary system. He investigated the effect of shock on cardiac function and assessed the consequences of various congenital heart defects. He also looked at the action of drugs, notably the digitalin type, on the heart.

In 1945 Cournand introduced an improved catheter with two branches through which simultaneous pressures in two adjacent heart chambers could be recorded. This led to greatly improved diagnoses of anatomical abnormalities, which consequently provided a better guide to treatment.

For his "discoveries concerning heart catheterization" Cournand shared the 1956 Nobel Prize for physiology or medicine with Forssmann and Richards.

COURTOIS, Bernard (b. Feb. 8, 1777; Dijon, France; d. Sept. 27, 1838; Paris) French chemist.

Courtois was the son of a saltpeter manufacturer and as a small boy he worked in the plant showing an alert interest. He was later apprenticed to a pharmacist and subsequently studied at the Ecole Polytechnique under Antoine Fourcroy. During his military service as a pharmacist he became the first to isolate morphine in its pure form from opium.

Meanwhile his father's saltpeter business had been running into difficulties because the product could be manufactured more cheaply in India, and Courtois returned to help his father. Saltpeter was obtained from the seaweed washed ashore in Normandy; the ashes (known as 'varec') were leached for sodium and potassium salts. Courtois noticed that the copper vats in which the lye was stored were becoming corroded by some unknown substance. By chance, in 1811, during the process of extracting the salts, he added excess concentrated sulfuric acid to the lye (the solution obtained by leaching) and was astonished to see "a vapor of a superb violet color" that condensed on cold surfaces to form brilliant crystalline plates. Courtois suspected that this was a new element but lacked the confidence and the laboratory equipment to establish this and asked Charles Bernard Désormes and Nicolas Clément to continue his researches. His discovery was announced in 1813, and Joseph Gay-Lussac and Humphry Davy soon verified that it was an element, Gay-Lussac naming it 'iodine' (from the Greek for 'violet') for its color.

COUSTEAU, Jacques Yves (b. June 11, 1910; Saint-André-de-Cubzac, France) French oceanographer.

Cousteau studied at the Ecole Navale in Brest and on graduation entered the French navy. During World War II he served in the French resistance and was awarded the Légion d'Honneur and the Croix de Guerre. During the war he also made his first two underwater films and, despite German occupation of France, designed and tested an aqualung. For this he adapted a valve (hitherto used by Emile Gagnan to enable car engines to work with cooking gas) into an underwater breathing apparatus. Using compressed air, the *Cousteau–Gagnan aqualung* allows long periods of underwater investigation at depths of more than 200 feet (61 m) and frees the diver of the need for a heavy suit and lifeline.

In 1946 Cousteau became head of the French navy's Underwater Research Group and the following year set a world record of 300 feet (91 m) for free-diving. In 1951–52 he traveled to the Red Sea in a converted British minesweeper, the *Calypso*, and made the first underwater color film to be taken at a depth of 150 feet (46 m). Later he helped Auguste Piccard in the development of the first bathyscaphes. Cousteau also designed and worked on a floating island off the French coast that enabled long-term study of marine life. He is the designer of an underwater diving

'saucer' capable of descents to more than 600 feet (183 m) and able to stay submerged for 20 hours. More significantly, he has worked on the future exploitation of the sea bed as a living environment for man, conducting various experiments on short-term undersea living.

Cousteau may be said to have made more significant contributions to undersea exploration and study than any other individual. His work has been brought to a wide audience by means of cinephotography and television, and a number of his films, for example, *The Silent World*, have won Academy Awards. His many books, such as *The Living Sea* (1963), and his television documentaries in the series *The Undersea World of Jacques Cousteau* have captured the imagination of millions.

CRAFTS, James Mason (b. Mar. 8, 1839; Boston, Massachusetts; d. June 20, 1917; Ridgefield, Connecticut) American chemist.

Crafts initially studied engineering and mining at Lawrence Scientific School, graduating in 1858. He then went to Europe, where he studied chemistry at Freiburg and worked with Robert Bunsen and Charles Adolphe Wurtz before returning to America in 1866. He became professor of chemistry at Cornell (1868) and held the same post at the Massachusetts Institute of Technology (1871). He returned to Europe in 1874 for health reasons and worked with Charles Friedel (q.v.) at the mining school in Paris. Here in 1877 they discovered the *Friedel–Crafts reaction*, a versatile synthetic method involving the alkylation or acylation of aromatic hydrocarbons with aluminum chloride as catalyst. Crafts returned to MIT in 1891, becoming president (1898–1900) before retiring through ill health. His other work included research on silicon derivatives, catalysis, and thermometry.

CRAIG, Lyman Creighton (b. June 12, 1906; Palmyra, Iowa; d. July 7, 1974; Glen Rock, New Jersey) American biochemist.

Craig was educated at Iowa State University where he obtained his PhD in 1931. After two years at Johns Hopkins University he moved to Rockefeller University, New York, where he was appointed professor of chemistry in 1949.

Craig concentrated on devising and improving techniques for separating the constituents of mixtures. His development of a fractional extraction method named countercurrent distribution (CCD) proved to be particularly good for preparing pure forms of several antibiotics and hormones. The method also established that the molecular weight of insulin is half the weight previously suggested. Craig also used CCD to separate the two protein chains of hemoglobin.

During work on ergot alkaloids Craig, with W. A. Jacobs, isolated an unknown amino acid, which they named lysergic acid. Other workers managed to prepare the dimethyl amide of this acid and found the compound, LSD, to have considerable physiological effects.

CRAM, Donald James (b. Apr. 22, 1919; Chester, Vermont) American chemist.

Cram, a lawyer's son, was educated at Rollins College and the University of Nebraska. After working for Merck and Company on streptomycin and penicillin, he entered Harvard where he obtained his PhD in 1947. He then joined the University of California at Los Angeles, becoming professor of chemistry there in 1956.

Cram has coauthored with George Hammond a standard textbook, *Organic Chemistry* (1959). He also produced *Fundamentals of Carbanion Chemistry* (1965), the first general work on the subject. Carbanions or carbon anions are negatively-charged organic ions, highly reactive but existing only as short-lived intermediates in organic reactions. Cram discussed their generation, structure, and reaction capabilities.

CRICK, Francis Harry Compton (b. June 8, 1916; Northampton, England) British molecular biologist.

Crick graduated from University College, London, and during World War II worked on the development of radar and magnetic mines. Later he changed from physics to biology and in 1947 began work at the Strangeways Research Laboratory, Cambridge, transferring to the Medical Research Council unit at the Cavendish Laboratory in 1949.

In 1951 a young American student, James Watson (q.v.), arrived at the unit. Watson suggested to Crick that it was necessary to find the molecular structure of the hereditary material, DNA, before its function could be properly understood. Much was already known about the chemical and physical nature of DNA from the studies of such scientists as Phoebus Levene, Erwin Chargaff, Alexander Todd, and Linus Pauling. Using this knowledge and the x-ray diffraction data of Maurice Wilkins (q.v.) and Rosalind Franklin, Crick and Watson had built, by 1953, a molecular model incorporating all the known features of DNA. Fundamental to the model was their conception of DNA as a double helix. The model served to explain how DNA replicates — by the two spirals uncoiling and each acting as a template — and how the hereditary information might be coded — in the sequence of bases along the chains. Crick received his PhD in 1953.

Ten years' intensive research in many laboratories around the world all tended to confirm Crick and Watson's model. For their work, which has been called the most significant discovery of this century, they were awarded, with Wilkins, the 1962 Nobel Prize for physiology or medicine.

Crick, in collaboration with Sydney Brenner, made important contributions to the understanding of the genetic code and introduced the term 'codon' to describe a set of three adjacent bases that together code for one amino acid. He also formulated the adaptor hypothesis in which he suggested that, in protein synthesis, small adaptor molecules act as intermediaries between the messenger RNA template and the amino acids. Such adaptors, or transfer RNAs, were identified independently by Robert Holley and Paul Berg in 1956. Crick is also known for his formulation of the Central Dogma of molecular genetics, which assumes that the passage of genetic information is from DNA to RNA to protein. David Baltimore (q.v.) was later to show that in certain cases, information can actually go from RNA to DNA.

In 1966 Crick published the book *Of Molecules and Men*, reviewing the recent progress in molecular biology. He remained in Cambridge until 1977, when he took up a professorship at the Salk Institute, San Diego, California.

CROLL, James (b. Jan. 2, 1821; Cargill, Scotland; d. Dec. 15, 1890; Perth, Scotland) British geologist.

Croll was the son of a stonemason and crofter and he started work as a millwright. He became caretaker at Anderson's College, Glasgow, in 1859, and was later made resident geologist in the Edinburgh office of the Geological Survey, where he remained until his retirement in 1880.

In 1864 he studied the work of A.J. Adhemar and began research into the idea of an astronomical causation of ice ages. He developed the theory that the answer lay in the orbital history of the Earth. Using work done by Urbain Leverrier in 1843, he found that the degree of eccentricity (the extent to which an elliptical orbit departs from circularity) had been subjected to substantial change — 100 000 years ago it was highly eccentric while 10 000 years ago its eccentricity was quite small. He concluded that if winter occurred when the Earth was furthest away from the Sun in its precessional cycle and if the orbit of the Earth was at its most eccentric then the two factors would produce an ice age. He followed Adhemar in seeing this as alternating between the two hemispheres and having a period of about 26 000 years.

This view was generally accepted by other geologists, notably by James Geikie in his pioneering work *The Great Ice Age* (1874–84), but tests made on the theory were too rudimentary to be conclusive.

Croll's work was published in his *Climate and Time* (1875) and *Climate and Cosmology* (1885).

CRONIN, James Watson (b. Sept. 29, 1931; Chicago, Illinois) American physicist.

Cronin was educated at the Southern Methodist University and at Chicago, where he obtained his PhD in 1955. After a period at the Brookhaven National Laboratory he moved to Princeton in 1958 and later served as professor of physics from 1965 until 1971 when he was appointed to a comparable chair at the University of Chicago.

In 1956 Tsung Dao Lee and Chen Ning Yang made the startling claim that parity (P) was not conserved in weak interactions. To the surprise of physicists their bold conjecture was confirmed in a matter of months. It was however widely assumed that in a reaction the combination of parity and a property called charge conjugation (C) was conserved. Cronin and Val Fitch, together with James Christenson and René Turlay, tested this CP conservation in 1964 by investigating the decay of neutral kaons. It was known that one type of kaon could decay into two pions; the other (K_2^0) could not without violating CP conservation. Cronin and his colleagues discovered a small number of decays of K_2^0 into two pions, clearly demonstrating that the conservation of CP is violated.

The result is of fundamental interest for it is known that the combined properties of charge conjugation (C), parity (P), and time (T) are conserved — so that if CP is violated then the decay of the kaons is not symmetrical with respect to time reversal.

Cronin and Fitch shared the 1980 Nobel Physics Prize for this work.

CRONSTEDT, Axel Frederic (b. Dec. 23, 1722; Södermanland, Sweden; d. Aug. 19, 1765; Stockholm) Swedish chemist and mineralogist.

Cronstedt studied chemistry at the University of Uppsala and the School of Mines until 1748, becoming a member of the Swedish Academy of Sciences soon after; he held no academic post.

Cronstedt used the blowpipe extensively for studying minerals and classified minerals according to chemical principles rather than the physical characteristics that had been used previously. This work was published (at first anonymously) in *An Essay toward a System of Mineralogy* (1758). In 1751 he discovered nickel by reducing a mineral known as devil's copper, or *kupfernickel*, and observed its magnetic properties.

CROOKES, Sir William (b. June 17, 1832; London; d. Apr. 4, 1919; London) British chemist and physicist.

Crookes studied at the Royal College of Chemistry, London, under August von Hofmann (1848). After working at the Radcliffe Observatory, Oxford, and the Chester College of Science, he returned to London in 1856, where, having inherited a large fortune, he edited *Chemical News* and spent his time on research.

Following the invention of the spectroscope by Robert Bunsen and Gustav Kirchhoff, Crookes discovered the element thallium (1861) by means of its spectrum. In investigating the properties and molecular weight of thallium, he noticed unusual effects in the vacuum balance that he was using. This led him to investigate effects at low pressure and eventually to invent the instrument known as the *Crookes radiometer* (1875). This device is a small evacuated glass bulb containing an arrangement of four light metal vanes. Alternate sides of the vanes are polished and blackened. When radiant heat falls on the instrument, the vanes rotate. The effect depends on the low pressure of gas in the bulb; molecules leaving the dark (hotter) surfaces have greater momentum than those leaving the bright (cooler) surfaces. Although the instrument had little practical use, it was important evidence for the kinetic theory of gases.

Crookes went on to investigate electrical discharges in gases at low pressure, producing an improved vacuum tube (the *Crookes tube*). He also investigated cathode rays and radioactivity. *Crookes glass* is a type of glass invented to protect the eyes of industrial workers from intense radiation.

From about 1870, Crookes became interested in spiritualism and became one of the leading investigators of psychic phenomena.

CROSS, Charles Frederick (b. Dec. 11, 1855; Brentford, England; d. Apr. 15, 1935; Hove, England) British industrial chemist.

Cross studied chemistry at King's College, London, in Zurich, and at Owens College, Manchester, where he met Edward Bevan (q.v.), whose partner he became and with whom he developed the viscose process of rayon manufacture. Cross was subsequently involved in the industrial development of this process. He wrote several books on cellulose and paper-making.

CRUM BROWN, Alexander (b. Mar. 26, 1838; Edinburgh, Scotland; d. Oct. 28, 1922; Edinburgh) British organic chemist.

The son of a Presbyterian minister, Crum Brown studied arts and then medicine and chemistry at Edinburgh, gaining an MA degree in 1858 and his MD in 1861. He was also awarded a doctorate from London University (1862) and worked with Robert Bunsen at Heidelberg and Hermann Kolbe at Marburg before returning to Edinburgh as a lecturer in 1863, becoming professor of chemistry in 1869.

Crum Brown was essentially a theoretician of organic chemistry and his structural formulae, introduced in his MD thesis *On the Theory of Chemical Combination* (1861) and taken up by Edward Frankland in 1866, are essentially the symbols used today. In 1867–68, with T.R. Fraser, he carried out pioneering work in what is now called structure/activity relationships in pharmacology. In 1892 (with J. Gibson) he proposed a rule (*Crum Brown's rule*) concerning the effect of substitution of an organic group into a benzene ring that already contains a group. The rule can be used to predict the position into which the existing group will direct the second group. Other research interests were physiology (the function of the semicircular canals in the ear), phonetics, mathematics, and crystallography.

CTESIBIUS of Alexandria (*fl.* 270 BC) Greek physicist and inventor.

Ctesibius is said to have first discovered the principle of air elasticity. He invented compressed-air weapons, suction pumps, force pumps, a water clock known as a *clepsydra*, and a pipe organ, the *hydraulis*, in which keys let air into pan pipes from mechanical pumps. The *hydraulis* was used until the sixth century and the *clepsydra* was used by Galileo.

CUGNOT, Nicolas-Joseph (b. Sept. 25, 1725; Poid, France; d. Oct. 2, 1804; Paris) French engineer.

Cugnot served as a military engineer in the Austro-Hungarian army during the Seven Years' War (1756–63). Following this he built what was probably the first fuel-driven vehicle. Independently of James Watt and Thomas Newcomen he designed, in 1770, a two-piston steam boiler, demonstrating that steam traction was feasible. It was intended for pulling heavy artillery and was the first engine to use high-pressure steam, although its application was limited by problems with the water supply.

CULPEPER, Nicholas (b. Oct. 18, 1616; London; d. Jan. 10, 1654; London) English medical writer and astrologer.

Culpeper studied briefly at Cambridge University, where he learned Latin and Greek, before being apprenticed to an apothecary. In 1640 he established himself as an astrologer and physician in Spitalfields, London. Culpeper invoked the indignation of the College of Physicians by publishing, in 1649, an unauthorized translation of their *Pharmacopeia*, which listed the preparation and uses of all major drugs. In 1652, he published, with Peter Cole, *The English Physician*, in which he attacked the medical establishment. The enlarged version, published the following year, listed many herbal medicines and became very popular, running into several editions and being dubbed 'Culpeper's Herbal'. His prolific output included works dealing with astrology, medicine, and politics. He was a fervent supporter of the Parliamentary side in the English Civil War and was apparently wounded in battle. This may have contributed to his early death.

CURIE, Marie Sklodowska (b. Nov. 7, 1867; Warsaw; d. July 4, 1934; Haute-Savoie, France) Polish–French chemist.

Marie Sklodowska's father was a physics teacher and her mother the principal of a girls' school. She acquired from her father a positivism and an interest in science although to aid the family finances she was forced, in 1885, to become a governess. She seems to have been on the fringe of nationalist revolutionary politics at a time when Polish language and culture were very much under Russian domination, but her main interest at this time appears to have been science. There was no way in which a girl could receive any form of higher scientific education in Poland in the 1880s, and so in 1891 she followed her elder sister to Paris. Living in poverty and working hard she graduated in physics from the Sorbonne in 1893, taking first place. She received a scholarship from Poland, which enabled her to spend a year studying mathematics; this time she graduated in second place.

In 1894 she met Pierre Curie and they married the following year. He was a physicist of some distinction, having already made several important discoveries, and was working as chief of the laboratory of the school of Industrial Physics and Chemistry. Marie was at this time looking for a topic for research for a higher degree. Her husband was in full sympathy with her desire to continue with research, by no means a common attitude in late 19th-century France. She was also fortunate in her timing and choice of topic — the study of radioactivity. In 1896 Henri Becquerel had discovered radioactivity in uranium. Marie Curie had reason to believe that there might be a new element in the samples of uranium ore (pitchblende) that Becquerel had handled, but first she needed a place to work and a supply of the ore. It was agreed that she could work in her husband's laboratory. Her first task was to see if substances other than uranium were radioactive. Her method was to place the substance on one of the plates of Pierre's sensitive electrometer to see if it produced an electric current between the plates. In a short time she found that thorium is also radioactive.

Her next discovery was in many ways the most fundamental. She tried to see whether different compounds of uranium or thorium would have differing amounts of radioactivity. Her conclusion was that it made no difference what she mixed the uranium with, whether it was wet or dry, in powder form or solution; the only factor that counted was the amount of uranium present. This meant that radioactivity must be a property of the uranium itself and not of its interaction with something else. Radioactivity had to be an atomic property; it would soon be recognized as an effect of the nucleus.

One further advance was made by Marie Curie in 1898; she found that two uranium minerals, pitchblende and chalcolite, were more active than uranium itself. She drew the correct conclusion from this, namely that they must contain new radioactive elements. She immediately began the search for them. By the end of the year she had demonstrated the existence of two new elements, radium and polonium, both of which were highly radioactive. No precautions were taken at this time against the levels of radiation, as their harmful effects were not recognized. (Indeed, her notebooks of this period are still too dangerous to handle.)

Her next aim was to produce some pure radium. The difficulty here was that radium is present in pitchblende in such small quantities that vast amounts of the ore were needed. The Curies managed to acquire, quite cheaply, several tons of pitchblende from the Bohemian mines thanks to the intercession of the Austrian government. As there was too much material for her small laboratory she was offered the use of an old dissecting room in the yard of the school. It was freezing in winter and unbearably hot in summer — Wilhelm Ostwald later described it as a cross between a stable and a potato cellar. The work was heavy and monotonous. The limitations of her equipment meant that she could only deal with batches of 20 kilograms at a time, which had to be carefully dissolved, filtered, and crystallized. This procedure went on month after month, in all kinds of weather. By early 1902 she had obtained one tenth of a gram of radium chloride. She took it to Eugene Demarçay who had first identified the new elements spectroscopically. He now had enough to determine its atomic weight, which he calculated as 225.93.

The crucial question arising from the discovery of these new elements was, what was the nature of the radiation emitted? It was thought that there were at least two different kinds of rays. One kind could be deflected by a magnetic field while the other was unaffected and would only travel a few centimeters before disappearing. (These were identified as the alpha and beta rays by Ernest Rutherford.) A further question was the nature of the source of the energy. Pierre Curie showed that one gram of radium gave out about a hundred calories per hour. One further mystery at this time was the discovery of induced radioactivity — they had found that metal plates that had been close to, but not in contact with, samples of radium became radioactive themselves and remained so for some time.

The mysteries of radioactivity were explained not by the Curies but by Rutherford and his pupils. Although Marie Curie was no great theorist, she was an industrious experimentalist who with great strength and singlemindedness would pursue important but basically tedious experimental procedures for years. Her thesis was presented in 1903 and she became the first woman to be awarded an advanced scientific research degree in France. In the same year she was awarded the Nobel Prize for physics jointly with her husband and Becquerel for their work on radioactivity.

In 1904, when her husband was given a chair at the Sorbonne, Marie was offered a part-time post as a physics teacher at a girls' Normal School at Sèvres. In the same year her second daughter Eve was born. It is also about this time that she first appears to have suffered from radiation sickness. Given all these distractions it is not surprising that for a few years after the completion of her thesis she had little time for research. In 1906 Pierre Curie died in a tragic accident. The Sorbonne elected her to her husband's chair and the rest of her life was largely spent in organizing the research of others and attempting to raise funds. She made two long trips to America in 1921 and 1929. On her first trip she had been asked what she would most like to have. A gram of radium of her own was her reply, and she returned from America with a gram, valued at $100000. She also received $50000 from the Carnegie Institution. In 1912 the Sorbonne founded the Curie laboratory for the study of radioactivity. It was opened in 1914 but its real work could only begin after the war, during which Marie Curie spent most of her time training radiologists. Later her laboratory,

with its gram of radium, was to become one of the great research centers of the world.

Her position in France was somewhat odd. As a foreigner and a woman France was never quite sure how to treat her. She was clearly very distinguished for in 1911 she was awarded her second Nobel Prize, this time in chemistry for her discovery of radium and polonium. Her eminence was recognized by the creation of the Curie laboratory, yet at almost the same time she found herself rejected by the Académie des Sciences. She allowed her name to go forward in 1910 as the first serious female contender but was defeated. There is no doubt that this offended her. She refused to allow her name to be submitted for election again and for ten years refused to allow her work to be published in the proceedings of the Académie.

The following year, 1911, worse was to happen and she became the center of a major scandal. The physicist and former pupil of her husband, Paul Langevin was accused of having an affair with her. Langevin had left his wife and four children, but although he was close to Madame Curie it is by no means clear that there were grounds for the accusations. Some of her letters to Langevin were stolen and published in the popular press and doubts were raised about Pierre Curie's death. Most of the attacks seem to have emanated from Gustave Téry, editor of L'Oeuvre and a former classmate of Langevin. Langevin retaliated by challenging Téry to a duel. Langevin faced Téry late in 1911 at 25 yards with a loaded pistol in his hand. Both refused to fire and shortly afterward the scandal died down.

One final honor was bestowed on her. The unit of measurement of the activity of a radioactive substance was named the curie for her in 1910. Characteristically she insisted on defining the unit herself. Her major published work was the massive two-volume Treatise on Radioactivity (1910). The Curies' daughter Irène and her husband Frédéric Joliot-Curie continued the pioneering work on radioactivity and themselves received the Nobel Prize for physics.

CURIE, Pierre (b. May 15, 1859; Paris; d. Apr. 19, 1906; Paris) French physicist.

Pierre Curie was the son of a physician. He was educated at the Sorbonne where he became an assistant in 1878. In 1882 he was made laboratory chief at the School of Industrial Physics and Chemistry where he remained until he was appointed professor of physics at the Sorbonne in 1904. In 1895 he married Marie Sklodowska with whom he conducted research into the radioactivity of radium and with whom he shared the Nobel Prize for physics in 1903.

His scientific career falls naturally into two periods, the time before the discovery of radioactivity by Henri Becquerel, when he worked on magnetism and crystallography, and the time after when he collaborated with his wife Marie Curie on this new phenomenon.

In 1880 with his brother Jacques he had discovered piezoelectricity. 'Piezo' comes from the Greek for 'to press' and refers to the fact that certain crystals when mechanically deformed will develop opposite charges on opposite faces. The converse will also happen; i.e. an electric charge applied to a crystal will produce a deformation. The brothers used the effect to construct an electrometer to measure small electric currents. Marie Curie later used the instrument to investigate whether radiation from substances other than uranium would cause conductivity in air. Pierre Curie's second major discovery was in the effect of temperature on the magnetic properties of substances, which he was studying for his doctorate. In 1895 he showed that at a certain temperature specific to a substance it will lose its ferromagnetic properties; this critical temperature is now known as the *Curie point*.

Shortly after this discovery he began to work intensively with his wife on the new phenomenon of radioactivity. Two new elements, radium and polonium, were discovered in 1898. The rays these elements produced were investigated and enormous efforts were made to produce a sample of pure radium.

He received little recognition in his own country. He was initially passed over for the chairs of physical chemistry and mineralogy in the Sorbonne and was defeated when he applied for membership of the Académie in 1902. He was however later admitted in 1905. The only reason he seems eventually to have been given a chair (in 1904) was that he had been offered a post in Geneva and was seriously thinking of leaving France. Partly this may have been because his political sympathies were very much to the left and because he was unwilling to participate in the science policies of the Third Republic.

Pierre Curie was possibly one of the first to suffer from radiation sickness. No attempts were made in the early days to restrict the levels of radiation received. He died accidentally in 1906 in rather strange circumstances — he slipped while crossing a Paris street, fell under a passing horse cab, and was kicked to death.

The Curies' daughter Irène Joliot-Curie carried on research in radioactivity and also received the Nobel Prize for work done with her husband Frédéric.

CURTIS, Heber Doust (b. June 27, 1872; Muskegon, Michigan; d. Jan. 9, 1942; Ann Arbor, Michigan) American astronomer.

Curtis obtained his AB (1892) and AM (1893) from the University of Michigan, where he studied classics. He moved to California in 1894 where he became professor of Latin and Greek at Napa College. There his interest in astronomy was aroused and from 1897 to 1900 he was professor of mathematics and astronomy after the college merged with the University of the Pacific. After obtaining his PhD from the University of Virginia in 1902 he joined the staff of the Lick Observatory where he remained until 1920 when he became director of the Allegheny Observatory of the University of Pittsburg. Finally, in 1930 he was appointed director of the University of Michigan's observatory.

Curtis's early work was concerned with the measurement of the radial velocities of the brighter stars. From 1910 however he was involved in research on the nature of 'spiral nebulae' and became convinced that these were isolated independent star systems. In 1917 he argued that the observed brightness of novae found by him and by George Ritchey on photographs of the nebulae indicated that the nebulae lay well beyond our Galaxy. He also maintained that extremely bright novae (later identified as supernovae) could not be included with the novae as distance indicators. He estimated the Andromeda nebula to be 500 000 light-years away.

Curtis's view was opposed by many, including Harlow Shapley who proposed that our Galaxy was 300 000 light-years in diameter, far larger than previously assumed, and that the spiral nebulae were associated with the Galaxy. In 1920, at a meeting of the National Academy of Sciences, Curtis engaged in a famous debate with Shapley over the size of the Galaxy and the distance of the spiral nebulae. Owing to incomplete and incorrect evidence the matter was not settled until 1924 when Edwin Hubble redetermined the distance of the Andromeda nebula and demonstrated that it lay well beyond the Galaxy.

CURTIUS, Theodor (b. May 27, 1857; Duisburg, now in West Germany; d. Feb. 8, 1928; Heidelberg, now in West Germany) German organic chemist.

Curtius gained his doctorate under Adolph Kolbe at Leipzig and later became professor at Kiel (1889), Bonn (1897), and Heidelberg (1898). Two reactions are named for Curtius; the first, discovered in 1894, is a method for the conversion of an acid into an amine via the azide and urethane, and the second, discovered in 1913, is a method of converting an azide into an isocyanate. Curtius also discovered diazoacetic ester, which was the first known aliphatic diazo compound (1883), hydrazine (1887), and hydrazoic acid (1890).

CUSHING, Harvey Williams (b. Apr. 8, 1869; Cleveland, Ohio; d. Oct. 7, 1939; New Haven, Connecticut) American surgeon.

Cushing received his MD from Harvard Medical School in 1895 and joined Massachusetts General Hospital, Boston, before moving to Johns Hopkins Hospital, where he progressed to associate professor of surgery. In 1912 he was appointed professor of surgery at Harvard. Cushing's specialty was brain surgery and he pioneered several important techniques in this field, especially in the control of blood pressure and bleeding during surgery. From his many case histories, he distinguished several classes of brain tumors and made great improvements in their treatment. Cushing also demonstrated the vital role of the pituitary gland in regulating many bodily functions. He was the first to associate adenoma (tumor) of the basophilic cells of the anterior pituitary with the chronic wasting disease now known as *Cushing's syndrome*. The characteristic symptoms include thin arms and legs, atrophied skin with red lines, obesity of the trunk and face, and high blood pressure. This syndrome is now known to be caused by any of several disorders that result in the increased secretion of corticosteroid hormones by the adrenal glands.

Cushing had a lifelong interest in the history of medicine and wrote the *Life of Sir William Osler* (1925), which won him a Pulitzer Prize. He donated his large collection of books and papers to the Yale Medical Library.

CUVIER, Baron Georges Léopold Chrétien Frédéric Dagobert (b. Aug. 23, 1769; Montbéliard, now in France; d. May 13, 1832; Paris) French anatomist and taxonomist.

As a child Cuvier was greatly influenced by Georges Buffon's books. In 1795 he became assistant to the professor of comparative anatomy at the Museum of Natural History in Paris — then the world's largest scientific research establishment. During his lifetime he greatly enlarged the comparative anatomy section from a few hundred skeletons to 13 000 specimens. Cuvier extended Linnaeus's classification, creating another level, the phylum, into which he grouped related classes. He recognized four phyla in the animal kingdom and his work on one of these, the fishes, is recognized as the foundation for modern ichthyology. Together with Achille Valenciennes, Cuvier compiled the lengthy *Histoire des poissons*, nine volumes of which had appeared by his death. The fish families delimited in this work remain as orders or suborders in today's classification. Cuvier was the first to classify fossils and named the pterodactyl. His results from investigations of the Tertiary formations near Paris are published in four volumes as *Recherches sur les ossements fossiles des quadrupèdes* (1812).

In 1799 Cuvier became professor of natural history at the Collège de France and in 1802 was also made professor at the Jardin des Plantes. In his later life he became increasingly involved in educational administration and played a large part in organizing the new Sorbonne.

D

D'ABANO, Pietro (b. *c.* 1250; Abano, near Padua, Italy; d. 1316; Padua) Italian physician and philosopher.

D'Abano studied in Greece and Constantinople before learning medicine in Paris. He became professor of medicine at Padua University in 1306 and soon became a celebrated teacher and physician.

His knowledge of Greek enabled him to study the texts of the ancient scholars and physicians and to attempt to reconcile medicine and philosophy in his most famous book known as the *Conciliator.* This rationalist stance together with his interest in astrology brought D'Abano into conflict with the Catholic Church. In 1315 he was accused of being a heretic and was twice brought before the Inquisition. Acquitted the first time, he died before a second trial was completed and his body was hidden by friends. He was nevertheless found guilty and the Inquisition ordered that his effigy be burned instead.

DAGUERRE, Louis-Jacques-Mandé (b. Nov. 18, 1789; Cormeilles, near Paris; d. July 10, 1851; Bry-sur-Marne, France) French physicist, inventor, and painter.

Daguerre, the inventor of the daguerreotype (the first practical photograph), first became interested in the effect of light on films from the artistic point of view. After working first as a tax officer he became a painter of opera scenery. Working with Charles-Marie Bouton he invented the diorama — a display of paintings on semi-transparent linen that transmitted and reflected light — and opened a diorama in Paris (1822).

From 1826 Daguerre turned his attention to heliography and he was partnered in this by Joseph-Nicéphore Niepce until Niepce's death in 1833. Daguerre continued his work and in 1839 presented to the French Academy of Sciences the daguerreotype, which needed only about 25-minutes exposure time to produce an image, compared with over 8 hours for Niepce's previous attempts. In the daguerreotype a photographic image was obtained on a copper plate coated with a light-sensitive layer of silver iodide and bromide.

D'AILLY, Pierre (b. 1350; Compiègne, France; d. Aug. 9, 1420; Avignon, France) French geographer, cosmologist, and theologian.

D'Ailly studied at the University of Paris serving as its chancellor from 1389 until 1395 when he became a bishop, first of Le Puy and subsequently of Cambrai. He became a cardinal in 1411.

Primarily concerned with church affairs, in which he advocated reform, d'Ailly was also interested in science and was the leading geographical theorist of his time. He was the author of the influential work *Imago mundi* (Image of the World), which was completed by 1410 and printed in about 1483. This was a scholastic summary of the classical and Arabian geographers, typical of the medieval period, and was influenced by Roger Bacon. D'Ailly's underestimate of the Earth's circumference and exaggeration of the size of Asia may well have influenced Columbus, whose copy of d'Ailly's work, with his marginal annotations, still survives.

D'Ailly's work had been written without the benefit of Ptolemy's *Geography*, which only became available in a Latin version shortly afterward. He produced, in 1413, the *Compendium cosmographiae*. This was basically a summary of Ptolemy, reviving uncritically the full fabric of Ptolemaic geography, which was already being dismantled by such travelers as Marco Polo.

DAIMLER, Gottlieb Wilhelm (b. Mar. 17, 1834; Schorndorf, now in West Germany; d. Mar. 6, 1900; Cannstatt, now in West Germany) German engineer and inventor.

Daimler patented the first internal-combustion engine in 1885 and developed the carburetor that made the gasoline engine possible. His first engines were used on bicycles (1885) — the first two-wheeled motor cycles in the world. In 1890 he founded the Daimler-Motoren-Gesellschaft company, which, in 1899, built the first Mercedes car.

DAINTON, Sir Frederick Sydney (b. Nov. 11, 1914; Sheffield, England) British physical chemist and scientific administrator.

Dainton was educated at the universities of Oxford and Cambridge. After World War II he remained in Cambridge until 1950, when he was appointed professor of physical chemistry at the University of Leeds. Apart from a brief period (1970–73) as professor of physical chemistry at Oxford, most of Dainton's time since 1965 has been spent as an administrator.

Dainton's early work in physical chemistry was on the kinetics and thermodynamics of polymerization reactions. From about 1945 he turned his attention to studies of radiolysis — i.e. chemical changes produced by high-energy radiation (alpha, beta, or gamma rays). In particular, he has studied the properties and reactions of hydrated electrons in liquids.

From 1965 he was a member of the Council for Scientific Policy and was its chairman from 1969. While holding this office he was influential in decisions made about the way British academic research is financed.

DALE, Sir Henry Hallett (b. June 9, 1875; London; d. July 23, 1968; Cambridge, England) British physiologist.

Educated at Cambridge University and St. Bartholomew's Hospital, Dale became, in 1904, director of the Wellcome Physiological Research Laboratories. His work there over the next ten years included the isolation (with Arthur Ewins) from ergot fungi of a pharmacologically active extract — acetylcholine — which he found had similar effects to the parasympathetic nervous system on various organs. It was later shown by Otto Loewi that a substance released by electrical stimulation of the vagus nerve was responsible for effecting changes in heartbeat. Following up this work, Dale showed that the substance is in fact acetylcholine, thus establishing that chemical as well as electrical stimuli are involved in nerve action. For this research, Dale and Loewi shared the 1936 Nobel Prize for physiology or medicine. Dale also worked on the properties of histamine and related substances, including their actions in allergic and anaphylactic conditions. He was the chairman of an international committee responsible for the standardization of biological preparations, and from 1928 to 1942 was director of the National Institute for Medical Research.

D'ALEMBERT, Jean Le Rond (b. Nov. 16, 1717; Paris; d. Oct. 29, 1783; Paris) French mathematician, encyclopedist, and philosopher.

D'Alembert was the illegitimate son of a Parisian society hostess, Mme de Tenzin, and was abandoned on the steps of a Paris church, from which he was named. He was brought up by a glazier and his wife and his father, the chevalier Destouches, made sufficient money available to ensure that d'Alembert received a good education although he never acknowledged that d'Alembert was his son. He graduated from Mazarin College in 1735 and was admitted to the Academy of Sciences in 1741.

D'Alembert's mathematical work was chiefly in various fields of applied mathematics, in particular dynamics. In 1743 he published his *Traité de dynamique*, in which the famous *d'Alembert principle* is enunciated. This principle is a generalization of Newton's third law of motion, and it states that Newton's law holds not only for fixed bodies but also for those that are free to move. D'Alembert wrote numerous other mathematical works on such subjects as fluid dynamics, the theory of winds, and the properties of vibrating strings. His most significant purely mathematical innovation was his invention and development of the theory of partial differential equations. Between 1761 and 1780 he published eight volumes of mathematical studies.

Apart from his mathematical work he is perhaps more widely known for his work on Denis Diderot's *Encyclopédie* as editor of the mathematical and scientific articles, and his association with the philosophes. D'Alembert was a friend of Voltaire's and he had a lively interest in theater and music, which led him to conduct experiments on the properties of sound and to write a number of theoretical treatises on such matters as harmony. He was elected to the French Academy in 1754 and became its permanent secretary in 1772 but he refused the presidency of the Berlin Academy.

DALÉN, Nils Gustaf (b. Nov. 30, 1869; Stenstorp, Sweden; d. Dec. 9, 1937; Stockholm) Swedish engineer.

Dalén graduated in mechanical engineering in 1896 from the Chalmers Insti-

tute at Göteborg and then spent a year at the Swiss Federal Institute of Technology at Zurich. For several years he researched and improved hot-air turbines, compressors, and air pumps and from 1900 to 1905 worked with an engineering firm, Dalén and Alsing. He then became works manager for the Swedish Carbide and Acetylene Company, which in 1909 became the Swedish Gas Accumulator Company with Dalén as managing director.

Dalén is remembered principally for his inventions relating to acetylene lighting for lighthouses and other navigational aids, and in particular an automatic light-controlled valve, for which he received the 1912 Nobel Prize for physics. The valve, known as 'Solventil', used the difference in heat-absorbing properties between a dull black surface and a highly polished one to produce differential expansion of gases, and thus to regulate the main gas valve of an acetylene-burning lamp. The lamp could thus be automatically dimmed or extinguished in daylight, and this allowed buoys and lighthouses to be left unattended and less gas to be used. The system soon came into widespread use and is still in use today.

Another invention of Dalén's was a porous filler for acetylene tanks, 'Agamassan', that prevented explosions. It was ironic that in 1912 he was himself blinded by an explosion during the course of an experiment. This did not, however, deter him from continuing his experimental work up to his death.

DALTON, John (b. Sept. 6, 1766; Eaglesfield, England; d. July 27, 1844; Manchester, England) British chemist and physicist.

The son of a Cumbrian hand-loom weaver, Dalton was born into the nonconformist tradition of northern England and he remained a Quaker all his life. He was educated at the village school until the age of 11, and received tuition from Elihu Robinson, a wealthy Quaker, meteorologist, and instrument maker, who first encouraged Dalton's interest in meteorology. At the age of only 12, Dalton himself was teaching in the village. He then worked on the land for two years before moving to Kendal with his brother to teach (1781). In 1793 he moved to Manchester where he first taught at the Manchester New College, a Presbyterian institute. In 1794 he was elected to the Manchester Literary and Philosophical Society at which most of his papers were read.

From 1787 until his death Dalton maintained a diary of meteorological observations of the Lake District where he lived. His first published work, *Meteorological Observations and Essays* (1793), contained the first of his laws concerning the behavior of compound atmospheres: that the same weight of water vapor is taken up by a given space in air and in a vacuum. Both Dalton and his brother were color blind and he was the first to describe the condition, sometimes known as daltonism, in his work *Extraordinary Facts Relating to the Vision of Colours* (1794).

In 1801 Dalton read four important papers to the Manchester Philosophical Society. *On the Constitution of Mixed Gases* contains what is now known as the law of partial pressures and asserts that air is a mixture, not a compound, in which the various gases exert pressure on the walls of a vessel independently of each other. *On the Force of Steam* includes the first explanation of the dew point and hence the founding of exact hygrometry. It also demonstrates that water vapor behaves like any other gas. The third paper, *On Evaporation*, shows that the quantity of water evaporated is proportional to the vapor pressure. *On the Expansion of Gases by Heat* contains the important conclusion that all gases expand equally by heat. This law had been discovered by Jacques Charles in 1787 but Dalton was the first to publish.

During this time, Dalton was developing his atomic theory, for which he is best known. A physical clue to the theory was provided by the solubility of gases in water. Dalton expected to find that all gases had the same solubility in water but the fact

that they did not helped to confirm his idea that the atoms of different gases had different weights. The first table of atomic weights was appended to the paper *On the Absorption of Gases by Water* read in 1802 but not printed until 1805. In another paper read in 1802 and printed in 1805 he showed that when nitric oxide is used to absorb oxygen in a eudiometer they combine in two definite ratios depending on the method of mixing. This was the beginning of the law of multiple proportions and led Dalton to much work on the oxides of nitrogen and the hydrocarbons methane and ethylene to confirm the law.

The atomic theory was first explicitly stated by Dalton at a Royal Institution lecture in December 1803 and first appeared in print in Thomas Thomson's *System of Chemistry* (1807). Dalton's own full exposition appeared in *A New System of Chemical Philosophy* (1808), with further volumes in 1810 and 1827. The basic postulates of the theory are that matter consists of atoms; that atoms can neither be created nor destroyed; that all atoms of the same element are identical, and different elements have different types of atoms; that chemical reactions take place by a rearrangement of atoms; and that compounds contained in 'compound atoms' formed from atoms of the constituent elements.

Using this theory, Dalton was able to rationalize the various laws of chemical combination (conservation of mass, definite proportions, multiple proportions) and show how they followed from the theory. He did, however, make the mistake of assuming "greatest simplicity:" i.e. that the simplest compound of two elements must be binary (e.g. water was HO). His system of atomic weights, although based on the analytical work of the best chemists, was not very accurate (e.g. he gave oxygen an atomic weight of seven rather than eight). Dalton's theory remained open to dispute until 1858 when Stanislao Cannizzaro's rediscovery of Amedeo Avogadro's work removed the last objections to the theory. Dalton's symbols for atoms and molecules were spherical representations and he used wooden molecular models similar to the modern version.

DAM, Carl Peter Henrik (b. Feb. 21, 1895; Copenhagen) Danish biochemist.

Dam was educated in Copenhagen at the Polytechnic and the University, where he obtained his doctorate in 1934. He taught at the university from 1923 until 1941, when — although stranded in America because of the war — he was appointed professor of biochemistry at the Copenhagen Polytechnic. From 1956 until 1963 Dam served as director of the Biochemical Division of the Danish Fat Research Institute.

From 1928 to 1930 Dam worked on the problem of cholesterol metabolism in chickens. Cholesterol, first analyzed by Heinrich Wieland is a sterol with an important role in mammalian physiology. It was known that many mammals could readily synthesize it, but it was assumed that chickens lacked this ability. To test this assumption Dam began to rear chickens on a cholesterol-free diet enriched with vitamins A and D.

As it turned out he found that chickens could synthesize cholesterol but, more importantly, he also found that if kept on such a diet for two to three weeks the chickens developed hemorrhages under the skin, and blood removed for examination showed delayed coagulation. Supplementing the diet with fat, vitamin C, and cholesterol made no appreciable difference, so Dam concluded that the condition was due to lack of a hitherto unrecognized factor in the diet.

The missing factor, found to be present in green leaves and pig liver, was designated vitamin K by Dam in 1935 (K being the initial letter of 'koagulation', the Scandinavian and German form of the word). Using ether Dam went on to extract the fat-soluble vitamin K from such sources as alfalfa, and in 1939 succeeded, with Paul Karrer (q.v.), in isolating it. It was for this work that Dam shared the 1943 Nobel Prize for physiology or medicine with Edward Doisy.

DANA, James Dwight (b. Feb. 12, 1813; Utica, New York; d. Apr. 14, 1895; New Haven, Connecticut) American geologist, mineralogist, and zoologist.

Dana was educated at Yale (1830–33) where he became interested in geology. He worked initially as assistant to Benjamin Silliman and published, in 1837, *A System of Mineralogy*, one of the major textbooks on the subject.

He sailed as geologist and naturalist on the Wilkes expedition (1838–42) visiting the Antarctic and Pacific. On his return, Dana published a series of research reports on the voyage during the period 1844–54, which established his reputation as an important scientist. These included *Zoophytes* (1846), *Geology* (1849), and *Crustacea* (1852).

In 1847 Dana formulated his geosynclinal theory of the origin of mountains. He introduced the term geosyncline to refer to troughs or dips in the Earth's surface that became filled with sediment. These huge deposits of sediment could then, Dana proposed, be compressed and folded into mountain chains.

He was appointed to the chair of natural history at Yale in 1856 and in 1864 to the chair of geology and mineralogy where he remained until his retirement in 1890. He published several important books while at Yale, including his most notable textbook, *Manual of Geology* (1863), and the synthesis of his work on coral reefs in *Corals and Coral Islands* (1872). In agreement with Charles Darwin's ideas, published in 1842, Dana argued that coral islands are the result of subsidence of the island together with the upward growth of corals.

DANIELL, John Frederic (b. Mar. 12, 1790; London; d. Mar. 13, 1845; London) British chemist and meteorologist.

Daniell was the son of a lawyer. He started work in the sugar-refining factory of a relative and, on the basis of early researches, he was elected to the Royal Society at the age of 23. He was appointed as first professor of chemistry at the newly opened King's College, London, in 1831.

Daniell invented a number of scientific instruments, including a hygrometer (1820) to measure humidity in the atmosphere. His theories on the atmosphere and wind movements were published in *Meteorological Essays and Observations* (1823). He also stressed the importance of moisture in hothouse management.

Daniell is best remembered for his introduction in 1836 of a new type of electric cell. The voltaic cell, introduced by Alessandro Volta in 1797, lost power once the current was drawn. This was due to bubbles of hydrogen collecting on the copper plate and producing resistance to the free flow of the circuit. With the growth of telegraphy there was a real need for a cell that could deliver a constant current over a long period of time. In the *Daniell cell* a zinc rod is immersed in a dilute solution of sulfuric acid contained in a porous pot, which stands in a solution of copper sulfate surrounded by copper. Hydrogen reacts with the copper sulfate. The porous pot prevents the two electrolytes from mixing, and at the positive (copper) electrode, copper is deposited from the copper sulfate. Thus, no hydrogen bubbles can form on this electrode.

DANIELS, Farrington (b. Mar. 8, 1889; Minneapolis, Minnesota; d. June 23, 1972; Madison, Wisconsin) American chemist.

Daniels was educated at the University of Minnesota and at Harvard, where he obtained his PhD in 1914. He moved to the University of Wisconsin in 1920, spending his whole career there and serving as professor of chemistry from 1928 until his retirement in 1959.

Daniels worked on a wide variety of chemical problems. In addition to a textbook, *Outlines of Physical Chemistry*

(1931), he wrote on photochemistry, nitrogen fixation, and thermoluminescence.

He was also interested in the utilization of solar energy, publishing a book on the subject, *Direct Use of the Sun's Energy* (1964), and organizing a symposium on it in 1954, many years before the discussion of solar energy had become fashionable.

DANSGAARD, Willi (b. Aug. 30, 1922; Copenhagen) Danish meteorologist.

Dansgaard was educated at the University of Copenhagen, obtaining his PhD in 1961. He has studied the applications of environmental isotopes to meteorological, hydrological, and glaciological problems, and in particular to the climate of the last 100 000 years. Oxygen is present in two stable isotopes — the normal oxygen–16 and a much smaller proportion of oxygen–18 with two extra neutrons in its nucleus. In 1947 Harold Urey demonstrated that the variation of the two isotopes in sea water depended on temperature; i.e. the colder the temperature the smaller the oxygen–18 content of the seas. He had further established that a slight change of temperature would produce a measurable alteration in oxygen–18 levels.

In the early 1960s the US army drilled down into the Greenland icecap, producing an ice core 4600 feet (1400 m) long and with a 100 000 year history. Dansgaard realized that by making careful measurement of the core's varying oxygen–18 level he should be able to reconstruct the climatic history of the last 100 000 years. The most recent ice age, ending 10 000 years ago, was clearly marked, as was evidence of a weather cycle during the last 1000 years.

DARBY, Abraham (b. *c.* 1678; near Dudley, England; d. Mar. 8, 1717; Madley Court, England) British metallurgist.

Darby developed the first successful method of smelting iron ore with coke, and in doing so made possible the large-scale production of good quality iron castings.

Previously only wood charcoal had been used but supplies of this were depleted and there were insufficient fuel supplies to provide the growing volume of iron. Attempts to use coal were unsuccessful because the sulfur impurities it contained spoiled the iron. By coking the coal the sulfur could be removed and Darby founded a factory at Coalbrookdale to smelt iron using coke. Abundant coal supplies and Darby's process meant that brass could be replaced by iron from large furnaces. Thomas Newcomen's new steam engine (1712) needed hard-wearing metal parts for cylinders etc., and the iron castings soon became an integral part of the industrial developments of the day.

Darby's grandson, also named Abraham, built the world's first iron bridge at Coalbrookdale (1779).

DARLINGTON, Cyril Dean (b. Dec. 12, 1903; Chorley, England; d. Mar. 26, 1981) British geneticist.

Darlington graduated in agriculture from Wye College, London, in 1923 and joined the John Innes Horticultural Institution, which was then under the directorship of William Bateson. He studied nuclear division, comparing mitosis (normal cell division) with meiosis (the reduction division that halves the chromosome number prior to gamete formation). He demonstrated that the chromosomes have already replicated by the first stage of mitosis whereas the chromosomes are still single in the earliest stage of meiosis, a discovery basic to nuclear cytology.

Darlington was also extremely interested in the crossing over of chromosomes that occurs at meiosis. He saw it as a mechanism that not only allows for recombination of genes between chromosomes but also accounts for the complete succession of meiotic events.

Darlington became director of the John Innes Institute in 1939 and presided over the move of the Institute from Merton to Bayfordbury in 1949. He became professor of botany at Oxford in 1953, attaining emeritus status in 1971. He wrote a number of books, including *Evolution of Genetic Systems* (1939) and, with Ronald Fisher, founded the journal *Heredity* in 1947.

DART, Raymond Arthur (b. Feb. 4, 1893; Toowong, Australia) Australian anatomist.

Dart was educated at the universities of Queensland and Sydney where he qualified as a physician in 1917. After a short period (1919–22) at University College, London, Dart moved to South Africa to serve as professor of anatomy at the University of the Witwatersrand, Johannesburg, a post he held until his retirement in 1958.

In 1924 Dart was privileged to make one of the great paleontological discoveries of the century, the Taung skull. For this he was indebted to his student Josephine Salmons who brought him in the summer of 1924 a fossil collected from a mine at Taung, Bechuanaland. Dart named it *Australopithecus africanus*, meaning southern African ape, and declared it to be intermediate between anthropoids and man. Such a claim was far from acceptable to many scholars at the time who, like Arthur Keith, dismissed the skull as that of a young anthropoid. Other and older australopithecine remains were later discovered by Robert Broom in South Africa, East Africa, and Asia, making it clear that they were in fact hominid. It is still however a matter of controversy whether *Australopithecus* lies in the direct line of descent to *Homo sapiens* or whether it represents a quite separate and unsuccessful evolutionary sideline.

DARWIN, Charles Robert (b. Feb. 12, 1809; Shrewsbury, England; d. Apr. 19, 1882; Down, England) British naturalist.

Darwin began his university education by studying medicine at Edinburgh (1825), but finding he had no taste for the subject he entered Cambridge University to prepare for the Church. At Cambridge his interest in natural history, first stimulated by the geologist Adam Sedgwick, was encouraged by the professor of botany John Henslow. Their friendship led to Henslow's recommending Darwin to the admiralty for the position of naturalist on HMS *Beagle*, which was preparing to survey the coast of South America and the Pacific.

The *Beagle* sailed in 1831 and Darwin, armed with a copy of Charles Lyell's *Principles of Geology*, initially concerned himself more with the geological aspects of his work. However, his observations of animal species — particularly the way in which they gradually change from region to region — also led him to speculate on the development of life. He was particularly struck by the variation found in the finches of the Galápagos Islands, where he recorded some 14 different species, each thriving in a particular region of the islands. Darwin reasoned that it was highly unlikely that each species was individually created; more probably they had evolved from a parent species of finch on mainland Ecuador. Further considerations, back in England, as to the mechanism that brought this about resulted in probably the most important book in the history of biology.

On returning to England in 1836, Darwin first concerned himself with recording his travels in *A Naturalist's Voyage on the Beagle* (1839), which received the acclaim of Alexander von Humboldt. His interest in geology was reflected in *Structure and Distribution of Coral Reefs* (1842) and *Geological Observations on Volcanic Islands* (1844). These early works, which established his name in the scientific community and won the respect of Lyell, were fundamental to the development of his theories on evolution.

Early on Darwin had perceived that many questions in animal geography, comparative anatomy, and paleontology could only be answered by disregarding the theory of the immutability of the species (an idea widely held at the time) and accepting that one species evolved from another. The idea was not original but Darwin's contribution was to propose a means by which evolution could have occurred and to present his case clearly, backed up by a wealth of evidence. In 1838 he read Thomas Malthus's *An Essay on the Principle of Population* and quickly saw that Malthus's argument could be extended from man to all other forms of life. Thus environmental pressures, particularly the availability of food, act to select better adapted individuals, which survive to pass on their traits to subsequent generations. Valuable characteristics that arise through natural variability are therefore preserved while others with no survival value die out. If environmental conditions change, the population itself will gradually change as it adapts to the new conditions, and with time this will lead to the formation of new species. Darwin spent over 20 years amassing evidence in support of this theory of evolution by natural selection, so as to provide a buffer against the inevitable uproar that would greet his work on publication. In this period the nature of his studies was divulged only to close friends, such as Joseph Hooker, T.H. Huxley (q.v.), and Charles Lyell.

The stimulus to publish came in June 1858 when Darwin received, quite unexpectedly, a communication from Alfred Russel Wallace (q.v.) that was effectively a synopsis of his own ideas. The question of priority was resolved through the action of Lyell and Hooker, who arranged for a joint paper to be read to the Linnean Society in July 1858. This consisted of Wallace's essay and a letter, dated 1857, from Darwin to the American botanist Asa Gray outlining Darwin's theories. Darwin later prepared an 'abstract' of his work, published in November 1859 as *On The Origin of Species by Means of Natural Selection*.

As expected the work made him many enemies among orthodox scientists and churchmen since beliefs in the Creation and divine guidance were threatened by Darwin's revelations. Darwin, a retiring man, chose not to defend his views publicly — a task left to (and seemingly immensely enjoyed by) Huxley, 'Darwin's bulldog', notably at the famous Oxford debate in 1860. Darwin continued quietly with his work, publishing books that extended and amplified his theories. One of these was *The Descent of Man* (1871), in which he applied his theory to the evolution of man from subhuman creatures. Many of his books are seen as pioneering works in various fields of biology, such as ecology and ethology.

Darwin was, however, troubled by one flaw in his theory — if inheritance were blending, i.e., if offspring received an average of the features of their parents (the then-held view of heredity), then how could the variation, so essential for natural selection to act on, come about? This problem was put in a nutshell by Fleeming Jenkin, professor of engineering at University College, London, who wrote a review of the *Origin* in 1867. In this Jenkin pointed out that any individual with a useful trait, assuming it mated with a normal partner, would pass on only 50% of the character to its children, 25% to its grandchildren, 12½% to its greatgrandchildren, and so on until the useful feature disappeared. The logic of this drove Darwin to resort to Lamarckian ideas of inheritance (of acquired characteristics) as elaborated in his theory of *pangenesis* in the sixth edition of the *Origin*. The question was not resolved until the rediscovery, nearly 20 years after Darwin's death, of Gregor Mendel's work (q.v.), which demonstrated the particulate nature of inheritance.

Darwin was troubled through most of his life by continuous illness, which most probably was due to infection by the trypanosome parasite causing Chagas' disease, contracted during his travels on the *Beagle*. On his death he was buried, despite his agnosticism, in Westminster Abbey.

DARWIN, Erasmus (b. Dec. 12, 1731; Elston, England; d. Apr. 18, 1802; Breadsall, England) British physician.

Darwin studied medicine at the universities of Cambridge and Edinburgh, obtaining his MB from Cambridge in 1755. He set up practice in Lichfield, where he soon established a reputation such that George III asked him to move to London to become his personal physician — an offer Darwin declined. He remained in Lichfield and founded, with friends, the Lunar Society of Birmingham — so called because of the monthly meetings held at members' houses. It included such eminent men as Joseph Priestley, Josiah Wedgwood, James Watt, and Matthew Boulton.

Darwin was something of an inventor, but is best remembered for his scientific writings, which often appeared in verse form. These were generally well received until the politician George Canning produced a very damaging parody of his work. This was part of a general campaign by the government against the Lunar Society for its support of the French and American revolutions and its denouncement of slavery.

In his work *Zoonomia* (1794–96), Darwin advances an evolutionary theory stating that changes in an organism are caused by the direct influence of the environment, a proposal similar to that proposed by Jean Baptiste Lamarck some 15 years later.

Darwin was the grandfather, by his first wife, of Charles Robert Darwin and, by his second wife, of Francis Galton.

DARWIN, Sir George Howard (b. July 9, 1845; Down, England; d. Dec. 7, 1912; Cambridge, England) British astronomer and geophysicist.

Darwin was the second son of the famous biologist, Charles Darwin. He was educated at Clapham Grammar School, where the astronomer Charles Pritchard was headmaster, and Cambridge University. He became a fellow in 1868 and, in 1883, Plumian Professor of Astronomy, a post he held until his death. He was knighted in 1905.

His most significant work was on the evolution of the Earth–Moon system. His basic premise was that the effect of the tides has been to slow the Earth's rotation thus lengthening the day and to cause the

Moon to recede from the Earth. He gave a mathematical analysis of the consequences of this, extrapolating into both the future and the past. He argued that some 4.5 billion years ago the Moon and the Earth would have been very close, with a day being less than five hours. Before this time the two bodies would actually have been one, with the Moon residing in what is now the Pacific Ocean. The Moon would have been torn away from the Earth by powerful solar tides that would have deformed the Earth every 2.5 hours.

Darwin's theory, worked out in collaboration with Osmond Fisher in 1879, explains both the low density of the Moon as being a part of the Earth's mantle, and also the absence of a granite layer on the Pacific floor. However, the theory is not widely accepted by astronomers. It runs against the Roche limit, which claims that no satellite can come closer than 2.44 times the planet's radius without breaking up; there are also problems with angular momentum. Astronomers today favor the view that the Moon has formed by processes of condensation and accretion. Whatever its faults, Darwin's theory is important as being the first real attempt to work out a cosmology on the principles of mathematical physics.

DAUBRÉE, Gabriel Auguste (b. June 25, 1814; Metz, France; d. May 29, 1896; Paris) French geologist.

Daubrée was educated at the University of Strasbourg. After investigating the tin mines of England he was employed, in 1838, as an engineer for Bas-Rhin and prepared a geological map of the area (1840–48). He was then appointed professor of geology at the University of Strasbourg, becoming professor of geology at the Museum of Natural History, Paris, in 1861. Finally, in 1862 he became director of the Imperial School of Mines.

Daubrée was a pioneer of experimental geology, publishing his research in his most significant work, *Etudes synthétiques de géologie expérimentale* (1879; Synthesis

Studies on Experimental Geology), in which he tried to show that an understanding of geochemical processes can be attained by reproducing them in the laboratory. In particular he worked on the effect that heating water at great depths in the Earth would have on the production of metamorphic rocks.

Daubrée also built up an extensive collection of meteorites and published his findings in *Météorites et la constitution géologique du globe* (1886; Meteorites and the Geological Constitution of the World). He concluded from his study of the composition of meteorites that the Earth has an iron core.

DAUSSET, Jean (b. Oct. 19, 1916; Toulouse, France) French physician and immunologist.

Dausset, the son of a doctor, gained his MD from the University of Paris in 1945 following wartime service in the blood transfusion unit. He was professor of hematology at the University of Paris from 1958 and professor of immunohematology from 1968. In 1977 he was elected professor of experimental medicine at the Collège de France.

Dausset's war experience stimulated his interest in transfusion reactions, and in 1951 he showed that the blood of certain universal donors (those of blood group 0), which had been assumed safe to use in all transfusions, could nonetheless be dangerous. This was because of the presence of strong immune antibodies in their plasma, which develop following antidiptheria and antitetanus injections. Donor blood is now systematically tested for such antibodies.

In the 1950s Dausset noticed a peculiar feature in the histories of patients who had received a number of blood transfusions: they developed a low white blood cell (leukocyte) count. He suspected that the blood transfused could well have contained antigens that stimulated the production of antibodies against the leukocytes. With insight and considerable courage Dausset went on to claim that the antigen on the blood cells, soon to be known as the HLA or human lymphocyte antigen, was the equivalent of the mouse H-2 system, described by George Snell (q.v.).

The significance of Dausset's work was enormous. It meant that tissues could be typed quickly and cheaply by simple blood agglutination tests as opposed to the complicated and lengthy procedure of seeing if skin grafts would take. Such work made the technically feasible operation of kidney transplantation a practical medical option for at last the danger of rejection could be minimized by rapid, simple, and accurate tissue typing. Further confirmation of Dausset's work was obtained when the specific regions of the HLA gene complex were later identified by J. van Rood and R. Ceppellini as a single locus on human chromosome 6.

Dausset later shared the 1980 Nobel Physiology or Medicine Prize with Snell and Baruj Benacerraf.

DAVAINE, Casimir Joseph (b. Mar. 19, 1812; St. Amand-les-Eaux, France; d. Oct. 14, 1882; Garches, France) French physician.

Davaine studied medicine and worked for most of his life in general practice in Paris. Around 1850 he began studying anthrax in cattle and became, arguably, the first scientist to recognize the role of a specific bacteria as the causal agent of an identifiable disease.

The rodlike organisms of anthrax were first described by Franz Pollender in 1849. Found in the blood of cattle killed by anthrax, Pollender could not be sure if they were the cause or consequence of the disease. In 1863 Davaine took the crucial step of demonstrating that the disease could be transmitted to other cattle by inoculating them with the blood of diseased animals. However if the blood was heated the disease could no longer be transmitted. Further, Davaine found, if the blood was mixed with water and the mixture allowed to stand then fluid taken from the top of the vessel proved harmless but anthrax could still be transmitted with a sample from the bottom. Such was the evidence assembled by Davaine to support the existence of disease transmitting 'bactéridies'.

His theory however did not explain the well-established fact that anthrax could break out in apparently uncontaminated areas. It was only when Robert Koch was able to show in 1876 that the bacillus formed spores, which could exist unchanged in the soil, that the full force of Davaine's work became clear.

DAVENPORT, Charles Benedict (b. June 1, 1866; Stamford, Connecticut; d. Feb. 18, 1944; Cold Spring Harbor, New York) American zoologist and geneticist.

Davenport obtained a zoology doctorate at Harvard in 1892, where he taught until 1899. From 1901 until 1904 he was curator of the Zoological Museum at the University of Chicago, and from 1904 until 1934 was director of the Carnegie Institution's Department of Genetics at Cold Spring Harbor. In 1910 Davenport founded the Eugenics Record Office, directing it until 1934.

Davenport's early studies of animal genetics, using chickens and canaries, were carried out at the turn of the century, and he was among the first to accept Gregor Mendel's rediscovered theory of heredity. He later turned his attention to man, and in *Heredity in Relation to Eugenics* (1912) offered evidence for the inheritance of particular human traits, suggesting that the application of genetic principles to human breeding might improve the race (eugenics). From 1898 Davenport was assistant editor of the *Journal of Experimental Zoology*; he was also editor of both *Genetics* and the *Journal of Physical Anthropology*.

DAVIS, William Morris (b. Feb. 12, 1850; Philadelphia, Pennsylvania; d. Feb. 5, 1934; Pasadena, California) American physical geographer.

Davis was educated at Harvard where he returned to teach in 1877 after a period as a meteorologist in Argentina and as an assistant with the North Pacific Survey. He became professor of physical geography in 1890 and of geology in 1898.

Davis is acknowledged as the founder of the science of geomorphology, the study of landforms. In his *The Rivers and Valleys of Pennsylvania* (1889) he first introduced what later became known as the Davisian system of landscape analysis. His aim was to provide an explanatory description of how landforms change in an ideal situation and his most important contribution to this was his introduction of the 'cycle of erosion' into geographical thought.

He proposed a complete cycle of youth, maturity, and old age to describe the evolution of a landscape. In youth rivers occupy steep V-shaped valleys while in old age the valleys are broad. The end product would be a flat featureless plain he called a 'peneplain'. This was an ideal cycle but in practice the cycle would invariably be interrupted by Earth movements. It was nevertheless strongly attacked by the German geographers who objected to it on the grounds that it neglected such vital factors as weathering and climate in transforming the landscape. They also believed him to be undermining their argument that landforms could only be discovered by local fieldwork and the production of regional monographs.

Davis also produced an influential work, *Elementary Meteorology* (1894), which was used as a textbook for over 30 years, and, in 1928, published *The Coral Reef Problem*.

DAVISSON, Clinton Joseph (b. Oct. 22, 1881; Bloomington, Illinois; d. Feb. 1, 1958; Charlottesville, Virginia) American physicist.

Davisson was educated at the University of Chicago, and at Princeton where he obtained his PhD in 1911. After working for a short period at the Carnegie Institute of Technology, Pittsburgh, Davisson joined the Bell Telephone Laboratory (then Western Electric) in 1917 and remained there until his retirement in 1946.

Davisson began his work by investigating the emission of electrons from a platinum oxide surface under bombardment by positive ions. He moved from this to studying the effect of electron bombardment on surfaces, and observed (1925) the angle of reflection could depend on crystal orientation. Following Louis de Broglie's theory of the wave nature of particles, he realized that his results could be due to diffraction of electrons by the pattern of atoms on the crystal surface.

In 1927 he performed a classic experiment with Lester Germer in which a beam of electrons of known momentum (p) was directed at an angle onto a nickel surface. The angles of reflected (diffracted) electrons were measured and the results were in agreement with de Broglie's equation for the wavelength ($\lambda = h/p$). In 1937 he shared the Nobel Physics Prize with George Thomson for "their experimental discovery of the diffraction of electrons by crystals."

DAVY, Sir Humphry (b. Dec. 17, 1778; Penzance, England; d. May 29, 1829; Geneva, Switzerland) British chemist.

The son of a small landowner and woodcarver, Davy went to school in Penzance and Truro and at the age of 17 he was apprenticed to an apothecary and surgeon with a view to qualifying in medicine. He was self-reliant and inquisitive from an early age and taught himself chemistry from textbooks. In 1798 he was appointed to Thomas Beddoes's Pneumatic Institute at Clifton, Bristol, to investigate the medicinal properties of gases. Davy's first papers were published by Beddoes in 1799. In one he concluded, independently of Count Rumford, that heat was a form of motion; the other contained some fanciful speculations on oxygen, which he called phosoxygen. Davy soon discovered the inebriating effect of nitrous oxide and his paper *Researches, Chemical and Philosophical; chiefly concerning Nitrous Oxide* (1800), and the subsequent fashion for taking the 'airs', made him famous. At Clifton he met many eminent people, including the poets William Wordsworth, Samuel Taylor Coleridge, and Robert Southey (Davy was himself a Romantic poet), and his flirtation with fashionable society began.

In 1801 Davy moved to London, to the Royal Institution, where his lectures were spectacularly successful. At Clifton he had begun to experiment in electrochemistry, following William Nicholson's electrolysis of water, and this was to prove his most fruitful field. In the early years at the Royal Institution, however, he did much work of an applied nature, for example on tanning and on agricultural chemistry. In his 1806 Bakerian Lecture to the Royal Society he predicted that electricity would be capable of resolving compounds into their elements and in the following year he was able to announce the isolation of potassium and sodium from potash and soda. This result cast doubts on Antoine Lavoisier's oxygen theory of acidity. Davy was essentially a speculative and manipulative chemist, not a theorist, and he reasoned incorrectly that ammonia (because of its alkaline properties), and hence nitrogen, might contain oxygen. He remained sceptical about the elementary nature of bodies for many years and tried to show that sulfur and phosphorus contained hydrogen.

Davy's work in the years immediately following the discovery of sodium was hindered by his social success and competition for priority with the French chemists Joseph Gay-Lussac and Louis Thenard. He prepared boron, calcium, barium, and strontium by electrolysis but his priority was disputed. In 1810 he published a paper on chlorine, which established that it contained no oxygen — another blow against the oxygen theory of acidity — and was in fact an element. The name 'chlorine' was proposed by Davy.

In 1812 Davy was knighted, married a wealthy widow, and published his book *Elements of Chemical Philosophy*. In 1813 he appointed Michael Faraday as his assistant and the Davys and Faraday visited France. Working in Michel Chevreul's laboratory, he established that iodine, discovered two years before by Bernard Courtois, was an element similar in many properties to but heavier than chlorine. On his return to England, Davy was commissioned to investigate the problem of firedamp (methane) explosions in mines. In 1816, only six months after beginning the investigation, he produced the famous safety lamp, the *Davy lamp*, in which the flame was surrounded by a wire gauze.

Davy became president of the Royal Society in 1820 and the rest of his life was much taken up by traveling on the Continent. Depite his successes there is something incomplete about his life. He never accepted the atomic theory of Dalton, his great contemporary. He had in fact more in common with his Romantic poet friends than he did with Dalton. Jöns Berzelius said of him that his work consisted of "brilliant fragments."

DAWES, William Rutter (b. Mar. 19, 1799; London; d. Feb. 15, 1868; Haddenham, England) British astronomer.

Dawes's father was an astronomer, often on colonial service, and later taught mathematics in a London school. Dawes was originally intended for the Church but finding the views of the established church uncongenial, studied medicine at St. Bartholomew's Hospital, London, instead. He practiced for some time in Berkshire and in 1826 went to Liverpool where he was persuaded to exchange medicine for the post of a Dissenting minister in Ormskirk, Lancashire.

It was in Ormskirk that Dawes took up the serious study of astronomy in 1829. He built his own observatory and equipped it with a Dollond refractor. In 1839 Dawes moved to London to take charge of George Bishop's observatory in Regent's Park. Bishop had made a fortune in the wine trade and hoped to gain recognition by sponsoring some important discovery in his observatory. A second marriage to a wealthy widow in 1842 allowed Dawes to leave the somewhat disagreeable service of Bishop in 1844 and, despite persistent ill health, to devote himself to his own private astronomical researches first in Kent at Cranbrook and Maidstone and after 1857 at Haddenham in Oxfordshire.

Dawes, the keenest of observers, worked for many years on double stars. During his Ormskirk period he published details on over 200 of them. Basic data on a further 250 was published in 1852 in Bishop's *Astronomical Observations at South Villa*. In November 1850 he narrowly missed an important discovery when he reported that while observing Saturn's rings he noted in the ansa, that part visible at the side of the planet and sticking out like a handle, "a light ... at both ends." Dawes had in fact observed the faint inner 'crepe ring' of Saturn, Ring C, but had been narrowly anticipated in this by the American astronomer William C. Bond.

DAWKINS, Richard (b. 1941) British ethologist.

Dawkins was educated at Oxford University where he worked for his doctorate under Niko Tinbergen. He initially taught at the University of California, Berkeley, before returning to Oxford in 1970 as lecturer in animal behavior.

In *The Selfish Gene* (1976) Dawkins did much to introduce the work of such scholars as William Hamilton, Robert L. Trivers, and John Maynard Smith to a wider public. He tried to show that such apparently altruistic behavior as birds risking their lives to warn the flock of an approaching predator can be seen as the 'selfish' gene ensuring its own survival (by ensuring the survival of the descendents and relatives of the 'heroic' bird) — indeed that such behavior is as relentlessly under the control of the selfish gene as the compulsive rutting of the dominant stag.

DAY, David Talbot (b. Sept. 10, 1859; East Rockport, Ohio; d. Apr. 15, 1925; Washington DC) American chemist.

Day was educated at Johns Hopkins University, gaining his PhD in 1884. He started his career as a demonstrator in chemistry at the University of Maryland but left to become head of the Mineral Resources Division of the US Geological Survey in 1886.

Day investigated the reasons for the differences found in the composition of various petroleum deposits and concluded that percolation through mineral deposits affected the nature of the underlying petroleum. His experiments, in which he ran crude petroleum through fuller's earth, anticipated the later development of adsorption chromatography by Mikhail Tsvet.

Day did much to stimulate the growth of the petroleum industry and in 1922 produced one of its basic texts, *Handbook of the Petroleum Industry*. From 1914 to 1920 he was a consultant chemist with the Bureau of Mines.

DEACON, Henry (b. July 30, 1822; London; d. July 23, 1876; Widnes, England) British industrial chemist.

Deacon started his career as an apprentice with an engineering firm at the age of 14. He later joined the firm of Nasmyth and Gaskell, near Manchester, before joining Pilkington's glassworks at St. Helens. There he introduced, in 1844, a new method for grinding and smoothing glass. Leaving the glassworks in 1851, Deacon went into partnership with the younger William Pilkington in 1853 to manufacture alkali at Widnes. When Pilkington withdrew in 1853 Holbrook Gaskell took his place.

Deacon made a significant improvement in the Leblanc process for producing alkali, using one of its by-products, hydrochloric acid, to produce chlorine. William Gossage had introduced his tower to condense and collect the toxic hydrochloric acid fumes in

1836. In 1870 Deacon patented his method where the hydrochloric acid was passed over clay balls soaked in copper chloride, which, in air, oxidized the acid yielding chlorine. The chlorine was used in making bleaching powder for the textiles industry. The process was supplanted by an alternative method of converting the hydrochloric acid into chlorine introduced by Walter Weldon (1866–69).

DE BARY, Heinrich Anton (b. Jan. 26, 1831; Frankfurt am Main, now in West Germany; d. Jan. 19, 1888; Strassburg, now Strasbourg in France) German botanist.

De Bary gained his medical degree from Berlin in 1853 and practiced briefly in Frankfurt before devoting all his time to botany. He became *Privatdozent* in botany at Tübingen and then professor of botany, first at Freiburg im Breisgau (1855), then Halle (1867), and finally Strassburg (1872), where he remained until his death.

When de Bary began working on fungi some people still believed in the spontaneous generation of fungi, and the general ignorance of fungal life cycles severely impeded the development of intelligent control measures against fungal epidemics of crops. De Bary's first mycological publication, *Researches on Fungal Blights* (1853), dealt with the rust and smut diseases of plants and maintained that fungi are the cause, and not the effect, of these diseases. In 1865 he demonstrated that the fungus that causes stem rust of wheat, *Puccinia graminis*, needs two hosts — wheat and barberry — to complete its life cycle. De Bary showed in 1866 that individual lichens consist of a fungus and an alga in intimate association and in 1879 he introduced the term 'symbiosis' to describe mutually advantageous partnerships between dissimilar organisms.

De Bary's work was instrumental in encouraging a more developmental approach to mycology and his research on host–parasite interactions greatly helped in the fight against plant diseases.

DE BEER, Sir Gavin Rylands (b. Nov. 1, 1899; London; d. June 21, 1972; Alfriston, England) British zoologist.

De Beer graduated from Oxford University, where he was a fellow from 1923 to 1938. He served in both World Wars; during World War II he landed in Normandy in 1944, where he was in charge of psychological warfare. He was professor of embryology at University College, London, 1945–50, and then director of the Natural History Museum in London (1950–60).

In an early publication, *Introduction to Experimental Biology* (1926), de Beer finally disproved the germ-layer theory. Embryological investigations had indicated that vertebrate structures such as cartilage and certain bone cells were formed from the ectoderm, or outer layer of the embryo, and not, as was previously thought, from the mesoderm. As this goes against the germ-layer theory, orthodox embryologists argued that the experimental manipulations involved in such work altered the normal course of development. De Beer's contribution was to find a system that does not involve such manipulations so establishing the validity of earlier work.

De Beer has also done work to show that adult animals retain some of the juvenile characters of their evolutionary ancestors (*pedomorphosis*), thus refuting Ernst Haeckel's theory of recapitulation. He has suggested that gaps in the evolutionary development of animals may be accounted for by the impermanence of the soft tissues of young ancestors. Studies of *Archeopteryx*, the earliest known bird, led him to propose piecemeal evolutionary changes in such animals, thus explaining the combination of reptilian and avian characters (e.g. teeth and feathers). De Beer also carried out research into the functions of the pituitary gland. In the field of ancient history, de Beer applied scientific methods to various problems, for example, the origin of the Etruscans and Hannibal's journey across the Alps. His other books include *Embryology and Evolution of Chordate Animals* (1962), (with Julian

Huxley), *The Elements of Experimental Embryology* (1962), and a biography of Charles Darwin (1961). He was knighted in 1954.

DEBIERNE, André Louis (b. July 14, 1874; Paris; d. Aug. 31, 1949; Paris) French chemist.

Debierne was educated at the Ecole de Physique et Chemie. After graduation he worked at the Sorbonne and as an assistant to Pierre and Marie Curie, finally succeeding the latter as director of the Radium Institute. On his retirement in 1949 he in turn was succeeded by Marie Curie's daughter, Irène Joliot-Curie.

Debierne was principally a radiochemist; his first triumph came in 1900 with the discovery of a new radioactive element, actinium, which he isolated while working with pitchblende. In 1905 he went on to show that actinium, like radium, formed helium. This was of some significance in helping Ernest Rutherford to appreciate that some radioactive elements decay by emitting an alpha particle (or, as it turned out to be, the nucleus of a helium atom). In 1910, in collaboration with Marie Curie, he isolated pure metallic radium.

DE BROGLIE, Prince Louis Victor Pierre Raymond (b. Aug. 15, 1892; Dieppe, France) French physicist.

De Broglie is descended from a French family ennobled by Louis XIV. He was educated at the Sorbonne, originally as a historian but his interest in science was aroused in World War I when he was posted to the Eiffel Tower as a member of a signals unit. He pursued this interest after the war and finally obtained his doctorate in physics from the Sorbonne in 1924. He taught there from 1926, serving as professor of theoretical physics at the newly founded Henri Poincaré Institute (1928–62).

De Broglie is famous for his theory that particles (matter) can have wavelike pro-

perties. At the start of the 20th century physicists explained phenomena in terms of particles (such as the electron or proton) and electromagnetic radiation (light, ultraviolet radiation, etc.). Particles were 'matter' — conceived as discrete entities forming atoms and molecules; electromagnetic radiation was a wave motion involving changing electric and magnetic fields.

In 1905 two papers by Albert Einstein began a change in this conventional view of the physical world. His work on the special theory of relativity led to the idea that matter is itself a form of energy. More specifically he explained the photoelectric effect by the concept that electromagnetic radiation (a wave) can also behave as particles (photons). Later, in 1923, Arthur Compton produced further evidence for this view in explaining the scattering of x-rays by electrons.

In 1924 de Broglie, influenced by Einstein's work, put forward the converse idea — that just as waves can behave as particles, particles can also behave as waves. He proposed that an electron, for instance, can behave as if it were a wave motion (a *de Broglie wave*) with wavelength h/p, where p is the momentum of the electron and h is Planck's constant. This revolutionary theory was put forward in de Broglie's doctoral thesis. Experimental support for it was obtained independently by George Thomson and by Clinton J. Davisson and the wavelike behavior of particles was used by Erwin Schrödinger in his formulation of wave mechanics.

The fact that particles can behave as waves, and vice versa, is known as wave–particle duality and has caused intense debate as to the 'real' nature of particles and electromagnetic radiation (*see* Niels Bohr, Max Born, Erwin Schrödinger). De Broglie has always taken the view that there is a true deterministic physical process underlying quantum mechanics — i.e. that the current inderterminate approach in terms of probability can be replaced by a more fundamental theory. He bases his ideas on the concept of particles that are concentrations of energy guided through space by a real wave, and exchanging energy with a 'subquantum medium'.

De Broglie received the 1929 Nobel Physics Prize for his "discovery of the wave nature of the electron."

DEBYE, Peter Joseph William (b. Mar. 24, 1884; Maastricht, Netherlands; d. Nov. 2, 1966; Ithaca, New York) Dutch–American physicist and physical chemist.

Debye studied electrical engineering at Aachen and gained his PhD at Munich in 1910. He held chairs of physics at Zurich (1911–12 and 1919–27), Utrecht (1912–14), Göttingen (1914–19), and Leipzig. He was director of the Kaiser Wilhelm Institute for Theoretical Physics (1935–40) before emigrating to America where he was professor of chemistry at Cornell (1940–50).

Debye was essentially a theoretician and most of his work, although varied, had a common theme: the application of physical methods to problems of molecular structure. An early work was the derivation of a relation governing the change of the specific heat capacity of solids with temperature. In 1915 he gave a theoretical treatment of electron diffraction by gases, not realized in practice until 1930. At Göttingen, Debye and P. Scherrer discovered a method of producing x-ray diffraction patterns from powders. This was later extended to the production of diffraction patterns from simple molecules such as CCl_4 (1928).

A major part of Debye's work was devoted to dipole moments, beginning in 1912. He used these to determine the degree of polarity of covalent bonds and to determine bond angles. Together with his x-ray work and results from rotational spectra, this enabled the precise spatial configuration of small molecules to be deduced. For example, the planarity of the benzene molecule was confirmed by dipole moment measurements. Debye is probably better known, however, for the *Debye–Hückel theory* of electrolytes (1923). This was a theory that could be applied to con-

centrated solutions of ionic compounds, and was a great advance on the theories of the time, which applied only to very dilute solutions. The Debye–Hückel theory takes account of the fact that an ion in solution tends to attract other ions of opposite charge.

DEDEKIND, (Julius Wilhelm) Richard (b. Oct. 6, 1831; Brunswick, now in West Germany; d. Feb. 12, 1916; Brunswick) German mathematician.

Dedekind's life was long but outwardly uneventful. He studied in Brunswick (Braunschweig) at the Caroline College and then at the University of Göttingen where his teachers included Karl Gauss. He taught briefly at Göttingen and at the Federal Institute of Technology, Zurich, and then returned to Brunswick to take up a post at the Technical Institute. Dedekind remained in this relatively obscure position for nearly fifty years.

His most important contribution to mathematics was in his work on the foundations of the theory of numbers. The axioms for the natural number system, which are now known as the *Peano axioms*, were in fact first formulated by Dedekind in his seminal essay *Was sind und was sollen die Zahlen* (1888; What Numbers Are and Should Be). His best-known contribution was the rigorous definition of irrational numbers as classes of fractions by means of *Dedekind cuts* (or *sections*).

Dedekind's work marks an extremely important step forward in the movement in 19th-century mathematics toward modern standards of rigor. Dedekind was a close friend of Georg Cantor and one of the few mathematicians to recognize immediately the value of Cantor's work on the transfinite.

DE DUVE, Christian René (b. Oct. 2, 1917; Thames Ditton, England) Belgian biochemist.

De Duve was educated at the Catholic University of Louvain where he obtained his MD in 1941. After holding brief appointments at the Nobel Institute in Stockholm and at Washington University he returned to Louvain in 1947 and was appointed professor of biochemistry in 1951. Since 1962 he has also held a similar appointment at Rockefeller University in New York.

In 1949 de Duve was working on the metabolism of carbohydrates in the liver of the rat. By using centrifugal fractionation techniques to separate the contents of the cell, he was able to show that the enzyme glucose-6-phosphatase is associated with the microsomes — organelles whose role was only speculative until de Duve began this work. He also noted that the process of homogenization led to the release of the enzyme acid phosphatase, the amount of which seemed to vary with the degree of damage inflicted on the cells. This suggested to de Duve that the enzyme in the cell was normally enclosed by some kind of membrane. If true, the supposition would remove a problem that had long troubled cytologists — namely how it was that such powerful enzymes did not attack the normal molecules of the cell. This question could now be answered by proposing a self-contained organelle, which neatly isolated the digestive enzymes. Confirmation for this view came in 1955 with the identification of such a body with the aid of the electron microscope. As its role is digestive or lytic, de Duve proposed the name *lysosome*. The peroxisomes (organelles containing hydrogen peroxide in which oxidation reactions take place) were also discovered in de Duve's laboratory.

For such discoveries de Duve shared the 1974 Nobel Prize for physiology or medicine with Albert Claude and George Palade.

DE FOREST, Lee (b. Aug. 26, 1873; Council Bluffs, Iowa; d. June 30, 1961; Hollywood, California) American physicist and inventor.

De Forest was interested in science from the age of 13. His father, a congregational minister, wanted him to study for the Church, but De Forest refused, going instead, in 1893, to the Sheffield Scientific School at Yale University. His PhD thesis, *Hertzian Waves from the Ends of Parallel Wires* (1899), was probably the first PhD thesis on radio in America, and drew on the work of Heinrich Hertz and Guglielmo Marconi. While working for the Western Electric Company in Chicago, he developed an electrolytic detector and an alternating-current transmitter.

In 1907 De Forest patented the Audion tube, a thermionic grid-triode vacuum tube that was a very sensitive receiver of electrical signals. This invention was crucial to the development of telecommunications equipment. In 1912 he had the idea of 'cascading' these to amplify high-frequency radio signals, making possible the powerful signals needed for long-distance telephones and for radio broadcasting. His invention formed the basis of radio, radar, telephones, and computers until the advent of solid-state electronics.

Throughout his career De Forest pushed for the acceptance of radio broadcasting. He was not a very good business manager, however, and had to sell many of his patents. Later he worked on a sound film system that was similar to the one eventually adopted. In the 1930s he designed Audion diathermy machines for medical use and during World War II he worked on military research at the Bell Telephone Laboratories.

DE GEER, Charles (b. Jan. 30, 1720; Finspang, Sweden; d. Mar. 8, 1778; Stockholm) Swedish entomologist.

De Geer was educated in the classics at the University of Utrecht and then studied under Linnaeus at Uppsala. His extensive *Mémoires pour servir à l'histoire des insectes* (7 vols. 1752–78) include excellent drawings and probably the earliest published accounts of the maternal instinct in such nonsocial insects as the earwig *Forficula auriculara* and the shield bug *Elasmucha griseus*. He also initiated a system of insect classification based on the wings and mouthparts.

DE LA BECHE, Sir Henry Thomas (b. Feb. 10, 1796; d. Apr. 13, 1855; London) British geologist.

De La Beche entered the army but at the end of the Napoleonic Wars he chose to devote himself to geology instead. After traveling extensively in Europe and Jamaica on his own research work, he became, in 1835, director of the Geological Survey of Great Britain, which had been recently formed largely on his initiative. He was also instrumental in setting up the Royal School of Mines in 1851, of which he was the first principal.

He wrote extensively on the geology of southwest England and Jamaica, publishing the first account of the geology of Jamaica in 1827 and his report on the geology of Devon during the period 1832–35.

In 1834, while working in Devon, he made his most significant discovery. He observed that some rock strata contained fossil plants similar to those of the Carboniferous system, discovered by William Conybeare in 1822, but did not contain any of the fossils of the preceding Silurian system, recently discovered by Roderick Murchison. The Silurian was believed to merge directly into the Carboniferous and De La Beche assumed the strata he had discovered came before the Silurian. However, William Lonsdale, librarian of the Geological Society, convincingly argued for a system, later named the Devonian, which overlay the Silurian and underlay the Carboniferous.

De La Beche wrote extensively on geology; his *A Geological Manual* (1831), *How to Observe* (1835), and *Geological Observer* (1851), were in part aimed at satisfying the growing popular interest in geology.

DELAMBRE, Jean Baptiste Joseph (b. Sept. 19, 1749; Amiens, France; d. Aug. 19, 1822; Paris) French astronomer and mathematician.

Delambre was most unusual for a mathematician and astronomer in that he did not begin the serious study of his subject until he was well over 30 years old. As a student he had been interested in the classics and only turned to the exact sciences when he was 36. He published tables of Jupiter and Saturn in 1789 and of Uranus in 1792. He also measured an arc of the meridian between Dunkirk and Barcelona to establish a basis for the new metric system. He succeeded Joseph de Lalande as professor of astronomy at the Collège de France in 1795. In his later years he devoted himself to a monumental six-volume *Histoire de l'astronomie* (1817–27).

DE LA RUE, Warren (b. Jan. 18, 1815; Guernsey, Channel Islands; d. Apr. 19, 1889; London) British astronomer.

De la Rue was the son of a printer and worked most of his life in his father's business. He was educated in Paris and studied science privately. He was initially interested in chemistry, being a friend of and working with August Hofmann, but later, at the suggestion of James Nasmyth, he took up astronomy, building a small observatory for himself.

De la Rue devoted himself to problems of photographic astronomy. He was the first to apply the collodion process (invented by Frederick Archer in 1851) to photographing the Moon. In 1852, he took some photographs that were sharper than any previously produced and that could be enlarged without blurring. Ten years later he was producing photographs that could show as much as could be seen through any telescope. In 1854 he designed the photoheliograph, a device for taking telescopic photographs of the Sun. In 1860 he used it to take dramatic photographs of prominences during the total eclipse in Spain, proving that they were solar (and not, as had been thought, lunar) in origin.

De la Rue gave up active astronomical investigation in 1873 donating his telescope to the observatory at Oxford and devoting the rest of his life to his business and to his chemical researches.

DELBRÜCK, Max (b. Sept. 6, 1906; Berlin; d. Mar. 9, 1981) German biophysicist.

Delbrück received his PhD in physics from the University of Göttingen in 1930, and, after working in Copenhagen and Zurich on a Rockefeller Foundation physics fellowship, became a research assistant at the Kaiser Wilhelm Institute for Chemistry in Berlin. In 1937 he joined the California Institute of Technology on another Rockefeller fellowship, this time in biology, and became involved in bacteriophage research. He remained in America, becoming physics instructor at Vanderbilt University in 1939 and taking American citizenship in 1945.

In 1943 Delbrück published an important paper with Salvador Luria in which he produced an equation describing the mutation rate in bacterial cultures from virus-susceptible to virus-resistant forms. In 1946 both he and Alfred Hershey, working independently, found evidence that viruses can exchange (recombine) genetic material. Delbrück designed an experiment to see whether two different types of virus could reproduce in the same bacterial cell. He not only found that they could but also saw that the offspring contained characters of both types. This was the first evidence of recombination in such primitive organisms. Delbrück was one of the pioneers in the new fields of biophysics and molecular biology and, with Hershey and Luria, received the 1969 Nobel Prize for physiology or medicine for his contributions to these sciences.

D'ELHUYAR, Don Fausto (b. Oct. 11, 1755; Logroño, Spain; d. Jan. 6, 1833; Madrid) Spanish chemist and mineralogist.

D'Elhuyar studied mineralogy with his brother, Juan José, at the Freiberg Mining Academy under Abraham Werner. He then studied chemistry in Paris (1772–77). He returned to Spain shortly after and was sent to Mexico in 1788 to supervise mining operations. On his return to Spain in 1821 he was made director general of mines.

The D'Elhuyar brothers working together in 1783 discovered the element tungsten (formerly also known as wolfram). Two very dense minerals were known to chemists in the 18th century: 'tungsten' (Swedish meaning 'heavy stone') and wolframite. In 1781 Carl Scheele had discovered that 'tungsten' (now known as scheelite) contained tungstic acid. The brothers proved that the same acid is present in wolframite, from which mineral they succeeded in isolating the element tungsten.

DEL RIO, Andrès Manuel (b. Nov. 10, 1764; Madrid; d. Mar. 23, 1849; Mexico City) Spanish mineralogist.

After graduating in Spain in 1781 Del Rio studied in France, England, and Germany, where he was a pupil of Abraham Werner at the Freiberg Mining Academy. He had been chosen by Charles III to acquire the new scientific learning and to introduce it into the Spanish empire in order to develop and modernize the mining industry. Consequently he was sent to Mexico City to become, in 1794, professor of mineralogy at the School of Mines set up by Fausto D'Elhuyar. While there he published the *Elementos de orictognosia* (1795), which has some claim to being the first mineralogical textbook published in the Americas. He was forced into exile in the period 1829–34 after Mexico's war of independence but on his return he tried to reestablish the scientific tradition he had first introduced.

As a scientist he is best remembered for his independent discovery of the element vanadium in 1801. He had found what he took to be a new metal in some lead ore from the Mexican mines and named it 'erythronium' (from the Greek *erythros*, red) as its salts turned red when ignited. However, he failed to press his claim, being persuaded by other scientists that it was probably a compound of lead and chromium. Nils Gabriel Sefström rediscovered the metal in 1830 and named it vanadium. Its identity with Del Rio's erythronium was demonstrated by Friedrich Wohler in 1831.

DE LUC, Jean André (b. Feb. 8, 1727; Geneva, Switzerland; d. Nov. 7, 1817; Windsor, England) Swiss geologist and meteorologist.

De Luc came from an Italian family, which had moved to Switzerland from Tuscany in the 15th century. He initially concentrated on commercial activities with science as a side line but, in 1773, after the collapse of his business, he moved to England where he devoted himself to science. He was appointed as reader to Queen Charlotte, retaining that post until his death.

In a series of letters *Sur l'histoire de la terre* (On the History of the Earth) addressed to Queen Charlotte in 1779, James Hutton in 1790, and Johann Blumenbach in 1798, De Luc, following in the tradition of Thomas Burnet, tried to write a history of the Earth that took account of the advances in geology yet was still compatible with the Creation as described in Genesis.

De Luc proposed that the Earth itself was old though the flood was recent. The flood was caused by a collapse of the existing lands causing their inundation by the oceans and the emergence of the present continents. As these had been the prediluvial ocean floor it was only reasonable to suppose that they should contain marine fossils. De Luc thus explained one of the puzzles facing early geologists — the presence of marine fossils in the center of continents. De Luc opposed Hutton's fluvial theory that such major terrestrial features as valleys are the result of the still continuing action of the rivers. He pointed out that many valleys contain no rivers, that rivers far from eroding actually deposit material, and that there seems to be no relation between the size of the river and the valley it is supposed to have created. His main objection was over downstream lakes, for in this case, when the enormous amount of material eroded from the valley is considered, De Luc argued that the lake should have been filled in long before. Hutton's unsatisfactory answer was that such infilling does take place but that the lakes are much younger than the rivers. This issue was not resolved until the crucial role of glaciation was established by Louis Agassiz some 50 years later.

De Luc was also a major figure in meteorological research. His two works, *Recherches sur la modification de l'atmosphère* (1772) and *Idées sur la météorologie* (1786–87), made important suggestions for advances in instrumental design. His most important achievement was his formula, in 1791, for converting barometric readings into height, which provided the first accurate measurements of mountain heights.

DEMARÇAY, Eugene Anatole (b. Jan. 1, 1852; Paris; d. 1904; Paris) French chemist.

Demarçay was a research chemist who also maintained his own private laboratory in Paris. In 1901, while working with a sample of the newly discovered element samarium (discovered by Paul Lecoq de Boisbaudran in 1879) he found traces of an additional element, europium. More dramatic however was his earlier work with the Curies in 1898. They had discovered one new radioactive element, polonium, early in the year. But they found further radioactivity in their sample of pitchblende after the removal of polonium. They took the small sample they had extracted to Demarçay, an expert spectroscopist, who was able to find a new line in the spectrum. This enabled the Curies to announce the existence of a much more strongly radioactive element, radium.

DEMEREC, Milislav (b. Jan. 11, 1895; Kostajnica, Yugoslavia; d. Apr. 12, 1966; Laurel Hollow, New York) Yugoslavian-American geneticist.

Demerec graduated from the College of Agriculture in Krizevci, Yugoslavia, in 1916 and, after a few year's work at the Krizevci Experimental Station, moved to America. He gained his PhD in genetics from Cornell University in 1923 and then worked at the Carnegie Institution, Cold Spring Harbor, where he remained for most of his career, becoming director in 1943.

Demerec was concerned with gene structure and function, especially the effect of mutations. He found that certain unstable genes are more likely to mutate than others and that the rate of mutation is affected by various biological factors, such as the stage in the life cycle. He also demonstrated that chromosome segments that break away and rejoin in the wrong place may cause suppression of genes near the new region of attachment. This lent additional support to the idea of the 'position effect', first demonstrated by Alfred Sturtevant.

Demerec's work with the bacterium *Salmonella* revealed that genes controlling related functions are grouped together on the chromosome rather than being randomly distributed through the chromosome complement. Such units were later termed 'operons'. His radiation treatment of the fungus *Penicillium* yielded a mutant strain producing much larger quantities of penicillin — a discovery of great use in World War II. He showed that antibiotics should be administered initially in large doses, so that resistant mutations do not develop, and should be given in combinations, because any bacterium resistant to one is most unlikely to have resistance to both.

Demerec greatly increased the reputation of Cold Spring Harbor while director there and also served on many important committees. He founded the journal *Advances in Genetics* and wrote some 200 scientific articles.

DEMOCRITUS of Abdera (b. *c.* 460 BC; Abdera, Greece; d. *c.* 370 BC) Greek philosopher.

Although reputedly a prolific author, only fragments of Democritus's work survive and little is known of his life. He is believed to have been a wealthy citizen of Abdera and to have traveled in Egypt and Persia. He wrote on many subjects, and was reputedly the most learned man of his time.

Democritus is best known for his atomic theory. Despite the fact that Leucippus is generally regarded as the originator of the atomic theory, and the difficulty in separating Democritus's contribution from that of the later Epicurus and Lucretius, Democritus was acknowledged by Aristotle (the principle source for Democritus's ideas) to be the leading exponent of the theory. In the 'classical' atomic theory, coming into being and dissolution were explained by the linking and flying apart of small hard indestructible particles. Conservation of matter was recognized ("nothing is created out of nothing") and the important doctrine of primary and secondary qualities (later taken up by Galileo and John Locke) was enunciated by Democritus in the memorable aphorism: "Ostensibly there are sweet and bitter, hot and cold, and color; in reality only atoms and the void." The primary qualities were size, shape, and position. Whether or not Democritus attributed weight to atoms is controversial. The theory was deterministic in that the atomic interactions were thought to be ordered by 'necessity'. Atomism was ignored from the time of Aristotle until the mid-17th century when it was reintroduced by Pierre Gassendi and Galileo.

DE MOIVRE, Abraham (b. May 26, 1667;

Vitry, France; d. Nov. 27, 1754; London)
French mathematician.

Although born in France De Moivre was
a Huguenot and consequently was forced
to flee to England to escape the religious
persecution that flared up in 1685 after the
revocation of the Edict of Nantes. In
England De Moivre came to know both
Isaac Newton and Edmond Halley, eventually becoming a fellow of the Royal
Society of London himself in 1697.

De Moivre made important contributions to mathematics in the fields of probability and trigonometry. His interest in
probability was no doubt stimulated by the
fact that despite his abilities he was unable
to find a permanent post as a mathematician and so was forced to earn his living by,
among other things, gambling. De Moivre
was the first to define the concept of
statistical independence and to introduce
analytical techniques into probability. His
work on this was published in *The
Doctrine of Chances* (1718), later followed
by *Miscellanea analytica* (1730; Analytical Miscellany). De Moivre also introduced
the use of complex numbers into trigonometry.

DEMPSTER, Arthur Jeffrey (b. Aug. 14,
1886; Toronto, Ontario; d. Mar. 11, 1950;
Stuart, Florida) Canadian–American physicist.

Dempster was educated at the University of Toronto. He emigrated to America
in 1914, attended the University of Chicago, obtained his PhD in 1916, and began
teaching in 1919. In 1927, he was made professor of physics.

He is noted for his early developments of
and work with the mass spectrograph
(invented by Francis W. Aston). In 1935,
he was able to show that uranium did not
consist solely of the isotope uranium–238,
for seven out of every thousand uranium
atoms were in fact uranium–235. It was
this isotope ^{235}U that was later predicted
by Niels Bohr to be capable of sustaining a

chain reaction that could release large
amounts of atomic fission energy.

DESAGULIERS, John Theophilus (b. Mar.
13, 1683; La Rochelle, France; d. Feb. 29,
1744; London) French–English physicist.

Desaguliers, the son of a Huguenot
refugee, began giving popular lectures on
science and its applications in Oxford in
1710. In 1713 he moved to London where
he continued to lecture and became experimental assistant to Isaac Newton until
Newton's death in 1727. He is important in
spreading Newtonian theory both in
England and on the Continent. He was also
an experimenter — particularly on the
flow of electricity, being the first to use the
terms 'conductor' and 'insulator' — and an
inventor, improving the design of Thomas
Savery's steam engine by adding a safety
valve and an internal water jet.

DESARGUES, Girard (b. Mar. 2, 1591;
Lyons, France; d. October 1661; France)
French mathematician and engineer.

Little is known of Desargues's early life.
He served as an engineer at the siege of La
Rochelle (1628) and later became a technical adviser to Cardinal de Richelieu and
the French government. He is said to have
known René Descartes.

Around 1630 Desargues joined a group
of mathematicians in Paris and concentrated on geometry. In his most famous
work, *Brouillon projet d'une atteinte aux
événements des rencontres d'une cône
avec un plan* (1639; Proposed Draft of an
Attempt to deal with the Events of the
Meeting of a Cone with a Plane), he
applied projective geometry to conic sections. *Desargues's theorem* states that if
the corresponding points of two triangles
in nonparallel planes in space are joined
by three lines that intersect at a single
point, then the pairs of lines that are the
extensions of corresponding sides will each
intersect on the same line. Blaise Pascal
was greatly influenced by Desargues,

whose contribution to projective geometry was not recognized until a handwritten copy of his work was found in 1845. This oversight probably arose because he used obscure botanical symbols instead of the better-known Cartesian symbolism.

DESCARTES, René du Perron (b. Mar. 31, 1596; La Haye, France; d. Feb. 11, 1650; Stockholm, Sweden) French mathematician, philosopher, and scientist.

Descartes's father was a counselor of the Britanny *parlement* while his mother, who died shortly after his birth, left him sufficient funds to make him financially independent. He was educated by the Jesuits of La Flèche (1604–12) and at the University of Poitiers, where he graduated in law in 1616. For the next decade Descartes spent much of his time in travel throughout Europe and in military service, first with the army of the Prince of Orange, Maurice of Nassau, and later with the Duke of Bavaria, Maximilian, with whom he was present at the battle of the White Mountain outside Prague in 1620. In the years 1628–49 Descartes settled in the freer atmosphere of Holland. There, living quietly, he worked on the exposition and development of his system. Somewhat unwisely, he allowed himself to be enticed into the personal service of Queen Christina of Sweden in Stockholm in 1649. Forced to indulge the Queen's passion for philosophy by holding tutorials with her at 5 am on icy Swedish mornings Descartes, who normally loved to lie thinking in a warm bed, died within a year from pneumonia and the copious bleeding inflicted by the enthusiastic Swedish doctors.

Descartes is in many ways, in mathematics, philosophy, and science, the first of the moderns. The moment of modernity can be dated precisely to 10 November, 1619, when, as later described in his *Discours de la méthode* (1637; Discourse on Method), he spent the whole day in seclusion in a *poêle* (an overheated room). He began systematically to doubt all sup-posed knowledge and resolved to accept only "what was presented to my mind so clearly and distinctly as to exclude all ground of doubt."

Descartes thus managed to pose in a single night the problem whose solution would obsess philosophers for the next 300 years. The same night also provided him with one of the basic insights of modern mathematics — that the position of a point can be uniquely defined by coodinates locating its distance from a fixed point in the direction of two or more straight lines. This was revealed in his *La Geométrie* (1637), published as an appendix to his *Discourse*, and describing the invention of analytic or coordinate geometry, by which the geometric properties of curves and figures could be written as and investigated by algebraic equations. The system is known as a *Cartesian coordinate* system.

His theories on physics were published in his *Principia philosophiae* (1644; Principles of Philosophy). "Give me matter and motion and I will construct the universe," Descartes had proclaimed. The difficulty for him arose from his account of matter which, on metaphysical grounds, he argued, "does not at all consist in hardness, or gravity or color or that which is sensible in another manner, but alone in length, width, and depth," or, in other words, extension. From this initial handicap Descartes was forced to deny the existence of the void and face such apparently intractable problems as how bodies of the same extension could possess different weights. With such restrictions he was led to describe the universe as a system of vortices. Matter came in three forms — ordinary matter opaque to light, the ether of the heavens transmitting light, and the subtle particles of light itself. With considerable ingenuity and precious little concern for reality Descartes used such a framework within which he was able to deal with the basic phenomena of light, heat, and motion. Despite its initial difficulties it was developed by a generation of Cartesian disciples to pose as a viable alternative to the mechanics worked out later in the century by Newton. Unlike many less radical thinkers Descartes did not shrink from applying his mechanical principles to physiology, seeing the human body purely in terms of a physico-mechanical system (with the mind as a separate entity, interacting with the body via the pineal gland — the supposed seat of the soul.

The fundamental impact of Descartes's work was basically one of demystification. Apart from the residual enigma of the precise relationship between mind and body, the main areas of physics and physiology had been swept clear of such talk as that of occult powers and hidden forms.

DESCH, Cyril Henry (b. Sept. 7, 1874; London; d. June 19, 1958; London) British metallurgist.

Desch, the son of a surveyor, was educated at King's College, London. He taught in Glasgow from 1909 until 1920, when he took up an appointment at the University of Sheffield where he served as professor of metallurgy from 1920 to 1931. Desch then moved to the National Physical Laboratory at Teddington, Middlesex, where he was in charge of the metallurgy department until his retirement in 1939.

Desch is mainly known for his publication in 1910 of his *Textbook of Metallography*, a work that served as the standard account of the subject for the first half of the century.

DE SITTER, Willem (b. May 6, 1872; Sneek, Netherlands; d. Nov. 20, 1934; Leiden, Netherlands) Dutch astronomer and mathematician.

De Sitter, the son of a judge, studied mathematics and physics at the University of Groningen, his interest in astronomy being aroused by Jacobus Kapteyn. After serving at the Cape Town Observatory from 1897 to 1899 and, back at Groningen, as assistant to Kapteyn from 1899 to 1908, he was appointed to the chair of astronomy at the University of Leiden. He also served

as director of Leiden Observatory from 1919 to 1934.

De Sitter is remembered for his proposal in 1917 of what came to be called the 'de Sitter universe' in contrast to the 'Einstein universe'. Einstein had solved the cosmological equations of his general relativity theory by the introduction of the cosmological constant, which yielded a static universe. But de Sitter, in 1917, showed that there was another solution to the equations that produced a static universe if no matter was present. The contrast was summarized in the statement that Einstein's universe contained matter but no motion while de Sitter's involved motion without matter.

The Russian mathematician Alexander Friedmann in 1922 and the Belgian George Lemaître independently in 1927 introduced the idea of an expanding universe that contained moving matter. It was then shown in 1928 that the de Sitter universe could be transformed mathematically into an expanding universe. This model, the 'Einstein–de Sitter universe', comprised normal Euclidean space and was a simpler version of the Friedmann–Lemaître models in which space was curved.

De Sitter also worked on celestial mechanics and stellar photometry. He spent much time trying to calculate the mass of Jupiter's satellites from the small perturbations in their orbits. The results were published in 1925 in his *New Mathematical Theory of Jupiter's Satellites*.

DESMAREST, Nicolas (b. Sept. 16, 1725; Soulaines-Dhuys, France; d. Sept. 28, 1815; Paris) French geologist.

Desmarest was the son of a school teacher. He first came to notice when he won a prize essay set by the Amiens Academy in 1751 on whether England and France had ever been joined together. Working for a while in Paris as an editor of scholarly works, he eventually started work for the department of commerce in 1757 investigating and reporting on various trades and industries. He served as inspector-general of manufactures (1788–91).

In 1763, following the work of Jean Guettard, he noticed large basalt deposits and traced these back to ancient volcanic activity in the Auvergne region. He mapped the area and worked out the geology of the volcanoes and their eruptions in great detail, publishing his work in the *Encyclopédie* of 1768. This work disproved the theory that all rocks were sedimentary by revealing basalt's igneous origins. He later produced an influential work, *Géographie physique* (1794; Physical Geography).

DESORMES, Charles Bernard (b. June 3, 1777; Dijon, France; d. Aug. 30, 1862; Verberie, France) French chemist.

Désormes studied at the Ecole Polytechnique and was an assistant to Guyton de Morveau until 1804. With Jacques and Joseph Montgolfier and his son-in-law, Nicolas Clément, he was co-owner of a chemical factory at Verberie.

Clément and Désormes discovered carbon monoxide (1801), investigated the catalytic effect of nitric oxide in the lead-chamber process of sulfuric acid manufacture, and were involved in the early work on iodine, which was discovered by Bernard Courtois in 1811. Their most important work, however, was in physical chemistry on the specific heats of gases. In 1819 they published an important paper on the determination of the ratio of the principal specific heats (i.e. the ratio of the specific heat of a gas at constant pressure to that at constant volume).

DEVILLE, Henri Etienne Sainte-Claire (b. Mar. 11, 1818; St. Thomas, West Indies; d. July 1, 1881; Boulogne, France) French chemist.

The son of a wealthy shipowner in the West Indies, Deville studied medicine in Paris but became interested in chemistry by attending Louis Thenard's lectures. He isolated toluene and methyl benzoate from

tolu balsam and investigated other natural products before turning to inorganic chemistry, following his appointment as professor of chemistry at Besançon (1845).

Deville's first major discovery was that of nitrogen pentoxide (1849). Following this success he became professor of chemistry at the Ecole Normale Supérieure (1851) and also lectured at the Sorbonne from 1853. Deville is best known for his work on the large-scale production of aluminum. This had been obtained by Kaspar Wöhler in 1827 but had been produced only in small quantities. Deville developed a commercially successful process involving reduction of aluminum chloride by sodium; the first ingot was produced in 1855. Deville was an expert on the purification of metals and produced (among others) crystalline silicon (1854) and boron (1856), pure magnesium (1857), and pure titanium (1857; with Wöhler). He did much work on the purification of platinum and in 1872 was commissioned to produce the standard kilogram.

After his work on aluminum, Deville's most important researches were those on dissociation. Working with L. J. Troost, he discovered that many molecules were dissociated at high temperature, giving rise to anomalous vapor-density results. Deville's work explained these results and helped to confirm Amedeo Avogadro's hypothesis. His other work included the production of artificial gemstones and improved furnaces.

DE VRIES, Hugo (b. Feb. 16, 1848; Haarlem, Netherlands; d. May 21, 1935; Amsterdam) Dutch plant physiologist and geneticist.

The son of a Dutch politician, de Vries studied botany at Leiden and Heidelberg. He became an expert on the Netherlands flora and later turned his attention from classification to physiology and evolution. He entered Julius von Sachs's laboratory at Würzburg University, where he conducted important experiments on the water of plant cells. He demonstrated that the pressure (turgor) of the cell fluid is responsible for about 10% of extension growth, and introduced the term *plasmolysis* to describe the condition in non-turgid cells in which the cell contents contract away from the cell wall. His work in this field led to Jacobus Van't Hoff's theory of osmosis.

During the 1880s, de Vries became interested in heredity. In 1889 he published *Intracellular Pangenesis*, in which he critically reviewed previous research on inheritance and advanced the theory that elements in the nucleus, 'pangenes', determine hereditary traits. To investigate his theories, he began breeding plants in 1892 and by 1896 had obtained clear evidence for the segregation of characters in the offspring of crosses in 3:1 ratios. He delayed publishing these results, proposing to include them in a larger book, but in 1900 he came across the work of Gregor Mendel (q.v.), published 34 years earlier, and announced his own findings. This stimulated both Karl Correns and Erich von Tschermak-Seysenegg to publish their essentially similar observations.

De Vries's work on the evening primrose, *Oenothera lamarckiana*, began in 1886 when he noticed distinctly differing types within a colony of the plants. He considered these to be mutants and formulated the idea of evolution proceeding by distinct changes such as those he observed, believing also that new species could arise through a single drastic mutation. He published his observations in *The Mutation Theory* (1901–03). It was later shown that his *Oenothera* 'mutants' were in fact triploids or tetraploids (i.e. they had extra sets of chromosomes) and thus gave a misleading impression of the apparent rate and magnitude of mutations. However, the theory is still important for demonstrating how variation, essential for evolution, can occur in a species.

De Vries was professor of botany at Amsterdam from 1878 to 1918 and was elected a fellow of the Royal Society in 1905.

DEWAR, Sir James (b. Sept. 20, 1842; Kincardine-on-Forth, Scotland; d. Mar. 27, 1923; London) British chemist and physicist.

Dewar was the son of a wine merchant. He was educated at Edinburgh University where he was a pupil of Lyon Playfair. In 1869 he was appointed lecturer in chemistry at the Royal Veterinary College, Edinburgh, and from 1873 also held the post of assistant chemist to the Highland and Agricultural Society of Scotland. In 1875 Dewar became Jacksonian Professor of Experimental Philosophy at Cambridge University, England, and from 1877 he was also Fullerian Professor of Chemistry at the Royal Institution, London. He did most of his work in London where the facilities for experimental work were much better.

Dewar conducted his most important work in the field of low temperatures and the liquefaction of gases. In 1878 he demonstrated Louis Cailletet's apparatus for the liquefaction of oxygen and by 1891 he was able to produce liquid oxygen in quantity. In about 1872 he devised a double-walled flask with a vacuum between its highly reflective walls, the *Dewar flask*, and used this to store liquefied oxygen at extremely low temperatures. This vessel (the thermos flask) has come into everyday use for keeping substances either hot or cold.

Hydrogen had so far resisted liquefaction and Dewar now turned his attention to this. Using the Joule–Thomson effect together with Karl von Linde's improvements of this he produced a machine with which he obtained temperatures as low as 14 K and he produced liquid hydrogen in 1898 and solid hydrogen in 1899. Only helium now resisted liquefaction; this was achieved by Heike Kamerlingh-Onnes in 1908.

From about 1891 Dewar also studied explosives and with Frederick Abel he developed the smokeless powder, cordite. He was knighted in 1904.

DEWAR, Michael James Stewart (b. Sept. 24, 1918; Ahmednagar, India) British–American chemist.

Dewar was educated at Oxford University where he obtained his DPhil in 1942. After research at Oxford he worked in industry as a physical chemist for the Courtauld company from 1945 until his appointment in 1951 as professor of chemistry at Queen Mary College, London. In 1959 Dewar moved to America and has served successively as professor of chemistry at the University of Chicago and since 1963 at the University of Texas.

Dewar is noted for his contributions to theoretical chemistry. In his *Electronic Theory of Organic Chemistry* (1949) he argued strongly for the molecular-orbital theory introduced by Robert Mulliken. He did much to improve molecular-orbital calculations and by the 1960s he was able to claim that he and his colleagues could rapidly and accurately calculate a number of chemical and physical properties of molecules.

D'HERELLE, Felix (b. Apr. 25, 1873; Montreal, Quebec; d. Feb. 22, 1949; Paris) French–Canadian bacteriologist.

D'Herelle, the son of a Canadian father and Dutch mother, went to school in Paris and later studied medicine at the University of Montreal. He worked as a bacteriologist in Guatemala and Mexico from 1901 until 1909, when he returned to Europe to take up a position at the Pasteur Institute in Paris. D'Herelle moved to the University of Leiden in 1921 but after only a short stay resigned to become director of the Egyptian Bacteriological Service (1923). Finally, in 1926, d'Herelle was appointed to the chair of bacteriology at Yale, a position he held until his retirement in 1933.

D'Herelle is best known for his discovery of the bacteriophage — a type of virus that destroys bacteria. This work began in 1910 in Yucatan, when he was investigating diarrhea in locusts as a means of locust control. While developing cultures of the causative agent, a coccobacillus, d'Herelle found that occasionally there would develop on a culture a clear spot, completely free of any bacteria. The cause of these clear spots became clear to him in 1915, while investigating a more orthodox form of dysentry in a cavalry squadron in Paris. He mixed a filtrate from the clear area with a culture of the dysentry bacilli and incubated the resulting broth overnight. The next morning the culture, which had been very turbid, was perfectly clear: all the bacteria had vanished. He concluded that this was the action of "a filterable virus, but a virus parasitic on bacteria."

A similar discovery of what d'Herelle termed a 'bacteriolytic agent' was announced independently by Frederick Twort in 1915. D'Herelle published his own account first in 1917, followed by his monograph *The Bacteriophage, Its Role in Immunity* (1921). He spent the rest of his career attempting to develop bacteriophages as therapeutic agents. Thus, he tried to cure cholera in India in 1927 and bubonic plague in Egypt in 1926 by administering to the patients the appropriate phage. D'Herelle himself claimed good results with his treatment, although in the hands of other workers the effect of phage on such diseases as cholera and plague appeared to be minimal. This conclusion d'Herelle continued to resist until his death, claiming that no proper test using his methods had ever been carried out.

However, the importance of the bacteriophage as a research tool in molecular biology cannot be disputed. It was the so-called phage group, centered on Max Delbrück, that made many of the early advances in this discipline in the 1940s.

DICEARCHUS of Messina (*fl.* 310 BC; Messina, now in Italy) Greek geographer and philosopher.

Dicearchus was a pupil of Aristotle and spent most of his life in Sparta. As none of his works have survived it is difficult to be sure of his contributions to geography. He wrote on a large number of topics including the soul, prophecy, and political theory.

His main work in geography was entitled *Periodos ges* (Tour of the Earth) and he also wrote a history of Greek civilization entitled *Bios Hellados* (Life of Greece). As Dicearchus was writing so soon after Alexander the Great's campaigns it is assumed that his works would have contained much new information on the geography of Asia. He is variously reported to have been the first to establish lines of latitude on maps, to have included the heights of mountains, and to have made a reasonable attempt at measuring the size of the Earth using methods that Eratosthenes was later to perfect.

DICKE, Robert Henry (b. May 6, 1916; St. Louis, Missouri) American physicist.

Dicke graduated in 1939 from Princeton University and obtained his PhD in 1941 from the University of Rochester. He spent the war at the radiation laboratory of the Massachusetts Institute of Technology, joining the Princeton faculty in 1946. In 1957 he was appointed professor of physics and has served since 1975 as Albert Einstein Professor of Science.

In 1964, unaware that he was repeating a line of thought pursued earlier by George Gamow, Ralph Alpher, and Robert C. Herman in 1948, Dicke began to think about the consequences of a big-bang origin of the universe. Assuming a cataclysmic explosion some 18 billion years ago with a temperature one minute after of about 10 billion degrees, then intense radiation would have been produced in addition to particles of matter. As the universe expanded this radiation would gradually lose energy. Could there still be any trace left of this 'primeval fireball'? It would in fact be detected as black-body radiation, characteristic of the temperature of the black body, a perfect emitter of radiation. At Dicke's instigation his colleague P.J.E. Peebles made the necessary calculations and concluded that the remnant radiation

should now have a temperature of only about 10 K, later corrected to about 3 K, i.e. −270°C. At this temperature a black body should radiate a weak signal at microwave wavelengths from 0.05 millimeter to 50 centimeters with a peak at about 2 mm. Further, the signal should be constant throughout the entire universe.

Dicke began to organize a search for such radiation and had actually begun to install an antenna on his laboratory roof when he heard from Arno Penzias and Robert Wilson that they had detected background microwave radiation at a wavelength of 7 cm. It was this confluence of theory, calculation, and observation that really established the big-bang theory.

Another major area of study for Dicke is gravitation. In the 1960s he carried out a major evaluation of the experiment originally performed by Roland von Eötvös to confirm that the gravitational mass of a body is equal to its inertial mass. Dicke was able to establish the accuracy of the equivalence to one part in 10^{11}. This equivalence is basic to Einstein's theory of general relativity.

In 1961, following a suggestion of Paul Dirac in 1937, Dicke and Carl Brans proposed that the gravitational constant was not in fact a constant, but slowly decreases at a rate of one part in 10^{11} per year. The resulting *Brans–Dicke theory* differs somewhat from Einstein's general relativity at a number of points. Thus while Einstein predicts that a ray of light should be deflected by the Sun's gravitational field 1.75 seconds of arc, the Brans–Dicke theory leads to a figure of 1.62″; such a difference is within the range of observational error and so is not readily detectable. Again the perihelion of Mercury should advance for Einstein by 43″ per century, for Brans–Dicke a mere 39″. A value of 43″ has in fact been measured but Dicke maintains that part of this value, 4″, could be explained by the Sun's nonspherical shape. It has however been claimed that very precise measurements of radio pulses from pulsars appear to favor Einstein. The theory was concurrently and independently developed by Pascual Jordan, and is thus sometimes known as the *Brans–Dicke–Jordan theory*. The idea of a changing gravitational constant was put forward by Paul Dirac (q.v.).

DIELS, Otto Paul Hermann (b. Jan. 23, 1876; Hamburg, now in West Germany; d. Mar. 7, 1954; Kiel, West Germany) German organic chemist.

The son of Hermann Diels, a famous classical scholar, Diels gained his doctorate under Emil Fischer in Berlin (1899), and became professor there in 1906. From 1916 until his retirement in 1948 he was professor at Kiel. In 1906 he made an extremely unexpected discovery, that of a new oxide of carbon, carbon suboxide (C_3O_2), which he prepared by dehydrating malonic acid with phosphorus pentachloride. Diels's second major discovery was a method of removing hydrogen from steroids by means of selenium. He used this method in research on cholesterol and bile acids, obtaining aromatic hydrocarbons that enabled the structures of the steroids to be deduced.

In 1928 Diels and his assistant Kurt Alder discovered a synthetic reaction in which a diene (compound containing two double bonds) is added to a compound containing one double bond flanked by carbonyl or carboxyl groups to give a ring structure. The reaction proceeds in the mildest conditions, is of general application, and hence of great utility in synthesis. It has been used in the synthesis of natural products such as sterols, vitamin K, and cantharides, and of synthetic polymers. For this discovery Diels and Alder were jointly awarded the Nobel Prize for chemistry in 1950.

DIESEL, Rudolph Christian Carl (b. Mar. 18, 1858; Paris; d. Sept. 29, 1913; English Channel) German engineer and inventor.

Diesel, the designer of the *diesel engine*, was brought up by his German parents in Paris until the age of 12. He was academi-

cally talented, but his schooling was interrupted in August 1870, when the Franco-Prussian war broke out and the Diesels were deported to London. His cousin, a teacher in Augsburg, Bavaria, invited Diesel to go there to study and he later won a scholarship to the Munich Institute of Technology.

After graduating, Diesel worked as a mechanic for two years in Switzerland and then worked in Paris as a thermal engineer. He was a devout Lutheran and a dedicated pacifist, believing in international religious liberation. In the laboratory that he set up in 1885, an accident with ammonia gas gave him the idea of using chemical firework-type weapons instead of lethal bombs and bullets on the battlefields. In 1893, he demonstrated his first engine and, although the first few attempts failed, within three years he had developed a pressure-ignited heat engine with an efficiency of 75.6%. (Equivalent steam engines had an efficiency of 10%.) The engine named for him is now used universally, for example in powering boats and in running generators.

By 1898 Diesel was a millionaire but his fortune soon disappeared. He toured the world giving lectures and visited America in 1912. His health was bad, he suffered from gout, and was depressed by the build-up to World War I. On the ferry returning from London in 1913, after dining apparently happily with a friend, he disappeared and was assumed to have drowned in the English Channel.

DIOPHANTUS of Alexandria (*fl.* 250) Greek mathematician.

Diophantus was one of the outstanding mathematicians of his era but almost nothing is known of his life and his writings survive only in fragmentary form. His most famous work was in the field of number theory and of the so-called 'Diophantine' equations named after him. His major work, the *Arithmetica*, contains many new methods and results in this field. It originally consisted of 13 books but only 6 of these survived to be translated by the

Arabs. However Diophantus was not solely interested in equations with only integral (whole number) solutions and also considered rational solutions. Diophantus made considerable innovations in the use of symbolism in Greek mathematics — the lack of suitable symbolism had previously hampered work in algebra.

DIOSCORIDES, Pedanius (b. *c.* AD 40; Anazarbus, now in Turkey; d. unknown) Greek physician.

Little is known of Dioscorides' life except that he was a surgeon with Emperor Nero's armies and most probably learned his skills at Alexandria and Tarsus. Many writings are attributed to him but the only book for which his authorship is undisputed is *De materia medica*. This pharmacopeia remained the standard medical text until the 17th century, undergoing many revisions and additions through the years and greatly influencing both Western and Islamic cultures. It describes animal derivatives and minerals used therapeutically but is most important for the description of over 600 plants, including notes on their habitat and the methods of preparation and medicinal use of the drugs they contain. Many of the common and scientific plant names in use today originate from Dioscorides, and the yam family, Dioscoreaceae, is named for him.

DIRAC, Paul Adrien Maurice (b. Aug. 8, 1902; Bristol, England) British mathematician and physicist.

Dirac's father was Swiss by birth. After graduating in 1921 in electrical engineering at Bristol University, Dirac went on to read mathematics at Cambridge University, where he obtained his PhD in 1926. After several years lecturing in America he was appointed (1932) to the Lucasian Professorship of Mathematics at Cambridge, a post he held until his retirement in 1969. In 1971 he became professor of physics at Florida State University.

Dirac is acknowledged as one of the most creative of the theoreticians of the early 20th century. In 1926, slightly later than Max Born and Pascual Jordan in Germany, he developed a general formalism for quantum mechanics. In 1928 he produced his relativistic theory to describe the properties of the electron. The wave equations developed by Erwin Schrödinger to describe the behavior of electrons were nonrelativistic. A significant deficiency in the Schrödinger equation was its failure to account for the electron spin discovered in 1925 by Samuel Goudsmit and George Uhlenbeck. Dirac's rewriting of the equations to incorporate relativity had considerable value for it not only predicted the correct energy levels of the hydrogen atom but also revealed that some of those levels were no longer single but could be split into two. It is just such a splitting of spectral lines that is characteristic of a spinning electron.

Dirac also predicted from these equations that there must be states of negative energy for the electron. In 1930 he proposed a theory to account for this that was soon to receive dramatic confirmation. He began by taking negative energy states to refer to those energy states below the lowest positive energy state, the ground state. If there were a lower energy state for the electron below the ground state then, the question arises, why do some electrons not fall into it? Dirac's answer was that such states have already been filled with other electrons and he conjured up a picture in which space is not really empty but full of particles of negative energy. If one of these particles were to collide with a sufficiently energetic photon it would acquire positive energy and be observable as a normal electron, apparently appearing from nowhere. But it would not appear alone for it would leave behind an empty hole, which was really an absence of a negatively charged particle or, in other words, the presence of a positively charged particle. Further, if the electron were to fall back into the empty hole it would once more disappear, appearing to be annihilated together with the positively charged particle, or positron as it was later called.

Out of this theory there emerged three predictions. Firstly, that there was a positively charged electron, secondly, that it could only appear in conjunction with a normal electron, and, finally, that a collision between them resulted in their total common annihilation. Such predictions were soon confirmed following the discovery of the positron by Carl Anderson in 1932. Dirac had in fact added a new dimension of matter to the universe, namely antimatter. It was soon appreciated that Dirac's argument was sufficiently general to apply to all particles.

In 1937 Dirac published a paper entitled *The Cosmological Constants* in which he considered 'large-number coincidences'; i.e. certain relationships that appear to exist between the numerical properties of some natural constants. An example is to compare the force of electrostatic attraction between an electron and a proton with the gravitational attraction due to their masses. The ratio of these is about 10^{40}:1. Similarly, it is also found that the characteristic 'radius' of the universe is 10^{40} times as large as the characteristic radius of an electron. Moreover, 10^{40} is approximately the square root of the number of particles in the universe.

These coincidences are remarkable and many physicists have speculated that these apparently unrelated things may be connected in some way. The ratios were first considered in the 1930s by Arthur Eddington, who believed that he could calculate such constants and that they arose from the way in which physics observes and interprets nature. Dirac used the 10^{40} number above in a model of the universe. He argued that there was a connection between the force ratio and the radius ratio. Since the radius of the universe increased with age the gravitational 'constant', on which the force ratio depends, may decrease with time.

Above all else however Dirac was a quantum theorist. In 1930 he published the first edition of his classic work *The Principles of Quantum Mechanics*. In 1933 he

shared the Nobel Prize for physics with Schrödinger for his work on electron theory.

DIRICHLET, (Peter Gustav) Lejeune (b. Feb. 13, 1805; Düren, now in West Germany; d. May 5, 1859; Göttingen, now in West Germany) German mathematician.

Dirichlet studied mathematics at Göttingen where he was a pupil of Karl Gauss and Karl Jacobi. He also studied briefly in Paris where he met Joseph Fourier, who stimulated his interest in trigonometric series. In 1826 he returned to Germany and taught at Breslau and later at the Military Academy in Berlin. He then moved to the University of Berlin, which he only left 27 years later when he returned to Göttingen to fill the chair left vacant by Gauss's death.

Dirichlet's work in number theory was very much inspired by Gauss's great work in that field, and Dirichlet's own book, the *Vorlesungen über Zahlentheorie* (1863; Lectures on Number Theory), is of comparable historical importance to Gauss's *Disquisitiones*. He made many important discoveries in the field and his work on a problem connected with primes led him to make the fundamentally important innovation of using analytical techniques to obtain results in number theory.

His stay in Paris had stimulated Dirichlet's interest in Fourier series and in 1829 he was able to solve the outstanding problem of stating the conditions sufficient for a Fourier series to converge. (The other problem of giving necessary conditions is still unsolved.) Fourier also gave the young Dirichlet an interest in mathematical physics, which led him to important work on multiple integrals and the boundary-value problem, now known as the *Dirichlet problem*, concerning the formulation and solution of those partial differential equations occurring in the study of heat flow and electrostatics. These are of great importance in many other areas of physics. The growth of a more rigorous understanding of analysis owes to Dirichlet what is essentially the modern definition of the concept of a function.

DÖBEREINER, Johann Wolfgang (b. Dec. 13, 1780; Hof an der Saale, now in West Germany; d. Mar. 24, 1849; Jena, now in East Germany) German chemist.

The son of a coachman, Döbereiner had little formal education but was an assistant to apothecaries in several places from the age of 14. He was largely self-taught in chemistry and was encouraged by Leopold Gmelin whom he met at Strasbourg. After several failures in business, he was appointed assistant professor of chemistry at Jena (1810).

In 1823 he discovered that hydrogen would ignite spontaneously in air over platinum sponge, and subsequently developed the *Döbereiner lamp* to exploit this phenomenon. Döbereiner was interested in catalysis in general and discovered the catalytic action of manganese dioxide in the decomposition of potassium chlorate. His law of triads (1829), based on his observation of regular increments of atomic weight in elements with similar properties, was an important step on the way to Dmitri Mendeleev's periodic table. Thus in triads such as calcium, strontium, and barium or chlorine, bromine, and iodine, the middle element has an atomic weight that is approximately the average of the other two. It is also intermediate in chemical properties between the other two elements. Döbereiner also worked in organic chemistry.

DOBZHANSKY, Theodosius (b. Jan. 25, 1900; Nemirov, now in the Soviet Union; d. Dec. 18, 1975; Davis, California) Russian-American geneticist.

Dobzhansky graduated in zoology from Kiev University in 1921, remaining there to teach zoology before moving to Leningrad, where he taught genetics. In 1927 he took up a fellowship at Columbia University, New York, where he worked with T. H. Morgan. Morgan was impressed by Dobzhansky's ability and, when the fellowship was completed, offered him a teaching post at the California Institute of Technology. Dobzhansky accepted and became an American citizen in 1937.

Dobzhansky studied the fruit fly (*Drosophila*) and demonstrated that the genetic variability within populations was far greater than had been imagined. The high frequency of potentially deleterious genes had previously been overlooked because their effects are masked by corresponding dominant genes. Dobzhansky found that such debilitating genes actually conferred an advantage to the organism when present with the normal type of gene, and therefore they tended to be maintained at a high level in the population. Populations with a high genetic load — i.e. many concealed lethal genes — proved to be more versatile in changing environments. This work profoundly influenced the theories on the mathematics of evolution and natural selection with regard to Mendelism.

In addition, Dobzhansky wrote many influential books, including *Genetics and the Origin of Species* (1937), a milestone in evolutionary genetics.

DOISY, Edward Adelbert (b. Nov. 13, 1893; Hume, Illinois) American biochemist.

Doisy was educated at the University of Illinois and at Harvard, where he obtained his PhD in 1920. From 1919 to 1923 he worked at the Washington University School of Medicine. In 1923 he was appointed to the chair of biochemistry at the St. Louis University Medical School, a position he retained until his retirement in 1965.

In 1939 Doisy succeeded in synthesizing vitamin K, recently discovered by Carl Dam. He discovered that the vitamin existed in two forms, the physiologically active form K_1, extracted from alfalfa, and K_2, differing in a side chain and derivable from rotten fish. For his discovery of the chemical nature of vitamin K, technically a naphthoquinone, Doisy shared the 1943 Nobel Prize for physiology or medicine with Dam.

DOKUCHAEV, Vasily Vasilievich (b. Mar. 1, 1846; Milyukovo, Smolensk, now in the Soviet Union; d. Nov. 8, 1903; St. Petersburg, now Leningrad in the Soviet Union) Russian soil scientist.

Dokuchaev, the son of the village priest, was originally trained for the priesthood but later turned to the study of science at St. Petersburg University where he graduated in 1871. He was immediately appointed to the faculty, initially as curator of the geological collection but he also served as professor of geology until poor health forced him to retire in 1897.

Dokuchaev made the first comprehensive scientific study of the soils of Russia, details of which are to be found in his *Collected Works* (9 vols. 1949–61). He also, in the 1890s, set up at the Kharkov Institute of Agriculture and Forestry, the first department of soil science in Russia.

In the West he is mainly known for his work on the classification of soils, his insistence that soil is a geobiological formation, and his use of soil to define the different geographical zones.

It is also owing to Dokuchaev that the Russian term 'chernozem', used to describe a black soil rich in humus and carbonates, has entered most languages.

DOLLFUS, Audouin Charles (b. Nov. 12, 1924; Paris) French astronomer.

Dollfus, the son of an aeronaut, studied at the University of Paris. In 1946 he joined the staff of the astrophysical division of the Paris Observatory at Meudon and is now head of the Laboratory for Physics of the Solar System.

Dollfus has established a reputation as an authority on the solar system and a leading planetary observer. He began a study of Saturn's rings in 1948 and soon noted the presence of occasional brightness ripples. Work in the 1950s showed that they could not be explained by the effects of the known satellites and Dollfus concluded that other forces seemed to be acting, possibly attributable to an unknown satellite very close to the rings. A favorable viewing time, with the rings appearing edge-on to an Earth-bound observer, came in 1966. Although early visual attempts to detect the satellite failed, Dollfus was more successful when he examined photographic plates taken with the 43-inch (1.1-m) reflecting telescope of the Pic du Midi Observatory in December 1966, virtually the last opportunity for favorable viewing before 1980. On these he found the image of an unknown satellite.

Following independent confirmation, the satellite was named Janus and was widely accepted as Saturn's 10th satellite, its period having been calculated by Dollfus as 18 hours. When no such satellite was found by the Pioneer II and Voyager I spacecraft in 1979 and 1980, Dollfus rechecked his measurements. It now appears that he photographed one of the 'twin' satellites that appeared in the spacecraft pictures and that recent calculations have shown to move in nearly identical orbits with periods of about 16.7 hours.

DÖLLINGER, Ignaz Christoph von (b. May 24, 1770; Bamberg, now in West Germany; d. Jan. 14, 1841; Munich, now in West Germany) German biologist.

A medical student at Bamberg, Würzburg, Vienna, and Pavia (Italy), Döllinger gained his doctorate at Bamberg in 1794. In 1796 he was appointed professor of medicine at the University of Bamberg, and in 1803 became professor of physiology and normal and pathological anatomy at Würzburg. From 1823 Döllinger was curator of academic sciences at Munich and then became (1826) professor of anatomy and physiology and director of the anatomical museum of the University of Munich. He was one of the pioneers of the use of the microscope in medical studies and made investigations of blood circulation, the spleen and liver, glandular secretions, and the eye, as well as comparative anatomy studies. His embryological work exercised a considerable influence on Louis Agassiz.

DOLLOND, John (b. June 10, 1706; London; d. Nov. 30, 1761; London) British optician.

Dollond, the son of Huguenot refugees, started life as a silk weaver but later joined his eldest son, Peter, in making optical instruments, and devoted years of experiment to developing an achromatic lens. The problem confronting lens makers at the time was chromatic aberration — the fringe of colors that surrounds and disturbs images formed by a lens. This put a limit on the power of lenses (and of refracting telescopes), for the stronger the lens, the more chromatically disturbed the images became. Chromatic aberration is caused by the different wavelengths that make up white light being refracted differently by the glass, each being focused at a different point.

In 1758 Dollond succeeded in making lenses without this defect by using two different lenses, one of crown glass and one of flint glass (one convex and one concave), so made that the chromatic aberration of one was neutralized by the aberration of the other. In fact he was not the first to make such a lens, since Chester Hall had already done so in 1753, but Dollond managed to patent the idea because he was the first to publicize the possibility.

In 1761 he was appointed optician to George III but died of apoplexy later that year.

DOMAGK, Gerhard (b. Oct. 30, 1895; Lagow, now in Poland; d. Apr. 24, 1964; Burberg, West Germany) German biochemist.

Domagk graduated in medicine from the University of Kiel in 1921 and began teaching at the University of Greifswald and later at the University of Münster. At this time he carried out important researches into phagocytes — special cells that attack bacteria in the body. He became interested in chemotherapy and in 1927 he was appointed director of research in experimental pathology and pathological anatomy at the giant chemical factory I.G. Farbenindustrie at Wuppertal-Elberfeld. Pursuing the ideas of Paul Ehrlich, Domagk tested new dyes produced by the Elberfeld chemists for their effect against various infections. In 1935 he reported the effectiveness of an orange-red dye called prontosil in combating streptococcal infections. For the first time a chemical had been found to be active *in vivo* against a common small bacterium. Earlier dyes used as drugs were active only against infections caused by the much larger protozoa. The work was followed up in research laboratories throughout the world — Alexander Fleming neglected penicillin to work on prontosil in the early 1930s — but the most significant ramifications were discovered by Daniele Bovet and his coworkers. Prontosil and the sulfa drugs that followed were effective in saving many lives, including those of Franklin D. Rooseveldt Jr., Winston Churchill, and Domagk's own daughter. In 1939 Domagk was offered the Nobel Prize for physiology or medicine. The Nazis forced him to withdraw his acceptance because Hitler was annoyed with the Nobel Committee for awarding the 1935 Peace Prize to a German, Carl von Ossietzky, whom Hitler had imprisoned. In 1947 Domagk was finally able to accept the prize. In his later years he undertook drug research into cancer and tuberculosis.

DONATI, Giovanni Battista (b. Dec. 16, 1826; Pisa, Italy; d. Sept. 20, 1873; Florence, Italy) Italian astronomer.

Donati worked at the Florence Observatory, becoming its director in 1864. He was best known as a discoverer of comets, including (in 1858) the very bright comet that bears his name. In 1864 he was the first to observe the spectrum of a comet and discover the gaseous composition of comet tails.

DONDI, Giovanni de (b. 1318; Chiogga, Italy; d. 1389; Genoa, Italy) Italian astronomer and clockmaker.

Dondi, the son of a professor of medicine and clock designer, taught medicine and astronomy at the universities of Padua and Pavia. He became famous throughout the whole of Europe for his construction of a marvelous astronomical clock that he began in 1348 and that took him 16 years to complete. It was built for the duke of Milan and was put in his library in Pavia. Although the clock has long been destroyed, Dondi wrote a treatise on it, which has survived. It was weight driven, had a verge and foliot escapement, and was made of brass and bronze. It was completely unlike a modern clock being so unconcerned with the time of day that it did not even have hands. It was intended to show the movements of the planets and the time of the movable and fixed ecclesiastical festivals. It involved advanced gear work and showed mechanical skill of a high order. Such was his fame that Dondi was known throughout Europe as 'John of the Clock'.

DONNAN, Frederick George (b. Sept. 5, 1879; Colombo, Ceylon; d. Dec. 16, 1956; Canterbury, England) British chemist.

Donnan, the son of a Belfast merchant, was educated at Queen's College, Belfast, and the universities of Leipzig and Berlin where he obtained his PhD in 1896 and some of the German expertise in physical chemistry. On his return to England he worked at University College, London, with William Ramsay from 1898 until 1904, when he accepted the post of professor of physical chemistry at the Univer-

sity of Liverpool. In 1913 Donnan returned to succeed Ramsay at University College, remaining there until his retirement in 1937.

Donnan is mainly remembered for the *Donnan membrane equilibrium* (1911) — a theory describing the equilibrium which arises in the passage of ions through membranes.

DOODSON, Arthur Thomas (b. Mar. 31, 1890; Worsley, England; d. Jan. 10, 1968; Birkenhead, England) British mathematical physicist.

Doodson, the son of a manager of a cotton mill, was educated at the University of Liverpool. After working at University College, London, from 1916 to 1918 he joined the Tidal Institute, Liverpool, in 1919 as its secretary. Doodson remained through its re-formation as the Liverpool Observatory and Tidal Institute as assistant director (1929–45) and as director until his retirement in 1960.

Much of Doodson's early work was on the production of mathematical tables and the calculation of trajectories for artillery. Proving himself an ingenious, powerful, and practical mathematician he found an ideal subject for his talents in the complicated behavior of the tides. He made many innovations in their accurate computation and, with H. Warburg in 1942, produced the *Admiralty Manual of Tides*.

DOPPLER, Christian Johann (b. Nov. 29, 1803; Salzburg, Austria; d. Mar. 17, 1853; Venice, Italy) Austrian physicist.

Christian Doppler, the son of a stonemason, studied mathematics at the Vienna Polytechnic. In 1835 he started teaching at a school in Prague and six years later was appointed professor of mathematics at the Technical Academy there.

Doppler's fame comes from his discovery in 1842 of the *Doppler effect* — the fact that the observed frequency of a wave depends on the velocity of the source relative to the observer. The effect can be observed with sound waves. If the source is moving toward the observer, the pitch is higher; if it moves away, the pitch is lower. A common example is the fall in frequency of a train's whistle or a vehicle siren as it passes. Doppler's principle was tested experimentally in 1843 by Christoph Buys Ballot, who used a train to pull trumpeters at different speeds past musicians who had perfect pitch.

Doppler also tried to apply his principle to light waves, with limited success. It was Armand Fizeau in 1848 who suggested that at high relative velocities the apparent color of the source would be changed by the motion: an object moving toward the observer would appear bluer; one moving away would appear redder. The shift in the spectra of celestial objects (the *Doppler shift*) is used to measure the rate of recession or approach relative to the Earth.

DORN, Friedrich Ernst (b. July 27, 1848; Guttstadt, now Dobre Miasto in Poland; d. June 13, 1916; Halle, now in East Germany) German physicist.

Dorn studied at Königsberg and in 1873 was made professor of physics at Breslau. In 1886 he transferred to a professorship at Halle and started working with x-rays. He is noted for his discovery, in 1900, that the radioactive element radium gives off a radioactive gas, which Dorn called 'radium emanation'. The gas was isolated in 1908 by William Ramsay, who named it 'niton'. The name radon was adopted in 1923. Dorn's discovery is the first established demonstration of a transmutation of one element into another.

DOUGLAS, Donald Wills (b. Apr. 6, 1892; New York city; d. Feb. 1, 1981; Palm Springs, California) American aircraft engineer.

Douglas, the son of an assistant bank cashier, was educated at the US Naval Academy and the Massachusetts Institute of Technology. He gained his first experience of aircraft design working for the Glenn L. Martin Company of California on the development of a heavy bomber.

In 1920 he set up on his own with $600 and the backing of David Davis, a wealthy sportsman willing to invest $40 000 to produce a plane capable of flying non stop across America. Although the *Cloudster*, the result of their venture, only reached Texas it was in fact the first aircraft in history capable of lifting a useful load exceeding its own weight.

By 1928, on the strength of some profitable navy contracts, Douglas was ready to go public with his new Douglas Aircraft Company. The company had many years of success, with such planes as the DC-3, first flown in 1935, contributing substantially to their profits. In 1967 the company was taken over by the McDonnell Aircraft Company and reformed as the McDonnell–Douglas Corporation.

DOUGLASS, Andrew Ellicott (b. July 5, 1867; Windsor, Vermont; d. Mar. 20, 1962; Tucson, Arizona) American astronomer and dendrochronologist.

Douglass came from a family of academics with both his father and grandfather being college presidents. He graduated from Trinity College, Hartford, Connecticut in 1889 and in the same year was appointed to an assistantship at Harvard College Observatory. In 1894 he went with Percival Lowell to the new Lowell Observatory in Flagstaff, Arizona, moving to the University of Arizona in 1906 as professor of astronomy and physics.

Douglass's first interest was the 11-year sunspot cycle. In trying to trace its history he was led to the examination of tree rings in the hope that he would find some identifiable correlation of sunspot activity with terrestrial climate and vegetation. Soon the tree rings became the center of his studies.

The only previously established method of dating the past, except by inscriptions, was the geological varve-counting technique, which was developed from 1878. But this was of no use if there were no varves (thin seasonally deposited layers of sediment in glacial lakes) to be found. Douglass soon found that he could identify local tree rings with confidence and use them in dating past climatic trends. He thus founded the field of dendrochronology. By the late 1920s he had a sequence of over a thousand tree rings with six thin rings, presumably records of a severe drought, correlated with the end of the 13th century. In 1929 he found some timber that contained the six thin rings and a further 500 in addition. This took him to the eighth century and over the years he managed to get as far as the first century. This was extended still further and by careful analysis scholars have now established a sequence going back almost to 5000 BC.

The dated rings of Arizona and New Mexico were found however not to correlate with sequences from other parts of the world: the tree-ring clock was a purely local one. The search for a more universal clock continued, and the method of radiocarbon dating was developed by Willard Libby in 1949.

DRAKE, Frank Donald (b. May 28, 1930; Chicago, Illinois) American astronomer.

Drake graduated in 1952 from Cornell University and obtained his PhD in 1958 from Harvard. He worked initially at the National Radio Astronomy Observatory (NRAO), West Virginia (1958–63) and at the Jet Propulsion Laboratory, California (1963–64) before returning to Cornell and being appointed professor of astronomy in 1966.

Although Drake has made significant contributions to radio astronomy, including radio studies of the planets, he is perhaps best known for his pioneering search for extraterrestrial intelligence. In April 1959 he managed to gain approval from the director at NRAO, Otto Struve, to proceed with his search, which was called 'Project Ozma'. The name was taken from the Oz stories of Frank Baum. Drake began in 1960, using the NRAO 26-meter radio telescope to listen for possible signals from planets of the Sunlike stars Tau Ceti and Epsilon Eridani, both about 11 light-years away. He decided to tune to the frequency of 1420 megahertz at which radio emission from hydrogen occurs. This would have considerable significance for any civilization capable of building radio transmitters.

No signals were received although at one time excitement was generated when signals from a secret military radar establishment were received while the antenna was pointed at Epsilon Eridani. In July 1960 the project was terminated to allow the telescope to fulfill some of its other obligations. Drake revived the project in 1975, in collaboration with Carl Sagan, when they began using the Arecibo 1000-foot (305-m) radio telescope to listen to several nearby galaxies on frequencies of 1420, 1653, and 2380 megahertz. No contact was made nor was it likely they declare for "A search of hundreds of thousands of stars in the hope of detecting one message would require remarkable dedication and would probably take several decades."

DRAPER, Henry (b. Mar. 7, 1837; Prince Edward County, Virginia; d. Nov. 20, 1882; New York City) American astronomer.

Draper was the son of the distinguished physician and chemist John W. Draper. He studied at the City University of New York, completing the course in medicine in 1857 before he was old enough to graduate. He obtained his MD in 1858, spending the preceding months in Europe where his interest in astronomy was aroused by a visit to the observatory of the third earl of Rosse at Parsonstown, Ireland. On his return to New York he joined the Bellevue Hospital and was later appointed professor of natural science at the City University in 1860. Draper later held chairs of physiology, 1866–73, and analytical chemistry, 1870–82, and in 1882 succeeded his father briefly as professor of chemistry. He retired from the university in 1882 in order to devote himself to astronomical research but died prematurely soon after.

One of the most important events in Draper's life was his marriage in 1867 to Anna Palmer, daughter and heiress to Courtlandt Palmer who had made a fortune in hardware and New York real estate. His wife's money allowed him to purchase a 28-inch (71-cm) reflecting telescope and to begin a 15-year research partnership.

Draper was interested in the application of the new technique of photography to astronomy. He started by making daguerrotypes of the Sun and Moon but in 1872 succeeded for the first time in obtaining a photograph of a stellar spectrum, that of Vega. In 1879 he found that dry photographic plates had been developed and that these were more sensitive and convenient than wet collodion. By 1882 he had obtained photographs of over a hundred stellar spectra plus spectra of the Moon, Mars, Jupiter, and the Orion nebula. He also succeeded in directly photographing the Orion nebula, first with a 50-minute exposure in 1880 and then, using a more accurate clock-driven telescope, with a 140-minute exposure. He thus helped to establish photographic astronomy as an important means of studying the heavens.

At the time of his death his widow hoped to continue his work herself, but with prompting from Edward Pickering at the Harvard College Observatory, she set up the Henry Draper Memorial Fund. It was with the aid of this fund that the famous *Henry Draper Catalogue*, some nine volumes with details of the spectra of 225 000 stars, was published from 1918 to 1924 through the labors of Pickering and Annie Cannon.

DRAPER, John William (b. May 5, 1811; St. Helens, England; d. Jan. 4, 1882; Hastings-on-Hudson, New York) British–American chemist.

Draper was educated at University College, London, before he emigrated to America in 1833. He qualified in medicine at the University of Pennsylvania in 1836. After a short period teaching in Virginia he moved to New York University (1838) where he taught chemistry and in 1841 helped to start the medical school of which he became president in 1850.

Most of his chemical work was done in the field of photochemistry. He was one of the first scientists to use Louis Daguerre's new invention (1837) of photography. He took the first photograph of the Moon in 1840 and in the same year took a photograph of his sister, Dorothy, which is the oldest surviving photographic study of the human face. In 1843 he obtained the first photographic plate of the solar spectrum. He was also one of the first to take photographs of specimens under a microscope. On the theoretical level Draper was one of the earliest to grasp that only those rays that are absorbed produce chemical change and that not all rays are equally powerful in their effect. He also, in a series of papers (1841–45), showed that the amount of chemical change is proportional to the intensity of the absorbed radiation multiplied by the time it has to act. Draper's work was continued and largely confirmed by the work of Robert Bunsen and Henry Roscoe in 1857. Draper's work also resulted in the development of actinometers (instruments to measure the intensity of light) which he named 'tithonometers'. He also wrote on a wide variety of other topics.

Draper's son Henry was an astronomer of note after whom the famous Harvard catalog of stellar spectra was named.

DREYER, Johann Louis Emil (b. Feb. 13, 1852; Copenhagen; d. Sept. 14, 1926; Oxford, England) Danish astronomer.

Dreyer, the son of a general of the Danish Army, studied at Copenhagen University where he obtained his MA in 1874 and his PhD in 1882. He began his career in 1874 as an assistant at the observatory of William Parsons, third earl of Rosse, in Parsonstown, Ireland, moving in 1878 to another assistantship at the Dunsink Observatory, Dublin. In 1882 Dreyer was appointed director of the Armagh Observatory, in what is now Northern Ireland, a post he occupied until his retirement in 1916 when he settled in Oxford, England.

Dreyer's major contribution to astronomy was his three catalogs. He began by preparing in 1878 a supplement to John Herschel's catalog of 5000 nebulae. The work naturally led to the production of a totally new work, the *New General Catalogue of Nebulae and Clusters of Stars* (1888) containing details of 7840 celestial objects and known invariably as the NGC. It listed all the nebulae and clusters that had been discovered up to 1888 and included many galaxies, which had not yet been identified as such. This in turn was followed by the two *Index Catalogues* (IC), the first in 1895 containing details of a further 1529 nebulae and clusters (and galaxies) and the second in 1908 adding a further 3857. The catalogs with over 13 000 nebulae, galaxies, and clusters were reissued in a single volume in 1953. Many of the objects listed are still referred to by their NGC or IC numbers.

Dreyer is also remembered as a historian of astronomy. In 1890 he published a biography of his countryman, *Tycho Brahe*, and followed this with Brahe's *Omnia opera* (15 vols; 1913–29). He had earlier published his *History of Planetary Systems from Thales to Kepler* (1906), a work, despite its age, still without any competitor in the English language.

DRICKAMER, Harry George (b. Nov. 19, 1908; Cleveland, Ohio) American physicist.

Drickamer was educated at the University of Michigan where he obtained his PhD in 1946. He then joined the staff of the University of Illinois, Urbana, serving first as professor of physical chemistry and, after 1953, as professor of chemical engineering. He has specialized in the study of the structure of solids by means of high pressures, producing in the course of

his researches pressures of the order of some 500 000 atmospheres.

DRIESCH, Hans Adolf Eduard (b. Oct. 28, 1867; Bad Kreuznach, now in West Germany; d. Apr. 16, 1941; Leipzig, now in East Germany) German biologist.

Driesch held professorships at Heidelberg, Cologne, and Leipzig, and was visiting professor to China and America. A student of zoology at Freiburg, Jena, and Munich, he was for some years on the staff of the Naples Zoological Station.

Driesch carried out pioneering work in experimental embryology. He separated the two cells formed by the first division of a sea-urchin embryo and observed that each developed into a complete larva, thus demonstrating the capacity of the cell to form identical copies on division. He was also the first to demonstrate the phenomenon of embryonic induction, whereby the position of and interaction between cells within the embryo determine their subsequent differentiation.

Driesch is perhaps best known for his concept of entelechy — a vitalistic philosophy that postulates the origin of life to lie in some unknown vital force separate from biochemical and physiological influences. This also led him to investigate psychic research and parapsychology.

DUBOIS, Marie Eugène François Thomas (b. Jan. 28, 1858; Eijsden, Netherlands; d. Dec. 16, 1940; Halen, Belgium) Dutch physician and paleontologist.

After studying medicine at the University of Amsterdam and briefly working there as a lecturer in anatomy, Dubois served as a military surgeon in the Dutch East Indies, now Indonesia, from 1887 to 1895. On his return to Amsterdam he held the chair of geology, paleontology, and mineralogy from 1899 until his retirement in 1928.

The decision to go to the Indies was no accident. Dubois was determined to find the 'missing link' and had reasoned that such a creature would have originated in proximity to the apes of Africa or the orang-utang of the Indies. After several years fruitless search in Sumatra, Dubois moved to Java and in 1890 discovered his first humanoid remains (a jaw fragment) at Kedung Brubus. The following year, at Trinil on the Solo river, he found the skullcap, femur, and two teeth of what he was later to name *Pithecanthropus erectus*, more commonly known as Java man. He published these findings in 1894.

Although Dubois's estimate of the cranial capacity of *Pithecanthropus* was, at 850 cubic centimeters (later estimates ranged up to 940 cubic centimeters), on the low side for a hominid, the femur it had been found with indicated to Dubois that it must be a form with a very erect posture. However many doubted this, stating the usual objections that the remains belonged to different creatures, to apes or (Rudolf Virchow's view) to deformed humans. So irritated did Dubois become by this reception that he withdrew the fossils from view, keeping them locked up for some 30 years.

When they were once more made available to scholars in 1923 and Peking man was discovered in 1926 it at last became widely agreed that *Pithecanthropus* was, as Dubois had earlier claimed, a link connecting apes and man. By this time however Dubois would have no part of such a consensus and began to insist the bones were those of a giant gibbon, a view he maintained until his death.

DU BOIS-REYMOND, Emil Heinrich (b. Nov. 7, 1818; Berlin; d. Dec. 26, 1896; Berlin) German neurophysiologist.

Of Swiss and Huguenot descent, Du Bois-Reymond was educated at Berlin and Neuchâtel (Switzerland) universities and is famous as the first to demonstrate how electrical currents in nerve and muscle fibers are generated. He began his studies under the eminent physiologist Johannes Müller at Berlin with work on fish capable of discharging electric currents as an external shock (e.g. eels). Turning his attention to nerve and muscle activity he then showed (1843) that applying a stimulus to the nerve brings about a drop in the electrical potential at the point of stimulus. This reduction in potential is the impulse, which travels along the nerve as waves of 'relative negativity'. This variation in negativity is the main cause of muscle contraction. Du Bois-Reymond's pioneering research, for which he devised a specially sensitive galvanometer capable of measuring the small amounts of electricity involved, was published as *Untersuchungen über tierische Elektricität* (2 vols. 1848–84; Researches on Animal Electricity): a landmark in electrophysiology, although subject to later elaboration. Du Bois-Reymond's collaboration with fellow physiologists Hermann von Helmholtz, Carl Ludwig, and Ernst von Brücke was of great significance in linking animal physiology with physical and chemical laws.

Du Bois-Reymond was elected a member of the Berlin Academy of Sciences in 1851 and succeeded Müller as professor of physiology at Berlin in 1858. He was also instrumental in establishing the Berlin Physiological Institute, opened in 1877, then the finest establishment of its kind.

DUBOS, René Jules (b. Feb. 20, 1901; Saint Brice, France) French-American microbiologist.

Dubos graduated in agricultural science from the National Agronomy Institute in 1921 and after a period with the International Institute of Agriculture in Rome as assistant editor, he emigrated to America in 1924.

Dubos was awarded his PhD in 1927 from Rutgers University for research on soil microorganisms, continuing his work in this field at the Rockefeller Institute for Medical Research. Reports that soil microorganisms produce antibacterial substances particularly interested him and in 1939 he isolated a substance from *Bacillus brevis* that he named tyrothricin. This is effective against many types of bacteria but unfortunately also kills red blood cells and its medical use is therefore limited. However, the discovery stimulated such workers as Selman Waksman and Benjamin Duggar to search for useful antibiotics and led to the discovery of the tetracyclines.

DU FAY, Charles François de Cisternay (b. Sept. 14, 1698; Paris; d. July 16, 1739; Paris) French chemist.

Du Fay started his career in the French army, rising to the rank of captain. He left to become a chemist in the Académie Française and in 1732 became superintendent of the Jardin du Roi. His great achievement was to discover the two kinds of electricity, positive and negative, which he named 'vitreous' and 'resinous'. This was based on his discovery that a piece of gold leaf charged from an electrified glass rod would attract and not repel a piece of electrified amber. This was the 'two-fluid theory' of electricity, which was to be opposed by Benjamin Franklin's 'one-fluid theory' later in the century.

DUGGAR, Benjamin Minge (b. Sept. 1, 1872; Gallion, Alabama; d. Sept. 10, 1956; New Haven, Connecticut) American plant pathologist.

Duggar was born into a farming community and soon developed an interest in agriculture. He graduated with honors from the Mississippi Agricultural and Mechanical College, in 1891. He devoted his career to studying plant diseases, and while professor of plant physiology at Cornell University wrote *Fungus Diseases of Plants* (1909), the first publication to deal purely with plant pathology.

Duggar is known for his work on cotton diseases and mushroom culture, but he made his most important discovery after retiring from academic life. In 1945 he became consultant to the American Cyanamid Company, and soon isolated the fungus *Streptomyces aureofaciens*. Three years' work with this organism resulted in Duggar extracting and purifying the compound chlortetracycline, (marketed as Aureomycin), the first of the tetracycline antibiotics. This drug was on the market by December 1948, and has proved useful in combating many infectious diseases.

Duggar was one of the foremost coordinators of plant science research in America and was editor of many important publications.

DUHAMEL DU MONCEAU, Henri-Louis (b. 1700; Paris; d. Aug. 23, 1782; Paris) French agriculturalist and technologist.

Duhamel first took an interest in science following lectures at the Jardin du Roi in Paris during the 1720s. His study of the parasitic fungus found to attack saffron bulbs earned him admission to the French Academy of Sciences in 1728. In 1739 Duhamel was appointed inspector-general of the navy, his duties including supervision of the timber used by the French fleet.

During the 1730s he undertook a series of chemical investigations in collaboration with the chemist Jean Grosse. His most important work during this period was *Sur la base du sel marin* (1736; On the Composition of Sea Salt) in which he distinguished between potassium and sodium salts.

His major work was his contribution to agriculture with studies of French and English methods of practice. He published a series of writings entitled *Traité de la culture des terres* (1775; Treatise on Land Cultivation) in which he adapted Jethro Tull's system to France taking into account his own readings, experiments, and case histories.

DUJARDIN, Félix (b. Apr. 5, 1801; Tours, France; d. Apr. 8, 1860; Rennes, France) French biologist and cytologist.

Largely self-educated, Dujardin studied geology, botany, optics, and crystallography while working variously as a hydraulics engineer, librarian, and teacher of geometry and chemistry at Tours. In 1839 he was elected to the chair of geology and mineralogy at Toulouse, and in the following year was appointed professor of botany and zoology and dean of the Faculty of Sciences at Rennes. As a skilled microscopist, Dujardin carried out extensive studies of the microorganisms (infusoria) occurring in decaying matter. These led him, in 1834, to suggest the separation of a new group of protozoan animals, which he called the rhizopods (i.e. rootfeet). He was the first to recognize and appreciate the contractile nature of the protoplasm (which he termed the *sarcode*) and also demonstrated the role of the vacuole for evacuating waste matter. Such studies enabled Dujardin to refute the supposition, reintroduced by Christian Ehrenberg, that microorganisms have organs similar to those of the higher animals. Dujardin also investigated the cnidarians (jellyfish, sea anemones, corals, etc.), echinoderms (sea-urchins, starfish, etc.), as well as the platyhelminths, or flatworms, the last mentioned providing the basis for subsequent parasitological investigations.

DULBECCO, Renato (b. Feb. 22, 1914; Catanzaro, Italy) Italian–American physician and molecular biologist.

Dulbecco obtained his MD from the University of Turin in 1936 and taught there until 1947 when he moved to America. He taught briefly at Indiana before moving to California in 1949, where he served as professor of biology (1952–63) at the California Institute of Technology. Dulbecco then joined the staff of the Salk Institute where, apart from the period 1971–74 at the Imperial Cancer Research Fund in London, he has remained.

Beginning in 1959 Dulbecco introduced the idea of cell transformation into biology. In this process special cells are mixed *in vitro* with such tumor-producing viruses as the polyoma and SV40 virus. With some

cells a 'productive infection' results, where the virus multiplies unchecked in the cell and finally kills its host. However in other cells this unlimited multiplication does not occur and the virus instead induces changes similar to those in cancer cells; that is, the virus alters the cell so that it reproduces without restraint and does not respond to the presence of neighboring cells. A normal cell had in fact been transformed into a 'cancer cell' *in vitro*.

The significance of this work was to provide an experimental set up where the processes by which a normal cell becomes cancerous can be studied in a relatively simplified form. It was for this work that Dulbecco was awarded the Nobel Prize for physiology or medicine in 1975, sharing it with Howard Temin and David Baltimore.

DULONG, Pierre-Louis (b. Feb. 12, 1785; Rouen, France; d. July 18, 1838; Paris) French chemist and physicist.

Dulong studied chemistry at the Ecole Polytechnique (1801–03) and later studied medicine. He was an assistant to Claude-Louis Berthollet before becoming professor of physics at the Ecole Polytechnique (1820), and later its director (1830).

In 1813 Dulong accidentally discovered the highly explosive nitrogen trichloride, losing an eye and nearly a hand in the process. He is best known for the law of atomic heats (1819), discovered in collaboration with Alexis-Thérèse Petit (q.v.).

DUMAS, Jean Baptiste André (b. July 14, 1800; Alais, France; d. Apr. 11, 1884; Cannes, France) French chemist.

Dumas was educated in classics at the college of Alais and intended to serve in the navy. However, after Napoleon's final defeat he changed his mind and became apprenticed to an apothecary. In 1816 he went to Geneva, again to work for an apothecary. His first research was in physiological chemistry, investigating the use of iodine in goiter (1818). He also studied chemistry in Geneva and was encouraged by Friedrich von Humboldt to go to Paris, where he became assistant lecturer to Louis Thenard at the Ecole Polytechnique (1823). He subsequently worked in many of the Parisian institutes, becoming professor at the Ecole Polytechnique (1835) and at the Sorbonne (1841).

Dumas's early work included a method for measuring vapor density (1826), the synthesis of oxamide (1830), and the discoveries of the terpene cymene (1832), anthracene in coal tar (1832), and urethane (1833). In 1834 Dumas and Eugène Peligot discovered methyl alcohol (methanol) and Dumas recognized that it differed from ethyl alcohol by one $-CH_2$ group. The subsequent discovery that Chevreul's 'ethal' was cetyl alcohol (1836) led Dumas to conceive the idea of a series of compounds of the same type (this was formalized into the concept of homologous series by Charles Gerhardt).

Dumas was both a prolific experimentalist and a leading theorist and he took a vigorous part in the many controversies that bedeviled organic chemistry at the time. He was originally an exponent of the 'etherin' theory (in which ethyl alcohol (ethanol) and diethyl ether were considered to be compounds of etherin (ethene) with one and two molecules of water, respectively). However he was converted to the radical theory (an attempt to formulate organic chemistry along the dualistic lines familiar in inorganic chemistry) by Justus von Liebig in 1837. He then introduced his own theory — the *substitution theory* — which was his greatest work. It had been noticed that candles bleached with chlorine gave off fumes of hydrogen chloride when they burned. Dumas discovered that during bleaching the hydrogen in the hydrocarbon oil of turpentine became replaced by chlorine. This seemed to contradict Jöns Berzelius's electrochemical theory and the latter was bitterly opposed to the substitution theory. Liebig, too, was hostile at first. Dumas then prepared trichloroacetic acid (1838) and showed that its properties were similar to those of the parent acetic acid. This con-

vinced Liebig but not Berzelius. Further work on this series of acids, combined with the substitution theory, led him to a theory of types (1840), essentially similar to the modern concept of functional groups, although the credit for this theory was disputed between Dumas and Auguste Laurent.

Dumas also carried out important work on atomic weights. He had been an early supporter of Amedeo Avogadro but he never properly distinguished between atoms and molecules and the problems this raised caused him to abandon the theory. He also supported William Prout's hypothesis that atomic weights were whole-number multiples of that of hydrogen. In 1840, working with Jean Stas, he obtained the figure 12.000 for carbon instead of the figure 12.24 in use at that time.

Following the revolution of 1848 Dumas became involved in administration, becoming minister of agriculture and commerce (1849–51), minister of education, and permanent secretary of the Academy of Sciences (1868).

DUNNING, John Ray (b. Sept. 24, 1907; Shelby, Nebraska; d. Aug. 27, 1975; Key Biscayne, Florida) American physicist.

Dunning was educated at Wesleyan University, Nebraska, and at Columbia University, New York, where he obtained his PhD in 1934. He took up an appointment at Columbia in 1933, being made professor of physics in 1950.

Dunning was one of the key figures in the Manhattan project to build the first atomic bomb. It had been shown by Niels Bohr that the isotope uranium–235 would be more likely to sustain a neutron chain reaction than normal uranium. Only 7 out of every 1000 uranium atoms occurring naturally are uranium–235, which presents difficulties in extraction. Various techniques were tried and Dunning was placed in charge of the process of separation known as gaseous diffusion. This involved turning the uranium into a voltatile compound (uranium hexafluoride, UF_6) and passing the vapor through a diffusion 'filter'. As ^{235}U atoms are slightly less massive than the normal ^{238}U they pass through the filter a little faster and can thus be concentrated. The difference in mass is so small, however, that simply to produce a gas enriched with ^{235}U atoms required its passage through thousands of filters.

As early as 1939 Dunning had shown that the process would work but to produce ^{235}U in the quantities required by the Manhattan project was a daunting prospect and the engineering problems were immense. The gas is extraordinarily corrosive and a single leak in one of the hundreds of thousands of filters would lose the precious ^{235}U. But as the other projects ran into even more formidable difficulties it was largely through gaseous diffusion that sufficient enriched uranium was made available for the bomb to be built.

DURAND, William Frederick (b. Mar. 5, 1859; Beacon Falls, Connecticut; d. Aug. 9, 1958) American engineer.

Durand graduated from the US Naval Academy in 1880 and entered the Engineering Corps of the US Navy (1880–87). He then took a post as professor of mechanical engineering at Michigan State College in 1887. He moved to Cornell in 1891 to the chair of marine engineering and, in 1904, he accepted the professorship of mechanical engineering at Stanford, a position he held until his retirement in 1924.

Durand worked mainly on problems connected with the propeller, both marine and, after 1914, aeronautical. He was general editor of an important standard work, *Aerodynamic Theory*, produced in six volumes (1929–36). He also served on the National Advisory Committee for Civil Aeronautics (NACA) (1915–33) and, in 1941, was recalled to advise the government on the construction of an American jet-propelled airplane.

DU TOIT, Alexander Logie (b. Mar. 14, 1878; Rondebosch, near Cape Town, South Africa; d. Feb. 25, 1949; Cape Town) South African geologist.

Du Toit studied at the South Africa College, now the University of Cape Town, and at the Royal Technical College, Glasgow, and the Royal College of Science, London.

After a short period teaching at Glasgow University (1901–03) he returned to South Africa and worked with the Geological Commission of the Cape of Good Hope (1903–20), during which he explored the geology of South Africa. For the next seven years he worked for the Irrigation Department and produced six detailed monographs on South African geology. He served as a consulting geologist to De Beers Consolidated Mines during the period 1927–41.

Following a visit to South America in 1923, du Toit became one of the earliest supporters of Alfred Wegener's theory of continental drift, publishing his observations in *A Geological Comparison of South America with South Africa* (1927). He noted the similarity between the continents and developed his ideas in *Our Wandering Continents* (1937), in which he argued for the separation of Wegener's Pangaea into the two super-continents, Laurasia and Gondwanaland.

DUTROCHET, René Joachim Henri (b. Nov. 14, 1776; Neón, France; d. Feb. 4, 1847; Paris) French physiologist.

Dutrochet began medical studies while serving in the army in Paris in 1802. After graduating in 1806 he served as an army surgeon in Spain. However, through illness he resigned his post in 1809 and thereafter devoted his time to natural science.

In 1814 he published his investigations into animal development, suggesting a unity of the main features during the early stages. Later research into plant and animal physiology led to his assertion that respiration is similar in both plants and animals. In 1832, Dutrochet showed that gas exchange in plants was via minute openings (stomata) on the surface of leaves and the deep cavities with which they communicate. He further demonstrated that only cells containing chlorophyll can fix carbon and thus transform light energy into chemical energy. Dutrochet studied osmosis and suggested it may be the cause of ascent and descent of sap in plants. Although sometimes lacking in accuracy, the importance of his work lies mainly in his endeavor to demonstrate that the vital phenomena of life can be explained on the basis of physics and chemistry.

DUTTON, Clarence Edward (b. May 15, 1841; Wallingford, Connecticut; d. Jan. 4, 1912, Englewood, New Jersey) American geologist.

Dutton graduated from Yale in 1860 and then entered the Yale Theological Seminary. He joined the army in 1862 during the Civil War and remained in the army although not always on active service. He became interested in geology and joined the Geographical and Geological Survey of the Rocky Mountains and the West in 1875.

The term 'isostasy' was introduced into geology by Dutton in 1889. This described a theory propounded by George Airy in which it is supposed that mountain ranges and continents rest on a much denser base. As mountains are eroded or snow melts from the continents the land rises while the settling sediment will compensate by depressing some other part of the Earth.

After his return to the army in 1890 Dutton turned to the study of earthquakes and volcanoes. His research was published in 1904 in his *Earthquakes in the Light of the New Seismology*.

DUVE, Christian René de *See* DE DUVE, Christian René.

DU VIGNEAUD, Vincent (b. May 18, 1901; Chicago, Illinois) American biochemist.

Du Vigneaud graduated from the University of Illinois in 1923 and remained there to take his master's degree before going to the University of Rochester. There he studied the hormone insulin, gaining his PhD in 1927. The research on insulin marked the beginning of his interest in sulfur compounds, particularly the sulfur-containing amino acids — methionine, cystine, and cysteine.

In 1938 Du Vigneaud became head of the biochemistry department of Cornell University Medical College. Two years later he had isolated vitamin H (biotin) and by 1942 had determined its structure. He then went on to examine the hormones secreted by the posterior pituitary gland, especially oxytocin and vasopressin. He found oxytocin to be composed of eight amino acids, worked out the order of these, and in 1954 synthesized artificial oxytocin, which was shown to be as effective as the natural hormone in inducing labor and milk flow. This was the first protein to be synthesized and for this achievement Du Vigneaud received the Nobel Prize for chemistry in 1955.

Du Vigneaud's other work has included research on penicillin and on methyl groups. From 1967 to 1975 he was professor of chemistry at Cornell University and is presently emeritus professor of biochemistry at Cornell.

DYSON, Sir Frank Watson (b. Jan. 8, 1868; Ashby-de-la-Zouche, England; d. May 25, 1939; at sea, returning from Australia) British astronomer.

Dyson, the son of a Baptist minister, graduated in mathematics from Cambridge University in 1889 and in 1891 was elected to a fellowship. After first working as chief assistant at the Royal Observatory at Greenwich from 1894 to 1905, he was Astronomer Royal for Scotland from 1905 to 1910 and then returned to Greenwich as

Astronomer Royal, serving from 1910 to 1933. He was knighted in 1915.

Dyson's early observational work was done in collaboration with William G. Thackeray: they measured the positions of over 4000 circumpolar stars that had first been observed by Stephen Groombridge at the beginning of the 19th century. They were thus able to determine the proper motions of the stars. Dyson could then extend the work of Jacobus Kapteyn on star streaming to fainter stars.

Dyson observed the total solar eclipses of 1900, 1901, and 1905, obtaining spectra of the atmospheric layers of the Sun. He also organized the detailed observations of the total solar eclipse in 1919, sending expeditions to Principe in the Gulf of Guinea and Sobral in Brazil. The measured positions of stars near the Sun's rim during the eclipse provided evidence for the bending of light in a gravitational field, as predicted by Einstein in his theory of general relativity; this was the first experimental support for the theory.

DYSON, Freeman John (b. Dec. 15, 1923; Crowthorne, England) British–American theoretical physicist.

Dyson, the son of George Dyson the director of the Royal College of Music, was educated at Cambridge University. During World War II he worked at the headquarters of Bomber Command. In 1947 he went on a Commonwealth Fellowship to Cornell University and joined the Institute of Advanced Studies, Princeton, in 1953.

Dyson has worked on a number of topics but is best-known for his contribution to quantum electrodynamics; i.e. the application of quantum theory to interactions between particles and electromagnetic radiation. The observation in 1946 by Willis Lamb of a small difference between the lowest energy levels of the hydrogen atom was an experimental result against which such theories could be tested. In the period 1946–48 independent formulations of quantum electrodynamics were put forward by Julian Schwinger, Sin-Itiro Tomonaga, and Richard Feynman. Dyson showed that the three methods were all consistent and brought them together into a single general theory.

Dyson later became known to a wider public through his work on the nuclear test ban treaty and for his quite serious considerations of space travel and the 'greening of the galaxy'.

E

EASTMAN, George (b. July 12, 1854; Waterville, New York; d. Mar. 14, 1932) American inventor.

Eastman began his career in banking and insurance but turned from this to photography. In 1880 he perfected the dry-plate photographic film and began manufacturing this. He produced a transparent roll film in 1884 and in the same year founded the Eastman Dry Plate and Film Company. In 1888 he introduced the simple hand-held box camera that made popular photography possible. The Kodak camera with a roll of transparent film was cheap enough for all pockets and could be used by a child. It was followed by the Brownie camera, which cost just one dollar.

Eastman gave away a considerable part of his fortune to educational institutions, including the Massachusetts Institute of Technology. He committed suicide in 1932.

EBASHI, Setsuro (b. Aug. 31, 1922; Tokyo) Japanese biochemist.

Ebashi received his MD from the University of Tokyo in 1944 and his PhD in 1954. He became professor of pharmacology in 1959 and, since 1963, has held the chair of biochemistry.

Ebashi has, for many years, been one of the leading workers in the field of muscle contraction. His work has thrown considerable light on the identity and workings of the so-called 'relaxing factor'. As early as 1952 B. Marsh had isolated a substance from muscle that produces relaxation in muscle fibers, and he noted that its effect could be neutralized by the presence of calcium ions.

While the process of muscle contraction appeared to be initiated by the release of calcium ions from the sarcoplasmic reticulum, Ebashi and his colleagues were able to show in the 1960s that such ions were not enough. The presence of two globular proteins, troponin and tropomyosin, is also necessary. Neither protein alone is sufficient as only the complex sensitizes muscle to calcium ions.

The globular proteins appear to prevent the interaction of myosin and actin as first described by Hugh Huxley. However, once a certain level of calcium is reached such inhibition is prevented and contraction occurs. Later x-ray analysis by many workers seems to have confirmed Ebashi's model.

ECCLES, Sir John Carew (b. Jan. 27, 1903; Melbourne, Australia) Australian physiologist.

Eccles was educated at the University of Melbourne and in England at Oxford University, working at Oxford with Charles Sherrington on muscular reflexes and nervous transmission across the synapses (nerve junctions). For a time he taught in Australia and New Zealand and in 1966 began working at the Institute for Biomedical Research in Chicago. While professor of physiology at the Australian National University, Canberra (1951–66), Eccles carried out work on the chemical changes that take place at synapses, pursuing the findings of Alan Hodgkin and Andrew Huxley, with whom he subsequently shared the 1963 Nobel Prize for physiology or medicine. Eccles showed that excitation of different nerve cells causes the synapses to release a substance (probably acetylcholine) that promotes the passage of sodium and potassium ions and effects an alternation in the polarity of the electric charge. It is in this way that nervous impulses are communicated or inhibited by nerve cells. Eccles is the author of *Reflex Activity of the Spinal Cord* (1932) and *The Physiology of Nerve Cells* (1957).

EDDINGTON, Sir Arthur Stanley (b. Dec. 28, 1882; Kendal, England; d. Nov. 22, 1944; Cambridge, England) British astrophysicist and mathematician.

Eddington's father died in 1884 and he moved with his mother and sister to Somerset. He was a brilliant scholar, graduating from Owens College (now the University of Manchester) in 1902 and from Cambridge University in 1905. From 1906 to 1913 he was chief assistant to the Astronomer Royal at Greenwich after which he returned to Cambridge as Plumian Professor of Astronomy. He was a Quaker throughout his life and was knighted in 1930.

Eddington was the major British astronomer of the interwar period. His early work on the motions of stars was followed, from 1916 onward, by his work on the interior of stars, which was published in his first major book, *The Internal Constitution of the Stars* (1926). He introduced "a phenomenon ignored in early investigations, which may have considerable effect on the equilibrium of a star, viz. the pressure of radiation." He showed that for equilibrium to be maintained in a star, the inwardly directed force of gravitation must be balanced by the outwardly directed forces of both gas pressure and radiation pressure. He also proposed that heat energy was transported from the center to the outer regions of a star not by convection, as thought hitherto, but by radiation.

It was in this work that Eddington gave a full account of his mass-luminosity relationship, which was discovered in 1924 and shows that the more massive a star the more luminous it will be. The value of the relation is that it allows the mass of a star to be determined if its intrinsic brightness is known. This is of considerable significance since only the masses of binary stars can be directly calculated. Eddington realized that there was a limit to the size of stars: relatively few would have masses exceeding 10 times the mass of the Sun while any exceeding 50 solar masses would be unstable owing to excessive radiation pressure.

Eddington wrote a number of books for both scientists and laymen. His more popular books, including *The Expanding Universe* (1933), were widely read, went through many editions, and opened new worlds to many enquiring minds of the interwar years. It was through Eddington that Einstein's general relativity theory reached the English-speaking world. He was greatly impressed by the theory and was able to provide experimental evidence for it. He observed the total solar eclipse of 1919 and submitted a report that captured the intellectual imagination of his generation. He reported that a very precise and unexpected prediction made by Einstein in his general theory had been successfully observed; this was the very slight bending of light by the gravitational field of a star — the Sun. Further support came in 1924 when Einstein's prediction of the reddening of starlight by the gravitational field of the star was tested: at Eddington's request Walter Adams detected and measured the shift in wavelength of the spectral lines of Sirius B, the dense white-dwarf companion of the star Sirius. Eddington thus did much to establish Einstein's theory on a sound and rigorous foundation and gave a very fine presentation of the subject in his *Mathematical Theory of Relativity* (1923).

Eddington worked for many years on an obscure but challenging theory, which was only published in his posthumous work, *Fundamental Theory* (1946). Basically, he claimed that the fundamental constants of science, such as the mass of the proton and mass and charge of the electron were a "natural and complete specification for constructing a universe" and that their values were not accidental. He then set out to develop a theory from which such values would follow as a consequence, but never completed it.

EDELMAN, Gerald Maurice (b. July 1, 1929; New York City) American biochemist.

Edelman was educated at Ursinus College, the University of Pennsylvania, and Rockefeller University, where he obtained his PhD on human immunoglobulins in 1960. He remained at Rockefeller and in 1966 was appointed professor of biochemistry.

Edelman was interested in determining the structure of human immunoglobulin. However the molecule is very large and it was first necessary to break it into smaller portions, which was achieved by reducing and splitting the disulfide bonds. Following this, Edelman proposed that the molecule contained more than one polypeptide chain and moreover that two kinds of chain exist, light and heavy. Such studies helped Rodney Porter propose a structure for the antibody immunoglobulin G (IgG) in 1962.

Edelman was more interested in attempting to work out the complete amino-acid sequence of IgG. As it contained 1330 amino acids it was by far the largest protein then attempted. By 1969 Edelman was ready to announce the results of his impressive work, the complete sequence, and was able to show that while much of the molecule was unchanging the tips of the Y-like structure were highly variable in their amino-acid sequence. It thus seemed obvious that such an area would be identical with the active antigen binding region in Porter's structure and that such variability represented the ability of IgG to bind many different antigens. It was for this work that Edelman and Porter shared

the 1972 Nobel Prize for physiology or medicine.

Edelman has also speculated on antibody formation and the mechanism behind the spurt in production after contact with an antigen. In the former area he argued in 1966 for a major modification of the clonal theory of Macfarlane Burnet; in the latter case he suggested, in 1970, that the signal to the immune system to increase production is set off by the change in shape of the antibody molecule as it combines with its antigen.

EDISON, Thomas Alva (b. Feb. 11, 1847; Milan, Ohio; d. Oct. 18, 1931; West Orange, New Jersey) American physicist and inventor.

Edison was taught at home by his mother. He had been expelled from school as 'retarded', perhaps because of his deafness. From the age of seven he lived in Port Huron, Michigan, and when he was twelve years old began to spend much of his time on the railroad between Port Huron and Detroit, selling candy and newspapers to make money. However he was also fascinated by the telegraph system, designing his own experiments and training himself in telegraphy. He became a casual worker on telegraphy (1862–68), reading and experimenting as he traveled.

At the age of 21 he bought a copy of Faraday's *Experimental Researches in Electricity* and was inspired to undertake serious systematic experimental work.

While Edison was living in a Wall Street basement (1869) he was called in to carry out an emergency repair on a new telegraphic gold-price indicator in the Gold Exchange. He was so successful that he was taken on as a supervisor. Later he remodeled the equipment and, soon after being commissioned to improve other equipment, his skill became legendary.

For a while Edison had a well-paid job with the Western Union Telegraph Company, but he gave it up to set up a laboratory of his own at Menlo Park, New Jersey. This he furbished with a wide range of scientific equipment, costing $40 000, and an extensive library. He employed 20 technicians and later a mathematical physicist. The laboratory was the first organized research center outside a university and produced many inventions. In 1877 Edison became known internationally after the phonograph was invented. In 1878, after seeing an exhibition of glaring electric arc lights, he declared that he would invent a milder cheap alternative that could replace the gas lamp. Because of his past successes, he managed to raise the capital to do this and the Edison Electric Light Company was set up. It took 14 months to find a filament material but by October 1899, Edison was able to demonstrate 30 incandescent electric lamps connected in parallel with separate switches. Three years later a power station was opened in New York and this was the start of modern large-scale electricity generation. In 1887 Edison's laboratory moved to larger premises in West Orange, now a national monument.

EDLÉN, Bengt (b. Nov. 2, 1906; Gusum, Sweden) Swedish physicist.

Edlén studied at the University of Uppsala where he gained his PhD in 1934 and also served on the faculty from 1928 until 1944. He was then appointed professor of physics at the University of Lund, a post he retained until his retirement in 1973.

Edlén is recognized for his research on atomic spectra and its applications to astrophysics. In the early 1940s he carried out important work on the emission lines, first described in 1870, in the Sun's corona, i.e. the outermost layer of the solar atmosphere. The problem with the 20 'well-measured lines' was that none had ever been observed in a laboratory light source. At one time they were thought to indicate the presence of an unknown element, conveniently described as 'coronium', but it had become apparent when Edlén began his work that the periodic table no longer contained any suitable gaps.

Edlén succeeded in showing in 1941 that the coronal lines were mainly caused by iron, nickel, calcium, and argon atoms deprived of 10–15 electrons; i.e. by highly charged positive ions. The implications of such extreme ionization were not lost on Edlén who was quick to point out that it must indicate temperatures of over a quarter of a million degrees in the solar corona.

EDSALL, John Tileston (b. Nov. 3, 1902; Philadelphia, Pennsylvania) American biochemist.

Edsall was educated at Harvard and at Cambridge University, England. He joined the Harvard faculty in 1928 and from 1951 to 1973 served there as professor of biochemistry.

Edsall is basically a protein chemist. He spent much time establishing basic data on the constitution and properties of numerous proteins — information that has since been reproduced in innumerable textbooks. With Edwin Cohn he was the author of the authoritative work *Proteins, Amino Acids and Peptides* (1943).

In later years Edsall turned his attention to the history of biochemistry, his books in this field including *Blood and Hemoglobin* (1952).

EGAS MONIZ, Antonio Caetanio de Abreu Freire (b. Nov. 29, 1874; Avanca, Portugal; d. Dec. 13, 1955; Lisbon) Portuguese neurologist.

Egas Moniz was educated at the University of Coimbra, where he gained his MD in 1899. After postgraduate work in Paris and Bordeaux he returned to Coimbra, becoming a professor in the medical faculty in 1902. He moved to Lisbon in 1911 to a newly created chair of neurology, a post he retained until his retirement in 1944. At the same time he was pursuing a successful political career, being elected to the National Assembly in 1900. He served as ambassador to Spain in 1917 and in the following year became foreign minister, leading his country's delegation to the Paris Peace Conference.

Egas Moniz achieved his first major success in the 1920s in the field of angiography (the study of the cardiovascular system using dyes that are opaque to x-rays). In collaboration with Almeida Lima, he injected such radioopaque dyes into the arteries, enabling the blood vessels of the brain to be photographed. In 1927 he was able to show that displacements in the cerebral circulation could be used to infer the presence and location of brain tumors, publishing a detailed account of his technique in 1931.

Egas Moniz is better known for his introduction in 1935 of the operation of prefrontal leukotomy. It was for this work, described by the Nobel authorities as "one of the most important discoveries ever made in psychiatric therapy," that they awarded him the 1949 Nobel Prize for physiology or medicine.

The operation consisted of inserting a sharp knife into the prefrontal lobe of the brain, roughly the area above and between the eyes; it required the minimum of equipment and lasted less than five minutes. The technique was suggested to Egas Moniz on hearing an account (by John Fulton and Carlyle Jacobsen in 1935) of a refractory chimpanzee that became less aggressive after its frontal lobes had been excised. Egas Moniz believed that a similar surgical operation would relieve severe emotional tension in psychiatric patients. He claimed that 14 of the first 20 patients operated upon were either cured or improved. The operation generated much controversy, since the extent of the improvement in the patients' symptoms was not easy to judge and the procedure often produced severe side-effects. Today a more refined version of the operation, in which selective incisions are made in smaller areas of the brain, is still quite widely practiced.

EHRENBERG, Christian Gottfried (b. Apr. 19, 1795; Delitzsch, now in East Germany;

d. June 27, 1876; Berlin) German biologist and microscopist.

Ehrenberg took an MD degree at the University of Berlin in 1818, and in the same year was elected a member of the Leopoldine German Academy of Researchers in Natural Sciences. Two years later he took part in a scientific expedition to Egypt, Libya, the Sudan, and the Red Sea, sponsored by the Prussian Academy of Sciences and the University of Berlin. During these travels (1820–25) Ehrenberg collected and classified some 75 000 plant and animal specimens, both terrestrial and marine, including microorganisms. On a further expedition in 1829 to Central Asia and Siberia, sponsored by Czar Nicholas 1, he was accompanied by Alexander von Humboldt. In 1827 Ehrenberg was appointed assistant professor of zoology at Berlin and was elected a member of the Berlin Academy of Sciences. He became professor of natural science at Berlin in 1839.

Ehrenberg's studies in natural science were primarily concerned with microorganisms, especially the protozoans. His paleontological investigations led him to demonstrate the presence of single-celled fossils in certain rock layers of various geological formations, and he was also able to show that marine phosphorescence (strictly, bioluminescence) was due to the activity of species of animal plankton. He described fungal development from spores, as well as their sexual reproduction, and also carried out detailed studies of corals. His most important thesis lay in the belief that microorganisms were complete in the sense of sharing the same organs as higher animals, and that social behavior provided the basis for a new approach to animal classification. Ehrenberg's theory was demolished, with the help of experimental evidence, by Félix Dujardin. His publications include *Travels in Egypt, Libya, Nubia and Dongola* (1828) and *The Infusoria as Complete Animals* (1838). His descriptions and classification of fossil protozoans were published as *Microgeology* (1854).

EHRLICH, Paul (b. Mar. 14, 1854; Strehlen, now Strzelin, Poland; d. Aug. 20, 1915; Bad Homburg, now in West Germany) German physician, bacteriologist, and chemist.

Ehrlich studied medicine at the universities of Breslau, Strasbourg, and Freiburg, gaining a physician's degree at Breslau in 1878. For the next nine years he worked at the Charité Hospital, Berlin, on many topics including typhoid fever, tuberculosis, and pernicious anemia. He was awarded the title of professor by the Prussian Ministry of Education in 1884 for his impressive work in these fields. In 1887 he became a teacher at the University of Berlin but was not paid because of the anti-Semitic feeling at the time — Ehrlich would not renounce his Jewish upbringing. As a result of his laboratory work he contracted tuberculosis and was not restored to health until 1890, when he set up his own small research laboratory at Steglitz on the outskirts of Berlin.

In 1890 Robert Koch announced the discovery of tuberculin and suggested its use in preventing and curing tuberculosis. He asked Ehrlich to work on it with him at the Moabit Hospital in Berlin. Ehrlich accepted and for six years studied TB and cholera. In 1896 he accepted the post of director of the new Institute for Serum Research and Serum Investigation at Steglitz and in 1899 moved to the Institute of Experimental Therapy in Frankfurt. Here he investigated African sleeping sickness and syphilis along with his other studies. In 1908 he was awarded the Nobel Prize for physiology or medicine for his work on immunity and serum therapy.

Two years later he announced his most famous discovery, Salvarsan — a synthetic chemical that was effective against syphilis — and until the end of his life he worked on the problems associated with the treatment of patients using this compound of arsenic.

Ehrlich is considered to be the founder of modern chemotherapy because he developed systematic scientific techniques to search for new synthetic chemicals that could specifically attack disease-causing microorganisms. Ehrlich sought for these 'magic bullets' by carefully altering the chemical structure of dye molecules that selectively stained the microorganisms observable in his microscope but did not stain cells in the host. He was persevering and optimistic — Salvarsan (compound number 606) was not 'rediscovered' until almost 1000 compounds had been synthesized and tried. He made and tested about 3000 compounds based on the structure of Salvarsan in an attempt to make a drug that was bacteriocidal to streptococci.

EICHLER, August Wilhelm (b. Apr. 22, 1839; Neukirchen, now in West Germany; d. Mar. 2, 1887; Berlin) German botanist.

After studying natural science and mathematics at the University of Marburg, gaining his PhD in 1861, Eichler became assistant to Karl von Martius at Munich. With Martius he began editing the 15-volume *Flora of Brazil*, continuing this work single-handed after Martius's death in 1868. In 1878 he succeeded Alexander Braun as professor of systematic and morphologic botany at Berlin and also became director of the university's herbarium. The same year he published the second volume of his two-volume *Diagrams of Flowers*, describing the comparative structure of flowers.

In 1886, the year before his death, Eichler developed a plant classification system in which the plant kingdom is split into four divisions: Thallophyta (algae, fungi), Bryophyta (mosses, liverworts), Pteridophyta (ferns, horsetails), and Spermatophyta (seed plants). He further subdivided the Spermatophyta into the Gymnospermae (conifers, cycads, gingkos) and Angiospermae (flowering plants). This system was later adopted by nearly all botanists, but because of his early death from leukemia Eichler did not live to see the general acceptance of his work.

EIGEN, Manfred (b. May 9, 1927; Bochum,

now in West Germany) German physical chemist.

Eigen, the son of a musician, was educated at the University of Göttingen where he obtained his PhD in 1951. He joined the staff of the Max Planck Institute for Physical Chemistry at Göttingen in 1953 and has served as its director since 1964.

In 1954 Eigen introduced the so-called relaxation techniques for the study of extremely fast chemical reactions (those taking less than a millisecond). Eigen's general technique was to take a solution in equilibrium for a given temperature and pressure. If a short disturbance was applied to the solution the equilibrium would be very briefly destroyed and a new equilibrium quickly reached. Eigen studied exactly what happened in this very short time by means of absorption spectroscopy. He applied disturbances to the equilibrium by a variety of methods, such as pulses of electric current, sudden changes in temperature or pressure, or changes in electric field.

The first reaction he investigated was the apparently simple formation of a water molecule from the hydrogen ion, H^+, and the hydroxyl radical, OH^-. Calculations of reaction rates made it clear that they could not be produced by the collision of the simple ions H^+ and OH^-. Eigen went on to show that the reacting ions are the unexpectedly large $H_9O_4^+$ and $H_7O_4^-$, a proton hydrated with four water molecules and a hydroxyl ion with three water molecules. For this work Eigen shared the 1967 Nobel Chemistry Prize with George Porter and Ronald Norrish.

Eigen later applied his relaxation techniques to complex biochemical reactions. He has also become interested in the origin of nucleic acids and proteins; with his colleague R. Winkler he has proposed a possible mechanism to explain their formation.

EIJKMAN, Christiaan (b. Aug. 11, 1858; Nijkerk, Netherlands; d. Nov. 5, 1930; Utrecht, Netherlands) Dutch physician.

Eijkman qualified as a physician from the University of Amsterdam in 1883. He served as an Army Medical Officer in the Dutch East Indies from 1883 to 1885, when he was forced to return to Holland to recuperate from a severe attack of malaria. In 1886 he returned to the East Indies as a member of an official government committee to investigate beriberi. After the completion of the committee's work, Eijkman remained in Batavia (now Djakarta) as director of a newly established bacteriological laboratory. In 1896 he took up the post of professor of public health at the University of Utrecht.

Eijkman was responsible for the first real understanding of the nature and possible cure of beriberi. For this work he shared the 1929 Nobel Prize in physiology or medicine with Frederick Gowland Hopkins. Beriberi is a disorder caused by dietary deficiency, producing fatal lesions in the nervous and cardiovascular systems. Physicians of the late 19th century, however, were not trained to recognize its cause: with the clear success of the germ theory recently demonstrated by Robert Koch it was difficult to realize that symptoms could be produced by the absence of something rather than by the more obvious presence of a visible pathogen.

Eijkman's discovery was prompted by the outbreak of a disease very similar to human beriberi among the laboratory chickens. Despite the most thorough search no causative microorganism could be identified, and then, for no obvious reason, the disease disappeared.

On investigation, Eijkman discovered that the symptoms of the disease had developed during a period of five months in which the chickens' diet was changed to hulled and polished rice. With a return to their normal diet of commercial chicken feed the symptoms disappeared. Eijkman subsequently found that he could induce the disease with a diet of hulled and polished rice and cure it with one of whole rice. However, he failed to conclude that beriberi was a deficiency disease. He argued that the endosperm of the rice produced a toxin that was neutralized by the outer hull: by eating polished rice the toxin would be released in its unneutralized form.

Thus although Eijkman had clearly demonstrated how to cure and prevent beriberi it was left to Hopkins to identify its cause as a vitamin deficiency. It was not until the early 1930s that Robert Williams identified the vitamin as vitamin B_1 (thiamine).

EINSTEIN, Albert (b. Mar. 14, 1879; Ulm, now in West Germany; d. Apr. 18, 1955; Princeton, New Jersey) German–Swiss–American theoretical physicist.

Einstein's father was a manufacturer of electrical equipment. Business failure led him to move his family first to Munich, where Einstein entered the local gymnasium in 1889, and later to Milan. There were no early indications of Einstein's later achievements for he did not begin to talk until the age of three, nor was he fluent at the age of nine, causing his parents to fear that he might even be backward. It appears that in 1894 he was expelled from his Munich gymnasium on the official grounds that his presence was 'disruptive'. At this point he did something rather remarkable for a fifteen-year-old boy. He had developed such a hatred for things German that he could no longer bear to be a German citizen. He persuaded his father to apply for a revocation of his son's citizenship, a request the authorities granted in 1896. Until 1901, when he obtained Swiss citizenship, he was in fact stateless.

After completing his secondary education at Aarao in Switzerland he passed the entrance examination, at the second attempt, to the Swiss Federal Institute of Technology, Zurich, in 1896. He did not appear to be a particularly exceptional student finding the process of working for examinations repellent. Disappointed not to be offered an academic post, he survived

as a private tutor until 1902, when he obtained the post of technical expert, third class, in the Swiss Patent Office in Bern. Here he continued to think about and work on physical problems. In 1905 he published four papers in the journal *Annalen der Physik* — works that were to direct the progress of physics during the 20th century.

The first, and most straightforward, was on Brownian motion — first described by Robert Brown in 1828. Einstein derived a formula for the average displacement of particles in suspension, based on the idea that the motion is caused by bombardment of the particles by molecules of the liquid. The formula was confirmed by Jean Perrin in 1908 — it represented the first direct evidence for the existence of atoms and molecules of a definite size. The paper was entitled *Über die von molekularkinetischen Theorie der Wärme gerforderte Bewegung von in ruhenden Flüssigkeiten suspendierten Teilchen* (On the Motion of Small Particles Suspended in a Stationary Liquid According to the Molecular Kinetic Theory of Induction).

His second paper of 1905 was *Über einen die Erzeugung und Verwandlung des Lichtes betreffenden heuristischen Gesichtspunkt* (On a Heuristic Point of View about the Creation and Conversion of Light). In this Einstein was concerned with the nature of electromagnetic radiation, which at the time was regarded as a wave propagated throughout space according to Clerk Maxwell's equations. Einstein was concerned with the difference between this wave picture and the theoretical picture physicists had of matter. His particular concern in this paper was the difficulty in explaining the photoelectric effect, investigated in 1902 by Philipp Lenard. It was found that ultraviolet radiation of low frequency could eject electrons from a solid surface. The number of electrons depended on the intensity of the radiation and the energy of the electrons depended on the frequency. This dependence on frequency was difficult to explain using classical theory.

Einstein resolved this by suggesting that

electromagnetic radiation is a flow of discreet particles — quanta (or photons as they are now known). The intensity of the radiation is the flux of these quanta. The energy per quantum, he proposed, was hv, where v is the frequency of the radiation and h is the constant introduced in 1900 by Max Planck. In this way Einstein was able to account for the observed photoelectric behavior. The work was one of the early results introducing the quantum theory into physics and it won for Einstein the 1921 Nobel Physics Prize.

The third of his 1905 papers is the one that is the most famous: *Zur Electrodynamik bewegter Korper* (On the Electrodynamics of Moving Bodies). It is this paper that first introduced the special theory of relativity to science. The term 'special' denotes that the theory is restricted to certain special circumstances — namely for bodies at rest or moving with uniform relative velocities.

The theory was developed to account for a major problem in physics at the time. Traditionally in mechanics, there was a simple procedure for treating relative velocities. A simple example is of a car moving along a road at 40 mph with a second car moving toward it at 60 mph. A stationary observer would say that the second car was moving at 60 mph relative to him. The driver of the first car would say that, relative to him, the second car was approaching at 100 mph. This common-sense method of dealing with relative motion was well established. The mathematical equations involved are called the Galilean transformations — they are simple equations for changing velocities in one frame of reference to another frame of reference. The problem was that the method did not appear to work for electromagnetic radiation, which was thought of as a wave motion through the ether, described by the equations derived by Maxwell. In these, the speed of light is independent of the motion of the source or the observer. At the time, Albert Michelson and Edward Morley had performed a series of experiments to attempt to detect the Earth's motion through the ether, with negative results. Hendrik Lorentz proposed that this result could be explained by a change of size of moving bodies (the Lorentz–Fitzgerald contraction).

Although Einstein was unaware of the Michelson–Morley experiment, he did appreciate the incompatibility of classical mechanics and classical electrodynamics. His solution was a quite radical one. He proposed that the speed of light *is* a constant for all frames of reference that are moving uniformly relative to each other. He also put forward his 'relativity principle' that the laws of nature are the same in all frames of reference moving uniformly relative to each other. To reconcile the two principles he abandoned the Galilean transformations — the simple method of adding and subtracting velocities for bodies in relative motion. He arrived at this rejection by arguments about the idea of simultaneity — showing that the time between two events depends on the motions of the bodies involved. In his special theory of relativity, Einstein rejected the ideas of absolute space and absolute time. Later it was developed in terms of events specified by three spacial coordinates and one coordinate of time — a space–time continuum.

The theory had a number of unusual consequences. Thus, the length of a body along its direction of motion decreases with increasing velocity. The mass increases as the velocity increases, becoming infinitely large in theory at the speed of light. Time slows down for a moving body — a phenomenon known as time dilation. These effects apply to all bodies but only become significant at velocities close to the speed of light — under normal conditions the effects are so small that classical laws appear to be obeyed. However, the predictions of the special theory — unusual as they may seem — have been verified experimentally. Thus, increase in mass is observed for particles accelerated in a synchrocyclotron. Similarly, the lifetimes of unstable particles are increased at high velocities.

In that same year of 1905 Einstein had one more fundamental paper to contribute:

Ist der Trägheit eins Körpers von seinem Energieinhalt abhängig? (Does the Inertia of a Body Depend on its Energy Content?). It was in this two-page paper that he concluded that if a body gives off energy E in the form of radiation, its mass diminishes by E/c^2 (where c is the velocity of light), obtaining the celebrated equation $E = mc^2$ relating mass and energy.

Within a short time Einstein's work on relativity was widely recognized to be original and profound. In 1908 he obtained an academic post at the University of Bern. Over the next three years he held major posts at Zurich (1909), Prague (1911), and the Zurich Federal Institute of Technology (1912) before taking a post in Berlin in 1914. This was probably due in part to the respect in which he held the Berlin physicists, Max Planck and Walther Nernst.

By 1907 Einstein was ready to remove the restrictions imposed on the special theory showing that, on certain assumptions, accelerated motion could be incorporated into his new, general theory of relativity. The theory begins with the fact that the mass of a body can be defined in two ways. The inertial mass depends on the way it resists change in motion, as in Newton's second law. The gravitational mass depends on forces of gravitational attraction between masses. The two concepts — inertia and gravity — seem dissimilar yet the inertial and gravitational masses of a body are always the same. Einstein considered that this was unlikely to be a coincidence and it became the basis of his principle of equivalence.

The principle states that it is impossible to distinguish between an inertial force (that is, an accelerating force) and a gravitational one; the two are, in fact, equivalent. The point can be demonstrated with a thought experiment. Consider an observer in an enclosed box somewhere in space far removed from gravitational forces. Suppose that the box is suddenly accelerated upward, followed by the observer releasing two balls of different weights. Subject to an inertial force they will both fall to the floor at the same rate. But this is exactly how they would behave if the box was in a gravitational field and the observer could conclude that the balls fall under the influence of gravity. It was on the basis of this equivalence that Einstein made his dramatic prediction that rays of light in a gravitational field move in a curved path. For if a ray of light enters the box at one side and exits at the other then, with the upward acceleration of the box, it will appear to exit at a point lower down than its entrance. But if we take the equivalence principle seriously we must expect to find the same effect in a gravitational field.

In 1911 he predicted that starlight just grazing the Sun should be deflected by 0.83 seconds of arc, later increased to 1″.7, which, though small, should be detectable in a total eclipse by the apparent displacement of the star from its usual position. In 1919 such an eclipse took place; it was observed by Arthur Eddington at Principe in West Africa, who reported a displacement of 1″.61, well within the limits of experimental error. It was from this moment that Einstein became known to a wider public, for this dramatic confirmation of an unexpected phenomenon seemed to capture the popular imagination. Even the London *Times* was moved to comment in an editorial, as if to a recalcitrant government, that "the scientific conception of the fabric of the universe must be changed."

In 1916 Einstein was ready to publish the final and authoritative form of his general theory: *Die Grundlagen der allgemeinen der Relativitätstheorie* (The Foundation of the General Theory of Relativity). It is this work that gained for Einstein the reputation for producing theories that were comprehensible to the very few. Eddington on being informed that there were only three people capable of understanding the theory is reported to have replied, "Who's the third?" It is true that Einstein introduced into gravitational theory a type of mathematics that was then unfamiliar to most physicists thus presenting an initial impression of incomprehension. In his theory Einstein used the space–time continuum introduced by Hermann Minkowski in 1907, the non-Euclidean geometry developed by Bernhard Riemann in 1854, and the tensor calculus published by Gregorio Ricci in 1887. He was assisted in the mathematics by his friend Grossmann. The theory of gravitation produced is one that depends on the geometry of space–time. In simple terms, the idea is that a body 'warps' the space around it so that another body moves in a curved path (hence the notion that space is curved). Einstein and Grossmann in 1915 succeeded in deriving a good theoretical value for the small (and hitherto anomalous) advance in the perihelion of mercury; Einstein wrote at the time, "I was beside myself with ecstasy for days."

The theory also predicted (1907) that electromagnetic radiation in a strong gravitation field would be shifted to longer wavelengths — the *Einstein shift*. This was used by Walter Adams in 1925 to explain the spectrum of Sirius B. In 1959 Robert Pound and Glen Rebka demonstrated it on Earth using the Mossbauer effect. They found that at a height of 75 feet (23 m) above the ground gamma rays from a radioactive source had a longer wavelength than at ground level.

Einstein was less successful in applying his theory to the construction of a cosmological model of the universe, which he assumed to be uniform in density, static, and lacking infinite distances. He found himself forced to complicate his equations with a cosmological constant, λ. It was left to Aleksandr Friedmann in 1922 to show that the term could be dropped and a solution found that yielded an expanding universe, a solution that Einstein eventually adopted.

By the early 1920s Einstein's great work was virtually complete. He wrote in 1921 that: "Discovery in the grand manner is for young people ... and hence for me a thing of the past." From the early 1920s he rejected quantum theory — the theory he had done much to establish himself. His basic objection was to the later formulation that included the probability interpretation. "God does not play dice," he said, and, "He may be subtle, but he is not malicious." He felt, like Louis de Broglie, that although the new quantum mechanics was clearly a powerful and successful theory it was an imperfect one, with an underlying undiscovered deterministic basis. For the last 30 years of his life he also pursued a quest for a unified field theory — a single theory to explain both electromagnetic and gravitational fields. He published several attempts at such a theory but all were inadequate. This work was carried out right up to his death.

Einstein was also involved in a considerable amount of political activity. When Hitler came to power in 1933 Einstein made his permanent home in America where he worked at Princeton. In 1939 he was persuaded to write to President Roosevelt warning him about the possibility of an atomic bomb and urging American research. He was, in later years, a convinced campaigning pacifist. He was also a strong supporter of Zionist causes and, on the death of Chaim Weizmann in 1952 was asked to become president of Israel, but declined.

EINTHOVEN, Willem (b. May 21, 1860; Semarang, Java; d. Sept. 28, 1927; Leiden, Netherlands) Dutch physiologist.

Einthoven, the son of a physician, was educated at the University of Utrecht, where he gained his MD in 1885. In the following year he moved to Leiden as professor of physiology.

As early as 1887 the English physiologist Augustus Waller had recorded electric currents generated by the heart. He had used the capillary electrometer invented by Gabriel Lippmann in 1873, which — although sensitive to changes of a millivolt — turned out to be too complicated and inaccurate for general use. In 1901 Einthoven first described a recording system using a string galvanometer, which he claimed would overcome the inadequacies of Waller's device.

A string galvanometer consists of a fine wire thread stretched between the poles of a magnet. When carrying a current it is displaced at right angles to the directions of the magnetic lines of force to an extent proportional to the strength of the current. By linking this up to an optical system the movement of the wire can be magnified and photographically recorded. As the differences in potential developed in the heart are conducted to different parts of the body it was possible to lead the current from the hands and feet to the recording instrument to obtain a curve that was later called an *electrocardiogram* (ECG).

Having demonstrated the potentiality of such a machine two further problems needed solution. Einthoven first had to standardize his ECG so that different machines or two recordings of the same machine would produce comparable readings. It was therefore later established that a 1 mv potential would deflect a recording stylus 1 cm on standardized paper. The second problem was how to interpret such a curve in order to distinguish normal readings from recordings of diseased hearts. By 1913 Einthoven had worked out the interpretation of the normal tracing and, by correlating abnormal readings with specific cardiac defects identified at post mortem, was able to use the ECG as a diagnostic tool.

For his development of the electrocardiogram Einthoven was awarded the 1924 Nobel Prize in physiology or medicine.

EKEBERG, Anders Gustaf (b. Jan. 16, 1767; Stockholm; d. Feb. 11, 1813; Uppsala, Sweden) Swedish chemist.

Ekeberg graduated from the University of Uppsala in 1788 and, after traveling in Europe, began teaching chemistry at Uppsala in 1794. He was an early convert to the system of Antoine Lavoisier and introduced this new chemistry to Sweden. He was partially deaf from a childhood illness but the further loss of an eye (1801) caused by an exploding flask did not impede his work.

Ekeberg is remembered chiefly for his discovery of the element tantalum. In 1802, while analyzing minerals from Ytterby quarry, Sweden, he isolated the new metal. The name supposedly comes from its failure to dissolve in acid, looking like Tantalus in the waters of Hell. It was a long time before it was recognized as a separate element as it was difficult to distinguish from niobium, isolated by Charles Hatchett in 1801. Wollaston failed to distinguish between them and it was as late as 1865 that Jean Marignac conclusively demonstrated the distinctness of the two new metals.

EKMAN, Vagn Walfrid (b. May 3, 1874; Stockholm; d. Mar. 9, 1954; Gostad, Sweden) Swedish oceanographer.

Ekman was the son of an oceanographer and was educated at the University of Uppsala, graduating in 1902. He worked at the International Laboratory for Oceanographic Research in Oslo (1902–08) before he moved to Lund, Sweden, as a lecturer in mathematical physics, being made a professor in 1910.

In 1905 Ekman published a fundamental paper, *On the Influence of the Earth's Rotation on Ocean Currents*. This work originated from an observation made by the explorer Fridtjof Nansen that in the Arctic, drift ice did not follow wind direction but deviated to the right. He showed that the motion, since known as the *Ekman spiral*, is produced as a complex interaction between the force of the wind on the water surface, the deflecting force due to the Earth's rotation (Coriolis force), and the frictional forces within the water layers.

Ekman also studied the phenomenon of dead water, a thin layer of fresh water from melting ice spreading over the sea, which could halt slow-moving ships. This, he established, resulted from the waves formed between water layers of different densities. The *Ekman current meter*, invented by him, is still in use.

ELHUYAR, Don Fausto D' *See* D'ELHUYAR, Don Fausto.

ELLET, Charles (b. Jan. 1, 1810; Penns Manor, Pennsylvania; d. June 21, 1862; Cairo, Illinois) American civil engineer.

Ellet began work as a surveyor and assistant engineer, and then traveled to Europe to study engineering, returning to America in 1832. He concentrated on designing suspension bridges and built his first in 1842 over the Schuylkill River in Pennsylvania, with a span of 358 feet (109 m). He went on to build the world's first long-span wire-cable suspension bridge, with a central span of 1010 feet (308 m), over the Ohio River (1846–49). The bridge failed in 1854 because of aerodynamic instability.

Ellet also devised a steam-powered ram that helped to win the Mississippi River for the Union in the Battle of Memphis on 6 June, 1862. Ellet was mortally wounded in this battle.

ELLIOTT, Thomas Renton (b. Oct. 11, 1877; Durham, England; d. Mar. 4, 1961; Broughton, Scotland) British physician.

Elliott, the son of a retailer, was educated at Cambridge University and University College Hospital, London, where he later served as professor of clinical medicine from the end of World War I until his retirement in 1939.

It was as a research student under John Langley at Cambridge that Elliott made his greatest discovery. In 1901 Langley had injected animals with a crude extract from the adrenal gland and noted that the extract stimulated the action of the sympathetic nerves. Adrenaline (epinephrine) had earlier (1898) been isolated by John Abel at Johns Hopkins University. Elliott therefore decided to inject adrenaline into animals to see if he got the same response as Langley had with the adrenal gland extract. He did indeed achieve increases in heart beat, blood pressure, etc., characteristic of stimulation of the sympathetic nervous system. Elliott is remembered for his subsequent suggestion that adrenaline may be released from sympathetic nerve endings — the first hint of neurotransmitters. Langley discouraged such speculation but later work by Henry Dale and Otto Loewi on acetylcholine supported Elliott's early work.

ELSASSER, Walter Maurice (b. Mar. 20, 1904; Mannheim, now in West Germany) German-American geophysicist.

Elsasser was educated at the University of Göttingen where he obtained his doctorate in 1927. He worked at the University of Frankfurt before leaving Germany in 1933 following Hitler's rise to power. He taught at the Sorbonne, Paris, before emigrating to America (1936) where he joined the staff of the California Institute of Technology. He became professor of physics at the University of Pennsylvania (1947–50) and at the University of Utah (1950–58). In 1962 he became professor of geophysics at Princeton and he was appointed research professor at the University of Maryland from 1968 until his retirement in 1974.

Elsasser made fundamental proposals on the question of the origin of the Earth's magnetic field. It had been known for some time that this could not be due to the Earth's iron core for its temperature is too high for it to serve as a simple magnet. Instead he proposed that the molten liquid core contains eddies set up by the Earth's rotation. These eddies produce an electric current that causes the familiar terrestrial magnetic field.

Elsasser also made predictions of electron diffraction (1925) and neutron diffraction (1936). His works include *The Physical Foundation of Biology* (1958) and *Atom and Organism* (1966).

ELTON, Charles Sutherland (b. Mar. 29, 1900; Liverpool, England) British ecologist.

Elton graduated in zoology from Oxford University in 1922. He was assistant to Julian Huxley on the Oxford University expedition to Spitzbergen (1921), where

Elton carried out ecological studies of the region's animal life. Further Arctic expeditions were made in 1923, 1924, and 1930. Such experience prompted his appointment as biological consultant to the Hudson's Bay Company, for which he carried out investigations into variations in the numbers of fur-bearing animals, using trappers' records dating back to 1736. In 1932 Elton helped establish the Bureau of Animal Population at Oxford — an institution that subsequently became an international center for information on and research into animal numbers and their ecology. In the same year he became editor of the new *Journal of Animal Ecology*, launched by the British Ecological Society, and in 1936 was appointed reader in animal ecology as well as a senior research fellow by Oxford University.

Elton was one of the first biologists to study animals in relation to their environment and other animals and plants. His demonstration of the nature of food chains and cycles, as well as such topics as the reasons for differences in animal numbers, were discussed in *Animal Ecology* (1927). In 1930 *Animal Ecology and Evolution* was published in which he advanced the notion that animals were not invariably at the mercy of their environment but commonly, perhaps through migration, practiced environmental selection by changing their habitats. Work on the rodent population of Britain, and how it is affected by a changing environment, was turned to eminently practical account at the outbreak of World War II when Elton conducted intensive research into methods of controlling rats and mice and thus conserving food for the war effort. *Voles, Mice and Lemmings: Problems in Population Dynamics* was published in 1942, and *The Control of Rats and Mice* in 1954, the latter becoming accepted as the standard work on the subject.

ELVEHJEM, Conrad Arnold (b. May 27, 1901; McFarland, Wisconsin; d. July 27, 1962; Mahia, Wisconsin) American biochemist.

Elvehjem, the son of a farmer, graduated from and spent his whole career at the University of Wisconsin. He obtained his PhD in 1927, and served as professor of biochemistry from 1936 until 1958, when he became president of the university, a position held until his retirement in 1962.

In 1937, following discoveries by Casimir Funk and Joseph Goldberger, Elvehjem succeeded in producing a new treatment for pellagra. In the 1920s Goldberger had postulated that this disease was caused by a deficiency of 'P-P' (pellagra preventive) factor present in milk. In 1913 Funk, while searching for a cure for beriberi, came across nicotinic acid in rice husks. Although it was of little use against beriberi, Elvehjem found that even in minute doses it would dramatically remove the symptoms of blacktongue, the canine equivalent of pellagra. Tests on humans revealed the same remarkable effects on pellagra.

Elvehjem, a prolific author with over 800 papers to his credit, also worked on the role of trace elements in nutrition, showing the essential role played by such minerals as copper, zinc, and cobalt.

EMBDEN, Gustav George (b. Nov. 10, 1874; Hamburg, now in West Germany; d. July 25, 1933; Frankfurt, now in West Germany) German physiologist.

Embden, the son of a lawyer, was educated at the universities of Freiburg, Munich, Berlin, and Strasbourg. From 1904 he was director of the chemical laboratory in the medical clinic of the Frankfurt hospital, becoming in 1907 director of the Physiological Institute (which evolved from the medical clinic) and in 1914 director of the Institute for Vegetative Physiology (which in its turn evolved from the Physiological Institute).

In 1918 Otto Meyerhof (q.v.) threw considerable light on the process of cellular metabolism by showing that it involved the breakdown of glucose to lactic acid. Embden spent much time in working out the precise steps involved in such a breakdown, as did many other chemists and physiologists. By the time of his death the details of the metabolic sequence from glycogen to lactic acid, later known as the Embden–Meyerhof pathway, had been worked out.

Embden's earlier work concentrated on the metabolic processes carried out by the liver. In his experiments he used a new perfusion technique to maintain the condition of the dissected livers. In this way he discovered the breakdown of amino acids by oxidative deamination, realized that abnormal sugar metabolism can lead to the formation of acetone and acetoacetic acid, and showed that sugar is synthesized from lactic acid.

EMELEUS, Harry Julius (b. June 22, 1903; London) British inorganic chemist.

Emeleus was educated at Imperial College, London, and at Karlsruhe and Princeton. He returned to Imperial College in 1931 and taught there until 1945 when he moved to Cambridge University, where he served as professor of inorganic chemistry until his retirement in 1970.

In 1938, in collaboration with John Anderson, he published the well-known work, *Modern Aspects of Inorganic Chemistry*. He also worked on fluorine, publishing a monograph on the subject in 1969: *The Chemistry of Fluorine and its Compounds*.

EMILIANI, Cesare (b. Dec. 8, 1922; Bologna, Italy) Italian-American geologist.

Emiliani was educated at the University of Bologna. He moved to America in 1948, obtaining his PhD from the University of Chicago in 1950. After teaching at Chicago (1950–56) he moved to the University of Miami where he was appointed professor of geology in 1963 at the Institute of Marine Science.

Emiliani has specialized in using oxygen isotopic analysis of pelagic microfossils from ocean sediments. Albrecht Penck and

Eduard Brückner had, in 1909, established the long-held orthodox view that four ice ages had occurred during the Pleistocene. In his fundamental paper *Pleistocene temperatures* (1955) Emiliani produced evidence that there had been more. Using the principle established by Harold Urey that the climate of past ages can be estimated by the ratio of oxygen–16 to oxygen–18 present in water (i.e. the less oxygen–18 present the colder the climate must have been), he examined the oxygen–18 content of fossils brought up from the mud of the Caribbean. By choosing fossils that he knew had lived near the surface he could reconstruct the climatic history, and consequently identified seven complete glacial cycles.

EMPEDOCLES of Acragas (b. *c.* 490 BC; Acragas, now Agrimento in Sicily; d. *c.* 430 BC) Greek philosopher.

Empedocles was a poet and a physician as well as a philosopher and he was probably a pupil of Parmenides. Much legend surrounds what is known of his life. Styling himself as a god, he reputedly brought about his own death in an attempt to persuade his followers of his divinity by throwing himself into the volcanic crater of Mount Etna. Fragments of two poems by Empedocles survive: *On Nature* and *Purifications*. There is some difficulty in reconciling the two because the first is purely physical while the second deals with the progress of the soul from fall to redemption.

Empedocles is best known as the originator of the four-element theory of matter (earth, fire, air, and water), which had a persuasive influence until the beginning of modern chemistry in the 18th century. Empedocles was noted for his keen observation and was the first to demonstrate that air has weight.

ENCKE, Johann Franz (b. Sept. 23, 1791; Hamburg, now in West Germany; d. Aug. 26,

1865; Spandau, now in East Germany) German astronomer.

Encke was a student of Karl Gauss at the University of Göttingen and, after serving as an artillery officer in the Napoleonic wars, he worked at the Seeberg Observatory and later became director of the Berlin Observatory. In 1819 he computed the orbit of a comet, since called *Encke's comet*, that had been discovered in 1786. Encke showed that it had the shortest known period (3.3 years) and successfully predicted its return. Using data collected from the transits of Venus of 1761 and 1769 he worked out the solar parallax (and thus the Sun's distance from the Earth) as 8.57 arc seconds (compared with today's measurement of 8.79 arc seconds). He also noted *Encke's division* — a fine rift in the outer ring of Saturn.

ENDERS, John Franklin (b. Feb. 10, 1897; West Hartford, Connecticut) American microbiologist.

Enders, the son of a wealthy banker, was educated at Yale and Harvard where he obtained his PhD in 1930. His career was somewhat delayed by the war, in which he served as a flying instructor, and also by his initial intention to study Germanic and Celtic languages. This was upset by the influence of the bacteriologist Hans Zinsser who 'seduced' Enders into science in the late 1920s.

In 1946 Enders set up an Infectious Diseases Laboratory at the Boston Children's Hospital; it was here that he did the work to be later described as opening up a "new epoch in the history of virus research." This referred to his success, in collaboration with Thomas Weller and Frederick Robbins, in 1949 in cultivating polio virus in test tube cultures of human tissue for the first time. They further demonstrated that the virus could be grown on a wide variety of tissue and not just nerve cells.

This at last allowed the polio virus to be studied, typed, and produced in quantity.

Without such an advance the triumphs of Albert Sabin and Jonas Salk in developing a vaccine against polio in the 1950s would have been impossible. In 1954 Enders, Weller, and Robbins were awarded the Nobel Physiology or Medicine Prize.

By this time Enders had already begun to work on the cultivation of the measles virus. This time, working with T. Peebles, they followed up their success in cultivating the virus with, in 1957, the production of the first measles vaccine.

ENGELMANN, George (b. Feb. 2, 1809; Frankfurt, now in West Germany; d. Feb. 4, 1884; St. Louis, Missouri) American botanist.

Engelmann, the son of a schoolmaster, was educated at the universities of Heidelberg, Berlin, and Würzburg where he obtained his MD in 1831. In the following year he visited America to invest in some land for a wealthy uncle and decided in 1835 to settle and practice medicine in St. Louis.

Engelmann was not only a plant collector of some importance, he also did much to initiate and organize major collecting expeditions of the flora of the West. It was thus through Engelmann that many of the newly collected specimens passed on their way to such eastern scholars as Asa Gray at Harvard. Engelmann's role became more official with the setting up of the Missouri Botanical Garden in 1859 with the backing of the St. Louis businessman Henry Shaw.

He is also remembered for his demonstration that some stocks of American vine were resistant to the pest *Phylloxera*, which had begun to devastate the vineyards of Europe from 1863 onward.

ENGELMANN, Theodor Wilhelm (b. Nov. 14, 1843; Leipzig, now in East Germany; d. May 20, 1909; Berlin) German physiologist.

Engelmann, the son of a publisher, was educated at Jena, Heidelberg, Göttingen, and Leipzig where he obtained his PhD in 1867. He immediately joined the faculty of the University of Utrecht, serving there as professor of physiology from 1888 until 1897 when he returned to Germany to a similar chair at the University of Berlin, where he remained until his retirement in 1908.

Between 1873 and 1895 Engelmann published a number of papers on muscle contraction. By this time, following the work of such physiologists as William Bowman, the main anatomical details of striated muscle had been established. However an explanation was needed as to why the anisotropic or A bands refract polarized light quite differently to the isotropic or I bands. Engelmann had noted that in contraction the A bands increased in volume while the I bands decreased. He consequently proposed his 'imbibition' theory in which the contraction of striped muscle is attributed to a flow of fluid from the I to the A bands.

Engelmann also worked on the nature and mechanism of the heartbeat and in 1875 devised an experiment that proved the heartbeat is myogenic; that is, the contraction originates in the heart muscle and not from an external nerve stimulus. In 1881 he discovered the chemotactic response of certain bacteria to oxygen, and he also demonstrated that red and blue light is far more effective in stimulating plant chloroplasts during photosynthesis than other parts of the spectrum.

ENGLER, Heinrich Gustav Adolf (b. Mar. 25, 1844; Sagan, now in Poland; d. Oct. 10, 1930; Dahlem, now in West Germany) German botanist.

Engler studied botany at Breslau University, gaining his PhD in 1866 for his thesis on the genus *Saxifraga*. After teaching natural history he became custodian of the Munich botanical collection and then professor of botany at Kiel University; in 1884 he returned to Breslau to succeed his former teacher in the chair of botany. At Breslau Engler replanned the botanic garden, ordering the plants accor-

ding to their geographical distribution. In 1887 he took up the important chair of botany at Berlin and successfully reestablished the garden in Dahlem.

Between 1878 and his retirement from Berlin in 1921, Engler contributed greatly to the development of plant taxonomy with his classifications, presented in such books as *The Natural Plant Families* (1887–1911) and *The Plant Kingdom* (1900–37). Much of his work was drawn from first-hand observation gained during travels through Africa, Europe, India, China, Japan, and America.

EÖTVÖS, Baron Roland von (b. July 27, 1848; Budapest, Hungary; d. Apr. 8, 1919; Budapest) Hungarian physicist.

Eötvös studied at the University of Königsberg and at Heidelberg where he obtained his PhD in 1870 for a thesis concerning a method of detecting motion through the ether by measuring light intensity. At Königsberg in 1886 he introduced the *Eötvös law* — an equation approximately relating surface tension, temperature, density, and relative molecular mass of a liquid.

He then started teaching at Budapest University, where he was appointed professor in 1872. His work from then on centered on gravitation. In 1888 he developed the *Eötvös torsion balance* — an instrument of exceptional accuracy. Using this, he was able to prove almost conclusively Galileo's hypothesis that all bodies have the same acceleration in a gravitational field. This experiment became one of the foundation stones of general relativity, since it shows that gravitational and inertial mass are the same. Einstein called this the *equivalence principle*.

Eötvös spent much of his time trying to improve the Hungarian education system and for a short time was minister of instruction. He was also an excellent mountain climber and a peak in the Dolomites is named for him.

EPICURUS (b. *c.* 341 BC; Samos, Greece; d. 270 BC; Athens) Greek philosopher.

Epicurus traveled to Athens when he was about 18 years old, and received military training. He then taught at Mytilene and Lampsacus before returning to Athens (305 BC) where he founded a school of philosophy and attracted a substantial following.

Epicurus revived Democritean atomism and was little influenced by his predecessors, Plato and Aristotle. His work is known through substantial fragments in the writings of Diogenes Laërtius and especially through the long poem, *De rerum natura* (On the Nature of Things), by his Roman disciple Lucretius. The Epicurean philosophy aimed at the attainment of a happy, though simple, life and used the atomic theory to sanction the banishment of the old fears and superstitions. Epicurus also made important additions to the atomic theory, asserting the primacy of sense-perception where Democritus had distrusted the senses, and he introduced the concept of random atomic 'swerve' to preserve free will in an otherwise deterministic system.

ERASISTRATUS of Chios (b. *c.* 304 BC; Chios, Greece; d. *c.* 250 BC; Mycale, Greece) Greek anatomist and physician.

Erasistratus came from a distinctly medical background and studied in Athens, Cos, and Alexandria. Following Herophilus he became the leading figure in the Alexandrian School of Anatomy.

It is possible with Erasistratus, unlike his contemporaries, to make out at least the outline of his physiological system. Every organ and part of the body was served by a 'three-fold network' of vein, artery, and nerve. Indeed he believed the body tissues were a plaiting of such vessels, which at their extremities became so fine as to be invisible. The veins carried blood and the nerves and arteries transported nervous and animal spirits respectively.

As an atomist he rejected all attractive and occult forces seeking instead to explain everything in terms of atoms and the void. He thus accounted for the bleeding of severed arteries by assuming the escaped pneuma left a vacuum that was filled by blood from adjoining veins.

One of the most interesting aspects of his thought was his unusual rejection of the humoral theory of disease which, formulated by the Hippocratics and authorized by Galen became the sterile orthodoxy of Western medicine for 2000 years. Instead he seems to have argued for a more mechanical concept of disease, attributing it to a 'plethora' of blood, vital spirit, or food, which produces a blocking and inflammation of the various vessels.

His objection to the humoral theory found little support and with the passing of Erasistratus the great innovative period of Alexandrian medicine came to an end.

ERATOSTHENES of Cyrene (b. *c.* 276 BC; Cyrene, now in Libya; d. *c.* 194 BC; Alexandria, Egypt) Greek astronomer.

Eratosthenes was educated at Athens and taught in Alexandria where he became tutor to the son of Ptolemy III and librarian. He was prominent in history, poetry, mathematics, and astronomy and was known by the nickname 'beta' because, some say, he was the second Plato.

In number theory he introduced the procedure named for him to collect the prime numbers by filtering out all the composites. The method, called the *sieve of Eratosthenes*, was to write down a list of ordered numbers and to strike out every second number after 2, every third number after 3, and so on. The numbers remaining are primes.

Eratosthenes achieved his greatest fame by using a most ingenious and simple method to measure the circumference of the Earth. He was aware that on a certain day the Sun at Syene (now Aswan) was exactly at its zenith (it was known to shine directly down a deep well on that day). He found that on the same day at Alexandria it was south of its zenith by an angle corresponding to 1/50 of a circle (7° 12′). He also knew that the distance between Syene and Alexandria was 5000 stadia. Therefore, 5000 stadia must be 1/50 of the circumference of the Earth; that is, 250 000 stadia. (Since the exact length of a stade is not known it is impossible to work out exactly how accurate his measurement was but it has been thought to be within 50 miles of the presently accepted value.) Eratosthenes also established an improved figure for the obliquity of the ecliptic (the tilt of the Earth's axis) of 23°51′20″. Finally, he produced the first map of the world, as he knew it, based on meridians of longitude and parallels of latitude.

ERCKER, Lazarus (b. *c.* 1530; Annaberg, now in West Germany; d. *c.* 1594; Prague) Bohemian metallurgist.

Ercker studied at the University of Wittenberg (1547–48). In 1554 he was made assayer in Dresden, Saxony, and later he became control tester of coins in a town near Prague.

Ercker's main contribution to metallurgy was to write the first systematic account of analytical and metallurgical chemistry. This manual, *Beschreibung allerfürnemisten mineralischen Ertzt und Berckwercksarten* (1574; Description of Leading Ore Processing and Mining Methods), described the testing of alloys, minerals, and compounds containing silver, gold, copper, antimony, mercury, bismuth, and lead.

ERLANGER, Joseph (b. Jan. 5, 1874; San Francisco, California; d. Dec. 5, 1965; St. Louis, Missouri) American neurophysiologist.

Erlanger, the son of a German immigrant drawn to California in the gold rush, was educated at the University of California and Johns Hopkins University in Baltimore, where in 1899 he obtained his MD. After working on the staff for a few years Erlanger moved to the University of Wisconsin (1906) to accept the chair of physiology. In 1910 he moved to Washington University, St. Louis, where he held the chair of physiology in the Medical School until his retirement in 1944.

Between 1921 and 1931 Erlanger carried out some fundamental research on the functions of nerve fibers with his former pupil and colleague, Herbert Gasser. They investigated the transmission of a nerve impulse along a frog nerve kept in a moist chamber at constant temperature. Their innovation was to study the transmission with the cathode-ray oscillograph, invented by Ferdinand Braun in 1897, which enabled them to picture the changes the impulse underwent as it traveled along the nerve.

Erlanger and Gasser found that on stimulating a nerve, the resulting electrical activity indicating the passage of an impulse was composed of three waves, as observed on the oscillograph. They explained this by proposing that the one stimulus activated three different groups of nerve fibers, each of which had its own conduction rate. They went on to measure these rates, concluding that the fastest fibers (the A-fibers) conduct with a speed of up to 100 meters per second (mps) while the slowest (the C-fibers) could manage speeds of no more than 2 mps. The intermediate B-fibers conducted in the range 2–14 mps. Erlanger and Gasser were able to relate this variation to the thickness of the different nerve fibers, A-fibers being the largest.

It was a short step from this to the theory of differentiated function, in which it was proposed that the slender C-fibers carry pain impulses whereas the thicker A-fibers transmit motor impulses. But it was soon demonstrated that while such propositions may be broadly true the detailed picture is more complex.

Erlanger and Gasser produced an account of their collaboration in *Electrical Signs of Nervous Activity* (1937); they were awarded the 1944 Nobel Prize in physiology or medicine for their work.

ERLENMEYER, Richard August Carl Emil (b. June 28, 1825; near Wiesbaden, now in West Germany; d. Jan. 22, 1909; German chemist.

Erlenmeyer studied at Giessen and practiced at first as a pharmacist. In 1855 he became a private pupil of August Kekulé at Heidelberg and later was appointed professor at the Munich Polytechnic (1868–83). He synthesized guanidine and was the first to give its correct formula (1868). He also synthesized tyrosine and formulated the *Erlenmeyer rule*, which states the impossibility of two hydroxy groups occurring on the same carbon atom or of a hydroxy group occurring adjacent to a carbon–carbon double bond (chloral hydrate is an exception to this rule). His son F. G. C. E. Erlenmeyer introduced the Erlenmeyer synthesis of amino acids and synthesized cystine, serine, and phenylalanine.

ESAKI, Leo (b. Mar. 12, 1925; Osaka, Japan) Japanese physicist.

Esaki graduated in physics at the University of Tokyo in 1947, where he later gained his doctorate in 1959. His doctoral work was on the physics of semiconductors, and in 1958 he reported an effect known as 'tunneling', which he had observed in narrow p–n junctions of germanium that were heavily doped with impurities. The phenomenon of tunneling is a quantum-mechanical effect in which an electron can penetrate a potential barrier through a narrow region of solid, where classical theory predicts it could not pass.

Esaki was quick to see the possibility of applying the tunnel effect, and in 1960 reported the construction of a device with diodelike properties — the tunnel (or *Esaki*) diode. With negative bias potential, the diode acts as a short circuit, while under certain conditions of forward bias it can have effectively negative resistance (the current decreasing with increasing voltage). Important characteristics of the tunnel diode are its very fast speed of operation, its small physical size, and its low power consumption. It has found application in many fields of electronics, principally in computers, microwave devices, and where low electronic noise is required. Esaki shared the Nobel Physics Prize in 1973 with Brian Josephson and Ivar Giaever.

Esaki now works for the computer firm International Business Machines at the Thomas J. Watson Research Center, Yorktown Heights, New York.

ESCHENMOSER, Albert (b. Aug. 5, 1925; Erstfeld, Switzerland) Swiss chemist.

Eschenmoser was educated at the Federal Institute of Technology, Zurich, where he has taught since 1956 and where, in 1960, he was appointed professor of organic chemistry.

He is best known for his work in synthesizing a number of complex organic compounds. His first success came with colchicine — an alkaloid found in the autumn crocus — which has important applications in genetical research. He also collaborated with Robert Woodward on the synthesis of vitamin B12 (cyanocobalamin), which had first been isolated and crystallized by Karl Folkers in 1948. Its empirical formula was soon established and in 1956 Dorothy Hodgkin established its structure. It took many years with samples passing between Zurich and Harvard before Eschenmoser and Woodward were finally able to announce its synthesis in 1965.

ESPY, James Pollard (b. May 9, 1785; Washington County, Pennsylvania; d. Jan. 24, 1860; Cincinnati, Ohio) American meteorologist.

Espy graduated from Transylvania University in Lexington, Kentucky, in 1808. He became principal of the Academy in Cumberland, Maryland, (1812–17) and, after teaching mathematics and physics in Philadelphia, he became a full-time meteorologist in 1835. He was made state meteorologist in 1839 and from 1842 took up a national appointment, being attached at various times to the War Department, the Navy, and, after 1852, the Smithsonian, which eventually took over his network of observers and out of which the Weather Bureau was later to grow.

In addition to collecting and issuing basic data, Espy also wrote on questions of theoretical meteorology. He was the first to argue for the convectional theory of precipitation in which the ascent and cooling of moist air with the release of latent heat leads to condensation and the formation of clouds. Much of the evidence for this came from his 'nephelescope', a device whereby he could simulate cloud behavior and measure cooling rates. Espy published, in 1841, his *Philosophy of Storms* and then became involved in a prolonged and bitter controversy with William Redfield on the cause and nature of storms. Here he argued that storms consisted of radially convergent winds with the air escaping up the middle. Although his views on storms were influential in Europe, Redfield and Elias Loomis were able to produce convincing contrary evidence.

EUCLID (b. *c.* 330 BC; d. *c.* 260 BC) Greek mathematician.

Euclid is one of the best known and most influential of classical Greek mathematicians but almost nothing is known about his life. He was a founder and member of the academy in Alexandria, and may have been a pupil of Plato in Athens. Despite his great fame Euclid was not one of the greatest of Greek mathematicians and not of the same caliber as Archimedes.

Euclid's most celebrated work is the *Elements*, which is primarily a treatise on geometry contained in 13 books. The influence of this work not only on the future development of geometry, mathematics, and science, but on the whole of Western thought is hard to exaggerate. Some idea of the importance that has been attached to the *Elements* is gained from the fact that there have probably been more commentaries written on it than on the Bible. The *Elements* systematized and organized the work of many previous Greek geometers, such as Theaetetus and Eudoxus, as well as containing many new discoveries that Euclid had made himself. Although mainly concerned with geometry it also deals with such topics as number theory and the theory of irrational quantities. One of the most celebrated number theoretic results is Euclid's proof that there are an infinite number of primes. The *Elements* is in many ways a synthesis and culmination of Greek mathematics. Euclid and Apollonius of Perga were the last Greek mathematicians of any distinction, and after their time Greek civilization as a whole soon became decadent and sterile.

Euclid's *Elements* owed its enormously high status to a number of reasons. The most influential single feature was Euclid's use of the axiomatic method whereby all the theorems were laid out as deductions from certain self-evident basic propositions or axioms in such a way that in each successive proof only propositions already proved or axioms were used. This became accepted as the paradigmatically rigorous way of setting out any body of knowledge, and attempts were made to apply it not just to mathematics, but to natural science, theology, and even philosophy and ethics.

However, despite being revered as an almost perfect example of rigorous thinking for almost 2000 years there are considerable defects in Euclid's reasoning. A number of his proofs were found to contain mistakes, the status of the initial axioms themselves was increasingly considered to be problematic, and the definitions of such basic terms as 'line' and 'point' were found to be unsatisfactory. The most celebrated case is that of the parallel axiom, which states that there is only one straight line passing through a given point and parallel to a given straight line. The status of this axiom was long recognized as problematic, and many unsuccessful attempts were made to deduce it from the remaining axioms. The question was only settled in the 19th century when Janos Bolyai and Nicolai Lobachevski showed that it was perfectly possible to construct a consistent geometry in which Euclid's other axioms were true but in which the parallel axiom was false. This epoch-making discovery displaced Euclidean geometry from the privileged position it had occupied. The question of the relation of Euclid's geometry to the properties of physical space had to wait until the early 20th century for a full answer. Until then it was believed that Euclid's geometry gave a fully accurate description of physical space. No less a thinker than Immanuel Kant had thought that it was logically impossible for space to obey any other geometry. However when Albert Einstein developed his theory of relativity he found that the appropriate geometry for space was not Euclid's but that developed by Georg Riemann. It was subsequently experimentally verified that the geometry of space is indeed non-Euclidean.

In mathematical terms too, the discovery of non-Euclidean geometries was of great importance, since it led to a broadening of the conception of geometry and the development by such mathematicians as Felix Klein of many new geometries very different from Euclid's. It also made mathematicians scrutinize the logical structure of Euclid's geometry far more closely and in 1899 David Hilbert at last gave a definitively rigorous axiomatic treatment of geometry and made an exhaustive investigation of the relations of dependence and independence between the axioms, and of the consistency of the various possible geometries so produced.

Euclid wrote a number of other works besides the *Elements*, although many of them are now lost and known only through references to them by other classical authors. Those that do survive include *Data*, containing 94 propositions, *On Divisions*, and the *Optics*. One of his sayings has come down to us. When asked by Ptolemy I Soter, the reigning king of Egypt, if there was any quicker way to master geometry than by studying the

Elements Euclid replied "There is no royal road to geometry."

EUDOXUS of Cnidus (b. *c.* 400 BC; Cnidus, now in Turkey; d. *c.* 350 BC; Cnidus) Greek astronomer and mathematician.

Eudoxus is reported as having studied mathematics under Archytas, a Pythagorean. He also studied under Plato and in Egypt. Although none of his works have survived they are quoted extensively by Hipparchus. Eudoxus was the first astronomer who had a complete understanding of the celestial sphere. It is only this understanding that reveals the irregularities of the movements of the planets that must be taken into account in giving an accurate description of the heavens. For Eudoxus the Earth is at rest and round this center 27 concentric spheres rotate. The outermost sphere carries the fixed stars, each of the planets requires four spheres, and the Sun and the Moon three each. All these spheres are necessary to account for the daily and annual relative motions of the heavenly bodies. He also described the constellations and the changes in the rising and setting of the fixed stars in the course of a year.

In mathematics, Eudoxus is thought to have contributed the theory of proportion to be found in book V of Euclid — the importance of this being its applicability to irrational as well as rational numbers. The method of exhaustion in book XII is also attributed to Eudoxus. This tackled in a mathematical way for the first time the difficult problem of calculating an area bounded by a curve.

EULER, Leonhard (b. Apr. 15, 1707; Basel, Switzerland; d. Sept. 18, 1783; St. Petersburg, now Leningrad in the Soviet Union) Swiss mathematician.

Euler was one of the outstanding figures of 18th-century mathematics, and also the most prolific. He studied at the University of Basel where he came to the notice of the

Bernoulli family and became, in particular, a friend of Daniel Bernoulli. Having completed his studies Euler applied unsuccessfully for a post at Basel University. He was encouraged by his friend Bernoulli to join him at the St. Petersburg Academy of Science. Bernoulli obtained for Euler a post in the medical section of the academy and in 1727 Euler left for Russia to find on arriving that the empress had just died and that the future of the academy was doubtful. Fortunately it survived intact and he managed to find his way into the mathematical section. In 1733 Bernoulli left Russia to return to Switzerland and Euler was appointed to replace him as head of the mathematical section of the academy. Euler was not particularly happy in the highly repressive political climate and devoted himself almost exclusively to his mathematics. In 1740 he eventually left Russia to join Frederick the Great's Berlin Academy. He returned to Russia in 1766 at the invitation of Catherine the Great, remaining there for the rest of his life. He had lost the sight of his right eye through observing the Sun during his first stay in Russia and shortly after returning there his blindness became total. However, such was his facility for mental calculation and the power of his memory that this did not affect his mathematical creativity.

Euler contributed to almost all areas of mathematics, and did equally important work in both pure and applied mathematics. One of his most significant contributions was to the development of analysis. Although he was working before the development of modern standards of rigor by such mathematicians as Karl Friedrich Gauss and Augustin Cauchy and thus lacked a rigorous treatment of such key topics as convergence, nonetheless his work in analysis constitutes a major advance over previous work in the area. He wrote three treatises on different aspects of analysis, which together collect, systematize, and develop what the mathematicians of the 17th century had achieved in this area. These treatises became important and influential textbooks. It is worth noting that unlike some great mathematicians, such as Gauss, Euler was a highly successful and effective teacher. It is a measure of his intuitive insight into mathematics that even though he did lack truly rigorous analytical techniques he was still able to arrive at so many novel and important results. His phenomenal ability for calculation came to his aid here, for he frequently arrived at results, for example about infinite series, by induction from a great many calculations and gave only a highly dubious proof leaving future mathematicians to give properly rigorous proofs of results that were indeed quite correct.

Outside analysis Euler made extremely important contributions both to the calculus of variations and mechanics. Mechanics was transformed by his treatment of it in his treatise of 1736. In essence he transformed the subject into one to which the full resources of analytical techniques could be applied. In doing so he paved the way for the work of mathematicians such as Joseph Lagrange.

Euler put his expertise in mechanics to practical use in his work on the three-body problem. He was interested in this problem because he wished to investigate the motion of the Moon. He published his first lunar-motion theory in 1753 and then a second theory in 1772. The problem is not fully solved to this day and Euler did not solve it, but he was able to invent methods of approximating solutions, which were accurate enough to be of practical use in navigation. Here his prodigious ability as a sheer calculator came into its own.

In addition to these pieces of work Euler made notable contributions to number theory and geometry. Numerous theorems and methods are named for him.

EULER, Ulf Svante von *See* VON EULER, Ulf Svante.

EULER-CHELPIN, Hans Karl August Simon von (b. Feb. 15, 1873; Augsburg, now in West Germany; d. Nov. 7, 1964; Stockholm) German–Swedish biochemist.

Euler-Chelpin was educated at the universities of Berlin, Strasbourg, and Göttingen and at the Pasteur Institute. In 1898 he moved to Sweden being appointed to the staff of the University of Stockholm, where in 1906 he became professor of general and inorganic chemistry. In 1929 he also became director of the Institute of Biochemistry where he remained until his retirement in 1941. Although he became a Swedish citizen in 1902 he served Germany in both world wars.

In 1904 important work by Arthur Harden had shown that enzymes contained an easily removable nonprotein part, a coenzyme. In 1923 Euler-Chelpin worked out the structure of the yeast coenzyme. He showed that the molecule was made up from a nucleotide similar to that found in nucleic acid. It was named diphosphopyridine nucleotide.

Euler-Chelpin shared the 1929 Nobel Prize for chemistry with Harden for this work. His son, Ulf von Euler, was also a Nobel prizewinner.

EUSTACHIO, Bartolommeo (b. *c.* 1524; San Severino, Italy; d. Aug. 27, 1574; Fossombrone, Italy) Italian anatomist.

Eustachio, the son of a physician, received a sound humanist education acquiring a good knowledge of Latin, Greek, and Arabic. In the early 1540s he was appointed physician to the duke of Urbino and, from 1547, served the duke's brother, Cardinal Rovere, with whom he moved to Rome in 1549. While there he also served from 1562 as professor of anatomy at the Sapienza or Papal College.

In 1564 he collected some of his earlier work in his *Opuscula anatomica* (Anatomical Works). It contains his *De auditus organis* (On the Auditory Organs), which describes the eustachian tubes connecting the middle ear to the pharynx and named in his honor (although these were first described by Alcmaeon). It also contained the *De renum structura* (On the Structure of the Kidney), in which he published the first description of the adrenal glands.

Eustachio was not in fact as influential an anatomist as he might have been for his anatomical plates, prepared for a text never completed, were lost and only rediscovered in the early 18th century. They were finally published as the *Tabulae anatomica* in 1714 and republished with full notes by Bernhard Albinus in 1744. It has been claimed that the plates manifest an originality equaled only by Andreas Vesalius and Leonardo da Vinci and that Eustachio's plates of the sympathetic nervous system are the best yet produced.

EVANS, Robley Dunglison (b. May 18, 1907; University Place, Nebraska) American physicist.

Evans was educated at the California Institute of Technology where he obtained his PhD in 1932. He went to the Massachusetts Institute of Technology in 1934 and was appointed professor of physics there in 1945.

In 1940 Evans suggested that radioactive potassium–40 could be of use in geologic dating. It is widespread in the Earth's crust and has an exceptionally long halflife of over a thousand million years. It decays to the stable isotope argon–40 and determination of the ratio of ^{40}K to ^{40}Ar allows estimations of the age of potassium-bearing rocks ranging from 100000 to about 10 million years. This proved to be particularly valuable as it permitted accurate dating beyond the limits of Willard Libby's carbon–14 technique.

EWING, Sir James Alfred (b. Mar. 27, 1855; d. Jan. 7, 1935; Cambridge) British physicist.

The son of a minister of the Free Church of Scotland, Ewing was educated at the University of Edinburgh where he studied engineering. He served as professor of engineering at the Imperial University, Tokyo, from 1878 until 1883 when he returned to Scotland to a similar post at the University of Dundee. In 1890 he was appointed professor of applied mechanics at Cambridge, but in 1903 moved into higher levels of administration, first as director of naval education and from 1916 until his retirement in 1929 as principal and vice-chancellor of Edinburgh University.

In Japan he worked on problems in seismology and in 1883 published *Treatise on Earthquake Measurement*. However, His most important achievement as a physicist was his discovery of the phenomenon of hysteresis, first described by him in 1881. Hysteresis is an effect in which there are two properties, M and N, such that cyclic changes of N cause cyclic variations of M. If the changes of M lag behind those of N, there is hysteresis in the relation of M to N. Ewing came across the phenomena when working on the effects of stress on the thermoelectric properties of a wire. The hysteresis effect was later shown to apply to many aspects of the behavior of materials, in particular in the field of magnetism.

Ewing was put in charge of the cryptologists at the admiralty from 1914 to 1916 and described his work there in the book *The Man in Room 40* (1939).

EWING, William Maurice (b. May 12, 1906; Lockney, Texas) American oceanographer.

Ewing was educated at the Rice Institute, Houston, obtaining his PhD in 1931. He taught at Lehigh University, Pennsylvania, from 1934 until moving in 1944 to Columbia University, New York, where he organized the new Lamont Geological Observatory into one of the most important research institutions in the world.

Ewing pioneered seismic techniques to obtain basic data on the ocean floors. He was able to establish that the Earth's crust below the oceans is only about 3–5 miles (5–8 km) thick while the corresponding continental crust averages 25 miles (40 km).

Although the Mid-Atlantic Ridge had been discovered when cables were laid across the Atlantic, its dimensions were unsuspected. In 1956 Ewing and his colleagues were able to show that it constituted a mountain range extending throughout the oceans of the world and was some 40 000 miles (64 000 km) long. In 1957, working with Marie Tharp and Bruce Heezen, he revealed that the ridge was divided by a central rift, which was in places twice as deep and wide as the Grand Canyon.

His group found that the oceanic sediment, expected to be about 10 000 feet (3000 m) thick, was nonexistent on or within about 30 miles (50 km) of the ridge. Beyond this it had a thickness of about 130 feet (40 m) — much less than the depth of the corresponding continental sediment. All this seemed to be consistent with the new sea-floor spreading hypothesis of Harry H. Hess. Ewing was however reluctant to support it until Frederick Vine and Drummond H. Matthews showed how the magnetic reversals discovered by B. Brunhes in 1909 could be used to test the theory.

Ewing also proposed, with William Donn, a mechanism to explain the periodic ice ages. If the Arctic waters were icefree and open to warm currents this source of water vapor would produce greater accumulations of snowfall. This would increase the Earth's reflectivity and reduce the amount of solar radiation absorbed. Temperatures would fall and glaciers move south, but with the freezing of the Arctic seas the supply of water vapor would be cut off and the ice sheets would retreat. This would cause an increase in solar radiation absorbed and the cycle would begin again. No hard evidence has yet been found in support of the theory.

EWINS, Arthur James (b. Feb. 3, 1882; Norwood, near London; d. Dec. 24, 1957; Leigh-on-Sea, England) British pharmaceutical chemist.

Ewins went straight from school to the brilliant team of researchers at the Wellcome Physiological Research Laboratories at Beckenham. He worked on alkaloids with George Barger and in 1914, with Henry Dale, isolated the important neurotransmitter acetylcholine from ergot. Following wartime experience in manufacturing arsenicals with the Medical Research Council, he became head of research with the pharmaceutical manufacturers May and Baker, where he remained until retirement in 1952. Under Ewins in 1939, the team produced sulfapyridine, one of the most important of the new sulfonamide drugs. An important later discovery was the antiprotozoal drug pentamidine (1948). He was elected a fellow of the Royal Society in 1943.

EYDE, Samuel (b. Oct. 29, 1866; Arendal, Norway; d. June 21, 1940; Aasgaardstrand, Norway) Norwegian engineer and industrialist.

Eyde was a civil engineer, trained in Berlin. Up until 1900 he worked in Germany and also on harbor and railroad-station projects in Scandinavia. Here he became interested in industrial electrochemical processes — a subject of some potential in Scandinavia because of the availability of cheap hydroelectric power.

In 1901 Eyde met Kristian Birkeland with whom he developed a process (1903) for the fixation of atmospheric nitrogen by reaction of oxygen in an electric arc. The *Birkeland–Eyde process* needed plentiful and cheap supplies of electricity, leading to an explosive growth in the production of hydroelectric power. In 1900 Norway had an output of little more than 100 000 kilowatts; by 1905 production had jumped to 850 000 kilowatts. In the same year he started the company Norsk Hydro-Elektrisk Kvaelstof, with the help of French capital, to produce fertilizers by the Birkeland–Eyde process. As a result of this Norway's export of chemicals was to treble before the start of World War I. Eyde retired from the firm in 1917. As well as his industrial interests, he was also a member of the Norwegian parliament.

EYRING, Henry (b. Feb. 20, 1901; Colonia Juarez, Mexico) Mexican–American physical and theoretical chemist.

Eyring was a grandson of American missionaries who had become Mexican citizens. He thus first came to America in 1912 as a Mexican citizen and did not take American citizenship until 1935. He was educated at the University of Arizona and the University of California, where he obtained his PhD in 1927. He then held a number of junior appointments before joining the Princeton faculty in 1931, becoming professor of chemistry there in 1938. Eyring moved to a similar chair at the University of Utah, holding the post until his retirement in 1966.

Eyring, the author of 9 books and over 600 papers, has been as creative a chemist as he has been productive. His main work has probably been in the field of chemical kinetics with his transition-state theory. Since the time of Sven Arrhenius it had been appreciated that the rate constant of a chemical reaction depended on temperature according to an equation of the form:

$$k = A\exp(-E_A/RT)$$

The constant A is the frequency factor of the reaction; E_A is the activation energy. The values of A and E_A can be found experimentally for given reactions. Eyring's contribution to the field was to develop a theory capable of predicting reaction rates.

The method of treating reaction rates is to use potential-energy surfaces. In a reaction, the atoms move — i.e. molecules break and new molecules form. If the potential energy of a set of atoms is plotted against the distances between atoms for chosen arrangements, the result is a surface. Positions of low energy on the surface correspond to molecules; a reaction can be thought of as a change from a low-energy point, over a higher-energy barrier, to another low-energy position.

A. Marcelin, in 1915, had shown that reactions could be represented in this way, and in 1928 Fritz London pointed out that it was possible to calculate potential surfaces using quantum mechanics. Eyring, with Michael Polyani, first calculated such a surface (1929–30) for three hydrogen atoms and Eyring later went on to calculate the potential surfaces for a number of reactions. The activation energy of the reaction is the energy barrier that the system must surmount.

Eyring later (1935) showed how to calculate the frequency factor (A). He assumed that the configuration of atoms at the top of the energy barrier — the 'activated complex' — could be treated as a normal molecule except for a vibrational motion in the direction of the reaction path. Assuming that the activated complex was in equilibrium with the reactants and applying statistical mechanics, Eyring derived a general expression for reaction rate. Eyring's theory, called absolute-rate theory, is described in his book (with Samuel Glasstone and Keith J. Laidler) *The Theory of Rate Processes* (1941). It can also be applied to other processes, such as viscosity and diffusion.

Eyring has also worked on the theory of the liquid state and has made contributions in molecular biology.

F

FABRE, Jean Henri (b. Dec. 21, 1823; Saint-Léons, France; d. Oct. 11, 1915; Sérignan, France) French entomologist.

Although world famous for his detailed studies of insect habits and life histories, Fabre's stature as a field entomologist was only attained late in life, his earlier years being spent under great difficulty and comparative poverty. Described by Darwin, with whom he corresponded, as "an inimitable observer", Fabre's best-known entomological observations were largely made in his native Provence and the Rhône valley. His enthusiasm for his subject had been stimulated by reading an essay on the habits of the *Cerceris* wasp, which prompted Fabre to make his own detailed observations of these and other parasitic wasps, as well as many other insect groups. His descriptions of their development and behavior, written in a clear simple style, still stand as models of accurate observation. Fabre's earliest entomological observations appeared in *Annales des sciences naturelles*, but his major publication is the classic *Souvenirs entomologiques* (10 vols. 1879–1907).

FABRICIUS, David (b. Mar. 9, 1564; Esens, now in West Germany; d. May 7, 1617; Ostfriesland, now in West Germany) German astronomer.

Fabricius was a clergyman and amateur astronomer who engaged in a prolonged correspondence with Johannes Kepler but remained unconvinced by Kepler's Copernican arguments. In 1596 he noticed the variability of the star Omicron Ceti and called it 'Mira' (the marvelous). Fabricius was murdered by one of his parishioners. His son Johannes Fabricius was also an astronomer and was one of the discoverers of sunspots.

FABRICIUS ab Aquapendente, Hieronymus (b. May 20, 1537; Aquapendente, Italy; d. May 21, 1619; Padua, Italy) Italian anatomist and embryologist.

Fabricius was educated at the University of Padua where he studied under Gabriel Fallopius, succeeding him, in 1565, as professor of anatomy.

As an anatomist his most significant work was his *De venarum ostiolis* (1603; On the Valves of the Veins), which contains a clear and detailed description of the venous system and which exercised a considerable influence on his most famous pupil, William Harvey. Fabricius himself entertained no such idea as the circulation of the blood, explaining the role of the valves as retarding the blood flow, thus allowing the tissues to absorb necessary nutriment.

He spent much time observing the development of the chick embryo and published two works *De formato foetu* (1600; On the Formation of the Fetus) and *De formatione ovi et pulli* (1612; On the Development of the Egg and the Chick). These were hailed as elevating embryology into an independent science but they still contain many incorrect assumptions.

Thus for Fabricius semen did not enter the egg but rather initiated the process of generation from a distance in some mysterious way. He also made a now totally unfamiliar distinction between what nourishes and what produces the embryo. Thus he believed both the yolk and albumen merely nourished the embryo. Having eliminated the sperm, yolk, and albumen, Fabricius claimed that the chalaza — the spiral threads holding the yolk in position — produces the chick.

It was while engaged upon this work that he discovered and described the bursa of Fabricius. This is a small pouch in the oviduct of the hen, which Fabricius thought to be a store for semen. In the 1950s however the young research student B. Glick showed that this obscure organ plays a key role in the immune system of chickens, and by implication of humans who must possess a comparable system.

FAHRENHEIT, (Gabriel) Daniel (b. May 24, 1686; Danzig, now Gdańsk, Poland; d. Sept. 16, 1736; The Hague, Netherlands) German physicist.

Possibly owing to a business failure, Fahrenheit emigrated to Amsterdam to become a glass blower and instrument maker. He specialized in the making of meteorological instruments, and proceeded to develop a reliable and accurate thermometer. Galileo had invented the thermometer in about 1600, using changes in air volume as an indicator. Since the volume of air also varied considerably with changes in atmospheric pressure liquids of various kinds were quickly substituted. Fahrenheit was the first to use mercury in 1714. He fixed his zero point by using the freezing point of a mixture of ice and salt as this gave him the lowest temperature he could reach. His other fixed point was taken from the temperature of the human body, which he put at 96°. Given these two fixed points the freezing and boiling points of water then work out at the familiar 32° and 212°. One advantage of the system is that, for most ordinary purposes, negative degrees are rarely needed.

Using his thermometer, Fahrenheit measured the boiling point of various liquids and found that each had a characteristic boiling point, which changed with changes in atmospheric pressure.

FAJANS, Kasimir (b. May 27, 1887; Warsaw, Poland) Polish–American physical chemist.

Fajans gained his doctorate at Heidelberg (1909) and was professor of physical chemistry at Munich (1925–35) before emigrating to America in 1936. He was a member of the Faculty of the University of Michigan (1936–57) and emeritus professor from 1957.

He is best known for *Fajan's laws* (1913), which state that elements emitting alpha particles decrease in atomic number by two whilst those undergoing beta emission gain in atomic number by one. These were independently discovered by Frederick Soddy. In 1917 Fajans discovered, with Otto Gohring, uranium X_2 — a form of protactinium-234.

FALLOPIUS, Gabriel (b. 1523; Modena, Italy; d. Oct. 9, 1562; Padua, Italy) Italian anatomist.

Fallopius originally intended to enter the Church and served as a canon in Modena for some time before turning to the study of medicine at Ferrara and Padua where he was a pupil of the great Andreas Vesalius. He held the chair of anatomy at the University of Pisa from 1548 until 1551 when he moved to a similar post at the University of Padua, remaining there until his early death at the age of 39.

On the strength of his masterpiece *Observationes anatomicae* (1561) he has been described as a better and more accurate anatomist than his teacher, Vesalius. His main innovations were in the anatomy of the skull and the generative system. In the former area he introduced the terms cochlea and labyrinth, going on to give a clear account of the auditory system.

In his account of the reproductive system he described the clitoris and introduced the term 'vagina' into anatomy. He is mainly remembered today, however, for his description of the eponymous fallopian tubes. The tubes, connecting the uterus and the ovaries, were described by him as resembling at their extremity a 'brass trumpet' (tuba). This somehow became mistranslated into English as tube. It was many years before their function was understood.

FARADAY, Michael (b. Sept. 22, 1791; Newington, England; d. Aug. 25, 1867; London) British physicist and chemist.

Faraday's father was a blacksmith who suffered from poor health and could only work irregularly. Faraday knew real poverty as a child and his education was limited for he left school at the age of 13. He began work for a bookseller and binder in 1804 and was apprenticed the following year. His interest in science seems to have been aroused by his reading the 127-page entry on electricity in an Encyclopaedia Brittanica he was binding and this stimulated him to buy the ingredients to make a Leyden jar and to perform some simple experiments. He joined the City Philosophical Society, which he attended regularly, broadening his intellectual background still further. The turning point in his life came when he attended some lectures by Humphry Davy at the Royal Institution in 1812. He took very full notes of these lectures, which he bound himself.

By now he was no longer satisfied with his amateur experiments and evening lectures and wanted desperately to have a full-time career in science. He wrote to the president of the Royal Society, Joseph Banks, asking for his help in obtaining any post but received no reply. Faraday now had a little luck. Davy had had an accident and needed some temporary assistance. Faraday's name was mentioned and proved acceptable. While working with Davy he showed him the lecture notes he had taken and bound. When a little later, in 1813, a vacancy for a laboratory assistant arose, Davy remembered the serious young man and hired him at a salary of a guinea a week (less than Faraday had been earning as a bookbinder).

Faraday was to spend the rest of his working life at the Royal Institution, from which he finally resigned in 1861. In 1815 he was promoted to the post of assistant and superintendent of the apparatus of the laboratory and meteorological collection. In 1825 he was made director of the laboratory and, in 1833, he was elected to the newly endowed Fullerian Professorship of Chemistry at the Royal Institution. He had earlier turned down the offer of the chair of chemistry at University College, London, in 1827.

The paucity of the salary paid him was made up by Faraday with consultancy fees and a part-time lectureship he held at the Royal Military Academy, Woolwich. These extra sources took up his time and in 1831, when he was working as hard as he could on his electrical experiments, he gave up all his consultancies. This left him in some financial difficulties and moves were made to arrange for a government pension. He called on the prime minister of the day, Lord Melbourne, who made some sneering remark about such pensions being, in his view, a "gross humbug." This was enough to make Faraday refuse the pension. In fact, Faraday was one of nature's great refusers. Apart from the pension and the chair at University College, he also refused a knighthood and, what must surely be a record, the presidency of the Royal Society, not once, but twice. Faraday also had strong views on awards — "I have always felt that there is something degrading in offering rewards for intellectual exertion, and that societies or academies, or even kings and emperors, should mingle in the matter does not remove the degradation." He had become a fellow of the Royal Society in 1824 but not without some friction between himself and the president, Davy. He was asked to withdraw his application by Davy. Just why Davy behaved in this way is not clear. Some have seen it as jealousy by Davy of someone whose talents so clearly surpassed his own. There is no evidence of this but it is reasonably clear that when Faraday insisted on going ahead with his application Davy voted against him.

Faraday's financial problems were solved when, in 1835, Melbourne apologized, enabling him to accept the pension. After his labors of the 1830s he suffered some kind of breakdown in 1841 and went into the country to rest. Just what was wrong is not known; he wrote in 1842 that he could see no visitors because of "ill health connected with my head." For two years he did no work at all until in 1844 he seemed to be able to resume his experiments. Faraday continued to work but by the 1850s his creativity was in decline. He gave his last childrens' lectures at the Royal Institution in 1860 and resigned from it the following year, taking up residence in a house at Hampton Court made available to him by Prince Albert in 1858.

Faraday's first real successes were made in chemistry. In 1823 he unwittingly liquefied chlorine. He was simply heating a chlorine compound in a sealed tube and noticed the formation of some droplets at the cold end. He realized that this was the result of both temperature and pressure and on and off over the years applied the method to other gases. In 1825 he discovered benzene (C_6H_6) when asked to examine the residue collecting in cylinders of illuminating gas; he called the new compound 'bicarburet of hydrogen' because he took its formula to be C_2H. As a working chemist Faraday was one of the best analysts of his day. All his working life he was working and publishing as a chemist but in 1820 he also turned to a new field that was to dominate his life.

Faraday had begun by accepting the view that electricity is composed of two fluids. It was common in the 18th century to see such phenomena as light, heat, magnetism, and electricity to be the result of weightless fluids. In 1820 Hans Christian Oersted made a most surprising discovery: he had found that a wire carrying a current is capable of deflecting a compass needle; the direction in which the needle turned depended on whether the wire was under or over the needle and the direction in which the current was flowing. André Marie Ampère found that two parallel wires attract each other if the current in each is traveling in the same direction but repel each other if the currents are moving in opposite directions. Finally François Arago discovered that a copper disk rotating freely on its own axis would produce rotation in a compass needle suspended over it.

These phenomena were difficult to fit into fluid theories of electricity and magnetism. They enabled Faraday to make his first important discovery in 1821, that of electromagnetic rotation. A magnet was placed upright in a tube of mercury and secured firmly at the bottom with the pole of the magnet above the surface. A wire dipping into the mercury but free to rotate was suspended over the pole. When a current was passed through the mercury and through the wire, the wire rotated around the magnet. If the wire was secured and the magnet allowed to move, then the current caused the magnet to rotate. The first electric motor had been constructed.

When Faraday published his results they were to cause him much distress. William Wollaston had spoken of the possibility of such rotation and many concluded that Faraday had stolen his ideas. Faraday was only too aware of the stories about him but found there was little he could do about them. It may well have been this that Davy thought disqualified him from membership of the Royal Society.

In any case it was not really electromagnetic rotation that interested Faraday. All the new results involved the production of a magnetic force by an electric current and Faraday, with many others, was sure that it should also be possible to induce an electric current by magnetic action. He tried intermittently for ten years without success until in 1832 he hit upon an apparatus in which an iron ring was wound with two quite separate coils of wire. One was connected to a voltaic cell; the other to a simple galvanometer. He showed that on making and breaking the current in the cell circuit, the galvanometer momentarily registered the presence of a current in its circuit. The following few months were some of the most active of his life. He showed that the same results can be obtained without a battery: a magnet moved in and out of a coil of wire produced a current. A steady current could be produced by rotating a copper disk between the poles of a powerful magnet. His results were published in his *Experimental Researches in Electricity, first series* (1831).

Faraday found this deeply satisfying for it reinforced one of his strongest convictions about nature "that the various forms under which the forces of matter are made manifest have one common origin." That electricity and magnetism could interact made this view more plausible. At the time it was by no means clear that the various types of electricity — static, voltaic, animal, magnetic, and thermoelectric — were the same and Faraday spent the period 1833–34 on this problem publishing his results in the third series of his *Experimental Researches*.

Faraday had also continued the work of Davy on electrolysis — i.e. on the chemical reaction produced by passing an electric current through a liquid. He applied his ideas on the quantity of electricity to this chemical effect and produced what are now known as *Faraday's laws of electrolysis*. By careful analysis he showed that the chemical action of a current is constant for a constant quantity of electricity. This was his first law, that equal amounts of electricity produce equal amounts of decomposition. In the second law he found that the quantities of different substances deposited on the electrode by the passage of the same quantity of electricity were proportional to their equivalent weights.

In his explanations of magnetic and electrical phenomena Faraday did not use the fluid theories of the time. Instead he introduced the concept of lines of force (or tension) through a body or through space. (A similar earlier idea had been put forward by R. J. Boscovich with his picture of point atoms surrounded by shells of force.)

Thus, Faraday saw the connection between electrical and magnetic effects as vibrations of electrical lines communicated to magnetic lines. His experiments on induction were described in terms of the cutting of magnetic lines of force, which induces the electrical current. He explained electrical induction in dielectrics by the strain in 'tubes of induction' — and electrolysis was complete breakdown under such strain.

Faraday was no mathematician, relying instead on his wonderful experimental skill and his imagination. His lines of force were taken up by others more skillful mathematically. In the latter half of the century Clerk Maxwell (q.v.) developed Faraday's ideas into a rigorous and powerful theory, creating an orthodoxy in physics that lasted until the time of Einstein. Faraday's greatness rests in his courage and insight in rejecting the traditional physics and creating an entirely new one. Few can compete with Faraday at the level of originality.

One further effect discovered by Faraday lay in optics. His discovery of *Faraday rotation* in 1845 was one that gave him pleasure for it seemed to be further evidence for the unity of nature by showing that "magnetic force and light were proved to have a relation to each other." Here, he showed that if polarized light is passed through a transparent medium in a magnetic field its plane of polarization will be rotated.

Not the least of Faraday's achievements was as a lecturer and popularizer of science. In 1826 he started the famous Christmas lectures to children at the Royal Institution in London and gave 19 of these lecture courses. For most only the notes exist but a couple of lectures were taken down in shorthand and later published: *The Chemical History of a Candle* and *Lectures on Various Forces of Matter*. The children's Christmas lectures still continue to be given every year by eminent scientists.

FECHNER, Gustav Theodor (b. Apr. 19, 1801; Gross-Särchen, now in East Germany; d. Nov. 18, 1887; Leipzig, now in East Germany) German physicist and psychologist.

Fechner studied medicine at the University of Leipzig but, after graduating, his interest turned toward physics. He did some research on the galvanic battery and, on the strength of this, was appointed professor of physics at Leipzig in 1834. However, partial blindness, caused by overlong study of the Sun, and mental illness forced him to resign five years later.

It was after his recovery that he started trying to put psychology on a scientific basis. He studied the relationship between the intensities of external stimulae and subjective sensations, and elaborated Ernst Weber's (q.v.) work to develop the *Weber–Fechner law* governing this connection. This work, published in 1860, founded the science of psychophysics.

Fechner also became interested in spiritualism, like many scientists of his day, and wrote much on mystical and philosophical subjects. He also wrote satirical poems under the pseudonym of Dr. Mises.

FEHLING, Hermann Christian von (b. June 9, 1812; Lübeck, now in West Germany; d. July 1, 1885; Stuttgart, now in West Germany) German organic chemist.

Fehling gained his doctorate at Heidelberg in 1837 and studied with Justus von Liebig at Giessen. He was professor of chemistry at the polytechnic school at Stuttgart from 1839 to 1882.

Fehling did much work in organic chemistry, including the preparation and hydrolysis of benzonitrile and the discovery of succinosuccinic ester. However, he is best known for his invention of *Fehling's solution*, used as a test for aldehydes and reducing sugars (e.g. glucose, fructose, lactose). It consists of a solution of copper(II) sulfate (Fehling's I) and an alkaline solution of a tartaric acid salt (Fehling's II). The solutions are boiled with the test material and a positive result is a brick-red precipitate (insoluble copper(I) oxide), formed by the reduction of copper(II) sulfate.

FERMAT, Pierre de (b. Aug. 17, 1601; Beaumont-de-Lomagne, France; d. Jan. 12, 1665; Castres, France) French mathematician and physicist.

Fermat was one of the leading mathematicians of the early 17th century although not a professional mathematician. He studied law and spent his working life as a magistrate in the small provincial town of Castres. Although mathematics was only a spare-time activity, Fermat was an extremely creative and original mathematician who opened up whole new fields of enquiry.

Fermat's work in algebra built on and greatly developed the then new theory of equations, which had been largely founded by François Viète. With Pascal, Fermat stands as one of the founders of the mathematical theory of probability. In his work on methods of finding tangents to curves and their maxima and minima he anticipates some of the central concepts of Isaac Newton's and Gottfried Leibniz's differential calculus.

Another area of mathematics that Fermat played a major role in founding, independently of René Descartes, was analytical geometry. This work led to violent controversies over questions of priority with Descartes. Nor were Fermat's disagreements with Descartes limited to mathematics. Descartes had produced a major treatise on optics — the *Dioptrics* — which Fermat greatly disliked. He particularly objected to Descartes' attempt to reach conclusions about the physical sciences by purely *a priori* rationalistic reasoning without due regard for empirical observation. By contrast Fermat's view of science was grounded in a thoroughly empirical and observational approach, and to demonstrate the errors of Descartes' ways he set about experimental work in optics himself. Among the important contributions that Fermat made to optics are his discovery that light travels more slowly in a denser medium, and his formulation of the principle that light always takes the quickest path.

Fermat is probably best known for his work in number theory, and he made numerous important discoveries in this field. But he also left one of the famous unsolved problems of mathematics — *Fermat's last theorem*. This theorem states that the algebraic analog of Pythagoras's theorem has no whole number solution for a power greater than 2, i.e. the equation

$$a^n + b^n = c^n$$

has no solutions for n greater than 2 if a, b, and c are all integers. Fermat himself thought he had found a proof of this result, but this proof was subsequently lost. As mathematicians' attempts to re-prove the 'last theorem' since then have been unsuccessful, it is generally thought that Fermat's proof must have been mistaken.

FERMI, Enrico (b. Sept. 29, 1901; Rome; d. Nov. 28, 1954; Chicago, Illinois) Italian–American physicist.

Fermi was without doubt the greatest Italian scientist since Galileo and in the period 1925–50 was one of the most creative physicists in the world. Unusually in an age of ever-growing specialization he excelled as both an experimentalist and a theoretician.

He was brought up in the prosperous home of his father who, beginning as a railroad official, progressed to a senior position in government service. Fermi's intelligence and quickness of mind were apparent from an early age and he had little difficulty in gaining admission in 1918 to the Scuola Normale in Pisa, a school for the intellectual élite of Italy. He later completed his education at the University of Pisa where he gained his PhD in 1924. After spending some time abroad in Göttingen and Leiden, Fermi returned to Italy where, after some initial setbacks, he was appointed to a professorship of physics at the University of Rome. This in itself was a considerable achievement for one so young, considering the traditional

and bureaucratic nature of Italian universities. It was no doubt due to the reputation he had already established with the publication of some 30 substantial papers, and the support of O. M. Corbino, the most distinguished Italian physicist at the time and also a senator. Corbino was determined to modernize Italian physics and had the good sense to see that Fermi, despite his youth, was the ideal man to advance his cause.

Fermi began by publishing the first Italian text on modern physics, *Introduzione alla Fisica Atomica* (1928). Soon his reputation attracted around him the brightest of the younger Italian physicists. But the growth of fascism in Italy led to the dispersal of its scientific talent. By 1938 Fermi, with a Jewish wife, was sufficiently alarmed by the growing anti-Semitism of the government to join the general exodus and move to America.

However, before his departure, his period in Rome turned out to be remarkably productive, with major advances being made in both the theoretical and the experimental field. His experimental work arose out of attempts to advance the efforts of Irène and Frédéric Joliot-Curie who had announced in 1934 the production of artificial radioactive isotopes by the bombardment of boron and aluminum with helium nuclei (alpha particles). Fermi realized that the neutron, discovered by James Chadwick in 1932, was perhaps an even better tool for creating new isotopes. Although less massive than an alpha particle, the neutron's charge neutrality allowed it to overcome the positive charge of a target nucleus without dissipating its energy.

Fermi reported that in 1934 he had impulsively and for no apparent reason interposed paraffin between the neutron source and the target. "It was with no advance warning, no conscious prior reasoning ... I took some odd piece of paraffin" and placed it in front of the incident neutrons. The effect was to increase the activation intensity by a factor that ranged from a few tens to a few hundreds. Fermi had stumbled on the phenomenon of slow neutrons. What was happening was that the neutrons were slowing down as the result of collisions with the light hydrocarbon molecules. This in turn meant that they remained in the vicinity of the target nucleus sufficiently long to increase their chance of absorption.

The production of slow neutrons was later to have a profound impact in the field of nuclear energy, both civil and military. However Fermi's immediate task was to use them to irradiate as many of the elements as possible and to produce and investigate the properties of a large number of newly created radioactive isotopes. It was for this work, for "the discovery of new radioactive substances ... and for the discovery of the selective power of slow neutrons" that Fermi was awarded the 1938 Nobel Physics Prize.

He did however miss one significant phenomenon. In the course of their systematic irradiation of the elements Fermi and his colleagues naturally bombarded uranium with slow neutrons. This would inevitably lead to nuclear fission, but Fermi thought that transuranic elements were being produced and in his Nobel address actually referred to his production of elements 93 and 94, which he named 'ausonium' and 'hesperium'. In 1938 Otto Frisch and Lise Meitner first realized that nuclear fission was taking place in such reactions.

On the theoretical level Fermi's major achievement while at Rome was his theory of beta decay. This is the process in unstable nuclei whereby a neutron is converted into a proton with the emission of an electron and an antineutrino ($n \longrightarrow p + e^- + \nu$). Fermi gave a detailed analysis which introduced a new force into science, the so-called 'weak' force. An account was published in Italian in 1933 as an original English version was rejected by the journal *Nature* as being too speculative.

In America Fermi soon found himself caught up in the attempt to create a controlled nuclear chain reaction. In 1942 he succeeded in building the first atomic pile in the stadium of the University of Chicago at Stagg Field. Using pure graphite as a moderator to slow the neutrons, and enri-

ched uranium as the fissile material, Fermi and his colleagues began the construction of the pile. It consisted of some 40 000 graphite blocks, specially produced to exclude impurities, in which some 22 000 holes were drilled to permit the insertion of several tons of uranium. At 2.20 p.m. on 2 December, 1942, the atomic age began as Fermi's pile went critical, supporting a self-supporting chain reaction for 28 minutes. In an historic telephone call afterwards Arthur Compton informed the managing committee that "the Italian navigator has just landed in the new world," and that the natives were friendly.

Fermi continued to work on the project and was in fact present in July 1945 when the first test bomb was exploded in the New Mexico desert. He is reported to have dropped scraps of paper as the blast reached him and, from their displacement, to have calculated the force as corresponding to 10 000 tons of TNT.

After the war Fermi accepted an appointment as professor of physics at the University of Chicago where he remained until his untimely death from cancer. His name has been commemorated in physics in various ways. Element 100, *fermium*, and the unit of length of 10^{-13} cm, the *fermi*, were named for him, as was the National Accelerator Laboratory, Fermilab, at Batavia, near Chicago.

FERNEL, Jean Francois (b. 1497; Clermont, France; d. Apr. 26, 1558; Fontainebleau, France) French physician.

Fernel, the son of an innkeeper, was educated at the Collège de Sainte Barbe in Paris where he graduated in 1519. After some years devoted to such subjects as philosophy and cosmology, Fernel took up the study of medicine, qualifying in 1530 and being appointed professor of medicine in 1534 at the University of Paris. He was also appointed as physician to Henri II after successfully treating Henri's mistress Diane de Poitiers, although his failure to cure Henri's father, Francis I, of syphilis appears not to have been held against him.

In 1554 Fernel published his *Medicina*, which went through some 30 editions and was one of the standard texts of the late 16th century. It is here that he introduced the terms 'physiology' and 'pathology' into medicine. The work was however mainly traditional describing the physiology of Galen with but a few modifications.

Fernel also wrote an interesting account of the status of medicine in his *On the Hidden Causes of Things* (1548) in which he began to question long accepted magical and astrological accounts of diseases. He fell back on the standard medical objection to therapies offered by competitors, namely that any relief obtained would be only superficial and temporary.

Before turning to medicine Fernel had published his *Cosmotheria* (1528) a work that contained one of the earliest measurements of a meridian, measured with an odometer between Paris and Amiens.

FERREL, William (b. Jan. 29, 1817; Fulton County, Pennsylvania; d. Sept. 18, 1891; Maywood, Kansas) American meteorologist.

Ferrel moved with his family to farm in West Virginia in 1829. Receiving only the most rudimentary education, his early scientific knowledge was entirely self acquired. Despite this he developed an interest in mathematical physics and, after graduating from Bethany College in West Virginia in 1844, began to study the *Principia* of Isaac Newton and the *Mécanique céleste* of Pierre Simon de Laplace. He earned his living as a schoolteacher from 1844 until 1857 when, having established his scientific reputation, he was appointed to the staff of the American Ephemeris and Nautical Almanac. He worked there until 1867 when he joined the US Coast and Geodetic Survey.

In 1856 he published his most significant work, *Essay on the Winds and Currents of the Oceans*. He showed that all atmospheric motion, as well as ocean currents, are deflected by the Earth's rotation. He went on in 1858 to formulate his law, which

states that if a mass of air is moving in any direction there is a force arising from the Earth's rotation that always deflects it to the right in the northern hemisphere and to the left in the southern hemisphere. The air tends to move in a circle whose radius depends upon its velocity and distance from the equator. Ferrel went on to show how this law could be used to explain storms and the pattern of winds and currents. He was in some ways anticipated by Gustave-Gaspard Coriolis whose name is much better known.

Ferrel also did fundamental work on the solar system. He was able to correct Laplace and show that the tidal action of the Sun and Moon on the Earth is slowly retarding the Earth's rotation. In 1864 he provided the first mathematical treatment of tidal friction. His other works included his three-volume *Meteorological Researches* (1877–82). In 1880 he invented a machine to predict tidal maxima and minima.

FERRIER, Sir David (b. Jan. 13, 1843; Aberdeen, Scotland; d. Mar. 19, 1928; London) British neurologist.

Ferrier graduated in philosophy from the University of Aberdeen in 1863 and then spent some time at Heidelberg studying psychology. He returned to Scotland to study medicine at Edinburgh University and graduated in 1868. Initially he worked in private practice until his appointment as professor of forensic medicine at King's College Hospital, London (1872–89). The chair of neuropathology was created for him in 1889, a post he retained until his retirement in 1908.

Following the fundamental paper of Gustav Fritsch and Eduard Hitzig on cerebral localization, Ferrier began, in 1873, a series of experiments that both confirmed and extended their work. Whereas they had worked only with dogs, Ferrier used a wide variety of mammals, including primates. He was thus able to identify many more different areas in the cerebral hemispheres capable of eliciting movement. This work was soon shown to have practical implications. The surgeon William Macewen saw that the technique could be reversed and that disturbances of movement in a patient could be used to indicate the site of a possible brain tumor.

Ferrier was an important figure in the newly emerging discipline of neurophysiology. He was one of the first editors of the influential journal *Brain* (founded 1878) and was also a founder member of the Physiological Society.

FESSENDEN, Reginald Aubrey (b. Oct. 6, 1866; Milton, Quebec; d. July 22, 1932; Hamilton, Bermuda) Canadian electrical engineer.

After an education in Canada, Fessenden worked for Edison as an engineer and later as head chemist (1886–90) and as an engineer (1890–91) for Westinghouse, Edison's great rival. He was professor of electrical engineering at Purdue University, Indiana, (1882–83) and the Western University of Pennsylvania (now the University of Pittsburgh) from 1893 to 1900. He was then appointed special agent for the US Weather Bureau, adapting the technique of radio telegraphy, newly developed by Guglielmo Marconi, to weather forecasting and storm warning. In 1902 he became general manager of the National Electric Signaling Company, a company formed by two Pittsburgh financiers to exploit his ideas. From 1910 he was consultant engineer at the Submarine Signal Company.

Fessenden's inventions were prolific and varied: at the time of his death he held over 500 patents. In 1900 he developed an electrolytic detector that was sufficiently sensitive to make radio telephony feasible. His most significant invention was the technique of amplitude modulation. This involved the use of 'carrier waves' to transmit audio signals; he varied the amplitude of a steady high-frequency radio signal so that it corresponded to variations in the sound waves and thus 'carried' the audio information. Using this principle he transmitted on Christmas Eve, 1906, what was probably the first program of music and speech broadcast in America. The program was heard by ships' radio operators up to distances of several hundred miles.

Fessenden had a choleric temperament and a fear of being outwitted by businessmen. He was involved in various lawsuits, one of which was against his financial backers in the National Electric Signaling Company: Fessenden won a judgment of 406 000 dollars and sent the company into bankruptcy.

FEYNMAN, Richard Phillips (b. May 11, 1918; New York City) American theoretical physicist.

Feynman graduated from the Massachusetts Institute of Technology in 1939 and studied for his doctorate at Princeton University. After working on the atomic bomb during World War II, he later joined the California Institute of Technology, where he is now a professor.

In the late 1940s Feynman did important work in quantum electrodynamics — the part of quantum mechanics dealing with the theory of electromagnetic interactions. It is concerned, for example, with interactions between electrons or between electrons and photons (electromagnetic radiation). Prior to the period of his work the detailed theory of such interactions had been unsatisfactory. In his approach they are treated as exchanges of virtual particles. For instance, the interaction of two electrons is explained as an exchange of virtual photons between the two; i.e. by a photon thought of as emitted by one electron and absorbed by the other after a very brief period of time. Thus, electron–electron scattering can be described quantitatively by a matrix written as a sum of terms corresponding to all the ways in which the photons can be exchanged. Each term is illustrated by a *Feynman diagram*, built up from *Feynman propagators*, representing the exchange of virtual photons or electrons. For his work he received the 1965 Nobel Prize for physics, jointly with Julian S. Schwinger and Sin-Itiro Tomonaga (workers in the same field).

Feynman is a notable teacher of physics, known for his clear exposition of abstract matters in lectures and writing. He is also noted for his colorful character.

FIBIGER, Johannes Andreas Grib (b. Apr. 23, 1867; Silkeborg, Denmark; d. Jan. 30, 1928; Copenhagen) Danish physician.

Fibiger, the son of a physician, was educated at the University of Copenhagen, completing his medical studies in 1890. After some hospital work and further study in Berlin under Robert Koch and Emil von Behring, Fibiger joined the Institute of Pathological Anatomy at the University of Copenhagen in 1897, serving there as its director from 1900.

It was realized that cancers could be chemically induced by factors in the environment but all attempts to induce such cancers artificially had failed. Fibiger thought he could change this when, in 1907, he observed extensive papillomatous tumors virtually filling the stomachs of three wild rats. Microscopic examination showed the presence in the stomachs of formations similar to nematode worms, and Fibiger naturally concluded that these parasites were the cause of the tumors. A search of a further 1200 wild rats, however, produced no additional cases of cancer. This suggested to him that the nematodes were transmitted by an intermediate host, and a report published in 1878 confirmed that such nematodes had been found as parasites of a common kind of cockroach. Before long Fibiger found rats from a sugar refinery that fed regularly on the cockroaches there: examination of 61 of these rats showed that 40 had nematodes in their stomachs and 7 of these 40 had the earlier identified tumor.

By 1913 Fibiger was able to claim that he could induce such malignancies in rats by feeding them with cockroaches infested with nematode larvae, noting a proportional relationship between the number of parasites and the degree of anatomic

change in the stomach. It was for this work, described somewhat extravagantly by the Nobel Committee as the "greatest contribution to experimental medicine in our generation", that Fibiger was awarded the 1926 Nobel Prize in physiology or medicine.

Although no one disputed that Fibiger had induced cancer it was never completely accepted that such growths were caused by the nematodes. In any case Fibiger's work had little impact on experimental cancer research: simpler methods of carcinogenesis were almost universally preferred.

FIBONACCI, Leonardo (b. *c.* 1170; d. *c.* 1250) Italian mathematician.

Fibonacci lived in Pisa and is often referred to as Leonardo of Pisa. Although he was probably the most outstanding mathematician of the Middle Ages virtually nothing is known of his life. The modern system of numerals, which originated in India and had first been introduced to the West by al-Khwarizmi, first became widely used in Europe owing to Fibonacci's popularization of it. His father served as a consul in North Africa and it is known that Fibonacci studied with an Arabian mathematician in his youth, from whom he probably learned the decimal system of notation.

Fibonacci's main work was his *Liber abaci* (1202; Book of the Abacus) in which he expounded the virtues of the new system of numerals and showed how they could be used to simplify highly complex calculations. Fibonacci also worked extensively on the theory of proportion and on techniques for determining the roots of equations, and included a treatment of these subjects in the *Liber abaci*. In addition it contains contributions to geometry and Fibonacci later published his *Practica geometriae* (1220; Practice of Geometry), a shorter work that was devoted entirely to geometry.

Fibonacci was fortunate in being able to gain the patronage of the Holy Roman

Emperor, Frederick II, and a later work, the *Liber quadratorum* (1225; Book of Square Numbers) was dedicated to his patron. This book, which is generally considered Fibonacci's greatest achievement, deals with second order Diophantine equations. It contains the most advanced contributions to number theory since the work of Diophantus, which were not to be equaled until the work of Fermat. He discovered the 'Fibonacci sequence' of integers in which each number is equal to the sum of the preceding two $(1, 1, 2, 3, 5, 8, ...)$.

FINCH, George Ingle (b. Aug. 4, 1888; Orange, Australia; d. Nov. 22, 1970) Australian physical chemist.

Finch was educated at Wolaroi College in Australia and the Ecole de Médecine in Paris. Finding the study of medicine unappealing, Finch moved to Switzerland where he studied physics and chemistry, first at the Federal Institute of Technology in Zurich and afterward at the University of Geneva. On moving to Britain in 1912 he worked briefly as a research chemist at the Royal Arsenal, Woolwich, joining the staff of Imperial College, London, in 1913. Finch remained there until his retirement in 1952, having been appointed professor of applied physical chemistry in 1936. After his retirement Finch spent the period 1952–57 in India as director of the National Chemical Laboratory.

Finch worked mainly on the properties of solid surfaces. In the 1930s he developed the technique of low-energy electron diffraction, using the wavelike properties of electrons, demonstrated by George Thomson and Clinton J. Davisson in 1927, to investigate the structure of surfaces. X-rays are neutral and too penetrating to provide much information about surfaces or thin films; electrons, however, are charged and are deflected after penetrating no more than a few atoms below the surface. With this new and powerful tool Finch began the study of lubricants and the Beilby layer — a thin surface layer pro-

duced by polishing, and differing in its properties from the underlying material. Finch had earlier worked on the mechanism of combustion in gases as initiated by an electric discharge.

Finch was also widely known as a mountaineer. As one of the leading climbers of his generation he was a member of the 1922 Everest expedition, climbing to the then unequaled height of 27 300 feet (8321 m).

FINLAY, Carlos Juan (b. Dec. 3, 1833; Puerto Principe, now Camagüey, Cuba; d. Aug. 20, 1915; Havana) Cuban physician.

Finlay's father was a Scottish physician who had fought with Simon Bolivar. Carlos was educated in Paris and at the Jefferson Medical College, Philadelphia, where he graduated in 1855. He then returned to Cuba where he spent his life in general practice.

In 1881 Finlay published a prophetic paper *The Mosquito Hypothetically Considered as the Agent of the Transmission of Yellow Fever*, naming the species *Culex fasciatus* (now *Aëdes aegypti*) as the vector. He had been struck by the presence of *Aëdes* in houses during epidemics and noted that the yellow fever and mosquito seasons seemed to coincide. Although he campaigned vigorously for his theory he only succeeded in turning himself into a figure of mild ridicule.

There were a number of complicating factors that undermined Finlay's work. Firstly yellow fever is caused by a virus, a microorganism only discovered in 1898 and far too small to be detected by the microscopic techniques of the late 19th century. Further with the newly established germ theory of Robert Koch, scientists were demanding visual evidence for the existence of the supposed pathogen. As Finlay could not isolate the causative organism he attempted to demonstrate its existence by such clinical techniques as transmitting the disease from a sick patient via *Aëdes* to a healthy individual. But here too, although he repeated such experiments many times, he failed to produce any coherent results. As it turned out, it was only the female mosquito, and then only one who had bitten a victim in the first three days of infection who could, two weeks later, transmit the disease. Consequently many of Finlay's failures could be explained by using the wrong type of mosquito or the right type at the wrong time. But to discover such facts required more ambitious resources than Finlay commanded.

He did however live long enough to see such resources come to Cuba with the arrival of the 4th US Yellow Fever Commission in 1900 under the command of Walter Reed. Finlay interested Reed in his views, and Reed, in a classic series of trials, completely vindicated him.

FINSEN, Niels Ryberg (b. Dec. 15, 1860; Thorshavn, Faeroe Islands, Denmark; d. Sept. 24, 1904; Copenhagen) Danish physician.

Finsen, the son of a leading civil servant, was educated in Reykjavik and at the University of Copenhagen, where he qualified as a physician in 1890. After teaching anatomy for some time Finsen founded (1895) the Institute of Phototherapy, which he directed until his early death at the age of 43.

In the 1890s, following up some earlier work suggesting that light had the ability to kill bacteria, Finsen began a systematic appraisal of its therapeutic effects. Arguing that it was light, acting slowly and weakly, rather than heat that was effective, he devised various filters and lenses to separate and concentrate the different components of sunlight. He found that it was the short ultraviolet rays, either natural or artificial, that turned out to have the greatest bactericidal power.

Finsen found phototherapy to be of most use against lupus vulgaris, a skin infection produced by the tubercle bacillus. He claimed that on exposure to ultraviolet rays the skin regained its normal color and the ulcerations began to heal. For this Finsen received the third

Nobel Prize in physiology or medicine in 1903.

It was, however, an avenue that few physicians were willing to explore. The use of ultraviolet radiation was mainly restricted to the treatment of lupus vulgaris and even this was superseded by x-rays and, more importantly, by such drugs as cortisone when they became available in the 1950s.

FISCHER, Emil Hermann (b. Oct. 9, 1852; Euskirchen, now in West Germany; d. July 15, 1919; Berlin) German organic chemist and biochemist.

The son of a successful businessman, Fischer joined his father's firm on leaving school (1869) but left in 1871 to study chemistry with August Kekulé at Bonn. He was not happy with the chemistry instruction there and came close to abandoning chemistry for physics. In 1872, however, he moved to Strasbourg to study with Adolf von Baeyer and the baton of the leadership of organic chemistry eventually passed from Baeyer to Fischer. He gained his doctorate in 1874 for work on phthaleins. The same year he made the vital discovery of phenylhydrazine, a compound that was later to prove the vital key for unlocking the structures of the sugars.

Fischer became Baeyer's assistant and together they moved to Munich (1875). At Munich, working with his cousin, Otto Fischer, he proved that the natural rosaniline dyes are derivatives of triphenylmethane. In 1879 Fischer became assistant professor of analytical chemistry and soon after became financially independent. He was then professor at Erlangen (1882), Würzburg (1885), and Berlin (1892).

Fischer has some claim to be called the father of biochemistry. He carried out extremely comprehensive work in three main fields: purines, sugars, and peptides, the last two effectively founding biochemistry on a firm basis of organic chemistry. The work on purines, begun in 1882, resulted in the synthesis of many important compounds, including the alkaloids caffeine and theobromine, and purine itself (1898). Fischer's early structures were incorrect but from 1897 the correct structures were used.

In 1884 Fischer discovered that phenylhydrazine produces well-defined crystalline compounds with sugars, thus affording a reliable means of identification. In 1887 he synthesized first fructose (from acrolein dibromide) and later mannose and glucose. By 1891 he was able to deduce the configurations of the 16 possible aldohexoses, which he represented in the form of the famous *Fischer projection formulae*.

In 1899 Fischer turned to amino acids and peptides and devised a peptide synthesis that eventually produced a polypeptide containing 18 amino acids (1907). Fischer's other work included the first synthesis of a nucleotide (1914), the 'lock-and-key' hypothesis of enzyme action, work on tannins, and attempts to prepare very high-molecular-weight compounds. He was awarded the 1902 Nobel Prize for chemistry for his work on purines and sugars.

FISCHER, Ernst Otto (b. Nov. 10, 1918; Munich, now in West Germany) German inorganic chemist.

Fischer, the son of a physics professor, was educated at the Munich Institute of Technology, where he obtained his PhD in 1952. He taught at the University of Munich serving as professor of inorganic chemistry from 1957 to 1964, when he became the director of the Institute for Inorganic Chemistry at the Institute of Technology.

Fischer is noted for his work on inorganic complexes. In 1951 two chemists, T. Kealy and P. Pauson, were attempting to join two five-carbon (cyclopentadiene) rings together and discovered a compound $C_5H_5FeC_5H_5$, which they proposed had an iron atom joined to a carbon atom on each ring.

Fischer, on reflection, considered such a structure inadequate for he failed to see how it could provide sufficient stability with a carbon–iron–carbon bond. The British chemist Geoffrey Wilkinson suggested a more novel structure in which the iron atom was sandwiched between two parallel rings and thus formed bonds with the electrons in the rings, rather than with individual carbon atoms. Compounds of this type are called 'sandwich compounds'.

By careful x-ray analysis Fischer confirmed the proposed structure of ferrocene, as the compound was called, and for this work shared the Nobel Prize for chemistry

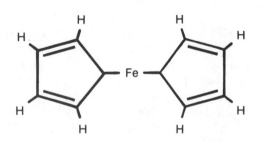
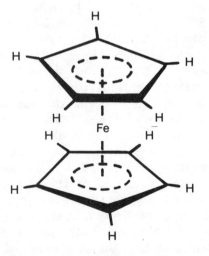

FERROCENE Originally the structure was thought to be that on the left. Later it was found to be a 'sandwich compound', with the iron atom positioned between two parallel rings.

with Wilkinson in 1973. Fischer went on to do further work on transition-metal complexes with organic compounds and is one of the leading workers in the field of organometallic chemistry.

FISCHER, Hans (b. July 27, 1881; Höchst-am-Main, now in West Germany; d. Mar. 31, 1945; Munich, now in West Germany) German organic chemist.

Fischer, the son of a chemicals industrialist, gained his doctorate in chemistry at the University of Marburg in 1904. He also studied medicine at the University of Munich, gaining his MD in 1908. He was assistant to Emil Fischer before occupying chairs of medical chemistry at Innsbruck (1916) and Vienna (1918). In 1921 he succeeded Heinrich Wieland as professor at the Technical Institute in Munich.

Fischer's life work was the study of the immensely important biological molecules hemoglobin, chlorophyll, and the bile pigments, especially bilirubin. He showed that hemin — the nonprotein, iron-containing portion of the hemoglobin molecule — consists of a system of four pyrrole rings, linked by bridges, with iron in the center. He synthesized hemin in 1929 and extensively investigated similar molecules — the porphyrins. He was awarded the Nobel Prize for chemistry for this work in 1930. He then turned to the chlorophylls and showed that they are substituted porphins with magnesium rather than iron in the center. The bile acids were shown by Fischer to be degraded porphins, and he synthesized bilirubin in 1944. Fischer took his own life at the end of World War II, after his laboratories had been destroyed in the bombing of Munich.

FISCHER, Otto Philipp (b. Nov. 28, 1852; Euskirchen, now in West Germany; d. Apr. 4, 1932; Erlangen, now in West Germany) German organic chemist.

Otto Fischer was the cousin of Emil Fischer, with whom he collaborated in some of his work. He gained his doctorate at Strasbourg (1874) and was professor of chemistry at Erlangen from 1885 to 1925. His most notable work was with dyestuffs: he discovered malachite green, a triphenyl-methane dye (1877), determined the structures of pararosaniline (with Emil) (1880), and mauveine (1890).

FISHER, Sir Ronald Aylmer (b. Feb. 17, 1890; London; d. July 29, 1962; Adelaide, Australia) British statistician and geneticist.

Fisher studied mathematics and physics at Cambridge University, graduating in 1912. In the years before joining Rothamsted Experimental Station in 1919 he undertook a variety of jobs, including farm work in Canada, employment with an investment company, and teaching in various private schools. In this period he also produced two important papers marking his interest in both statistics and genetics. The first, published in 1915, described a solution for the exact distribution of the correlation coefficient, a problem that had been perplexing other statisticians. The second paper was *The Correlation between Relatives on the Supposition of Mendelian Inheritance* (1918). This demonstrated that the inheritance of continuous variation, which had been thought of as non-Mendelian, is in fact governed by many additive genes, each of small effect and each inherited in a Mendelian manner. Thus continuous variation may be analyzed following Mendelian rules. This work later led to the development of the science of biometric genetics. At Rothamsted, Fisher was appointed to sort out the accumulation of over 60 years' data on field trials. He modified the significance test, enabling more confident conclusions to be drawn from small samples of data, and developed the analysis of variance technique. He emphasized the need for random rather than systematic experimental design so that error due to environmental variation could be analyzed quantitatively. His book *Statistical Methods for Research Workers* (1925) is one of the most influential works in statistics.

Fisher's major researches in genetics at Rothamsted were brought together in *The Genetical Theory of Natural Selection* (1930). In this book he argued that Mendelism, far from contradicting Darwinism as some people believed, actually provides the missing link in the theory of evolution by natural selection by showing that inheritance is particulate rather than blending. (In 1936 Fisher published a paper arguing that probabilistically Mendel's famous results were 'too good to be true'.) The book also summarizes his views on eugenics and on genes controlling dominant characteristics. He believed that dominance develops gradually by selection, showing selection rather than mutation to be the driving force in evolution.

The Genetical Theory of Natural Selection led to Fisher's appointment as Galton Professor of Genetics at University College, London, in 1933. Here he did important work clarifying the genetics of the Rhesus blood groups. He accepted the chair of genetics at Cambridge University in 1943, remaining there until 1959 although he retired officially in 1957. He spent the last three years of his life working for the Commonwealth Scientific and Industrial Research Organization (CSIRO) in Adelaide.

Fisher was knighted in 1952.

FITCH, Val Logsdon (b. Mar. 10, 1923; Merriman, Nebraska) American physicist.

Fitch was educated at McGill and Columbia universities, and obtained his PhD from Columbia in 1954. He then joined the Princeton staff, being appointed professor of physics there in 1960.

Working with Leo James Rainwater, Fitch was the first to observe radiation from muonic atoms; i.e. from species in which a muon is orbiting a nucleus rather than an electron. This work indicated that the sizes of atomic nuclei were smaller than had been supposed. He went on to study kaons and in 1964 collaborated with James

Cronin (q.v.), James Christenson, and René Turley in an experiment that disproved CP conservation. In 1980 Fitch and Cronin shared the 1980 Nobel Physics Prize for this fundamental work.

FITTIG, Rudolph (b. Dec. 6, 1835; Hamburg, now in West Germany; d. Nov. 19, 1910, Strasbourg, now in France) German organic chemist.

Fittig gained his doctorate at Göttingen in 1858 and became a professor at Tübingen (1870) and Strasbourg (1876–1902). He was a prolific experimentalist with many discoveries and syntheses to his credit, including pinacol, diphenyl, mesitylene, cymene, coumarone, and phenanthrene in coal tar. He also did extensive work on lactones and unsaturated acids. His name is remembered in the *Wurtz–Fittig reaction*, a variation of the Wurtz reaction for synthesizing alkylaryl hydrocarbons. An example is the reaction to form methylbenzene (toluene):

$$CH_3Cl + C_6H_5Cl + 2Na \longrightarrow C_6H_5CH_3 + 2NaCl.$$

FITZGERALD, George Francis (b. Aug. 3, 1851; Dublin; d. Feb. 21, 1901; Dublin) Irish physicist.

Fitzgerald graduated from Trinity College, Dublin, in 1871 and then joined the staff there, rising to the position of professor in 1881. His work was mainly concerned with the development of electromagnetism from James Clerk Maxwell's equations, in which he became interested after Heinrich Hertz had demonstrated the existence of the radio waves predicted by theory. Like Hendrik Lorentz, he constructed an electromagnetic theory of the reflection and refraction of light.

His name is best known for the *Lorentz–Fitzgerald contraction* — an effect suggested to explain the negative result of the Michelson–Morley experiment (*see* A. A. Michelson). The suggestion was that a body moving relative to an observer contracted slightly in the dimension parallel to the direction of motion, the amount of the contraction being dependent on the velocity. Thus, light emitted by a moving body would have a different speed, but would travel over a different path length. The contraction in size was supposed to result from the effect of the ether on the electromagnetic forces holding the atoms together. The Lorentz–Fitzgerald contraction received an alternative explanation in Einstein's theory of relativity.

FITZROY, Robert (b. July 5, 1805; near Bury St. Edmunds, England; d. Apr. 30, 1865; Norwood, England) British hydrographer and meteorologist.

Fitzroy was educated at the Royal Naval College, Portsmouth, and in 1828 took command of the *Beagle*, on a survey of the South American coast. In 1831 he made a second voyage in the *Beagle* to complete his survey, taking with him as naturalist the then unknown Charles Darwin. After his return in 1836 he devoted himself to the publication, in 1839, of his *Narrative*, a three-volume account of the voyage. The third volume, known as *The Voyage of the Beagle*, was the work of Darwin.

Fitzroy served as a member of Parliament (1841–43) and was then appointed governor of New Zealand until his dismissal in 1845. He retired from active duty in 1850 but later (1854) took up the newly created post of meteorological statist and remained there until his death. He organized a number of observation stations, designed the barometer named for him, and began the publication of storm warnings that evolved into daily weather forecasts. One of the earliest textbooks on meteorology, *The Weather Book* (1863), was published by him.

He had a reputation for having a quick temper and, while suffering from depression, committed suicide.

FIZEAU, Armand Hippolyte Louis (b. Sept. 23, 1819; Paris; d. Sept. 18, 1896; Venteuil, France) French physicist.

Fizeau started by studying medicine but his interest turned to optics before he finished the course. In collaboration with Léon Foucault he first tried to improve the newly developed process of photography and, in 1845, they took the first clear pictures of the Sun.

In 1849 he obtained a value for the speed of light in air, using an ingenious toothed-wheel apparatus. Light was directed through a gap between two teeth and reflected back between the teeth from a distant mirror. The wheel was rotated, the rate of rotation being changed until the reflected flashes were blocked by the tooth of the wheel. The speed of light could then be calculated from the rate of rotation of the wheel. Fizeau's experiment was performed using a path of 8 kilometers (5 mi) between Suresnes and Montmartre.

The next year both he and Foucault simultaneously proved that light traveled faster in air than in water, thus giving experimental support to the wave theory of light. Fizeau is also known for analyzing the Doppler effect for light waves (*see* Christian Doppler). The change in wavelength with relative speed is sometimes called the *Doppler–Fizeau shift*.

FLAMMARION, Nicolas Camille (b. Feb. 25, 1842; Montigny-le-Roi, France; d. June 4, 1925; Paris) French astronomer.

Owing to his family's poverty, Flammarion was forced to leave school and abandon his intention of going into the priesthood. Instead he got a post in the Paris Observatory in 1858 but eventually was dismissed by Urbain Leverrier who accused him of being a poet rather than a scientist. Flammarion made serious contributions to astronomy, including founding the French Astronomical Society in 1887, and built himself a private observatory at Juvisy. However he is best known as a popularizer of astronomy. His general attitude to astronomy was made clear when he published at the age of 19 *Plurality of Inhabited Worlds* (1862). This was translated into 12 languages, including Chinese and Arabic, and became a best seller in France, making Flammarion famous. His *Popular Astronomy* (1879) was one of the most popular books of the late 19th century. Giovanni Schiaparelli's discovery of 'canals' on Mars in 1877 received enthusiastic support from Flammarion. He went even further, claiming that he could discern changes in the lunar craters that could be cultivated fields.

FLAMSTEED, John (b. Aug. 19, 1646; Denby, England; d. Dec. 31, 1719; Greenwich, England) English astronomer.

Because of ill health, which was to dog his career, Flamsteed was forced to leave school early and was therefore largely self educated. He started his scientific career under the patronage of William Brouncker, the first president of the Royal Society, having impressed him by computing an almanac of celestial events for 1670.

A major problem of the time — one tackled at some time by all major astronomers of the 17th century — was the determination of longitude at sea. A suggestion had been made that the motion of the Moon against the stellar background could be used to determine standard time. Flamsteed, asked by Brouncker to comment on this proposal, pointed out that the scheme was impractical because of the inaccuracy of contemporary tables. Charles II subsequently commanded that accurate tables should be constructed, appointing Flamsteed as first Astronomer Royal with this responsibility in 1675, and building the Royal Greenwich Observatory for him, which was opened in 1676. The limited nature of the royal patronage is indicated by the fact that Flamsteed was paid a salary of £100 a year but was expected to provide his own instruments and staff. He eventually managed to put together two small telescopes and then began his

decades of observation, made more difficult by his lack of staff and the crippling headaches from which he suffered. In order to make ends meet he was forced to become a clergyman at Burstow in Surrey from 1684 until his death.

The results of his labors were eventually published posthumously in 1725 as the *Historia coelestis Britannica* (British Celestial Record). It contains the position of over 3000 stars calculated to an accuracy of ten seconds of arc. It was the first great modern comprehensive telescopic catalog and established Greenwich as one of the leading observatories of the world. The publication of the work was not without its difficulties. It involved Flamsteed in a long and bitter dispute with Newton. Flamsteed was reluctant to rush into print with his catalog, claiming, it seemed to Newton, far too much time for the checking of his numerous observations. The dispute lasted from Newton's assumption of the presidency of the Royal Society in 1703 until Flamsteed's death. It involved the virtual seizure of Flamsteed's papers by Newton, the editing and partial publication by Edmond Halley, and their total rejection by Flamsteed who even went so far as to acquire 300 of the 400 printed copies of his own work and burn them. He managed, however, to revise the first volume to his satisfaction before his death in 1719.

FLEMING, Sir Alexander (b. Aug. 6, 1881; Lochfield, Scotland; d. Mar 11, 1955; London) British bacteriologist.

After his early education at Kilmarnock Academy and the London Polytechnic Institute, Fleming began his career at the age of 16 as a shipping clerk in a London office. With encouragement from his brother, who was a doctor, he became a medical student at St. Mary's Hospital Medical School in 1902 and graduated from the University of London in 1908. He worked at St. Mary's all his life apart from 1914–18, when he served in the Royal Army Medical Corps. During this time he became interested in the control of wound infections and was a vigorous supporter of the physiological treatment of wounds rather than treatment using harsh chemicals, such as carbolic acid. In the 1920s he studied various body secretions and their effects on bacteria. Thus he discovered lysozyme, a bacteriolytic enzyme that is present in serum, saliva, and tears, publishing his findings in 1922.

In 1928 Fleming was appointed professor of bacteriology and in the same year he made his most important discovery. After accidentally leaving a dish of staphylococcus bacteria uncovered, Fleming noticed certain clear areas in the culture. He found these areas were due to contamination by a mold he identified as *Penicillium notatum*, which produced a substance that killed the bacteria. Fleming named this substance 'penicillin' and tested the bactericidal effect of the mold on various different bacteria, observing that it killed some but not others. He appreciated the potentialities of his discovery but was unable to isolate and identify the compound. It was not until World War II, with the urgent need for new antibacterial drugs, that penicillin — the first antibiotic — was finally isolated by Howard Florey (q.v.) and Ernst Chain.

Fleming was awarded the 1945 Nobel Prize for physiology or medicine jointly with Florey and Chain for his discovery, which initiated a whole new range of lifesaving antibiotics. He received a knighthood in 1944 and many other honors.

FLEMING, Sir John Ambrose (b. Nov. 29, 1849; Lancaster, England; d. Apr. 18, 1945; Sidmouth, England) British physicist and electrical engineer.

Fleming studied for a short time at University College, London, but left before graduating. However, he continued his work for a science degree in his leisure hours while employed first in a shipwright's drawing office and later as a stockbroker's clerk. Between 1871 and 1880 he had alternate periods of school science teaching and further study, including

working under James Clerk Maxwell from 1877 at the new Cavendish Laboratory in Cambridge. In 1881 he was appointed professor of mathematics and physics at University College, Nottingham. From 1882 to 1885 he worked as consultant to the Edison Electric Light Company in London. He was then appointed professor of electrical technology at University College, London, a post he held for 41 years.

At University College Fleming gave special courses and experimented on wireless telegraphy, cooperating a great deal with Guglielmo Marconi. One of Fleming's outstandingly important inventions was the thermionic vacuum tube, a rectifying device based on an effect discovered by Thomas Edison. Fleming's diode consisted of a glass bulb containing two electrodes. One, a metal filament, was heated to incandescence by an electric current, so that it emitted electrons by thermionic emission. The second electrode (the anode) could collect electrons if held at a positive potential with respect to the filament (the cathode) and a current would flow. Current could not flow in the opposite direction — hence the name 'valve' for such devices. Lee de Forest developed the device into the triode for amplifying current.

Other scientific contributions by Fleming included investigations into the property of materials, transformer design, electrical measurements, and photometry. He was an outstanding teacher and highly successful as a popular lecturer. *Fleming's left hand rule* and *right hand rule* are mnemonics for relating the direction of motion, magnetic field, and electric current in electric motors and generators respectively.

FLEMING, Williamina (b. May 15, 1857; Dundee, Scotland; d. May 21, 1911; Boston, Massachusetts) Scottish–American astronomer.

Williamina Paton, as she was born, worked for several years as a schoolteacher. In 1877 she married James Fleming and emigrated with him to Boston, Massachusetts, in 1878. Her marriage broke up and, forced to support her young son, she worked for Edward Pickering, director of the Harvard College Observatory, as a maid. As it was his policy to employ young women at the observatory as computers, Pickering, who quickly recognized her intelligence, offered her temporary employment as a copyist and computer in 1879. She was given a permanent post in 1881. She remained at the observatory for the rest of her life, serving as curator of astronomical photographs from 1899 until her death.

She worked with Pickering on the basic classification of stars into spectral types and was thus involved in the introduction of the original 17 classes arranged alphabetically from A to Q in terms of the intensity of the hydrogen spectral lines. This system was later modified and improved by her colleagues Annie Cannon and Antonia Maury.

Fleming was largely responsible for the classification of over 10000 stars, published in 1890 in the *Draper Catalogue of Stellar Spectra*. In the course of her work she discovered 10 novae and over 200 variable stars, and estimated that by 1910 she had examined nearly 200000 photographic plates.

FLEMMING, Walther (b. Apr. 21, 1843; Sachsenberg, now in East Germany; d. Aug. 4, 1905; Kiel, now in West Germany) German cytologist.

Flemming graduated in medicine from the University of Rostock in 1868 but, after a short period working in a hospital, turned to physiology and became assistant to Willy Kuhne at the Institute of Physiology in Amsterdam. After serving as a physician in the Franco-Prussian War he held professional posts at Prague (1873) and Kiel (1876).

By making use of the newly synthesized aniline dyes Flemming was able to discern the threadlike structures in the cell nucleus, which Heinrich Waldeyer was later to term chromosomes. The new staining techniques made it possible for Flemming to follow in far greater detail the process of cell division, which he named 'mitosis' from the Greek for thread. Most importantly, Flemming detailed the fundamental process of mitosis, that is, the splitting of the chromosomes along their lengths into two identical halves. These results were published in the seminal book *Zell substanz, Kern und Zelltheilung* (1882; Cytoplasm, Nucleus and Cell Division). It was another 20 years before the significance of Flemming's work was truly realized with the rediscovery of Gregor Mendel's rules of heredity.

FLEROV, Georgii Nikolaevich (b. Feb. 17, 1913; Rostov-on-Don, now in the Soviet Union) Soviet nuclear physicist.

Educated at the Leningrad Industrial Institute of Science, Flerov started his career at the Leningrad Institute of Physics and Technology in 1938. He later became chief of the laboratory of multicharged ions at the Kurchatov Institute of Atomic Energy, Moscow. Throughout his life, Flerov has been involved in the search for new elements and isotopes through synthesis and discovery. In many ways his work parallels that of Glenn Theodore Seaborg in America.

Flerov and his co-workers have synthesized and analyzed isotopes of elements 102, 103, 104, 105, 106, and 107 (members of the actinide group and transactinides) by bombarding nuclei of heavy elements with heavy ions in a cyclotron. In particular, they have a claim to the first discovery or identification of transactinide elements 104 (1964) and 107 (1968). The correct attribution of these discoveries is still in dispute. Besides his work on the transuranic elements, Flerov has also been involved in the search, both by synthesis and discovery in nature (possibly in cosmic rays), of the postulated superheavy elements. Many theorists believe that although elements beyond the actinides in the periodic table would be highly unstable, there may be 'islands of stability' at higher atomic numbers, if they can only be reached.

Flerov is now director of the nuclear radiation laboratories of the Joint Institute for Nuclear Research, Dubna, near Moscow, a post he has held since 1960.

FLOREY, Howard Walter, Baron Florey of Adelaide (b. Sept. 24, 1898; Adelaide, Australia; d. Feb. 21, 1968; Oxford, England) Australian experimental pathologist.

Florey was educated in Adelaide and graduated in medicine from the University of Adelaide in 1921. Early in 1922 he arrived in Oxford, England, on a Rhodes scholarship and studied physiology for two years under Charles Sherrington. He then moved to Cambridge University where he studied the various roles and behavior of cells and their constituents for his PhD degree.

In 1931 he was appointed professor of pathology at Sheffield University and for four years studied mucus secretions and the role of the cell in inflammation. He was especially interested in the chemical action of lysozyme (an enzyme discovered in 1921 by Alexander Fleming). which is an antibacterial agent that catalyzes the destruction of the cell walls of certain bacteria.

In 1935 Florey became head of the Sir William Dunn School of Pathology at Oxford. Here, along with the biochemist Ernst Chain, he took up Fleming's neglected studies on *Penicillium* mold and in 1939 they succeeded in extracting an impure form of the highly reactive compound penicillin. Florey's work on penicillin was a natural extension of his earlier antibacterial work, inspired by the necessity for efficient antibiotics in wartime. Work continued over the next few years on the purification of the drug. The main problem was that vast quantities of mold needed to be grown for just a few milligrams of penicillin. In wartime Britain the necessary financial backing for these

innovative biochemical engineering developments could not be obtained, and permission was given to use companies in the US for the manufacture of the drug. The considerable problems of large-scale production were overcome and from 1943 onward sufficient penicillin was available to treat war casualties as well as cases of pneumonia, meningitis, syphilis, and diphtheria.

Florey is important as a scientist who took Fleming's discovery and made it into a workable treatment for disease — 15 years after the original discovery. He shared the Nobel Prize for physiology or medicine with Chain and Fleming in 1945. He had been knighted in 1944, and in 1965 he was awarded a life peerage.

FLORY, Paul John (b. June 19, 1910; Sterling, Illinois) American polymer chemist.

Flory was educated at Ohio State University, where he obtained his PhD in 1934. His career has been divided between industry and university. He worked with Du Pont from 1934 until 1938 on synthetic polymers and then spent the next two years at the University of Cincinnati. After working for Standard Oil from 1940 until 1943, Flory served as director of fundamental research for the Goodyear Tire Company in Akron, Ohio, until 1948. He was then appointed to the chair of chemistry at Cornell. He left Cornell in 1957 to become director of research of the Mellon Institute in Pittsburgh and, finally, in 1961, accepted the chair of chemistry at Stanford University, California.

Flory was one of the people who, in the 1930s, began working on the properties of polymers. A particular problem at the time was that polymer molecules do not have a definite size and structure; a given polymeric material consists of a large number of macromolecules with different chain lengths. Flory approached this problem using statistical methods, obtaining expressions for the distribution of chain lengths.

In further work he developed a theory of

nonlinear polymers, which involve cross linkages between molecular chains. He showed how such extended structures can form from a solution of linear polymers. A particular innovation was the concept of *Flory temperature* — a temperature for a given solution at which meaningful measurements can be made of the properties of the polymer.

In later work Flory considered the elasticity of rubbers and similar polymeric materials. He has published two authoritative books: *Principles of Polymer Chemistry* (1953) and *Statistical Mechanics of Chain Molecules* (1969). For his major contribution in the field Flory was awarded the Nobel Prize for chemistry in 1974.

FLOURENS, Jean Pierre Marie (b. Apr. 13, 1794; Maureilhan, France; d. Dec. 8, 1867; Montgeron, near Paris) French physician and anatomist.

Flourens studied medicine at the University of Montpellier, graduating in 1813. Moving to Paris he was fortunate enough to be taken in hand by the powerful Georges Cuvier, serving as his deputy at the Collège de France from 1828. After Cuvier's death in 1832, Flourens succeeded him as professor of anatomy and secretary of the Académie des Sciences.

In 1824 Flourens published his highly influential *Recherches expérimentales sur les propriétés et les fonctions du système nerveux dans les animaux vertébrés* (Experimental Researches on the Properties and Functions of the Nervous System in Vertebrates) in which he demonstrated the main roles of different parts of the central nervous system. Extending the work of the Italian anatomist Luigi Rolando on the nervous system, Flourens removed various parts of the brain and carefully observed the resulting changes. Thus he found that removal of the cerebral hemispheres of a pigeon destroyed the sense of perception. Removal of the cerebellum destroyed coordination and equilibrium and excision of the medulla oblongata caused respiration to cease. He also exposed the spinal cord of a dog from head to tail and found that while stimulation lower down would produce movement there came a point higher up where no muscular reaction could be elicited. Flourens is also known for important work on the semicircular canals in the ear, demonstrating their function in balance.

Although Flourens assigned different roles to different anatomical parts of the brain he was not prepared to go further and localize different roles and powers within each part. It was not until 1870 that Gustav Fritsch and Eduard Hitzig were able to break this unitary picture and establish cerebral localization experimentally.

Flourens is also remembered for his attack on Darwin in his *Examen du livre de M. Darwin* (1864; Examination of Mr. Darwin's Book) in which he poured scorn on Darwin's "childish and out of date personifications."

FLOYER, Sir John (b. 1649; Hintes, England; d. Feb. 1, 1734; Lichfield, England) English physician.

Floyer graduated MD from Oxford University in 1680, after which he spent most of his life in Lichfield in general practice. In *The Physician's Pulse Watch* (2 vols. 1707–10) he described measuring the pulse with a special pulse watch made to run for exactly one minute, a considerable improvement over the 'string pendulum' of Sanctorius.

He also published a number of works on the therapeutic powers of cold baths, a topic on which he became somewhat obsessive. His work on asthma was important in recognizing the lung condition emphysema in connection with one of the forms of asthma.

FOCK, Vladimir Alexandrovich (b. Dec. 22, 1898) Soviet theoretical physicist.

Fock was educated at the University of Petrograd (now Leningrad) where he graduated in 1922. He later worked at the Leningrad Institute of Physics (1924–36) and in 1939 joined the academy's Institute of Physics. He was also appointed professor of physics at Leningrad University in 1961.

Although Erwin Schrödinger had published a solution of the wave equation for the hydrogen atom in 1926 it was by no means clear how it could be applied to atoms with more than one electron. The problem was solved between 1927 and 1932 by Fock and, independently, R. Hartree who developed the method known as the *Hartree–Fock approximation*. Fock has also worked extensively on problems in general relativity.

FOLKERS, Karl August (b. Sept. 1, 1906; Decatur, Illinois) American organic chemist.

Folkers graduated in chemistry from the University of Illinois in 1928 and gained his PhD from the University of Wisconsin in 1931. After postdoctoral work at Yale he joined the pharmaceutical manufacturers Merck and Company in 1934, becoming director of organic and biochemical research in 1945. He was president of the Stanford Research Institute from 1963 to 1968, and then director of the Institute for Biomedical Research at the University of Texas.

In 1948 Folkers's team isolated the antipernicious anemia factor, vitamin B_{12} (cyanocobalamin) and they played a major role in the lengthy process of determining the structure of this molecule. Folkers has been involved in many investigations of biologically active compounds, especially antibiotics, and the structure of streptomycin was largely determined by his group in 1948.

FORBES, Edward (b. Feb. 12, 1815; Douglas, Isle of Man; d. Nov. 18, 1854; Wardic, near Edinburgh) British naturalist.

Forbes's education was primarily in medicine at Edinburgh University; his interests however included natural history, and in 1833 he visited Norway, collecting mollusks and plants. In 1841–42 he went as naturalist on the HMS *Beacon* to investigate the botany and geology of the Mediterranean and Asia Minor. After lecturing for the Geological Society, Forbes became its curator, and in 1843 was elected to the chair of botany at King's College, London. From 1844 he was paleontologist to the Geological Survey, and subsequently became professor of natural history both at the Royal School of Mines and Edinburgh University.

Forbes traveled widely over Europe, North Africa, and the Middle East, collecting plants and animals (especially mollusks) and studying their relationships. His observations of the littoral zones produced evidence of oceanic sedimentation, while he also investigated molluskan migration, and speculated on the origin and distribution of animal and vegetable life — stimulating later research along these lines. Some of Forbes's most important work was concerned with the starfishes, the British species of which he was the first to classify systematically (*History of British Starfishes*; 1842). His dredging up of a starfish from a depth of a quarter of a mile in the Mediterranean confounded previously held views that life was largely confined to the upper layers of the sea. Forbes also wrote *A History of British Mollusca* (1848–52) and *Naked-eyed Medusae* (1848). His geological investigations of the Purbeck Beds (1849) proved them to be of the Oolitic series.

FORD, Edmund Brisco (b. Apr. 23, 1901; Papcastle, England) British geneticist.

Ford studied at Oxford University and began research there, in collaboration with Julian Huxley, on the genetic control of growth. Together they demonstrated that one type of gene action is to affect the rate rather than nature of chemical reactions. During the same period (1923–26) Ford was also working with Ronald Fisher and was stimulated by Fisher's work on genetic dominance to expand his own work on adaptation and evolution in natural populations.

Having gained his MA in 1927, Ford developed techniques to identify the conditions that promote rapid adaptation and evolution, and then subjected such conditions to ecological investigation. He termed these methods 'ecological genetics' and the application of his methods was later to show that selection for beneficial characters is some 30 to 40 times greater than had been believed — an important consideration in evolutionary studies.

Most of Ford's work was conducted on moths and butterflies. He showed that in a given moth population the amount of genetic diversity corresponds to the population size, proportionally greater variation occurring when numbers are higher. He studied the existence of distinct forms in populations of the butterfly *Maniola jartina* and formulated a definition of such genetic polymorphisms. He speculated that the different human blood groups, which are an example of polymorphism, are maintained by the association of certain blood groups with specific diseases, a theory that was proved correct in 1953.

Ford became professor of ecological genetics at Oxford in 1963 and emeritus professor in 1969. His publications include *Ecological Genetics* (1964) — the culmination of over 30 years' research — and *Genetic Polymorphism* (1965).

FOREST, Lee de *See* DE FOREST, Lee.

FORSSMANN, Werner Theodor Otto (b. Aug. 29, 1904; Berlin; d. June 1, 1979; Schopfheim, West Germany) German surgeon and urologist.

Forssmann was educated at the University of Berlin where he qualified as a physician in 1929. He then worked in the 1930s as a surgeon in various German hospitals. After the war he practiced as a urologist at Bad Kreuznach from 1950 until 1958 when he moved to Düsseldorf as head of surgery at the Evangelical Hospital.

In 1929 Forssmann introduced the procedure of cardiac catheterization into medicine. He was struck by the danger inherent in the direct injection of drugs into the heart frequently demanded in an emergency. The alternative that he proposed sounded no less alarming — introducing a catheter through the venous system from a vein in the elbow directly into the right atrium of the heart. Drugs could then be introduced through this.

After practice on cadavers and an unsuccessful attempt on himself made with the aid of a nervous colleague, Forssmann decided to do the whole thing himself. He consequently introduced a 65-centimeter (25.6-in) catheter for its entire length, walked up several flights of stairs to the x-ray department and calmly confirmed that the tip of the catheter had in fact reached his heart. There had been no pain or discomfort.

Unfortunately further development was inhibited by criticism from the medical profession, which assumed that the method must be dangerous. Consequently it was left to André Cournand and Dickinson Richards to develop the technique into a routine clinical tool in the 1940s; for this work they shared the Nobel Prize in physiology or medicine with Forssmann in 1956.

FOSTER, Sir Michael (b. Mar. 8, 1836; Huntingdon, England; d. Jan. 28, 1907; London) British physiologist.

Foster, the son of a surgeon, was educated at University College, London, where he obtained his MD in 1859, and after several years in private practice with his father, returned in 1867 as a lecturer in physiology. He moved to Cambridge University in 1870 where he later served as the first professor of physiology from 1883 until his retirement in 1903.

Foster's greatest achievement was undoubtedly the Cambridge school of physiology. Just as the late 19th century saw the emergence in Cambridge of a major physics laboratory, the Cavendish, so too did it witness the creation of a major center for physiological research. Foster did much to establish physiology as a major scientific discipline in Cambridge and, indeed, in Britain. He pressed for the construction of new laboratories, produced the *Textbook of Physiology* (1877), and founded the Physiological Society (1875) and the *Journal of Physiology* (1878). From Foster's laboratory there emerged, as clear proof of his success, such scholars as Charles Sherrington, Henry Dale, John Langley, and Walter Gaskell.

Much of Foster's work as a research physiologist was devoted to the problem of the genesis of the heartbeat, namely whether it was under nervous control. The role of the vagus nerve in inhibiting the heartbeat had been known since the 1840s, as had the presence of nervous ganglia in the heart itself. Against such impressive evidence Foster pointed out, in 1859, that in the snail's heart neither the inhibitory nerve or ganglia could be found, yet small pieces taken from it would continue to contract rhythmically for some time. He concluded from this that the cause of the heartbeat was a 'peculiar property of general cardiac tissue'. Several years later this work was extended and confirmed by Gaskell.

After 1880 Foster did little original work, being more concerned with the demands of his growing organization. When he began there were 20 students studying physiology at Cambridge; when he retired there were over 300.

FOUCAULT, Jean Bernard Léon (b. Sept. 19, 1819; Paris; d. Feb. 11, 1868; Paris) French physicist.

Foucault, the son of a bookseller, originally intended to study medicine, but transferred his interest to physical science. In 1855 he became a physicist at the Paris Observatory.

His main work was on measurements of the speed of light. He helped Armand Fizeau in his toothed-wheel experiment and, in 1850, took over D.F.J. Arago's experiments on comparing the speed of light in air with that in water. The experiment was important for distinguishing between the wave and particle theories of light: the wave theory predicted that light should travel faster in air than in water; the particle theory predicted the opposite. In 1850, Foucault showed that the wave-theory prediction was correct. In 1862 he obtained the first accurate value for the speed of light using a rotating-mirror apparatus.

Foucault also worked on other topics. Thus he noted (1849) that a bright yellow line in the spectrum of sodium corresponded to a dark line in the Fraunhofer spectrum, although he failed to follow this up.

His most famous experiments began in 1850 and involved pendulums. While trying to construct an accurate timing device for his work on light, he noticed that a pendulum remained swinging in the same plane when he rotated the apparatus. He then used a pendulum to demonstrate the rotation of the Earth. Over a long period of time the plane in which a pendulum is swinging will appear to rotate. In fact the pendulum swings in a fixed plane relative to the fixed stars, and the Earth rotates 'underneath' it.

At the Earth's poles, the plane of the pendulum will make one full rotation every 24 hours; this period increases as the equator is approached. Foucault derived an equation relating the time of rotation to the latitude. He also gave public exhibitions of the effect, including one in which he suspended an iron ball of 28 kilograms (62 lbs) by steel wire 67 meters (222 ft) long from the dome of the Panthéon in Paris. Foucault also invented the gyroscope.

FOURCROY, Antoine François de (b. June 15, 1755; Paris; d. Dec. 16; 1809; Paris) French chemist.

Fourcroy grew up in poverty and began to study medicine in 1773. Graduating in 1780, he became professor of chemistry at the Jardin du Roi in 1784. He was an excellent lecturer, a prolific writer, and played a leading role in the scientific life of France. He helped to found the Ecole de Santé (1795) and the Ecole Polytechnique (1795) and was minister of public instruction under Napoleon (1802–08). With Louis Nicolas Vauquelin he carried out many researches, especially on natural products, and they were the first to prepare a relatively pure form of urea and to name this compound. Fourcroy was an important advocate of the chemical system of Antione Lavoisier, which he taught from 1786. Among his many writings was the massive *Système de connaissance chimique* (1801–02; System of Chemical Knowledge).

FOURIER, Baron (Jean Baptiste) Joseph (b. Mar. 21, 1768; Auxerre, France; d. May 16, 1830; Paris) French mathematician.

Fourier, the son of a tailor, was educated at the local military school and later at the Ecole Normale in Paris. He held posts at both the Ecole Normale and the Ecole Polytechnique where he was a very effective and influential teacher. In 1798 he accompanied Napoleon on the invasion of Egypt and later contributed to and oversaw the publication of the *Description de l'Egypte* (1808–25), a massive compilation of the cultural and scientific materials brought back from the expedition.

Fourier's most important mathematical work is contained in his *Théorie analytique de la chaleur* (1822; The Analytical Theory of Heat), a pioneering analysis of the conduction of heat in solid bodies in terms of infinite trigonometric series, now known as *Fourier series*. Fourier was led to consider these series when attempting to solve certain boundary-value problems in physics and his interest was always in the physical applications of mathematics rather than in its development for its own sake. His work continues to be extremely important in many areas of mathematical physics, but it has also been developed and generalized to yield a whole new branch of mathematical analysis, namely, the theory of harmonic analysis.

FOURNEAU, Ernest François Auguste (b. Oct. 4, 1872; Biarritz, France; d. Aug. 5, 1949; Ascain, France) French medicinal chemist and pharmacologist.

After graduating from the Lyceum of Bayonne, Fourneau worked in a Paris hospital pharmacy (1892–96) before becoming director of the research laboratories at the pharmaceutical manufacturers Poulenc Frères (1900–1912). From 1912 to 1942 he was head of the therapeutic chemistry laboratories at the Pasteur Institute. In 1924 he synthesized suramin, an effective drug against African sleeping sickness, which had first been discovered by the German Bayer company in 1920 but had not been published by them. This was followed by acetarsol (1926), an amebicide, and plasmocid (1930), an antimalarial agent. In 1935, working with the newly discovered antibacterial dye, Prontosil, he showed that its metabolite, now known as sulfanilamide, was the active part of the molecule.

FOURNEYRON, Benoît (b. Oct. 31, 1802; Saint-Etienne, France; d. July 31, 1837; Paris) French engineer and inventor.

Fourneyron, whose father was a mathematician, studied at the then newly opened Saint-Etienne engineering school until 1816. His professor, Claude Burdin, had written a paper describing a new kind of waterwheel called a 'turbine'. This design principle is now basic to electricity generators and many propulsion engines, but Burdin's paper was rejected by the French Academy of Sciences and by the Society for the Encouragement of Industry. Fourneyron, while he was working in an ironworks at Le Creuset, studied the idea and, in 1827, actually built a six-horsepower unit, in which the force of water flowing outward from a central source on to angled blades turned a rotor.

Ten years later, Fourneyron built a turbine with a one-foot- (30-cm-) diameter wheel, which could turn at 2300 revolutions per minute and had an efficiency of 80%. Weighing only 40 pounds (18 kg), it was very much smaller than an equivalent waterwheel and could be mounted horizontally with a vertical shaft. Fourneyron thought of building steam turbines but was unable to do so because, at that time, no suitable materials and manufacturing techniques were available.

FOWLER, Alfred (b. Mar. 22, 1868; Bradford, England; d. June 24, 1940; London) British astrophysicist.

Fowler's parents were poor but he gained a scholarship and in 1882 went to the Normal School of Science (later to become the Royal College of Science and now part of Imperial College, London). After graduating with a diploma in mechanics, he became assistant to Norman Lockyer at the Solar Physics Observatory in South Kensington, London. He remained there after Lockyer's retirement in 1901, being made professor of astrophysics in 1915. Finally, from 1923 to 1934 he served as Yarrow Research Professor of the Royal Society. Fowler was one of the leading figures behind the founding of the International Astronomical Union in 1919, serving as its first general secretary until 1925.

Not surprisingly Fowler worked very much in the Lockyer tradition of solar and stellar spectroscopy. He became particularly skilled in identifying difficult spectra, using his experience in producing different spectra in the laboratory. He thus detected magnesium hydride in sunspots and carbon monoxide in the tails of comets, and showed that the band spectra of cool M-type stars were due to titanium oxide. In addition, following the announcement in 1913 of the Bohr theory of the atom (see Niels Bohr), Fowler was out-standing in analyzing the structure of atoms from their spectral characteristics.

FOWLER, William Alfred (b. Aug. 9, 1911; Pittsburgh, Pennsylvania) American physicist.

Fowler graduated in 1933 from Ohio State University and obtained his PhD in 1936 from the California Institute of Technology. He was immediately appointed to the Cal Tech staff, was professor of physics there from 1946 to 1970, and since 1970 has been Institute Professor.

Fowler has worked mainly in nuclear physics, especially on the nuclear reactions that occur in stars and by which energy is produced and the elements synthesized, on nuclear forces, and on nuclear spectroscopy. In 1957 Margaret and Geoffrey Burbidge, Fred Hoyle, and Fowler published a key paper dealing with the problem of the creation of the chemical elements. Their aim was to show how the elements could be produced in the interiors of stars without having to introduce such singularities as the hot 'big bang' proposed by George Gamow. The synthesis involved nuclear reactions that could occur at the immense temperatures of stellar cores; the type of process changed, and hence changed the elements being produced, as the temperature increased and conditions altered inside the stars. A later and fuller version was published by Fowler and Hoyle in their *Nucleosynthesis in Massive Stars and Supernovae* (1965).

Fowler has since worked on such fundamental questions as the amount of helium and deuterium in the universe, the answers to such questions having profound implications for knowledge of the age and future development of the universe.

FOX, Harold Munro (b. Sept. 28, 1889; London; d. Jan. 29, 1967; London) British zoologist.

Fox (originally Fuchs) the son of an officer in the Prussian army, was educated at

FOX

Cambridge University, England, where, after war service, he served as a fellow from 1920 to 1928. He then moved to Birmingham as professor of zoology, a post he held until 1941 when he accepted a similar chair at Bedford College, London, where he remained until his retirement in 1954.

Fox, a zoologist of wide interests, is best known for his work on invertebrate blood pigments. In 1871 Ray Lankester had noted that the red blood of the water flea *Daphnia*, a crustacean, was due to the presence of the pigment hemoglobin. Other crustaceans, such as lobsters, were blue-blooded with the pigment hemocyanin in their blood.

It had been observed that the transparent *Daphnia* could become redder or paler by synthesizing or breaking down blood hemoglobin. This was done at a rate far in excess of that noted in any other creature. Fox showed by laboratory experiments in the 1940s that the response was controlled by the level of dissolved oxygen in the water. If this were low, hemoglobin, with its affinity for oxygen, was synthesized; if high, *Daphnia* lose their hemoglobin and become colorless.

Earlier, in 1923, Fox had repeated the controversial experiments of Paul Kammerer on the supposed elongations produced in the siphons of the sea squirt *Ciona intestinalis*. He reported that in none of the operated animals was there any further growth of the siphons once the original length had been attained, and went on to suggest that Kammerer's results could have been produced by keeping the animals in a highly nutritious solution, an explanation Kammerer was quick to dismiss.

FOX, Sidney Walter (b. Mar. 24, 1912; Los Angeles, California) American biochemist.

Fox was educated at the University of California, Los Angeles, and at the California Institute of Technology, where he obtained his PhD in 1940. He taught briefly at Berkeley and the University of Michigan before moving to Iowa State

University in 1943, serving as professor of biochemistry from 1947 until 1954. Fox then moved to Florida State University as professor of chemistry, joining the University of Miami in 1964 to take up an appointment as director of the Institute of Molecular and Cellular Evolution.

Biochemists dealing with the origin of life at some time or other have to face the problem of which came first, proteins or nucleic acids? In this classic dispute Fox has placed himself firmly in favor of the protein-first hypothesis.

He demonstrated in 1958 the existence of what he termed 'proteinoids', polymers of amino acids produced by the application of heat alone. Furthermore he found that on cooling, the proteinoids produce microspheres — tiny spheres, a micrometer or two in diameter, apparently resembling bacteria and supposed by Fox to be protocells. Since they appeared to develop some kind of membrane, produced buds, and sometimes divided, the comparison was far from outrageous. One further significant consideration is that the proteinoids are not just a random grouping of amino acids; a selection principle of some kind operates to give preference to some amino acids over others. There is, however, a major difficulty implicit in Fox's work. To construct the proteinoids he has been forced to use an above-average concentration of the amino acids lysine, glutamic acid, and aspartic acid, and it is unlikely that the early terrestrial environment consisted of such a specialized distribution of amino acids.

FRACASTORO, Girolamo (b. *c.* 1478; Verona, Italy; d. Aug. 6, 1553; Verona) Italian physician.

Fracastoro was educated at the University of Padua where he graduated in 1502. He taught logic there until 1508, when he returned to the family estates at Incaffi, near Verona. He thereafter seems to have divided his time between practicing medicine in Verona and attending to the family estates.

278

Fracastoro was the author of two important medical works. The first, written as the poem, *Syphilis sive morbus Gallicus* (1530; Syphilis or the French Disease) introduced the term 'syphilis' into most European languages. Syphilis seems to have appeared first in Europe at the end of the 15th century with the siege of Naples by the French army of Charles VIII. Called the 'Mal de Naples' by the French and the 'Mal Francese' by the Neapolitans, the disease spread rapidly throughout Europe. It was because of this rapidity that Fracastoro rejected the even then popular view attributing the infection to the New World. His descriptions of the symptoms suggest syphilis was then more virulent that it is now.

The second work of Fracastoro, *De contagione et contagiosis morbis* (1546; On Contagion and Contagious Diseases), is claimed to be a precursor of the germ theory of disease. He distinguished three types of infection: by direct contact, by indirect contact through an intermediary, and those, like some fevers, that appear to operate at a distance. He spoke of 'seeds of contagion', imperceptible and passing from person to person, which he believed could generate more identical germs. Having made such a theoretical advance in introducing his 'seminaria contagium' it was difficult to see what further steps could be taken at that time. Consequently his work remained an isolated curiosity rather than a part of the main tradition of medicine.

Fracastoro also, in 1538, published an astronomical work, *Homocentrica sive de stellis liber* (Homocentricity or the Book of Stars), which attempted to eliminate the epicycles and eccentrics from the geocentric system of Ptolemy and replace them with the original concentric spheres of Eudoxus. This work influenced Copernicus, a contemporary of Fracastoro at Padua.

FRAENKEL-CONRAT, Heinz L. (b. July 29, 1910; Breslau, now Wroclaw in Poland) German–American biochemist.

Fraenkel-Conrat, son of the noted gynecologist Ludwig Fraenkel, left Germany for Britain after graduating MD from the University of Breslau in 1934. He gained his PhD for work on ergot alkaloids and thiamine from the University of Edinburgh in 1936 and then moved on to America, where he settled and became an American citizen in 1941. He joined the faculty of the University of California at Berkeley in 1951, becoming professor of virology in 1958 and later professor of molecular biology.

Fraenkel-Conrat, working with the tobacco mosaic virus (TMV), an RNA virus, provided evidence that RNA, like DNA, can act as the genetic material. This he did by separating the RNA and protein portions of the virus, and then reassembling them to make a fully infective virus. Moreover Fraenkel-Conrat demonstrated that, while the isolated protein was quite dead, the isolated RNA showed slight signs of infectivity. This work was reported in a paper by Fraenkel-Conrat and Robley C. Williams *Reconstitution of Tobacco Mosaic Virus from Its Inactive Protein and Nucleic Acid Components* (1955). In later work with Wendell Stanley the complete amino-acid sequence, consisting of 158 amino acids, of the TMV protein was established.

Fraenkel-Conrat has written a number of virology texts and has also done important work on snake neurotoxins.

FRANCIS, Thomas Jr. (b. July 15, 1900; Gas City, Indiana; d. Oct. 1, 1969; Ann Arbor, Michigan) American virologist.

Francis, the son of a methodist clergyman, was educated at Allegheny College and Yale where he obtained his MD in 1925. He worked with the Rockefeller Institute from 1925 to 1938 and, after serving as professor and chairman of bacteriology at the New York University College of Medicine, moved to the University of Michigan in 1941 as professor of epidemology, a post he retained until his death.

Francis became known to a wide public when, in 1954, he reported on the Salk polio vaccine trial. Before this however he had worked for over 20 years on the epidemiology of the influenza virus. The first such virus, the A-type, had been detected by Christopher Andrewes and his colleagues in 1933. In the following year Francis found a further strain of the A-type, the PR 8, present in the Puerto Rican epidemic of 1934. In 1940 he went on to detect a completely distinct type, B, with no immunological relationship to the A-type.

The US Army, fearful of a repeat of the 1918 flu epidemic, set up in 1941 a commission to develop a vaccine and asked Francis to be its chairman. By 1942 he was ready to vaccinate 8000 soldiers with his vaccine but, perversely, flu was scarce that year. It was not until 1943 that he was able to report that those vaccinated were 70% less likely to be hospitalized compared with the control group. This encouraged the army to vaccinate some 1 250 000 troops in 1947 but this time it disconcertingly seemed to offer no protection at all.

It soon became clear to Francis why the vaccine had failed — the arrival of a new strain of A-type virus, known as A^1. Francis was thus able to present the dilemma facing flu epidemologists, namely that while it was certainly possible to develop a vaccine against flu it was more than likely that it would end up as a vaccine against yesterday's flu.

FRANCK, James (b. Aug. 26, 1882; Hamburg, now in West Germany; d. May 21, 1964; Göttingen, West Germany) German-American physicist.

Franck, the son of a banker, was educated at Heidelberg and Berlin where he obtained his doctorate in 1906. After distinguished war service, in which he won two iron crosses, he was appointed to the chair of experimental physics at Göttingen. Although exempt from the 1933 Nazi law that excluded Jews from public office because of his military service, he insisted on publicly resigning. After spending a year in Copenhagen, he emigrated to America in 1935 where he served as professor of physical chemistry at the University of Chicago from 1938–49.

In collaboration with Gustav Hertz he produced experimental evidence of the quantized nature of energy transfer, work that won them the 1925 Nobel Physics Prize. Their experiment, conducted in 1914, consisted of bombarding mercury atoms with electrons. Most of the electrons simply bounced off losing no energy in the process. When the velocity of electrons was increased it was found that on collision with mercury atoms they lost precisely 4.9 electronvolts of energy. If an electron possessed less energy than 4.9 eV it lost none at all on collision; if it had more than 4.9 eV it made no difference — only 4.9 eV was absorbed by the mercury atoms. Franck and Hertz had thus succeeded in showing that energy can only be absorbed in quite definite and precise amounts. For mercury the minimum amount was 4.9 eV. Their results were quickly confirmed and shown to hold for other atoms.

In America Franck worked mainly on the physical chemistry involved in photosynthesis although he is better known as the author of the *Franck report* published in 1946. This report, actually produced by a number of distinguished scientists of whom Leo Szilard was probably the most important, was sent to the Secretary of State for War in June 1945. It argued that it was unnecessary to drop the recently produced atomic bomb on Japan as its explosion on a barren island would be sufficient to force the Japanese into submission.

FRANK, Ilya Mikhailovich (b. Oct. 23, 1908; St. Petersburg, now Leningrad in the Soviet Union) Soviet physicist.

Frank was educated at Moscow University and, after working at the State Optical Institute from 1930 to 1934, was made an associate of the Physics Institute of the Soviet Academy of Sciences. In 1944 he was appointed professor of physics at Moscow University.

Frank and Igor Tamm first gave an explanation of the radiation discovered in 1934 by Pavel Cherenkov (q.v.). This occurs when a charged particle is traveling through a medium faster than the speed of light in that medium. The particle displaces electrons in the atoms of a medium and an electromagnetic wave is produced. The effect is similar to the sonic boom produced when a body moves faster than sound in air.

Frank, Cherenkov, and Tamm shared the Nobel Physics Prize in 1958.

FRANKLAND, Sir Edward (b. Jan. 18, 1825; Churchtown, near Lancaster, England; d. Aug. 9, 1899; Golaa, Norway) British organic chemist.

Frankland was first apprenticed to a pharmacist at Lancaster but was encouraged to go to London to study chemistry under Lyon Playfair at the Royal College of Engineers (1845). He became Playfair's assistant in 1847 and studied extensively in Europe with Robert Bunsen and Justus von Liebig. He succeeded Playfair as professor of chemistry in 1850, holding the same position at Owens College, Manchester, (1851–57) and in London at St. Bartholomew's Hospital (1857), the Royal Institution (1863), and the Royal School of Mines (1865), later the Royal College of Science.

Frankland's first important work was on methylalkyls (1849). He prepared zinc methyl and zinc ethyl but, being at that time an adherent of the radical theory, was led into the error of believing that 'methyl hydride' and 'ethyl hydride' (actually both ethane) were different compounds.

Frankland is generally credited as the originator of the theory of valence — valence being the number of chemical bonds that an atom or group can make with other atoms or groups in forming a compound. In 1852 he noticed that coordination with an alkyl group could change the combining power of a metal. He

showed that the concept of valence could reconcile the radical and type theories and in 1866 he elaborated the concept of a maximum valence for each element.

In 1864, working with B.F. Duppa, Frankland pointed out that the carboxyl group (which he called 'oxatyl') is a constant feature of the series of organic acids. He was also interested in applied chemistry: he investigated the luminosity of flames and his later work was in the field of coal-gas supply and water purification. He was knighted in 1897.

FRANKLIN, Benjamin (b. Jan. 17, 1706; Boston, Massachusetts; d. Apr. 17, 1790; Philadelphia, Pennsylvania) American scientist, statesman, diplomat, printer, and inventor.

Franklin's father left England in 1682 and settled in Boston in the following year where he worked as a candle maker and soap boiler. Although originally intended for the clergy, Franklin was forced to leave school at the age of ten for financial reasons and after helping his father for some time was apprenticed to his brother, a printer, in 1718.

He continued his trade as a printer in London (1724–26), and thereafter in Philadelphia where he published, from 1729, the *Pennsylvania Gazette* and, from 1733, the hugely successful *Poor Richard's Almanac*. Shortly afterward Franklin began his life in public affairs serving as clerk of the State Assembly (1736–51) and as deputy postmaster representing the colonies (1753–74), during which he saw further service in London (1757–62; 1764–75). On his return to America Franklin played an active role in the revolution and was one of the five who drafted the Declaration of Independence in 1776. He was sent to France in 1776 to seek military and financial aid for the colonies and largely through his own popularity succeeded in achieving an alliance in 1778. Returning to America in 1785, he performed his last public duty as a member of the Constitution Convention in 1787 before retiring from public life in 1788.

Despite such an active political and public life Franklin also made a number of important contributions to 18th-century physical theory in the period 1743–52. By conversation with scholars in London, reading, and correspondence with friends his interest in the newly discovered phenomena of electricity had been aroused.

Franklin would have known of the work of Stephen Gray and Charles Dufay and the basic distinction established between electrics (such as glass and amber), which could be electrified by rubbing, and nonelectrics (such as metals), which resisted such treatment. Electrics were further divided into vitreous, such as glass, and resinous, such as amber. Dufay had concluded that there were two distinct electric fluids — the vitreous and the resinous — in his two-fluid theory.

Franklin agreed with Dufay that electricity was a fluid. More significant properties of electricity emerged out of Franklin's experiments from 1747 onward. From these experiments, including those on the Leyden jar, Franklin devised his one-fluid theory of electricity. He also introduced the terminology of 'positive' and 'negative' into the science.

Practical gains emerged from Franklin's discovery that lightning is an electric charge. He knew that the electric fluid was attracted by points but wondered if lightning would also be attracted. In 1752 he performed his famous, yet hazardous, experiment with a kite during a thunderstorm and established the identity of lightning with electricity. Following this he suggested the use of lightning rods on tall buildings to conduct electricity away from the building and direct to ground.

Franklin also published works on the problems of light, heat, and dynamics. Outside of physics Franklin's most important scientific work was in oceanography with his study of the Gulf Stream. He measured its temperature at different places and depths, estimated the current's velocity, and analyzed its effects on the weather. From reports supplied to him by Nantucket sea captains he also constructed the first printed chart of the Gulf Stream. Franklin is also remembered for his large number of inventions that included (in addition to his lightning rod) bifocal spectacles, the rocking chair, and an efficient stove.

FRANKLIN, Rosalind (b. July 25, 1920; London; d. Apr. 16, 1958; London) British x-ray crystallographer.

After graduating from Cambridge University, Franklin joined the staff of the British Coal Utilisation Research Association in 1942, moving in 1947 to the Laboratoire Centrale des Services Chimique de L'Etat in Paris. She returned to England in 1950 and held research appointments at London University, initially at King's College from 1951 to 1953 and thereafter at Birkbeck College until her untimely death from cancer at the age of 37.

Franklin played a major part in the discovery of the structure of DNA by James Watson and Francis Crick. With the unflattering and distorted picture presented by Watson in his *The Double Helix* (1968) her role in this has become somewhat controversial. At King's, she had been recruited to work on biological molecules and her director, John Randall, had specifically instructed her to work on the structure of DNA. When she later learned that Maurice Wilkins, a colleague at King's, also intended to work on DNA, she felt unable to cooperate with him. Nor did she feel much respect for the early attempts of Watson and Crick in Cambridge to establish the structure.

The causes of friction were various ranging from simple personality clashes to, it has been said, male hostility to the invasion of their private club by a woman. Despite this unsatisfactory background Franklin did obtain results without which the structure established by Watson and Crick would have been at the least delayed. The most important of these was her x-ray photograph of hydrated DNA, the so-called

B form, the most revealing such photograph then available. Watson first saw it in 1952 at a seminar given by Franklin, and recognized that it clearly indicated a helix. Franklin also appreciated, unlike Watson and Crick, that in the DNA molecule the phosphate groups lie on the outside rather than inside the helix.

Despite such insights it was Watson and Crick who first realized that DNA has a double helix. By March 1953 Franklin had overcome her earlier opposition to helical structures and was in fact producing a draft paper on 17 March, 1953, in which she proposed a double-chain helical structure for DNA. It did not, however, contain the crucial idea of base pairing, nor did she realize that the two chains must run in opposite directions. She first heard of the Watson–Crick model on the following day.

FRASCH, Herman (b. Dec. 25, 1851; Gaildorf, now in West Germany; d. May 1, 1914; Paris) German–American industrial chemist.

The son of a wealthy apothecary, Frasch was educated in Halle and was apprenticed to an apothecary before emigrating to America in 1868. He worked in the field of petroleum chemistry and in 1876 he joined the Standard Oil Company in Cleveland.

In 1882 Frasch developed a process for reducing the sulfur content of poor-quality crude oil through the use of metallic oxides, thus making it commercially acceptable, and in 1884 he bought such a field at London, Ontario. When, in 1886, Standard Oil discovered high-sulfur oil in Ohio Frasch rejoined them as a part-time consultant to solve the problem. From sulfur as an impurity he turned to the problems of extracting sulfur as a product in its own right. In 1894 he was the first to raise sulfur from deep underground by means of superheated water. In the *Frasch process* three concentric pipes are sunk down to the sulfur deposit. Superheated water is pumped down the outside pipe to liquefy the sulfur, which is forced up the middle pipe by compressed air passed down the center pipe. The process became a commercial proposition in 1900 thanks largely to the availability of cheap local oil to heat the water. Frasch had a 50% share in the company, Union Sulfur, and the Sicilian sulfur monopoly was broken. Eventually other companies used the process, Frasch lost his patent-infringement actions, and his company faded away.

FRAUNHOFER, Josef von (b. Mar. 6, 1787; Straubing, now in West Germany; d. June 7, 1826; Munich, now in West Germany) German physicist and optician.

Fraunhofer's family was in the optical trade and he was apprenticed to an optician in Munich after his parents died. He subsequently moved to the Utzschneider optical institute near Munich.

His great ambition was to perfect the achromatic lens, which John Dollond had developed a century earlier, and his scientific discoveries came as by-products of this work. The major difficulty was to measure the refractive indices of the different types of glass used in these lenses. In 1814, while testing prisms in order to determine these constants, he observed that the Sun's spectrum was covered with fine dark lines. He also noticed that these *Fraunhofer lines* occurred in the spectra of bright stars, but that their positions were different. The lines had been observed earlier by William Wollaston, but Fraunhofer studied them in detail, measuring the positions of 576 of them and giving the main ones letters A–G. He also found the lines to be present in spectra produced by reflection from a grating (1821–22), thus proving them to be a characteristic of the light, not the glass of the prism.

Fraunhofer had in his grasp the key to finding the composition of the stars, but this step was taken half a century later by Gustav Kirchhoff (q.v.), who showed that lines in the solar spectrum resulted from characteristic absorption by elements in the atmosphere of the Sun.

FREDHOLM, Erik Ivar (b. Apr. 7, 1866; Stockholm; d. Aug. 17, 1927; Stockholm) Swedish mathematician.

Fredholm, who was a pioneer in the theory of integral equations, studied at the Stockholm Polytechnic Institute, the University of Stockholm and the University of Uppsala, from which he received his doctorate in 1898. The same year he was appointed lecturer in mathematical physics at the University of Stockholm, becoming professor there in 1906.

In the field of mathematical physics Fredholm's work on the deformation of anisotropic media (such as crystals) led him to the study of partial differential equations. His most important work was on integral equations establishing the field in which David Hilbert was to do some of his greatest work. A number of results and concepts are named for him including the *Fredholm integral equations* and the *Fredholm operator*.

FREGE, (Friedrich Ludwig) Gottlob (b. Nov. 8, 1848; Wismar, now in East Germany; d. July 26, 1925; Bad Keinen, now in East Germany) German philosopher and mathematician.

Frege studied at the universities of Jena and Göttingen, where he obtained his PhD in 1873. He then returned to Jena as a lecturer, where he remained for the rest of his working life, rising to the position of professor in 1896.

In a series of seminal works Frege laid the foundations of modern mathematical logic, transforming logic with an understanding of and notation for the problem of multiple generality — propositions containing predicates, quantifiers, and variables — and showing how the basic concepts and operations of mathematics could be formalized. He also revolutionized modern philosophy through his influence on the philosophy of language. However Frege's work was almost completely ignored, misunderstood, or treated with hostility by his contemporaries — notable

exceptions were Bertrand Russell and Giuseppe Peano.

In *Die Grundlagen der Arithmetik* (1884; The Foundations of Arithmetic) Frege gave a formal definition of cardinal number and showed how basic properties of numbers could be logically derived from it. In *Grundgesetze der Arithmetik* (1893 and 1903; Basic Laws of Arithmetic) he went further in attempting to derive arithmetic from formal logic. The *Grundgesetze* is still regarded as a massive achievement, but his main aim was doomed to failure. On the eve of the publication of the second volume Russell wrote to Frege pointing out a contradiction — Russell's paradox (see Bertrand Russell) — that could be derived from his system. This, as Frege acknowledged, vitiated his whole project.

FRESNEL, Augustin Jean (b. May 10, 1788; Broglie, France; d. July 14, 1827; Ville-d'Avray, France) French physicist.

Fresnel grew up in the time of the French Revolution but, by the time he was 26, Napoleon had been exiled and Louis XVIII was on the throne. At this time Fresnel was a qualified engineer but, when Napoleon returned from Elba, Fresnel supported the royalists and lost his job as a result.

Fresnel started studying optics in 1814 and was one of the major supporters of the wave theory of light. He worked on interference, at first being unaware of the work of Thomas Young (q.v.), and produced a number of devices for giving interference effects. *Fresnel's biprism* is a single prism formed of two identical narrow-angled prisms base-to-base. Placed in front of a single source it splits the beam into two parts, which can produce interference fringes. Initially, Fresnel believed that light was a longitudinal wave motion, but he later decided that it must be transverse to account for the phenomenon of polarization.

Another important part of Fresnel's work was his development of optical systems for lighthouses. He invented the

Fresnel lens — a lens with a stepped surface — to replace the heavy metal mirrors that were in use at the time.

Fresnel became a member of the French Academy of Sciences in 1823 and four years later, shortly before he died, the Royal Society awarded him the Rumford medal.

FREUD, Sigmund (b. May 6, 1856; Freiberg, now Příbor in Czechoslovakia; d. Sept. 23, 1939; London) Austrian psychoanalyst.

The son of a wool merchant, Freud graduated from the University of Vienna with an MD in 1881 having also spent much time in the study of physiology. He worked at the Vienna General Hospital until 1885 and, after a further period of study in Paris under the neurologist Jean-Martin Charcot, set up in private practice in Vienna in the same year. He took the post of part-time head of the neurological outpatients clinic at the Children's Hospital and also held the position of *Privatdozent* in neuropathology at the University of Vienna.

Before Freud worked out the basic principles of psychoanalysis in the 1890s he had produced a substantial body of research in more orthodox fields. In addition to early work on comparative neuroanatomy, he discovered the euphoric effects of cocaine in 1884 and produced two sizable monographs — one on aphasia (1891) and the other on paralysis in children (1893).

By this time he had developed a more ambitious research program, clearly stated in his unpublished *Project for a Scientific Psychology* (1895). In this unfinished work he aimed to explain 'the theory of mental functioning' in terms of quantitative physical concepts that would apply to both normal and abnormal psychology. To this end he went into considerable detail, even supposing the existence of three types of neurones with different physiological properties.

Freud however drew back from such a neurological approach. In 1893 he collaborated with Josef Breuer on *The Psychical Mechanism of Hysterical Phenomena*, later expanded into *Studien über Hysterie* (1895; Studies in Hysteria, 1955), a work that marked the beginning of psychoanalysis. During the period 1892–95 Freud evolved his psychoanalytical method using the technique of free association. Following this he developed his theory that neuroses were rooted in suppressed sexual desires.

Freud's major work, *Die Traumdeutung* (1899; The Interpretation of Dreams, 1953), is regarded as his most original. In this he analyzed dreams in terms of unconscious desires and experiences. His other works included *Zur Psychopathologie des Alltagslebens* (1904; Psychopathology of Everyday Life, 1960), *Totem und Tabu* (1913; Totem and Taboo, 1955), *Jenseits des Lustprinzips* (1920; Beyond the Pleasure Principle, 1955), and *Das Ich und das Es* (1923; The Ego and the Id, 1961).

In 1902 Freud established a circle of colleagues who met to discuss psychoanalytical matters once a week at his house. The group's original members were Alfred Adler, Max Kahane, Rudolf Reitler, and Wilhelm Stekel. This grew, and later became the Vienna Psycho-Analytical Society (1908), and finally, the International Psycho-Analytical Association (1910). Freud, now becoming famous in Europe, made a tour of America in 1909 where he was well received. By 1911 the International Psycho-Analytical Association had begun to break up through differences of opinion, Carl Jung and Adler being among the most significant to leave. However, by the 1920s Freud had become one of the most famous thinkers of the century.

In 1923 Freud was diagnosed as having cancer of the jaw. During the next 16 years he was to suffer more than 30 operations and be compelled to live with a prosthesis which, by substituting for his excised jaw and palette, allowed him to eat, drink, smoke, and talk. In 1938 he was forced to leave Vienna by the Nazis for exile in London. He continued to see patients and to work on his last book, *Der Mann Moses und die monotheistische Religion* (1939; Moses and Monotheism, 1960), but within a matter of months it was clear to him that he could work no more. It was then that he reminded his doctor: "My dear Schur ... you promised you would help me when I could no longer carry on." Schur honored his pledge with morphine ensuring a peaceful death.

FREUNDLICH, Herbert Max Finlay (b. Jan. 28, 1880; Charlottenburg, now in West Berlin; d. Mar. 30, 1941; Minneapolis, Minnesota) German–American physical chemist.

Freundlich studied physical chemistry at Munich and at Leipzig where he became assistant to Wilhelm Ostwald. From 1911 to 1917 he was professor at the Institute of Technology in Brunswick. He was professor at the Kaiser Wilhelm Institute, Berlin-Dahlem, from 1917 to 1934 when he left Germany because of the Nazi regime. He traveled first to Britain and worked at University College, London, and from 1938 to his death was professor of colloid chemistry at the University of Minnesota.

Freundlich's life work was in colloid chemistry. He showed how colloid stability was changed by the addition of electrolytes and he is well known for the *Freundlich adsorption isotherm*, a theoretical formula for the amount of adsorption on a surface at constant temperature.

FREY-WYSSLING, Albert Friedrich (b. Nov. 8, 1900; Küsnacht, Switzerland) Swiss botanist.

Frey-Wyssling graduated in biology from the Federal Institute of Technology, Zurich, in 1923 and gained his PhD the following year. He then studied optics at the University of Jena followed by plant physiology at the Sorbonne. From 1928 to 1932 he was plant physiologist at the Rubber Experimental Station in Medan, Sumatra, where he investigated latex flow.

On his return to Switzerland he took up a lectureship at the Federal Institute of Technology becoming professor of botany in 1938.

Frey-Wyssling was concerned about the rift in biology between histologists and biochemists and decided to help unite the two camps by promoting research in the intermediate area of submicroscopic morphology. To this end he reintroduced research with the polarizing microscope, using it to study, indirectly, the structure of macromolecules, which are beyond the resolving power of the light microscope. Many of his results were corroborated by the work of x-ray crystallographers, such as William Astbury, and later verified directly when the electron microscope was introduced in 1940. His work on 'macromolecular chemistry' helped lay the foundations of ultrastructural research and molecular biology.

Frey-Wyssling published a number of books, including (with K. Mühlethaler) *Ultrastructural Plant Cytology* (1959) and *Plant Cell Walls* (1976).

FRIEDEL, Charles (b. Mar. 12, 1832; Strasbourg, now in France; d. Apr. 20, 1899; Montauban, France) French chemist.

After studying at Strasbourg with Louis Pasteur and at the Sorbonne with Charles Adolphe Wurtz, Friedel became curator of the mineral collections at the mining school in Paris (1856). Although his most important work was in organic chemistry, he also did much work on the synthesis of minerals. In 1862 he discovered secondary propyl alcohol, thus verifying Hermann Kolbe's prediction of its existence. His most notable work was that carried out with James Crafts on the alkylation and acylation of aromatic hydrocarbons — the *Friedel–Crafts reaction* (1877). This was a method of synthesizing hydrocarbons or ketones from aromatic hydrocarbons using aluminum chloride as a catalyst. Friedel and Crafts also did much work on the synthesis of organosilicon compounds. Friedel was professor of mineralogy at the mining school in Paris (1876–84) and professor of organic chemistry at the Sorbonne (1884–99).

FRIEDLÄNDER, Paul (b. 1857; d. 1923) German organic chemist.

Friedländer was assistant to Adolf von Baeyer at Munich during the latter's great researches on indigo, and much of Friedländer's work was concerned with indigo derivatives. He synthesized many derivatives and showed that the ancient dyestuff Tyrian purple is dibromoindigo (1909). He also developed a useful quinoline synthesis (1882). He was the holder of 235 patents concerned with dyestuffs.

FRIEDMAN, Herbert (b. June 21, 1916; New York City) American physicist and astronomer.

Friedman graduated from Brooklyn College in 1936 and obtained his PhD in 1940 from Johns Hopkins University, Baltimore. Shortly afterwards he joined the US Naval Research Laboratory in Washington where he has spent his whole career, being appointed in 1958 as superintendent of the atmosphere and astrophysics division and in 1963 superintendent of the space science division. Also in 1963 he became chief scientist at the E. O. Hulbert Center for Space Research. In addition he has served as adjunct professor at the universities of Maryland and Pennsylvania.

Friedman has been a pioneer in both rocket astronomy and in the study of the x-ray sky. The two went hand in hand in the early days of x-ray astronomy for without rockets it would have been impossible to detect any significant x-ray activity in space since x-rays are absorbed by the Earth's atmosphere. Solar x-rays were detected as early as 1948 by T. R. Burnright and were systematically investigated from 1949 by Friedman and his colleagues, who observed x-ray activity throughout a full solar cycle of 11 years. Friedman also studied ultraviolet radiation from the Sun and in 1960 produced the first x-ray and ultraviolet photographs of the Sun.

X-ray astronomy really came of age in 1962 when nonsolar x-ray activity was first discovered by Bruno Rossi. The x-rays came from a source in Scorpio, since named Sco X–1. A second source was discovered in 1963 in Taurus and named Tau X–1. Friedman made the first attempt to locate accurately an x-ray source two years later: when the Moon passed in front of the Crab nebula, a luminous supernova remnant in Taurus, the x-ray activity of Tau X–1 was found to fade out gradually. Tau X–1 was therefore identified with the Crab nebula and seemed to be a source about a light-year across lying in the center of the nebula.

Since then satellites carrying x-ray equipment have been launched, including Uhuru in 1970 and the Einstein Observatory in 1978. These have enormously extended the scope of x-ray astronomy and shown its value in the search for neutron stars and black holes.

FRIEDMANN, Aleksandr Alexandrovich (b. June 29, 1888; St. Petersburg, now Leningrad in the Soviet Union; d. Sept. 16, 1925; Leningrad) Soviet astronomer.

The son of a composer, Friedmann was educated at the University of St. Petersburg. He began his scientific career in 1913 at the Pavlovsk Observatory in St. Petersburg and, after war service, was appointed professor of theoretical mechanics at Perm University in 1918. In 1920 he returned to the St. Petersburg Observatory where he became director shortly before his early death from typhoid at the age of 37.

Friedmann established an early reputation for his work on atmospheric and meteorological physics. He is, however, better known for his 1922 paper on the expanding universe. This arose from work of Einstein in 1917 in which he attempted to apply his equations of general relativity to cosmology. Friedmann developed a theoretical model of the universe using Einstein's theory, in which the average mass density is constant and space has a constant curvature. Different cosmological models are possible depending on whether the curvature is zero, negative, or positive. Such models are called *Friedmann universes*.

FRIEDMANN, Herbert (b. Apr. 22, 1900; New York City) American biologist and ornithologist.

Friedmann gained a PhD in ornithology from Cornell University in 1923 and then held a fellowship at Harvard for three years during which he spent much time in Argentina and Africa. After a series of academic posts he became, in 1929, curator of birds of the Smithsonian Institution, Washington, and was its head curator of zoology from 1957 to 1961.

Friedmann was especially interested in reproductive parasitism, particularly of birds, studying for example the African cuckoos and parasitic weaverbirds. He also investigated the parasitic honey guides, one species of which was observed to guide people to wild bees' nests. It had been thought that such birds fed on the honey and bee larvae and eggs but Friedmann demonstrated the birds were actually after the beeswax. This discovery was particularly interesting as it had been assumed wax was indigestible. Friedmann went on to find that a wax-breaking bacterium *Micrococcus cerolyticus* was present in the birds' intestine.

Friedmann has also investigated the systematics of birds of Africa, North America, and South America. His other work has included studies of animal and plant symbolism in European medieval and Renaissance art.

FRIES, Elias Magnus (b. Aug. 15, 1794; Femsjö, Sweden; d. Feb. 8, 1878; Uppsala, Sweden) Swedish mycologist.

Fries grew up in a region particularly abundant in fungi, which — together with botanical instruction he received from his father — resulted in his lifelong interest in mycology (the study of fungi). Fries entered Lund University in 1811, graduating in 1814 with a dissertation on the flora of Sweden. He continued at Lund until 1835, producing the three-volume *Systema Mycologicum* (1821–32), which classifies the fungi by their developmental stages and morphological relationships. This work remains the foundation of mycological taxonomy today for all but three groups of fungi.

Fries also produced an important work on the European lichens and issued floras spanning all of Scandinavia. In 1835 he took up the chair of botany at Uppsala University, becoming a member of the Linnean Society in the same year, and in 1875 he was elected a fellow of the Royal Society.

FRISCH, Karl von (b. Nov. 20, 1886; Vienna) Austrian zoologist, entomologist, and ethologist.

Educated at home and at convent school, Frisch began his academic career by studying medicine at the University of Vienna, but gave this up to study zoology at the Zoological Institute in Munich, an internationally recognized center for research in experimental zoology. He also studied marine biology at the Trieste Biological Institute for Marine Research, taking his PhD for work on the color adaptation and light perception of minnows (1910). Frisch taught at the Munich Zoological Institute and in 1919 became assistant professor of zoology. He then held academic posts at the universities of Rostock and Breslau before returning to Munich in 1925 as director of the Zoological Institute where he continued to work until the end of World War II. In 1946 he assumed the chair of zoology at Graz but returned to Munich where he remained until his retirement in 1958.

Interested in animals from childhood,

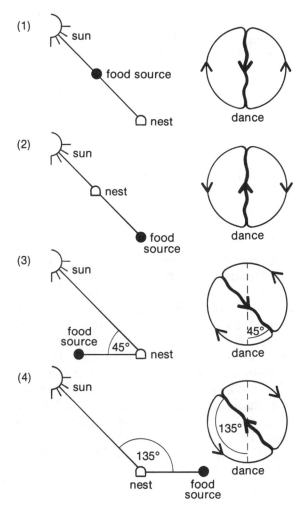

THE TAIL-WAGGING DANCE OF THE BEE
The relationship between the angle of the straight run of the tail-wagging dance on the vertical surface of the comb and the angle between sun, nest, and food source.

Frisch has devoted 40 years to an intense study of the senses, communication, and social organization of honey (or hive) bees. By means of ingenious experiments he has shown that bees can find their way back to the hive, even when the sun is obscured by cloud, by using polarized or ultraviolet light, and that they are able to communicate discovery of a new food source by means of a special 'dance'. The bee performs its dance on the vertical surface of the comb. Depending on the distance of the food supply, the bee may perform either the round dance — food within

about 80 feet (24 m) — or the tail-wagging dance — food beyond about 325 feet (99 m). At intermediate distances various transitional dance forms between these are seen. In the tail-wagging dance the bee makes a straight run over a short distance, wagging its abdomen rapidly, and then makes a semicircle back to the starting point. This movement is repeated, making a semicircle in the opposite direction. The dance gives information on the direction of the food supply because the angle that the straight run makes with the vertical surface of the comb is the same as the angle between the direction of the food and the Sun at the hive or nest. Frisch also showed that the bees are unable to distinguish between certain shapes, that they have a limited range of color perception, but can see light of longer wavelength than man. They do not, for example, distinguish red but can see ultraviolet, which is reflected by many flowers. Red poppies are seen as wholly ultraviolet, while many yellow flowers are seen either as yellow or in varying shades of ultraviolet. Frisch's discoveries have proved of practical benefit to beekeepers in that if hives are painted certain colors — a yellow hive next to a blue one for example — this aids the bees' homing. His major contribution to ethology was recognized in 1973 when he was awarded the Nobel Prize for physiology or medicine, jointly with Konrad Lorenz and Niko Tinbergen.

FRISCH, Otto Robert (b. Oct. 1, 1904; Vienna; d. Sept. 22, 1979) Austrian–British physicist.

Frisch, the son of a printer and publisher, was educated at the University of Vienna where he obtained his doctorate in 1926. He was employed in Berlin (1927–30) at the German national physical laboratory, the Physikalisch Technische Reichsanstalt, and moved to the University of Hamburg in 1930. However, with the introduction of Hitler's racial laws, he was sacked in 1933 and consequently he traveled via Copenhagen to England. After working at the universities of Birmingham and Liverpool (1939–43) he moved to America and spent the period 1943–45 at Los Alamos, working on the development of the atom bomb. With the end of the war Frisch worked briefly at the Atomic Energy Research Establishment at Harwell, England, leaving in 1947 to take up the Jackson Chair of Physics at Cambridge, a post he held until his retirement in 1972.

In 1939 Frisch, with his aunt, Lise Meitner (q.v.), was closely involved in the crucial discovery of nuclear fission. He spent Christmas in Sweden visiting Meitner, who reported to him some strange results obtained by her former colleague Otto Hahn. Hahn found that when uranium was bombarded with neutrons, one of its decay products was the much lighter element barium. Frisch said that his first reaction was that Hahn had made a mistake, but Meitner was more inclined to trust Hahn's qualities as a good chemist. After some thought and calculation they concluded that this must in fact be what was later called nuclear fission. Frisch rushed back to Copenhagen to inform Niels Bohr who was able to confirm Hahn's experiments. But in all this excitement the most important point had been missed — the mechanism of the neutron chain reaction. However the thought did occur independently to many others.

Frisch did further work on fission while at Birmingham, collaborating with Rudolph Peierls in confirming Bohr's suggestion that a chain reaction would be more likely to result with uranium–235 rather than with the more common isotope, uranium–238. After much work Frisch came to the basic and frightening conclusion that an 'explosive chain reaction' could be produced with a pound or two of uranium–235 rather than the tons of it which he first thought would be necessary. Frisch and Peierls were therefore probably the first two people in the world to be aware not just of the possibility of a nuclear bomb but of its practicality. They immediately wrote a report that was sent to Henry Tizard, a scientific adviser to the British Government, which Frisch claimed was decisive in getting the British Government to take the atomic bomb seriously.

In 1979 Frisch produced his fascinating and witty memoirs, *What Little I Remember*.

FRITSCH, Felix Eugen (b. Apr. 26, 1879; London; d. May 23, 1954; Cambridge, England) British algologist.

Fritsch, the son of a headmaster, was educated at the University of London and at Munich, where he obtained his DPhil in 1899. He taught at University College, London, from 1902 until 1911, when he moved to Queen Mary College, London, where he served as professor of botany from 1924 until his retirement in 1948.

Before Fritsch there was no comprehensive work on algae. He remedied this with his classic work *The Structure and Reproduction of the Algae* (2 vols. 1935–45). He was also instrumental in the foundation of the Freshwater Biological Association in 1929.

FRITSCH, Gustav Theodor (b. Mar. 5, 1838; Cottbus, near Berlin; d. June 12, 1927; Berlin) German ethnographer, anatomist, and neurologist.

Fritsch, the son of a building inspector, was educated at the gymnasium in Breslau and the University of Berlin where he obtained his MD in 1862. From 1867 to 1900 Fritsch worked at the Institute of Anatomy in Berlin, also becoming head of the histological section at the Physiological Institute.

Fritsch was a much traveled ethnographer. From 1863 to 1866 he was in South Africa where he made a careful study of the anatomy and culture of the Bushmen. He also made research expeditions to Egypt, Syria, and Persia. He is however best known for his collaboration with Eduard Hitzig (q.v.) in 1870 in which they clearly demonstrated the phenomenon of cerebral localization.

FRONTINUS, Sextus Julius (b. *c.* AD 35; d. *c.* AD 104) Roman engineer.

Frontinus was responsible in AD 97, for constructing the aqueducts of Rome, many of which are still standing. His writings are the main source of information on the water-supply system of the time and he devised a method of measuring water flow with a standard pipe called a *quinaria*. Based on his figures, one estimate of the water supply to each Roman citizen is about the same as that of modern European cities. Frontinus also wrote on land-surveying techniques.

FUCHS, Leonhard (b. Jan. 17, 1501; Wemding, now in West Germany; d. May 10, 1566; Tübingen, now in West Germany) German botanist and physician.

Fuchs was professor of medicine at Tübingen University from 1535 until his death, his main interest being the medicinal properties of plants. He is remembered for his herbal manual *De historia stirpium* (1542), in which about four hundred native and a hundred foreign plants are arranged alphabetically, with original descriptions of the form, habitat, and best season for collection of each plant. The herbal is notable for its glossary of botanical terms, accurate woodcut illustrations, and detailed descriptions.

A genus of ornamental shrubs, *Fuchsia*, is named after him.

FUCHS, Sir Vivien Ernest (b. Feb. 11, 1908; Freshwater, England) British explorer and geologist.

Fuchs was the son of a farmer of German origin. He was educated at Cambridge University where he obtained his MA in geology in 1929 and his PhD (1935). From 1929 he traveled on a series of expeditions

as geologist, the first being the Cambridge East Greenland Expedition (1929). In 1947 he became a member of the Falkland Islands Dependencies Survey and in 1950 its director.

As a result of his involvement with the survey, Fuchs led an expedition to Graham Land in Antarctica (1948) to reassert the British claim to the territory, which was being challenged by Argentina. He was stranded on Storington Island by bad weather until 1950.

Fuchs is best known for the Commonwealth Trans-Antarctic Expedition he jointly led with Edmund Hillary in the International Geophysical Year (1957–58). Leaving Shackleton Base on the Weddele Sea on 24 November, 1957, he reached the South Pole and met Hillary on 19 January, 1958, then continued to reach Scott Base, Victoria Land, on 2 March. From the scientific studies made during this it was established that a single continent exists below the polar ice cap.

Fuchs was knighted in 1958.

FUNK, Casimir (b. Feb. 23, 1884; Warsaw; d. Nov. 20, 1967; Albany, New York) Polish–American biochemist.

Funk, the son of a dermatologist, obtained his doctorate from the University of Bern in 1904. He worked at the Pasteur Institute in Paris, the University of Berlin, and the Lister Institute in London, before emigrating to America in 1915. Although he became naturalized in 1920, Funk returned to Poland in 1923 as director of the Warsaw Institute of Hygiene, but finding the political conditions unattractive moved to Paris in 1927, where he acted as a consultant to a drug company and founded a private research institute, the Casa Biochemica. In 1939 Funk returned to America, where he served as consultant to the US Vitamin Corporation and as president of the Funk Foundation for medical research.

It was while working at the Lister Institute in 1912 that Funk first clearly formulated his crucial idea that certain diseases are caused by food deficiencies. He was working on the antiberiberi factor, which he succeeded in extracting from rice husks. He went on to postulate that there were comparable ingredients whose absence from a regular diet would produce scurvy, rickets, and pellagra.

Noting that the antiberiberi factor contained an amine ($-NH_2$) group, Funk proposed to call such ingredients 'vital amines', or 'vitamines'. When it became clear that the amine group was not present in all 'vitamines' the term 'vitamin' came to be preferred.

G

GABOR, Dennis (b. June 5, 1900; Budapest; d. Feb. 8, 1979; London) Hungarian–British physicist.

Gabor, the son of a businessman, was educated at the technical universities of Budapest and of Berlin where he obtained a doctorate in engineering in 1927. He worked initially as a research engineer for Siemens and Halske from 1927 until 1933 when, with the rise of Hitler, he decided to leave Germany and took a post with the British Thomson–Houston Company, Rugby. In 1948 he joined the staff of Imperial College, London, later serving as professor of applied electron physics from 1958 until his retirement in 1967.

Gabor is credited with the invention of the technique of holography — a method of photographically recording and reproducing three-dimensional images. The modern technique uses lasers to form such images, but the invention came out of work by Gabor on improving the resolution of the electron microscope — work done in 1948, twelve years before the introduction of the laser.

The electron microscope has theoretically much higher resolution than the optical microscope because of the shorter wavelength of electrons (resolution is limited by diffraction effects). One method of improving the resolution of the electron microscope is to improve the electron lenses used to deflect and focus the beam of electrons. Gabor was interested in increasing the resolution to the point at which atoms in a lattice could be 'seen'. Rather than work on the electron optics of the system he had the idea of extracting more information from the electron micrographs produced by existing instruments, and to do this he proposed forming a diffraction pattern between the incident beam of electrons and a background beam that was coherent with it (the same wavelength and phase). The principle was that the image produced would have information on the phase of the electrons as well as the intensity and that it would be possible to reconstruct a true image from the resulting electron micrograph.

Gabor began experiments to investigate the technique (which he named holography from the Greek *holos* meaning whole — the record contained the whole information about the specimen). He used a mercury lamp and pinhole to form the first, imperfect, holograms. Subsequently, in 1961, E. Leith and J. Upatnieks produced holograms using laser light. The technique is to illuminate a specimen with light from a laser and form an interference pattern between light reflected from the specimen and direct light from the source, the pattern being recorded on a photographic plate. If the photographic record is then illuminated with the laser light, a three-dimensional image of the specimen is generated.

Gabor received the Nobel Physics Prize for his work in 1971.

GABRIEL, Siegmund (b. Nov. 7, 1851; Berlin; d. Mar. 22, 1924; Berlin) German chemist.

Gabriel studied under August von Hofmann in Berlin and under Robert Bunsen in Heidelberg. He returned to Berlin in

1874 being appointed to the chair of chemistry there in 1886.

In 1880 Zdenko Skraup had succeeded in synthesizing the heterocyclic compound quinoline. Gabriel helped work out the chemistry of such structures by synthesizing isoquinoline in 1885. Isoquinoline is the parent substance of several opium alkaloids. In 1887, Gabriel also worked out methods for the synthesis of primary amines from haloalkanes and potassium phthalimide with subsequent hydrolysis.

GADOLIN, Johan (b. June 5, 1760; Åbo, now Turku in Finland; d. Aug. 15, 1852; Wirmo, Finland) Finnish chemist.

Gadolin was the son of an astronomer and physicist. He studied under Torbern Bergman at Uppsala and taught at Åbo from 1785, becoming professor of chemistry from 1797 until 1822.

In 1794 Gadolin examined a black mineral from Ytterby, a quarry in Sweden. The rocks from this quarry were found to contain a dozen or so new elements. Gadolin isolated the first lanthanoid element from it in the form of its oxide and named it yttria. The element was named gadolinium after him in 1886 by Lecoq de Boisbaudran. Gadolin also worked on specific heat and published a set of standard tables.

GAFFKY, Georg Theodor August (b. Feb. 17, 1850; Hannover, now in West Germany; d. Sept. 23, 1918; Hannover) German bacteriologist.

Gaffky was educated at the University of Berlin where, after service in the Franco-Prussian War, he obtained his MD in 1873. He served as Robert Koch's assistant from 1880 to 1885 and, after holding the chair of hygiene at the University of Giessen (1888–1904), succeeded Koch in Berlin as director of the Institute for Infectious Diseases, renamed the Koch Institute in 1912.

In 1880 Carl Eberth had first described the microorganism responsible for typhoid fever. As it was easily confused with several other intestinal organisms, it was only when Gaffky succeeded in obtaining a pure culture in 1884 that Eberth's work could be confirmed.

Gaffky also served on a number of important field investigations. He was with Koch on his trips to Egypt and India in 1883–84, during which the vibrio responsible for cholera was discovered, and wrote the official report of the investigation. Gaffky made a further trip to Egypt in 1897 to work on the bubonic plague.

GAHN, Johan Gottlieb (b. Aug. 19, 1745; Voxna, Sweden; d. Dec. 8, 1818; Stockholm) Swedish chemist and mineralogist.

Gahn graduated from the University of Uppsala in 1770, and then taught at the College of Mines. Working with Carl Scheele, he showed that phosphorus is present in bones (1770). He also first isolated the element manganese, suspected by Scheele to be present in pyrolusite — an oxide known to the ancients and used chiefly to color glass. Gahn's extraction involved igniting a paste of pyrolusite (manganese(IV) oxide) and charcoal. Gahn also contributed to the discovery of selenium by Jöns Berzelius (q.v.) in 1818.

He became superintendent of mines in 1782 and later became a mine owner himself. The mineral ghanite (zinc spinel) is named for him.

GAJDUSEK, Daniel Carleton (b. Sept. 9, 1923; Yonkers, New York) American virologist.

Gajdusek was educated at the University of Rochester and at Harvard, where he obtained his MD in 1946. He specialized in pediatrics, working at Harvard, the Pasteur Institute in Teheran, and the Walter and Eliza Hall Institute for Medical Research in Melbourne, before joining the National Institutes of Health in Bethesda, Maryland, in 1958. Since 1970 he has been with the National Institute of Neurological Diseases.

In 1963 he made an intriguing discovery that could well have profound consequences for the control of a number of serious but little-understood diseases. In the 1950s he began studying the Fore people of New Guinea, a supposedly cannibalistic tribe who suffered from a very localized neurological complaint they called 'kuru'. With the aid of the district medical officer, who first drew his attention to the disease, Gajdusek spent much of the next ten years among the Fore looking for the cause of kuru. He suspected the disease was transmitted by the Fore custom of ritually eating parts of the brain of their deceased relatives so he collected samples from the brains of several kuru victims.

Failing to detect any obvious signs of an organism in the brain tissue he injected filtered extracts into the brains of chimpanzees and waited. After about 12 months the disease at last appeared. This was the first of the so-called 'slow virus infections' to be observed in humans. By 1968 Gajdusek and his colleagues had shown that kuru was not unique and that the rare neurological complaint Creutzfeldt-Jakob disease, a presenile dementia, is transmitted after a comparable delay. This immediately opened the still unresolved question as to whether such complaints as Parkinson's disease and multiple sclerosis are also due to slow viruses.

For his work on kuru Gajdusek shared the 1976 Nobel Prize for physiology or medicine with Baruch Blumberg. The prize itself he used to set up a trust for the education of the Fore people. Gajdusek, who is unmarried, has adopted 16 boys while on his expeditions to the Pacific, and is bringing them up in America.

GALEN (b. *c.* 130; Pergamum, now Bergama in Turkey; d. *c.* 200; Rome?) Greek physician.

Galen's father apparently decided to educate his son as a doctor as the result of a dream in which Asklepios, the god of medicine, appeared to him. Thus after an initial period of training in Pergamum, Galen spent the years 148–57 traveling and studying at Corinth, Smyrna, and Alexandria. He then returned home and took the post of surgeon to the Pergamum gladiators. Eventually Galen left for Rome where he made a considerable reputation for himself serving the emperors Marcus Aurelius and Commodus.

In addition to his imperial duties Galen wrote extensively and more than 130 of his texts have survived. Even though some are undoubtedly spurious, there still remains an impressive opus on virtually every aspect of the medicine of his times.

It is this opus that acquired an unprecedented authority, which persisted, unopposed, for another 1500 years. It was not until William Harvey proposed his new theory of the circulation of the blood (1628) that anatomists were presented with a viable alternative to the traditional system of Galen.

Galen made few advances in pathology believing as he did in Hippocrates' humoral theory — that disease is caused by an imbalance of the four body humors; phlegm, black bile, yellow bile, and blood. It was as an anatomist that Galen's true originality lay. He stressed the importance of dissecting personally and frequently, and combined his anatomical studies with a number of neat and conclusive experiments. Thus he clearly demonstrated the falsity of Erasistratus's view that the arteries carry air not blood by placing ligatures both above and below the point of incision and noting the absence of any air escaping before the discharge of blood. Also, by similar experiments he was able to show that urine passes from the kidneys to the bladder irreversibly down the ureters.

Galen however was less successful in describing the complete system and operation of the body. He thought that blood was made in the liver from the food brought by the portal vein from the stomach. This was then transported by the venous system to nourish all parts of the body. Some of the blood however passed along the vena cava to the right side of the heart where it passed to the left side by some supposed perforations in the dividing wall or septum. Belief in such perforations persisted well into the 16th century. In the left ventricle the blood was mixed with air brought from the lungs and distributed round the body via the arterial system carrying the vital spirit or innate heat. Some of this blood was carried by the arteries to the head where in the *rete mirabile* (a vascular network not actually found in man) it was mixed with animal spirit and distributed to the senses and muscles by the supposedly hollow nerves. It was this spirit or pneuma that produced consciousness.

Thus instead of a single basic circulation Galen has a tripartite system in which the liver, heart, and brain each inject into the body three different spirits — natural, vital, and animal, which travel through the body via the venous, arterial, and nervous channels respectively. Although such a scheme is now recognized as totally misguided it possessed sufficient plausibility and experimental support to persist into the 17th century.

GALILEO (Galileo Galilei) (b. Feb. 15, 1564; Pisa, Italy; d. Jan. 8, 1642; Florence, now in Italy) Italian astronomer and physicist.

Galileo made major contributions to most branches of physics especially mechanics, invented and so deployed the telescope to change our view of the nature of the universe completely, and became engaged in a highly dramatic confrontation with the Church.

Galileo was the son of a scholar and musician of some distinction. He entered the University of Pisa in 1581 to study medicine — a subject in which he showed little interest — and failed to complete the course, developing instead a passion for mathematics. He is thought to have made his first important observation in 1583, two years before he left the university. While in Pisa cathedral he noticed that the lamps swinging in the wind took the same time

for their swing whatever its amplitude. He timed the swing against his pulse. In 1586 he invented a hydrostatic balance for the determination of relative densities. In 1589 he was appointed to the chair of mathematics at Pisa and later moved to the chair in Padua, in 1592.

It was while in Padua in 1610 that he designed and constructed a simple refracting telescope. He may not have been the first to do so, and there are many other claimants, but he was certainly the first to use the instrument constructively. His initial reaction was sheer amazement at the number of stars in the sky, "So numerous as to be almost beyond belief" he asserted. Merely looking at the Moon immediately revealed that it is not the smooth unchangeable object of Aristotelian theory. He also discovered sunspots. His most exciting moment came in January 1610, when he observed Jupiter for the first time telescopically. To his astonishment he found that the planet has four satellites. Contrary to received opinion as to what was possible, these were new bodies, unmentioned in Aristotle, and certainly not circling the Earth. He published his observations immediately, in 1610, in *Sidereus nuncius* (Starry Messenger), dedicating them to his patron and former pupil Cosimo II of Tuscany, in whose honor he named the satellites Sidera Medicea (Medici Stars). Within weeks he had received an invitation to a well-paid research chair in Pisa and returned there at the end of 1610.

In a series of works he was also tackling the problem of motion. His mature views were expressed in his *Discorsi ... a due nuove scienze...* (1638; Discourse on Two New Sciences). In a series of brilliant experiments rolling balls down inclined planes (and not, as is commonly thought, by dropping weights from the leaning tower of Pisa) he showed that the speed with which bodies fall is independant of their weight and correctly formulated the law $s = \frac{1}{2}at^2$ (where s is speed, a acceleration, and t time). He lacked the concept of inertia and could only accept circular motion as being natural since, for Galileo, a body without any force acting on it would move in perfect circular motion. This was one aspect of his medieval heritage from which he was unable to break away.

After his return to Pisa, Galileo was beginning to meet opposition. Some of this was merely personal; in his criticism of others he wrote with a wit and savagery that many found wounding and impossible to forgive. He also found himself in dispute with many over his numerous discoveries. In these he was never inclined to take a charitable view over the claims of others, and there were many waiting for a chance to humiliate him on his return from the safety of Padua (then part of the independent Venetian republic). Their chance was his open support for the Copernican system. That the Earth moves round the Sun was so contrary to Scripture for many churchmen that those who enthusiastically campaigned for such a view were seen as heretics if not atheists. Galileo made no secret of his views in his writings, talk, and lectures. He openly ridiculed the Aristotelian scholars and supporters of the Ptolemaic (geocentric) system, many of whom were, or were to become, high officers of the Church. To stop the squabbling, Pope Paul V, on the advice of Cardinal Bellarmine, placed Copernicus on the Index (a list of books banned by the Catholic Church) in 1616, summoned Galileo to Rome, and informed him that he could no longer support Copernicus publicly. At this point Galileo had no choice; continued support for Copernicus would be to call the authority of the pope into question and to send him to the stake as it had sent Giordano Bruno in 1600.

In 1623 an old friend of Galileo's, Cardinal Barberini, was elected pope as Urban VIII. Galileo wasted no time in dedicating his new book *Il saggiatore* (1623; The Assayer) to him. It was a work that was savagely critical of Aristotle's account of comets. Although Urban was not prepared to go back on the decision of 1616 publicly, Galileo seems to have thought that he would be safe unless he supported Copernicus specifically. One thing that should have made him more prudent was

the death of his patron, Cosimo, and the succession of a powerless minor to the duchy of Tuscany.

Galileo thought he could avoid the problem by writing a dialogue between a (Ptolemaic-) Aristotelian and a Copernican without ostensibly committing himself to either side, and the Church gave him permission to do so. Thus he wrote the *Dialogue Concerning the Two Chief World Systems* (1632). However, the form of the dialogue fooled no one. The Aristotelian, Simplicius, is no match for the brilliance of the Copernican, Salviati. It was even suggested to the pope that the bumbling Simplicius was a portrait of Urban himself. Galileo was once more summoned to Rome, threatened with torture and forced to renounce Copernicus in the most abject terms. There is a tradition that after his renunciation he whispered, "Eppur si muove" ("Yet it moves"), but this is unlikely. Galileo was truly frightened, and it must be remembered that he was nearly 70 years old and facing a powerful body, which might have tortured and burned him at the stake. In the end he was treated reasonably well. He was allowed to return to his villa at Arcetri in isolation. Later, after he became blind and after the death of his daughter, his disciples Vincenzo Viviani and Evangelista Toricelli were allowed to stay with him.

GALL, Franz Joseph (b. Mar. 9, 1758; Tiefenbronn, now in West Germany; d. Aug. 22, 1828; Paris) German physician and anatomist.

Gall studied medicine at Strasbourg and then Vienna where he obtained his MD in 1785 and set up practice. In 1805, seeking a less restrictive scientific community, he left Vienna, where his lectures had been forbidden by the chancellor and after a European tour settled in Paris in 1807.

Although Gall is largely remembered as the founder of phrenology, now a totally discredited system, his crucial place in the development of cerebral localization is little known. Gall began as a conventional anatomist and established that the white matter of the brain consists of nerve fibers. However he was distracted from such work by a couple of chance observations.

He noted that the two acquaintances of his with the best memory both had prominent staring eyes. This impressed him to search for cases of distinct traits or skills being linked with a distinctive physiognomy. This path led to him linking specific parts of the brain with specific behavior, a theory that could have been a major advance in anatomy, if properly handled. Unfortunately Gall went too far, recognizing 27 faculties. His collaborator Johann Spurzheim, who worked closely with him for several years and actually coined the term phrenology, added a further eight faculties. The evidence for these was largely anecdotal and uncritically accepted. Thus, paintings of the great depicting the appropriate bump would confirm the theory; if, however, the bump was missing this would merely show the painter was working according to standards of beauty not truth.

Operations to test the theory were later performed by Pierre Flourens and tended not to support Gall. It was not in fact until 1861 that Paul Broca obtained any hard surgical evidence for the localization of cerebral faculties while the full proof of the hypothesis had to wait for the work of Gustav Fritsch and Eduard Hitzig in 1870.

GALLE, Johann Gottfried (b. June 9, 1812; Pabsthaus, now in East Germany; d. July 10, 1910; Potsdam, now in East Germany) German astronomer.

Galle was chief assistant to Johann Encke at the Berlin Observatory at a crucial moment in the history of planetary astronomy. Urbain Leverrier had worked out what he considered to be the position of an as yet undiscovered planet. Having had some contact with Galle, Leverrier wrote to him on 18 September, 1846, asking him to try and check his prediction. Galle started observing on 23 September. He was favored by having an unpublished copy of a new star chart covering the right part of the sky and, aided by Louis D'Arrest, he found a star that was not on the chart. A wait of 24 hours showed that it had moved against the background of the fixed stars and so was a planet — it was the planet Neptune.

Galle also made an important contribution to determine the mean distance of the Sun from the Earth (the astronomical unit or AU). Conventional means of determining the AU had leaned heavily on the two transits of Venus in each century. In practice it turned out to be difficult to measure accurately the moment of first contact. Galle proposed instead, in 1872, that measuring the parallax of the planetoids would give a more reliable figure. (Harold Spencer Jones followed this procedure in 1931 when the planetoid Eros came within 16 million miles of the Earth. He was able to calculate the AU to within 10 000 miles.) In 1851 Galle became director of the Breslau Observatory. He lived long enough to receive the congratulations of the astronomical world on the 50th anniversary of the discovery of Neptune in 1896.

GALOIS, Evariste (b. Oct. 25, 1811; Bourg-la-Reine, near Paris; d. May 31, 1832; Paris) French mathematician.

Galois was born during the rule of Napoleon. He entered the Collège Royale de Louis-le-Grand in Paris in 1823 and it was here that his precocious mathematical genius first emerged. He published several papers while still a student and at the age of about 16 embarked upon his noted work on algebraic equations. But his career was marred by lack of advancement, associated with political bitterness. Twice, in 1827 and 1829, he was rejected by the Paris Ecole Polytechnique, and three papers submitted to the Academy of Sciences were rejected or lost. In 1830 he entered the Ecole Normale Supérieure to train as a teacher. That year revolution in Paris caused the abdication of Charles X who was succeeded by Louis Philippe. Galois —

fiercely republican — was expelled for writing an antiroyalist newspaper letter. In 1831 he was arrested twice: once for a speech against the king and the second time for wearing an illegal uniform and carrying arms — for this he received six-months' imprisonment. In the spring of 1832 he died in a duel; the details are uncertain but it may have been provoked by political opponents.

Galois seems to have anticipated that he was to die, for the night before was spent desperately recording his mathematical ideas in a letter to his former schoolmaster, Auguste Chevalier. Here he outlined his work on elliptic integrals and set out a theory of the roots (solutions) of equations, in which he considered the properties of permutations of the roots. Admissible permutations — ones in which the roots obey the same relations after permutation — form what is now known as a *Galois group*, having properties that throw light on the solvability of the equations. The manuscripts were published in 1846 and his work recognized. With the equally tragic Norwegian, Niels Henrik Abel, he is regarded as the founder of modern group theory.

GALTON, Sir Francis (b. Feb. 16, 1822; Birmingham, England; d. Jan. 17, 1911; Haslemere, England) British anthropologist and explorer.

Even though Galton's exceptional intelligence was apparent at an early age, his higher education was unremarkable. After reading mathematics at Cambridge University, he studied medicine in London but abandoned his studies on inheriting his father's fortune, which enabled him to indulge his passion for travel. Following consultations with the Royal Geographical Society, Galton set out to cover various uncharted regions of Africa, and became known as an intrepid explorer. He collected much valuable information and was elected first a fellow of the Royal Geographical Society and three years later, in 1856, a fellow of the Royal Society.

Galton made important contributions to the science of meteorology, identifying and naming anticyclones and developing the present techniques of weather mapping. This work was published as *Meteorographica* (1863). He was also instrumental in establishing the Meteorological Office and the National Physical Laboratory, but he is remembered chiefly for his researches on human heredity, which were stimulated by the publication of *The Origin of Species* by his cousin, Charles Darwin. This led Galton to speculate that the human race could be improved by controlled breeding and he later gave the name *eugenics* to the study of means by which this might be achieved.

Galton studied the histories of notable families to determine whether intelligence is inherited, and concluded that it is. This aroused much controversy amongst those who believed environment is all important. Galton was the first to use identical twins to try to assess environmental influences. His work was characterized by its quantitative approach and he was also the first to stress the importance to biology of statistical analysis, introducing regression and correlation into statistics.

At a time when most scientists believed in blending inheritance, Galton deviated from contemporary thought and, in a letter to Darwin, outlined a theory of particulate inheritance, which anticipated Gregor Mendel's work, then still undiscovered. Galton also discussed a concept similar to the phenotypes and genotypes of Wilhelm Johannsen, under the terms patent and latent characteristics.

Galton was knighted in 1909. In his will he left a large sum of money to endow a chair of eugenics at University College, London, which was first held by Karl Pearson, an energetic advocate of Galton's ideas on eugenics.

GALVANI, Luigi (b. Sept. 9, 1737; Bologna, Italy; d. Dec. 4, 1798; Bologna) Italian anatomist and physiologist.

Galvani studied medicine at the University of Bologna, gaining his MD in 1762 for his thesis on the structure and development of bones. He stayed at Bologna to teach anatomy and in the late 1770s began his experiments in electrophysiology. He observed that the muscles of a dissected frog twitched when touched by a spark from an electric machine or condenser, such as a Leyden jar. Similar responses could be obtained when such muscles were laid out on metal during a thunderstorm, or even by simple contact with two different metals, without the deliberate application of an electric current. Galvani concluded that the source of the electricity therefore lay in the living tissue, and did not derive from outside. His finding was later disproved by Alessandro Volta. However Galvani is celebrated for his discovery of Galvanic electricity (the metallic arc), as well as for applications of his principle to the galvanization of iron and steel and the invention of the galvanometer, named in Galvani's honor by André Ampère. Galvani's animal electricity theory was published as *De viribus electricitatis in motu musculari commentarius* (1791; Commentary on the Effect of Electricity on Muscular Motion).

GAMBLE, Josias Christopher (b. 1776; Enniskillen, Scotland; d. Jan. 27, 1848; St. Helens, England) British industrial chemist.

Gamble came from a Presbyterian background and was educated at Glasgow University, graduating in 1797. He first became a minister, going to Belfast in that capacity in 1804, but soon entered the bleaching industry. He had picked up enough knowledge of Charles Tennant's St. Rollox process to open a factory in Dublin to manufacture chlorine bleach powder. He also produced sulfuric acid, potash, and alum. In 1829 he returned to England and partnered James Muspratt to open the first chemical works in St. Helens, a Leblanc soda works, which became a highly profitable business.

GAMOW, George (b. Mar. 4, 1904; Odessa, now in the Soviet Union; d. Aug. 20, 1968; Boulder, Colorado) Soviet–American physicist.

Gamow, the son of a teacher, was educated at the University of Leningrad where he obtained his doctorate in 1928 and later served as professor of physics (1931–34). Before his move to America in 1934 he spent long periods at Göttingen, Copenhagen and Cambridge, England, the major centers of the revolution then taking place in physics. In America he spent his career as professor of physics at George Washington University (1934–68) and then at the University of Colorado (1956–68).

Gamow made many contributions to nuclear and atomic physics, but is mainly noted for his work on interesting problems in cosmology and molecular biology.

In cosmology he revised and extended the big-bang theory of the creation of the universe (first formulated by Georges Lemaître). This postulates that the universe expanded from a single point in space and time. It was first announced in Gamow's famous 'alpha beta gamma' paper in 1948, which he wrote in collaboration with Ralph Alpher and Hans Bethe. A fuller account was later published by Gamow in his *Creation of the Universe* (1952). Gamow dated the expansion to about 17 billion years ago, probably the result of an earlier contraction. The difficulty with any such theory was in accounting for the formation of the chemical elements. He supposed the primeval atom to consist of 'Ylem', an old word used by Gamow to refer to a mixture of protons, electrons, and neutrons. Under the conditions of temperature and density prevailing in the first half hour of the universe's history he tried to work out ways in which the elements could be formed by nuclear aggregation. There was no difficulty in showing that ^{1}H, ^{2}H, ^{3}H, ^{3}He, and ^{4}He would be formed but at that point he could see no way to advance the chain further, for there is no stable element with an atomic weight of 5. Add either a proton or a neutron to the nucleus of ^{4}He and either ^{5}Li or ^{5}He will be formed, both of which are unstable and decay in less than 10^{-20} second back to the original ^{4}He.

The only solution was to suppose that more than one particle collided with the ^{4}He nucleus simultaneously but, as Gamow realized, the universe by this time would be insufficiently dense and hot enough to permit such collisions to occur with the required frequency. He was therefore forced to conclude in 1956 that most of the heavy elements have been formed later in the hot interior of stars. One prediction that did emerge from his work and was to have important consequences for cosmology was his claim that the original explosion would produce a uniform radiation background; the discovery of such radiation in 1964 by Arno Penzias and Robert Wilson did more than anything else to stimulate interest once more in Gamow's theory.

Gamow later moved from showing how the universe began to the no less interesting question of how life began. He was quick to see the significance of the DNA model proposed by James Watson and Francis Crick in 1953. The problem was to show how the sequences of the four nucleic acid bases that constitute the DNA chain could control the construction of proteins, which may be made from 20 or more amino acids. Gamow had the insight to see that the bases must contain a code for the construction of amino acids. But the question of how this worked still remained. It could not be one base to one amino acid for then there would be only four amino acids. Nor would two bases be sufficient for they could produce only $4 \times 4 = 16$ amino acids. It would therefore need a sequence of three bases to produce one amino acid, a language with a capacity of $4 \times 4 \times 4 = 64$ words, which was more than adequate for the construction of all proteins. Gamow also produced convincing arguments to show that the code was not overlapping; that is, the three consecutive bases had to be read as a unit independent of its neighbors on either side.

The work on DNA allowed Gamow to indulge his passion for science fantasy. He founded the RNA tie club for which he actually designed a tie. It was restricted to 20 members, one for each amino acid. Each member took the name of one of the acids — Gamow was 'phe' (the usual abbreviation for phenylalanine) while Crick was 'tyr' (tyrosine). Meetings were held, information was exchanged, and considerable progress was made.

Gamow was also well known as one of the most successful popular science writers of his day. He wrote many books, most of which are still in print, which convey much of the excitement of the revolution in physics that he lived through.

GARROD, Sir Archibald Edward (b. Nov. 25, 1857; London; d. Mar. 28, 1936; Cambridge, England) British physician.

Garrod's father was also a physician, a specialist in joint diseases who in 1848 demonstrated the presence of uric acid in the joints of his gouty patients. His son graduated in natural science from Oxford University in 1880, and qualified in medicine from St. Bartholomew's Hospital, London. Garrod remained at St. Bartholomew's until 1920 when he returned to Oxford to succeed William Osler as professor of medicine, a post he retained until his retirement in 1927.

In a lecture he gave to the Royal College of Physicians in 1908, *Inborn Errors of Metabolism*, Garrod introduced to the medical world an entirely new and unsuspected class of disease. An early interest in the pathological aspects of urinary pigments led Garrod to investigate alkaptonuria, a complaint in which the urine turns black on exposure to air. This was known to be due to the presence of large amounts of alkapton or homogentisic acid, a breakdown product of the amino acids tyrosine and phenylalanine. It was at first thought that some intestinal microbe was responsible for the disorder but Garrod's initial researches quickly disposed of this supposition when he found a tendency for siblings to be affected while their parents remained quite normal. He therefore argued that the disease was genetically determined and inherited as a recessive Mendelian trait.

He went on to propose a mechanism whereby in a normal individual the homogentisic acid derived from the breakdown of amino acids was itself further reduced to its harmless ingredients. In some individuals however there was a 'metabolic block'. They lacked the specific enzyme that breaks down homogentisic acid into harmless carbon dioxide and water, so allowing the acid to accumulate and overflow into the urine.

Nor was alkaptonuria the only such metabolic disorder; others identified by Garrod included cystinuria, pentosuria and, the cause of George III's madness, porphyria.

Garrod's daughter Dorothy, a distinguished archeologist, was appointed to the Disney Professorship at Cambridge University in 1939, thus becoming the first woman to hold a Cambridge chair. Of his three sons, two died in action in World War I and the third died of pneumonia.

GASKELL, Walter Holbrook (b. Nov. 1, 1847; Naples, Italy; d. Sept. 7, 1914; Cambridge, England) British physiologist.

Gaskell, a lawyer's son, graduated in mathematics from Cambridge University in 1869. He then studied medicine at University College Hospital, London, but returned to Cambridge to serve as lecturer in physiology from 1883 until his death. His first studies investigated whether the heartbeat is under external nervous control or is an inherent property of the cardiac musculature (myogenic). Skillful work with tortoises and crocodiles showed that the heart's rhythm is indeed myogenic.

Gaskell also greatly increased knowledge of the structure of the autonomic (involuntary) nervous system. In 1886 he noted three major 'outflows' of nerves from the spinal cord and lower part of the brain: the cervico-cranial, thoracic, and sacral. On leaving the central nervous system each nerve passes through a ganglion, or relay station, sited alongside the spine. Gaskell discovered two key properties of the system. He first noted that the nerves of all three groups are enclosed in a white sheath of myelin before entering their adjacent ganglion; on leaving the ganglion however the nerves of the thoracic outflow have lost their sheath in contrast to the still myelinated nerves of the other two outflows. He had thus succeeded in finding a simple anatomical distinction between the myelinated nerves, sacral and cervicocranial, of the parasympathetic system, and the unmyelinated nerves, thoracic, of the sympathetic nervous system.

He also noted that most parts of the body receive nerves of both types and that their actions seem to be antagonistic. That is, while the myelinated nerves of the parasympathetic system inhibited the action of involuntary muscle, those of the sympathetic system seemed to increase its activity. Although much of Gaskell's work was done on reptiles he realized it had wider implications and boldly predicted that it would apply also to mammals, a prediction soon confirmed. His work was published posthumously in *The Involuntary Nervous System* (1916).

Much of Gaskell's later life was spent studying mammalian evolution. He tried to show how mammals could have evolved from arthropods rather than echinoderms (the orthodox view). His ideas were published in *The Origin of the Vertebrates* (1908), which contains the results of 20 years work, but his theories have been largely ignored.

GASSENDI, Pierre (b. Jan. 22, 1592; Champtercier, France; d. Oct. 21, 1655; Paris) French physicist and philosopher.

After being educated in Aix and Paris, Gassendi gained a doctorate in theology from Avignon in 1616, was ordained in 1617 and in the same year was appointed to the chair of philosophy at Aix. In 1624 Gassendi moved to Digne where he served as provost of the cathedral until 1645 when he was elected to the professorship of mathematics at the Collège Royale in Paris, resigning because of illness in 1648.

As a practicing astronomer Gassendi made a large number of observations of comets, eclipses, and such celestial phenomena as the aurora borealis — a term he introduced himself. His most significant observation was of the 1631 transit of Mercury, the first transit to be observed, which he recorded in 1632 as support for the astronomical system of Johannes Kepler.

In physics Gassendi attempted to measure the speed of sound and obtained the (too high) figure of 1473 feet per second. He also, in 1640, performed the much-contemplated experiment of releasing a ball from the mast of a moving ship; as he expected, it fell to the foot of the mast in a straight line.

Gassendi's importance to science rests with his role as a propagandist and philosopher rather than as an experimentalist. Even though the Paris parliament declared in 1624 that on penalty of death "no person should either hold or teach any doctrine opposed to Aristotle," Gassendi published in the same year the first of his many works attacking both medieval scholasticism and Aristotelianism. Nor did Gassendi find much attraction in the then emerging system of René Descartes. Instead he sought to revive the classical atomism of Epicurus, suitably modified to ensure its compatibility with 17th-century Christianity. Unlike Epicurus he insisted that the atoms were created by God who also bestowed on man an immaterial soul; against Descartes he admitted the existence of the void within which his atoms could interact.

Gassendi's works were well known in England and exercised considerable influence on such leading scientists as Robert Boyle.

GASSER, Herbert Spencer (b. July 5, 1888; Platteville, Wisconsin; d. May 11, 1963; New York City) American physiologist.

Gasser, the son of a country doctor, was educated at the University of Wisconsin and at Johns Hopkins University, qualifying as a physician in 1915. He then moved to Washington University, St. Louis, to take up an appointment as professor of pharmacology. Here he joined his old teacher, Joseph Erlanger (q.v.), in a famous collaboration that resulted in their sharing the 1944 Nobel Prize for physiology or medicine for work on the differentiated function of nerve fibers. In 1931 Gasser was appointed to the chair of physiology at Cornell Medical School. Finally, in 1935, he was made director of the Rockefeller Institute in New York, a post he retained until his retirement in 1953.

GATTERMANN, Ludwig (b. Apr. 20, 1860; Goslar, now in West Germany; d. June 20, 1920; Freiburg, now in West Germany) German organic chemist.

Gattermann studied chemistry at Göttingen University, where he became Victor Meyer's assistant, moving with Meyer to Heidelberg in 1889. In 1900 Gattermann was appointed professor of chemistry at Freiburg University.

Gatterman is noted for his work on derivatives of benzene and a number of reactions are named for him. The *Gattermann–Koch synthesis* (with J.C. Koch, 1897) is a method of introducing the formyl group (CHO) onto a benzene ring using a mixture of carbon monoxide and hydrogen chloride with a metal chloride catalyst. The *Gattermann synthesis* (1907) uses liquid hydrogen cyanide in place of carbon monoxide to achieve the same result. The *Gattermann–Sandmeyer reaction* (1890) is a method of promoting the conversion of diazonium compounds into other benzene derivatives using freshly precipitated copper powder.

GAUSS, Karl Friedrich (b. Apr. 30, 1777; Brunswick, now in West Germany; d. Feb.

23, 1855; Göttingen, now in West Germany)
German mathematician.

Gauss came of a peasant background and his extraordinary talent for mathematics showed itself at a very early age. By the age of three, he had discovered for himself enough arithmetic to be able to correct his father's calculations when he heard him working out the wages for his laborers. Gauss retained a staggering ability for mental calculation and memorizing throughout his life. At the age of ten he astonished his schoolteacher by discovering for himself the formula for the sum of an arithmetical progression. As a result of such precocity the young Gauss obtained the generous patronage of the duke of Brunswick. The duke paid for Gauss to attend the Caroline College in Brunswick and the University of Göttingen, and continued to support him until his death in 1806. Gauss then accepted an offer of the directorship of the observatory at Göttingen. This post probably suited him better than a more usual university appointment since he had little enthusiasm for teaching. Working at the observatory no doubt also stimulated his interest in applied mathematics and astronomy.

Gauss's life was uneventful. He remained director of the observatory for the rest of his life and indeed only rarely left Göttingen. Apart from mathematics he had a very keen interest in languages and at one stage hesitated between a career in mathematics and one in philology. His linguistic ability was evidently very great for he was able to teach himself fluent Russian in under two years. He also had a lively interest in world affairs, although in politics as in literature his views were somewhat conservative.

Gauss's contributions to mathematics were profound and they have affected almost every area of mathematics and mathematical physics. In addition to being a brilliant and original theoretician he was a practical experimentalist and a very accurate observer. His influence was naturally very great, but it would have been very much greater had he published all his discoveries. Many of his major results had to be rediscovered by some of the best mathematicians of the 19th century, although the extent to which this was the case was only revealed after Gauss's death. To give but two of many examples — Janos Bolyai and Nikolai Lobachevsky are both known as the creators of non-Euclidean geometry, but their work had been anticipated by Gauss 30 years earlier. Cauchy's great pioneering work in complex analysis is justly famous, yet Gauss had proved but not published the fundamental Cauchy theorem years before Cauchy reached it. The reason for Gauss's extreme reluctance to publish seems to have been the very high standard he set himself and he was unwilling to publish any work in a field unless he could present a complete and finished treatment of it.

Gauss received his doctorate in 1799 from the University of Helmstedt for a proof of the fundamental theorem of algebra, i.e. the theorem that every equation of degree n with complex coefficients has at least one root that is a complex number. This was the first genuine proof to be given; all the supposed previous proofs had contained errors, and it is this standard of rigor that really marks Gauss's work out from that of his predecessors. (Mathematicians of the 18th century and earlier had often possessed an intuitive ability to conjecture mathematical theorems that were in fact true, but their ideas of rigorous mathematical proof fell short of modern standards.)

Gauss's first publication is generally accepted as his finest single achievement. This is the *Disquisitiones Arithmeticae* of 1801. Appropriately it was dedicated to Gauss's patron the duke of Brunswick. The *Disquisitiones* is devoted to the area of mathematics that Gauss always considered to be the most beautiful, namely the theory of numbers or 'higher arithmetic'. Gauss's prodigious ability for mental calculation enabled him to arrive at many of his theorems by generalizing from large numbers of examples. Among many other striking results Gauss was able to prove in the *Disquisitiones* the impossibility of constructing a regular heptagon with straight edge and compass — a problem that had baffled geometers since antiquity.

Gauss's interest was not confined to pure mathematics and he made contributions to many areas of applied mathematics and mathematical physics. Thus he discovered the *Gaussian error curve* and also the method of least squares, which he used in his work on geodesy. In his work on electromagetism he collaborated with Wilhelm Weber on studies that led to the invention of the electric telegraph. The invention of the bifilar magnetometer for his own experimental work was another practical consequence of Gauss's interest in electromagnetism. His interest in mathematical astronomy resulted in many valuable innovations; he obtained a formula for calculating parallax in 1799 and in 1808 he published a work on planetary motion. When in 1801 the asteroid Ceres was first observed and then 'lost' by Giuseppe Piazzi, Gauss was able to predict correctly where it would reappear. He also made improvements in the design of the astronomical instruments in use at his observatory.

Gauss's work transformed mathematics and he is generally considered to be, with Newton and Archimedes, one of the greatest mathematicians of all time. The cgs unit of magnetic flux density is named in his honor.

GAY-LUSSAC, Joseph-Louis (b. Dec. 6, 1778; St. Léonard, France; d. May 9, 1850; Paris) French chemist and physicist.

Gay-Lussac was the son of a judge who was later imprisoned during the French Revolution. He entered the recently founded Ecole Polytechnique in 1797 and graduated in 1800. His career was thereafter one of steady promotion. Originally studying engineering, in 1801 he attracted the attention of the chemist Claude-Louis Berthollet who made him his assistant at Arcueil, near Paris. The science of chemistry was then in its infancy. Few chemists were actively engaged in research, and the equipment used was primitive. Chemical symbols had just been introduced, and no chemical formulae were known with certainty. During his career Gay-Lussac contributed to the advancement of all branches of chemistry by his discoveries, and greatly improved and developed experimental techniques.

In 1802, following the researches of the chemist Jacques Charles, Gay-Lussac formulated the law now alternatively attributed to himself and Charles — that gases expand equally with the same change of temperature, provided the pressure remains constant. Using superior experimental techniques, Gay-Lussac largely eliminated the errors of his predecessors in this field, in particular by developing a method of drying the gases. He measured the coefficient of expansion of gases between 0°C and 100°C, thus forming the basis for the theory of the absolute zero of temperature. His law was received with satisfaction as complementary to Boyle's law. It was later shown that Gay-Lussac's and Boyle's laws applied exactly only to a hypothetical 'ideal gas'; real gases obey the law approximately.

Gay-Lussac made his first daring balloon ascent in 1804 with Jean Biot, during which they made scientific observations and established that there was no change in either the composition of the air or in the Earth's magnetic force at the heights they reached. Gay-Lussac made a second ascent alone, reaching a height of 23018 feet.

In 1805, by exploding together given volumes of hydrogen and oxygen, Gay-Lussac discovered that one volume of oxygen combined with two volumes of hydrogen to form water. In 1808, after researches using other gases, he formulated his famous law of combining volumes — that when gases combine their relative volumes bear a simple numerical relation to each other (e.g. 1:1, 2:1) and to the volumes of their gaseous product, provided pressure and temperature remain constant. The English chemist John Dalton was immediately interested in Gay-Lussac's discovery, but when, on investigation, the law appeared to conflict with his own theory of the indivisibility of atoms Dalton rejected the law and sought to discredit Gay-Lussac's experimental methods. The reason for the apparent conflict was that the difference between an atom and a molecule was not clearly understood, and it was left to the Italian chemist Amadeo Avogadro to formulate a theory reconciling the two laws, thus laying the basis of modern molecular theory.

From 1808 Gay-Lussac worked with the chemist Louis Thenard. Following Humphry Davy's isolation of minute amounts of sodium and potassium, the two chemists in 1808 prepared these metals in reasonable quantities. It was during his experiments with potassium as a reagent that Gay-Lussac blew up his laboratory, temporarily blinding himself. In collaboration with Thenard he isolated and named the element boron. Simultaneously with Davy, Gay-Lussac investigated in 1813 a substance first isolated by Bernard Courtois and established that it was an element similar to chlorine. He named it iodine from the Greek 'iode' meaning 'violet'. In 1815 he prepared cyanogen and described it as a compound radical. He proved that prussic acid (hydrogen cyanide) was made up of this radical and hydrogen, completing the overthrow of Lavoisier's theory that all acids must contain oxygen. His recognition of compound radicals laid the basis of modern organic chemistry.

Gay-Lussac also investigated fermentation, the phenomenon of supercooling, the growth of alum crystals in solution, the compounds of sulfur, and the various stages of oxidation of nitrogen. With the young student Justus von Liebig he investigated the fulminates. In his later years he improved on experimental techniques, and laid the basis of modern volumetric analysis. In 1827 he devised the *Gay-Lussac tower*. Oxides of nitrogen arising from the preparation of sulfuric acid by the lead-chamber process, which formerly escaped into the atmosphere, are absorbed by passing them up a chimney packed with coke, over which concentrated sulfuric acid is trickled. This tower and its

modifications are used in many chemically-based industries today.

Gay-Lussac was a chemist of brilliance and determination. Although said to be cold and reserved as a man, as a researcher he was bold and energetic. Shortly before his death he expressed regret at the experiments that he would never be able to perform.

GEBER (*fl.* 14th century) Spanish alchemist.

The name Geber, the Latinized form of Jabir, was adopted by an anonymous medieval writer, probably because of the reputation of the great Arabian alchemist, Jabir ibn Hayyan, who is also known better as Geber.

Four of Geber's works are known, the longest being the *Summi perfectionis magisterii*, which was translated into English as *The Sum of Perfection* or *The Perfect Magistery*. The other works are *De investigatione perfectionis* (The Investigation of Perfection), *De inventione veritatis* (The Invention of Verity), and *Liber fornacum* (Book of Furnaces). The four manuscripts were translated into English in 1678.

Geber's major contribution was to spread Arabian alchemical theories throughout Europe where they had considerable influence.

GEBER or **Jabir ibn Hayyan** (b. *c.* 721; Tus, now in Iran; d. *c.* 815; Kufah, now in Iraq) Arabian alchemist.

Geber's life seems to have been spent among the political uncertainties of the decline of the Umayyad dynasty. His father was executed for his part in a plot to oust the caliph and Geber was sent to southern Arabia. He became a courtier to Harun al-Rashid (of *Arabian Nights* fame) but fell out of favor in 803 and left Baghdad for Kufah, where he probably remained for the rest of his life. He was a

Sufi as well as being connected with the Isma'ilite sect.

A large number of works carry his name, which is now usually taken to refer to a corpus as a whole without implying actual authorship by one individual. The most important works are *The 112 Books*, *The 70 Books*, *The 10 Books of Rectification*, and *The Books of the Balances*. Geber believed that everything is composed of a combination of earth, water, fire, and air. These elements combined to form mercury and sulfur from which he believed all metals are formed, a view that continued until Robert Boyle. He further held that if the right proportions of each were combined they would produce gold. Geber's theory was of considerable influence on alchemy and the early development of chemistry.

Geber is regarded as the father of Arabian chemistry. In the 14th century his name was adopted by an anonymous Spanish alchemist to add authority to his work.

GEER, Charles de *See* DE GEER, Charles.

GEER, Gerard Jacob de (b. Oct. 20, 1858; Stockholm; d. July 24, 1943; Stockholm) Swedish geologist.

Geer came from a noble family and both his father and brother served as prime minister of Sweden. He graduated from Uppsala University in 1879 and worked initially with the Geological Survey on the problem of raised beaches before taking up an appointment as professor of geology at Uppsala in 1897. In 1924 he became the first director of the Stockholm Geochronological Institute.

Geer originated the varve-counting method for dating the geological past in years, a system that gave unprecedented accuracy in age determinations. In 1878 he had begun a study of the Quaternary Period in Sweden and soon became aware of the layered deposits, known as varves, laid down in glacial lakes. Seasonal differences in the material deposited enabled individual years to be identified, the summer layer consisting of light-colored coarse-grained material and the winter layer of dark-colored fine material, and Geer noticed the analogy of the varves to tree rings.

He tried to see if the sequence of varves from one region would correlate in any way with those of other areas and found that this could be done for most parts of Sweden. However, this would only allow him to say that two samples came from the same time without being able to say whether that time was a century or a millenium in the past. He was able eventually to establish a base year at 6839 BC from which point individual years could be counted in either direction.

Geer's work was a major breakthrough although it was soon to be overshadowed by radioactive dating and was limited to certain glaciated areas. In his later years, Geer tried to apply his techniques and to establish correlations with other areas of the world, but with varying success.

GEGENBAUR, Karl (b. Aug. 21, 1826; Würzburg, now in West Germany; d. June 14, 1903; Heidelberg, now in West Germany) German comparative anatomist.

Educated at the University of Würzburg, Gegenbaur was professor of zoology and comparative anatomy at the University of Jena from 1855 to 1873, and from then until 1901 held a similar post at Heidelberg.

Gegenbaur's work was noteworthy in emphasizing the importance of comparative anatomy to the concept of evolution. One of the leading champions of Darwinism in Europe, he may be said to have laid the foundations of modern comparative anatomy with his embryological investigations, which led to his demonstration (1861) that all vertebrate eggs and sperm are unicellular, thus developing an earlier supposition of Theodor Schwann. Like T. H. Huxley, Gegenbaur denied that the vertebrate skull derived from expanded vertebrae, basing his opinion on studies of cartilaginous fishes. He also investigated the disappearance of the gill clefts in mammalian development and evolution. In his standard textbook on evolutionary morphology, *Grundriss der vergleichenden Anatomie* (1859; Elements of Comparative Anatomy), Gegenbaur expounded his view that the most reliable clues to animal evolutionary relationships lay in homology, e.g. the arm of a man as compared to the foreleg of a horse or the wing of a bird. Gegenbaur was editor of the *Morphologisches Jahrbuch* (Morphology Yearbook) from 1875, and published his autobiography in 1901.

GEIGER, Hans Wilhelm (b. Sept. 30, 1882; Neustadt, now in West Germany; d. Sept. 24, 1945; Potsdam, now in East Germany) German physicist.

Geiger studied physics at the universities of Munich and Erlangen, obtaining his doctorate (1906) for work on electrical discharges in gases. He then took up a position at the University of Manchester, England, where he worked with Ernest Rutherford from 1907 to 1912. In 1912 he returned to Germany, from then until his death holding a series of important university positions, including director of the German physical laboratory, the Physikalisch Technische Reichsanstalt, in Berlin (1912), and professor of physics at Kiel University (1925).

Geiger, a pioneer in nuclear physics, developed a variety of instruments and techniques for detecting and counting individual charged particles. In 1908 Rutherford and Geiger, investigating the charge and nature of alpha particles, devised an instrument to detect and count these particles. The instrument consisted of a tube containing gas with a wire at high voltage along the axis. A particle passing through the gas caused ionization, and initiated a brief discharge in the gas, and the resulting pulse of current could be detected on a meter. This was the prototype, which Geiger subsequently improved and made more sensitive; in 1928 he

produced, with W. Müller, a design of counter that is now widely used (and known as the *Geiger–Muller counter*). With their primitive counter Rutherford and Geiger established that alpha particles are doubly charged helium atoms.

Other important work of Geiger was his investigation with E. Marsden in 1909, of the scattering of alpha particles by gold leaf; this led Rutherford (q.v.) to propose a nuclear theory for the atom.

GEIKIE, Sir Archibald (b. Dec. 28, 1835; Edinburgh; d. Nov. 10, 1924; Haslemere, England) British geologist.

Geikie, the son of a musician, was intended to be a banker, but was allowed to pursue his interests in natural history and fossils by attending Edinburgh University. With the help of Hugh Miller he joined the staff of the Geological Survey of Great Britain in 1855 under Roderick Murchison. In 1867 he became director of the Scottish branch of the Geological Survey, a position he continued to hold after becoming professor of geology at Edinburgh in 1871. Geikie moved to London to become head of the Geological Survey in 1882, a post he occupied until his retirement in 1901.

Geikie was especially concerned with erosion processes and believed that rivers were a major factor in soil erosion. His studies were confined chiefly to the Scottish landscape and he was an early supporter of the role of glaciation in its formation.

A prolific writer, Geikie published works on the geology of Edinburgh (1861) and of Fife (1900) for the Geological Survey. His other works include his *Textbook of Geology* (1882), and a fine historical survey, *Founders of Geology* (1897). Perhaps his most original geological work was contained in his *Ancient Volcanoes of Great Britain* (1897).

From 1908 until 1913 Geikie served as president of the Royal Society. He was knighted in 1907.

GELFAND, Izrail Moiseevich (b. Sept. 2, 1913; Krasnye Okny, now in the Soviet Union) Soviet mathematician and biologist.

Gelfand's mathematical ability revealed itself early, and although he had not completed the usual university education course his mathematical expertise was sufficient for him to be admitted to do postgraduate work at the Moscow State University at the age of 19. He began teaching there in 1932 and was appointed an assistant professor in 1935. From 1939 Gelfand worked at the V. A. Steklov Institute of Mathematics of the Soviet Academy of Sciences, and since 1943 he has been professor at the Moscow State University.

Gelfand is one of the most fertile and brilliant Soviet mathematicians of his generation, and his work has been equally influential in both pure and applied mathematics. His first major original contribution was made in his doctoral dissertation, presented in 1940, in which he made advances of great importance in the theory of commutative normed rings. Other outstanding achievements of Gelfand's include his contributions to group theory, in particular his work on infinite dimensional representations of continuous groups, and on the harmonic analysis of noncompact groups.

Gelfand carried out very important studies on the theory of generalized functions. This work focused on the application of such functions to be found in dealing with differential equations. As a result of this research the whole theory of integral transformations was placed on a geometrical basis, and thus became amenable to a whole new range of techniques. In applied mathematics Gelfand's work has provided key mathematical tools needed in developing a theory of symmetry for elementary particles.

From about 1958 Gelfand became interested in biology and physiology and he made studies of the nervous system and of cell biology. He applied mathematical techniques to these studies, for example devising mathematical models of neurophysiological systems.

GELLIBRAND, Henry (b. Nov. 17, 1597; London; d. Feb. 16, 1636; London) English mathematician and astronomer.

Gellibrand was educated at Oxford University. He was described by the diarist John Aubrey as, "good for little a great while, till at last it happened accidentally, that he heard a Geometrie lecture. He was so taken with it, that immediately he fell to studying it, and quickly made great progress in it." In 1626 he became Gresham Professor of Astronomy at Oxford. He did important work on evidence for the variation of the Earth's magnetic field publishing, in 1635, his observation of the 7° shift in direction of the compass needle over the previous 50 years.

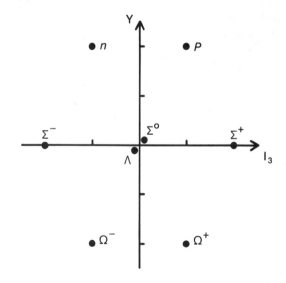

UNITARY SYMMETRY An example of an octect consisting of the neutron, proton, sigma, lambda, and omega particles.

GELL-MANN, Murray (b. Sept. 15, 1929;

New York City) American theoretical physicist.

Gell-Mann graduated from Yale University in 1948 and gained his PhD from the Massachusetts Institute of Technology in 1951. He spent a year at the Institute of Advanced Study in Princeton, before joining the Institute for Nuclear Studies at the University of Chicago, where he worked with Enrico Fermi. In 1955 he went to the California Institute of Technology, where he became a full professor in theoretical physics in 1956.

Gell-Mann's chosen subject was the theoretical study of elementary particles. His first major contribution in 1953 (at the age of only 24) was to introduce the idea of 'strangeness'. The concept came from the fact that certain mesons were 'strange particles' in the sense that they had unexpectedly large lifetimes. This concept was also advanced independently by the Japanese physicist Kazuhiko Nishijima. Strangeness, as defined by Gell-Mann and Nishijima, is a quantum property conserved in any 'strong' interaction of elementary particles.

The search for order among the known elementary particles led Gell-Mann and Israeli physicist Yuval Ne'eman to advance, independently, a mathematical representation for the classification of hadrons (particles that undergo strong interactions). Using group theory they showed that mesons and baryons could be classified into multiplets according to various properties. The mathematical group SU(3) — symmetry unitary theory of dimension 3 — is used. Particles are grouped into multiplets of 1, 8, 10, or 27 members and all particles in the same multiplet can be regarded as different states of the same basic particle. A major triumph for the theory was the prediction of the existence and properties of the omega-minus particle before it was observed at the Brookhaven National Laboratory in 1964. The theory was consolidated in Gell-Mann and Ne'eman's book *The Eightfold Way* (1964); the title refers to the octets of particles and, humorously, to the Buddhist eightfold path of morality designed to achieve nirvana.

Gell-Mann felt that it should be possible to explain many of the properties of the known elementary particles by postulating even more basic particles, later to be called 'quarks'. (The name is from a quotation in *Finnegan's Wake* by James Joyce — "Three quarks for Master Marks.") These would have electric charges and baryon numbers that were integral numbers of one third. Quarks, together with their antiparticles, would normally be in combination as constituents of the more familiar nucleons and mesons. This idea challenged established thinking, and has greatly influenced the direction of high-energy theory and experiment.

The quark hypothesis was further extended with the postulation of a fourth type of quark by Sheldon Glashow (q.v.), and more recently other properties ('color') of quarks have been assigned. The unitary symmetry theory has been extended to a higher group SU(4).

Gell-Mann received the 1969 Nobel Prize for physics, cited for his "contributions and discoveries concerning the elementary particles and their interactions." He is currently professor of theoretical physics at the California Institute of Technology's Lauritsen High-Energy Physics Laboratory.

GERARD, John (b. 1545; Nantwich, England; d. February 1612; London) British herbalist.

Gerard was educated at Willaston, Cheshire, and at the age of 16 took up an apprenticeship as barber-surgeon in London. Thereafter he traveled, probably as ship's surgeon, aboard a merchant ship trading in Scandinavia, Russia, and the Baltic. He then settled in London and began his study of plants, paying particular attention to those with medicinal properties. By 1577 he had become superintendent of the gardens of Lord Burghley, a post he held for over 20 years. His knowledge and practical experience led to his appointment as curator of the gardens of the College of Physicians between 1586 and 1603 or 1604, and in 1597 his election as warden of the Barber-Surgeon's Company.

Gerard had cultivated his own extensive garden in London and in 1596 issued a catalog listing over a thousand different plants in his possession. In 1597, he published his most famous work, the *Herball*, a survey of plants then available in western Europe. Although probably an adaptation of an earlier work by Rembertus Dodoens and of questionable accuracy, its descriptive style and over 1800 woodcut illustrations make it the most famous of English herbals.

GERHARDT, Charles Frédéric (b. Aug. 21, 1816; Strasbourg, France; d. Aug. 15, 1856; Strasbourg) French chemist.

Gerhardt was the son of an Alsatian chemical manufacturer. He was educated at the universities of Karlsruhe, Leipzig, and Giessen where he studied under Justus von Liebig. From 1838 he worked in Paris as assistant to Jean Dumas before becoming professor of chemistry at Montpellier (1844). He returned to Paris in 1848 and worked with Auguste Laurent in their private laboratory until he was appointed to the chair at Strasbourg in 1855. He published two original works: *Précis de chimie organique* (1844–45) and his *Introduction à l'étude de la chimie par le système unitaire* (1848).

Gerhardt is best known for his attempts to rationalize organic chemistry. Like most chemists he was aware that the dualistic system of Jöns Berzelius was unsatisfactory and tried to create an alternative. He adopted what became known as 'type theory' in which he saw all organic compounds with reference to four 'types' — hydrogen, hydrogen chloride, ammonia, and water. Organic compounds were referred to these types by replacing a hydrogen atom in one of these compounds by a radical (i.e. by a group of atoms).

GERMER, Lester Halbert (b. Oct. 10, 1896; Chicago, Illinois; d. Oct. 3, 1971; Gardiner, New York) American physicist.

Germer began research at the Western Electric and the Bell Telephone Laboratories. Later he moved to Cornell University, New York. In 1927 he assisted Clinton J. Davisson (q.v.) in the celebrated *Davisson–Germer experiment*, which first demonstrated the wavelike behavior of electrons. Germer's other interests were in thermionics, the erosion of metals, contact physics, and the plating of molybdenum and tungsten, by thermal decomposition of metal carbonyl compounds.

GESNER, Conrad (b. Mar. 26, 1516; Zurich, Switzerland; d. Dec. 13, 1565; Zurich) Swiss naturalist, encyclopedist, and physician.

Although Gesner graduated in medicine from the University of Basel (1541), his main interest was natural history. In the comprehensive survey *Historiae animalium* (1551–87), he attempted in five volumes, to present the facts rather than the myths then known about the animal kingdom. A comparable work that he planned on plants was never written owing to his untimely death from the plague. He nevertheless collected more than 500 plant species not described in ancient texts, mainly alpine species found while indulging his hobby of mountain climbing. The notes and engravings made in preparation for his botanical encyclopedia were used by botanists for the following 200 years.

Gesner also wrote a major bibliographical work on Latin, Greek, and Hebrew writers, a work on comparative philology, and a book on fossils, containing the first illustrations of these 'stony concretions' as Gesner regarded them.

GIAEVER, Ivar (b. Apr. 5, 1929; Bergen, Norway) Norwegian–American physicist.

Giaever studied electrical engineering at the Norwegian Institute of Technology. He did service with the Norwegian Army (1952–53) and worked as a patent examiner in the Norwegian Patent Office (1953–54). In 1954 he emigrated to Canada to take up the post of mechanical engineer with the Canadian General Electric Company, transferring to General Electric's Research and Development Center in Schenectady, New York, in 1956. He gained his doctorate in 1964 from the New York Rensselear Polytechnical Institute.

At General Electric, Giaever worked on tunneling effects in superconductors, a phenomenon explored by Leo Esaki (q.v.). In 1960 he performed experiments with metals separated by a thin insulating film through which electrons tunneled, and found that if one of the metals was in the superconducting state, the current–voltage characteristics of such junctions were highly nonlinear and revealed much about the superconducting state. This laid the foundation for Brian Josephson's (q.v.) important discovery of the Josephson effect.

Giaever, Josephson, and Esaki shared the 1973 Nobel Prize for physics for their various contributions to knowledge of the phenomenon of tunneling and superconductivity. Their work has had important application in microelectronics and in the precise measurement of electromotive force.

Subsequently, Giaever has also published work in the field of visual observation of the antibody–antigen reaction.

GIAUQUE, William Francis (b. May 12, 1895; Niagara Falls, Canada) Canadian-American physical chemist.

Giauque has spent his whole academic life at the University of California. He began as a student, obtaining his PhD in 1922, and was immediately appointed to the staff at Berkeley, becoming professor of chemistry in 1934.

Giauque was one of the pioneer workers in low-temperature phenomena. His early work in the 1920s concerned the experimental measurement of entropies at very low temperature — work that depended on use of the third law of thermodynamics introduced in 1906 by Walther Nernst (the Nernst heat theorem). At the same time, Giauque used statistics to calculate the absolute entropies using the energy levels of molecules obtained from spectroscopy. This method, developed by Josiah Willard Gibbs and others, is known as statistical mechanics. Giauque's work provided support for the validity of both statistical thermodynamics and the third law.

Moreover, it led him to a method of attaining very low temperatures, close to absolute zero. The lowest temperature achieved at that time was $0.8\,K$, reached by Heike Kamerlingh-Onnes in 1910 by pumping away the vapor of liquid helium and causing it to evaporate under reduced pressure. Giauque, and independently Peter Debye, proposed in 1925 a completely different method known as adiabatic demagnetization.

The basic idea is to take a paramagnetic substance surrounded by a coil of wire in a gas-filled container. The sample can be cooled by surrounding the container by liquid helium and magnetized by a current through the coil. It is thus possible to produce a magnetized specimen at liquid-helium temperature, and then to isolate it in a vacuum by removing the gas from the container. In the magnetized specimen the 'molecular magnets' are all aligned. If the magnetic field on the specimen is reduced to zero the sample is demagnetized, and in this process the molecular magnets become random again. The entropy increases and work is done against the decreasing external field, causing a decrease in the temperature of the specimen.

There were considerable problems in putting this theory into practice, not least in measuring the temperatures produced. In 1933 Giauque had a working apparatus that improved on Kamerlingh-Onnes's in achieving a temperature of $0.1\,K$. Giauque received the 1949 Nobel Chemistry Prize for his work on low-temperature phenomena.

He also worked on isotopes, showing in 1929 (with H. L. Johnson) that oxygen was a mixture of ^{16}O, ^{17}O, and ^{18}O.

GIBBS, Josiah Willard (b. Feb. 11, 1839; New Haven, Connecticut; d. Apr. 28, 1903; New Haven) American mathematician and theoretical physicist.

Gibbs came from an academic family. He entered Yale in 1854, graduated in 1858, and in 1863 received a PhD for research on the design of gears. The same year he traveled to Europe, returning in 1869 to Yale where he remained until his death. In 1871 he was appointed professor of mathematical physics.

His initial work on the theory of James Watt's steam-engine governor led him into a study of the thermodynamics of chemical systems. In a series of long papers published between 1873 and 1876 he developed, and indeed virtually completed, the theory of chemical thermodynamics. Gibbs's most famous paper, *On the Equilibrium of Heterogeneous Substances* (1876), contains the celebrated *Gibbs phase rule*, describing the equilibrium of heterogeneous systems. His name is also associated with the *Gibbs free energy* — a function that determines the conditions in which a chemical reaction will occur — and with several other equations in thermodynamics.

Gibbs was also active in mathematics and physics. He worked on the theory of William Hamilton's quaternions and introduced the simpler, widely used, vector notation. Between 1882 and 1889 he published a series of papers on the electromagnetic theory of light. He also made important contributions to statistical mechanics, introducing the fundamental concept of *Gibbsian ensembles* — collections of large numbers of macroscopic systems with the same thermodynamic properties, used in relating thermodynamic properties to statistical properties.

Gibbs, who never married, lived a quiet retiring life at Yale; he was a poor teacher but a brilliant and productive theorist. His work, carried out far from the European mainstream of science, was largely published in the obscure *Transactions of the Connecticut Academy of Sciences*. However, James Clerk Maxwell understood the importance of his ideas as early as 1875 and in later life Gibbs was widely recognized. Many regard him as the greatest native-born American scientist.

GIBBS, William Francis (b. Aug. 24, 1886; Philadelphia, Pennsylvania; d. Sept. 7, 1967; New York City) American naval architect and marine engineer.

Gibbs was educated at Harvard (1906–10) and Columbia (1910–13) where he studied law. His interest in ship design was aroused by the rapid sinking of the *Empress of Ireland* following a collision in 1914 with the loss of 1000 lives. He argued that simple compartmentalization and properly designed bulkheads could have prevented such a tragedy. Gibbs consequently joined the International Mercantile Marine Company with whom he stayed until 1922 when, with his brother, Frederick, he founded the company Gibbs Brothers, later (1929) Gibbs and Cox.

Beginning in 1933, Gibbs did much to modernize the US Navy, and persuaded it to adopt high-pressure and high-temperature steam turbines into the design of its destroyers. It was largely due to plans laid down by Gibbs that large numbers of Liberty ships could be rapidly built when America entered World War II. During the war Gibbs served as controller of shipbuilding.

Gibbs is probably best-known as the designer of the SS *United States*, a passenger ship launched in 1952, which set new speed records across the Atlantic, achieving an average speed of 35.05 knots (40.3 statute miles per hour).

GILBERT, Walter (b. Mar. 21, 1932; Boston, Massachusetts) American molecular biologist.

Gilbert was educated at Harvard and in England at Cambridge University where he obtained his PhD in physics in 1957. He returned to America to take up an appointment in theoretical physics at Harvard. He changed to molecular biology in 1960 under the influence of James Watson and in 1968 became professor of molecular biology at Harvard.

In 1961 Jacques Monod (q.v.) and François Jacob (q.v.) proposed a theoretical answer to one of the most pressing problems of molecular biology, that of genetic control. If the common bacteria *Escherichia coli* is grown in the presence of milk sugar (lactose) it will produce an enzyme, beta-galactosidase, to split it into its component sugars. However, if grown in the absence of lactose, the enzyme will not be produced. There must therefore presumably be a mechanism whereby the gene controlling the production of the enzyme can be switched on and off. Monod and Jacob proposed a detailed account of such a mechanism, part of which involves the existence of a repressor molecule, which could bind itself to the gene and switch it off in the absence of lactose. The lac repressor, as it was called, would be inactivated, thus switching the gene on, by an inducer molecule produced by the lactose itself.

Plausible and powerful though the Monod–Jacob model appeared, it was still only a model until the basic confirmation provided by the isolation and identification of the lac repressor was achieved. Gilbert began such a search in 1965. This was a formidable task as the repressor was known to exist in small quantities only; nor was its chemical nature known. Gilbert himself likened the task to isolating the neutrino.

By 1966, in collaboration with Benno Muller-Hill, Gilbert had devised an ingenious experimental procedure, known as equilibrium dialysis. They used a specially active inducer, isopropyl thiogalactoside (IPTG), discovered by Melvin Calvin. Cells of *E. coli* were ground up and placed in a bag with a cellular membrane, allowing the passage of water and IPTG molecules but excluding such larger molecules as proteins. The bag was then placed in water containing radioactive IPTG.

As IPTG can pass through the bag an equal concentration of the inducer should be achieved. But if IPTG should bind itself to the lac repressor inside the bag then it will be too large to pass freely through the bag membrane. Consequently the concentration of the IPTG bound to the repressor should start to build up inside the bag and, being radioactive, should be readily detectable. Eventually they were able to report a concentration of IPTG 4% greater inside the bag than out. This was enough to encourage Gilbert and Muller-Hill to proceed to the next stage of fractionating, purifying, and isolating the repressor. This proved more difficult than they had expected but in late 1966 they were able to report the existence of a large protein molecule, the lac repressor. The following year their Harvard colleague M. Ptashne obtained a similar result with the lambda phage repressor.

Gilbert has also developed techniques for determining the sequence of bases in DNA, which though similar to Frederick Sanger's (q.v.) method differs in that it can be applied to single as well as double-stranded DNA. It was for this work that he shared the 1980 Nobel Chemistry Prize with Sanger and Paul Berg.

GILBERT, William (b. May 24, 1544; Colchester, England; d. Dec. 10, 1603; either London or Colchester) English physicist and physician.

Gilbert was educated at Cambridge University, where he took his degree in 1569 and later became a fellow. He moved to London in 1573, became a member of the Royal College of Physicians, and served as physician to Queen Elizabeth I and briefly to James I. In 1600 he published the first great English scientific work *De magnete, magnetisque corporibus, et de magno magnete tellure* (On the Magnet, Magnetic Bodies, and the Great Magnet Earth) in which he presented his investigations into magnetic bodies and electrical attractions. It is a remarkably 'modern' work — rigorously experimental, emphasizing observation, and rejecting as unproved many popular beliefs on magnetism, such as the supposed ability of diamond to magnetize iron. He showed that a compass needle was subject to magnetic dip (pointing downward) and, reasoning from experiments with a spherical lodestone, explained this by concluding that the Earth acts as a bar magnet. He also introduced the term 'magnetic pole'. The book was widely available on the Continent, there being five editions in Germany and Holland alone before 1628, and was very influential in the creation of the new mechanical view of science.

GILCHRIST, Percy Carlyle (b. Sept. 27, 1851; Lyme Regis, England; d. Dec. 15, 1935) British industrial chemist.

Gilchrist was educated at the Royal School of Mines in London. In 1875 he was appointed chemist at the Cwm Avon works in South Wales, and here in his spare time he assisted his cousin Sidney Gilchrist Thomas in trials of a new process of smelting iron ore. In the *Gilchrist–Thomas process* the furnace was lined with a basic material (such as magnesium oxide), which combined with phosphate impurities in the iron. Gilchrist later made other improvements to the process, which was extremely important at the time in allowing exploitation of phosphoric ores.

GILL, Sir David (b. June 12, 1843; Aberdeen, Scotland; d. Jan 24, 1914; London) Scottish astronomer.

Gill was educated at Marischal College and Aberdeen University. He was in charge of the Earl of Crawford's private observatory at Dunecht before becoming royal astronomer at the Cape of Good Hope, where he remained until 1907. He was knighted in 1900.

Gill spent much time and thought on improving the accuracy of the astronomical unit (AU — the mean distance between the Earth and the Sun, one of the basic measurements of astronomy), then determined from measurements of the distances of Venus and Mars. In 1874 he went to Mauritius to observe the transit of Venus. The difficulty with this method is that Venus, on magnification, presents a disk whose edges are not absolutely sharp, thus making it difficult to estimate the moment of first contact. In 1877 Gill went to Ascension Island to measure the distance of Mars using the distance from Greenwich as a base line. Although he obtained reasonable results he realized (as had Johann Galle) that a more accurate figure could be obtained if the planetoids were used instead for they came closer to the Earth and on magnification presented a starlike appearance. (This idea was taken up with great success later by Harold Spencer Jones.) In 1897, with the cooperation of astronomers in Leipzig and New Haven, Gill made a very accurate determination of the solar parallax.

His other main research was extending Friedrich Argelander's catalog to the southern skies. This began in 1882 when he photographed a comet and was impressed with the clarity of the stars visible in the background. Consequently he started photographing the southern skies, collaborating with the Dutch astronomer Jacobus Kapteyn. In 1904 the *Cape Photographic Dorchmusterung* was published cataloging over 450 000 stars to within 19° of the southern celestial pole.

GILMAN, Henry (b. May 9, 1893; Boston, Massachusetts) American chemist.

Gilman was educated at Harvard, where he obtained his PhD in 1918. After working briefly at the University of Illinois he moved to Iowa State University in 1919, spending the rest of his career there and serving as professor of organic chemistry from 1923 until his retirement in 1962. He has worked extensively in the field of organometallic chemistry.

GLASER, Donald Arthur (b. Sept. 21, 1926; Cleveland, Ohio) American physicist.

Glaser took his degree in physics and mathematics at the Case Institute of Technology, Cleveland, graduating in 1946, and went on to gain his doctorate for cosmic-ray research from the California Institute of Technology in 1950. From 1949 to 1959, Glaser worked in the physics department of the University of Michigan, becoming professor in 1957. In 1959 he moved to the University of California at Berkeley as a professor of physics and subsequently (1964) as a professor of physics and biology.

While at the University of Michigan, Glaser became interested in techniques for the visualization and recording of elementary particles. The Wilson cloud chamber, using supersaturated vapor, had been in use since the 1920s, but was unsuited to the detection of the highly energetic particles emerging from the new accelerators of the 1950s.

Glaser considered other unstable systems that could be used, and experimented with superheated liquids, in which ionizing particles would leave a trail of vapor bubbles. In 1952 he produced the first radiation-sensitive bubble chamber, in which he used diethyl ether under pressure and controlled temperature. A sudden brief reduction in pressure was used and trails of bubbles forming along the tracks of particles could be captured by high-speed photography before the bulk of the liquid boiled. For this invention, and its subsequent development into a useful research tool, Glaser received the 1960 Nobel Prize for physics.

The bubble chamber, using liquid hydrogen at low temperature, is now a basic component of almost all high-energy physics experiments, and has been the instrument of detection of many strange new particles and phenomena. Present-day bubble chambers are much bigger (and more expensive) than Glaser's original, which was only three cubic centimeters in volume. More recently, at the University of California at Berkeley, Glaser's interest has turned to methods of applying physics to molecular biology.

GLASHOW, Sheldon Lee (b. Dec. 5, 1932; New York City) American physicist.

Glashow graduated from the Bronx High School in New York in 1950 and went on to Cornell University, gaining his bachelor's degree in 1954. His MA (1955) and PhD in physics (1959) were gained at Harvard University, and his postdoctoral research took him to the Bohr Institute, the European Organization for Nuclear Research (CERN) in Geneva, and the California Institute of Technology. After a year at Stanford he joined the faculty of the University of California at Berkeley (1961–66). In 1967 he returned to Harvard as a professor of physics, and has remained there since.

The award of the 1979 Nobel Physics Prize, shared with Abdus Salam (q.v.) and Steven Weinberg (q.v.), was for the explanation of the forces that bind together elementary particles of matter. The citation was "for their contribution to the theory of the unified weak and electromagnetic interaction between elementary particles, including *inter alia* the prediction of the weak neutral current."

The Weinberg–Salam theory was a major step in unifying two of the four fundamental forces of physics: the electromagnetic interaction and the weak interaction. The theory was originally applied only to the class of particles known as leptons (electrons and neutrinos). Glashow extended the theory to other elementary particles (including the baryons and mesons) by introducing a new property that he called 'charm'. The quark theory of Murray Gell-Mann could be extended by the introduction of a fourth quark — the 'charmed quark' — and combinations of the four types of quark could lead to a group of particles with symmetry SU4. The idea of charm can be used to explain the properties of the J/psi particle, discovered in 1974 by Burton Richter and Samuel Ting.

Other extensions of the quark theory

have since been made involving 'colored quarks' — the theory is known as 'quantum chromodynamics'.

GLAUBER, Johann Rudolf (b. 1604; Karlstadt, now in West Germany; d. Mar. 10, 1668; Amsterdam) German chemist.

Glauber was the son of a barber. He spent the first half of his life traveling and working in Germany, and later settled in Amsterdam. There he made his living chiefly through selling chemicals and medicinals. He made important contributions to chemistry and his fame is largely based on his discovery of a salt called *sal mirabile* (sodium sulfate). He had found that the action of sulfuric acid on common salt produced a new acid, hydrochloric, and a salt, sodium sulfate. This became known as *Glauber's salt* and was originally sold to treat everything from typhus to constipation. It is still widely used, together with Epsom salt (magnesium sulfate), as a laxative.

Glauber's chief work, *Philosophical Furnaces* (1646–48), has been described as the first comprehensive treatise on industrial chemistry outside metallurgy. He seems to have been something of a consultant developing new products and advising on chemical processes in industry. He also speculated on the nature and rules of chemical affinity. His technical works were published as *Opera omnia chymica* (1658) in seven volumes. His *Prosperity of Germany*, written after the Thirty Years' War, looked forward to a peaceful Europe ruled by a Germany whose power arose from a science-based military technology.

GLAZEBROOK, Sir Richard Tetley (b. Sept. 18, 1854; Liverpool, England; d. Dec. 15, 1935; Limpsfield Common, England) British physicist.

Glazebrook graduated from Cambridge University in 1876 and at once joined the Cavendish Laboratory, Cambridge, under the directorship of James Clerk Maxwell. He became lecturer in physics and mathematics and in 1891 was appointed assistant director of the Cavendish. He left to become first principal of University College, Liverpool (1898–99) and then director of the newly established National Physical Laboratory at Teddington (1900–19). He was knighted in 1917.

Glazebrook conducted a considerable amount of research on electrical standards involving very precise electrical measurements. He also made contributions to the fields of optics and thermometry. From 1909 the National Physical Laboratory undertook research into aeronautics. This work included wind-tunnel experiments for aircraft development and the adoption of scientific apparatus for military and aeronautical engineering purposes.

After his retirement in 1919 Glazebrook took on new teaching and administrative responsibilities, serving for many years as chairman of the Aeronautical Research Committee. He was the author of several books on physics and science in general and also edited the *Dictionary of Applied Physics*.

GLISSON, Francis (b. 1597; Rampisham, England; d. Oct. 16, 1677; London) English physician.

Glisson was educated at Cambridge University where he obtained his MD in 1634. He was appointed professor of physics at Cambridge in 1636 and retained the post until his death. However most of his time was spent in private practice in London, so an assistant was employed to fulfill his Cambridge teaching obligations.

Glisson was a member of the group that, beginning in 1645, met regularly in London and out of which the Royal Society was later to emerge. From this 'Invisible College' as it was later known, came one of the earliest examples of cooperative research. A committee of nine was set up in 1645 to investigate rickets but, as Glisson's contribution far exceeded that of any other contributor, it was agreed that he should publish the report *De rachitide* (1650) under his own name. However as the nature of rickets could only begin to be comprehended with the discovery of vitamins by Casimir Funk in 1912, Glisson must yet be credited for his clear description of the disease.

He was more original and influential in his account of irritability, first formulated in his work on the liver, *Anatomia hepatis* (1654). He argued that muscular irritability, that is their tendency to respond to stimuli, was independent of any external input, nervous or otherwise. This was a considerable improvement over the orthodox position adopted by the followers of René Descartes who believed that muscle could only respond by being pumped up like a tire, with a subtle nervous spirit rather than air. Glisson later reported a simple experiment where he placed his arm in a tube filled with water and noted that when his muscles contracted the level of water actually fell. This showed quite clearly, he claimed, that there had been no flow of anything into the limb.

It was this idea of irritability which, picked up by Albrecht von Haller in the following century, was to find a permanent place in physiology.

GMELIN, Leopold (b. Aug. 2, 1788; Göttingen, now in West Germany; d. Apr. 13, 1853; Heidelberg, now in West Germany) German chemist.

Gmelin, whose father and grandfather were botanists, studied at the universities of Tübingen, Göttingen, and Vienna. In 1817 he was appointed to the first chair of chemistry at Heidelberg, where he remained until 1851. In 1817 he published the first edition of what was to become the major chemical textbook of the first half of the 19th century, *Handbuch der Chemie*, in three volumes. By 1843 the book was in its fourth edition and had been expanded to nine volumes. In this edition Gmelin adopted the atomic theory and devoted much more space to the growing discipline of organic chemistry. The terms *ester* and *ketone* were introduced by him. His book was translated into English in 1848.

He also worked on the chemistry of digestion, discovering several of the constituents of bile, and introduced *Gmelin's test* for bile pigments. In 1822 he discovered potassium ferrocyanide.

GODDARD, Robert Hutchings (b. Oct. 5, 1882; Worcester, Massachusetts; d. Aug. 10, 1945; Baltimore, Maryland) American physicist.

Goddard was educated in his hometown gaining his BSc in 1908 from the Polytechnic Institute and his PhD in 1911 from Clark University. He did postgraduate work at Princeton, 1912–13. He returned to Clark in 1914 where he was made professor of physics in 1919 and where he remained until his retirement in 1943.

Goddard is remembered as the designer of the first successful liquid-fuel rocket. He had been interested in space travel as a boy and his early views were first publicly revealed in his famous pamphlet *A Method of Reaching Extreme Altitudes*, published in 1919. He had most of the basic ideas of rocket design and travel clear in his mind in his 1919 paper. He realized that a reaction engine would be necessary and that sufficient thrust could only be developed with liquid fuels. In 1923 he therefore started to design rockets powered by liquid oxygen.

Unlike his Russian contemporary Konstantin Tsiolkovsky, he was fortunate to attract almost immediate and generous backing. The Smithsonian Institution supported him until 1929 when, through the influence of Charles Lindbergh, the Guggenheim family backed him with 15 000 dollars a year up to the mid-1940s. His first successful rocket flight was made in 1926 when a four-foot rocket flew for two seconds and reached an altitude of 40 feet (12 m). This was followed by bigger faster and inevitably noisier and smellier rockets. To escape the complaints and threatened litigation he set up a research and testing station at Roswell, New Mexico, in 1929, financed by the Guggenheim Foundation.

He continued to make improvements in his design. In 1931 he introduced the now familiar automatic launch sequential system and in 1932 gyroscopic steering. In 1935 his liquid-fuel rockets flew at supersonic speeds. The greatest altitude reached was 12½ miles (20 km).

Goddard's New Mexico station closed down during the war even though he offered his work to the military. He lived just long enough to inspect the captured German V–2 rockets, which, though much bigger than his, were based on the same principles. He was also prudent enough to take out about 100 patents on rocket design. His widow was later to receive 1 000 000 dollars for their use from the Department of Defense.

GÖDEL, Kurt (b. Apr. 28, 1906; Brünn, now Brno in Czechoslovakia; d. Jan. 14, 1978; Princeton, New Jersey) Austrian–American mathematician.

Gödel initially studied physics at the University of Vienna, but his interest soon turned to mathematics and mathematical logic. He obtained his PhD in 1930 and the same year joined the faculty at Vienna. He became a member of the Institute for Advanced Study, Princeton, in 1938 and in 1940 emigrated to America. He was a professor at the Institute from 1953 to 1976, and received many scientific honors and awards including the National Medal of Science in 1975.

In 1930 Gödel published his doctoral dissertation, the proof that first-order logic is complete — that is to say that every sentence of the language of first-order logic is provable or its negation is provable. The completeness of logical systems was then a concept of central importance owing to the various attempts that had been made to reveal a logical axiomatic basis for mathematics. Completeness can be thought of as ensuring that all logically valid statements that a formal (logical) system can produce can be proved from the axioms of the system, and that every invalid statement is disprovable.

In 1931 Gödel presented his famous incompleteness proof for arithmetic. He showed that in any consistent formal system complicated enough to describe simple arithmetic there are propositions or statements that can neither be proved nor disproved on the basis of the axioms of the system — intuitively speaking, there are logical truths that cannot be proved within the system. Moreover, as a corollary Gödel showed (what is known as his second incompleteness theorem) that the *consistency* of any formal system including arithmetic cannot be proved by methods formalizable within that system; consistency can only be proved by using a stronger system — whose own consistency has to be assumed. This latter result showed the impossibility of carrying out Hilbert's program (*see* David Hilbert), at least in its original form.

Gödel's second great result concerned two important postulates of set theory, whose consistency mathematicians had been trying to prove since the turn of the century. Between 1938 and 1940 he showed that if the axioms of (restricted) set theory are consistent then they remain so upon the addition of the axiom of choice and the continuum hypothesis, and that these postulates cannot, therefore, be disproved by restricted set theory. (In 1963 Paul Cohen showed that they were independent of set theory.)

Gödel has also worked on the construction of alternative universes that are models of the general theory of relativity, and has produced a rotating-universe model.

GODWIN, Sir Harry (b. May 9, 1901; Rotherham, England) British botanist.

Godwin was educated at Cambridge University and remained there for his whole career serving as demonstrator, lecturer, and reader before becoming director of the subdepartment of Quaternary research in 1948. He held the chair of botany from 1960 until his retirement in 1968.

Godwin's early investigations concerned the development of fen and bog vegetation using the technique of pollen analysis. During these studies he compiled a card index of higher plants with information about their Quaternary history. This led to his *History of the British Flora* (1956), which has become a standard reference for archeological, climatic, geological, and botanical investigations of the Quaternary period in Europe.

GOEPPERT-MAYER, Maria (b. June 18, 1906; Kattowitz, Poland; d. Feb. 20, 1972, San Diego, California) German-American physicist.

Maria Goeppert was educated at the University of Göttingen where she obtained her PhD in 1930. (She changed her name on marrying the physical chemist, Joseph Mayer.) Emigrating to America in 1931 she was employed at Johns Hopkins University, Baltimore (1931–39), Columbia University, New York (1939–46), and the Argonne National Laboratory (1946–60). Finally, in 1960 she took a post at the University of California, San Diego, at La Jolla.

In 1963 she was awarded the Nobel Physics Prize together with Hans Jensen and Eugene P. Wigner for their work on nuclear shell theory. The shell theory of the nucleus is analogous to the shell model of the atom. The theory could help explain why some nuclei were particularly stable and possessed an unusual number of stable isotopes. In particular, in 1948, she argued that the so-called magic numbers — 2, 8, 20, 50, 82, and 126 — which are the numbers of either protons or neutrons in particularly stable nuclei, can be explained in this way. She supposed that the protons and neutrons are arranged in the nucleus in a series of nucleon shells. The magic numbers thus describe those nuclei in which certain key shells are complete. In this way helium (with 2 protons and 2 neutrons), oxygen (8 of each), calcium (20

of each), and the ten stable isotopes of tin with 50 protons all fit neatly into this pattern. Also significant was the fact that, in general, the more complex a nucleus becomes the less likely it is to be stable (although there are two complex stable nuclei, lead 208 and bismuth 209, both of which have the magic number of 126 neutrons).

GOLD, Thomas (b. May 22, 1920; Vienna) Austrian–American astronomer.

Gold, a refugee from the Austrian Anschluss, gained his BA in 1942 from Cambridge University, England. He lectured there in physics from 1948 to 1952 before he joined the Royal Greenwich Observatory as chief assistant to the Astronomer Royal. He moved to America in 1956, becoming professor of astronomy at Cornell and director of the Center for Radiophysics and Space Research in 1959.

Gold is best known for his contribution to cosmology, the study of the origin, evolution, and large-scale structure of the universe. In the 1940s the prevailing cosmological model was the big-bang theory originally proposed by Georges Lemaître. Since this theory postulated a 'beginning of time' when the incredibly compact universe exploded into being, it was regarded with suspicion and alarm by many astronomers. In 1948 Gold published with Hermann Bondi *The Steady-State Theory of the Expanding Universe*. At the heart of this paper was the adoption of what became known as the 'perfect cosmological principle'. This was an extension of the cosmological principle, which states that the universe looks basically the same from whichever point one observes it; Gold and Bondi added to this that the time of observation was as irrelevant as the place. Thus the universe, on a large scale, is unchanging in time and space. It had no beginning, will never end, and a constant density of matter throughout space will always be maintained. This needed to be reconciled with the work of Edwin Hubble, which Gold and Bondi accepted and which showed that the galaxies are receding and the universe is expanding. To maintain the steady state of their universe Gold and Bondi had to introduce an original and startling proposition, namely, that there must be continuous creation of new matter from nothing. They calculated the amount needed as about one hydrogen atom per cubic kilometer of space every ten years, an amount too small to be detected. Although this proposition conflicted with such deep physical assumptions as the conservation of matter and the laws of thermodynamics they found that it was compatible with all astronomical data.

Consequently the steady-state theory proved attractive to a number of cosmologists and crucial evidence only emerged against it in the 1960s. Then Arno Penzias (q.v.) and Robert Wilson discovered the background microwave radiation in 1965 and Maarten Schmidt produced a survey of the distribution of quasars that seemed to support the evolving universe of the big-bang theory.

In 1968 news of a new type of star, a 'pulsar', was published by Jocelyn Bell and Antony Hewish. The distinguishing features of the pulsar were its high-frequency radio signals that had a periodicity of the order of a second or less. Gold quickly proposed a structure capable of producing such an effect: rapidly rotating neutron stars. The same theory was proposed independently by Franco Pacini. Neutron stars are extraordinarily dense stars that have undergone such extreme gravitational collapse following exhaustion of their nuclear fuel that their constituent protons and electrons have combined to form neutrons. These stars would be small and dense enough to rotate with a period equivalent to that of the radio pulses. It had also been shown that they would radiate energy in a narrow beam. If the Earth happened to be in the direction of the beam it would be picked up as a source of pulses, much as the beam of a lighthouse is observed as a series of flashes. The theory of Gold and Pacini was eventually accepted once pulsars rotating even faster

than the original one were detected in the Crab and Vela nebulae.

Gold was able to make a prediction that has since been confirmed. He argued that pulsars should be slowing down by a small but measurable amount, because of the loss of energy. Following careful observation of the pulsar in the Crab nebula it was found to be slowing down and its period increasing by 3.46×10^{-10} second per day.

GOLDBERGER, Joseph (b. July 16, 1874; Giralt, Hungary; d. Jan. 17, 1929; Washington DC) American physician.

Goldberger, the son of Jewish immigrants, was brought to America at the age of six. He was educated at the College of the City of New York and at Bellevue Hospital Medical School. After a brief period in private practice Goldberger joined the US Public Health Service in 1899, remaining there for the rest of his life.

Goldberger worked as a field officer for many years, making contributions to the understanding and control of such diseases as yellow fever, typhus, and dengue. He is, however, mainly remembered for his authoritative investigation of the nature, causation, and treatment of pellagra. This disease, which became widely known in America after the Civil War, is typified by chronic diarrhea, roughening of the skin, a sore tongue, and involvement of the nervous system. Death from secondary infection or general emaciation was not uncommon.

When Goldberger began his work in 1913 it was thought that the disease — prevalent in grain-eating communities, was caused by an unknown toxin produced by bacterial fermentation during storage of grain. But stimulated by the work of Frederick Gowland Hopkins and Casimir Funk, Goldberger directed his attention to deficiency diseases. He began a classic investigation into the connection between pellagra and diet in various asylums and orphanages of the southern states. He was immediately struck by the fact that the staff of such institutions — with a diet containing milk, eggs, cheese, and meat — remained free of the disease while the inmates, subsisting virtually on cereals alone, frequently suffered from epidemics of pellagra.

It was a relatively simple matter to show that the disease could be eliminated by supplementing the inmates' diet with milk. He was further able to trade the offer of a pardon with 11 inmates of a Mississippi prison for their adoption of a diet of corn, rice, sugar, pork fat, potatoes, and turnips. Within a few months 7 of the 11 were showing early symptoms of pellagra. Attempts to transmit the disease by contact with the clothes, excreta, and vomit of the patients ended in failure. All this led Goldberger to propose the existence of a P-P, or pellagra-preventive, factor. Whatever such a factor might be, he was able to show by 1920 that sufficient of it was contained in a daily dose of 15–30 gm of yeast, and by this means alone Goldberger was able to prevent the 10 000 deaths a year attributable to pellagra in the USA.

The active ingredient involved was shown in 1937 by Conrad Elvehjem to be nicotinic acid (niacin), part of the vitamin B complex.

GOLDHABER, Maurice (b. Apr. 18, 1911; Lemberg, now Lvov in the Soviet Union) Austrian–American physicist.

Goldhaber was educated at the universities of Berlin and Cambridge, where he obtained his PhD in 1936. He emigrated to America in 1938 where he first taught at the University of Illinois, becoming professor there in 1945. He moved to the Brookhaven National Laboratory in 1950, serving as its director from 1961 until 1973.

In 1934, while at the Cavendish Laboratory of Cambridge University, Goldhaber codiscovered the nuclear photoelectric effect with James Chadwick. This is the disintegration of a nucleus by high-energy x-rays or gamma rays. From this it was later established that the neutron is slightly heavier than the proton. Following Enrico Fermi's discovery of slow neutrons, Chadwick and Goldhaber also discovered (1934–35) the neutron disintegration reactions for lithium, boron, and nitrogen. The nitrogen reaction is the major source of radioactive carbon–14 on Earth.

At the University of Illinois (1938) Goldhaber and his wife, Gertrude Scharff-Goldhaber, demonstrated that electrons and beta particles are the same. In 1940 he discovered that beryllium is a good moderator, i.e. it slows down fast neutrons so they more readily split uranium atoms.

He has also proposed a cosmological theory in which an initial 'universon' broke up into a 'cosmon' (matter) and an 'anticosmon' (antimatter), with the anticosmon forming a second universe made of antimatter.

GOLDSCHMIDT, Johann (Hans) Wilhelm (b. Jan. 18, 1861; Berlin; d. May 21, 1923; Baden-Baden, now in West Germany) German chemist.

Goldschmidt was the son of an Essen industrialist. After studying at Berlin and Heidelberg he joined the family business in 1888.

In 1905 Goldschmidt introduced cheaper methods for the reduction of metallic oxides to metals (the 'Thermit process'). It had been common for the reduction process to use highly reactive but expensive metals, such as potassium and sodium. Goldschmidt showed that if a mixture of the metal oxide and aluminum powder is ignited with magnesium in contact with barium peroxide, great heat is generated and the pure metal produced. The technique was important in the production of certain metals used in alloy steels. It was also used for localized welding of steel (using iron oxide and aluminum).

GOLDSCHMIDT, Victor Moritz (b. Jan. 27, 1888; Zurich, Switzerland; d. Mar. 20, 1947; Oslo) Swiss–Norwegian chemist.

Goldschmidt was the son of H. J. Goldschmidt, a physical chemist. He attended Christiania (now Oslo) University where he obtained his PhD in 1911, remaining in Norway as director of the Mineralogical Institute until 1929 when he moved to the University of Göttingen in Germany. Being a Jew he returned to Norway in 1935, following the rise of anti-Semitism and the Nazi party. He was later sent to a concentration camp but was released by the Norwegian authorities on the grounds of ill health and escaped to England (1942). His time in England was spent first at the Macaulay Institute for Soil Research near Aberdeen, and later at the Rothamsted Experimental Station, Harpenden. He returned to Oslo after the war.

Goldschmidt is acknowledged as the founder of modern geochemistry. Following the work of Max von Laue and W. H. and W. L. Bragg, Goldschmidt laid the foundation for his work by working out the crystal structure of over 200 compounds. His interest was directed to more practical work when, as a result of the naval blockade in World War I, he was called upon to investigate Norway's mineral resources.

By the mid-1920s the atomic radii of elements in various stages of ionization had been established. Using this information, together with his detailed knowledge of crystal structure, Goldschmidt began predicting in which minerals and rocks various elements could or could not be found. His results were published over the years in his eight-volume *Geochemische Verteilungsgesetze der Elemente* (1923–38; The Geochemical Laws of the Distribution of the Elements). His book *Geochemistry* was published posthumously in 1954.

GOLDSTEIN, Eugen (b. Sept. 5, 1850; Gleiwitz, now Gliwice in Poland; d. Dec. 25, 1930; Berlin) German physicist.

Goldstein studied for a year at the University of Breslau (1869–70) then worked with Hermann von Helmholtz at the University of Berlin. He was appointed physicist at the Berlin Observatory in 1878, took his doctorate in 1881, and later established his own laboratory. In 1927 he became head of the astrophysical section of the Potsdam Observatory.

Goldstein's best-remembered scientific work is his studies of electrical discharges in gases at low pressures. He gave the name 'cathode rays' to the invisible emanations coming from the cathode of an evacuated discharge tube, showed that the rays could cast sharp shadows, and demonstrated that they were emitted perpendicular to the cathode surface. He later showed that they could be deflected by magnetic fields. Like most German scientists Goldstein believed that cathode rays were waves like light. J. J. Thomson later identified cathode rays as a stream of electrons. In 1886 Goldstein announced his discovery of *kanalstrahlen* (canal rays), rays that emerged from channels in the anode in a low-pressure discharge tube. These were identified as positively charged particles by Jean Baptiste Perrin in 1895, and later exploited in mass spectroscopy.

GOLGI, Camillo (b. July 7, 1843; Corteno, near Brescia, now in Italy; d. Jan. 21, 1926; Pavia, Italy) Italian cytologist and histologist.

Golgi studied medicine at Pavia University and thereafter mainly concerned himself with research on cells and tissues. In 1873 while serving as physician at the home for incurables, Abbiategrasso, he devised a method of staining cells by means of silver salts. This allowed the fine processes of nerve cells to be distinguished in greater detail than before and enabled Golgi to confirm Wilhelm von Waldeyer's view that nerve cells do not touch but are separated by gaps called synapses. Golgi also found a specialized type of nerve cell, later called the Golgi cell, which, by means of fingerlike projections (dendrites), serves to connect many other nerve cells. This discovery led to the formulation (by Waldeyer) and establishment (by Santiago

Ramón y Cajal) of the neuron theory — a theory that Golgi was nevertheless strongly opposed to.

Golgi was also the first to draw attention to the Golgi bodies: flattened cavities parallel to the cell's nuclear membrane whose function appears to be packaging and exporting various materials from the cell. Apart from work on the sense organs, muscles, and glands, Golgi studied varying forms of malaria. He found that different species of the protozoan parasite *Plasmodium* are responsible for the two types of intermittent fever — the tertian and quartan. He also established that the onset of fever coincides with the release into the blood of the parasitic spores from the red blood cells.

Golgi served as professor of histology (1876) and then of general pathology (1881) at Pavia University. In 1906 he shared with Ramón y Cajal the Nobel Prize for physiology or medicine for his work on the structure of the human nervous system.

GOMBERG, Moses (b. Feb. 8, 1866; Elizavetgrad, now Kirovgrad in the Soviet Union; d. Feb. 12, 1947; Ann Arbor, Michigan) Ukrainian–American chemist.

Gomberg's father, an estate owner in the Ukraine, fled with his family from Russia in 1884 when accused of plotting against the czar. Gomberg was educated at the University of Michigan where he obtained his doctorate in 1894. After a period abroad at Munich and Heidelberg he returned to Michigan where he spent his whole career serving as professor of organic chemistry from 1904 until his retirement in 1936.

Gomberg is noted for the first preparation of a stable free radical — i.e. a group of atoms with an unpaired electron. In 1900, he was trying to make hexaphenylethane, which is simply an ethane molecule (C_2H_6) in which all the hydrogen atoms have been replaced by phenyl groups (C_6H_5). Gomberg found to his surprise, and everyone else's disbelief, that he was obtaining the free radical, triphenylmethyl — $(C_6H_5)_3C$ — which clearly has a carbon atom with only three phenyl groups attached to it; that is, with a forbidden valence of three. In general free radicals are highly reactive short-lived entities. Gomberg's compound, a colorless crystalline substance, was stabilized by the three benzene rings.

Gomberg later discovered a suitable antifreeze for automobile radiators, ethylene glycol.

GOOD, Robert Alan (b. May 21, 1922; Crosby, Minnesota) American pathologist and immunologist.

Good, the son of a high school principal who died of cancer when Good was five, was educated at the University of Minnesota where he simultaneously obtained an MD and PhD in 1947. After this triumph he joined the Minnesota staff and served as professor of pediatrics from 1954 until 1973 when he moved to New York as director of the Sloan-Kettering Institute for Cancer Research.

One of the great achievements of modern immunology has been the demonstration that the immunological system is not a simple unity but rather a complex interrelationship of a number of different units. The unraveling of this particular tangle was not the work of any one man or, indeed, any one group; Good's contribution was, however, as great as any other.

In the 1940s he showed a link between plasma cells, cells found in lymphoid tissue, and antibodies. Later he noted a simple tendency to recurrent infection amongst his patients suffering from myeloma (a tumor of bone marrow cells) despite an abundance of plasma cells. This suggested to Good that there must be more to the immune system than simply the ability to make antibodies. This was reinforced when examining patients with agammaglobulinemia, who had no plasma cells at all, yet who were immunologically active enough to reject foreign skin grafts.

In the mid 1950s Good realized that

there are two parts to the immune system: one dealing with defenses against typical bacterial infections; the other more concerned with clearing up 'foreign' or unusual cells. By 1961, independently of Jacques Miller, Good was beginning to suspect that the thymus gland was deeply implicated in providing the latter type of immunity.

Work on chickens' defense mechanisms against bacterial infection had demonstrated that if the bursa (a gland found in the chicken's alimentary canal) was removed, the creature lost the ability to make antibodies in any real quantity. They were in fact just like Good's agammaglobulinemic patients. Good therefore postulated that there must be two types of immunity — one related to the thymus and the other related to the human equivalent of the chicken bursa producing antibodies. The details of the two systems and their evolution and interrelationship called for major, and as yet far from complete, research programs by immunologists.

Since then Good has become a leading proponent of the view that cancer is somehow the result of an immunological defect, a failure of the system to recognize and destroy the cancerous cell before it has begun to proliferate.

GOODPASTURE, Ernest William (b. Oct. 17, 1886; Montgomery County, Tennessee; d. Sept. 20, 1960; Nashville, Tennessee) American pathologist.

Goodpasture, the son of a lawyer, was educated at Vanderbilt University, Nashville, and at Johns Hopkins University, where he gained his MD in 1912. After working as a pathologist for some years at Johns Hopkins and at Harvard, Goodpasture returned to Vanderbilt in 1924 as professor of pathology, a post he retained until his retirement in 1955.

In 1931 Goodpasture devised a method of virus culture that provided an enormous stimulation to virology. Before this, as viruses will grow only in living tissue, they could be studied experimentally either in a living host, or, after the work of Alexis Carrel in 1911, *in vitro* in a tissue culture. The first method was expensive and difficult to control while the second, before the advent of antibiotics, was susceptible to contamination by bacteria.

Goodpasture, in collaboration with Alice Woodruff, avoided such difficulties by providing a cheap living environment for viral growth — a fertile egg. Their first success was with fowl pox but within a year they had also grown both cowpox and cold-sore viruses. Goodpasture went on in 1933 to show that attenuated cowpox vaccine could be produced in a purer and cheaper form in eggs than by the customary method of production in calf lymph.

Within a few years Goodpasture's technique had made possible the production of vaccines against yellow fever by Max Theiler and influenza by Thomas Francis. Thereafter eggs became as standard a part of the virologist's laboratory as the test tube.

GOODRICH, Edwin Stephen (b. June 21, 1868; Weston-super-Mare, England; d. Jan. 6, 1946; Oxford, England) British zoologist.

Goodrich's father, a clergyman, died when his son was only two weeks old. He was brought up in France by his mother and, as he intended to be an artist, attended the Slade School of Art at University College, London. His interest in zoology was aroused by Ray Lankester with whom he moved to Oxford as an assistant in 1892. Goodrich remained at Oxford for the rest of his career, serving as professor of comparative anatomy from 1921 to 1945.

Goodrich produced two important works, *Evolution of Living Organisms* (1912) and *Studies on the Structure and Development of Vertebrates* (1930). His main achievement in the latter work was to distinguish clearly, for the first time, between the nephridium and the coelomoduct, or the primitive kidney and primitive reproductive tract.

More generally his labors are comparable to those of such other paleontologists and comparative anatomists as David Watson and Alfred Romer who, building on the efforts of previous workers, managed to sort out the muddled story of vertebrate evolution.

GOODRICKE, John (b. Sept. 17, 1764; Groningen, Netherlands; d. Apr. 20, 1786; York, England) Dutch–British astronomer.

Goodricke was a deaf mute who, although he died when he was 21, had already done work of such importance as to receive the Copley medal of the Royal Society three years before he died. Variable stars had been discovered by Fabricius nearly 200 years before but Goodricke was the first scientist to offer a plausible explanation. Noticing the rapid variation in magnitude of Algol he proposed, in 1782, that it was being regularly eclipsed by a dark companion that passed between it and the Earth. His suggestion was confirmed a century later.

GORDAN, Paul Albert (b. Apr. 27, 1837; Breslau, now in Poland; d. Dec. 21, 1912; Erlangen, now in West Germany) German mathematician.

Gordan studied at Breslau, Königsberg, and Berlin and became professor of mathematics at the University of Erlangen. For most of his mathematical career his research was concentrated on a single field, the study of indeterminates. The central problem in the field, which Gordan eventually solved, was to prove the existence of a finite basis for binary forms of any given degree. His result was subsequently refined and extended by many workers including Gordan himself. Gordan's proof was long and complicated and the result was re-proved in 1888 by David Hilbert using new and far simpler methods. In collaboration with Rudolph Clebsch, Gordan also wrote a book on Abelian functions which included the central theorem now known as the *Clebsch–Gordan theorem*. This work was influential in giving a new direction to algebraic geometry.

GORER, Peter Alfred (b. Apr. 14, 1907; London; d. May 11, 1961; London) British immunologist.

Gorer, the son of a wealthy father who died on the Lusitania, was educated at Guy's Hospital, London where he graduated in 1929. After studying genetics under J.B.S. Haldane at University College, London from 1933 to 1934 Gorer worked at the Lister Institute until 1940 when he returned to Guy's as morbid histologist and hematologist. In 1948 he became reader in experimental pathology.

As early as 1936 Gorer tried to see if red cells of mice could be divided into antigenic groups similar to the blood groups of humans. Using his own blood serum he distinguished three kinds of mouse red cell on the basis of their ability to agglutinate his serum. He further found that such a property was inherited by the mice in a Mendelian dominant manner. Such work was supported by comparable results obtained in 1937 with the transplantation of a spontaneously appearing tumor amongst the various distinguished genetic strains of mice.

Gorer had in fact discovered the histocompatibility antigens and established their control at the genetic level, an outstanding result little appreciated in his lifetime but later to be recognized as of fundamental importance in immunology, genetics, and transplantation surgery. One who did recognize the significance of Gorer's work was George Snell who worked with him in 1948. For his later work Snell was to receive the 1980 Nobel Prize for physiology or medicine, a prize Gorer would have undoubtedly shared with him if he had not died some 19 years before from lung cancer.

GORGAS, William Crawford (b. Oct. 3, 1854; Toulminville, Alabama; d. July 3, 1920; London) American physician.

Gorgas, the son of an army ordnance officer who later served as a general in the Confederate Army, was educated at the University of the South and at Bellevue Hospital, New York, where he obtained his MD in 1879. In the following year he joined the Army Medical Corps, serving in a number of frontier posts before being appointed (1898) chief sanitary officer of Havana.

Gorgas was fortunate to be in Cuba at the time when Walter Reed and his colleagues identified the mosquito *Aedes aegypti* as the vector of yellow fever. Given this information Gorgas was able to introduce measures to so control the vector that the disease was virtually eliminated in Cuba. The strategy basically involved reducing mosquito breeding grounds by either draining or covering all standing sources of water, attacking the adult mosquitoes by fumigation, and isolating patients with the disease under netting. Such simple procedures, energetically and conscientiously carried out, worked remarkably quickly.

In 1899 the US Government had obtained the shares of the Panama Railroad Company for 40 million dollars, and when in 1903 they also obtained permission from the newly established state of Panama to attempt the construction of a canal, they realized the enormous medical problems facing them in such a task. The previous attempt (1881–89) by Ferdinand de Lesseps had failed, largely owing to yellow fever killing over 20 000 of his labor force in eight years. On the strength of his success in Cuba, the government appointed Gorgas chief sanitary officer of the Canal Zone in 1904. Unfortunately the chairman of the Canal Commission, Admiral John Walker, refused Gorgas's request for screening material and sulfur for fumigation on the grounds of economy; privately he tried to get Gorgas removed, proclaiming that "the whole idea of mosquitoes carrying fever is balderdash." Before long, however, Walker resigned. Under his successor, Gorgas was allowed to introduce the measures he had pioneered in Cuba. The extent of Gorgas's achievement is best seen in the mortality figures:

when he arrived the death rate from yellow fever was running at about 10%, but after 1906 no further cases were reported.

Gorgas remained in Panama until 1913. In the following year he was appointed surgeon-general of the US Army and was much in demand to advise on public health programs. It was in fact on his way to West Africa to advise on yellow fever control that Gorgas died, of a stroke, in London.

GOSSAGE, William (b. 1799; Burgh-in-the-Marsh, England; d. Apr. 9, 1877; Bowdon, England) British chemist.

Gossage was apprenticed to his uncle, an apothecary, in Chesterfield and later set himself up in business in Leamington selling the spa salt. He moved to Stoke Prior to manufacture salt and alkali by the Leblanc process.

In 1836 Gossage introduced a basic improvement into the manufacture of alkali. One of the disadvantages of the Leblanc process was the production of large quantities of hydrochloric acid fumes as a waste product. This was released into the atmosphere and as a result polluted the surrounding area. Gossage constructed towers in which the gas was passed up through layers of coke, and then condensed by cold water flowing down. This fluid was fed into streams and rivers where it still acted as a pollutant until Henry Deacon discovered a method for producing chlorine from the solution. Gossage's tower made possible the introduction of the Alkali Act in 1865, which made it a legal obligation for manufacturers to absorb 95% of their waste hydrochloric acid.

Gossage also tried to invent a process to recover the sulfur from calcium sulfide, a waste product of the Leblanc process. He introduced a technique in 1837 that recovered some by partial oxidation. The thiosulfate resulting could be sold to paper mills. In 1850 Gossage moved to Widnes to open a soap and alkali factory and in 1854 he patented a process for introducing sodium silicate into soap, which produced a soap with improved detergent powers.

GOUDSMIT, Samuel Abraham (b. July 11, 1902; The Hague, Netherlands) Dutch–American physicist.

Goudsmit was educated at the universities of Amsterdam and Leiden, where he obtained his PhD in 1927. He emigrated to America shortly afterward, serving as professor of physics at the University of Michigan (1932–46) and North Western (1946–48). He then moved to the Brookhaven National Laboratory on Long Island, New York, where he remained until his retirement in 1970.

In 1925 Goudsmit, in collaboration with George Uhlenbeck, put forward the proposal of electron spin. They discovered that electrons rotate about an axis and, as they are charged, set up a magnetic field. This model was successful in clearing up a number of anomalies that were becoming apparent in the fine structure of atomic spectra. A theory of spin was later given by Paul Dirac.

During World War II Goudsmit worked on radar and then became head of a top-secret mission codenamed *Alsos* in 1944. The mission was for Goudsmit to follow the front-line Allied troops in Europe, and even in some cases to precede them, looking for any evidence of German progress in the manufacture of an atomic bomb. He found that the German scientists had, in fact, made little progress and it was clear that Hitler would not be presented with such a weapon before the end of the war. For this war service Goudsmit was awarded the Medal of Freedom from the US Department of Defense and he published his account of the mission in his book *Alsos* (1947).

GOULD, Benjamin Apthorp (b. Sept. 27, 1824; Boston, Massachusetts; d. Nov. 26, 1896; Cambridge, Massachusetts) American astronomer.

Gould, the son of a merchant and teacher, graduated from Harvard in 1844, studied for a year at Berlin, and obtained his PhD from Göttingen University in 1848

under the great Karl Friedrich Gauss. On his return to America he served as head of the longitude department of the US Coast Survey from 1852 to 1867, pioneering the use of the telegraph in measuring longitude. At the same time Gould founded the *Astronomical Journal* in 1849 and edited it until 1861 when its publication was halted by the Civil War. He was also connected with the Dudley Observatory, Albany, from 1855 and served as its director briefly in 1858 before being forced to get out of town in the following year. After his traumatic expulsion from Albany he handled his father's business for some time. He set up a private observatory in Cambridge, financed by his wife, and in 1862 produced a star catalog that brought together measurements made at various observatories. He left for Argentina in 1870.

The 15 years spent in Cordoba were by far the most productive of Gould's career. He established the Argentine National Observatory there and began the first major survey of the southern skies. The Observatory's first survey of naked-eye stars, i.e. down to 7th magnitude, was published as the *Uranometria Argentina* (1879). This was followed by the fuller recording, published in 1884, of 73 160 stars from 23°S to 80°S and in 1886 by the publication of the *Catàlago General* containing the more accurate recording of 32 448 stellar coordinates. This important work was continued by Gould's successor, Juan Thomé An extended band of young stars, cloud, and dust that forms a spur off one of the spiral arms of our Galaxy and was revealed by the southern surveys was subsequently named *Gould's Belt*.

In 1885 Gould returned to Massachusetts where he restarted the *Astronomical Journal* in 1886 and worked on the 1000 photographic plates of star clusters he brought back with him from Cordoba.

GRAAF, Regnier de (b. July 30, 1641; Schoonhoven, Netherlands; d. Aug. 17, 1673; Delft, Netherlands) Dutch anatomist.

Graaf studied at the University of Leiden and later obtained a degree in medicine at the University of Angers, France (1665). He was the first to collect and study the secretions of the pancreas and gall bladder but is best known for his work on the mammalian sex organs. In 1668 he described the structure of the testicles and in 1673 described the minute follicles of the ovary, which have been called *Graafian follicles* since Haller coined the term in the mid-18th century. Graaf died of the plague aged 32.

GRAAFF, Robert Jemison van de *See* VAN DE GRAAFF, Robert Jemison.

GRAEBE, Karl (b. Feb. 24, 1841; Frankfurt, now in West Germany; d. Jan. 19, 1927; Frankfurt) German chemist.

Graebe graduated from Heidelberg in 1862. He worked as an assistant to Bunsen and Baeyer before accepting an appointment as professor of chemistry at Königsberg in 1870. In 1878 he moved to the University of Geneva.

With C. T. Liebermann, Graebe made a major contribution to the chemistry of synthetic dyes. While working as assistant to Baeyer he studied alizarin, the coloring matter taken from the madder plant. Graebe and Liebermann vaporized the pigment and passed it over zinc dust and to their surprise found that anthracene was produced. As they had earlier been working on the structure of anthracene, a coaltar derivative, they had little difficulty in seeing how to synthesize alizarin. They applied for a patent on 15 June, 1869, only a day before Sir William Henry Perkin, the discoverer of mauveine, had applied for a patent for the same product.

GRAHAM, Thomas (b. Dec. 20, 1805; Glasgow, Scotland; d. Sept. 11, 1869; London) Scottish chemist.

Graham was the son of a prosperous manufacturer. He entered Glasgow University at the age of 14 and attended the classes of the chemist Thomas Thomson. Graham's father was determined that he should enter the ministry and on Graham's persistence with his scientific studies his father withdrew his financial support. To continue in chemistry Graham made his living through teaching and writing. In 1829 he became a lecturer at the Mechanics Institution and in 1830 he was elected to the chair of chemistry at Glasgow University. In 1837 he was appointed professor in the recently founded University College, London. He was the first president of the Chemical Society of London, and of the Cavendish Society, which he founded. In 1854 he was made master of the mint.

In 1829 Graham published a paper on the diffusion of gases. Observations on this subject had been made by Joseph Priestley and Johann Döbereiner, but it was Graham who formulated the law of diffusion. He compared the rates at which various gases diffused through porous pots, and also the rate of effusion through a small aperture, and concluded that the rate of diffusion (or effusion) of a gas at constant pressure and temperature is inversely proportional to the square root of its density.

In 1860 Graham examined liquids. He noticed that a colored solution of sugar placed at the bottom of a glass of water gradually extends its color upwards. He called this spontaneous process diffusion. He also noticed that substances such as glue, gelatin, albumen, and starch diffuse very slowly. He divided substances into two types: colloids (from Greek *kolla*, glue), which diffuse slowly, and crystalloids, which diffuse quickly. He also found that substances of the two types differ markedly in their ability to pass through a membrane, such as parchment, and he developed the method of dialysis to separate them. Graham is regarded as the father of modern colloid science, and many terms that he invented, such as sol, gel, peptization, and syneresis, are still in use.

In 1833 Graham published the results of

his research on phosphates. The composition of the compound that was then called phosphoric acid was expressed by the formula PO_5. Graham proved the existence of three 'acid hydrates' to which he gave compositions PO_53HO, PO_52HO, and PO_5HO, thus laying the foundations for Justus von Liebig's theory of the polbasicity of acids. He carried out similar studies with the arsenic acids and the arsenates. Other work done by Graham includes research into the water of crystallization in hydrated salts and investigations into the absorption of hydrogen by palladium.

Graham was an excellent and successful teacher.

GRAM, Hans Christian Joachim (b. Sept. 13, 1853; Copenhagen; d. Nov. 14, 1938; Copenhagen) Danish bacteriologist.

Gram graduated in medicine at the University of Copenhagen in 1878 and from 1883 to 1885 traveled in Europe, studying pharmacology and bacteriology. While in Berlin (1884) he discovered the method of staining bacteria with which his name has become associated. He followed the method of Paul Ehrlich, using aniline-water and gentian violet solution. After further treatment with Lugol's solution (iodine in aqueous potassium iodide) and ethanol he found that some bacteria (such as pneumococcus) retained the stain (*Gram positive*) while others did not (*Gram negative*). This discovery is of great use in the identification and classification of bacteria. It is also useful in deciding the treatment of bacterial diseases, since penicillin is active only against Gram-positive bacteria; the cell walls of Gram-negative bacteria will not take up either penicillin or Gram's stain.

In 1891 Gram became professor of pharmacology at the University of Copenhagen, where he showed a keen interest in the clinical education of the students. During this time he had a large medical practice in the city. He was chairman of the Pharmacopoeia Commission from 1901 to 1921

and director of the medical department of Frederick's Hospital, Copenhagen, until he retired in 1923.

GRANIT, Ragnar Arthur (b. Oct. 30, 1900; Helsinki) Finnish neurophysiologist.

Granit qualified as a physician from the University of Helsinki in 1927 and taught there from 1927 until 1940, serving as professor of physiology from 1935. In 1940 Granit moved to the Karolinska Institute, Stockholm, becoming professor of neurophysiology at the newly founded Medical Nobel Institute in 1946.

In a long career Granit has been a prolific writer on all aspects of the neurophysiology of vision. He demonstrated that light not only stimulates but can also inhibit impulses along the optic nerve. By attaching microelectrodes to individual cells in the retina he showed that color vision does not simply depend on three different types of receptor (cone) cells sensitive to different parts of the spectrum. Rather, some of the eye's nerve fibers are sensitive to the whole spectrum while others respond to a much narrower band and so are color specific.

Granit has described his work in *Sensory Mechanisms of the Retina* (1947) and *The Visual Pathway* (1962); for such research he shared the 1967 Nobel Prize for physiology or medicine with George Wald and Haldan Hartline. Granit has also done important work on the control of muscle spindles by the gamma fibers.

GRASSI, Giovanni Battista (b. Mar. 27, 1854; Rovellasca, Italy; d. May 4, 1925; Rome) Italian zoologist.

The son of a municipal official, Grassi was educated at the University of Pavia, where he obtained his MD in 1878. He went on to study zoology at the universities of Heidelberg and Würzburg and on his return to Italy was appointed to the chair of zoology in 1883 at the University of Catania. He later moved to the University of Rome, where he served as professor of comparative anatomy from 1895 until his death.

Although Grassi made a number of contributions to zoology working on bees, termites, eels, and other species, he is mainly remembered for his work on malaria. Unfortunately his own contribution in this field is not precisely known, since not only was much of his work done in collaboration with a large number of colleagues but also virtually all his published results were claimed by Ronald Ross, as his own.

Despite the accusations by Ross of 'brigandage' by Grassi and his colleagues it would seem that they were undisputably involved in three major areas of the complex malaria story. Firstly it was the Italians Angelo Celli and Ettore Marchiafava who, together with Grassi, made the important point in 1889–90 that there were a number of protozoa producing malaria. *Plasmodium falciparum* had been discovered in 1889 and *P. vivax* in 1890: this was enough to allow them to suggest that the different varieties of malaria, the so-called quartan and tertian fevers, could be understood as due to infection with different species of *Plasmodium*.

Secondly it was Grassi, in 1898, who solved one of the major problems in implicating mosquitoes in the production of malaria. For centuries the association between marshes, malaria, and mosquitoes had been known but no-one could confidently make the obvious connection between mosquitoes and malaria as there were numerous areas in Italy that were free of malaria despite being plagued with mosquitoes. In 1897 Ross had shown that avian malaria was transmitted by the *Proteosoma* mosquito; in the following year, quite independently of this work, the Italians demonstrated that it was only the *Anopheles* mosquito that could transmit the disease to humans. Thus the connection was at last established between *Anopheles* mosquitoes and malaria.

Grassi's final major contribution was to collaborate with Patrick Manson in 1900 in providing the crucial experimental confirmation of their claim. Mosquitoes of the species *Anopheles maculipennis* that had bitten malaria patients were sent by Grassi to London, where they were allowed to feed on Manson's son; 15 days later the boy developed a clear case of tertian fever.

In 1900 Grassi published an account of his work in *Studi di uno zoologo sulla malaria* (Studies of a Zoologist on Malaria).

GRAY, Asa (b. Nov. 18, 1810; Sauquoit, New York; d. Jan. 30. 1888; Cambridge, Massachusetts) American botanist.

Gray studied at Fairfield Medical School, obtaining his MD in 1831. He spent the next five years developing his interest in botany, supporting himself by teaching and library work. During this period he met, and made a favorable impression on, John Torrey, a prominent American botanist with whom he later collaborated to produce the two-volume *Flora of North America* (1838–43).

In 1838 Gray made the first of many visits to Europe, in order to examine type specimens of American plants in various European herbaria so that the taxonomy of his flora could be based on original species descriptions. For the next four years Gray worked full-time on the flora, but with his appointment as professor of natural history at Harvard in 1842 further progress was slow due to the pressure of other commitments. Nevertheless the work was hailed in its time as being second only to A. P. de Candolle's *Prodromus* and its publication marked the adoption of natural systematics in American classification.

Gray helped promote specialization in natural history by accepting the professorship at Harvard only on the condition that he might limit his work to botany. He remained at Harvard until 1873, during which time he developed the library and botanical gardens from almost nothing. He donated his own vast collection of books and plants to the university in 1865 on the understanding that they would be housed in their own building.

During another visit to Europe in 1851, Gray met Charles Darwin. The two men later corresponded on matters of plant geography, and in 1857 Darwin wrote to Gray concerning his ideas on the origin of species. When Darwin's theory was published, Gray became his main advocate in America and wrote many essays reconciling Darwinism with Christian doctrine. These articles were collected together and published as *Darwinia* in 1876.

Gray's most widely used book is his *Manual of the Botany of the Northern United States* (1848) but he established his worldwide reputation with the publication in 1859 of a monograph on the flora of Japan and its relation to floras of other north temperate zones.

Gray was president of the American Association for the Advancement of Science from 1863 to 1873 and in 1900 was commemorated in the newly founded Hall of Fame for Great Americans.

GRAY, Harry Barkus (b. Nov. 14, 1935; Woodburn, Kentucky) American inorganic chemist.

Gray was educated at the University of West Kentucky and at Northwestern University, where he obtained his PhD in 1960. After a year at the University of Copenhagen, he joined the Columbia faculty in 1961 but moved to the California Institute of Technology in 1966 and has since served there as professor of chemistry.

As an inorganic chemist Gray has worked on the electronic structure of metal complexes and on inorganic reaction mechanisms. He has also studied the chemistry of biochemical compounds containing metal ions (e.g. proteins containing iron and copper). Later work on the photochemistry of inorganic compounds led to an interest in using complexes as a method of absorbing and storing solar energy.

GRAY, Stephen (b. *c.* 1670; d. Feb. 25, 1736; London) British physicist.

Gray made many studies of electrical phenomena and discovered that electricity could be transmitted from one substance to another. In 1729 he electrified a glass tube (by friction) and found that corks in the end of the tube became electrically charged. Further experiments showed that many other materials could conduct electricity, and that electric charges could be transferred over long distances. The results of Gray's investigations were published in the *Philosophical Transactions* of the Royal Society in the years 1731–32 and 1735–36.

GREENSTEIN, Jesse Leonard (b. Oct. 15, 1909; New York) American astronomer.

Greenstein graduated from Harvard in 1929 and then, as he puts it, "rode out four depression years as an operator in real estate and investments." He returned to Harvard and obtained his PhD in 1937. He worked at the Yerkes Observatory from 1937 until 1948 when he moved to the California Institute of Technology. In 1949 he became professor of astrophysics and a staff member at the Mount Wilson and Palomar Observatories.

Greenstein has worked on the constitution of stars, and on how and why the constitution can vary from one star to another, and has also made extensive studies of quasars. In 1963, following Maarten Schmidt, he interpreted the spectrum of the quasar 3C 48 and was able to show that its peculiarities resulted from a red shift over twice that obtained by Schmidt for the quasar 3C 273.

GREGOR, William (b. Dec. 25, 1761; Trewarthenick, England; d. July 11, 1817; Creed, England) British mineralogist.

Gregor was educated at Cambridge University. Although elected a fellow of his college he decided instead to pursue a career in the Church and became rector of Creed, Cornwall, in 1793.

In 1791 he found a strange black sand in Manaccan (then spelled Menacchan), Cornwall. This contained iron and manganese plus an additional substance that Gregor could not identify. He called it menacchanine and succeeded in extracting its reddish-brown oxide, which, when dissolved in acid, formed a yellow solution. Martin Klaproth isolated the same oxide from a different source in 1795 and demonstrated that it was a new element, naming it titanium.

GREGORY, James (b. November 1638; Drumoak, Scotland; d. October 1675; Edinburgh) Scottish mathematician and astronomer.

Gregory was one of the many 17th-century mathematicians who made important contributions to the development of the calculus, although some of his best work remained virtually unknown until long after his death.

He studied mathematics at the University of Padua in about 1665 and produced *Vera circuli et hyperbolae quadratura* (1667; The True Areas of Circles and Hyperbolas). He was particularly interested in expressing functions as series, and he sketched the beginnings of a general theory. It was Gregory who first found series expressions for the trigonometric functions. He introduced the terms 'convergent' and 'divergent' for series, and was one of the first mathematicians to begin to grasp the difference between the two kinds. Gregory also gave the first proof of the fundamental theorem of calculus.

In addition to his mathematical work Gregory's interests in astronomy led him to do some valuable practical work in optics. He anticipated Newton by recommending a reflecting telescope in his *Optica promota* (1663; The Advance of Optics). He realized that refracting telescopes would always be limited by aberrations of various kinds. His solution was to use a concave mirror that reflected (rather than a lens that refracted) to minimize these effects. He solved the problem of the observer by having a hole in the primary mirror through which the light could pass to the observer. However, he was unable to find anyone skilled enough actually to construct the telescope.

Gregory held chairs in mathematics at the University of St. Andrews (1669–74) and the University of Edinburgh (1674–75). He died at the age of 37 shortly after going blind.

GRIESS, Peter Johann (b. Sept. 6, 1829; Kirklosbach, near Kassel, now in West Germany; d. Aug. 30, 1888; Bournemouth, England) German chemist.

Griess, who came from a farming family, was educated at the universities of Jena and Marburg. In 1858 he became August Wilhelm Hofmann's assistant at the Royal College of Chemistry in London. In 1862 he took up a post in industry with Allsopp's brewery in Burton-on-Trent, where he stayed for the rest of his career.

In 1862 he made an important discovery concerned with a new class of dyes. He discovered that aromatic amines (such as aniline, $C_6H_5NH_2$) react with nitrous acid at low temperature to form diazonium salts (of the type $C_6H_5N_2^+X^-$). These would react with phenols to produce larger, colored molecules — the azo dyestuffs. Griess himself had no interest in these products and, in fact, received no reward from them. The first azo dye, Manchester or Bismarck brown, was discovered within a year.

GRIFFITH, Fred (b. 1881; Hale, England; d. 1941; London) British microbiologist.

Griffith, described variously as a 'virtual recluse' or 'quiet and retiring', worked as a bacteriologist at the Ministry of Health's pathology laboratory in London. He was killed working in his laboratory during an air-raid.

Despite the general obscurity of his

background Griffith has acquired long after his death an almost legendary role as one of the founding fathers of molecular biology by his discovery in 1928 of bacterial transformation in pneumococci. He had first succeeded in distinguishing two types of pneumococci, the nonvirulent R (rough) of serological type I and the virulent S (smooth) of type III.

He inoculated mice with both live nonvirulent R and heat-killed S pneumococci. Although when either were inoculated separately no infection resulted, together they produced in the mice lethal cases of pneumonia. Further, he recovered from the infected mice living, virulent S pneumococci of type III.

It was this awkward result that later led Oswald Avery and his colleagues in 1944 to carry out the experiments that succeeded in explaining Griffith's results by suggesting that the power to transform bacteria lay with the nucleic acid of the cell rather than its proteins or sugars.

GRIGNARD, François Auguste Victor (b. May 6, 1871; Cherbourg, France; d. Dec. 13, 1935; Lyons, France) French chemist.

Grignard first studied mathematics at the University of Lyons before he switched to chemistry. He was a lecturer at the universities of Besançon, Nancy, and Lyons before he was appointed professor of chemistry at Nancy in 1910. In 1919 he moved to the chair of chemistry at Lyons.

In 1901 he discovered an important class of organic reagents now known as *Grignard reagents*. For this work he shared the Nobel Prize for chemistry with Paul Sabatier in 1912. He was searching for a catalyst for a methylation reaction he was trying to induce; chemists had earlier tried to use zinc in combination with various organic compounds and found it moderately successful. Grignard used magnesium mixed with organic halides in ether solution and obtained compounds of the type $RMgX$, where X is a halogen (chlorine, bromine, or iodine) and R an organic group. These Grignard reagents are very versatile and permit the synthesis of a large number of different classes of compounds, particularly secondary and tertiary alcohols, hydrocarbons, and carboxylic acids.

In 1935 he began the publication of his *Traité de chimie organique*, which was continued after his death and is now a massive multivolume work.

GRIMALDI, Francesco Maria (b. Apr. 2, 1618; Bologna, now in Italy; d. Dec. 28, 1663; Bologna) Italian physicist.

Grimaldi became a Jesuit and in 1648 took the chair of mathematics at his order's college in Bologna, where he acted as assistant to Giovanni Riccioli. His discovery of the phenomenon that he named the diffraction of light was reported in his posthumous work *Physico-mathesis de lumine, coloribus, et iride* (1665; Physicomathematical Studies of Light, Colors, and the Rainbow). He showed that when a beam of light passed through two successive narrow apertures the pattern of light produced was a little bigger than it should have been if the light had traveled in an absolutely straight line. Grimaldi considered that the beam had bent outward very slightly, indicating that light must have a wave nature. Diffraction thus presented difficulties to all 17th-century corpuscular theories of light.

GROS CLARK, Sir Wilfrid Edward Le *See* LE GROS CLARK, Sir Wilfrid Edward.

GROVE, Sir William Robert (b. July 11, 1811; Swansea, Wales; d. Aug. 1, 1896; London) British physicist.

Grove was educated at Oxford and, after graduating in 1835, became a barrister (lawyer). However, ill health turned him away from law to science.

His research concentrated on the newly formed science of electrochemistry and in 1839 he produced an improved version of the voltaic battery, which came to be known as the *Grove cell*. He also constructed the first fuel cell and, in 1845, invented a type of electric bulb, which he hoped would be useful in coal mines.

Grove was elected to the Royal Society in 1840 and, the next year, was appointed professor of physics at the London Institution. However, soon after this he returned to the legal profession and rose to the position of a high court judge. He continued to publish books on science, mainly supporting the idea of energy conservation.

GUERICKE, Otto von (b. Nov. 20, 1602; Magdeburg, now in East Germany; d. May 11, 1686; Hamburg, now in West Germany) German physicist and engineer.

After a training in law and mathematics, Guericke became an engineer in the army of Gustavus Adolphus of Sweden. After the Thirty Years' War he returned to Magdeburg as mayor, there carrying out numerous dramatic experiments on vacuums and the power of the atmosphere.

In 1650 Guericke constructed the first air pump, which he used to create a vacuum in various containers. He showed that sound would not travel in a vacuum, and furthermore a vacuum would not support combustion or animal life. In 1654 Guericke gave an impressive demonstration in front of the emperor Ferdinand III, of the power of atmospheric pressure. Two identical copper hemispheres 12 feet (3.66 m) in diameter were joined together. When the air was pumped out, 16 horses could not pull them apart although when the air reentered the hemispheres they fell apart by themselves. He also showed that 20 men could not hold a piston in a cylinder once the air had been evacuated from one end of it. The results of these and other experiments were published in his *Experimenta nova Magdeburgica de vacuo spatio* (1672; New Magdeburg Experiments Concerning Empty Space). In 1663 he built the first electrical friction machine by rotating a sulfur globe against a cloth.

GUETTARD, Jean Etienne (b. Sept. 22, 1715; Etampes, France; d. Jan. 6, 1786; Paris) French geologist.

After a training in medicine and chemistry, Guettard worked under the royal patronage of the duc d'Orléans from 1747 as keeper of his natural-history collection. Following the duc's death (1752) he continued this work under the patronage of his son.

In 1751 he made a crucial observation that upset the neptunism theories of Abraham Werner and his followers. While traveling through the Auvergne region he noticed an abundance of hexagonal basalt rocks and, exploring the region, identified the surrounding mountain peaks as the cones of extinct volcanoes (which would explain the presence of basalt). However, Werner's theory stated that all volcanic activity is recent, only occurring after the land has completely emerged from the oceans. Therefore, according to Wernerian theory, no volcanoes as ancient as the Auvergne ones should exist. Guettard published his findings in 1752 in his memoir, *On Certain Mountains in France which once have been Volcanoes*. He later changed his mind, distinguishing basalt from lava as it was not to be found among the recent eruptions of Vesuvius and other active volcanoes. He also observed the lack of vitrification found in basalt, then taken to be a sure sign of volcanic origin, and explained its formation by crystallization from an aqueous fluid.

Guettard was the first to map France geologically, publishing in 1780 his *Atlas et description minéralogiques de la France*. In the preparation of this he discovered (1765) a source of kaolin in Alençon, which made possible the production of the celebrated Sèvres porcelain.

GUILLAUME, Charles Edouard (b. Feb. 15, 1861; Fleurier, Switzerland; d. June 13, 1938; Sèvres, France) Swiss metrologist.

As a child Guillaume learned a good deal of science from his father, a clockmaker with a considerable scientific knowledge. In 1878 he entered the Zurich Federal Institute of Technology, gaining his doctorate in 1882. In 1883 Guillaume became an assistant at the newly established International Bureau of Weights and Measures at Sèvres, near Paris. He was appointed director in 1915 and held this post until his retirement in 1936.

Guillaume's early work at the Bureau was concerned with thermometry; his treatise of 1889 on this subject became a standard text for metrologists. He was also involved in developing the international standards for the meter, kilogram, and liter. His research on thermal expansion of possible standards materials led him from 1890 to investigate various alloys. After a methodical study of nickel–steel alloys he devised an alloy that showed a very small expansion with temperature rise. Guillaume's new material ('invar') found immediate practical applications, particularly in clocks, watches, and other precise instruments. He also produced a nickel–chromium–steel alloy, known as 'elinvar', with an elasticity that remains nearly constant over a wide range of temperatures. It became widely used, for example, for the hairsprings of watches.

In 1920 Guillaume received the Nobel Prize for physics for his researches into nickel–steel alloys.

GUILLEMIN, Roger (b. Jan. 11, 1924; Dijon, France) French–American physiologist.

Guillemin was educated at the universities of Dijon, Lyons, and Montreal, where he gained his PhD in physiology and experimental medicine in 1953. The same year he moved to America to join the staff of the Baylor University Medical School, Houston. In 1970 Guillemin joined the staff of the Salk Institute in La Jolla, California.

Early in his career Guillemin decided to work on the hypothesis of Geoffrey Harris that the pituitary gland is under the control of hormones produced by the hypothalamus. As the anterior pituitary secretes a number of hormones it was far from clear which to begin with. He eventually decided to search for the hypothalamic factor that controls the release of the adrenocorticotrophic hormone (ACTH) from the pituitary, the corticotrophic releasing factor (CRF). As it turned out, this was an unfortunate choice for after seven years Guillemin had nothing to show for his not inconsiderable efforts. A further six years spent fruitlessly searching for the thyrotropin releasing factor (TRF) exposed Guillemin to skepticism from many in the endocrine field.

The main difficulty was that such hormones were present in very small quantities. When Guillemin finally did succeed in 1968 in isolating one milligram of TRF it had come from 5 million sheep's hypothalami. It turned out to be a small, relatively simple tripeptide, easy to synthesize. The development of the radioimmunoassay method for the detection of minute quantities by Rosalyn Yalow was also of considerable help. Other successes quickly followed. Andrew Schally isolated the luteinizing-hormone releasing factor in 1971 and Guillemin in 1972 succeeded with somatostatin, which controls the release of the growth hormone.

In 1977 Guillemin shared the Nobel Prize for physiology or medicine with Schally and Yalow.

GULDBERG, Cato Maximilian (b. Aug. 11, 1836; Christiania, now Oslo; d. Jan. 14, 1902; Christiania) Norwegian chemist.

Guldberg was educated at the University of Christiania and started his career teaching at the Royal Military School in Christiania in 1860. He was appointed to the chair of applied mathematics at the university in 1869.

Guldberg's main work was on chemical thermodynamics. In 1864 he formulated the law of mass action in collaboration with his brother-in-law, Peter Waage. The law states that the rate of a chemical change depends on the concentrations of the reactants. Thus for a reaction: $A + B \longrightarrow C$

the rate of reaction is proportional to [A] × [B], where [A] and [B] are concentrations. Guldberg and Waage also investigated the effects of temperature. They did not gain full credit for their work at the time, partly due to their first publishing the law in Norwegian. However, even when published in French (1867) the law received little attention until it was rediscovered by William Esson and Vernon Harcourt working at Oxford University.

In 1870 he investigated the way in which the freezing point and vapor pressure of a pure liquid are lowered by a dissolved component. In 1890 he formulated Guldberg's law. This relates boiling point and critical temperature (the point above which a gas cannot be liquefied by pressure alone) on the absolute scale. The law was discovered independently by Phillippe-Auguste Guye.

GULLSTRAND, Allvar (b. June 5, 1862; Landskrona, Sweden; d. July 21, 1930; Uppsala, Sweden) Swedish ophthalmologist.

Gullstrand, a physician's son, was educated at the universities of Uppsala, Vienna, and Stockholm, where he obtained his PhD in 1890. After working briefly at the Karolinska Institute in Stockholm Gullstrand moved to the University of Uppsala, where he served as professor of ophthalmology from 1894 until his retirement in 1927.

In 1911 Gullstrand was awarded the Nobel Prize in physiology or medicine for his work on the dioptrics of the eye. Hermann von Helmholtz had earlier shown that the eye solves the problem of accommodation (how to focus on both near and distant objects) by changing the surface curvature of the lens — the nearer the object, the more convex the lens becomes; the further the object, the more concave the lens. Gullstrand showed that this could in fact account for only two thirds of the accommodation a normal eye could achieve. The remaining third was produced by what Gullstrand termed the 'intracapsular mechanism' and depended

on the fact that the eye was not a homogeneous medium.

GUTENBERG, Beno (b. June 4, 1889; Darmstadt, now in West Germany; d. Jan. 25, 1960; Los Angeles, California) German–American geologist.

Gutenberg was educated at the Technical University in Darmstadt and the University of Göttingen, where he obtained his PhD in 1911. He then taught at the University of Freiburg becoming professor of geophysics in 1926. He emigrated to America in 1930, taking a post at the California Institute of Technology, and later served as director of the seismological laboratory (1947–58).

In 1913 Gutenberg suggested a structure of the Earth that would explain the data on earthquake waves. It was known that there were two main types of waves: primary (P) waves, which are longitudinal compression waves, and secondary (S) waves, which are transverse shear waves. On the opposite side of the Earth to an earthquake, in an area known as the shadow zone, no S waves are recorded and the P waves, although they do appear, are of smaller amplitudes and occur later than would be expected. Gutenberg proposed that the Earth's core, first identified by Richard Oldham in 1906, is liquid, which would explain the absence of S waves as they cannot be transmitted through liquids. Making detailed calculations he was able to show that the core ends at a depth of about 1800 miles (2900 km) below the Earth's surface where it forms a marked discontinuity, now known as the *Gutenberg discontinuity*, with the overlying mantle. Its existence has been confirmed by later work including precise measurements made after underground nuclear explosions.

In collaboration with Charles Richter, Gutenberg produced a major study, *On Seismic Waves* (1934–39), in which, using large quantities of seismic data, they were able to calculate average velocity distributions for the whole of the Earth.

GUTHRIE, Samuel (b. 1782; Brimfield, Massachusetts; d. Oct. 19, 1848; New York City) American chemist.

Guthrie was a student at the University of Pennsylvania, where he qualified as a doctor. In 1831 he discovered chloroform, which was used as an anesthetic by James Simpson in 1847. It was, however, discovered independently by the French pharmacologist E. Soubeiran in the same year and by Justus von Liebig in 1832. Guthrie also discovered percussion powder, a substance that explodes on impact.

GUYOT, Arnold Henry (b. Sept. 21, 1807; Boudevilliers, Switzerland; d. Feb. 8, 1884; Princeton, New Jersey) Swiss–American geologist and geographer.

Intending to enter the Church, Guyot studied at the universities of Neuchâtel, Strasbourg, and Berlin, where his interests in science began to absorb him. After teaching in Paris (1835–40) he was appointed professor of history and physical geography at Neuchâtel in 1839 where he remained until 1848, when he emigrated to America. He taught first at the Lowell Technological Institute in Boston before he was appointed, in 1854, to the chair of geology and physical geography at Princeton University.

While in Switzerland he had studied the structure and movement of glaciers, spending much time testing the new theories of Louis Agassiz (q.v.). In America, under the auspices of the Smithsonian Institution, he began to develop, organize, and equip a number of East Coast meteorological stations. He also surveyed and constructed topographical maps of the Appalachian and Catskill mountains. In 1849 he published his influential work *The Earth and Man*.

GUYTON DE MORVEAU, Baron Louis Bernard (b. Jan. 4, 1737; Dijon, France; d. Jan. 2, 1816; Paris) French chemist.

Guyton began his career as a lawyer but as a member of the Burgundy parliament (1755–82) he met the great Georges Buffon who encouraged his interest in science. In 1782 he gave up law to devote himself to science and he collaborated with Antoine Lavoisier. During the revolutionary period he reentered politics. He was a founder of and teacher at the Ecole Polytechnique (1795–1805) and in 1800 became master of the mint until his retirement in 1814.

In the period 1776–77 Guyton published his three-volume *Eléments de chimie théorique et pratique*, which was a major attempt to quantify chemical affinities. Guyton was a passionate Newtonian and tried to apply Newtonian laws to chemistry. He tried to do this by floating disks of various metals on mercury and measuring the force necessary to remove them. Thus he obtained figures such as gold needs a force of 446 grains to remove it, lead 397, zinc 204, iron 115, and cobalt 8. He attempted to correlate his figures with the chemical affinities of the elements.

H

HABER, Fritz (b. Dec. 9, 1868; Breslau, now Wroclaw in Poland; d. Jan. 29, 1934; Basel, Switzerland) German physical chemist.

Haber was the son of a merchant. He was educated at Berlin, Heidelberg, Charlottenburg, and Jena, and in 1894 he became an assistant in physical chemistry at the Technical Institute, Karlsruhe, where he remained until 1911, being promoted to a professorship in 1906. He moved to Berlin in 1911 becoming director of the Kaiser Wilhelm Institute of Physical Chemistry. Though an intensely patriotic German he was also a Jew and with the rise of anti-Semitism he resigned his post in 1933 and went into exile in England, where he worked at the Cavendish Laboratory, Cambridge. He died in Basel en route to Italy.

Haber is noted for his discovery of the industrial process for synthesizing ammonia from nitrogen and hydrogen. The need at the time was for nitrogen compounds for use as fertilizers — most plants cannot utilize free nitrogen from the air, and need 'fixed' nitrogen. The main source was deposits of nitrate salts in Chile, but these would have a limited life.

Haber, in an attempt to solve this problem, began investigating the reaction:

$$N_2 + 3H_2 = 2NH_3$$

Under normal conditions the yield is very low. Haber showed (1907–09) that practical yields could be achieved at high temperatures (250°C) and pressures (250 atmospheres) using a catalyst (iron is the catalyst now used). The process was developed industrially by Carl Bosch around 1913 and is still the main method for the fixation of nitrogen. Haber received the Nobel Prize for chemistry for this work in 1918.

During World War I, Haber turned his efforts to helping Germany's war effort. In particular he directed the use of poisonous gas. After the war he tried, unsuccessfully, to repay the indemnities imposed on Germany by a process for extracting gold from seawater.

HADFIELD, Sir Robert Abbott (b. Nov. 28, 1858; Sheffield, England; d. Sept. 30, 1940; Kingston-upon-Thames, England) British metallurgist.

Hadfield's father was a steel manufacturer who had opened a factory for the production of steel castings in Sheffield in 1872. Hadfield was educated locally and started work in the laboratory in his father's works, inheriting the business on his father's death (1880). It had been known for some years that if manganese was added to iron the result was hard but was too brittle to be commercially useful. Hadfield discovered that if a large quantity of manganese was added (about 12–14%) and the steel was heated and quenched in water, the resulting alloy was extremely hard and strong. He patented his discovery in 1883. He also worked on the development of other steel alloys and in 1899 was able to show that silicon steels have a high electrical resistance. This made them suitable for use in transformers as they could substantially reduce bulk.

Hadfield was also interested in the history of metallurgy, forming a fine collection, and out of this interest came his two books: *Faraday and his Metallurgical Researches* (1931) and *Metallurgy and its Influence on Modern Progress: With a Survey of Education and Research* (1925). He was knighted in 1908 and made a baronet in 1917.

HADLEY, George (b. Feb. 12, 1685; London; d. June 28, 1768; London) English meteorologist.

The younger brother of the inventor John Hadley, George Hadley was educated at Pembroke College, Oxford, and called to the bar in 1709. He became more interested in physics and was made responsible for producing the Royal Society of London's meteorological observations.

In 1686 Edmond Halley had offered a partial explanation of the trade winds, pointing out that heated equatorial air will rise and thus cause colder air to move in from the tropics, but could not explain why the winds blew from the northeast in the northern hemisphere and the southeast in the southern.

Hadley put forward the explanation, in his paper *Concerning the Cause of the General Trade Winds* (1735), that the airflow toward the equator was deflected by the Earth's rotation from west to east. This circulation is now known as the *Hadley cell.*

HADLEY, John (b. Apr. 16, 1682; England; d. Feb. 14, 1744; East Barnet, England) English mathematician and inventor.

Little is known of Hadley's life. He is chiefly remembered for developing the reflecting telescope, producing his first in 1721. He was an extremely skilled craftsman and his reflectors were the among the first to be useful in astronomy.

Hadley also invented, in 1730, the reflecting quadrant with which a ship's position at sea could be determined by measurements of the Sun or a star above the horizon. This instrument later developed into the sextant.

HAECKEL, Ernst Heinrich (b. Feb. 16, 1834; Potsdam, now in East Germany; d. Aug. 9, 1919; Jena, now in East Germany) German biologist.

Haeckel studied medicine at the Universities of Berlin, Würzburg, and Vienna, and was then lecturer in and later professor of zoology at Jena (1865–1909). Haeckel's contributions to zoological science were a mixture of sound research and speculation often with insufficient evidence. An advocate of monism, which postulated a totally materialistic view of life as a unity, he based his evolutionary ideas on the embryological laws expounded by Karl von Baer. Expanding the idea of the his mentor, Johannes Müller, Haeckel argued that the embryological stages of an animal were a recapitulation of its evolutionary history, and indeed that there had once been complete animals resembling the embryonic stages of higher animal forms living today. He formulated a scheme of evolution for the whole animal kingdom, from inorganic matter upward. His studies, with Müller, of marine life, particularly the crystalline radiolarians, encouraged him to compare the symmetry of crystals with the simplest animals, and led him to postulate an inanimate origin for animal life. In 1866 Haeckel anticipated later proof of the fact that the key to inheritance factors lies in the cell nucleus, outlining this theme in his *Die Perigenesis der Plastidule* (1876; The Generation of Waves in the Small Vital Particles).

Haeckel also proposed the idea that all multicellular animals derived from a hypothetical two-layered (ectoderm and endoderm) animal, the *Gastraea* — a theory that provoked much discussion. He engaged in much valuable research on marine invertebrates, such as the radiolarians, jellyfish, calcareous sponges, and medusae, and wrote a series of monographs on these groups based largely on specimens brought back by the Challenger Expedition. He was also the first to divide the animal kingdom into unicellular (pro-

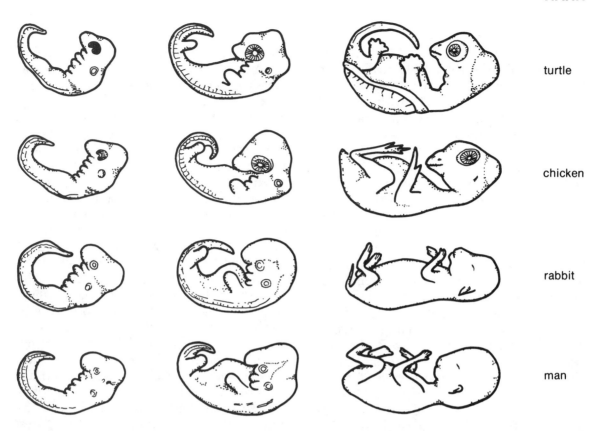

turtle

chicken

rabbit

man

SUCCESSIVE AND COMPARABLE STAGES OF DEVELOPMENT IN FOUR VERTEBRATE EMBRYOS These show the similarities, particularly in the early stages, that led Haeckel to suggest his theory of recapitulation.

tozoan) and multicellular (metazoan) animals.

An ardent Darwinist, Haeckel made several zoological expeditions and founded the Phyletic Museum at Jena and the Ernst Haeckel Haus, which contains his books, archives, and other effects.

HAHN, Otto (b. Mar. 8, 1879; Frankfurt, now in West Germany; d. July 28, 1968; Göttingen, West Germany) German chemist.

Hahn's father, a successful merchant, was keen for his son to train as an architect and it was against much family opposition that Hahn was finally allowed to study chemistry at the University of Marburg in 1897. After obtaining his doctorate in 1901 he studied abroad first with William Ramsay in London and then at McGill University, Canada, with Ernest Rutherford. Hahn returned to Germany in 1907, where he took up an appointment at the University of Berlin, being made professor of chemistry in 1910. Two years later he joined the Kaiser Wilhelm Institute of Chemistry where he served as director from 1928 to 1945.

Hahn had trained as an organic chemist and had really gone to London to learn English in order to prepare himself for an industrial career. Ramsay had however asked him to separate radium from some radioactive material he had recently acquired from Ceylon. In so doing Hahn found a new material, a highly active form of thorium which he named 'radiothorium'. So impressed was Ramsay with this work that he wrote to Emil Fischer in Berlin suggesting that he employ Hahn after he had acquired more experience of radioactivity with Rutherford at McGill.

Hahn was thus diverted into an academic career, most of which was spent in research on radioactivity and much of it in collaboration with Lise Meitner (q.v.).

341

With her he discovered a new element, protactinium, in 1917. He went on to define, in 1921, the phenomenon of nuclear isomerism. This arises when nuclei with different radioactive properties turn out to be identical in atomic number and mass.

Hahn's most important work however, was done in the 1930s when, with Meitner and Fritz Strassmann, he made one of the most important discoveries of the century, namely nuclear fission. One of the strange features about Hahn's work was that he was repeating experiments already done and formulating hypotheses already rejected as nonsense or due to some contamination of the materials used. Chemists at this time felt that they understood the process of nuclear transformation. After all it was some twenty years since Rutherford had first detected the transformation of nitrogen into oxygen, and a newer form of the same 'alchemy' had been described by Irène and Frédéric Joliot-Curie (q.q.v.) in 1934. Two basic rules were involved in this understanding. First, that nuclear transmutations always involved the emission of either an alpha particle (helium nucleus) or a beta particle (electron); and secondly, that the change could take place only between elements separated by no more than two places in the periodic table. If more substantial transformations appeared to occur, as in the transformation of uranium into lead, this was explained as the result of a series of such intermediate steps, each one taking place with the emission of the appropriate particle.

Thus, when in 1938 Hahn bombarded uranium with slow neutrons and detected some strange new half-lives, he assumed that the uranium had changed into radium, a close neighbor, with some undetected alpha particles. But when he tried to remove the radium all he could find was barium. This Hahn simply could not understand, for barium was far too low in the periodic table to be produced by the transmutation of uranium; and if the transformation *was* taking place it should be accompanied by the emission of a prodigious number of alpha particles, which Hahn could not have failed to

detect. The thought that the heavy uranium nucleus could split into two lighter ones was too outrageous for him to consider seriously. He could not dismiss it entirely for he asserted at the time that "we must really state that we are not dealing with radium but with barium." But to suppose the barium arose from what he then called nuclear 'bursting' he felt would be "in contradiction to all previous experience in nuclear physics." He did realize that something of importance was going on and quickly sent off for publication a joint paper with Strassmann even though, as he recalled twenty years later, "After the manuscript had been mailed, the whole thing once more seemed so improbable to me that I wished I could get the documents back out of the mail." Appropriately enough it was his old collaborator Meitner, in exile from the Nazis in Sweden, and her nephew Otto Frisch, who made the necessary calculations and announced fission to the world early in 1939. Hahn received the Nobel Prize for chemistry in 1944.

HALDANE, John Burdon Sanderson (b. Nov. 5, 1892; Oxford, England; d. Dec. 1, 1964; Bhudaneswar, India) British geneticist.

Haldane became involved in scientific research at an early age through helping in the laboratory of his father, the physiologist John Scott Haldane. His interest in genetics was first stimulated as early as 1901, when he heard a lecture on Mendel's work, and he later applied this by studying inheritance in his sister's (the writer Naomi Mitchison) 300 guinea pigs. On leaving school he studied first mathematics and then the humanities at Oxford University. He served in World War I with the Black Watch Regiment and was wounded at Loos and in Mesopotamia. Some work on gas masks, following the first German gas attacks, marked the beginning of his physiological studies.

In 1919 Haldane took up a fellowship at Oxford, where he continued research on respiration, investigating how the levels of carbon dioxide in the blood affect the muscles regulating breathing. He was next offered a readership in biochemistry at Cambridge, where he conducted some important work on enzymes. These experiments, and later work on conditions in submarines, aroused considerable public interest because he frequently used himself as a guinea pig.

In 1933 Haldane became professor of genetics at University College, London, a position he exchanged in 1937 for the chair of biometry. While at London he prepared a provisional map of the X sex chromosome and showed the genetic linkage between hemophilia and color blindness. He also produced the first estimate of mutation rates in humans from studies of the pedigrees of hemophiliacs, and described the effect of recurring deleterious mutations on a population. With the outbreak of the Spanish Civil War, Haldane joined the Communist Party and advised the republican government on gas precautions. In the 1950s he left the party as a result of Soviet acceptance and promotion of Trofim Lysenko. In protest at the Anglo-French invasion of Suez, Haldane emigrated to India in 1957, becoming an Indian citizen in 1961. He was director of the laboratory of genetics and biometry at Bhubaneswar from 1962 until his death.

Haldane's books include *Enzymes* (1930), *The Causes of Evolution* (1932), and *The Biochemistry of Genetics* (1954); he also wrote a number of books popularizing science.

HALDANE, John Scott (b. May 3, 1860; Edinburgh, Scotland; d. Mar. 15, 1936; Oxford, England) British physiologist.

Haldane, the son of a lawyer, was educated at the University of Edinburgh, where he obtained his MD in 1884. He worked first at the University of Dundee but moved to Oxford in 1887 to assist his uncle, John Burdon-Sanderson, the professor of physiology. Haldane was made reader in physiology in 1907 but resigned in 1913 to become director of the Mining Research Laboratory, initially sited in Doncaster but transferred to Birmingham in 1921.

From the beginning of his career Haldane sought to apply the results of physiological research to the solution of practical social and industrial problems. He was much concerned with problems of ventilation in mines and in 1896 published an important report, *Causes of Death in Colliery Explosions*. He was struck by the fact that in a serious explosion in 1896 only 4 out of 57 miners died from the blast and its effects, the vast majority succumbing to carbon monoxide poisoning. Haldane recommended the simple and effective safety procedure of taking mice down the pit: with their higher metabolic rate they would show the effects of carbon monoxide poisoning long before it reached levels dangerous to man.

He also worked for the admiralty on the problems faced by their divers at high pressures. It had been known for some time that rapid decompression produced the liberation of nitrogen bubbles into the bloodstream, with crippling and often lethal effects. Haldane showed how such effects could be minimized by pointing out that however long a diver had been exposed to compressed air it was always safe to halve the pressure; that is, it is just as safe to ascend from six to three atmospheres as from two to one. Using his technique over £5 000 000 of gold was recovered from the wreck of the *Lusitania* between 1917 and 1924.

Haldane also investigated the response of the human body to high temperatures. Haldane's main work as a pure physiologist, however, was on the mechanism of respiration. In 1906 he published his most significant paper, in collaboration with John Priestley, which demonstrated the key role of carbon dioxide in the regulation of breathing. They showed that it was not a deficiency in oxygen that triggers the respiratory reflex but an excess of carbon dioxide in the arterial blood, acting on the respiratory center in the midbrain. Their work was published in full in *Respiration* (1935; 2nd edition).

In much of his work Haldane used for an experimental subject his precocious son J. B. S. Haldane, later to become one of the leading biologists of the 20th century.

HALE, George Ellery (b. June 29, 1868; Chicago, Illinois; d. Feb. 21, 1938; Pasadena, California) American astrophysicist.

Hale's father, William Hale, was a wealthy manufacturer of elevators who stimulated in his son an early interest in designing and making his own scientific instruments. This interest was directed to astronomy by Sherburne W. Burnham, a neighbor and passionate observer of double stars, and increased during his four years at the Massachusetts Institute of Technology, where he studied physics. He built a solar observatory, financed by his father, at Kenwood, Chicago, and after graduating in 1890 became its director. In 1892 he was appointed assistant professor and later professor of astrophysics at the new University of Chicago and from 1895 to 1905 he was director of the university's Yerkes Observatory. From 1904 to 1923 he was director of the newly established Mount Wilson Observatory in California. The last 15 years of his life were spent organizing the equipping and building of the Palomar Observatory in California and in the pursuit of his solar researches in his private observatory in Pasadena.

Hale was undoubtedly one of the key figures in 20th-century astronomy. He saw very clearly and very early that astronomy could only develop if much more powerful telescopes were constructed. Thus with great vision and enormous persistence and energy he spent 40 years acting as midwife to a series of bigger and bigger telescopes. His insight was clearly justified for it was with his telescopes that Harlow Shapley, Edwin Hubble, and many others made their observations.

His first triumph came when he persuaded Charles T. Yerkes, a Chicago trolley-car magnate, to provide 349 000 dollars to build a 40-inch (1-m) refracting telescope for the University of Chicago. This was and still is the largest refractor ever built. It was first used in 1897. He was soon anxious however to build a large reflecting telescope. In 1896 his father acquired a 60-inch (1.5-m) mirror but the University of Chicago was unable to fund its mounting. Hale once more started raising money. This time he interested the Carnegie Institution of Washington in financing the Mount Wilson Observatory. The observatory was founded in 1904 and the 60-inch reflector eventually went into use in 1908. In 1918 this superb instrument was surpassed by the 100-inch (2.5-m) Hooker telescope, largely financed by a Los Angeles business man, John D. Hooker. For 30 years this was the world's largest telescope and it revolutionized astronomy.

Hale had resigned from his directorship of Mount Wilson Observatory in 1923 on the grounds of ill health but lost little time in seeking to interest the Rockefeller Foundation in building a reflecting telescope that would be the ultimate in size, 200 inches (5 m) across, for Earth-based instruments. In 1929 it was finally agreed that six million dollars would be donated for this purpose to an educational institute, the California Institute of Technology, rather than the Carnegie Institution. Hale became chairman of the group directing the planning, construction, and operation of the instrument that was to become his masterpiece.

Thus there began an epic struggle to complete the 200-inch telescope, which was to take nearly 20 years. The first mirror made from fused quartz proved to be a 600 000-dollar failure. Hale next tried Pyrex and the first experimental 200-inch disk cast proved satisfactory. The actual casting was made in December 1934 when the 65 tons of molten Pyrex began its carefully controlled 10 months' cooling. The mirror managed to survive the flooding of the factory, which required shutting down the temperature control for three days, and its long journey in the spring of 1936 from

Corning, New York, to California at a maximum speed of 25 mph. The grinding of the mirror was interrupted by the war and took so long that Hale had been dead for nine years when the instrument was finally commissioned as the Hale telescope in 1948. It was set up at the specially constructed Palomar Observatory, which together with the Mount Wilson Observatory was jointly operated by the California Institute of Technology and the Carnegie Institution. The two observatories were renamed the Hale Observatories in 1969. The Hale telescope was the world's largest telescope until the Soviet 6-meter (236-in) reflector went into operation in 1977 but is still considered by many to be the world's finest.

Hale was not just a highly successful scientific entrepreneur for he made major advances in the field of solar spectroscopy. As early as 1889 he had conceived of his spectroheliograph, an instrument that allowed the Sun to be photographed at a particular wavelength. He also designed an appropriate telescope to which it could be attached. In 1908 Hale made his most significant observation. He found that some of the lines in the spectra of sunspots were double. He realized that this demonstrated the presence of strong magnetic fields in sunspots, due to the effect discovered by Pieter Zeeman in 1896, and was the first indication of an extraterrestrial magnetic field.

HALES, Stephen (b. Sept. 7 or 17, 1677; Bekesbourne, England; d. Jan. 4, 1761; Teddington, England) English plant physiologist and chemist.

Hales entered Cambridge University in 1696 to study theology. He was ordained in 1703 and appointed curate at Teddington, near London, in 1708 (or 1709). During his time at Cambridge, he studied science and was influenced by Isaac Newton's ideas, which still dominated scientific thought at the university and probably accounted for Hales's consistent use of the quantitative method in his biological researches.

Hales was elected a fellow of the Royal Society in 1718 but his first work, *Vegetable Staticks*, was not published until 1727. In this book, which included his most important observations in plant physiology, Hales demonstrated that plant leaves absorb air and that a portion of air is used in plant nutrition. In addition, he realized that light is necessary for growth and investigated growth rates by marking plants at regular intervals. He measured the rate of water loss (transpiration) in plants, finding that it occurred through the leaves and was responsible for an upward flow of sap in plants. From additional measurements of sap flow he concluded that there was no circular movement of sap in plants analogous to blood circulation in animals.

Hales also made important contributions to the understanding of blood circulation by measuring such properties as blood pressure, output per minute from the heart, rate of flow and resistance to flow in vessels. The results were published in *Haemastaticks* (1733).

Other notable discoveries include the development of methods for collecting gases over water, distilling fresh water from sea water, and preserving foodstuffs with sulfur dioxide. He also invented a ventilator for introducing fresh air into prisons, ships, and granaries.

HALL, Asaph (b. Oct. 15, 1829; Goshen, Connecticut; d. Nov. 22, 1907; Annapolis, Maryland) American astronomer.

Hall had to leave school at the age of 13 and support his family as a carpenter, following the death of his father. He educated himself, and his interest in astronomy was strong enough for George Bond to employ him as his assistant at Harvard in 1857. In 1863 Hall became professor of mathematics at the Naval Observatory in Washington. He returned to Harvard as professor of astronomy in 1895.

In 1877 Mars was in opposition to the Sun at a distance of about 30 million miles from the Earth. Hall decided to search for

Martian satellites using the 26-inch (66-cm) refractor that the Clark firm had provided for the Naval Observatory. On 11 August he discovered a tiny satellite (the smaller moon) but was then compelled to wait a further six nights for the persistent cloud to clear before he could confirm his sighting and discover a further satellite. Both were very small, having diameters of 17 miles (27 km) and 9 miles (15 km) only. He named the larger 'Phobos' and the smaller 'Deimos' (Fear and Terror), after the sons of Mars. One curious feature of the two tiny satellites was that Jonathan Swift had spoken of two such Martian satellites in *Gulliver's Travels* (1726). Not only did Swift get their number correct but also spoke accurately of their size and orbital period.

In 1876, by noticing a white spot on the surface of Saturn, Hall was able to work out correctly the rotation period as 10.75 hours, which compares well with today's figure of 10 hours 14 minutes (for its equatorial region).

HALL, Charles Martin (b. Dec. 6, 1863; Thompson, Ohio; d. Dec. 27, 1914; Daytona Beach, Florida) American chemist.

Hall was educated at Oberlin College, graduating in 1885. He became interested in the costly process of manufacturing aluminum — until the late 19th century aluminum was a precious metal costing about 5.50 dollars an ounce. Napoleon III would have the majority of his guests served from gold plate; he and the chosen few he wished to impress were served from aluminum plates. Hall was stimulated by a remark of his teacher that anyone who could find a cheap way to make aluminum would win great wealth and fame.

Although the ore itself (bauxite, aluminum oxide) was cheap and plentiful, the metal could only be extracted by electrolysis of the molten ore, and aluminum oxide has a very high melting point. Hall tried various added compounds and, in 1886, found that adding 10–15% of cryolite (sodium aluminum fluoride)

reduced the melting point to a little over 1000°C. Hall produced his first sample in the form of buttons, which soon became known as the 'aluminum crown jewels'. Paul Héroult, working in France, discovered the process independently at about the same time. Hall helped to found the Pittsburgh Reduction Company (later the Aluminum Company of America) of which he became vice-president in 1890.

HALL, James (b. Sept. 12, 1811; Hingham, Massachusetts; d. Aug. 6, 1898; Bethlehem, New Hampshire) American geologist.

Hall, who came from a poor background, was educated at Rensselaer Polytechnic Institute, New York, where he became assistant professor in 1832. In 1837 he started work as a geologist on a survey of New York State, publishing an important report of these studies, *Geology of New York* (1843). In 1843 he became state paleontologist and was later, in 1865, made the curator and, in 1871, director of the New York State Museum in Albany.

Hall's major work was his massive 13-volume *The Palaeontology of New York* (1847–94). This important work became the standard for much of the later geological exploration of America in the 19th century. He was also active in the organization of the geological surveys of the Far and Midwest. He thus became a figure of some authority in the newly emerging geology profession, serving in 1888 as the first president of the Geological Society of the United States.

As a theorist, Hall is remembered for his account of mountain building published in 1859. This theory, known as the geosynclinal theory, was developed in a more comprehensive form by James Dana.

HALL, Sir James (b. Jan. 17, 1761; Dunglass, Scotland; d. June 23, 1832; Edinburgh) British geologist.

Hall succeeded to his father's baronetcy and fortune in 1776. He studied at Cambridge University (1777–79) but left without taking a degree. He spent two years traveling in Europe before returning to Edinburgh where he attended the university (1781–83). Following this he once more traveled extensively throughout Europe, meeting most of the scientists and scholars of his day.

Hall performed fundamental experiments to establish the plausibility of his friend James Hutton's uniformitarian and plutonist theories. The neptunist Abraham Werner had argued in criticism of James Hutton that great heat cannot have been a major factor in the formation of the Earth. He pointed out that when basalt cools it becomes glassy, not stony, and limestone, when subjected to heat, decomposes. The plutonist theories could therefore not account for the abundance of limestone and stony basalt on the Earth.

In 1798 Hall conducted his first experiment and succeeded in showing that if igneous rocks are allowed to cool slowly they form crystalline rather than glassy rocks. In 1805 he managed to refute Werner's second objection by showing that limestone when heated under pressure does not decompose on cooling but becomes marble.

Although Hall's experiments provided a good deal of plausibility for Hutton's views, Hall himself was only a moderate supporter. In his work *On the Revolutions of the Earth's Surface* (1812) he argued strongly, using his Alpine tours as evidence, for the need to assume the existence of enormous tidal waves and floods in the past to explain the present features of the Earth's surface.

HALL, Marshall (b. Feb. 18, 1790; Basford, England; d. Aug. 11, 1857; Brighton, England) British physician.

Hall, the son of a cotton manufacturer, obtained his MD from the University of Edinburgh in 1812. After a period of further study in Europe, Hall returned to England and set up in private practice, first in Nottingham in 1816 and, after 1826,

in London where he became one of the most successful and prosperous physicians of his day. His son, also named Marshall, was a famous lawyer who played a leading role in some of the most celebrated cases of his time.

In various publications from 1832 onward Hall described his investigations into reflex actions. He correctly believed that reflexes are controlled by the spinal cord, but this idea only met with ridicule from the Royal Society, who refused to publish his work. His claims were greeted more favorably by European scientists and were later used by such giants as Charles Sherrington to illuminate the workings of the nervous system.

Hall also worked on the function of the blood capillaries, denounced the practice of bloodletting, and introduced a form of artificial respiration for use in accidents involving drowning.

HALLER, Albrecht von (b. Oct. 16, 1708; Bern, Switzerland; d. Dec. 12, 1777; Bern) Swiss physiologist.

Haller studied under Hermann Boerhaave at Leiden, gaining his MD in 1727. He was later appointed professor of anatomy, botany, and medicine (1736–53) at the newly established University of Göttingen. He then retired to Bern to spend more time on his research and writing.

Between 1757 and 1766 Haller published in eight massive volumes his *Elementa physiologiae corporis humani* (Physiological Elements of the Human Body). The work described the advances in physiology made since the time of William Harvey, enriched with Haller's own experimental researches.

Before Haller, physiology followed the views of René Descartes — that bodily systems are essentially mechanical but require some vital principle to overcome their initial inertness. Haller, anticipated somewhat by Francis Glisson, broke radically with this tradition. When stimulated, muscles contract; such 'irritability', according to Haller, is inherent in the fiber and not caused by external factors.

The implications of this work were not immediately apparent to Haller. It was left to the philosophers of the Enlightenment to hammer home the conclusion that if such an inherent force resided in muscles then there no longer remained a need for the assumption of vital principles to imbue them with activity.

Haller also made important contributions to embryology and was a noted botanist, publishing a major work on the Swiss flora. However his attempt to construct an alternative classification scheme to that of Linnaeus, based on fruits rather than sexual organs, received little support despite being a more logical system.

HALLEY, Edmond or Edmund (b. Nov. 8, 1656; London; d. Jan. 14, 1742; Greenwich, England) British astronomer and physicist.

Halley was the son of a wealthy merchant. He was educated at St. Paul's School, London, and at Oxford University. He left Oxford without a degree in 1676, but having already published his first scientific paper in the *Philosophical Transactions* of the Royal Society on the theory of planetary orbits. Halley's scientific work and his life covered an enormous range. He started his active scientific career by spending two years on St. Helena mapping the southern skies. In 1679 he published *Catalogus stellarum australium* (Catalog of the Southern Stars) the first catalog of telescopically determined star positions. On his return he traveled extensively in Europe meeting such leading astronomers as Johannes Hevelius and Giovanni Cassini.

Halley now began his enormous contribution to just about all branches of physics and astronomy. He prepared extensive maps showing magnetic variation, winds, and tides. In atmospheric physics he formulated the mathematical law relating height and pressure (1686), making many advances in barometric design. He carried out important studies on evaporation and the salinity of lakes (1687–1694), which allowed him to draw conclusions about the age of the Earth. He used Newtonian mathematical techniques to improve and augment Descartes's work on the optics of the rainbow (1697–1721). He almost incidentally constructed mortality tables, estimated the acreage of England and the size of the atom, improved the design of the diving bell, and published numerous articles on natural history and classical studies.

These were sidelines compared to his work in astronomy and to the help he provided Newton. It is owing to Halley that Newton's *Principia* was published in the complete form we know it today. He pressed Newton to publish it, paid for the cost himself, saw it through the press, and even contributed some Latin verses in honor of the author. In 1695 he proposed the secular acceleration of the Moon, in 1718 he discovered the proper motion of the stars, but above all in his *Astronomiae cometicae synopsis* (1705; A Synopsis of the Astronomy of Comets) he laid the foundations of modern cometary study. His grasp of the geometry of cometary orbits allowed him to identify the comet (now known as Halley's comet) of 1531 with those of 1607 and 1682, and confidently to predict its return in 1758 — long after his death.

He held an equally varied and bewildering set of appointments. From 1696 until 1698 he was deputy controller of the Mint at Chester. From 1698 to 1700 he actually commanded a Royal Navy man-of-war, the *Paramour*, making prolonged and eventful ocean voyages. In 1702 and in 1703 he made two diplomatic missions to Vienna. In 1703 he was elected to the Savillian Chair of Geometry at Oxford, and in 1720 he succeeded John Flamsteed as Astronomer Royal. He held this post until his death, making observations of nearly 1500 lunar meridional transits and the full 18-year period of the Moon.

HALSTED, William Stewart (b. Sept. 23,

1852; New York City; d. Sept. 7, 1922; Baltimore, Maryland) American surgeon.

Halsted was educated at private schools, Yale, and the College of Physicians and Surgeons, New York. After graduating in 1877 he spent two years as a postgraduate student at the universities of Vienna, Leipzig, and Würzburg. Returning to America he worked as a surgeon in a number of New York hospitals before a growing addiction to cocaine forced him to leave in search of a cure in 1886. He eventually settled in Baltimore, where in 1892 he became professor of surgery at Johns Hopkins University.

The work that led to his addiction was probably his demonstration in 1885 of the localized anesthesia produced by the injection of cocaine into the appropriate nerve. The drug, introduced into medicine by Sigmund Freud in 1884, quickly became a valuable anesthetic for minor regional surgery.

As a surgeon Halsted pioneered two common operations. In 1889, independently of Eduardo Bassini in Padua, he devised a permanent surgical cure for inguinal hernia. Previous operative techniques involved such a high relapse rate — 40% in four years — that the operation had fallen into disrepute. He also introduced the operation of radical mastectomy, known in America as *Halsted's operation*. This involved treating breast cancer by the excision not only of the breast but also much of the underlying musculature and surrounding lymphatic tissue. He claimed a recurrence rate of 6%, as opposed to 50% produced by more conventional surgery.

One further important innovation by Halsted was his introduction, in 1889, of thin rubber gloves in operating theaters. This came about when he arranged for the Goodyear Rubber Company to make some gloves for a theater nurse, his future wife Caroline Hampton, whose hands were allergic to the antiseptic used. Over the next few decades rubber gloves gradually came to be used by all theater staff.

HAMILTON, William Donald (b. Aug. 1, 1936) British theoretical biologist.

Hamilton was educated at the universities of Cambridge and London. He served as a lecturer in genetics at Imperial College, London, from 1964 until 1977 when he moved to America to take up an appointment as professor of evolutionary biology at the University of Michigan.

In the *Origin of Species* (1859) Darwin raised a 'special difficulty', which at first he considered insurmountable. How could natural selection ever lead to the evolution of neuter or sterile insects? Darwin's answer was that selection may be applied to the family, as well as the individual. In a series of papers, beginning in 1964 with *The Genetical Theory of Social Behaviour*, Hamilton has pursued these implications and opened the way for the emergence of sociobiology. The key concept deployed by Hamilton is that of inclusive fitness, which covers not only an individual's fitness to survive but also the effects of his behavior on the fitness of his kin.

HAMILTON, Sir William Rowan (b. Aug. 3/4, 1805; Dublin; d. Sept. 2, 1865; Dublin) Irish mathematician.

Hamilton was a child prodigy, and not just in mathematics; he also managed to learn an extraordinary number of languages, some of them very obscure. In 1823 he entered Trinity College, Dublin, and four years later at the age of 22 was appointed professor of astronomy and astronomer royal for Ireland — posts given to him in order that he could continue to research unhampered by teaching commitments.

In 1827 he produced his first original work, in the theory of optics, expounded in his paper *A Theory of Systems of Rays*. In 1832 he did further theoretical work on rays, and predicted conical refraction under certain conditions in biaxial crystals. This was soon confirmed experimentally. In dynamics he introduced *Hamilton's equations* — a set of equations (similar to equations of Joseph Lagrange) describing the positions and momenta of a collection of particles. The equations involve the *Hamiltonian function*, which is used extensively in quantum mechanics. *Hamilton's principle* is the principle that the integral with respect to time of the kinetic energy minus the potential energy of a system is a minimum.

One of Hamilton's most famous discoveries was that of *quaternions*. These are a generalization of complex numbers with the striking property that the commutative law does not hold for them (i.e. $A \times B$ does not equal $B \times A$). Hamilton's discovery of an algebraic system for which this law does not hold is important for the development of abstract algebra; for instance, the introduction of matrices. Hamilton spent the last 20 years of his life trying to apply them to problems in applied mathematics, although the more limited theory of vector analysis of Josiah Willard Gibbs was eventually preferred. Toward the end of his life Hamilton drank increasingly, eventually dying of gout.

HÄMMERLING, Joachim August Wilhelm (b. Mar. 9, 1901; Berlin) German biologist.

Hämmerling was educated at the universities of Berlin and Marburg. After graduating he worked at the Kaiser Wilhelm Institute of Biology from 1922 until 1948 when he moved to Wilhelmshaven to serve as director of the Max Planck Institute for Marine Biology until his retirement in 1970.

In 1953 Hämmerling carried out a series of classic experiments on the unicellular alga, *Acetabularia*. It is shaped something like a mushroom with the nucleus included in the stem part, thus making the removal of the nucleus a relatively simple and harmless matter. This Hämmerling did. The aim of the experiment was to see if the nucleus itself actually produced the proteins necessary for the growth and development of an organism, or whether it merely produced the 'machinery' with which pro-

tein synthesis could take place outside the nucleus

Hämmerling's work seemed to confirm the latter alternative, for the enucleated alga continued to grow and develop, even proving capable in certain circumstances of regenerating a new cap.

HAMMOND, George Simms (b. May 22, 1921; Auburn, Maine) American chemist.

Hammond, the son of a farmer, was educated at Bates College and at Harvard where he obtained his PhD in 1947. He immediately afterward joined the faculty at Iowa State University, serving as professor of chemistry from 1956 until 1958. He then moved to California, being appointed first to the chair of organic chemistry at the California Institute of Technology and in 1972 to the chemistry chair at Santa Cruz. In 1978 he left academic life to become associate director for corporate research with the Allied Chemical Corporation.

Coauthor with Donald Cram of a widely used textbook, *Organic Chemistry* (1959), Hammond has worked mainly on the mechanism of photochemical reactions, particularly the behavior of energy-rich molecules.

HANSEN, Armauer Gerhard Henrik (b. July 29, 1841; Bergen, Norway; d. Feb. 12, 1912; Fluro, Norway) Norwegian bacteriologist.

Hansen, the son of a merchant, graduated in medicine from the University of Christiania, (now Oslo) in 1866. He began work in the Bergen leprosy hospital in 1868, an institution under the control of Daniel Danielssen, the leading European authority on leprosy and the future father-in-law of Hansen. Leprosy was thought to be a hereditary affliction, but Hansen concluded from epidemiological studies that it was infectious. He thus took the opportunity in 1870 to travel to Bonn and Vienna to extend his knowledge of bacteriology.

Back in Bergen he observed, in 1873, the rod shaped bacilli in specimen tissues from leprosy patients, since known variously as Hansen's bacillus or *Mycobacterium leprae*. He later proposed this to be the cause of leprosy but his claim was not appreciated for many years. Hansen however never managed to fulfil the postulates of Robert Koch and transmit the disease via the bacilli to animals or men, a difficulty also met with by all later workers. He was forced to resign from the leprosy hospital in 1880 for injudiciously injecting live leprosy bacilli into a patient without first obtaining her permission; he did, however, continue to advise the Norwegian government on their policy to leprosy and also carried on with his own research.

He succeeded, by a policy of limited isolation, in reducing the Norwegian incidence of leprosy from 2833 cases in 1850 to 140 in 1923. Hansen was also an ardent proponent of Darwinism and publicized Darwin's work in Norway.

HANTZSCH, Arthur Rudolf (b. Mar. 7, 1857; Dresden, now in East Germany; d. Mar. 14, 1935; Dresden) German chemist.

Hantzsch studied at Dresden Polytechnic and the University of Würzburg where he took his doctorate in 1880. He taught in Leipzig (1880), Zurich (1885), Würzburg (1893), and finally, in 1903, Leipzig. He retired to Dresden in 1927.

Hantzsch's first success came in 1882 when he announced his method for synthesizing substituted pyridines from aldehyde ammonia compounds and keto esters. In 1887 he synthesized thiazole and later prepared imidazole, oxazole, and selenazole. In 1890 he published with his pupil Alfred Werner an account of the stereochemistry of the organic nitrogen compounds, oximes. Hantzsch later tried to extend this work to the diazo compounds, which were being investigated by Eugen Bamberger.

Hantzsch was a prolific writer publishing over 450 papers. He wrote extensively on the theory of acids and bases, the absorption of light by different compounds, and on nitrophenols.

HARCOURT, Sir William Venables Vernon (b. June 1789; Sudbury, England; d. Apr. 1, 1871; Nuneham, England) British chemist.

Harcourt's father was the archbishop of York. Before entering Oxford University in 1807, Harcourt received a private education and spent five years in the Royal Navy. On graduation (1811) he moved to Yorkshire as a clergyman and in 1861, on the death of his elder brother, he succeeded to the family estates and retired to Nuneham in Oxfordshire.

Although he set up his own chemical laboratory he was basically an amateur scientist whose importance lies rather with those he stimulated and influenced than in the work he produced himself. He was a friend of John Kidd, William Wollaston, Humphry Davy, and other early 19th-century chemists. He played a crucial role in the establishment of the British Association for the Advancement of Science in 1830, serving as its first secretary, being responsible for drawing up its laws and constitution, and its president in 1839.

HARDEN, Sir Arthur (b. Oct. 12, 1865; Manchester, England; d. June 17, 1940; Bourne End, England) British biochemist.

Harden was educated at Owens College, Manchester, (where he subsequently taught) and at the University of Erlangen, Germany. He was professor of biochemistry at the Jenner (later Lister) Institute of Preventive Medicine, where he began research into alcoholic fermentation, continuing the work of Eduard Buchner who had discovered that such reactions took place in the absence of living cells.

Harden demonstrated that the activity of yeast enzymes was lost following dialysis (the separation of large from small molecules by diffusion of the smaller molecules through a semipermeable membrane). He went on to show that the small molecules are necessary for the successful action of the yeast enzyme and that, whereas the activity of the large molecules was lost on boiling, the activity of the small molecules remained after boiling. This suggested that the large molecules were proteins but the small molecules were probably nonprotein. This was the first evidence for the existence of *coenzymes* — nonprotein molecules that are essential for the activity of enzymes. Harden also discovered that yeast enzymes are not broken down and lost with time, but that the gradual loss of activity with time can be reversed by the addition of phosphates. He found that sugar phosphates are formed during fermentation as intermediates — phosphates are now known to play a vital part in biochemical reactions. Knighted in 1936, Harden shared the Nobel Prize for chemistry with Hans von Euler-Chelpin (q.v.) for his work on alcoholic fermentation and enzymes.

HARDY, Godfrey Harold (b. Feb. 7, 1877; Cranleigh, England; d. Dec. 1, 1947; Cambridge, England) British mathematician.

Hardy had his mathematical education at Cambridge University and remained there as a fellow of Trinity College until 1919 when he became Savilian Professor of Geometry at Oxford. From 1931 to 1942 he was back in Cambridge as Sadleirian Professor of Pure Mathematics.

His central field of interest was in analysis and such related areas as convergence and number theory. *Hardy classes* of complex functions are named for him. For 35 years, starting in 1911, Hardy collaborated with J. E. Littlewood and together they wrote nearly a hundred papers. The principal areas they covered were Diophantine approximations, the theory of numbers, inequalities, series and definite integrals, and the Riemann zeta-function.

Although primarily a pure mathematician Hardy made one lasting contribution to applied mathematics; the *Hardy–Wein-*

berg law was discovered independently by Hardy and the physician Wilhelm Weinberg in 1908 and proved to be fundamental to the whole science of population genetics. It gives a mathematical description of the genetic equilibrium in a large random-mating population and explains the surprising fact that, unless there are outside changing forces, the proportion of dominant to recessive genes tends *not* to vary from generation to generation. The law offered strong confirmation for the Darwinian theory of natural selection.

Hardy was one of the outstanding British mathematicians of his day, an excellent teacher, and one of the first to introduce modern work on the rigorous presentation of analysis into Britain. His *Course of Pure Mathematics* (1908) was influential on the teaching of mathematics in British universities. One of his achievements was his discovery of the young Indian mathematician Srinivasa Ramanujan. Partly through Hardy's efforts Trinity College made funds available for Ramanujan to go to Cambridge to pursue his mathematical researches under Hardy.

Hardy was a passionate devotee of cricket and an equally passionate enemy of the Christian religion. During World War I he was a staunch supporter of Bertrand Russell when Trinity set about depriving Russell of his fellowship on account of his pacifist activities. Hardy wrote a lively autobiographical sketch *A Mathematician's Apology*.

HARDY, Sir William Bate (b. Apr. 6, 1864; Erdington, England; d. Jan. 23, 1934; Cambridge, England) British biologist and chemist.

Hardy was educated at Cambridge University where he remained for the whole of his life, being appointed a lecturer in physiology in 1913 and superintendent of the Low Temperature Research Station in 1922. In addition Hardy served on a number of advisory bodies of which the most significant were his chairmanship of the Advisory Committee on Fisheries Development (1919–31) and his directorship of the Food Investigation Board (1917–34).

He began his research career as a histologist, publishing a number of papers in the 1890s on the morphology and behavior of the leukocytes (white blood cells). He began, however, to have considerable doubts about the value of staining and fixing living tissue suspecting that certain structures seen in cells after fixation might simply be artefacts caused by the fixing reagents themselves. He emphasized the point by the production of reticulated and fibrillar structures in his laboratory by fixing and staining albumin.

This led Hardy to work on colloid chemistry and the properties of proteins in solution. He later studied molecular films and lubrication. He reported on this work in his Croonian lecture *On Globulins* (1905) and his Bakerian lecture of 1925, *Boundary Lubrication*.

HARE, Robert (b. Jan. 17, 1781; Philadelphia, Pennsylvania; d. May 15, 1858; Philadelphia) American chemist.

Hare was the son of the owner of a brewery. He is best known for his invention of the oxyhydrogen blowpipe, which he demonstrated to Joseph Priestley in 1801. This became of great value in the welding process for it is the ancestor of the later welding torches.

HARGREAVES, James (d. Apr. 22, 1778; Nottinghamshire, England) British inventor.

Hargreaves was a poor and uneducated spinner and weaver when, in 1764, he had the idea of a hand-powered spinning machine that could spin many threads at once. The story is that he saw his daughter, Jenny, knock over a spinning wheel and noticed that it kept turning in a horizontal position. He built a machine, naming this the spinning jenny, and started to sell his invention. However, hand weavers who

were afraid of unemployment broke into his workshop and destroyed his machines. As a result of this he moved to Nottingham and together with a partner, Thomas James, set up a mill in 1768 in which he used the jennies to spin yarn for making hosiery. His machine was patented in 1770. Thereafter he was moderately successful and worked at his mill until his death.

HARIOT (or HARRIOT), Thomas (b. 1560; Oxford, England; d. July 2, 1621; London) English mathematician, astronomer, and physicist.

Hariot is best known as a pioneer figure in the British school of algebra, although his interests and activities were very wide ranging. He was an associate of Sir Walter Raleigh and accompanied Raleigh on a voyage to Virginia (1585–86) in the capacity of navigator and cartographer. He later wrote a book about this journey — *A Briefe and True Report of the New Found Land of Virginia* (1588). Among his many innovations in algebra Hariot introduced a number of greatly simplified notations. His central mathematical achievements were in the theory of equations where he discovered important relationships between the coefficients of equations and their roots. This work was published in his *Artis analyticae praxis ad aequationes algebraicas resolvendas* (1631; The Analytical Arts Applied to Solving Algebraic Equations).

Outside mathematics Hariot's achievements as a practical astronomer were noteworthy. He designed and constructed telescopes and made detailed studies of comets and sunspots. Independently of Galileo he discovered the moons of Jupiter. Hariot also discovered the law governing the refraction of light. He was granted a pension by the earl of Northumberland and was briefly imprisoned along with the earl during the Gunpowder Plot of 1605. Hariot conducted numerous experiments in a variety of fields including optics, ballistics, and meteorology. However he published few of his discoveries and it was only after his death that their extent was realized from his voluminous unpublished notes and papers.

HARKINS, William Draper (b. Dec. 28, 1873; Titusville, Pennsylvania; d. Mar. 7, 1951; Chicago, Illinois) American physical chemist.

Harkins, whose father was a pioneer in the Pennsylvania oil fields, was educated at Stanford University where he obtained his PhD in 1907. After studying abroad under Fritz Haber at Karlsruhe he taught briefly at the University of Montana before moving to Chicago in 1912, where he spent the rest of his career and was made professor of physical chemistry in 1917.

Harkins was one of the first Americans to establish an international reputation in the field of nuclear studies, although many of his results were independently established by his European counterparts. Thus in 1915 he proposed the 'whole number rule' at the same time as Francis Aston was publishing his theory of isotopes. In 1920 he predicted the existence of the neutron and an isotope of hydrogen, deuterium, which were also predicted by Ernest Rutherford in the same year.

In 1915 he demonstrated that the fusion of four atoms of hydrogen to form helium involved a mass excess which was available for conversion to energy in accordance with the famous formula $E = mc^2$ of Albert Einstein. He calculated that four grams of hydrogen could form four grams of helium with a release of energy of 10^{12} calories. Such facts of nuclear fusion were taken up by Arthur Eddington in 1920 and proposed as the source of energy in stars.

Harkins also worked on problems of surface tension and, in 1952 published a standard work on the topic, *The Physical Chemistry of Surface Tension.*

HARRIS, Geoffrey Wingfield (b. June 4, 1913; London; d. Nov. 29, 1971; Oxford, England) British endocrinologist.

Harris, the son of a physicist, was educated at Cambridge University and St. Mary's Hospital, London. After qualifying in 1939, Harris worked at Cambridge as an anatomy lecturer until 1952 when he moved to the Maudsley Hospital, London, to direct the Laboratory of Experimental Neuroendocrinology. In 1962 Harris was appointed Dr. Lee's Professor of Anatomy at Oxford where he remained until his sudden death in 1971.

In the period 1950–52 Harris published several papers that provided evidence for the important theory that the release of pituitary hormones is controlled by the hypothalamus. Such a mechanism had long been suspected but was only really made plausible when Harris showed that while nervous connection between the two glands could be severed without major effect, cutting the connecting blood supply severely restricted the production of pituitary hormones. (Solly Zuckerman announced conflicting results but Harris was able to show that in the experimental animal used, the ferret, the severed vessels tended to regenerate and restore the humoral connection.)

This led to a massive and prolonged search for the hypothalamic hormones or 'releasing factors'. As Harris was unwilling to devote himself exclusively to such a demanding and basically tedious exercise, the first hypothalamic hormones were isolated, purified, and synthesized by Roger Guillemin and Andrew Schally in the late 1960s.

HARRISON, Ross Granville (b. Jan. 13, 1870; Germantown, Philadelphia; d. Sept. 30, 1959; New Haven, Connecticut) American biologist and embryologist.

Harrison graduated from Johns Hopkins University in 1889 and continued studying experimental embryology for the next ten years at Bryn Mawr College, Johns Hopkins University, and in Germany at the University of Bonn. He had an excellent ear for languages and spoke German fluently. In 1899 he gained his MD degree from the University of Bonn and returned to America to become associate professor of anatomy at Johns Hopkins. From 1907 to 1938 he worked at Yale, first as professor of anatomy then from 1927 as professor of biology.

Harrison's work in experimental embryology formed a bridge between the morphological studies of the 19th century and the new molecular biology of the 20th century based on cell function and structure. In his most influential work (1910) he demonstrated the outgrowth of nerve fibers from ganglion cells in embryonic tissues by devising techniques so that the event could actually be observed. His early attempts used frog-embryo cells hanging in a nutrient medium from the underside of a special microscope slide. The method was gradually refined to give the important new technique of tissue culture. Although Harrison himself did not pursue tissue culture to any great extent the method has proved immensely useful in testing new drugs and in the production of vaccines.

Harrison founded the influential Journal of Experimental Zoology in 1906.

HARTLINE, Haldan Keffer (b. Dec. 22, 1903; Bloomsburg, Pennsylvania) American physiologist.

Hartline was educated at Lafayette College, Easton, Pennsylvania, and Johns Hopkins University, Baltimore, where he was professor of biophysics from 1949–53. In 1953 he became professor of physiology at the Rockefeller University, New York City. His work has been specially concerned with sense receptors and in particular with the neurophysiology of vision. Using minute electrodes to separate and study individual eye fibers of arthropod and vertebrate eyes, notably horseshoe crabs and frogs, he has been able to elucidate the fine working of individual cells in the retina and to show how the eye distinguishes between different shapes. His work in this field led to his sharing the Nobel Prize in physiology or medicine with George Wald and Ragnar Granit (1967).

HARTMANN, Johannes Franz (b. Jan. 11, 1865; Erfurt, now in East Germany; d. Sept. 13, 1936; Göttingen, now in West Germany) German astronomer.

Hartmann was the son of a merchant. He was educated at the universities of Tübingen, Berlin, and Leipzig where he obtained his PhD in 1891. He worked first at the Leipzig and Potsdam observatories before being appointed in 1909 as professor of astronomy and director of the Göttingen University Observatory. He remained there until 1921 when he became director of the La Plata Observatory in Argentina, only returning to Göttingen in 1935 a few months before his death.

Hartmann was responsible for the important observation in 1904 that provided the first clear evidence for the existence of interstellar gas. He noted that in the spectrum of the star Delta Orion, a binary system, the calcium lines failed to exhibit any periodic Doppler effect arising from the orbital motion of the stars: when a star moves in its orbit toward the Earth the wavelength of lines in its spectrum are shifted toward the blue, while as it moves away from the Earth its spectral lines are shifted toward the red. That there were what Hartmann described as 'stationary lines' of calcium in the spectrum could only mean that the calcium was not part of the atmosphere of Delta Orion and therefore was not participating in the orbital motion. It must occur somewhere between binary system and observer. The existence of interstellar matter and its significance in the estimation of stellar distances was finally demonstrated by Robert Trumpler in 1930.

HARVEY, William (b. Apr. 1, 1578; Folkestone, England; d. June 3, 1657; Roehampton, England) English physician.

Harvey was educated at King's School, Canterbury and Cambridge University. In 1599 he made the then customary visit to Italy where he studied medicine at the University of Padua under the anatomist

Fabricius ab Aquapendente, obtaining his MD in 1602. He was appointed physician at St. Bartholomew's Hospital, London, in 1609 and in 1618 began working at the court as physician extraordinary to James I. He also served Charles I, accompanying him on his various travels and campaigns throughout the English Civil War. He was rewarded briefly with the office of warden of Merton College, Oxford, in 1645 but with the surrender of Oxford to the Puritans in 1646 Harvey, suffering much from gout, took the opportunity to retire into private life.

In 1628 Harvey published *De motu cordis et sanguinis in animalibus* (On the Motion of the Heart and Blood in Animals). This announced the single most important discovery of the modern period in anatomy and physiology, namely, the circulation of the blood. The orthodox view, going back to Galen, saw blood originating in the liver and from there being distributed throughout the body. There was no circulation for Galen and he believed that the arteries and veins carried different substances. Harvey made a simple calculation that revealed the prodigious amounts of blood that would have to be produced if there was no circulation. Harvey also could not understand why the valves in the veins were placed so that they allowed free movement of blood to the heart but not away from it. It did however make sense if blood was pumped to the limbs through the arteries and returned through the veins.

Harvey then set about demonstrating his supposition. He examined the action of the heart of such cold-blooded creatures as frogs, snakes, and fishes as their slower heart rate allows clearer observations to be made. This enabled him to establish that blood passes from the right to the left side of the heart not through the wall, or septum, which was solid, but via the lungs. It was also clear that blood is pumped from the heart into the arteries for he observed that they begin to fill at the moment of systole or contraction. On the other hand diastole is related to the filling of the heart which is thus, Harvey declared, nothing more than a pump. To show that blood passes from the arteries to the veins rather than vice versa, Harvey resorted to a number of simple and compelling experiments with ligatures.

Harvey's 72-page masterpiece received considerable but by no means universal support. There was, as he was well aware one weak link in his argument, namely the precise connection, or anastomoses, between the arterial and venous system. He thus had to accept, without observation, that the hair thin capillaries of the two systems did in fact link up. Harvey only had a magnifying glass at his disposal and it was left to Marcello Malpighi to observe the implied anastomoses through his microscope in 1661. The importance of Harvey's discovery lay in providing an alternative to the Galenic theory, thus encouraging other scientists to question the authority of ancient texts.

Harvey also worked in embryology. He argued that all life arose from the egg thus denying spontaneous generation. To describe the process of generation he thought he had observed in chickens and deer, Harvey coined the term *epigenesis*. By this he meant the female egg possessed an independent existence and was capable of completing its development through the activity of its own vital principle. It did not join with the semen, nor was it fertilized by it. Harvey believed the semen acted by initiating the self-contained development of the egg through touch alone. However with the use of the microscope and the earlier identification of anatomical features within the egg by Malpighi in 1673 the alternative preformationist view began to gain ground.

Harvey became a figure of much influence within the College of Physicians. He served as treasurer in 1628 and although offered the presidency in 1654 felt compelled to decline it on grounds of health.

HASSELL, Odd (b. May 17, 1897; Oslo; d. May 15, 1981; Norway) Norwegian chemist.

Hassell was educated at the University of Oslo and in Berlin where he obtained his doctorate in 1924. He immediately returned to the University of Oslo and served there as professor of chemistry from 1934 until his retirement in 1964.

Early in his career, following studies on how organic dyes photosensitize silver halides, Hassell discovered adsorption indicators. In 1943 he published an important conformational analysis of cyclohexane but, as he refused to use the language of the German conquerors and published it in Norwegian, its influence was considerably reduced. The molecule exists in two main forms, the so-called boat and chair conformations; Hassell had little difficulty in showing the chair form to be the most stable. It was for his work on conformation that he shared the 1969 Nobel Chemistry Prize with Derek Barton.

HATCHETT, Charles (b. Jan. 2, 1765; London; d. Mar. 10, 1847; London) British chemist.

Hatchett was the son of a coachbuilder. He is noted as the discoverer of the element niobium, which he found in 1801 in a mineral from Connecticut. The following year, Anders Ekeberg found the element tantalum in Sweden and, for some time, it was unclear whether the elements were different. It was not until 1865 that Jean Marignac showed that the two were different elements. Hatchett's original name of columbium was replaced by niobium (for Niobe, daughter of Tantalus in mythology). Hatchett later served (1823) with Humphry Davy on a committee to investigate the corrosion of copper plates on ships. On his father's death he retired from research to take over his father's coachbuilding business.

HAUKSBEE, Francis (b. *c.* 1670; England; d. *c.* 1713; England) English physicist.

Hauksbee, a student of Robert Boyle, conducted numerous experiments on a wide range of topics. They are fully described in his *Physico-Mechanical Experiments* (1709). He worked as demonstrator at the Royal Society and became a fellow in 1705. Under the supervision of Newton he conducted a series of experiments on the capillary action (the movement of water through pores, caused by surface tension) of tubes and glass plates. He also made improvements to the air pump and made a thorough investigation of static electricity, showing that friction could, besides generating electricity, produce luminous effects in a vacuum.

HAUY, René Just (b. Feb. 28, 1743; St. Just, France; d. June 3, 1822; Paris) French mineralogist.

Haüy, whose father was a poor clothworker, was interested in church music. This attracted the attention of the prior of the abbey, who soon recognized Haüy's intelligence and arranged for him to receive a sound education. While in Paris, his interest in mineralogy was awakened by the lectures of Louis Daubenton. He became professor of mineralogy at the Natural History Museum in Paris in 1802. His *Traité de mineralogie* was published in five volumes in 1801 and *Traité de cristallographie* in three volumes in 1822.

Haüy is regarded as the founder of the science of crystallography through his discovery of the geometrical law of crystallization. In 1781 he accidentally dropped some calcite crystals onto the floor, one of which broke, and found, to his surprise, that the broken pieces were rhombohedral in form. Deliberately breaking other and diverse forms of calcite, he found that it always revealed the same form whatever its source. He concluded that all the molecules of calcite have the same form and it is only how they are joined together that produces different gross structures. Following on from this he suggested that other minerals should show different basic forms. He thought that there were, in fact, six different primitive forms from which all crystals could be derived by being linked in different ways. Using his theory he was able to predict in many cases the correct angles of the crystal face. Haüy's work aroused much controversy and was attacked by Eilhard Mitscherlich in 1819 when he discovered isomorphism in which two substances of different composition can have the same crystalline form. Haüy rejected Mitscherlich's arguments.

Haüy also conducted work in pyroelectricity. The mineral haüyne was named for him.

HAWKING, Stephen William (b. Jan. 8, 1942; Oxford, England) British theoretical physicist.

Hawking graduated from Oxford University and obtained his PhD from Cambridge University. After being connected with various Cambride institutes and departments he was appointed in 1977 to the chair of gravitational physics.

Hawking has worked mainly in the field of general relativity and in particular on the theory of black holes. He has objected to Einstein's treatment of gravity in his general theory since "it treats the gravitational field in a purely classical manner when all other observed fields seem to be quantized." A further objection, made with G. F. R. Ellis in their *Large Scale Structure of Space Time* (1973), was that the theory led inevitably to singularities that it could not describe adequately. Two such singularities they suggest are the totally collapsed form of stars known as black holes and the beginning of the expansion of the universe. For these reasons Hawking has been one of the leaders in the search for a theory of quantum gravity. Such a search has yet to find any general agreement and although a number of theories have been advanced it is quite clear that all still possess serious defects.

In the theory of black holes Hawking has been more successful, establishing a number of remarkable theorems. Black holes are celestial 'bodies' that, having had a mass in excess of three solar masses, have undergone a gravitational collapse so

extreme that they contract below the critical radius, calculated by Karl Schwarzschild, at which light or any other signal can escape. At first it appeared that absolutely nothing could be known about such bodies, or singularities, but Hawking has managed to construct many of their properties and show their relationship to more classical parts of physics.

Hawking showed however that black holes could originate in other circumstances. There could be "a number of very much smaller black holes scattered around the universe, formed not by the collapse of stars but by the collapse of highly compressed regions ... that are believed to have existed shortly after the 'big bang' in which the universe originated." These 'mini black holes' could weigh a billion tons and yet be no bigger than a proton with a radius of 10^{-15} meters.

His most exciting result, published in 1974, was one that he confessed he found hard to believe. This was the claim that black holes are not 'black' but emit particles at a steady rate. This result has been repeatedly confirmed mathematically and Hawking is able to propose a physical quantum process that would produce the effect. Quantum mechanics supposes space to be full of 'virtual' particles, i.e. particles that cannot be observed but do exist. They exist as pairs of particles and antiparticles that are constantly joining, separating, and annihilating each other. If one member of the pair were to be attracted into a black hole leaving its partner alone, then "The forsaken particle or antiparticle may fall into the black hole after its partner but it may also escape to infinity, where it appears to be radiation emitted by the black hole." If this is not clear he offers an alternative explanation involving one of the particles traveling backward in time. Such conclusions emerged when Hawking and his colleagues were able to link the physics of black holes with the laws of thermodynamics.

It should be said that since the early 1960s Hawking has been the victim of a progressive nervous disease. This has confined him to a wheelchair and has prevented him from writing or calculating in a direct and simple way. The bulk of his work, involving complex calculations, difficult mathematical proofs, and the introduction of new physical ideas, is thus interwoven into presentable form purely in his mind.

HAWKINS, Gerald Stanley (b. Apr. 20, 1928; Great Yarmouth, England) British–American astronomer.

Hawkins graduated from the University of Nottingham in 1949 and obtained his PhD in 1952 from the University of Manchester. He emigrated to America in 1954 and worked at the Harvard College Observatory. From 1957 to 1969 he was director of the observatory at Boston University, becoming professor of astronomy in 1964. Since 1962 he has also worked at the Smithsonian Astrophysical Observatory in Cambridge, Massachusetts.

Hawkins has made visual, photographic, and radar studies of meteors, has studied meteorites, tektites, and lunar craters, and has also investigated archeological sites with regard to their astronomical significance. In 1966 he published *Stonehenge Decoded*, which both aroused popular interest in archeo-astronomy and also succeeded in stimulating a new generation of scholars like Fred Hoyle to take the subject seriously and rescue it from the cranks and pedants. His great innovation was to program a computer to check pairs of stones from the famous prehistoric site of Stonehenge in England for possible alignments with celestial bodies. He found no detectable correlation with the stars and the planets, but discovered that many of the positions seemed to point to the maximum declinations (i.e. altitudes above or below the celestial equator) of the Sun and the Moon. More startling and controversial was his claim that the Aubrey holes, which number 56 and surround the main structure in a circle of 288-foot (88-m) diameter, could be used to predict lunar eclipses.

The success of his Stonehenge operation led Hawkins to make a computer analysis of other ancient monuments. The most significant conclusion established was the negative result for markings in the desert in Peru. Skeptics had felt that Hawkins and his computer were likely to find astronomical significance in any construction; his findings that the Peruvian lines could not be correlated with any celestial body between 5000 BC and AD 1900 did much to refute this argument.

HAWORTH, Sir (Walter) Norman (b. Mar. 19, 1883; Chorley, England; d. Mar. 19, 1950; Birmingham, England) British carbohydrate chemist.

Haworth began work in a linoleum factory managed by his father. This required some knowledge of dyes, which naturally led Haworth to chemistry. Despite his family's objections he persisted in private study until he was sufficiently qualified to gain admission to Manchester University in 1903, where he studied under and later worked with William Perkin, Jr. on terpenes. Haworth did his postgraduate studies at Göttingen where, in 1910, he gained his PhD. In 1912 he joined the staff of St. Andrews University where he worked with Thomas Purdie and James Irvine on carbohydrates. He remained there until 1920 when, after five years at the University of Durham, he was appointed Mason Professor of Chemistry at Birmingham where he remained until his retirement in 1948.

Emil Fischer had dominated late 19th-century organic chemistry and, beginning in 1887, had synthesized a number of sugars taking them to be open chain structures, most of which were built on a framework of six carbon atoms. Haworth however succeeded in showing that the carbon atoms in sugars are linked by oxygen into rings: either there are five carbon atoms and one oxygen atom, giving a pyranose ring, or there are four carbon atoms and one oxygen atom, giving a furanose ring. When the appropriate oxygen and hydrogen atoms are added to these rings the result is a sugar. He went on to represent the ring by what he called a 'perspective formula', today known as a *Haworth formula*.

With Edmund Hirst he went on to establish the point of closure of the ring using the technique of Irvine and Purdie of converting the sugar into its methyl ester. He later investigated the chain structure of various polysaccharides. In 1929 he published his views in *The Constitution of the Sugars*.

In 1933 Haworth and his colleagues achieved a further triumph. Albert Szent-Györgyi had earlier isolated a substance from the adrenal cortex and from orange juice, which he named hexuranic acid. It was in fact vitamin C and Haworth, again in collaboration with Hirst, succeeded in synthesizing it. He called it ascorbic acid.

For this work, the first synthesis of a vitamin, Haworth shared the 1937 Nobel Prize for chemistry with Paul Karrer.

HAYS, James Douglas (b. Dec. 26, 1933; Johnstown, New York) American geologist.

Hays was educated at Harvard, Ohio State, and Columbia universities, obtaining his PhD from the last in 1964. He joined Columbia's Lamont–Doherty Geological Observatory, New York, in 1967 as director of the deep-sea sediments core laboratory and in 1975 was appointed professor of geology.

In 1971 Hays reported that from his study of 28 deep-sea piston cores from high and low latitudes it was shown that during the last 2.5 million years eight species of radiolaria had become extinct. Prior to extinction these species were widely distributed and their sudden extinction, in six out of eight cases, was in close proximity to a magnetic reversal, a change in the Earth's magnetic polarity. Hays concluded that the magnetic reversals influenced the radiolarians' extinction.

HEAVISIDE, Oliver (b. Apr. 18, 1850; London; d. Feb. 3, 1925; Torquay, England) British electronic engineer and physicist.

Heaviside, a nephew of Charles Wheatstone, was very deaf so, hampered in school, he was largely self-taught. He was interested in the transmission of electrical signals and used Maxwell's equations (*see* James Clerk Maxwell) to develop a practical theory of cable telegraphy, introducing the concepts of self inductance, impedance, and conductance. However, his early results were not recognized, possibly because the papers were written using his own notation.

After radio waves had been transmitted across the Atlantic in 1901, he suggested (1902) the existence of a charged atmospheric layer that reflected the waves. The same year Arthur Kennelly independently suggested the same explanation. The *Heaviside layer* (sometimes called the Kennelly–Heaviside layer) was detected experimentally in 1924 by Edward Appleton.

Later in life his fame grew and he was awarded an honorary doctorate at Göttingen and was elected a fellow of the Royal Society in 1891.

HECATAEUS of Miletus (b. *c.* 550 BC; Miletus, now in Turkey; d. *c.* 476 BC; Miletus) Greek geographer.

Hecataeus flourished during the time of the Persian invasion of Ionia, and was one of the ambassadors sent to Persia. One of the earliest geographical works, the *Periegesis* (Tour Round the World), is attributed to him but only fragments of this now exist. It reportedly contained a map showing the world as Hecataeus believed it to be — a flat disk surrounded by ocean. The work was used by the ancients, notably by the Greek historian Herodotus (who also ridiculed it). Even fewer fragments remain of Hecataeus's other surviving work, *Historiai*, which gave an account of the traditions and mythology of the Greeks.

HECHT, Selig (b. Feb. 8, 1892; Glogow, Austria; d. Sept. 18, 1947; New York City) American physiologist.

Hecht was brought to America in 1898. He was educated at City College, New York, and Harvard where he obtained his PhD in 1917. After several junior posts and a prolonged traveling fellowship Hecht was appointed professor of biophysics at Columbia in 1926, a post he retained until his death.

Hecht is best remembered for his photochemical theory of visual adaptation formulated in the mid-1920s. That the eye can readily adapt to changes in brightness is a familiar experience but the exact mechanism behind this response is far from clear. Hecht proposed that in bright light the visual pigment rhodopsin is somewhat bleached while regeneration takes place in the dark. Under steady illumination the amount of rhodopsin bleached would be balanced by that regenerated. Adaptation is thus simply equated with the amount of rhodopsin in the retinal rods.

HEEZEN, Bruce Charles (b. Apr. 11, 1924; Vinton, Iowa; d. June 21, 1977; at sea) American oceanographer.

Heezen was educated at Iowa State University, graduating in 1948, and Columbia, New York, where he received his PhD in 1957. He worked at the Lamont Geological Observatory at Columbia from 1948.

Heezen's work has contributed significantly to knowledge of the ocean floor and the processes that operate within the oceans. In 1952 he produced convincing evidence for the existence of turbidity currents; i.e. currents caused by a mass of water full of suspended sediment. Their existence had been suggested by Reginald Daly in 1936 and proposed as the cause of submarine canyons. Heezen used precise records available from the 1929 Grand Bank earthquake to study these currents. As the area off the Grand Bank was rich with communication cables, exact records of the disturbance caused by the earthquake had been obtained. He was able to reconstruct the movement down the bank of about 25 cubic miles (100 cubic km) of sediment moving with speeds approaching 50 mph (85 km per hour).

In 1957, in collaboration with William Ewing and Marie Tharp, the existence of the worldwide ocean rift was demonstrated and its connection with seismic activity postulated. In 1960 Heezen argued for an expanding Earth in which new material is emerging from the rift, increasing the oceans' width and pushing the continents further apart. Such a view, based on the grounds that the gravitational constant decreases slowly with time, had been suggested earlier by Paul Dirac, but received little support in the early 1960s, particularly when a more plausible mechanism was suggested by Harry H. Hess (q.v.) in 1962.

HEIDELBERGER, Michael (b. Apr. 29, 1888; New York City) American immunologist.

Heidelberger was educated at Columbia where he obtained his PhD in 1911. He first worked at the Rockefeller Institute from 1912 until 1927 when he moved to Columbia, where he served as professor of immunochemistry from 1948 until his retirement in 1956.

Heidelberger in his long career has worked on many immunological problems. Between 1928 and 1950 he did much to reveal the chemical structure of antibody and complement, two of the key parts of the immune system.

He also collaborated with a colleague at Rockefeller, Oswald Avery, and in a famous experiment (1923) demonstrated that the specific antigenic properties of pneumococci are due to certain polysaccharides in their capsules.

HEISENBERG, Werner Karl (b. Dec. 5, 1901; Würzburg, now in West Germany; d.

361

Feb. 2, 1976; Munich, West Germany) German physicist.

Heisenberg's father was the professor of Greek at the University of Munich. He was himself educated at the universities of Munich and Göttingen where in 1923 he obtained his doctorate. After spending the period 1924–26 in Copenhagen working with Niels Bohr he returned to Germany to take up the professorship of theoretical physics at the University of Leipzig. In 1941 Heisenberg moved to Berlin where he was appointed director of the Kaiser Wilhelm Institute for Physics and where he played the key role in the German atomic bomb program. After the war he helped to establish the Max Planck Institute for Physics at Göttingen, serving as director and moving with it to Munich in 1955 where he was also appointed professor of physics.

In 1925 Heisenberg formulated a version of quantum theory that became known as matrix mechanics. It was for this work, which was later shown to be formally equivalent to the wave mechanics of Erwin Schrödinger, that Heisenberg was awarded the 1932 Nobel Physics Prize. Heisenberg began in a very radical way, much influenced by Ernst Mach. Considering the various bizarre results emerging in quantum theory, such as the apparent wave–particle duality of the electron, his first answer was that it is simply a mistake to think of the atom in visual terms at all. What we really know of the atom is what we can observe of it, namely, the light it emits, its frequency, and its intensity. The need therefore was to be able to write a set of equations that would permit the correct prediction of such atomic phenomena. Heisenberg succeeded in establishing a mathematical formalism that permitted accurate predictions to be made. The method was also developed by Max Born and Pascual Jordan. As they used the then relatively unfamiliar matrix mathematics to develop this system, it is not surprising that physicists preferred the more usual language of wave equations used in the equivalent system of Schrödinger.

In 1927 Heisenberg went on to explore a deeper level of physical understanding when he formulated his fundamental 'uncertainty principle': that it is impossible to determine exactly both the position and momentum of such particles as the electron. He demonstrated this by simple 'thought experiments' of the following type: if we try to locate the exact position of an electron we must use rays with very short wavelengths such as gamma rays. But by so illuminating it the electron's momentum will be changed by its interaction with the energetic gamma rays. Alternatively a lower-energy wave can be used that will not disturb the momentum of the electron so much but, as lower energy implies longer wavelength, such radiation will lack the precision to provide the exact location of the electron. There seems to be no way out of such an impasse and Heisenberg went on to express the limits of the uncertainty mathematically as:

$$\Delta x . \Delta p = h/4\pi$$

where Δx is the uncertainty in ascertaining the position in a given direction, Δp is the uncertainty in ascertaining the momentum in that direction, and h is the Planck constant. What the equation tells us is that the product of the uncertainties must always be about as great as the Planck constant and can never disappear completely. Further, any attempt made to reduce one element of uncertainty to the minimum can only be done at the expense of increasing the other. The consequence of this failure to know the *exact* position and momentum is an inability to predict accurately the future position of an electron. Thus, like Max Born, Heisenberg had found it necessary to introduce a basic indeterminacy into physics.

After his great achievements in quantum theory in the 1920s Heisenberg later turned his attention to the theory of elementary particles. Thus in 1932, shortly after the discovery of the neutron by James Chadwick, Heisenberg proposed that the nucleus consists of both neutrons and protons. He went further, arguing that they were in fact two states of the same basic entity — the 'nucleon'. As the strong nuclear force does not distinguish between them he proposed that they were 'isotopes' with nearly the same mass, distinguished instead by a property he called 'isotopic spin'. He later attempted the ambitious task of constructing a unified field theory of elementary particles. Although he published a monograph on the topic in 1966 it generated little support.

Unlike many other German scientists Heisenberg remained in Germany throughout the war and the whole Nazi era. He was certainly no Nazi himself but he thought it essential to remain in Germany to preserve traditional scientific values for the next generation. At one time he came under attack from the Nazis for his refusal to compromise his support for the physics of Einstein in any way. Thus when, in 1935, he wished to move to the University of Munich to succeed Arnold Sommerfeld he was violently attacked by the party press and, eventually, the post went to the little-known W. Müller.

With the outbreak of war in 1939 Heisenberg was soon called upon to come to Berlin to direct the program to construct an atom bomb. His exact role in the program has become a matter of controversy. He has claimed that he never had any real intention of making such a bomb, let alone giving it to Hitler. As long as he played a key role he was, he later claimed, in a position to sabotage the program if it ever looked like being a success. He even went so far as to convey such thoughts to Niels Bohr in 1941 when he met him in Copenhagen, hinting that the Allies' physicists should pursue a similar policy. Bohr later reported that if such comments had been made to him they were done so too cryptically for him to grasp; he was rather under the impression that Heisenberg was trying to find out the progress made by the Allies.

It is clear that the whole truth has not been told for when talking to a German audience Heisenberg was more inclined to explain the failure of the German scientists by the comparative lack of resources in the economy after 1942. By 1957 however his position was clear for he then declared publicly that he would not "in any way ... take part in the production, the tests, or the application of atomic weapons."

HELMHOLTZ, Hermann Ludwig Ferdinand von (b. Aug. 31, 1821; Potsdam, now in East Germany; d. Sept. 8, 1894; Charlottenburg, now in West Germany) German physiologist and theoretical physicist.

Helmholtz studied medicine at the Friedrich Wilhelm Institute in Berlin and obtained his MD in 1842. He returned to Potsdam to become an army surgeon, but returned to civilian life in 1848 and was appointed assistant at the Anatomical Museum in Berlin. He then held a succession of chairs at Königsberg (1849–55), Bonn (1855–58), Heidelberg (1858–71), and Berlin (1871–77) and later became director of the Physico-Technical Institute at Berlin Charlottenburg.

Helmholtz made major contributions to two areas of science: physiology and physics. In physiology he invented (1851) the ophthalmoscope for inspecting the interior of the eye and the ophthalmometer for measuring the eye's curvature. He investigated accommodation, color vision, and color blindness. His book *Handbuch der physiologische Optik* (Handbook of Physiological Optics) was published in 1867. Helmholtz also worked on hearing, showing how the cochlea in the inner ear resonates for different frequencies and analyzes complex sounds into harmonic components. In 1863 he published *Die Lehre von den Tönemfindungen als physiologische Grundlage für die Theorie der Musik* (The Sensation of Tone as a Physiological Basis for the Theory of Music). Another achievement was his measurement of the speed of nerve impulses (1850).

One of Helmholtz's interests had been muscle action and animal heat and this, inspired by his distaste for vitalism, led him to his best-known discovery — the law of conservation of energy. This was developed independently of the work of James Joule (q.v.) and Julius von Mayer (q.v.) and published as *Über die Erhaltung der*

Kraft (1847; On the Conservation of Force). He showed that the total energy of a collection of interacting particles is constant, and later applied this idea to other systems.

Helmholtz also worked in thermodynamics, where he introduced the concept of free energy (energy available to perform work). In electrodynamics he attempted to produce a general unified theory. Heinrich Hertz, who discovered radio waves in 1888, was Helmholtz's pupil.

HELMONT, Jan Baptista van (b. Jan. 12, 1579; Brussels; d. Dec. 30, 1644; Vilvoorde, now in Belgium) Flemish chemist and physician.

Helmont, who came from a noble family, was educated at the Catholic University of Louvain in medicine, mysticism, and chemistry, but declined a degree from them. Rejecting all offers of employment he devoted himself to private research at his home. In 1621 he was involved in a controversy with the Church over the belief that it was possible to heal a wound caused by a weapon by treating the weapon rather than the wound. Helmont did not reject this common belief but insisted that it was a natural phenomenon containing no supernatural elements. He was arrested, eventually allowed to remain under house arrest, and forbidden to publish without the prior consent of the Church. He wrote extensively and after his death his collected papers were published by his son as the *Ortus medicinae* (1648).

Helmont rejected the works of the ancients, although he did believe in the philosopher's stone. He carried out careful observations and measurements, which led him to discover the elementary nature of water. He regarded water as the chief constituent of matter. He pointed out that fish were nourished by water and that substantial bodies could be reduced to water by dissolving them in acid. To demonstrate his theory he performed his famous experiment where he grew a willow tree over a period of five years in a measured quantity of earth. The tree increased its weight by 164 pounds despite the fact that only water was added to it. The soil had decreased by only a few ounces.

Helmont also introduced the term 'gas' into the language, deriving it from the Greek for chaos. When a substance is burned it is reduced to its formative agent and its gas and Helmont believed that when 62 pounds of wood is burned to an ash weighing 1 pound, 61 pounds have escaped as water or gas. Different substances give off different gases when consumed and Helmont identified four gases, which he named gas carbonum, two kinds of gas sylvester, and gas pingue. These we would now call carbon dioxide, carbon monoxide, nitrous oxide, and methane.

HENCH, Philip Showalter (b. Feb. 28, 1896; Pittsburgh, Pennsylvania; d. Mar. 31, 1965; Ocho Rios, Jamaica) American biochemist.

Hench was educated at Lafayette College and the University of Pittsburgh, where he obtained his MD in 1920. He spent most of his career working at the Mayo Clinic, becoming head of the section for rheumatic diseases in 1926. Hench was also connected with the Mayo Foundation and the University of Minnesota, where he became professor of medicine in 1947.

For many years Hench had been seeking a method of treating the crippling and painful complaint of rheumatoid arthritis. He suspected that it was not a conventional microbial infection since, among other features, it was relieved by pregnancy and jaundice. Hench therefore felt it was more likely to result from a biochemical disturbance that is transiently corrected by some incidental biological change. The search, he argued, must concentrate on something patients with jaundice had in common with pregnant women. At length he was led to suppose that the antirheumatic substance might be an adrenal hormone, since temporary remissions are often induced by procedures that stimulate the adrenal cortex. Thus in 1948 he was ready to try the newly prepared 'compound E', later known as cortisone, of Edward Kendall on 14 patients. All showed remarkable improvement, which was reversed on withdrawing the drug.

For this development of the first steroid drug Hench shared the 1950 Nobel Prize for physiology or medicine with Kendall and Tadeusz Reichstein.

HENDERSON, Thomas (b. Dec. 28, 1798; Dundee, Scotland; d. Nov. 23, 1844; Edinburgh) British astronomer.

Henderson started as an attorney's clerk who made a reputation as an amateur astronomer. In 1831 he accepted an appointment as director of a new observatory at the Cape of Good Hope in South Africa. While observing Alpha Centauri he found that it had a considerable proper motion. He realized that this probably meant that the star was comparatively close and a good candidate for the measurement of parallax — the apparent change in position of a (celestial) body when viewed from spatially separate points, or one point on a moving Earth. All major observational astronomers had tried to detect this small angular measurement and failed. Henderson at last succeeded in 1882 and found that Alpha Centauri had a parallax of just less than one second of arc. The crucial importance of this was that once parallax was known, the distance of the stars could be measured successfully for the first time. Alpha Centauri turned out to be over four light years away. Unfortunately (for Henderson), he delayed publication of his result until it had been thoroughly checked and rechecked. By this time Friedrich Bessel had already observed and published, in 1839, the parallax of 61 Cygni.

In 1834 Henderson became the first Astronomer Royal of Scotland.

HENLE, Friedrich Gustav Jacob (b. July 17, 1809; Fürth, now in West Germany; d. May 13, 1885; Gottingen, now in West Germany) German physician, anatomist, and pathologist.

Henle, a merchant's son, was educated at the universities of Heidelberg and Bonn where he obtained his MD in 1832. He began his career as assistant to Johannes Müller in Berlin and, despite various political troubles, (he was tried for treason in Berlin) served as professor of anatomy and physiology at the universities of Zurich (1840–44) and Heidelberg (1844–52) before moving to a similar post at Göttingen where he remained until his death.

By the beginning of the 19th century the humoral theory of disease had been finally expelled from orthodox medicine. It was far from clear however what to put in its place. A cogent and comprehensive theory, as developed by Louis Pasteur and Henle's own pupil, Robert Koch, would not be available for a further 40 years. Henle however took some preliminary steps, notably his declaration that contagious substances are not only organic but indeed are living organisms. He distinguished between miasmas, which arise from the environment, and contagions, which spread from person to person. Such theorizing had little immediate impact on medicine largely because of the difficulty in providing experimental support. His work consequently was largely ignored as speculative.

Henle also produced two standard and highly influential textbooks. In them he first described and emphasized the microscopic structure of the epithelium, the cells that cover the internal and external surface of the human body. He has thus frequently been referred to as the founder of modern histology.

As an anatomist Henle's name has been preserved in the *loop of Henle*, a part of the nephron, or urine-secreting tubules, in the kidney.

HENRY, Joseph (b. Dec. 17, 1797; Albany, New York; d. May 13, 1878; Washington DC) American physicist.

One of the first great American scientists, Henry came from a poor background and had to work his way through college. He was educated at the Albany Academy, New York, where he first studied medicine, changing to engineering in 1825. A year later he was appointed a professor of mathematics and physics at Albany. In 1832 he became professor of natural philosophy at Princeton (then the College of New Jersey) where he taught physics, chemistry, mathematics, and geological sciences, and later astronomy and architecture as well.

Henry is noted for his work on electricity. In 1829 he developed a greatly improved form of the electromagnet by insulating the wire that was to be wrapped around the iron core, thus allowing many more coils wound closer together, and greatly increasing the magnet's power. Through this work he discovered, in 1830, the principle of electromagnetic induction. Soon after, and quite independently, Michael Faraday made the same discovery and published first. Faraday is thus credited with the discovery but Henry has the unit of inductance (the *henry*) named for him. However, he did publish in 1832 — prior to Faraday and Heinrich Lenz — his discovery of self-induction (in which the magnetic field from a changing electric current induces an electromotive force opposing the current). Earlier (in 1829) he had invented and constructed the first practical electric motor. In 1835 Henry developed the electric relay in order to overcome the problem of resistance that built up in long wires. This device had an immediate social impact for it was the key step in the invention of the long-distance telegraph, which played a large part in the opening up of the North American continent.

In 1846, Henry became the first secretary of the Smithsonian Institution, which he formed into an extremely efficient body for liaison between scientists and government support of their research. He also did work on solar radiation and on sunspots.

HENRY, William (b. Dec. 12, 1775; Manchester, England; d. Sept. 2, 1836; Pendlebury, England) British physician and chemist.

Henry's father, Thomas Henry, was a manufacturing chemist and an analytical chemist of some repute. Initially qualifying as a physician from Edinburgh University, Henry practiced for five years in the Manchester Infirmary. Later he took over the running of the chemical works established by his father.

In 1801 he formulated the law now known as *Henry's law*, which states that the solubility of a gas in water at a given temperature is proportional to its pressure. His close friend John Dalton was encouraged by this finding, seeing it as a confirmation of his own theory of mixed gases, and the two men discussed the methods of experimentation in detail.

Henry also researched into the hydrocarbon gases, following Dalton in clearly distinguishing methane from ethylene (ethene). He determined the molecular formula of ammonia by exploding it with oxygen. He also described the preparation, purification, and analysis of coal gas, and developed a method of analyzing gas mixtures by fractional combustion. His textbook, *Elements of Experimental Chemistry* (1799), went through 11 editions in 30 years.

HENSEN, Viktor (b. Feb. 10, 1835; Schleswig, now in West Germany; d. Apr. 5, 1924; Kiel, now in West Germany) German physiologist and oceanographer.

Hensen studied science and medicine at the universities of Würzburg, Berlin, and Kiel, graduating from the latter in 1858. He remained at Kiel to work in the physiology department and later became professor of physiology (1871–1911).

Hensen worked on comparative studies of vision and hearing but also discovered, independently of Claude Bernard, the compound glycogen. He is better remembered however for his work on plankton.

He introduced the term plankton in 1887 to describe the minute drifting animals and plants in the oceans. Moreover he advanced beyond the descriptive stage and introduced numerical methods into marine biology, notably in constructing the *Hensen net*, a simple loop net designed to filter a square meter of water. This enabled the number of plankton in a known area of water to be counted. Hensen tested his equipment in the North Sea and the Baltic in 1885.

Satisfied with his techniques he made a more ambitious trip in 1889 covering more than 15 000 miles of the Atlantic. One of his more surprising results was the greater concentration of plankton in temperate than in tropical waters.

HERACLEIDES of Pontus (b. *c.* 390 BC; Heraclea, now in Turkey; d. *c.* 322 BC; Athens) Greek astronomer.

Heracleides was an associate and possibly a pupil of Plato. Although none of his writings have survived, two views that were unusual for the time have been attributed to him. The philosopher Simplicius of Cilicia, a usually reliable source, reports that "Heracleides supposed that the Earth is in the center and rotates while the heaven is at rest." If this is accurate he must have been the first to state that the Earth rotates, a view that found as little support in antiquity as it did in the medieval period. The second doctrine attributed to him is that Mercury and Venus move around the Sun, which moves around the Earth — a view adopted later by Tycho Brahe in the 16th century.

HERACLITUS of Ephesus (*fl.* 500 BC) Greek natural philosopher.

Virtually nothing is known of the life of Heraclitus, and of his book *On Nature* only a few rather obscure fragments survive. His doctrines contrast with those of his near contemporary Parmenides for whom, on purely logical grounds, change of any kind was totally impossible. For Heraclitus, everything is continually in a state of change, hence his characteristic aphorism: "We cannot step twice into the same river," and his selection of fire as the fundamental form of matter. The mechanism behind such unremitting change was the constant tension or 'strife' between contraries or opposites.

HERELLE, Felix d' *See* D'HERELLE, Felix.

HERMITE, Charles (b. Dec. 24, 1822; Dieuze, France; d. Jan. 14, 1901; Paris) French mathematician.

Hermite's mathematical career was almost thwarted in his student days, since he was incapable of passing exams. Fortunately his talent had already been recognized and his examiners eventually let him scrape through. Hermite obtained a post at the Sorbonne where he was an influential teacher.

Hermite began his mathematical career with pioneering work on the theory of Abelian and transcendental functions, and he later used the theory of elliptic functions to give a solution of the general equation of the fifth degree — the quintic. One long-standing problem solved was proving that the number '*e*' is transcendental (i.e. not a solution of a polynomial equation). He also introduced the techniques of analysis into number theory. His most famous work is in algebra, in the theory of *Hermite polynomials*. Although Hermite himself had little interest in applied mathematics this work turned out to be of great use in quantum mechanics.

HERO of Alexandria (*fl.* AD 62) Greek mathematician and inventor.

Hero produced several written works on geometry, giving formulae for the areas and volumes of polygons and conics. His formula for the area of a triangle was contained in *Metrica*, a work that was lost until 1896. This book also describes a method for finding the square root of a number, a method now used in computers, but known to the Babylonians in 2000 BC. In another of Hero's books, *Pneumatica*, he wrote on siphons, a coin-operated machine, and the aeolipile — a prototype steam-powered engine that he had built. The engine consisted of a globe with two nozzles positioned so that steam jets from the inside made it turn on its axis. Hero also wrote on land-surveying and he designed war engines based on the ideas of Ctesibius. Yet another of his works, *Mechanica*, was quoted by Pappus of Alexandria.

HEROPHILUS of Chalcedon (*fl.* 300 BC) Greek anatomist and physician.

Herophilus, a pupil of Praxagoras of Cos, was one of the founders of the Alexandrian medical school set up at the end of the 4th century BC under the patronage of Ptolemy I Soter. Although none of his works have survived, Galen lists some eight titles of which the *Anatomica* was probably the most significant.

Herophilus is widely, even notoriously, remembered as the result of a famous passage in Celsus reporting that, with Erasistratus, he practiced vivisection on criminals. The passage has been regarded as suspect by many scholars on the grounds that no such reference occurs in any extant, earlier Greek text. It is however certain that from the results attributed to him he must have undertaken both human and animal dissection. For example, he described a passage from the stomach to the intestines as being '12 finger widths' (*dodekadaktylon*) or in its Latin form, the duodenum; he also named the retina and the prostate and did much work on the brain.

It has been claimed that Herophilus was the first to distinguish between sensory and motor nerves. Nerves, or neura, for Herophilus were simply channels that carried the pneuma or vital air to different parts of the body. Thus while he probably identified sensory nerves it is unlikely that he was able to distinguish between motor nerves and tendons.

Herophilus was reported to have advanced Praxagoras's work on the pulse by counting its frequency against a water clock. Also, according to Galen, he made the important observation that the arteries carried blood as well as pneuma.

HEROULT, Paul Louis Toussaint (b. Apr. 10, 1863, Thury-Harcourt, France; d. May 9, 1914; Antibes, France) French chemist.

Héroult was a student at the St. Barge Institute in Paris and later worked at the Paris School of Mines. In 1886 he discovered a process for extracting aluminum by electrolysis of molten aluminum oxide, with cryolite (sodium aluminum fluoride) added to lower the melting point. Charles Hall (q.v.) developed a similar process independently in America at about the same time.

HERRING, William Conyers (b. Nov. 15, 1914; Scotia, New York) American physicist.

Herring was educated at the University of Kansas where he obtained an AB in astronomy in 1933. He did research in mathematical physics at Princeton and obtained his PhD at Princeton in 1937. During World War II he worked on underwater warfare and then joined the Bell Telephone Laboratories in 1946. Herring remained with Bell as a research physicist until 1978 when he was appointed professor of applied physics at Stanford University, California.

Herring has worked on a wide range of theoretical problems in solid-state physics, including electrical conduction, surface tension of solids, anisotropic effects in superconducting materials, and the magnetic properties of solids.

HERSCHEL, Caroline Lucretia (b. Mar. 16, 1750; Hannover, now in West Germany; d. Jan. 9, 1848; Hannover) German-British astronomer.

Caroline Herschel was the sister and colleague of William Herschel, and she joined her brother as his housekeeper in Bath in 1772. She rapidly graduated from this to being his assistant and then to original astronomical research of her own. In 1786 she observed her first comet and before 1797 had detected seven more. She also discovered many new nebulae. Her devotion to her brother and his work must have been completely unconditional judging by the many hundreds of nights spent observing. There is a story that she once slipped and fell on a hook attached to the telescope but made no cry lest she disturb her brother's observations. After his death in 1822 she returned to Hannover where she prepared a catalog of about 2500 nebulae and star clusters. Although it was never published she received the Gold Medal of the Royal Astronomical Society in 1828 for it.

HERSCHEL, Sir John Frederick William (b. Mar. 7, 1792; Slough, England; d. May 11, 1871; Hawkhurst, England) British astronomer.

John Herschel read mathematics at Cambridge University and then began to study law. Although he was the son of the astronomer William Herschel he did not take up astronomy seriously until 1816 when he began, somewhat reluctantly, to assist his father with his observations.

John Herschel went to South Africa in 1834 to make a comprehensive survey of the skies of the southern hemisphere, and succeeded Thomas Henderson as director of the Cape of Good Hope Observatory, doing for the southern skies what his father had done for the northern. He discovered and described some 2000 nebulae and some 2000 double stars, publishing the results of his surveys in 1847. He seems to have given up astronomical observation on his return

from South Africa in 1838, instead becoming interested in photography (introducing the terms 'positive' and 'negative') and pioneering the use of photographic techniques in astronomy. He also experimented on the spectral lines discovered by Joseph von Fraunhofer because he began to see a connection between the absorption and emission lines. He was also a major figure in the regeneration and reorganization of British science in the first half of the 19th century. He was one of the founder members of the Royal Astronomical Society in 1830, and took on many public duties, becoming, like Newton, master of the mint from 1850 to 1855. This, however, proved too taxing for him and he suffered a nervous breakdown, which led to his retirement from public life. His study of scientific method *Discourse on the Study of Natural Philosophy* (1830) influenced the philosopher John Stuart Mill and Charles Darwin.

HERSCHEL, Sir (Frederick) William (b. Nov. 15, 1738; Hannover, now in West Germany; d. Aug. 25, 1822; Slough, England) German-British astronomer.

Herschel started life in the same occupation as his father — an oboist with the band of the Hannoverian footguards. He moved permanently to England in 1757, where he worked as a freelance itinerant musician until in 1767 he was appointed as organist of a church in Bath. His sister Caroline Herschel joined him in Bath in 1772. He was led by his interest in musical theory to a study of mathematics and ultimately astronomy. Herschel made his own telescopes and his early observations were significant enough to be drawn to the attention of George III in 1782. The king, who had a passionate interest in astronomy and clockwork, was sufficiently impressed with Herschel to employ him as his private astronomer at an initial salary of £200 a year and to finance the construction of very large telescopes. At first Herschel settled at Datchet, near

Windsor, but in 1786 he moved to Slough where he remained for the rest of his life.

Herschel's contributions, to astronomy were enormous. He was fortunate to live at a time when prolonged viewing with a large reflector could not but be fruitful and he took full advantage of his fortune. He made his early reputation by his discovery in 1781 of the first new planet since ancient times. He wished to name it after his patron as 'Georgium Sidus' (George's Star) but Johann Bode's suggestion of 'Uranus' was adopted. Herschel's work is notable for the unbelievable comprehensiveness with which he extended the observations of others. Thus he extended Charles Messier's catalog of just over 100 nebulae by a series of publications listing over 2000 nebulae. He not only began the study of double stars but cataloged 800 of them. He also discovered two satellites of Uranus — Titania and Oberon (1787) — and two of Saturn; Mimas and Enceladus (1789–90). He built a large number of telescopes of various sizes culminating in his enormous 40-foot (12-m) reflector. This cost George III £4000 plus £200 a year for its upkeep. The eyepiece was attached to the open end, thus eliminating the loss of light caused by the secondary mirror used in the Newtonian and Gregorian reflectors. The disadvantage was the danger of climbing up to the open end of the 40-foot instrument in the dark. One eminent astronomer, Giuseppe Piazzi, failing to master this skill, fell and broke his arm. It was finally dismantled in 1839 while William's son John conducted his family in a special requiem he had composed for the occasion.

Herschel produced not only observational work but theoretical contributions on the structure of the universe. He established the motion of the Sun in the direction of Hercules and tried to calculate its speed (1806). But, above all, he was the first to begin to see the structure of our Galaxy. Conducting a large number of star counts he established that stars are much more numerous in the Milky Way and the plane of the celestial equator, becoming progressively fewer towards the celestial poles. He explained this by supposing that the Galaxy is shaped like a grindstone. If we look through its short axis we see few stars and much dark space; through its long axis we see a stellar multitude. Herschel was supported in his astronomical life by his sister Caroline. His son John also became an astronomer of note.

HERSHEY, Alfred Day (b. Dec. 4, 1908; Owosso, Michigan) American biologist.

Hershey graduated from Michigan State College in 1930, and remained there to do his PhD thesis on the chemistry of *Brucella* bacteria, receiving his doctorate in 1934. He then taught at Washington University, St. Louis, until 1950, when he moved to the Genetics Research Unit of the Carnegie Institute, Washington.

Hershey is best known for the experiment, conducted in collaboration with Martha Chase in 1952, proving that DNA is the genetic material of bacteriophage (the viruses that infect bacteria). By using radioactive tracer techniques Hershey demonstrated that only the DNA enters the bacterial cell, the protein coat of the virus remaining attached to the outside of the cell wall. Nevertheless the viral DNA is capable of organizing the production of new phage particles complete with protein coat.

In 1945 Hershey and Salvador Luria independently showed that spontaneous mutations occur in bacteriophages, and the following year Hershey and Max Delbrück — again working separately — demonstrated genetic recombination between phages in the same cell.

For his fundamental contributions to molecular biology, Hershey received the 1958 Albert Lasker Award and the 1965 Kimber Genetics Award. However it was not until 1969 that Hershey, together with Delbrück and Luria, was awarded the Nobel Prize for physiology or medicine.

HERTZ, Gustav (b. July 22, 1887; Hamburg, now in West Germany; d. Oct. 30, 1975; East Germany) German physicist.

Hertz, a nephew of the distinguished physicist Heinrich Hertz, was educated at the universities of Munich and Berlin. He taught in Berlin and Halle before his appointment in 1928 to the professorship of experimental physics at the Technical University, Berlin. Hertz, as a Jew, was dismissed from his post in 1935. He worked for the Siemens company from 1935 until 1945, somehow managing to survive the war, when he was captured by the Russians. He reemerged in 1955 to become director of the Physics Institute in Leipzig, East Germany.

In 1925 Hertz was awarded the Nobel Physics Prize for his work with James Franck (q.v.) on the quantized nature of energy transfer.

HERTZ, Heinrich Rudolf (b. Feb. 22, 1857; Hamburg, now in West Germany; d. Jan. 1, 1894; Bonn) German physicist.

Hertz came from a prosperous and cultured family. In 1875 he went to Frankfurt to gain practical experience in engineering and after a year of military service (1876–77) spent a year at the University of Munich. He had decided on an academic and scientific career rather than one in engineering, and in 1878 chose to continue his studies at the University of Berlin under Hermann von Helmholtz. Hertz obtained his PhD in 1880 and continued as Helmholtz's assistant for a further three years. He then went to work at the University of Kiel. In 1885 he was appointed professor of physics at Karlsruhe Technical College and in 1889 became professor of physics at the University of Bonn. His tragic early death from blood poisoning occurred after several years of poor health and cut short a brilliant career.

Hertz's early work at Berlin was diverse but included several pieces of research into electrical phenomena and equipment. With no laboratory facilities at Kiel he had considered more theoretical aspects of physics and had become more interested in the recent work of James Clerk Maxwell on electromagnetic theory. Helmholtz had suggested an experimental investigation of the theory to Hertz in 1879 but it was not until 1885 in Karlsruhe that Hertz found the equipment needed for what became his most famous experiments. In 1888 he succeeded in producing electromagnetic waves using an electric circuit; the circuit contained a metal rod that had a small gap at its midpoint, and when sparks crossed this gap violent oscillations of high frequency were set up in the rod. Hertz proved that these waves were transmitted through air by detecting them with another similar circuit some distance away. He also showed that like light waves they were reflected and refracted and, most important, that they traveled at the same speed as light but had a much longer wavelength. These waves, originally called *Hertzian waves* but now known as radio waves, conclusively confirmed Maxwell's prediction on the existence of electromagnetic waves, both in the form of light and radio waves.

Once at Bonn Hertz continued his analysis of Maxwell's theory, publishing two papers in 1890. His experimental and theoretical work put the field of electrodynamics on a much firmer footing. It should also be noted that in 1887 he inadvertently discovered the photoelectric effect whereby ultraviolet radiation releases electrons from the surface of a metal. Although realizing its significance he left others to investigate it.

Hertz's results produced enormous activity among scientists but he died before seeing Guglielmo Marconi make his discovery of radio waves a practical means of communication. In his honor the unit of frequency is now called the hertz.

HERTZSPRUNG, Ejnar (b. Oct. 8, 1873; Frederiksberg, Denmark; d. Oct. 21, 1967; Roskilde, Denmark) Danish astronomer.

Hertzsprung was the son of a senior civil servant who had a deep interest in mathematics and astronomy but who was anxious to see that his son received a more practical education. Consequently Hertzsprung was trained as a chemical engineer at the Copenhagen Polytechnic, graduating in 1898. He worked as a chemist in St. Petersburg and then studied photochemistry under Wilhelm Ostwald in Leipzig before returning to Denmark in 1902. His first professional appointment as an astronomer was in 1909 at the Potsdam Observatory. The bulk of his career, from 1919 to 1944, was spent at the University of Leiden where from 1935 he served as director of the observatory. After his retirement in 1944 he returned to Denmark where he continued his studies for a further 20 years.

Hertzsprung's name is linked with that of Henry Russell as independent innovators of the Hertzsprung–Russell (H–R) diagram. In the late 19th and early 20th centuries, techniques used in photographic spectroscopy were being greatly improved. With his background in photochemistry, Hertzsprung was able to devise methods by which he could determine the intrinsic brightness, i.e. luminosity, of stars. He showed that the luminosity of most of the stars he studied decreased as their color changed from white through yellow to red, i.e. as their temperature decreased. He also found that a few stars were very much brighter than those of the same color. Hertzsprung thus discovered the two main groupings of stars: the highly luminous giant and supergiant stars and the more numerous but fainter dwarf or main-sequence stars. Hertzsprung published his results, although not in diagrammatic form, in 1905 and 1907 in an obscure photographic journal. His work therefore did not become generally known and credit initially went to Russell who published the eponymous diagram in 1913. It would be difficult to exaggerate the importance or usefulness of the H–R diagram, which has been the starting point for discussions of stellar evolution ever since.

Much of Hertzsprung's work concerned open clusters of stars. In 1911 he published the first color-magnitude diagrams of the Pleiades and Hyades clusters, showing how the color of member stars varied with observed brightness. He also measured the proper motions of stars, i.e. their angular motions in a direction perpendicular to the observer's line of sight, and used the results to establish membership of clusters.

One other major achievement of Hertzsprung was the development of a method for the determination of stellar and galactic distances. In the 19th century Friedrich Bessel and Friedrich Georg Struve had been the first to use measurements of annual parallax to calculate stellar distances but this was only accurate up to distances of about a hundred light-years. In 1913, when Hertzsprung announced his results, astronomers had made little progress in measuring distances. The work of Henrietta Leavitt in 1912 had shown that the period of light variation of a group of stars known as Cepheid variables was related to their observed mean brightness. These Cepheids lay in the Magellanic Clouds. Hertzsprung assumed that at the great distance of the Clouds all member stars could be considered to have approximately the same distance. Since observed and intrinsic brightness of a star are directly linked by its distance, the periods of light variation of Cepheids in the Clouds were thus also related to their intrinsic brightness. By extrapolation Cepheids could thus be an invaluable means of measuring the distance of any group of stars containing a Cepheid by observing the period and apparent brightness of the Cepheid.

The work of establishing the period-luminosity relation on a numerical basis was begun by Hertzsprung and continued by Harlow Shapley. Hertzsprung determined the distances of several nearby Cepheids from measurements of their proper motions. Using his results and Leavitt's values for the periods and apparent brightness of Cepheids in the Small Magellanic Cloud (SMC) he was then able to calculate the distance to the SMC. Although somewhat smaller than today's value this was the first measurement of an extragalactic distance.

HERZBERG, Gerhard (b. Dec. 25, 1904; Hamburg, now in West Germany) Canadian spectroscopist.

Herzberg was educated at the universities of Göttingen and Berlin. He taught at the Darmstadt Institute of Technology from 1930 until 1935 when, with the rise to power of the Nazis, he emigrated to Canada where he was research professor of physics at the University of Saskatchewan from 1935 until 1945. He returned to Canada in 1948 after spending three years as professor of spectroscopy at the Yerkes Observatory, Wisconsin. From 1949 until his retirement in 1969 he was director of the division of pure physics for the National Research Council in Ottawa.

Herzberg is noted for his extensive work on the technique and interpretation of the spectra of molecules. He has elucidated the properties of many molecules, ions, and radicals and also contributed to the use of spectroscopy in astronomy (e.g. in detecting hydrogen in space). His work includes the first measurements of the Lamb shifts (important in quantum electrodynamics) in deuterium, helium, and the positive lithium ion.

Herzberg has written a number of books, notably the two classic surveys *Atomic Spectra and Atomic Structure* (1937) and *Molecular Spectra and Molecular Structure* (4 vols. 1939–79). He received the Nobel Prize for chemistry in 1971 for his "contributions to the knowledge of electronic structure and geometry of molecules, particularly free radicals."

HESS, Germain Henri (b. Aug. 7, 1802; Geneva, Switzerland; d. Nov. 30, 1850; St. Petersburg, now Leningrad in the Soviet Union) Swiss-Russian chemist.

Hess was taken to Russia as a child by his parents. He studied medicine at the University of Dorpat (1822–25) and started his career by practicing medicine in Irkutsk. In 1830 he moved to St. Petersburg, becoming professor of chemistry at the Technological Institute of the university. While there he wrote a chemistry textbook in Russian, which became a standard work.

Hess worked on minerals and on sugars, but his main work was on the theory of heat. By carefully measuring the heat given off in various chemical changes, he was able to conclude in 1840 that in any chemical reaction, regardless of how many stages there are, the amount of heat developed in the overall reaction is constant. *Hess's law*, also called the law of constant heat summation, is in fact a special case of the law of conservation of energy.

HESS, Harry Hammond (b. May 24, 1906; New York City; d. Aug. 25, 1969; Woods Hole, Massachusetts) American geologist.

Hess was educated at Yale, graduating in 1927, and Princeton where he gained his PhD in 1932. He worked first as a field geologist in Northern Rhodesia (now Zambia) in the period 1928–29. After a year at Rutgers in 1932 he moved to Princeton in 1934, becoming professor of geology in 1948.

Hess was a key figure in the postwar revolution in the Earth sciences. He was the first to draw up theories using the considerable discoveries on the nature of the ocean floor that were made in the postwar period. Hess himself discovered about 160 flat-topped summits on the ocean bed, which he named guyots for an earlier Princeton geologist, Arnold Guyot. As they failed to produce atolls he dated them to the Precambrian, 600 million years ago, before the appearance of corals. But in 1956 Cretaceous fossils, from only 100 million years ago, were found in Pacific guyots. The whole of the ocean floor was discovered to be surprisingly young, dating only as far back as the Mesozoic, while the continental rocks were much older.

In 1962 Hess published his important paper, *History of Ocean Basins*. The ocean floors were young, he argued, as they were constantly being renewed by magma flowing from the mantle up through the oceanic rifts, discovered by William Morris Ewing, and spreading out laterally. This became known as the sea-floor spreading hypothesis and was a development of the

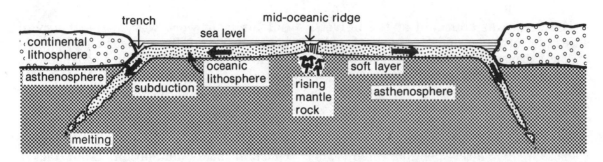

SEA-FLOOR SPREADING Magma rises from the Earth's mantle to the surface along the mid-oceanic ridge and cools to form the new oceanic crust. H. H. Hess estimated the oceanic crust to be spreading apart along the mid-oceanic ridge at the rate of about 1 to 2 inches (2.5–5cm) a year.

convection-currents theory proposed by Arthur Holmes (q.v.) in 1929. The hypothesis has been modified since its proposal, notably through the work of Drummond Hoyle Matthews and Frederick Vine on magnetic anomalies, but remains largely accepted.

HESS, Victor Francis (b. June 24, 1883; Waldstein, Austria; d. Dec. 17, 1964; Mount Vernon, New York) Austrian–American physicist.

Hess, the son of a forester, was educated at the University of Graz where he obtained his doctorate in 1906. He worked at the Institute for Radium Research, Vienna, from 1910 to 1920 and then took up an appointment at the University of Graz where he became professor in 1925. In 1931 he set up a cosmic-ray observatory near Innsbruck but in 1938 he was dismissed from all his official positions as he was a Roman Catholic. Leaving Nazi Austria, he emigrated to America where he served as professor of physics at Fordham University, New York, from 1938 to 1956.

In 1911–12 Hess made the fundamental discovery of cosmic rays, as they were later called by Robert Millikan in 1925. For this work he shared the Nobel Physics Prize with Carl Andersen in 1936. The work stemmed from an attempt to explain why gases are always slightly ionized; thus, a gold-leaf electroscope, however well

insulated it might be, will discharge itself over a period of time. Radiation was clearly coming from somewhere and the most likely source was the Earth itself. To test this, attempts were made to see if the rate of discharge decreased with altitude. But both T. Wulf, who took an electroscope to the top of the Eiffel Tower in 1910, and A. Gockel, who took one up in a balloon in 1912, failed to obtain any clear results.

However when Hess ascended in a balloon to a height of 16 000 feet (4880 m) he found that although the electroscope's rate of discharge decreased initially up to about 2000 feet (610 m), thereafter it increased considerably, being four times faster at 16 000 feet than at sea level. He concluded that his results were best explained by the assumption that a radiation of very great penetrating power enters our atmosphere from above.

He was able to eliminate the Sun as the sole cause for he found that the effect was produced both by day and at night. Further, in 1912, he made a balloon ascent during a total eclipse of the Sun and found that during the period when the Sun was completely obscured there was no significant effect on the rate of discharge. Hess however failed to convince everyone that cosmic rays came from outside the Earth's atmosphere as it could still be argued that the source of the radiation was such atmospheric disturbances as thunderstorms. It was left to Millikan in 1925 finally to refute this objection.

HESS, Walter Rudolf (b. Mar. 17, 1881; Frauenfeld, Switzerland; d. Aug. 16, 1973; Locarno, Switzerland) Swiss neurophysiologist.

Hess, the son of a physics teacher, was educated at the universities of Lausanne, Bern, Berlin, Kiel, and Zurich where he obtained his MD in 1906. Although he actually began as an ophthalmologist, building up a prosperous practice, he decided in 1912 to abandon it for a career in physiology. After junior posts in Zurich and Bonn he was appointed in 1917 to the directorship of the physiology department at the University of Zurich, where he remained until his retirement in 1951.

In the early 1920s Hess began an important investigation of the interbrain and hypothalamus. To do this he inserted fine electrodes into the brains of cats, and used these to stimulate specific groups of cells. His most startling discovery was that when electrodes in the posterior interbrain were switched on this would instantaneously turn a friendly cat into an aggressive spitting creature — a transformation instantly reversed by a further press of the switch. Other areas found by Hess would induce flight, sleep, or defecation.

Less dramatic perhaps but no less significant were the two main areas identified by Hess in the hypothalamus. Stimulation of the posterior region prepared the animal for action but stimulation of the anterior region tended to cause relaxation. Hess had discovered the control center for the sympathetic and parasympathetic nervous systems.

Hess's work was enormously influential and led to a detailed mapping of the interbrain and hypothalamus by many different workers in various centers over a number of years. For his discovery of "the functional organization of the interbrain" Hess was awarded the 1949 Nobel Prize for physiology or medicine, sharing it with Antonio Egas Moniz.

HEVELIUS, Johannes (b. Jan. 28, 1611; Danzig, now Gdansk in Poland; d. Jan. 28, 1687; Danzig) German astronomer.

Hevelius was the son of a prosperous brewer. He followed his father in the family business as well as devoting himself to civic duties. After studying in Leiden, he established his own observatory on the rooftops of several houses overlooking the Vistula, an observatory which soon gained him an international reputation.

He published several major works of observational astronomy. Four years' telescopic study of the Moon, using telescopes of long focal power, led to his *Selenographia* (1647; Pictures of the Moon). Making his own engravings of the Moon's surface he assigned names to the lunar mountains, craters, and plains taken from the Earth, placing with what the writer Sir Thomas Browne called 'witty congruity', "...the Mediterranean Sea, Mauritania, Sicily, and Asia Minor in the Moon." This system of naming, apart from the Alps, did not survive long, Giovanni Riccioli's alternative system of scientific eponomy being preferred. His star catalog *Prodromus astronomiae* (Guide to Astronomy) was published posthumously in 1690.

Hevelius is today best remembered for his 'aerial' telescopes of enormous focal length and his rejection of telescopic sights for stellar observation and positional measurement. He was widely criticized for the latter eccentricity and in 1679 was paid a famous visit by Edmond Halley who had been instructed by Robert Hooke and John Flamsteed to persuade him of the advantages of the new telescopic sights. Hevelius claimed he could do as well with his quadrant and alidade. Halley tested him thoroughly, finding to his surprise that Hevelius could measure both consistently and accurately. He is therefore the last astronomer to do major observational work without a telescope.

HEVESY, Georg Charles von (b. Aug. 1, 1885; Budapest; d. July 7, 1966; Freiburg-im-Breisgau, now in West Germany) Hungarian–Swedish chemist.

Hevesy came from a family of wealthy industrialists. He was educated in Budapest and at the University of Freiburg where he obtained his doctorate in 1908. He then worked in Zurich, Karlsruhe, Manchester, and Copenhagen, before his appointment to the chair of physical chemistry in 1926 at Freiburg. In 1935 he left Germany for Denmark, fleeing from the Nazis who caught up with him once more in 1942, when he sought refuge in Sweden at the University of Stockholm.

In 1923 Hevesy discovered the new element hafnium in collaboration with Dirk Coster. His most important work, however, began in 1911 in the Manchester laboratory of Ernest Rutherford, where he worked on the separation of 'radium D' from a sample of lead. In fact radium D was a radioactive isotope of lead (lead–210) and could not be separated by chemical means. Hevesy was quick to see the significance of this and began exploring the use of radioactive isotopes as tracers. In 1913, with Friedrich Adolph Pareth, he used radioactive salts of lead and bismuth to determine their solubilities. In 1923 Hevesy made the first application of a radioactive tracer — Pb–212 — to a biological system. The Pb–212 was used to label a lead salt that plants took up in solution. At various time intervals plants were burned and the amount of lead taken up could be determined by simple measurements of the amount of radioactivity present. The drawback of this technique was the high toxicity of lead to most biological systems and it was only with the discovery of artificial radioactivity by Irène and Frédéric Joliot-Curie in 1934 that Hevesy's radioactive tracers developed into one of the most widely used and powerful techniques for the investigation of living and of complex systems. For his work in the development of radioactive tracers Hevesy was awarded the 1943 Nobel Prize for chemistry.

HEWISH, Antony (b. May 11, 1924; Fowey, England) British radio astronomer.

Hewish studied at Cambridge University from where he obtained his BA in 1948 and his PhD in 1952 after wartime work with the Royal Aircraft Establishment, Farnborough. He lectured in physics at Cambridge until in 1969 he was made reader and in 1971 professor of radio astronomy. In 1974 he was awarded the Nobel Prize for physics jointly with Martin Ryle.

One of Hewish's research projects was the study of radio scintillation using the 4.5-acre telescope, which consisted of a regular array of 2048 dipoles operating at a wavelength of 3.7 meters. Radio scintillation is a phenomenon, similar to the twinkling of visible stars, arising from random deflections of radio waves by ionized gas. The three types of scintillation are caused by ionized gas in the interstellar medium, in the interplanetary medium, and in the Earth's atmosphere. All three types were discovered at Cambridge and Hewish was involved in their investigation. In 1967 a research student, Jocelyn Bell, noticed a rapidly fluctuating but unusually regular radio signal that turned out to have a periodicity of 1.337 301 13 seconds. She had discovered the first pulsar.

To determine the nature of the signal, Hewish's first job was to eliminate such man-made sources as satellites, radar echoes, and the like. Measurements indicated that it must be well beyond the solar system. It seemed possible that it had been transmitted by an alien intelligence and the LGM (Little Green Men) hypothesis, as it became known, was seriously considered at Cambridge, but with the rapid discovery of three more pulsars it was soon dropped.

Hewish did however manage to establish some of the main properties of the pulsar from a careful analysis of its radio signal. Apart from its phenomenal regularity, which was later shown to be slowing down very slightly, it was extremely small, no more than a few thousand kilometers, and was situated in our Galaxy.

By the end of February 1968 Hewish was ready to publish. His account received wide publicity in the popular press and stimulated much thought among astronomers as to the possible mechanism. There was also some criticism that he had not published earlier. The proposal made by Thomas Gold and others that pulsars were rapidly rotating neutron stars has since won acceptance.

HEYMANS, Corneille Jean François (b. Mar. 28, 1892; Ghent, Belgium; d. July 18, 1968; Knokke, Belgium) Belgian physiologist and pharmacologist.

Heymans was educated at the University of Ghent, where his father was professor of pharmacology, obtaining his MD in 1920. He began as a pharmacology lecturer there in 1923 and in 1930 succeeded his father, holding the chair until his retirement in 1963.

In 1924 Heymans began a series of important cross-circulation experiments. The relationship between respiration and blood pressure had been known for some time — high arterial pressure (hypertension) inhibited respiration while low pressure (hypotension) stimulated it — but the mechanism of such a response was far from clear. Heymans's basic experiment consisted of separating the head of a dog from its body in such a way that its only remaining contact with the body was the nervous supply to the heart. The body of the dog could be made to respire artificially while its head could be linked up to a blood supply of a second dog. Even in such circumstances, hypotension produced an increase in the rate of respiration while hypertension inhibited it. This suggested to Heymans that the process was due not to direct action of the blood pressure on the respiratory center but to nervous control.

Heymans went on to show the important role played in the regulation of heart rate and blood pressure by the carotid sinus, an enlargement of the carotid artery in the neck. By severing the sinus from its own blood supply while maintaining its nervous connection and linking it up to the blood supply of another animal he was able to show that changes of pressure initiated nervous reflexes that automatically reversed the process. The sinus was in fact a sensitive pressure receptor. He also demonstrated that a nearby glandlike structure, the glomus caroticum, was a chemoreceptor, responding to changes in the oxygen/carbon dioxide ratio in the blood.

For his work on the regulation of respiration Heymans was awarded the 1938 Nobel Prize for physiology or medicine.

HEYROVSKÝ, Jaroslav (b. Dec. 20, 1890; Prague; d. Mar. 27, 1967; Prague) Czech physical chemist.

Heyrovský, the son of an academic lawyer, was educated at Charles University, Prague, and University College, London. He joined the staff of Charles University in 1919 where he served as professor of physics from 1919 until 1954. From 1950 he was also head of the Central Polarographic Institute, which, since 1964, has borne his name.

Heyrovský is best known for his discovery and development of polarography, which he described in 1922. This is one of the most versatile of all analytical techniques. It depends on the fact that in electrolysis the ions are discharged at an electrode and, if the electrode is small, the current may be limited by the rate of movement of ions to the electrode surface. In polarography the cathode is a small drop of mercury (constantly forming and dropping to keep the surface clean). The voltage is increased slowly and the current plotted against voltage. The current increases in steps, each corresponding to a particular type of positive ion in the solution. The height of the steps indicates the concentration of the ion. For his work, Heyrovský was awarded the Nobel Prize for chemistry in 1959.

HIGGINS, William (b. 1763; Colooney, now

in the Republic of Ireland; d. 1825; Dublin)
Irish chemist.

As a young man Higgins worked in London with his uncle, Bryan Higgins, the chemist. He studied at Oxford University from 1786 and on his return to Ireland became, in 1791, chemist to the Apothecaries Company of Ireland. He moved to Dublin in 1795 to become chemist and librarian to the Royal Dublin Society, this post being made into a professorship in 1800. From 1795 to 1822 he was chemist to the Irish Linen Board.

Higgins is remembered for his contributions to the new atomic theory and for his claim to have anticipated John Dalton. His claim is based on his work *A Comparative View of the Phlogistic and Antiphlogistic Theories with Inductions* (1789), which was written as a reply to the work of Richard Kirwan (q.v.).

He introduced a clearer symbolism system than that of Dalton but did not follow up his work on atomism until he published a strong attack on Dalton's work in his eight-volume work *Experiments and Observations on the Atomic Theory and Electrical Phenomena* (1814).

Higgins spent the intervening years between these publications trying to introduce new chemical technology into Ireland. In 1799 he published an *Essay on the Theory and Practice of Bleaching*, a work written specifically for the bleachers themselves.

HILBERT, David (b. Jan. 23, 1862; Königsberg, now Kaliningrad, in the Soviet Union; d. Feb. 14, 1943; Göttingen, now in West Germany) German mathematician.

Hilbert studied at the universities of Königsberg and Heidelberg and also spent brief periods in Paris and Leipzig. He took his PhD in 1885, the next year became *Privatdozent* at Königsberg, and by 1892 had become professor there. In 1895 he moved to Göttingen to take up the chair that he occupied until his official retirement in 1930.

Hilbert's mathematical work was very wide ranging and during his long life there were few fields to which he did not make some contribution and many he completely transformed. His attention was first turned to the newly created theory of invariants and in the period 1885–88 he virtually completed the subject by solving all the central problems. However his work on invariants was very fruitful as he created entirely new methods for tackling problems, in the context of a much wider general theory. The fruit of this work consisted of many new and fundamental theorems in algebra and in particular in the theory of polynomial rings. Much of his work on invariants turned out later to have important application in the new subject of homological algebra.

Hilbert now turned to algebraic number theory where he did what is probably his finest work. Hilbert and Minkowski had been asked to prepare a report surveying the current state of number theory but Minkowski soon dropped out leaving Hilbert to produce not only a masterly account but also a substantial body of original and fundamental new discoveries. The work was presented in the *Zahlbericht* (1897) with an elegance and lucidity of exposition that has rarely been equalled.

Hilbert then moved to another area of mathematics and wrote a classic work, the *Grundlagen der Geometrie* (1899; Foundations of Geometry), giving an account of geometry as it had developed through the 19th century. Here his interest lay chiefly in expounding and illuminating the work of others in a systematic way rather than in making new developments of the subject. He devised an abstract axiomatic system that could admit many different geometries — Euclidean and non-Euclidean — as models and by this means go much further than had previously been done in obtaining consistency and independence proofs for various sets of geometrical axioms. Apart from its importance for pure geometry his work led to the development of a number of new algebraic concepts and was particularly important to Hilbert himself because his experience with the axiomatic method and his interest in consistency proofs shaped his approach to mathematical logic and the foundations of mathematics.

In mathematical logic and the philosophy of mathematics Hilbert is a key figure, being one of the major proponents of the formalist view, which he formulated with much greater precision than had his 19th-century precursors. This philosophical view of mathematics had a formative impact on the development of mathematical logic because of the central role it gave to the formalization of mathematics into axiomatic systems and the study of their properties by metamathematical means. Hilbert aimed at formalizing as much of mathematics as possible and finding consistency proofs for the resulting formal systems. It was soon shown by Kurt Gödel (q.v.) that *Hilbert's program*, as this proposal is called, could not be carried out, at least in its original form, but it is none the less true that Gödel's own revolutionary metamathematical work would have been inconceivable without Hilbert. Hilbert's contribution to mathematical logic was important, especially to the development of proof theory, as further developed by such mathematicians as Gerhard Gentzen.

Hilbert also made notable contributions to analysis, to the calculus of variations and to mathematical physics. His work on operators and on *Hilbert space* (a type of infinite-dimensional space) was of crucial importance to quantum mechanics. His considerable influence on mathematical physics was also exerted through his colleagues at Göttingen who included Minkowski, Hermann Weyl, Erwin Schrödinger, and Werner Heisenberg.

In 1900 Hilbert presented a list of 23 outstanding unsolved mathematical problems to the International Congress of Mathematicians in Paris. A number of these problems still remain unsolved and the mathematics that has been created in solving the others has fully vindicated his deep insight into his subject. Hilbert was an excellent teacher and during his time at Göttingen continued the tradition begun in the 19th century and built the university

into an outstanding center of mathematical research, which it remained until the dispersal of the intellectual community by the Nazis in 1933. Hilbert is generally considered one of the greatest mathematicians of the 20th century and indeed of all time.

HILDEBRAND, Joel Henry (b. Nov. 16, 1881; Camden, New Jersey) American chemist.

Hildebrand was educated at the University of Pennsylvania and at the University of Berlin, where he obtained his PhD in 1906. He returned to Pennsylvania in 1907, but moved to the University of California, Berkeley, in 1913 and served there as professor of chemistry from 1918 until his retirement in 1952.

Hildebrand, the author with R. Powell of a widely read textbook, *Principles of Chemistry* (1964; 7th edition), has been engaged in chemical research for virtually the whole of the century. He has worked on fluorine chemistry, intermolecular forces, and, above all, on the theory of solubility.

Even in his nineties Hildebrand has continued with his researches producing in 1976 a substantial monograph on the subject of viscosity and diffusion. He has, however, conceded that he can no longer ski adding that, "I am probably dying from my feet upward, which is better than starting from the top."

HILDITCH, Thomas Percy (b. Apr. 22, 1886; London; d. Aug. 9, 1965; Birkenhead, England) British chemist.

Hilditch was educated at the University of London where he was awarded a DSc in 1911. After further studies in Jena and Geneva he joined the research laboratories of Joseph Crosfield and Sons Ltd., a soap and chemical manufacturer (1911–25). There he began his studies of fat chemistry for which he is best known. Hilditch published over 300 papers in this field and produced two standard works, *The Chemical Constitution of Natural Fats* (1940) and *Industrial Chemistry of Fats and Waxes* (1927).

In 1926 Hilditch became the first John Campbell Brown Professor of Industrial Chemistry at Liverpool University, where he remained until his retirement in 1951. He established a large research school of fat chemistry at Liverpool, where with his co-workers he established the fatty acid and glyceride composition of a large number of fats and oils — over 1450 such substances were dealt with in the fourth edition of his 1940 work published in 1964.

HILL, Archibald Vivian (b. Sept. 26, 1886; Bristol, England; d. June 3, 1977; Cambridge, England) British physiologist and biochemist.

Hill was professor of physiology at Manchester University (1920–23) and then Jodrell Professor at University College, London, from 1923 to 1925 (and honorary professor from 1926 to 1951). He was Foulerton Research Professor of the Royal Society (1926–51), of which he was also for some years both secretary and foreign secretary. From 1940 until 1946 he was the Independent Conservative member of Parliament for Cambridge University and a member of the War Cabinet Scientific Advisory Committee.

Hill's major research was directed toward accurately recording the minute quantities of heat produced during muscle action. For this he used thermocouples, which recorded the smallest variations in heat generated after the muscle had completed its movement. He was able to show that oxygen was only consumed *after* muscular contraction, and not during it, indicating that molecular oxygen is required only for muscle recovery. In 1922 he shared the Nobel Prize for physiology or medicine (with Otto Meyerhoff) for this work on the physiology of muscular contraction.

HILL, James Peter (b. Feb. 21, 1873; Kennoway, Scotland; d. May 24, 1954; London) British embryologist.

Hill, the son of a farmer, was educated at the University of Edinburgh and the Royal College of Science, London. He taught in Australia at the University of Sydney from 1892 until 1906 when he returned to England as Jodrell Professor of Zoology at University College, London. In 1921 he became professor of embryology and histology, a post he retained until his retirement in 1938.

Beginning during his time in Australia, Hill spent most of his life working on monotreme and marsupial embryology, a virtually unexplored area. Hill totally dominated the field and in his numerous monographs on the subject revealed the evolutionary relationships between the primitive mammals.

HILLIER, James (b. Aug. 22, 1915; Brantford, Ontario) Canadian-American physicist.

Hillier was educated at the University of Toronto, where he gained successively his BA (1937), MA (1938), and PhD in physics (1941). He went to live and work in America in 1940 and became a naturalized citizen in 1945. From 1940 to 1953 he worked for the Radio Corporation of America (RCA) Laboratories as a research physicist, primarily on the development of the electron microscope.

Many efforts were being made around the world to develop a commercial electron microscope that could offer higher resolution than optical microscopes. It had been known since the 1920s that a shaped magnetic field could act as a 'lens' for electrons, and in the 1930s the first electron micrographs had been taken. Hillier and his colleagues at RCA designed and built the first successful high-resolution electron microscope in America in 1940; they had in fact been anticipated by Ernst Ruska and Max Knoll who had produced a similar machine for the Siemens and Halske Company in Germany in 1938. The outbreak of war prevented commercial development and exploitation of the German machine.

Hillier made many instrumental advances to the electron microscope. By 1946, he had achieved resolutions (magnifications) approaching close to the theoretical limits. He also involved himself in the development of techniques for the preparation of viral and bacteriological samples for examination.

Hillier's career at RCA continued with only a short break to his present position of executive vice-president for research engineering. He is now principally concerned with research management, and has served on various American governmental, research, and engineering committees.

HINSHELWOOD, Sir Cyril Norman (b. June 19, 1897; London; d. Oct. 9, 1967; London) British chemist.

Hinshelwood was educated at Oxford University, where he was elected to a fellowship in 1920 and obtained his doctorate in 1924. In 1937 he became Dr. Lee's Professor of Chemistry at Oxford. He retired in 1964 when he moved to Imperial College, London, as a senior research fellow.

Hinshelwood worked mainly in the field of chemical reaction kinetics. He produced a major text on the subject, *The Kinetics of Chemical Change in Gaseous Systems* (1926) and, in 1956, shared the Nobel Prize for chemistry with Nicolay Semenov (q.v.) for his work. He later applied his work to a relatively new field in his book, *The Chemical Kinetics of the Bacterial Cell* (1954).

In some papers published earlier, in 1950, Hinshelwood came very close to the true meaning of DNA, established by James Watson and Francis Crick three years later. He declared that in the synthesis of protein the nucleic acid guides the order in which the various amino acids are laid down. Little attention was paid to Hinshelwood's proposal at the time although Crick later declared it to be the first serious suggestion of how DNA might work.

Hinshelwood was a linguist and classical scholar as well as a scientist; he had the unique distinction of serving as president of both the Royal Society (1955–60) and the Classical Association. He was knighted in 1948.

HIPPARCHUS (b. *c.* 146 BC; Nicaea, now in Turkey; d. *c.* 127 BC) Greek astronomer and geographer.

Hipparchus worked in Rhodes, where he built an observatory, and in Alexandria. None of his works have survived but many of them were recorded by Ptolemy. In 134 BC he observed a new star in the constellation of Scorpio. This led him to construct a catalog of about 850 stars. By comparing the position of the stars of his day with those given 150 years earlier he found that Spica, which was then 6° from the autumn equinox, had previously been 8°. He used this observation to deduce not the movement of Spica but the east to west precession (motion) of the equinoctial point. He calculated the rate of the precession as about 45 seconds of arc a year — a value close to the 50.27 seconds now accepted. He also introduced the practice of dividing the stars into different classes of magnitude based on their apparent brightness. The brightest stars he classed as first magnitude and those just visible to the naked eye he classed as sixth magnitude.

As a theorist Hipparchus worked on the orbits of the Sun and Moon. He established more accurate lengths of both the year and the month and was able to produce more accurate eclipse predictions. One of his lasting achievements was the construction of a table of chords, which virtually began the discipline of trigonometry. The concept of a sine had not yet been developed. Instead, Hipparchus calculated the ratio of the chord to the diameter of its own circle, which was divided into 120 parts. Thus if a chord produced by an angle of 60° is half the length of the radius, it would have, for Hipparchus, 60 parts. He much improved the geography of Eratosthenes, fixing the parallels astronomically.

HIPPOCRATES of Cos (b. *c.* 460 BC; Cos, Greece; d. *c.* 370; near Larisa, Greece) Greek physician.

Very little is known of the life of Hippocrates. The main source, Soranus, dates from the second century AD and was clearly telling a traditional tale rather than writing a biography. Hippocrates is reported to have studied under his father Heraclides, also a physician, and with the atomist Democritus, and the sophist Gorgias. He then seems to have spent most of his life traveling around the Greek world curing the great of obscure diseases and ridding grateful cities of plagues and pestilence.

After the fantasy of his life there is the reality of the *Corpus hippocraticum* (The Hippocratic Collection). This consists of some 70 works though whether any were actually written by Hippocrates himself will probably always remain a matter of speculation. What is clear, on stylistic and paleographic grounds, is that the corpus was produced by many hands in the second half of the fifth century and the first part of the fourth. Nor do the works represent a single 'Hippocratic' point of view but, it has been suggested, probably formed the library of a physician and acquired the name of its first owner or collector.

Of more importance is the character of these remarkable works. They are surprisingly free of any attempt to explain disease in theological, astrological, diabolic, or any other spiritual terms. Diseases in the corpus are natural events, which arise in a normal manner from the food one has eaten or some such factor as the weather. The cause of the disease is for the Hippocratic basically a malfunction of the veins leading to the brain which, though no doubt false, is the same kind of rational, material, and verifiable claim that could be found in any late 20th-century neurological textbook.

Such rationality was not to rule for many years for in the fourth century new cults entered Greece and with them the dream, the charm, and other such superstitions entered medicine. More successful in the length of its survival was the actual theory of disease contained in the corpus. This was the view, first formulated by Alcmaeon in the fifth century BC, that health consists of an *isonomia* or equal rule of the bodily elements rather than a *monarchia* or domination by a single element. By the time of Hippocrates it was accepted that there were just four elements, earth, air, fire, and water with their corresponding qualities, coldness, dryness, heat, and wetness. If present in the human body in the right amounts in the right places health resulted, but if equilibrium was destroyed then so too was health.

A new terminology developed to describe such pathological conditions, a terminology still apparent in most western languages. Thus an excess of earth, the cold/dry element, produced an excess of black bile, or in Greek melancholic, in the body; too much water, the cold/moist element, made one phlegmatic.

One striking contrast between Hippocratic and later medicine is the curious yet impressive reluctance of the former to attempt cures for various disorders: the emphasis is rather on prognosis. For example, the *Epidemics* describes the course, but not treatment, of various complaints. At least knowing the expected course and outcome of an illness helped the practitioner to inform his patient what to expect, information that could be useful and reassuring. Further, if it is known which conditions lead to a disease such conditions could sometimes be avoided.

The works *Regimen in Acute Diseases* and *Regimen in Health*, which deal specifically with therapy, tend to restrict themselves to diet, exercise, bathing, and emetics. Thus the Hippocratic doctor may not have actually cured many of his patients but he was certainly less likely than his 18th-century counterpart to actually kill them.

HIRSCH, Sir Peter Bernhard (b. Jan. 16, 1925; Berlin) British metallurgist.

Hirsch gained his doctorate from Cambridge University in 1951. Continuing at Cambridge he lectured in physics from 1959 and took a readership in 1964. In 1966 he moved to the University of Oxford to become Isaac Wolfson Professor of Metallurgy. He is currently head of the department of metallurgy and the science of materials at Oxford. His research interests include the development of the Oxford field-emission scanning transmission electron microscope, the weak-beam technique of electron microscopy, and electron microscopy of the chemical behavior of metal oxides. Hirsch is known principally for his pioneering work in applying the electron microscope to the study of imperfections in the crystalline structure of metals, and in relating these defects to mechanical properties. He showed, for instance, that dislocations (faults) play an important part in theories of work-hardening.

HIRST, Sir Edmund Langley (b. July 21, 1898; Preston, England; d. Oct. 29, 1975; Edinburgh) British chemist.

Hirst, the son of a baptist minister, was educated at St. Andrews University where he worked with Norman Haworth (q.v.) and obtained his PhD in 1921. He continued working with Haworth at the universities of Durham and Birmingham, where Hirst served as reader in natural products from 1934 until 1936 when he was appointed professor of organic chemistry at Bristol University. He moved to Manchester in 1944 but held the chair of organic chemistry there only until 1947 when he accepted a similar post at the University of Edinburgh, where he remained until his retirement in 1968.

Hirst worked mainly in the field of carbohydrate chemistry, collaborating with Haworth over a long period in working out the structure and synthesis of various sugars. He succeeded in showing that the ring structure of stable methyl glycosides, for example of xylose, rhamnose, arabinose, and glucose, are actually six-membered and not, as previously assumed, five-membered. That is, they have the pyranose rather than the furanose ring structure.

Hirst is also known for determining the structure of vitamin C and, in collaboration with Haworth, managing to synthesize this compound. This was the first chemical synthesis of a vitamin.

HIS, Wilhelm (b. July 9, 1831; Basel, Switzerland; d. Mar. 1, 1904; Leipzig, now in East Germany) Swiss anatomist and physiologist.

His, a merchant's son, studied at a number of German and Swiss universities before he graduated from the University of Basel in 1854. He served on the staff there as professor of anatomy and physiology from 1857 until 1872 when he moved to a comparable post at the University of Leipzig, which he retained until his death.

His did much to redirect embryological research onto a more fruitful track by arguing powerfully against the so-called biogenetic law as formulated by Ernst Haeckel. His detailed how, starting from the assumption that the embryonic layers are basically elastic sheets, the principal organs could be constructed by such straightforward processes as cutting, bending, pinching, and folding. He was the first to describe accurately the development of the human embryo. His also worked on the development of the nervous system and was able to show that nerve fibers grow from specialized kinds of cell he termed 'neuroblasts'.

He had earlier, in 1866, introduced into science that invaluable instrument the microtome. This permitted the cutting of extremely thin slices, a few microns thick, for staining and microscopic examination.

One discovery frequently attributed to His, namely the bundles of His — a specialized bundle of fibers connecting the cardiac auricles and ventricles — are nothing to do with him. They were in fact first described by his son, also named

Wilhelm, professor of medicine at the University of Berlin.

HISINGER, Wilhelm (b. Dec. 22, 1766; Skinnatersberg, Sweden; d. June 28, 1852; Skinnatersberg) Swedish mineralogist.

Hisinger was the son of a wealthy iron-works owner. Following his father's death Hisinger ran the family business and also devoted himself to private geological research.

One of his iron mines at Bastnäs produced a mineral with an unexpectedly high density. Hisinger studied this mineral over the years, sending samples to some of the most expert analysts of Europe. Martin Klaproth who examined it in 1803 became convinced that it contained a new element. Shortly afterwards both Jöns Berzelius and Hisinger isolated a new element from it, which they called cerium, after the new minor planet Ceres, discovered by Giussepe Piazzi in 1801.

Hisinger also made major contributions to the growth of geological knowledge, publishing a geological map of southern and central Sweden (1832) and an account of the fossils of Sweden (1837–41).

HITCHINGS, George Herbert (b. Apr. 18, 1905; Hoquiam, Washington) American pharmacologist.

Hitchings, the son of a naval architect, was educated at the University of Washington and at Harvard where he obtained his PhD in 1933 and where he taught until 1939. He then moved briefly to the Western Reserve University until in 1942 he joined the Wellcome Research Laboratories where he spent the rest of his career, serving as vice president in charge of research from 1966 until his retirement in 1975.

Hitchings has been one of the most productive of modern chemical pharmacologists. He began in 1942 with the study of purines and pyrimidines on the grounds that as important ingredients in cell metabolism their manipulation could lead to the control of important diseases at the cellular level. This insight led to the synthesis in 1951 of the purine analog, 6-mercaptopurine (6MP), which, as it inhibited DNA synthesis and thus cellular proliferation, proved valuable in the treatment of cancer, particularly leukemia.

In 1959 6MP was found to inhibit the ability of rabbits to produce antibodies against foreign proteins. A less toxic form, azathioprine or Imuran, was quickly developed by Hitchings and used in 1960 by the surgeon Roy Calne to control rejection of transplanted kidneys.

One further drug was developed from work on 6MP when it was realized that it was broken down in the body by the enzyme xanthine oxidase, the same enzyme that converts purines into uric acid. As gout is caused by an excess of uric acid Hitchings developed allopurinol, which blocks uric acid production by competing for xanthine oxidase.

Other drugs developed by Hitchings include the malarial prophylactic pyrimethamine or Daraprim, and the antibacterial, trimethoprim.

HITTORF, Johann Wilhelm (b. Mar. 27, 1824; Bonn; d. Nov. 28, 1914; Münster, now in West Germany) German chemist and physicist.

Hittorf became professor of chemistry and physics at the University of Münster in 1852 and later became director of laboratories there (1879–89).

Hittorf carried out fundamental work on electrolytes, publishing, in 1853, his paper *The Migration of Ions during Electrolysis*. He showed that changes in concentration around electrodes during electrolysis could be understood if it was assumed that not all ions move with the same speed. He showed how the relative speeds of ions could be calculated from changes in concentration. He also introduced the ideas of complex ions and transport numbers (sometimes called the Hittorf numbers). The transport number of a given ion in an electrolyte is the fraction of total current carried by that ion.

Hittorf was also one of the first to experiment on cathode rays, noting as early as 1868 that obstacles put in their way would cast shadows.

HITZIG, Eduard (b. Feb. 6, 1838; Berlin; d. Aug. 28, 1907; St. Blasien, now in West Germany) German psychiatrist.

Hitzig, the son of an architect, was educated at the University of Berlin where he obtained his MD in 1862. He was later appointed, in 1875, director of the Berghölzi asylum and professor of psychiatry at the University of Zurich. In 1885 Hitzig moved to similar posts at the University of Halle, posts he retained until his retirement in 1903.

In 1870, in collaboration with Gustav Fritsch, Hitzig published a fundamental paper, *On the Excitability of the Cerebrum*, which provided the first experimental evidence for cerebral localization. Following the important work of Pierre Flourens in 1824 it was widely accepted that, despite the discoveries of Paul Broca and John Neethlings Jackson, the cerebral hemispheres constituted a unity, the seat of intelligence, sensation, and volition and not the source of movement.

This was shown to be false when Hitzig and Fritsch electrically stimulated the cerebral cortex of a dog and elicited distinct muscular contractions. They identified five localized centers, which produced various movements on the side of the dog opposite to the side of the brain stimulated. Their work was soon confirmed by David Ferrier and opened up a vast research program, still, a century later, unfinished.

Hitzig himself continued with this work and in 1874 tried to define what soon became known as the motor area of the dog and the monkey. He also tried to identify, though less successfully, the site of intelligence, in the sense of abstract ideas, in the frontal lobes.

HJELM, Peter Jacob (b. Oct. 2, 1746; Sunnerbo, Sweden; d. Oct. 7, 1813; Stockholm) Swedish chemist and metallurgist.

Hjelm studied at the University of Uppsala and became assay master of the Royal Mint in Stockholm in 1782. In the same year he discovered the element molybdenum. At the time, the term 'molybdaena' (a Latin form of a Greek word for 'lead') was used for a number of substances, including the substances now known as graphite and molybdenite. Carl Scheele showed that the mineral molybdenite with nitric acid produced sulfuric acid and an insoluble residue, which he suspected contained a new element. Lacking the appropriate equipment to reduce this, he called on the assistance of Hjelm, who obtained the metallic element molybdenum. This was later obtained in pure form by Jöns Berzelius in 1817.

HOAGLAND, Mahlon Bush (b. Oct. 5, 1921; Boston, Massachusetts) American biochemist.

Hoagland obtained his MD from Harvard in 1948 and then joined the Huntington Laboratories of the Massachusetts General Hospital. He served in the Harvard Medical School from 1960 until 1967 when he became professor of biochemistry at Dartmouth. In 1970 he was appointed scientific director of the Worcester Institute for Experimental Biology.

In early 1955 Francis Crick published his 'adaptor' hypothesis to explain protein synthesis by the cell. Unaware of this work Hoagland in 1956 in collaboration with Paul Zamecnick and Mary Stephenson provided the experimental confirmation. It had earlier been shown by George Palade that protein synthesis occurred outside the nucleus in the ribosomes. Hoagland and Zamecnick discovered that before the amino acids reach the ribosomes to be synthesized into protein they are first activated by forming a bond with the energy-rich adenosine triphosphate (ATP).

What happened in the ribosome was unveiled by forming a cell-free mixture of ATP, the radioactively labeled amino acid leucine, enzymes, and some of the small soluble RNA molecules found in the cytoplasm. At this point they discovered the crucial step, predicted by Crick, in between the activation of the amino acid and its appearance in the protein; the amino acid became tightly bound to the soluble RNA. Shortly afterward the labeled leucine was no longer bound to the RNA but present in the protein.

The discovery of transfer RNA or tRNA as it soon became known was also made independently by Paul Berg and Robert Holley.

HODGE, Sir William Vallance Douglas (b. June 17, 1903; Edinburgh; d. July 7, 1975; Cambridge, England) British mathematician.

Hodge studied at the universities of Edinburgh and Cambridge, then taught at Bristol University (from 1926) and in America at Princeton (1931–32). Most of his career was spent in Cambridge, England, where in 1936 he took up the Lowndean Chair in Mathematics.

Hodge's mathematical work belongs almost entirely to algebraic geometry and although no expert on analysis or physics his work had immense impact in both these fields. Hodge's principal contribution was to the theory of harmonic forms. One of his central results was a uniqueness theorem showing that there is a unique harmonic form with prescribed periods. In general Hodge helped to initiate the shift of focus in mathematics from a search for purely local results to the more ambitious global approach now so influential.

HODGKIN, Alan Lloyd (b. Feb. 5, 1914; Banbury, England) English physiologist.

Hodgkin graduated from Cambridge University, and became a fellow in 1936. He spent World War II working on radar for the Air Ministry. He then worked at the physiological laboratory at Cambridge, where he was appointed Foulerton Research Professor in 1952.

In 1951, with Andrew Huxley and Bernhard Katz, he worked out the sodium theory to explain the difference in action and resting potentials in nerve fibers. Using the single nerve fiber (giant axon) of a squid, they were able to demonstrate that there is an exchange of sodium and potassium ions between the cell and its surroundings during a nervous impulse, which enables the nerve fiber to carry a further impulse. Hodgkin also showed that the nerve fiber's potential for electrical conduction was greater during the actual passage of an impulse than when the fiber is resting. For their work on the 'sodium pump' mechanism and the chemical basis of nerve transmission Hodgkin, Huxley, and John Eccles shared the Nobel Prize for physiology or medicine in 1963. Hodgkin also did work on radar during World War II. He is the author of *Conduction of the Nervous Impulse* (1964).

HODGKIN, Dorothy Crowfoot (b. May 12, 1910; Cairo) British chemist.

Dorothy Crowfoot, as she was born, was educated at Somerville College, Oxford. After a brief period as a postgraduate student at Cambridge University, she returned to Oxford in 1934 and has spent her entire academic career there. She was appointed Wolfson Research Professor of the Royal Society from 1960 until 1977.

Hodgkin had the good fortune to fall under the influence of the inspiring and scientifically imaginative physicist J.D. Bernal at Cambridge. Bernal was keen to use the technique of x-ray diffraction analysis, introduced by Max von Laue in 1912, to investigate important complex organic molecules. He gathered around him a group of enthusiastic scientists to work out the appropriate techniques. Of the Bernal group, Hodgkin was probably the most talented; she also possessed a greater single-mindedness than Bernal himself and, despite the demands of three young children and a busy political life, it was her persistence and talent that produced some of the first great successes of x-ray analysis.

Her first major result came in 1949 when, with Charles Bunn, she published the three-dimensional structure of penicillin. This was followed by the structure of vitamin B_{12} (by 1956) and, in 1969, that of insulin. For her work on vitamin B_{12} she was awarded the Nobel Prize for chemistry in 1964.

HODGKIN, Thomas (b. Aug. 17, 1798; London; d. Apr. 5, 1866; Jaffa, Palestine) British pathologist.

Hodgkin, son of the grammarian John Hodgkin, graduated in medicine from Edinburgh in 1823. After further study abroad and practice in London he was appointed in 1825 as pathologist at Guy's Hospital. He resigned in 1837 to devote himself to his practice and, increasingly, to the affairs of the Aborigines' Protection Society, which he helped to found in 1838.

Hodgkin is widely known for his description of lymphadenoma, first described in his paper *On Some Morbid Appearances of the Absorbent Glands and the Spleen* (1832), and named Hodgkin's disease by Samuel Wilks in 1865. Hodgkin reported six cases, in all of whom he found enlargement of the glands in the neck, armpit, and groin together with, in five of the cases, a diseased spleen. However, later studies by Wilks employing the microscope, which Hodgkin did not use, revealed that some of Hodgkin's cases were actually different conditions.

HOFFMANN, Friedrich (b. Feb. 19, 1660; Halle, now in East Germany; d. Nov. 12, 1742; Halle) German physician.

Hoffmann, the son of a physician, studied medicine at the University of Jena where he qualified in 1681. After a period of travel and further study in Holland and England, Hoffmann returned to Germany where he practiced medicine in Minden and Halberstadt. In 1693 Hoffmann was appointed professor of medicine at the University of Halle where he remained for the rest of his life apart from two periods, 1709–12 and 1734, when he served as physician at the Brandenburg court.

Hoffmann belonged to the period of medical history that had come to reject the humoral theory of disease, being one of the new generation of theorists who tried to reconstruct some alternative scheme out of the mechanical philosophy of René Descartes. He declared that medicine can only be a science in so far as it uses the four mechanical principles of physics — size, shape, motion, and rest. All natural phenomena and effects may be explained by resort to these principles. However after this radical start he slipped back, believing the body consisted of an indeterminate number of elements. Various mixtures of these explained temperament, and imbalance accounted for disease.

It is clear that Hoffmann had simply translated ancient medicine into a modern terminology — there had in fact been no radical break with the past.

HOFFMANN, Roald (b. July 18, 1937; Zloczow, Poland) Polish-American chemist.

Hoffmann emigrated to America in 1949 and became naturalized in 1955. He was educated at Columbia and at Harvard where he remained after obtaining his PhD in 1962. He moved to Cornell in 1965 and was appointed first, in 1968, to a chair of chemistry and then in 1974 to the professorship of physical science.

Hoffmann is widely known to modern chemists for the collaboration with Robert Woodward that led in 1965 to the formulation of the Woodward–Hoffmann rules, fully discussed in their *Conservation of Orbital Symmetry* (1969). Using molecular orbital theory they showed how certain types of chemical reaction could be understood and predicted.

The basic assumption permitting such predictions was that in concerted reactions molecular orbitals of the reactant are continuously converted into molecular orbitals of the product. This imposed certain symmetries on the system and consideration of such symmetries allowed chemists to predict the result of reactions.

HOFMANN, Johann Wilhelm (b. Apr. 8, 1818; Giessen, now in West Germany; d. May 2, 1892; Giessen) German chemist.

Hofmann started as a law student but turned his attention to chemistry, becoming assistant to Justus von Liebig. In 1842 Liebig had visited England, where his impressive chemical knowledge drew attention to the lack of chemical skills and training in the UK. To overcome this problem a group led by Prince Albert opened the Royal College of Chemistry in London in 1845. Inevitably the college had to rely heavily on foreign staff to begin with, and Liebig recommended Hofmann as its director. He remained there until 1865, when he returned to Germany to take the chair at Berlin. His appointment in London was a great success; among his staff and pupils were William Henry Perkin, Edward Frankland, and William Odling.

It is partly owing to Hofmann that Perkin was able to develop the aniline dyes, since he was working under Hofmann's direction when he made his famous discovery of mauveine, the first synthetic dye, in 1856. Hofmann himself developed a series of violet dyes based on magenta. In theoretical chemistry he worked on type theory, trying to show that amines are derivatives of ammonia in which a hydrogen atom is replaced by a compound radical.

HOFMEISTER, Wilhelm Friedrich Benedict (b. May 18, 1824; Leipzig, now in East Germany; d. Jan. 12, 1877; Lindenau, now in East Germany) German botanist.

Hofmeister's father, a music and book publisher, was also a keen amateur botanist and encouraged his son's interest in botany. Wilhelm left school at 15 and served a two-year apprenticeship in a music shop before entering his father's business in 1841. He soon began to study botany seriously in his spare time and was greatly influenced by the views of Matthias Schleiden, who believed that botany could advance rapidly if researchers concentrated on studying cell structure and life histories.

Using procedures recommended by Schleiden, Hofmeister's first work was to disprove Schleiden's theory that the plant embryo develops from the tip of the pollen tube. He believed that a preexisting cell in the embryo sac gave rise to the embryo and his paper *The Genesis of the Embryo in Phanerogams* (1849) gained him an honorary doctorate from Rostock University.

Hofmeister's major discovery, however, was to demonstrate the alternation of generations between sporophyte and gametophyte in the lower plants. The work, published in 1851 as *Vergleichende Untersuchungen* (Comparative Investigations), showed the homologies between the higher seed-bearing plants (phanerogams) and the mosses and ferns (cryptogams) and demonstrated the true position of the gymnosperms between the angiosperms and the cryptogams. In 1863 Hofmeister was appointed professor at Heidelberg University and director of the botanic gardens there, and in 1872 moved to Tübingen University to succeed Hugo von Mohl.

HOFSTADTER, Robert (b. Feb. 5, 1915; New York City) American physicist.

Hofstadter graduated from the College of the City of New York in 1935 and gained his MA and PhD at Princeton University in 1938. From 1939 he held a fellowship at the University of Pennsylvania, and in 1941 returned to the College of the City of New York as an instructor in physics.

From 1943 to 1946 Hofstadter worked at the Norden Laboratory Corporation, and from there took on an assistant professorship in physics at Princeton University. In 1950 he moved to Stanford University as an associate professor and was made full professor in 1954.

His early research was in the fields of infrared spectroscopy, the hydrogen bond, and photoconductivity. One of his first notable achievements, in 1948, was the invention of a scintillation counter using sodium iodide activated with thallium. He is noted for his studies of the atomic nucleus, for which he received the 1961 Nobel Prize for physics (shared with Rudolf Mössbauer).

At Stanford, Hofstadter used the linear accelerator to study the scattering effects of high electrons fired at atomic nuclei. In many ways these experiments were similar in concept to Rutherford's original scattering experiments. He found that the distribution of charge density in the nucleus was constant in the core, and then decreased sharply at a peripheral 'skin'. The radial distribution of charge was found to vary in a mathematical relationship that depended upon the nuclear mass. Further, Hofstadter was able to show that nucleons (protons and neutrons) were not simply point particles, but had definite size and form. Both appeared to be composed of charged mesonic clouds (or shells) with the charges adding together in the proton, but canceling each other out in the neutral neutron. This led him to predict the existence of the rho-meson and omega-meson, which were later detected.

Hofstadter served as director of the high-energy physics laboratory at Stanford from 1967 to 1974.

HOLLEY, Robert William (b. Jan. 28, 1922; Urbana, Illinois) American biochemist.

After graduating in chemistry from Illinois University in 1942, Holley joined the team at Cornell Medical School that achieved the first artificial synthesis of penicillin. He remained at Cornell to receive his PhD in organic chemistry in 1947.

Two years (1955–56) spent at the California Institute of Technology marked the beginning of Holley's important research on the nucleic acids. He decided that to work out the structure of a nucleic acid he first needed a very pure specimen of the molecule. Back again at Cornell, his research team spent three years isolating one gram of alanine transfer RNA (alanine tRNA) from some 90 kilograms of yeast. In March, 1965 he was able to announce that they had worked out the complete sequence of 77 nucleotides in alanine tRNA. For this work Holley received the 1968 Nobel Prize for physiology or medicine, an award he shared with Marshall Nirenberg and Har Gobind Khorana.

HOLMES, Arthur (b. Jan. 14, 1890; Hebburn-on-Tyne, England; d. Sept. 20, 1965; London) English geologist.

Holmes came from a farming background. He graduated from Imperial College, London, in 1910, and went on to work with Lord Rayleigh on radioactivity. After an expedition to Mozambique in 1911 he taught at Imperial College until 1920 when he went to Burma as an oil geologist. In 1925 he returned to England to become professor of geology at Durham University, where he remained until 1943 when he moved to Edinburgh University.

Holmes conducted major work on the use of radioactive techniques to determine the age of rocks, leading to his proposal of the first quantitative geological time scale in 1913 and to his estimate of the age of the Earth being about 1600 million years. He continued to revise this estimate throughout his life, producing a figure in 1959 some three times larger.

Holmes also made a major contribution to the theory of continental drift proposed by Alfred Wegener (q.v.) in 1915. One of the early difficulties the theory faced was that geologists could not envisage a force capable of moving the continents in the way described by Wegener. In 1929 Holmes proposed the existence of convection currents in the Earth's mantle. Rocks in the Earth's interior are, according to Holmes, heated by radioactivity, causing them to rise and spread out and, when cold and dense, to sink back to the interior. It was only after World War II that hard evidence for such a view could be produced.

In 1944 Holmes published his *Principles of Physical Geology*, a major work on the subject. A substantially revised edition of this book was published in 1965, shortly before Holmes's death.

HOLMES, Oliver Wendell (b. Aug. 29, 1809; Cambridge, Massachusetts; d. Oct. 7, 1894; Boston, Massachusetts) American physician.

Holmes, the son of a congregational minister and the father of the identically named jurist and Supreme Court judge, graduated in law from Harvard in 1829 and in medicine in 1836. He was professor of anatomy and physiology at Harvard from 1847 until 1882.

In 1843 Holmes published the classic paper *The Contagiousness of Puerperal Fever* in which he repeated some of the earlier arguments of a number of notable physicians and anticipated some of the work of Ignaz Semmelweis and Joseph Lister. Puerperal (childbed) fever, a streptococcal infection of maternity wards in the early 19th century, had an average mortality of 5–10% occasionally rising to as much as 30% in particularly virulent outbreaks. Holmes stated that puerperal fever is frequently carried from patient to patient by physicians and nurses. He advised that no doctor or nurse who had recently participated in a post-mortem should treat a patient in labor, and he also recommended that they should always wash their hands before examining patients. So little attention was paid to Holmes' paper, however, that he felt it necessary to republish it in 1855.

In addition to being a distinguished man of American letters with numerous volumes of essays, verse, and fiction to his credit, Holmes is also remembered for a letter he wrote William Morton in 1846, proposing that the condition induced by Morton's ether inhalation should be called anesthesia, a term that had been employed in antiquity by Plato and Dioscorides.

HONDA, Kotaro (b. Jan. 24, 1870; Aichi, Japan; d. Feb. 12, 1954; Tokyo) Japanese metallurgist.

Honda was educated at the Imperial University, Tokyo, graduating in 1897. After studying abroad at the universities of Göttingen and Berlin, he returned to Japan to take up an appointment at the Tohoku Imperial University. In 1922 a research institute for iron and steel was attached to the university and Honda became its director. He finally, in 1931, became president of the university.

Honda is noted for his research on magnetic alloys. In 1917 he found that an alloy of 57% iron, 35% cobalt, 2% chrome, 5% tungsten, and 1% carbon was the most highly magnetic material then known. Its use in such instruments as magnetos and dynamos permitted a marked decrease in their size.

HOOKE, Robert (b. July 18, 1635; Freshwater, England; d. Mar. 3, 1703; London) English physicist.

Hooke, whose father was a clergyman, was educated at Oxford University. While at Oxford he acted as assistant to Robert Boyle, constructing the air pump for him. In 1662 Boyle arranged for Hooke to become first curator of experiments to the Royal Society. There he agreed to "furnish the Society every day they meet with three or four considerable experiments." Even though the society only met once a week the pressure on Hooke was still great and may explain why he never fully developed any of his ideas into a comprehensive treatise. He was also something of an invalid.

Hooke made numerous discoveries, perhaps the most well known being his law of elasticity, which states that, within elastic limits, the strain (fractional change in size) of an elastic material is directly proportional to the stress (force per unit area) producing that strain. He was the first to show that thermal expansion is a general property of matter. He also designed a balance spring for use in watches, built the first Gregorian (reflecting) telescope, and invented a number of scientific instruments including the compound microscope and the wheel barometer.

In 1665 he published his main work *Micrographia* (Small Drawings), which was an account — fully and beautifully illustrated — of the investigations he had made with his improved version of the microscope. It also contained theories of color, and of light, which he suggested was wavelike. This led to one of the major controversies — over the nature of light and the priority of theories — that he had with Isaac Newton. The other conflict was over the discovery of universal gravitation and the inverse square law. It is true that Hooke had revealed, in a letter to Newton in 1680, that he had an intuitive understanding of the form the inverse square law must take. Newton's reply to Hooke's charge of plagiarism was to distinguish between Hooke's general intuition that may have been well founded, and his own careful mathematical derivation of the law and detailed working out of its main consequences.

Hooke was also a capable architect, having written on the theory of the arch and designed parts of London after the great fire of 1666.

HOOKER, Sir Joseph Dalton (b. June 30, 1817; Halesworth, England; d. Dec. 10, 1911; Sunningdale, England) British plant taxonomist and explorer.

Hooker studied medicine at Glasgow University, where his father William Hooker was professor of botany. After graduating in 1839, he joined the Antarctic expedition on HMS *Erebus* (1839–43), nominally as assistant surgeon but primarily as naturalist. Between 1844 and 1860, using collections made on the expedition, Hooker produced a six-volume flora of the Antarctic Islands, New Zealand, and Tasmania.

When he returned from the Antarctic expedition Hooker was congratulated on his work by Charles Darwin, who had been following his progress, and in 1844 Darwin confided to Hooker his theory of evolution by natural selection. This communication later proved important in establishing Darwin's precedence when his theory — together with Alfred Russel Wallace's essentially identical conclusions — was presented by Hooker and George Lyell at the famous Linnaean Society meeting of July, 1858.

Following his unsuccessful application in 1845 for the botany chair at Edinburgh University, Hooker was employed to identify fossils for a geological survey, but he took time off between 1847 and 1850 to explore the Indian subcontinent. He visited Sikkim and Assam, Nepal, and Bengal, introducing the brilliant Sikkim rhododendrons into cultivation through the botanical gardens at Kew. Later (1872–97) he produced a seven-volume flora of British India.

In 1855 Hooker was appointed assistant director at Kew Gardens and in 1865 succeeded his father as director. In his 20 years as head of the institute he founded the Jodrell Laboratory and Marianne North Gallery, extended the herbarium, and developed the rock garden. His efforts established Kew as an international center for botanical research and in 1872 he successfully fought a move from the commissioner of works to relegate the gardens to a pleasure park. With George Bentham he produced a world flora, *Genera Plantarum* (1862–83) — a major work describing 7569 genera and 97000 species. The Kew herbarium is still arranged according to this classification.

Hooker retired from the directorship of Kew in 1885 owing to ill health but continued working until his death.

HOOKER, William Jackson (b. July 6, 1785; Norwich, England; d. Aug. 12, 1865; Kew, England) British botanist.

The son of a merchant's clerk, Hooker attended Norwich Grammar School but had little formal education. An interest in botany led to his first voyage, in 1809, to Iceland, which was followed by an extensive study of the English flora. From 1820 until 1842 Hooker held the botany chair at Glasgow. His main interest was in ferns, mosses, and fungi but his works also include some important regional floras and he was a pioneer of economic botany. Hooker's herbarium was accessible to all scholars, and with his publications (more than 20 major books and numerous articles) and journals he became the leading British botanist of his day.

In 1841 Hooker was appointed the first director of Kew Gardens, a position he held until his death. Under his direction Kew became the world's most important botanical institution and here he founded the Museum of Economic Botany in 1847.

HOPE, James (b. Feb. 23, 1801; Stockport, England; d. May 12, 1841; London) British cardiologist.

Hope, the son of a wealthy merchant, studied medicine at Edinburgh University and various London hospitals. He became assistant physician at St. George's Hospital in 1834 and in 1839, shortly before his early death from consumption (tuberculosis), was appointed full physician.

In the 1820s use of René Laennec's stethoscope became widespread in Britain. It still remained to link the sounds heard through the stethoscope and actual events in the heart, a task begun by Hope and reported in his influential *A Treatise on the Diseases of the Heart and Great Vessels* (1831), a work that went through three editions in his short life.

Hope made valuable observations on heart murmurs, valvular disease, and aneurism, and thus began the important work of transforming heart complaints from being merely a set of symptoms into identifiable and specific lesions of the heart.

HOPE, Thomas Charles (b. 1766; Edinburgh; d. June 13, 1844; Edinburgh) British chemist.

Hope's father, John Hope, was a professor of botany at Edinburgh University and founder of the new Edinburgh botanic gardens. Thomas studied medicine at Edinburgh and became professor of chemistry at Glasgow in 1787. He returned to Edinburgh in 1795 as joint professor of chemistry with Joseph Black, succeeding Black on his death in 1799. He remained as chemistry professor until 1843.

In 1787 Hope isolated the new element strontium and named it after the town of Strontian in Scotland where it was discovered. At first it was thought to be barium carbonate and was only established as a new metal in 1791. Martin Klaproth made the same discovery independently but a little later.

Hope was also the first to show the expansion of water on freezing and demonstrated that water attains a maximum density a few degrees above its freezing point (actually 3.98°C). He published his results in his paper *Experiment on the Contraction of Water by Heat* (1805).

HOPKINS, Sir Frederick Gowland (b. June 20, 1861; Eastbourne, England; d. May 16, 1947; Cambridge, England) British biochemist.

Hopkins was the son of a bookseller and publisher and a distant cousin of the poet Gerard Manley Hopkins. After attending the City of London School he was apprenticed as a chemist in a commercial laboratory, where for three years he performed routine analyses. An inheritance in 1881 allowed him to study chemistry at the Royal School of Mines and at University College, London. His work there brought him to the attention of Thomas Stevenson, who offered Hopkins the post of assistant in his laboratory at Guy's Hospital. Feeling the need of more formal qualifications he began to work for a medical degree at Guy's in 1889, finally qualifying in 1894. In 1898 Hopkins moved to Cambridge, where he remained for the rest of his long life and not only served as professor of biochemistry (1914–43) but also established one of the great research institutions of the century.

In 1901 Hopkins made a major contribution to protein chemistry when he discovered a new amino acid, tryptophan. He went on to show its essential role in the diet, since mice fed on the protein zein, lacking tryptophan, died within a fortnight; the same diet with the amino acid added was life-supporting. This work initiated vast research programs in biochemical laboratories.

In 1906–07 Hopkins performed a classic series of experiments by which he became convinced that mice could not survive upon a mixture of basic foodstuffs alone. This ran against the prevailing orthodoxy, which supposed as long as an animal received sufficient calories it would thrive. He began by feeding fat, starch, casein (or milk protein), and essential salts to mice, noting that they eventually ceased to grow. Addition of a small amount of milk, however, was sufficient to restart growth. It took several years of careful experiments before, in 1912, Hopkins was prepared to announce publicly that there was an unknown constituent of normal diets that was not represented in a synthetic diet of protein, pure carbohydrate, fats, and salts. Hopkins had in fact discovered what were soon to be called vitamins, and for this work he shared the 1929 Nobel Prize in physiology or medicine with Christiaan Eijkman.

At the same time Hopkins was working with Walter Fletcher on the chemistry of muscle contraction. In 1907 they provided the first clear proof that muscle contraction and the production of lactic acid are, as had long been suspected, causally connected. This discovery formed the basis for much of the later work done in this field. Hopkins later isolated the tripeptide glutathione, which is important as a hydrogen acceptor in a number of biochemical reactions.

In England Hopkins did more than anyone else to establish biochemistry as it is now practiced. He had to fight on many fronts to establish the discipline, since many claimed that the chemistry of life involved complex substances that defied ordinary chemical analysis. Instead he was able to demonstrate that it was a chemistry of simple substances undergoing complex reactions. Hopkins was knighted in 1925.

HOPPE-SEYLER, (Ernst) Felix Immanuel (b. Dec. 26, 1825; Freiberg, now in East Germany; d. Aug. 10, 1895; Wasserburg, now in West Germany) German biochemist.

Early in his career Hoppe-Seyler was assistant to Rudolf Virchow in Berlin. He became professor of physiological chemistry (biochemistry) at Strasbourg, where he established the first exclusively biochemical laboratory, and later founded the first biochemistry journal. In 1871 Hoppe-Seyler discovered the enzyme invertase, which aids the conversion of sucrose into the simpler sugars glucose and fructose. He was also the first to prepare hemoglobin in crystalline form. He isolated the fatlike compound lecithin, one of the class of compounds called phospholipids. Hoppe-Seyler's classification of the proteins (1875) is still accepted today.

HORROCKS, Jeremiah (b. *c.* 1617; Toxteth near Liverpool, England; d. Jan. 3, 1641; Toxteth) English astronomer and clergyman.

Horrocks studied at Cambridge University from 1632 to 1635 and became curate of Hoole in Lancashire in 1639, studying and practicing astronomy in his spare time. He very quickly saw the importance of Johannes Kepler's ideas, which was by no means common in the early 17th century.

Using Kepler's Rudolphine tables he became the first man both to predict accurately and to observe a transit of Venus across the face of the Sun. He realized the significance of this relatively rare event and set about using it to determine the solar parallax (distance) and diameter. Unfortunately these results, together with his defense of Kepler, were only published in full in 1678, many years after his early death.

HORSFALL, James Gordon (b. Jan. 9, 1905; Mountain Grove, Missouri) American plant pathologist.

Horsfall graduated in soil science from the University of Arkansas and gained his PhD in plant pathology from Cornell in 1929. He remained at Cornell until 1939 when he became chief of the department of plant pathology (1939–48) and director (1948–71) of the Connecticut Agricultural Experimental Station.

A leading plant pathologist, Horsfall coedited, with A. E. Dimond, the three-volume work *Plant Pathology* (1959–60). More recently he has, with Ellis Cowling, coedited *Plant Disease: An Advanced Treatise* (5 vols. 1977–80). He had earlier published extensively on fungicides.

HOUNSFIELD, Godfrey Newbold (b. Aug. 28, 1919; Newark, England) British engineer.

Hounsfield was educated in Nottinghamshire and went on to the City and Guilds College, London, and the Faraday House College of Electrical Engineering in London. He worked for Electrical and Musical Industries (EMI) from 1951 and led the design effort for Britain's first large solid-state computer. Later he worked on problems of pattern recognition. He is now head of the medical research division of EMI. Although he had no formal university education he was granted an honorary doctorate in medicine by the City University, London (1975).

Hounsfield was awarded the 1979 Nobel Prize for medicine, together with the South-African-born physicist Allan Cormack, for his pioneering work on the application of computer techniques to x-ray examination of the human body. Working at the Central Research Laboratories of EMI he developed the first commercially successful machines to use computer-assisted tomography, also known as computerized axial tomography (CAT). In CAT, a high-resolution x-ray picture of an imaginary slice through the body (or head) is built up from information taken from detectors rotating around the patient. These 'scanners' allow delineation of very small changes in tissue density. Introduced in 1973, early machines were used to overcome obstacles in the diagnosis of diseases of the brain, but the technique has now been extended to the whole body. Although Cormack worked on essentially the same problems of CAT the two men did not collaborate, or even meet.

New lines of research being pursued by Hounsfield include the possible use of nuclear magnetic resonance (NMR) as a diagnostic imaging technique.

HOUSSAY, Bernardo Alberto (b. Apr. 10, 1887; Buenos Aires, Argentina; d. Sept. 21, 1971; Buenos Aires) Argentinian physiologist.

Houssay was the founder and director of the Buenos Aires Institute of Biology and Experimental Medicine, and professor of physiology at Buenos Aires from 1910 until 1965, apart from the years 1943–55 when he was relieved of his post by the regime of Juan Perón.

Houssay's work centered upon the role of the pituitary gland in regulating the amount of sugar in the blood, as well as its effects in aggravating or inducing diabetes. Working initially with dogs, he found that diabetic sufferers could have their condition eased by extraction of the pituitary gland, since its hormonal effect is to increase the amount of sugar in the blood and thus counter the influence of insulin.

Deliberate injection of pituitary extracts actually increases the severity of diabetes or may induce it when the condition did not previously exist. He was also able to isolate at least one of the pituitary's hormones that had the reverse effect to insulin. Houssay's work on hormones led to his award, in 1947, of the Nobel Prize for physiology or medicine, which he shared with Carl and Gerty Cori. He was the author of *Human Physiology* (1951).

HOYLE, Sir Fred (b. June 24, 1915; Bingley, England) British astronomer.

Hoyle studied at Cambridge University, graduating in 1938. After the war he lectured in mathematics at Cambridge from 1945 to 1958 when he became Plumian Professor of Astronomy. He also served as director of the Cambridge Institute of Theoretical Astronomy from 1967. Hoyle left his Cambridge base in 1973, in dispute with the authorities on the development of astronomical research in the university. He has held numerous research and visiting posts at such institutions in America as the California Institute of Technology and Cornell University, and in England at Manchester University and the Royal Institution in London. From 1956 to 1958 he was a staff member of the Mount Wilson and Palomar Observatories.

He was one of the first to adopt the steady-state theory of Thomas Gold and Hermann Bondi and did much to introduce it to a wider audience in such works as his Reith lectures, *The Nature of the Universe* (1950). He was also one of the last to support the theory, still arguing for it in the 1970s despite the contrary evidence. He argued that the violations found in the homogeneity in both space and time of the universe were more apparent than real, for they could be simply small-scale effects, whereas the steady-state theory was concerned with uniformities of the order of a billion light-years or more. Eventually however the departures from the original theory became so numerous and extensive that the theory is no longer accepted.

Hoyle's contributions to cosmology and astrophysics have been numerous, deep, and extensive. One of his main achievements was to show how elements heavier than hydrogen and helium could have been produced. George Gamow and Ralph Alpher had shown in 1948 that hydrogen and helium were created in the big-bang in which the universe originated. With W. A. Fowler and Margaret and Geoffrey Burbidge, Hoyle gave in 1957 the first comprehensive account of how the elements are produced in the interior of stars. As a star evolves, the temperature in its core increases and different elements can be synthesized, beginning with helium then carbon and oxygen. The processes involve nuclear fusion reactions and ultimately, in massive and highly evolved stars, neutron capture. The elements formed are ejected into interstellar space by various means, including gigantic supernova explosions, and are eventually incorporated in new stars created from clouds of interstellar matter.

Hoyle has been a prolific writer on a wide variety of subjects. He has produced a number of science fiction novels beginning with *The Black Cloud* (1957), has written on the history of astronomy in his *Copernicus* (1973), on archeo-astronomy in *From Stonehenge to Modern Cosmology* (1972), on the origin of disease in *Lifecloud* (1978) with Chandra Wickramnsinghe, and on questions of social policy in *Commonsense in Nuclear Energy* (1980). Such works are noted for their originality, rigor, and a willingness to speculate and to argue in new and unexpected fields.

He has also written a prodigious number of lectures, papers, textbooks, and monographs of which some of the most significant are his *Frontiers of Astronomy* (1955), *Astronomy and Cosmology* (1975) and, with J. V. Narlikar, various papers on gravity.

HUBBLE, Edwin Powell (b. Nov. 20, 1889; Marshfield, Missouri; d. Sept. 28, 1953; San

Marino, California) American astronomer and cosmologist.

Hubble was the son of a lawyer. He was educated at the University of Chicago where he was influenced by the astronomer George Hale and, as a good athlete, was offered the role of Great White Hope in a match against the world heavyweight champion, Jack Johnson. Instead he went to England, accepting a Rhodes scholarship to Oxford University where, between 1910 and 1913, he studied jurisprudence, represented Oxford in athletics, and fought the French boxer, Georges Carpentier. On his return to America he practiced law briefly before returning in 1914 to the study of astronomy at the Yerkes Observatory of the University of Chicago. He obtained his PhD in 1917. After being wounded in France in World War I he took up an appointment in 1919 at the Mount Wilson Observatory in California where Hale was director and where he spent the rest of his career.

Hubble's early work involved studies of faint nebulae, which in the telescopes of the day appeared as fuzzy extended images. He considered that while some were members of our Galaxy and were clouds of luminous gas and dust, others, known as spiral nebulae, probably lay beyond the Galaxy. After the powerful 100-inch (2.5-m) telescope went into operation at Mount Wilson he produced some of the most dramatic and significant astronomy of the 20th century. In 1923 he succeeded in resolving the outer region of the Andromeda nebula into "dense swarms of images which in no way differ from those of ordinary stars." To his delight he found that several of them were Cepheids, which allowed him to use Harlow Shapley's calibration of the period-luminosity curve to determine their distance as the unexpectedly large 900 000 light-years. Although this conflicted sharply with the results of Adriaan van Maanen, Hubble continued with his observations. Between 1925 and 1929 he published three major papers showing that the spiral nebulae were at enormous distances, well outside our own Galaxy, and were in fact isolated systems of stars, now called spiral galaxies. This was in agreement with the work of Heber Curtis. In 1935 van Maanen reexamined his data and, appreciating their unsatisfactory nature, withdrew the final objection to Hubble's results.

In 1929 Hubble went on to make his most significant discovery and announced what came to be known as *Hubble's law*. Using his own determination of the distance of 18 galaxies and the measurements of radial velocities from galactic red shifts carried out by Vesto Slipher and Milton Humason, he saw that the recessional velocity of the galaxies increased proportionately with their distance from us, i.e. $v = Hd$, where v is the velocity, d the distance, and H is known as *Hubble's constant*. Further measurements made by Hubble in the 1930s seemed to confirm his earlier insight. It was this work that demonstrated to astronomers that the idea of an expanding universe, proposed earlier in the 1920s by Alexander Friedmann and Georges Lemaître, was indeed correct. The expansion of the universe is now fundamental to every cosmological model.

Hubble's law was soon seen as containing the key to the size, age, and future of the universe. Hubble's constant can be found from the mean value of v/d. Hubble himself gave it a value approximately ten times its presently accepted figure. Hubble's constant permits a calculation of the observable size of the universe to be made. The limiting value of recession must be the speed of light (c). If we divide this by H we get a 'knowable' universe with a radius of about 18 billion light-years. Beyond that no signal transmitted could ever reach us, for to do so it would need to exceed the speed of light.

It is also possible to calculate the time that must have elapsed since the original highly compact state of the universe, i.e. the age of the universe. Hubble's own estimate was 2 billion years but with revisions of his constant, cosmologists now, none too precisely, assign a value of between 12 and 20 billion years.

Hubble also made a major contribution

to the study of galactic evolution by producing the first significant classification of galaxies. William Herschel had simply classified them as bright or faint, large or small while his son John Herschel introduced five categories in terms of size, brightness, roundness, condensation, and resolvability, each with five subdivisions. Hubble published his scheme in 1926. It involved dividing galaxies into two classes, elliptical and spiral. Ellipticals could be subdivided on the basis of their degree of ellipticity, ranging from the circular form (E0) to the elongated (E7). Spirals could be either barred or normal spirals which were subdivided in terms of their degree of openness. Although anomalous objects were later discovered that failed to fit it, Hubble's scheme is still used as the basis for galactic classification.

HUBEL, David Hunter (b. Feb. 27, 1926; Windsor, Ontario) Canadian–American neurophysiologist.

Hubel was educated at McGill University and then worked at the Montreal Neurological Institute. He moved to America in 1954 and after working at Johns Hopkins joined the Harvard Medical School in 1959 where he was appointed professor of neurobiology in 1968.

Beginning in the 1960s, Hubel, in collaboration with Torsten Weisel, published a number of remarkable papers that explained for the first time the mechanism of visual perception at the cortical level.

Their work was made possible by a number of technical advances. From the early 1950s onward it became possible to use microelectrodes to monitor the activity of a single neuron. Further, the work of Louis Sokoloff allowed workers to identify precise areas of neural activity. Using this latter technique it was thus possible to identify the region known as the striate cortex, located at the back of the cortex in the occipital lobes, as one of the key centers of activity during the visual process.

The cells of the striate cortex seemed to

be arranged into columns, or 'hypercolumns' as they were soon described, that run the length of the cortex (3–4 mm) from the outer surface to the underlying white matter. Such hypercolumns were further clearly divided into distinct layers. Hubel and Weisel went on to probe the structure, function, and contents of such columns in great detail.

Above all they succeeded in establishing two crucial points. First that the retinal image was mapped in some way on to the striate cortex. That is, to each point on the retina there corresponded a group of cells in the striate cortex that would respond to a stimulation of that point and of no other.

Furthermore, the response could be evoked only by a relatively precise stimulus. Thus there were cells that would respond to a spot of light but not to a line. Cells that responded to lines would do so only to those lines with a specific tilt and if the angle of tilt was changed by as little as 10°, in either direction, the cells' ability to react would be diminished or even abolished.

As a result of such work the visual cortex has become the best known of all cortical regions.

HUGGINS, Charles Brenton (b. Sept. 22, 1901; Halifax, Nova Scotia) Canadian–American surgeon.

Huggins was educated at Acadia University and at the Harvard Medical School, where he obtained his MD in 1924. After graduate training at the University of Michigan he moved to the University of Chicago in 1927 where he has served as professor of surgery since 1936 and director of the May Laboratory of Cancer Research from 1951 until 1969.

In 1939 Huggins made a very simple inference that led to the development of new forms of cancer therapy. Noting that the prostate gland was under the control of androgens (male sex hormones) he concluded that cancer of the prostate might be treated by preventing the production of androgens. Admittedly his proposed treatment of orchiectomy (castration) might appear somewhat severe but it did lead to remissions in some cases and an alleviation of the condition in others.

Huggins soon appreciated however that the same results could probably be achieved by the less drastic procedure of the administration of female sex hormones to neutralize the effect of androgens produced by the testicles. Consequently in 1941 he began to inject his patients with the hormones stilbestrol and hexestrol. He was able to report later that of the first 20 patients so treated 4 were still alive after 12 years. Later workers, inspired by Huggins's work, treated women suffering from cancer of the breast with the male hormone testosterone and claimed improvement in some 20% of the cases.

It was for this work that Huggins shared the 1966 Nobel Prize for physiology or medicine with Peyton Rous.

HUGGINS, Sir William (b. Feb. 7, 1824; London; d. May 12, 1910; London) British astronomer and astrophysicist.

Huggins, the son of a silkmercer, attended school for a short period before being educated privately. After a few years in business he retired to devote himself exclusively to the study of science. His first interest was in microscopy but he became absorbed in the work of Gustav Kirchhoff and Robert Bunsen on spectroscopy and the solar spectrum and decided that he would try to do the same with the stars. He equipped himself with the best of instruments including a superb 8-inch (20-cm) glass from Alvan Clark. He spent some time making maps of the terrestrial elements before moving to the stars, collaborating with William Miller, professor of chemistry at King's College, London. He then began the first major intensive spectral investigation of the stars, which lasted until he was 84 years old, when he found that he could no longer see clearly enough. In later life he was also helped by his wife, Margaret, whom he married in 1875.

Huggins's first observations, published in 1863, showed the stars to be composed of known elements, occurring on the Earth and the Sun. His next great discovery came when he obtained the spectra of those nebula that earlier astronomers had failed to resolve into stars. His excitement is apparent in his report: "I looked into the spectroscope. No spectrum such as I expected! A single bright line only! ... The riddle of the nebula was solved ... Not an aggregation of stars, but a luminous gas." He quickly examined the spectra of over 50 nebulae and found that a third were gaseous. In the same year he obtained the spectra of a comet and found that it possessed hydrocarbons. In 1866 he showed that a nova was rich in hydrogen. He also discovered previously unidentified bright emission lines in the spectra of certain nebulae and attributed them to a new element 'nebulium'. The true explanation for these forbidden lines was not provided until the next century, by Ira Bowen (q.v.).

In 1868 Huggins successfully employed a use of spectroscopy that has had a more profound impact on cosmology than anything else. It had been shown by Christian Doppler and Armand Fizeau that the light waves of an object leaving an observer would have a lower frequency, and the frequency of an object approaching an observer should increase. In spectral terms this means that the spectra of the former object should be shifted toward the red and the latter toward the blue. In 1868 Huggins examined the spectrum of Sirius and found a noticeable red shift. As the degree of the shift is proportional to the velocity, Huggins was able to calculate that the speed of recession of Sirius was about 25 miles (40 km) per second. He quickly determined the velocity of many other stars. He and Lady Huggins published their spectral work in its entirety as the *Atlas of Representative Stellar Spectra* in 1899. Huggins had tried to photograph Sirius but was only successful in 1876 by which time the gelatine dry plate had been developed.

Huggins was knighted in 1897, and was president of the Royal Society from 1900 to 1905.

HUGHES, John Russell (b. Dec. 19, 1928; Du Bois, Pennsylvania) American neurophysiologist.

Hughes was educated at Oxford University and at Harvard, where he obtained his PhD in 1954. After some time at the National Institutes of Health and the State University of New York, Hughes moved to Northwestern University where he has served as professor of neurophysiology since 1964.

Among other problems Hughes has worked on the way in which information is transmitted within the central nervous system. In particular he has made a detailed study of the 'language' used by the olfactory bulb to inform the brain of the nature of the olfactory medium.

His method consisted of implanting electrodes in the olfactory bulb and recording their response to gauze soaked with a certain chemical held at a standard distance away. He found that the message transmitted essentially comprises a mixture of various frequency components.

HUISGEN, Rolf (b. June 13, 1920; Gerolstein, now in West Germany) German chemist.

Huisgen, the son of a surgeon, studied chemistry at the universities of Bonn and Munich where he obtained his PhD in 1943. Initially he taught at Tübingen before moving in 1957 to the University of Munich as professor of chemistry and director of the Institute of Physical Chemistry.

Huisgen has worked on the mechanisms of organic chemical reactions, and particularly on reactions leading to the formation of ring compounds. Many of his studies have been on reactions to which the principle of orbital symmetry, introduced by Robert Burns Woodward and Roald Hoffmann (q.v.), applies.

HULST, Hendrik Christoffell van de See VAN DE HULST, Hendrik Christoffell.

HUMASON, Milton La Salle (b. Aug. 19, 1891; Dodge Center, Minnesota; d. June 18, 1972; California) American astronomer.

Humason had no formal university training. He in fact began as a donkey driver moving supplies to the Mount Wilson Observatory in southern California. He quickly developed an interest in astronomy and its techniques, an interest that was stimulated by the staff of the observatory. He was taken on as janitor and by 1919 he was competent enough to be appointed assistant astronomer on the staff of the Mount Wilson Observatory and, after 1948, of the Palomar Observatory where he spent the rest of his career.

In the 1920s Edwin Hubble formulated his law that the distance of the galaxies was proportional to their recessional velocity. This work was based on the careful, painstaking, and difficult measurements of galactic red shifts made by Humason and also by Vesto Slipher. Humason developed extraordinary skill in this field. By 1936, using long photographic exposures of a day or more, he was able to measure a recessional velocity of 40000 kilometers per second, which took him to the limits of the 100-inch (2.5-m) reflecting telescope at Mount Wilson.

With the opening of the Palomar Observatory he was able to use the 200-inch (5-m) Hale reflector and by the late 1950s was obtaining velocities of over 100000 km per second; this corresponded to a distance, according to Hubble's law, of about six billion light-years.

HUMBOLDT, Baron (Friedrich Wilhelm Heinrich) Alexander von (b. Sept. 14, 1769; Berlin; d. May 6, 1859; Berlin) German explorer and scientist.

Humboldt initially showed little enthusiasm for his studies but while taking an engineering course in Berlin, he suddenly became interested in botany, and a year at the University of Göttingen further increased his interest in the sciences. Geology and mineralogy particularly intrigued him and he went on to join the School of Mines in Freiberg, Saxony, staying there for two years. He then worked for the mining department in Ansbach-Bayreuth, reorganizing and supervising the mines in the region.

In 1796, Humboldt inherited enough money to finance himself as a scientific explorer, and he gave up mining to do two years' intensive preparatory studies in geological measuring methods. Initially his expeditionary plans were thwarted by the Napoleonic Wars but, in 1799, he finally managed to sail with a ship bound for Latin America.

The French botanist, Aimé Bonpland, accompanied him on the five-year journey, during which they navigated the Orinoco River and traveled widely through Peru, Venezuela, Ecuador, and Mexico, collecting scientific specimens and data and covering over 6000 miles. Humboldt studied the Pacific coastal currents, the *Humboldt current* (now the Peru current) being named for him, and he was the first to propose building a canal through Panama. He investigated American volcanoes, noting their tendency to follow geological faults, and concluded that volcanic action had played a major part in the development of the Earth's crust, thus finally disproving the neptunist theory of Abraham Werner. He climbed the Chimborazo volcano to what was then a world record height of 19 280 feet (5876 m), and was the first to attribute mountain sickness to oxygen deficiency. He also measured changes in temperature with altitude and noted its effect on vegetation.

On his return to Europe in 1804, Humboldt settled in Paris and began to publish the data gathered on his travels, a task which took 20 years and filled 30 volumes. He introduced isobars and isotherms on his weather maps, so pioneering the subject of comparative climatology, and also helped initiate ecological studies with his discussions on the relationship between a region's geography and its flora and fauna.

By 1827 Humboldt's finances were severely depleted and he returned to Berlin as tutor to the Prussian crown prince.

Two years later he was invited by the Russian finance minister to visit Siberia, and Humboldt made use of the trip to take more geological and meteorological measurements. He also organized a series of meteorological and magnetic observatories through Russia, Asia, and the British Empire, to trace the fluctuations in the Earth's magnetic field.

Humboldt spent the last years of his life writing *Kosmos*, a synthesis of the knowledge about the universe then known, of which four volumes were published during his life.

HUME, David (b. May 7, 1711; Edinburgh, Scotland; d. Aug. 25, 1776; Edinburgh) British philosopher.

Hume was the younger son of a laird. Educated at Edinburgh university he intended to study law but found himself stricken with an "insurmountable aversion to everything but the pursuit of philosophy and general learning." He became a tutor, served in a variety of diplomatic posts, and spent the period 1752 to 1763 as librarian of the Edinburgh Faculty of Advocates where he wrote his *History of England* (6 vols. 1754–62) After another period of diplomatic service abroad in Paris, he retired to Edinburgh in 1769. In the spring of 1775 Hume contracted cancer. Shortly before his death in the summer of 1776 he was visited By James Boswell, eager to report back to Dr. Johnson that the notorious atheist, Hume, was facing death with apprehension. Instead he found Hume placid and cheerful, denying that death was to be feared and declaring survival to be "an unreasonable fancy." Boswell was most disturbed.

In 1738 Hume published his masterpiece, *A Treatise of Human Nature*, in which his aim was to do for the moral sciences, the science of man, what Newton had done for the natural sciences. In pursuing this aim Hume was lead into a profound study of causality and the idea of a 'necessary connection' between two physical events when one is said to be the cause of the other — work that carried important implications for science. Against Rationalists such as Descartes, Hume argued that empirical knowledge can never be deduced a priori, thus aiding the destruction of the Cartesian tradition in science. Hume put forward the basis of modern Empiricism — that all knowledge of matters of fact (and thus scientific knowledge) is based on experience and evidence and is therefore only probable, capable of denial, and can never be logically necessary. Thus, in his analysis of causation Hume argued that there is no necessary connection between physical events (e.g. when one is said to be the *cause* of the other); there is no mystical 'power' is one event that 'brings about' another. We merely observe that one type of event is invariably followed by another, and because of this association of ideas in our minds, when we observe an event of the first type we 'predict' an event of the second.

But such a practice will only be sound if the conjunctions we have observed in the past continue to hold in the future. How can, asked Hume, this latter assumption be justified? Not by pure reason, nor from experience, for we cannot conclude from the fact that nature has behaved uniformly in the past that it will continue to do so without assuming the truth of the very principle we are examining. In this way Hume presented the classical 'problem of induction' that has since been puzzled over by generations of philosophers and scientists.

HUNSAKER, Jerome Clarke (b. Aug. 26, 1886; Cheston, Iowa) American aeronautical engineer.

Hunsaker was educated at the US Naval Academy, graduating in 1908, and served in the navy from 1909 until 1926, reaching the rank of commander. Selected for the Construction Corps, he studied naval architecture at the Massachusetts Institute of Technology and aeronautical engineering in Europe. In 1914 he established the first course in aeronautical engineering at MIT. Recalled by the navy (1916) to put aeronautical engineering into practice, he worked on zeppelins, producing the *Shenandoah* (1923), and flying boats. Hunsaker worked in business from 1926, initially at the Bell Telephone Laboratories and then (1928–33) at Goodyear where he built zeppelins. In 1933 Hunsaker was appointed professor of mechanical engineering at MIT, also serving concurrently as head of the department of aeronautical engineering until his retirement in 1951.

He was the author of *Aeronautics at the Mid-century* (1952), a review of the problems facing the industry and the strategies open to it.

HUNTER, John (b. Feb. 13, 1728; Long Calderwood, Scotland; d. Oct. 16, 1793; London) British surgeon and anatomist.

Hunter joined his elder brother William, the famous obstetrician, in London in 1748. He there assisted his brother and attended surgical classes at Chelsea Hospital. Disputes with William over their research led John to branch out on his own and in 1759 he joined the army to serve as a surgeon in Portugal during the Seven Years' War. On his return to London in 1762 he set up as a private teacher and in 1767 was appointed surgeon at St. George's Hospital, London.

As a surgeon Hunter's major innovation was in the treatment of aneurysm, a bulge appearing at a weak spot in the wall of an artery. Rather than follow the drastic procedure of amputation Hunter instead tied the artery some distance from the diseased part and found that, with the pressure of circulation removed from the aneurismal sack, the progress of the disease is halted. He also made radical proposals, based on his military experience, for the treatment of gunshot wounds. He wisely argued in his *A Treatise on the Blood, Inflammation and Gunshot Wounds* (1794) that unless the missile in the body was actually endangering life the surgeon should leave it alone and under no circumstances enlarge the wound by opening it.

Hunter also wrote a famous work on venereal disease (1786) inadvertently producing much confusion. In the late 18th century it was still a matter of dispute whether syphilis with its chancre and gonorrhea with its purulent discharge were separate complaints. In 1767 Hunter decided to resolve the issue by inoculating himself with gonorrhea. He developed both gonorrhea and the typically hard chancre of syphilis, concluding therefore that discharge from a gonorrhea produces chancres. It seems not to have occurred to Hunter that his 'gonorrhea' was also infected with syphilis.

Hunter's main claim to fame however lay in his superb anatomical collection. He was supposed to have dissected over 500 different species and at his death his collection contained over 13 000 items. Included in his museum in Leicester Square, London, was the skeleton of the Irish giant, C. Byrne, who was so keenly aware of the desire of Hunter for his 7-foot-7-inch frame that he arranged to be secretly buried at sea. Hunter was widely reported to have paid the undertakers the sum of £500 for the corpse.

His collection was purchased by the government after his death and in 1795 was presented to the Royal College of Surgeons in London where, despite some losses from bombing in World War II, it has remained ever since.

HUNTER, William (b. May 23, 1718; Long Calderwood, Scotland; d. Mar. 30, 1783; London) British obstetrician.

A brother of John Hunter, the famous surgeon, William studied medicine at Edinburgh University before moving to London in 1740. Hunter went on to specialize in obstetrics and became an eminent practitioner, attending the royal family. He founded the Great Windmill Street School of Anatomy and his most famous work is *The Anatomy of the Human Gravid Uterus* (1774), a collation of 25 years' work, which contains 34 detailed plates produced from engravings of dissections.

Hunter built up a large and valuable collection of coins, medals, pictures, and books, which he bequeathed to Glasgow University. It is now housed in the Hunterian Museum.

HURTER, Ferdinand (b. Mar. 15, 1844; Schaffhausen, Switzerland; d. Mar. 5, 1898; Widnes, England) Swiss chemist.

Hurter was educated at the Federal Institute of Technology, Zurich and Heidelberg University, where he was a pupil of Robert Bunsen. In 1867 he moved to England and became the chief chemist at Holbrook Gaskell and Henry Deacon's alkali factory in Widnes. In 1890, when the United Alkali Company was formed, Hurter was appointed its chief chemist and set up one of the first industrial research laboratories. He collaborated with Georg Lunge in producing *The Alkali Maker's Handbook*, a work describing the Leblanc process in technical detail. Hurter also worked on photography with V.C. Driffield.

HUTCHINSON, George Evelyn (b. Jan. 30, 1903; Cambridge, England) American biologist.

Graduating from Cambridge University in 1924, Hutchinson was senior lecturer at the University of Witwatersrand (1926–28) before emigrating to America where he became Sterling Professor of Zoology at Yale in 1945. He received American citizenship in 1941.

Hutchinson's most important work has been concerned with aquatic ecosystems and the physical, chemical, meteorological, and biological conditions of lakes. He has made particular studies of the classification and distribution of aquatic bugs (Hemiptera), and has investigated water mixing and movement in stratified lakes, proving the circulation of phosphorus. He has also studied lake sediments and investigated certain aspects of evolution. His work has taken him to many different regions, including the lakes of western Transvaal, Tibet, and north-eastern North America.

HUTCHINSON, John (b. Apr. 7, 1884; Wark-on-Tyne, England; d. Sept. 2, 1972; London) British botanist.

Hutchinson, who was educated at the local village school, began work in 1900 under his father, the head gardener on a large estate. In 1904 he was appointed to a junior post at the Royal Botanic Gardens, Kew, where he remained for the rest of his career. Starting as an assistant in the herbarium he was in charge of the Africa section from 1919 until 1936 when he became keeper of the Museum of Economic Botany, a post he occupied until his retirement in 1948.

Hutchinson's most significant work was his *Families of Flowering Plants* (2 vols. 1926–34; 2nd edition 1959), which contains details of 342 dicotyledon and 168 monocotyledon families. Hutchinson drew most of the illustrations for this work himself. In it he concentrated on the different plant families that various workers had considered the most primitive. He concluded that bisexual flowers with free petals, sepals, etc., as seen in the magnolia and buttercup families, are more ancient than the generally unisexual, catkinlike flowers found in the nettle and beech families, which lack these parts. This conclusion supported the classification of George Bentham and Joseph Hooker and added weight to arguments against the system of Adolf Engler. Furthermore Hutchinson stated that families with apparently more simple flowers are in fact more advanced, and have evolved by reduction from more complex structures; that is, the families show retrograde evolution. In this, the now generally accepted view, Hutchinson was developing the earlier ideas of the German botanist, Alexander Braun.

An enormously prolific and industrious worker Hutchinson also published, with John Dalziel, the standard work, *Flora of West Tropical Africa* (1927–36) and at the time of his death was engaged in a revision of the *Genera Plantarum* of Bentham and Hooker.

HUTTON, James (b. June 3, 1726; Edinburgh; d. Mar. 26, 1797; Edinburgh) British geologist.

Hutton was the son of a merchant who became city treasurer of Edinburgh. He was educated at Edinburgh University, which he left in 1743 to be apprenticed to a lawyer. This did not retain his interest long for, in 1744, he returned to the university to read medicine. He studied in Paris for two years and finally gained his MD from Leiden in 1749. He next devoted several years to agriculture and industry, farming in Berwickshire and commercially producing sal ammoniac. In 1768 he returned to Edinburgh, financially independent, and devoted himself to scientific studies, especially of geology, for the rest of his life.

Hutton's uniformitarian theories were first published as a paper in 1788 and later extended into a two-volume work, *Theory of the Earth* (1795). This work proved difficult to read and it only reached a wide audience when his friend John Playfair edited and summarized it as *Illustrations of the Huttonian Theory* (1802). It marked a turning point in geology. The prevailing theory of the day, the neptunism of Abraham Werner, was that rocks had been laid down as mineral deposits in the oceans. However, Hutton maintained that water could not be the only answer for it was mainly erosive. The water could not account for the nonconformities caused by the foldings and intrusions characteristic of the Earth's strata. Hutton showed that the geological processes that had formed the Earth's features could be observed continuing at the present day. The heat of the Earth was the productive power, according to Hutton, that caused sedimentary rocks to fuse into the granites and flints, which could be produced in no other way. It could also produce the upheaval of strata, their folding and twisting, and the creation of mountains.

A long time scale is essential to Hutton's theory of uniformitarianism as the forces of erosion and combustion work, in general, only slowly, as demonstrated by the presence of visible Roman roads. He concluded that on the face of the Earth "we find no vestige of a beginning — no prospect of an end."

Hutton's work was accepted with little delay by most geologists, including the leading Edinburgh neptunist, Robert Jameson. In the 19th century Charles Lyell expanded the theories of uniformitarianism and these were to influence Charles Darwin in his theory of evolution.

HUXLEY, Andrew Fielding (b. Nov. 22, 1917; London) English physiologist.

Huxley, a grandson of T.H. Huxley, graduated in 1938 from Cambridge University, receiving his MA there three years later. He is best known for his collaboration with Alan Hodgkin (q.v.) in elucidating the 'sodium pump' mechanism by which nerve impulses are transmitted, for which they were awarded, with John Eccles, the Nobel Prize in physiology or medicine (1963). He has also done important work on muscular contraction theory and has been involved in the development of the interference microscope and ultramicrotome. Huxley was reader in experimental biophysics at Cambridge (1959–60), and since 1960 has been Jodrell Professor of Physiology at University College, London. In 1980 he succeeded Alexander Todd as president of the Royal Society.

HUXLEY, Hugh Esmor (b. Feb. 25, 1924; Birkenhead, England) British molecular biologist.

Huxley (no relation to T.H. Huxley or any of his descendants) read physics at Cambridge University where he obtained his PhD in 1952 after wartime research on the development of radar. Like many other physicists after the war Huxley was interested in applying physics to biological problems. After two years in America at the Massachusetts Institute of Technology and the period 1956–61 at the biophysics unit of the University of London, he returned to Cambridge to join the staff of the Medical Research Council's molecular biology laboratory.

In 1953, in collaboration with Jean Hanson, Huxley proposed the sliding filament theory of muscle contraction. This was based on his earlier study of myofibrils, the contractile apparatus of muscle, with the electron microscope. He found that myofibrils are made of two kinds of filament, one type about twice the width of the other. Each filament is aligned with other filaments of the same kind to form a band across the myofibril, and the bands of thick and thin filaments overlap for part of their length. The bands are also linked by an elaborate system of crossbridges. When the muscle changes length the two sets of filaments slide past each other. Further, the two sorts of filaments can be identified with the two chief proteins of muscle, myosin in the thick filament and actin in the thin. This made possible an elegant solution to how muscles contract at the molecular level.

In the areas where both kinds of protein are in contact, Huxley suggested that one, most probably myosin, serves as an enzyme, splitting a phosphate from ATP and so releasing the energy required for contraction. He concluded that the evidence of the combination of actin and myosin is seen in the bridges between the two kinds of filaments. The theory has since been much enlarged and taken to deeper levels of molecular understanding. Despite this the basic insight of Huxley and Hanson has remained intact.

HUXLEY, Sir Julian Sorell (b. June 22, 1887; London; d. Feb. 14, 1975; London) English biologist.

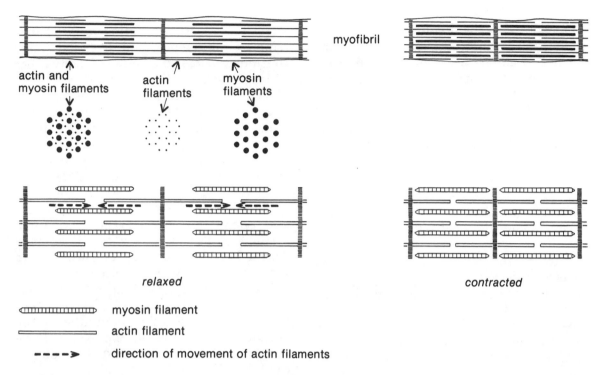

actin and
myosin filaments

actin
filaments

myosin
filaments

myofibril

relaxed

contracted

myosin filament

actin filament

- - - -> direction of movement of actin filaments

MUSCLE CONTRACTION The sliding filament theory proposed by Hugh Huxley and Jean Hanson.

A grandson of T. H. Huxley, Julian Huxley graduated in zoology from Oxford University in 1909. He did research on sponges (Porifera) at the Naples Zoological Station (1909–10) before taking up the post of lecturer in biology at Oxford (1910–12). From 1912 until 1916 he worked at the Rice Institute, Houston, Texas, where he met the famous American geneticist Hermann Muller. Before returning to Oxford to take up the post of senior demonstrator in zoology (1919–25) he saw war service in Italy. He was next appointed professor of zoology at King's College, London (1925–27), resigning from this post to devote more time to writing and research.

Huxley was a keen ornithologist and published, in 1914, a classic paper on the courtship of the great crested grebe. In the 1930s he was involved in the production of natural-history films, the most notable of which was the highly praised *Private Life of the Gannet* (1934), which he produced with the help of R. M. Lockley. One of the leading popularizers of science of modern times (especially the years before and just after World War II), Huxley spent much of his life explaining advances in natural science to the layman and in advocating the application of science to the benefit of mankind. To many he is best remembered as a most capable and lucid educationalist, but Huxley was also eminent in many other fields.

In 1946 he was appointed the first director-general of UNESCO, a post he held for two years. As an administrator, he also did much to transform the Zoological Society's collections at Regent's Park (London Zoo). Viewing man as 'the sole agent of further evolutionary advance on this planet', he caused considerable controversy by advocating the deliberate physical and mental improvement of the human race through eugenics. Huxley's biological research was also extensive, carrying out work on animal hormones, physiology, ecology, and animal (especially bird) behavior as it relates to evolution. He was president of the Institute of Animal

Behaviour and the originator of the term *ethology*, now in general use to define the science of animal behavior. He also introduced several other scientific terms, such as cline and clade.

Huxley's publications are extensive and include *Evolution: the Modern Synthesis* (1942, 1963). He was knighted in 1958.

HUXLEY, Thomas Henry (b. May 4, 1825; Ealing, England; d. June 29, 1895; Eastbourne, England) British biologist.

Huxley, the seventh child of a school teacher, received only two years' schooling; from the age of 10 he educated himself, doing sufficiently well to be admitted to Charing Cross Hospital to study medicine. He graduated in 1845 and the following year was employed as surgeon on HMS *Rattlesnake*, which was due to survey the Torres Strait between Australia and Papua. During the voyage Huxley studied the marine life of tropical waters and wrote an important paper on the medusae (jellyfish) and related species, naming a new phylum, the Coelenterata, into which these were placed. Recognizing the value of this work, the Royal Society elected Huxley a member in 1851. In 1854 he became lecturer in natural history at the Royal School of Mines (later the Royal College of Science) and while there gave a lecture on 'The Theory of the Vertebrate Skull', which disproved the idea that the skull originates from the vertebrae.

Huxley is best remembered as the main advocate of Charles Darwin's theory of evolution, and in 1860 — the year following the publication of *The Origin of Species* — he took part in the famous debate with the bishop of Oxford, Samuel Wilberforce, at the Oxford meeting of the British Association for the Advancement of Science. During the discussion Wilberforce asked whether Huxley traced his ancestry to the apes on his mother's or father's side of the family. Huxley answered witheringly that given the choice of a miserable ape and a man who could make such a remark at a serious scientific gathering, he would

select the ape. The meeting resulted in a triumph for science, and after it Huxley continued to gain the better of many other distinguished theologians in long academic wrangles. He introduced the term 'agnosticism' to describe his own view that since knowledge rested on scientific evidence and reasoning (and not blind faith) knowledge of the nature and certainty about the very existence of God was impossible.

Huxley worked hard to better educational standards for the working classes and spoke out against the traditional method of learning by rote. He opened Josiah Mason College (later Birmingham University), Owens College Medical School (later part of Manchester University), and Johns Hopkins University, Baltimore. Huxley was the grandfather of the author Aldous Huxley, the Nobel Prize winner Andrew Huxley, and the biologist Sir Julian Huxley.

HUYGENS, Christiaan (b. Apr. 14, 1629; The Hague, Netherlands; d. July 8, 1695; The Hague) Dutch physicist and astronomer.

Huygens, whose father was the Renaissance poet Constantin Huygens, studied at the University of Leiden and the College of Breda. He worked in Paris as one of the founding members of the French Academy of Sciences from 1666 to 1681 when, as a Protestant, he found the growing religious intolerance threatening, and returned to The Hague. His first work was in mathematics, but his greatest achievements were in physical optics and dynamics, and his importance to 17th-century science is second only to that of Newton.

Huygens's first great success was the invention of the pendulum clock. Galileo had noted in 1581 that a pendulum would keep the same time whatever its amplitude. Many, including Galileo himself, had tried unsuccessfully to use this insight to construct a more reliable clock. Huygens showed that a pendulum that moves in the arc of a circle does not move with an exactly equal swing. To produce an isochronous (equal-timed) swing it would need to move in a curve called a cycloid. It should be emphasized that Huygens worked this out largely from first principles. He also showed how the pendulum could be constructed so to move in a cycloidal path and how to make the connection to the escapement. The first clock was made to his design by Salomon Coster in 1657 and was described in Huygens's book *Horologium* (1658). The pendulum became one of the basic tools of 17th-century scientific investigation.

Huygens also made major contributions to astronomy as a designer of improved telescopes and as an observer of Saturn. He discovered Titan, Saturn's largest satellite, in 1655 and after prolonged observation was able to describe Saturn's rings correctly.

In 1673 Huygens published *Horologium oscillatorium*, a brilliant mathematical analysis of dynamics, including discussions of the relationship between the length of a pendulum and its period of oscillation, and the laws of centrifugal force. It also included an early formulation of Newton's first law of motion: that without some external force, such as gravity, a body once set in motion would continue in a straight line. His views on gravity were worked out in *Discours de la cause de la pesanteur* (1690; Discourse on the Cause of Gravity). As a Cartesian (a follower of René Descartes) he could not accept Newtonian action at a distance or, in fact, any talk of forces. Instead he would only accept a mechanical explanation, which meant a return to some kind of vortex theory. That is, bodies can only be heavy not because they are attracted by another body but because they are pushed by other bodies.

Huygens's greatest achievement was his development of the wave theory of light, described fully in his *Traité de la lumière* (1690; Treatise on Light). He assumed that space was pervaded by ether formed of particles, the disturbance of which constituted the radiation of light with the disturbance of one particle being passed on to its neighbor and so on. The disturbances

can be considered as waves spreading in a regular spherical form from the point of origin — the particles disturbed in phase constituting a wave front. Each point on a wave front may be regarded as a source of new secondary wavelets and a surface tangent joining such wavelets (i.e. the envelope of the secondary wavelets) can be considered as a new wave front. This method of treating light waves is known as the *Huygens construction*. Using it, Huygens dealt with reflection and refraction and predicted — as Newtonian theory did not — that light should travel more slowly in a denser medium. But as Huygens considered the waves to be longitudinal, the theory could not explain polarization.

Newton's *Opticks* (1704) presented a corpuscular (particle) theory of light, and the wave theory lay dormant until it was taken up by Thomas Young and his contemporaries.

HYMAN, Libbie Henrietta (b. Dec. 6, 1888; Des Moines, Iowa; d. Aug. 3, 1969; New York City) American zoologist.

Educated at the University of Chicago, Hyman also held a research post there from 1916 until 1931 where, under Charles Manning Child, she worked on the physiology and morphology of the lower invertebrates, particularly the planarians (flatworms). She published a number of works on invertebrate and vertebrate zoology, anatomy, physiology, and embryology, but her major compilation is *The Invertebrates*, a monumental work, six volumes of which had been published (1940–68) at the time of her death.

HYPATIA (b. *c.* 370; Alexandria, Egypt; d. 415; Alexandria) Greek mathematician.

Hypatia was the daughter of Theon of Alexandria, the author of a well-known commentary on Ptolemy. Although little is known about her, she appears to be, with the exception of the alchemist Marie the

Jewess, the only named woman scientist of the Greek world. In 400 she was reported to be head of the Neoplatonic school in Alexandria. To her have been attributed commentaries on Ptolemy's *Almagest*, Diophantus's *Arithmetic*, and Appolonius's *Conics*, none of which have survived.

Learning and science came to a violent conclusion in Alexandria and in the West, as did Hypatia. In conflict with Cyril, bishop of Alexandria, through her friendship with Orestes, the Roman prefect of the city, she was seized by the Christian mob and savagely mutilated and killed.

I

I-HSING (b. *c.* 681; d. *c.* 727) Chinese mathematician and astronomer.

I-Hsing was a Buddhist monk around whom many legends have grown. Only a small portion of his works has survived so it is difficult to appreciate his work in detail. There is, however, no reason to doubt his involvement in two major astronomical achievements. In the period 723–26 in collaboration with the Astronomer Royal, Nankung Yueh, expeditions were organized to measure, astronomically, the length of a meridional line. Over a distance of 1553 miles (2500 km) along this line simultaneous measurements of the Sun's solstitial shadow were made at nine stations. The estimated length of a degree, on the basis of their measurements, was far too large and it must be supposed that some systematic error in the method of observation was taking place. However, when it is appreciated that research expeditions to determine the length of a meridional degree were not organized in Europe until the 17th century, the amazing nature of I-Hsing's work can be appreciated. He also probably anticipated Su Sung in the use of an escapement in an astronomical clock. It was described in a 13th-century encyclopedia: "Water, flowing into scoops, turned a wheel automatically, rotating it one complete revolution in one day and one night." This turned various rings representing the motion of the celestial bodies. It was soon reported to be corroded, relegated to a musuem, and to have fallen into disuse.

IMBRIE, John (b. July 4, 1925; Penn Yan, New York) American geologist.

Imbrie was educated at Princeton and Yale, where he obtained his PhD in 1951. He joined the Columbia faculty in 1952 and after serving as professor of geology (1961–66) he moved to Brown University where he was professor of geology until 1975. He was then appointed to the chair of oceanography.

In his 1956 paper, *Biometrical Methods in the Study of Invertebrate Fossils*, Imbrie showed how statistical techniques could be applied to the analysis of variation in fossil assemblies. He has also worked on the paleoecology of the Great Bahamas Bank and in his *Ice Ages* (1979) produced a comprehensive and popular survey of the subject.

INGENHOUSZ, Jan (b. Dec. 8, 1730; Breda, Netherlands; d. Sept. 7, 1799; Bowood, England) Dutch plant physiologist and physician.

Ingenhousz studied medicine, chemistry, and physics at the universities of Louvain and Leiden, receiving his MD from Louvain in 1752. In 1765 he visited London and became expert at administering smallpox inoculations using Edward Jenner's method. News of his expertise spread and he was invited to Vienna in 1768 by the Empress Maria Theresa to inoculate her family and become court physician.

In 1779, Ingenhousz returned to England and published his work on gaseous exchange in plants. His experiments demonstrated that plants absorb carbon dioxide and give off oxygen (in his words, "purify the air") only in the light, and that the reverse process occurs in the dark. The light process later became known as photosynthesis. Ingenhousz also conducted research on soils and on plant nutrition, improved apparatus for generating static electricity, and studied heat conduction in metals.

INGOLD, Sir Christopher Kelk (b. Oct. 28, 1893; London; d. Dec. 8, 1970; London) British chemist.

Ingold was educated at the University of Southampton and Imperial College, London. After serving as professor of organic chemistry at the University of Leeds from 1924 until 1930, he moved to the chair of chemistry at University College, London, where he remained until his retirement in 1961.

With over 400 papers to his credit and as the author of the classic text, *Structure and Mechanism in Organic Chemistry* (1953), Ingold was one of the leading figures in British chemistry. The basic aim running through all his work was to understand the mechanism of the organic reaction, particularly the kinetics of elimination and substitution reactions. In 1926 he introduced the idea of mesomerism, fully explained in the famous paper *Principles of an Electronic Theory of Organic Reactions* (1934). This was similar to the concept of resonance proposed by Linus Pauling in the early 1930s. The basic idea was that if a molecule could exist in two electronic structures then its normal state was neither one nor the other but some 'hybrid' form. This theory was substantiated by measuring bond lengths in appropriate molecules.

INGRAM, Vernon Martin (b. May 19, 1924; Breslau, now Wroclaw in Poland) German–British–American biochemist.

Ingram, born Immerwahr, was brought to Britain as a refugee from Nazi Germany as a child. He was educated at Birkbeck College, London, where he obtained his PhD in 1949. After working briefly at Rockefeller and Yale he returned to England and joined the staff of the Medical Research Council's molecular biology unit at the Cavendish Laboratory, Cambridge, in 1952. In 1958 however he moved to the Massachusetts Institute of Technology where he has served as professor of biochemistry since 1961.

By the mid 1950s it was clear to Francis Crick that it should be possible, and was indeed essential, for molecular biology to be able to show that mutant genes produced changes in the amino acid sequences of proteins. Although such a claim was central to the supposed revolution in molecular biology, there was, as Crick realized in 1955, no direct evidence that proteins are in fact coded by genes.

Consequently Crick and Ingram attempted to reveal such a change in the lysozyme of fowl eggs. However, although they succeeded in distinguishing differences between lysozymes from such different birds as duck and pheasant, they failed to find any difference in lysozymes between two hens of the same species. At this point however Max Perutz gave Ingram some sickle-cell hemoglobin (hemoglobin S) to work with. (Hemoglobin S, possessed by sufferers of a crippling anemia, had been distinguished from normal hemoglobin A by Linus Pauling and his student Harvey Itano in 1949.) Ingram split the hemoglobin into smaller units by using the enzyme trypsin to break the peptide bonds. He then separated these units by electrophoresis and paper chromatography. This allowed him to show that hemoglobin S differs from normal hemoglobin at just one site where the amino acid valine replaces the glutamic acid of the A form. Although it came as a surprise that the alteration of one amino acid in over 500 could produce such lethal effects, it also dramatically established that molecular biology was not just an abstract and remote branch of structural chemistry.

Ingram went on to show that this and other point mutations of hemoglobin could be used to trace the evolutionary history of vertebrates, work reported in his *The Hemoglobins in Genetics and Evolution* (1963).

IPATIEFF, Vladimir Nikolayevich (b. Nov. 21, 1867; Moscow; d. Nov. 29, 1952; Chicago, Illinois) Russian–American chemist.

Ipatieff became an officer in the Imperial Russian Army in 1887 and was educated at the Mikhail Artillery Academy (1889–92) in St. Petersburg (now Leningrad). After further study in Germany and France he returned to the academy in 1898 and became professor of chemistry until 1906.

While in Munich (1897) Ipatieff achieved the synthesis of isoprene, the basic unit of the rubber molecule. On his return to Russia he carried out important work on high-pressure catalytic reactions. The first breakthrough in organic catalysis had been due to Paul Sabatier who had demonstrated the use of finely ground nickel to catalyze hydrogenation of unsaturated hydrocarbons (1897). Ipatieff greatly extended this work. He showed how it could be applied to liquids and demonstrated that the process became much more powerful and adaptable at high pressures. To this end he designed the so-called *Ipatieff bomb* — an autoclave that permitted the heating of substances under pressure to above their boiling point. Thus before World War I Ipatieff had synthesized methane and isooctane, and had polymerized ethylene.

During World War I and after the revolutionary years in Russia Ipatieff held a number of important advisory posts, in addition to continuing with his own research, despite his anti-Communist feelings. In 1930, worried for his own safety, he traveled to America. Despite being 64 when he arrived in America Ipatieff still had much to offer, publishing over 150 papers in this last phase of his career. He was appointed professor of chemistry at Northwestern University, Illinois, (1931–35) and also acted as a consultant to the Universal Oil Products Company of Chicago who, in 1938, established at Northwestern University the Ipatieff High Pressure Laboratory, which he directed. With the growth of the petrochemical industry after 1918, Ipatieff's techniques became widely used. Working in America he showed how low-octane gasolines could be converted to high-octane gasoline by 'cracking' hydrocarbons at high temperatures.

IRVINE, James Colquhoun (b. May 9, 1877; Glasgow, Scotland; d. June 12, 1952; St. Andrews, Scotland) British chemist.

Irvine studied chemistry at the Royal Technical College, Glasgow, and at Leipzig. His father was a manufacturer of light iron castings and appears to have been a capable mathematician. Irvine's whole career was spent at St. Andrews beginning in 1901 as a lecturer, being appointed professor of chemistry in 1909, and finally, in 1921, becoming vice-chancellor of the university.

Under Irvine the tradition of carbohydrate studies established by Thomas Purdie was to continue. Irvine's work involved the application of Purdie's methylation technique to carbohydrates. He realized that the constitution of disaccharides and other compound carbohydrates might be found by methylating them and he isolated the first methylated sugars, trimethyl and tetramethyl glucose. Irvine's fruitful line of research was to be continued at St. Andrews and later at Birmingham by Norman Haworth.

ISAACS, Alick (b. July 17, 1921; Glasgow, Scotland; d. Jan. 26, 1967; London) British virologist and biologist.

Isaacs graduated in medicine from the University of Glasgow in 1944. After three years' research work in the department of bacteriology he moved to Sheffield University for a year and then spent two years in Australia at the Hall Institute for Medical Research, Melbourne. During this time he studied influenza, in particular the genetic variation of the various strains of the virus and also the response of the body to attack by the virus. He continued with this work from 1950 at the National Institute for Medical Research in London, where he was director of the World Influenza Centre.

In 1957, together with the Swiss virologist Jean Lindenmann, Isaacs reported that a specific low-molecular-weight protein, which interfered with the multiplication of viruses, was produced by animal cells when under viral attack. This was *interferon*, which he studied closely for the rest of his life, investigating problems associated with its production and isolation, its mechanism of action, and its chemical and physical properties. Isaacs's work formed the basis for all present-day research on this potentially important drug, the full effects of which are still being closely studied.

In the early 1960s his health began to deteriorate but he continued work as head of the Laboratory for Research on Interferon at the National Institute.

IVANOVSKY, Dmitri Iosifovich (b. Nov. 9, 1864; Gdov, now in the Soviet Union; d. June 20, 1920; Soviet Union) Russian botanist.

Ivanovsky studied natural sciences at St. Petersburg University, graduating in 1888. He obtained his master's degree in botany in 1895 and worked (1896–1901) as an instructor in plant anatomy and physiology at the Technological Institute, St. Petersburg. In 1908 he was appointed professor at the University of Warsaw.

In 1892, following his investigations of tobacco mosaic disease in the Crimea, he demonstrated that a filtrate of the sap from infected tobacco plants had the ability to transmit the disease to healthy plants. Ivanovsky showed that minute crystalline particles were present in the filtrate and asserted that they were somehow linked to the disease. However, he wrongly attributed the cause of the disease to minute bacteria. Ivanovsky's work was confirmed in a publication by the Dutch bacteriologist Martinus Beijerinck in 1898. It was Beijerinck who stated that such infective agents are not bacterial and coined the term 'virus'. This, together with the work of the French bacteriologist Charles Chamberland on rabies, was one of the earliest pieces of evidence for the existence of viruses although it was not until 1935 that Wendell Stanley confirmed this.

J

JACKSON, Charles Thomas (b. June 21, 1805; Plymouth, Massachusetts; d. Aug. 28, 1880; Somerville, Massachusetts) American chemist.

Jackson studied medicine at Harvard and continued his education at the Sorbonne in Paris, working on chemistry and geology. He returned to America and set up a practice in Boston. Jackson's professional career consisted of a series of spectacular claims to the work of others. These started on his homeward voyage and were to persist until he finally became insane in 1873.

While sailing from France to America in 1832 Jackson befriended a fellow American, the portrait painter Samuel Morse, with whom he discussed the possibilities of electric telegraphy. When Morse exhibited his telegraph to Congress in 1837 he found that he had to establish a right to his own invention against Jackson's claim that Morse had stolen it from him. It took Morse seven years to prove the validity of his claim.

In July 1844 Jackson recommended to William Morton, a young dentist lodging with him, that he should try treating his patients using ether, which was commonly used by medical students as a joke. Morton took up his suggestion and found it promising. He experimented on himself, gave up his practice to work on dosages and systems of inhalation, and introduced the anesthetic to the medical profession. Nothing was heard from Jackson until it was clear that money and fame were going to be awarded to someone. When Morton went to Congress to ask for compensation for yielding his patent to the US govern-

ment he found some senators who took him for a thief. When he went to Paris in 1847 to lecture on his discovery he found that Jackson had already lodged a sealed envelope with the Académie claiming a priority going back to 1842. Committees were set up by governments, states, academies, and professional bodies but Jackson managed to so confuse the issue that when Morton collapsed and died in 1868 he was still fighting his claim and still penniless.

Jackson became obsessive about his 'discovery', ignored his other work, took to drink, and spent the last seven years of his life in a lunatic asylum. He even wrote a book on the subject, *A Manual of Etherisation* (1861). Curiously, both Morton and Jackson have monuments in the same cemetery, both proudly proclaiming their triumph in alleviating the misery of mankind.

JACKSON, John Neethlings (b. Apr. 4, 1835; Green Hammerton, England; d. Oct. 7, 1911; London) British neurologist.

Jackson was educated at York Hospital and St. Bartholomew's Hospital, London, and received his MD from St. Andrews University in 1860. He served on the staff of the London Hospital as assistant physician (1863) and physician (1874–94) and in 1862 began his long association with the National Hospital for the Paralysed and Epileptic, London. Here he specialized in neurology and ultimately exercised a profound influence on the development of clinical neurology. Through his work with epileptics, he described the condition, now called *Jacksonian seizure* or Jacksonian epilepsy, in which part of the leg, arm, or face undergoes spasmodic contraction due to local disease of the cerebral cortex in the brain.

Jackson's work supported the findings of Paul Broca and others — that different bodily functions are controlled by different regions of the cerebral cortex. Jackson also described a local paralysis of the tongue and throat caused by disease of the corresponding cranial nerves. This is now known as *Jackson's syndrome.*

JACOB, François (b. June 17, 1920; Nancy, France) French biologist.

Jacob served with the Free French forces during World War II and, although badly wounded, resumed his medical studies in 1945, obtaining his MD from the University of Paris in 1947. In 1950 he became André Lwoff's assistant at the Pasteur Institute, Paris, and, with Elie Wollman, began working on the bacteria, discovered by Lwoff, that carry a nonvirulent virus incorporated in their genetic material. In 1961 they introduced the term 'episomes' for genetic elements that become established in bacterial cells. Jacob and Wollman also studied conjugation in bacteria, the process by which genetic material is transferred from one cell to another. They found that the genes of the donor cell enter the recipient cell in a specific order and by interrupting the process, the position of given genes on the chromosome could be determined.

In 1958 Jacob began collaborating with Jacques Monod and Arthur Pardee on the control of bacterial enzyme production, research that culminated in a greatly increased understanding of the regulation of gene activity. In 1960 Jacob and Monod proposed the existence of the operon, consisting of an operator gene and structural genes that code for the enzymes needed in a given biosynthetic pathway. When the enzymes are not required another gene outside the operon, the regulator gene, produces a protein that binds with the operator and renders the operon ineffective.

Jacob and Monod received the 1965 Nobel Prize for physiology or medicine for this research, sharing the award with Lwoff.

Since 1964, Jacob has occupied the chair of cellular genetics at the Collège de France, which was created in his honor. He became a foreign member of the Royal Society in 1973 and a member of the Academy of Sciences, Paris, in 1977.

JACOBI, Karl Gustav Jacob (b. Dec. 10, 1804; Potsdam, now in East Germany; d. Feb. 18, 1851; Berlin) German mathematician.

Jacobi was a student in Berlin and became a lecturer at Königsberg where he managed to attract the favorable attention of Karl Friedrich Gauss. He was a superb teacher and had an astonishing manipulative skill with formulae. He made a brief but disastrous foray into politics that resulted in his losing a pension he had been granted by the king of Prussia.

Jacobi's most important contributions to mathematics were in the field of elliptic functions. Niels Hendrik Abel had partially anticipated some of Jacobi's work, but the two were equally important in the creation of this subject. Jacobi also worked on Abelian functions and discovered the hyperelliptic functions. He applied his work in elliptic functions to number theory.

Jacobi worked in many other areas of mathematics as well as the theory of functions. He was a pioneer in the study of determinants and a certain type of determinant arising in connection with partial differential equations is known as the *Jacobian* is his honor. This work was the result of his interest in dynamics, in which field he continued and developed the work of William Hamilton, and produced results that are important in quantum mechanics.

JANSKY, Karl Guthe (b. Oct. 22, 1905; Norman, Oklahoma; d. Feb. 14, 1950; Red Bank, New Jersey) American radio engineer.

Jansky was educated at the University of Wisconsin and started his career with the Bell Telephone Laboratories in 1928. He was given the task of investigating factors that could interfere with radio waves used for long distance communication. He designed a linear directional antenna, which, mounted on wheels from a Model T automobile, could scan the sky. He identified all the sources of interference, such as thunderstorms, except for one weak emission. This he found to be unconnected with the Sun and in 1931 he discovered that the radio interference came from the stars.

Jansky published his findings in the *Proceedings of the Institute of Radio Engineers* in December 1932, the date that marks precisely the beginnings of radio astronomy. In his paper Jansky made two astute comments: he suggested that the radio emission was somehow connected with the Milky Way and that it originated not from the stars but from interstellar ionized gas. He did not pursue his suggestions and it was left to Grote Reber, the amateur astronomer, to keep the subject alive until it developed into a major research field after 1945.

The unit of radio-wave emission strength was named the jansky in his honor.

JANSSEN, Pierre Jules César (b. Feb. 22, 1824; Paris; d. Dec. 23, 1907; Meudon, near Paris) French astronomer.

Janssen studied mathematics and physics at the University of Paris before becoming professor of general science at the school of architecture. He must have been one of the most widely traveled of the 19th-century astronomers, themselves a much traveled group. In 1857 he went to Peru to determine the magnetic equator. He observed the transits of Venus of 1874 and 1882 in Japan and Algeria and went on all the major eclipse expeditions. So keen was he to witness the 1870 eclipse in Algeria that he had to escape from the siege of Paris by balloon. While in India in 1868, observing the solar eclipse spectros-

copically, he noticed the hydrogen lines visible in the solar prominences and wondered if they could still be detected after the eclipse. The next day he found them still visible. This meant that while photography and observation would still depend on eclipse work the spectroscope could be used almost anywhere anytime. Janssen made one further important discovery on the same trip; he discovered lines in the solar spectrum that he could not identify. He sent his results to Norman Lockyer who suggested that they were produced by some element found only on the Sun, which Lockyer called 'helium'. In 1895 William Ramsay discovered a substance on Earth that matched exactly with Janssen's spectral lines.

In later life Janssen arranged for an observatory to be built on Mont Blanc in order to avoid as much atmospheric interference as possible. Using data from observations made there, he showed that absorption lines in the solar spectrum are caused by elements in the Earth's atmosphere.

JANSSEN, Zacharias (b. 1580; Middelburg, now in the Netherlands; d. *c.* 1638) Dutch instrument maker.

Together with his father, Hans Janssen, Zacharias is believed to have invented the first compound microscope in 1590. He is also credited with having made the first telescope in 1608, although Hans Lippershey, who also lived in Middelburg, and Jacobus Metius share claims to this invention.

JEANS, Sir James Hopwood (b. Sept. 11, 1877; London; d. Sept. 16, 1946; Dorking, England) British mathematician, physicist, and astronomer.

Jeans, the son of a journalist, graduated from Cambridge University in 1900 and obtained his MA in 1903. After lecturing at Cambridge, 1904–05, he became professor of applied mathematics at Princeton

University, 1905–09, and, back in England, Stokes Lecturer in applied mathematics at Cambridge (1910–12). There followed a period of writing and research during which his interest turned to astronomy. In 1923 he became a research assistant at the Mount Wilson Observatory, Pasadena, California, where he worked until 1944. Jeans was also professor of astronomy at the Royal Institution in London from 1935 until his death. He was knighted in 1928.

Jeans is best known as an astronomer and as a writer both of popular books on science and of several excellent textbooks. His earlier books were devoted to physics and included *Dynamical Theory of Gases* (1904) and *Mathematical Theory of Electricity and Magnetism* (1908). His serious astronomical works included *Problems of Cosmogeny and Stellar Dynamics* (1919) and *Astronomy and Cosmogeny* (1928) while among his popular books were *The Universe Around Us* (1929) and *The Mysterious Universe* (1930).

Jeans pioneered various ideas in astronomy and astrophysics. He showed that Pierre Simon Laplace's theory of the origin of the solar system, in which the Sun and planets condensed from a contracting cloud of gas and dust, was untenable. In collaboration with Harold Jeffreys he proposed a new view in its place. According to this 'tidal theory' a star had passed close by the newly formed Sun and the planets had been formed from the cigar-shaped filament of material drawn away from this star. Jeans and Jeffreys based their theory on a similar idea proposed earlier by Thomas Chamberlin and Forest Ray Moulton. The tidal theory was eventually superseded in the 1940s by revamped versions of Laplace's nebular theory.

Jeans also investigated other astronomical phenomena, among them spiral nebulae, binary and multiple star systems, and the source of energy in stars, which he concluded involved radioactivity.

JEFFREYS, Sir Harold (b. Apr. 22, 1891; Birtley, England) British astronomer and geophysicist.

Jeffreys was educated in Newcastle and at Cambridge University. After graduating in 1913 he was made a fellow of his college. He was reader in geophysics (1931–46) before being elected to the Plumian Professorship of Astronomy and Experimental Philosophy where he remained until his retirement in 1958.

In 1924 Jeffreys produced one of the fundamental works in geophysics of the first half of the 20th century, *The Earth: Its Origin, History, and Physical Constitution*. In this he argued forcibly against Alfred Wegener's proposed theory of continental drift. He demonstrated that the forces proposed by Wegener were inadequate. This did much to inhibit interest and research into drift theory for a while but much new evidence in its favor has since been uncovered.

Jeffreys was also joint author, with Keith Bullen, of the *Seismological Tables* (1935). These, more frequently known as the JB Tables, were revised in 1940 and are the present standard tables of travel times of earthquake waves. They allow observers to determine from the elapsed time between the arrival of the primary (P) waves and the secondary (S) waves the distance between the observer and the earthquake.

Jeffreys' work in astronomy included studies on the origins of the universe. He developed James Jeans's theory of tidal evolution. He also devised models for the planetary structure of Jupiter, Saturn, Uranus, and Neptune.

He was knighted in 1953.

JENNER, Edward (b. May 17, 1749; Berkeley, England; d. Jan. 24, 1823; Berkeley) British physician.

Jenner, a vicar's son, was apprenticed to the London surgeon John Hunter from 1770 to 1772. He then returned to country practice and established a reputation as a field naturalist. In 1787 Jenner observed that the newly hatched cuckoo, rather than the adult cuckoo, was responsible for removing the other eggs from the nest. He was elected a fellow of the Royal Society in 1789 partly on the basis of this work. Jenner's lasting contribution to science however is his investigations into the disease smallpox.

In 17th-century London some 10% of all deaths were due to smallpox. In response to this the practice of variolation, inoculation with material taken from fresh smallpox sores, was widely adopted. This was first described in England in 1713. However variolation suffered from two major defects for, if too virulent a dose was given, a lethal case of smallpox would develop and, secondly, the subject inoculated, unless isolated, was only too likely to start an epidemic amongst those in contact with him.

Jenner had heard reports that milkmaids once infected with cowpox developed a lifelong immunity to smallpox. On 14 May, 1796, he made the crucial experiment and took an eight-year-old boy and injected him with cowpox. He followed this on 1 July with injections taken from smallpox pustules, repeating the procedure several months later. On both occasions the boy did not develop smallpox and the same happy result was later observed with other experimental subjects. Jenner's conclusion that cowpox infection protects people from smallpox infection was first published in *An Inquiry into the Causes and Effects of the Variolae Vaccinae* (1798).

General acceptance of Jenner's work was almost immediate. In 1802 he was awarded £10 000 by a grateful House of Commons and in 1804 he was honored by Napoleon who made vaccination compulsory in the French army. Variolation was made illegal in England in 1840 and in 1853 further legislation made the vaccination of infants compulsory. As a consequence of this deaths from smallpox running at a rate of 40 per 10 000 at the beginning of the 19th century fell to 1 in 10 000 by the end.

JENSEN, Johannes Hans Daniel (b. June 25, 1907; Hamburg, now in West Germany; d. Feb. 11, 1973; Heidelberg, West Germany) German physicist.

Jensen was educated at the universities of Hamburg and Freiburg, where he obtained his doctorate in 1932. He worked at Hamburg and Hannover before his appointment in 1949 as professor of physics at Heidelberg. In 1963 Jensen was awarded the Nobel Physics Prize with Maria Goeppert-Mayer (q.v.) for their independent publication of the 'shell' theory of the nucleus.

JOHANNSEN, Wilhelm Ludwig (b. Feb. 3, 1857; Copenhagen; d. Nov. 11, 1927; Copenhagen) Danish botanist and geneticist.

On leaving school in 1872, Johannsen became apprenticed to a pharmacist as his father could not afford university fees. From his work in Danish and German pharmacies, Johannsen taught himself chemistry and developed an interest in botany. In 1881 he began work under Johan Kjeldahl in the chemistry department of the Carlsberg laboratories, investigating dormancy in seeds, tubers, and buds.

In 1892 Johannsen became lecturer at the Copenhagen Agricultural College. On reading Francis Galton's *Theory of Heredity* he was impressed by experiments demonstrating that selection is ineffective if applied to the progeny of self-fertilizing plants. Johannsen repeated this work using the Princess bean, but found that selection did work on the offspring of a mixed population of self-fertilizing beans. It was only when plants were derived from a single parent that selection had no effect. He called the descendants of a single parent a 'pure line' and argued that individuals in a pure line are genetically identical: any variation among them is due to environmental effects, which are not heritable. In 1905 he coined the terms 'genotype' to describe the genetic constitution of an individual, and 'phenotype', to describe the visible result of the interaction between genotype and environment.

Johannsen explained his ideas in *On Heredity and Variation* (1896), which he revised and lengthened with the rediscovery of Gregor Mendel's laws and reissued as *Elements of Heredity* in 1905. The enlarged German edition of this work became available in 1909 and proved the most influential book on genetics in Europe. In the same year Johannsen proposed the term 'genes' to describe Mendel's factors of inheritance. Johannsen's researches, with their emphasis on the quantitative variation of characters in populations and the application of statistical methods, played a major role in the development of modern genetics from 19th-century ideas.

In 1905 Johannsen became professor of plant physiology at Copenhagen University and was made rector of the University in 1917. He spent his later years writing on the history of science.

JOLIOT-CURIE, Frédéric (b. Mar. 19, 1900; Paris; d. Aug. 14, 1958; Paris) French physicist.

Frédéric Joliot, the son of a prosperous tradesman, was educated at the School of Industrial Physics and Chemistry. In 1923 he began his research career at the Radium Institute under Marie Curie, where he obtained his doctorate in 1930. He was appointed to a new chair of nuclear chemistry at the Collège de France in 1937 and, after World War II in which he played an important part in the French Resistance, was head of the new Commissariat à l'Energie Atomique (1946–50). In 1956 he became head of the Radium Institute.

In 1926 Joliot married the daughter of Marie Curie, Irène, and changed his name to Joliot-Curie. In 1931 they began research that was to win them the Nobel Physics Prize in 1935 for their fundamental discovery of artificial radioactivity (1934). His description of the crucial experiment is as follows: "We bombarded aluminum with alpha rays [the heavy nucleus of a helium atom, made of two protons and two neutrons] ... then after a certain period of irradiation, we removed the source of alpha rays. We now observed that the sheet of aluminum continued to emit positive electrons over a period of several minutes." What had happened was that the stable aluminum atom had absorbed an alpha-particle and transmuted into an (until then) unknown isotope of silicon, which was radioactive with a half-life of about 3.5 minutes. The significance of this was that it produced the first clear chemical evidence for transmutation and opened the door to a virtually new discipline. Soon large numbers of radioisotopes were created, and they became an indispensable tool in various branches of science. Dramatic confirmation of the Joliot-Curies' discovery was provided when Frédéric realized that the cyclotron at the laboratory of Ernest Lawrence in California would have been producing artificial elements unwittingly. He cabled them to switch off their cyclotron and listen. To their surprise the Geiger counter continued clicking away, registering for the first time the radioactivity of nitrogen–13.

In 1939 Joliot-Curie was quick to see the significance of the discovery of nuclear fission by Otto Hahn. He confirmed Hahn's work and saw the likelihood of a chain reaction. He further realized that the chain reaction could only be produced in the presence of a moderator to slow the neutrons down. A good moderator was the heavy water that was produced on a large scale only in Norway at Telemark. With considerable foresight Joliot-Curie managed to persuade the French government to obtain this entire stock of heavy water, 185 kilograms in all, and to arrange for its shipment to England out of the reach of the advancing German army.

JOLIOT-CURIE, Irène (b. Sept. 12, 1897; Paris; d. Mar. 17, 1956; Paris) French physicist.

Irène Curie was the daughter of Pierre and Marie Curie, the discoverers of radium. She received little formal schooling, attending instead informal classes where she was taught physics by her mother, mathematics by Paul Langevin, and chemistry by Jean Baptiste Perrin. She later attended the Sorbonne although she first served as a radiologist at the front during World War I. In 1921 she began work at her mother's Radium Institute with which she maintained her connection for the rest of her life, becoming its director in 1946. She was also, from 1937, a professor at the Sorbonne.

In 1926 Irène Curie married Frédéric Joliot and took the name Joliot-Curie. As in so many other things she followed her mother in being awarded the Nobel Prize for distinguished work done in collaboration with her husband. Thus in 1935 the Joliot-Curies won the physics prize for their discovery in 1934 of artificial radioactivity.

Irène later almost anticipated Otto Hahn's discovery of nuclear fission but like many other physicists at that time found it too difficult to accept the simple hypothesis that heavy elements like uranium could split into lighter elements when bombarded with neutrons. Instead she tried to find heavier elements produced by the decay of uranium.

Like her mother, Irène Joliot-Curie produced a further generation of scientists. Her daughter, Hélène, married the son of Marie Curie's old companion, Paul Langevin, and, together with her brother, Paul, became a distinguished physicist.

JOLY, John (b. Nov. 1, 1857; Hollywood, now in the Republic of Ireland; d. Dec. 8, 1933; Dublin) Irish geologist and physicist.

Joly was the son of a clergyman. He entered Trinity College, Dublin, in 1876 where he studied literature and engineering. He taught in the engineering school from 1883 and was appointed professor of geology and mineralogy in 1897, a post he held until his death.

Joly's major geological work was in the field of geochronology. He first tried to

estimate the age of the Earth by using Edmond Halley's method of measuring the degree of salinity of the oceans, and then by examining the radioactive decay in rocks. In 1898 he assigned an age of 80–90 million years to the Earth, later revising this figure to 100 million years. He published *Radioactivity and Geology* in 1909 in which he demonstrated that the rate of radioactive decay has been more or less constant through time.

Joly also carried out important work on radium extraction (1914) and pioneered its use for the treatment of cancer. His inventions in physics included a constant-volume gas thermometer, a photometer, and a differential steam calorimeter for measuring the specific heat capacity of gases at constant volume.

JONES, Sir Ewart Ray Herbert (b. Mar. 16, 1911; Wrexham, Wales) British chemist.

Jones was educated at the University College of Wales at Bangor and at Manchester University. He taught at Imperial College, London, from 1938 until 1947 when he returned to Manchester as professor of chemistry. In 1955 he moved to a similar chair at Oxford, in which post he remained until his retirement in 1978.

Jones has worked mainly on the structure, synthesis, and biogenesis of natural products, particularly the steroids, terpenes, and vitamins.

JONES, Sir Harold Spencer *See* SPENCER JONES, Sir Harold.

JORDAN, (Marie-Ennemond) Camille (b. Jan. 5, 1838; Lyons, France; d. Jan. 20, 1922; Milan, Italy) French mathematician.

Jordan studied in Paris at the Ecole Polytechnique where he trained as an engineer. Later he taught at both the Ecole Polytechnique and the Collège de France until his retirement in 1912. His interests lay chiefly in pure mathematics, although he made contributions to a wide range of mathematical subjects.

Jordan's most important and enduring work was in group theory and analysis. He was especially interested in groups of permutations and grasped the intimate connection of this subject with questions about the solvability of polynomial equations. This basic insight was one of the fundamental achievements of the seminal work of Evariste Galois, and Jordan was the first mathematician to draw attention to Galois's work, which had until then been almost entirely ignored. Jordan played a major role in starting the systematic investigation of the areas of research opened up by Galois. He also introduced the idea of an *infinite* group. Jordan also passed on his interest in group theory to two of his most outstanding pupils, Felix Klein and Sophus Lie, both of whom were to develop the subject in novel and important ways.

JORDAN, Ernst Pascual (b. Oct. 18, 1902; Hannover, now in West Germany) German theoretical physicist and mathematician.

Jordan was educated at the Hannover Institute of Technology and the University of Göttingen, where he obtained his doctorate in 1924. He left Göttingen in 1929 for the University of Rostock and after being appointed professor of physics there in 1935, later held chairs of theoretical physics at Berlin from 1944 to 1952 and at Hamburg from 1951 until his retirement in 1970.

Jordan was one of the founders of the modern quantum theory. In 1925 he collaborated with Max Born (q.v.) and in 1926 with Werner Heisenberg (q.v.) in the formulation of quantum mechanics. He also did early work on quantum electrodynamics. He developed a new theory of gravitation at the same time as Carl Brans and Robert Dicke (q.v.).

JOSEPHSON, Brian David (b. Jan. 4, 1940; Cardiff) British physicist.

Josephson was educated at Cambridge University where he obtained his PhD in 1964. He remained at Cambridge and in 1974 was appointed to a professorship of physics.

His name is associated with the *Josephson effects* described in 1962 while still a graduate student. The work came out of theoretical speculations on electrons in semiconductors involving the exchange of electrons between two superconducting regions separated by a thin insulating layer (a *Josephson junction*). He showed theoretically that a current can flow across the junction in the absence of an applied voltage. Furthermore, a small direct voltage across the junction produces an alternating current with a frequency that is inversely proportional to the voltage. The effects have been verified experimentally, thus supporting the BCS theory of superconductivity of John Bardeen and his colleagues. They have been used in making accurate physical measurements and in measuring weak magnetic fields. Josephson junctions can also be used as very fast switching devices in computers. For this work Josephson shared the 1973 Nobel Physics Prize with Leo Eskai and Ivar Giaevar.

More recently, Josephson has turned his attention to the study of the mind.

JOULE, James Prescott (b. Dec. 24, 1818; Salford, England; d. Oct. 11, 1889; Sale, England) British physicist.

Joule was the son of a brewer and received little formal education, was never appointed to an academic post, and remained a brewer all his life. He began work in a private laboratory that his father built near to the brewery.

His first major research was concerned with determining the quantity of heat produced by an electric current and, in 1840, Joule discovered a simple law connecting the current and resistance with the heat generated. For the next few years he carried out a series of experiments in which he investigated the conversion of electrical and mechanical work into heat. In 1849 he read his paper *On the Mechanical Equivalent of Heat* to the Royal Society. Joule's work (unlike that of Julius Mayer) was instantly recognized.

In 1848 Joule published a paper on the kinetic theory of gases, in which he estimated the speed of gas molecules. From 1852 he worked with William Thomson (later Lord Kelvin) on experiments on thermodynamics. Their best known result is the *Joule–Kelvin effect* — the effect in which an expanding gas, under certain conditions, is cooled by the expansion.

JUNG, Carl Gustav (b. July 26, 1875; Kesswil, Switzerland; d. June 6, 1961; Küsnacht, Switzerland) Swiss psychologist and psychiatrist.

The son of a pastor, Jung studied medicine at the universities of Basel (1895–1900) and Zurich, where he obtained his MD in 1920. From 1902 until 1909 he worked under the direction of Eugen Bleuler at the Burghölzi Psychiatric Clinic, Zurich, while at the same time lecturing in psychiatry at the University of Zurich (1905–13). In 1907 Jung met Sigmund Freud, whose chief collaborator he became. Following the formation of the International Psycho-Analytical Association (1910) he served as its first president from 1911 until his break with Freud in 1911.

Jung continued to practice in Zurich and to develop his own system of analytical psychology. He became professor of psychology at the Federal Institute of Technology in Zurich (1933–41) and was appointed professor of medical psychology at the University of Basel in 1943 but was forced to resign almost immediately for health reasons. He continued however to write, hold regular seminars, and take patients until well over 80.

Like Alfred Adler, who had broken away from Freudian orthodoxy earlier, Jung minimized the sexual cause of neuroses but, unlike Adler, he continued to emphasize the role of the unconscious. His final break with Freud followed publication of his *Wandlungen und Symbole de Libido* (1912) translated into English in 1916 as *Psychology of the Unconscious*. To the 'personal' unconscious of the Freudian he added the 'collective unconscious' stocked with a number of 'congenital conditions of intuition' or archetypes. In search of such archetypes Jung spent long periods with the Pueblo of Arizona, and visited Kenya, North Africa, and India, and also sought for them in dreams, folklore, and the literature of alchemy.

Jung also emphasized the importance of personality and in his *Psychologische Typen* (1921; Psychological Types) introduced his distinction between introverts and extroverts.

JUSSIEU, Antoine-Laurent de (b. Apr. 12, 1748; Lyons, France; d. Sept. 17, 1836; Paris) French plant taxonomist.

Jussieu was born into a family of eminent botanists. His uncles Antoine, Bernard, and Joseph de Jussieu all made important contributions to botany and his son, Adrien, subsequently continued the family tradition.

After graduating from the Jardin du Roi in 1770, Jussieu continued to work there, becoming subdemonstrator of botany in 1778. In his first publication in 1773, which reexamined the taxonomy of the Ranunculaceae, he advanced the idea of relative values of characters; the following year he applied this principle to other plant families.

Jussieu is remembered for introducing a natural classification system that distinguishes relationships between plants by considering a large number of characters, unlike the artificial Linnean system, which relies on only a few. In producing the famous *Genera Plantarum* (1789) Jussieu had access to a number of collections, including Linnaeus's herbarium and some of Joseph Banks's Australian specimens. He was also able to include many tropical angiosperm families thanks to the collection made by Philibert Commesson. From all this material he distinguished 15 classes and 100 families, and the value of his work can be seen in the fact that 76 of his 100 families remain in botanical nomenclature today. Both Georges Cuvier and Augustin de Candolle built on Jussieu's system.

Jussieu was in charge of the hospital of Paris during the French Revolution and was professor of botany at the National Natural History Museum (formerly the Jardin du Roi) from 1793 to 1826.

K

KAMEN, Martin David (b. Aug. 27, 1913; Toronto, Ontario) Canadian–American biochemist.

Kamen, the son of Russian immigrants, gained his BS (1933) and PhD (1936) from the University of Chicago. He then worked at the University of California Radiation Laboratory until 1944, and has held professorial posts at the universities of Washington (St. Louis), Brandeis, California, and Southern California.

At the Radiation Laboratory Kamen worked with the isotope oxygen–18, and, in collaboration with Samuel Ruben, showed that the source of the oxygen liberated in photosynthesis is water and not carbon dioxide. Better remembered however is his discovery, again with Ruben, of the long-lived isotope of carbon, carbon–14. In the hands of such scientists as Melvin Calvin, this isotope was to be a valuable tool in further investigations of photosynthesis and numerous other biochemical processes. Kamen has also done important work on the metabolism of photosynthetic bacteria, including the discovery that certain nitrogen-fixing bacteria evolve hydrogen in the light. His work with Sol Spiegelman indicated that there are polynucleotide intermediates involved in the transfer of genetic information. The discovery of messenger RNA confirmed this work. Kamen's later work has been on bacterial cytochromes (proteins involved in the electron transport chain, which operates during aerobic respiration).

KAMERLINGH-ONNES, Heike (b. Sept. 21, 1853; Groningen, Netherlands; d. Feb. 21, 1926; Leiden, Netherlands) Dutch physicist.

Kamerlingh-Onnes was educated at the University of Groningen, where he obtained a doctorate in 1879. In 1882 he was appointed professor of physics at Leiden, where he remained for the rest of his career. There he started the study of low-temperature physics, at first in order to gather experimental evidence for the atomic theory of matter. However, his interest turned to the problems involved in reaching extremely low temperatures and, in 1908, he became the first to succeed in liquefying helium. Matter at low temperatures — only a few degrees above absolute zero — has such strange properties that a completely new field of cryogenic physics was opened up. The first of these properties to be studied was superconductivity, which Kamerlingh-Onnes discovered in 1911. This phenomenon involves the total loss of resistance by certain metals at low temperatures.

Kamerlingh-Onnes was elected to the Royal Academy of Sciences in Amsterdam for this research and, in 1913, was awarded the Nobel Prize for physics.

KAMMERER, Paul (b. Aug. 17, 1880; Vienna; d. Sept. 23, 1926; Puchberg, Austria) Austrian zoologist.

Kammerer, the son of a prosperous factory owner, was educated at the University of Vienna where he obtained his PhD. He afterward joined the staff of the university's recently opened Institute of Experimental Biology, where he worked until the end of 1922 and soon established a reputation as a skilled experimentalist. Much of his work appeared to support the unorthodox doctrine of the inheritance of acquired characteristics associated with Jean Lamarck. The most famous of Kammerer's experiments concerned the breeding behavior of *Alytes obstetricans*, the midwife toad. Unlike most other toads this species mates on land; the male consequently lacks the nuptial pads, blackish swellings on the hand, possessed by water-breeding males in the mating season to enable them to grasp the female during copulation.

Kammerer undertook the experiment of inducing several generations of *Alytes* to copulate in water to see what changes resulted. This involved overcoming the difficult task of rearing the eggs in water and ensuring the developing tadpoles were kept free of fungal infection. After almost ten years following this line he noted that in the F$_3$ generation (great grandchildren of the original parents) grayish-black swellings, resembling rudimentary nuptial pads, could be seen on the upper, outer, and palmar sides of the first finger.

In 1923 Kammerer visited Britain in the hope of resolving a controversy that had arisen between himself and the leading Cambridge geneticist William Bateson. As virtually all his animals had been destroyed in the war he brought with him as evidence one preserved specimen and slides of the nuptial pads from the F5 generation made some ten years earlier. His lectures at Cambridge and to the Linnean Society were successful and none of the eminent biologists who examined Kammerer's specimen noticed anything suspect.

However when, early in 1926, G. Noble of the American Museum of Natural History came to examine the specimen in Vienna he found no nuptial pads, only blackened areas caused by the injection of ink. Despite the support of the institute's director, Hans Przibram, several possible explanations of the obvious fraud, and a still-open invitation from Moscow to establish an experimental institute there,

Kammerer shot himself some six months after Noble's visit.

Kammerer had in fact carried out a whole series of experiments of which the work with *Alytes* was but a part, and for him not the most important part. In 1909 he claimed to have induced inherited color adaptation in salamander, and by cutting the siphons of the sea squirt *Ciona intestinalis*, to have induced hereditary elongations. The few people who attempted to repeat Kammerer's results were unsuccessful although in certain cases Kammerer was able to claim, with some justification, that his protocols had not been scrupulously followed.

KAMP, Peter van de *See* VAN DE KAMP, Peter.

KANE, Sir Robert John (b. Sept. 24, 1809; Dublin; d. Feb. 16, 1890; Dublin) Irish chemist and educationalist.

Kane, the son of a manufacturing chemist, studied medicine at Trinity College, Dublin, and became professor of chemistry there in 1831. The following year he founded the *Dublin Journal of Medical Science*. He was president of Queen's College, Cork, from 1845 until 1873 and president of the Royal Irish Academy in 1877. In 1873 he was appointed the commissioner of national education and in 1880 he became vice-chancellor of Queen's University, Belfast. He was knighted in 1846.

In his books Kane did much to try and spread the new chemistry and show its relevance to industrial Ireland. After his early work *Elements of Practical Pharmacy*, he published his *Elements of Practical Chemistry* (1841–43). His most famous work, however, was his *Industrial Resources of Ireland* (1844), which caught the attention of Peel and led to his becoming an adviser to the government on the development of industry and education in Ireland and his sitting on the commission in 1846 to investigate the potato blight.

Kane's main work was that of administering and encouraging institutions rather than that of a creative scientist. His attempts to stimulate Irish industry and science were unfortunately held back by the famine and its consequences.

KANT, Immanuel (b. Apr. 22, 1724, Königsberg, now Kaliningrad in the Soviet Union; d. Feb. 12, 1804; Königsberg) German philosopher.

The son of a saddle maker and the grandson of a Scottish immigrant, Kant was educated at the University of Königsberg. Owing to interruptions necessary to fulfil family obligations it was not until 1755 that Kant, who had studied mathematics and physics, received his doctorate. He remained on the university staff, as a *Privatdozent* until 1770 when he was appointed to the chair of logic and metaphysics, a post he occupied until his retirement in 1797.

Apart from his influential philosophical works, Kant's first significant scientific publication was his *The Theory of the Heavens* (1755), which contained the first statement of the nebular hypothesis, an account of the origin of solar systems and perhaps better known in the later version of Pierre Simon Laplace (q.v.).

A more pervasive influence was exerted by Kant however in his *Metaphysische Angfangsgründe der Naturwissenschaft* (1786; Metaphysical Foundations of Natural Science). Here he squarely faced the problem of action at a distance arising from Newtonian mechanics. How could gravity act over the vast distances of space once the idea that causes act continuously in space had been rejected? He answered that there were two basic forces, attractive or gravitational and repulsive or elastic. While the latter required physical contact to operate, the former was "possible without a medium", acts immediately at a distance and "penetrates space without filling it."

Such ideas, together with his rejection of classical atomism in favor of the infinite divisibility of matter, were not just idle philosophical speculations. they were to exercise much influence over Michael Faraday in his later development of field theory, one of the great ideas of modern science.

KAPITZA, Pyotr (Peter) Leonidovich (b. July 9, 1894; Kronstadt, now in the Soviet Union) Soviet physicist.

Kapitza was educated at the Petrograd Polytechnic Institute and Petrograd Physical and Technical Institute (1918–21), and lectured at the Leningrad Polytechnic Institute from 1919 to 1921. From 1921 to 1924 he was involved in magnetic research at the Cavendish Laboratory of Cambridge University, England, under Ernest Rutherford and gained his PhD there in 1923. He was made director of the Royal Society Mond Laboratory at Cambridge in 1930. In 1934 he paid a visit to his homeland but was detained by the Soviet authorities. The next year Kapitza was made director of a newly founded research institute in Moscow — the Institute for Physical Problems — and was able to continue the line of his Cambridge research through the purchase of his original equipment. He worked there until 1946 when, apparently, he fell into disfavor with Stalin for declining to work on nuclear weapons. He was held under house arrest until 1955, when he was able to resume his work at the Institute.

Kapitza's most significant work in low-temperature physics was on the viscosity of the form of liquid helium known as He–II. This he (and, independently, J. F. Allen and A. D. Misener) found to exist in a 'superfluid' state — escaping from tightly sealed vessels and exhibiting unusual flow behavior. Kapitza found that He–II is in a macroscopic quantum state with perfect atomic order. In a series of experiments, he found also that a novel form of internal convection occurs in He–II.

Besides work on the unusual properties

of helium, Kapitza also devised a lique-faction technique for the gas, which is the basis of present-day helium liquefiers, and was able to produce large quantities of liquid hydrogen, helium, and oxygen. The availability of liquid helium has led to the production of electric superconductors and enabled much other work at extremely low temperatures to proceed. Kapitza also created very high magnetic fields for his experiments, and his record of 500 kilo-gauss in 1924 was not surpassed until 1956. Kapitza's low-temperature work was honored after almost forty years by the award of the 1978 Nobel Prize for physics.

From 1955, Kapitza headed the Soviet Committee for Interplanetary Flight and played an important part in the pre-parations for the first Soviet satellite laun-chings. In his career, Kapitza has collected many awards from scientific institutions of both East and West, including the Order of Lenin on six occasions.

KAPTEYN, Jacobus Cornelius (b. Jan. 19, 1851; Barneveld, Netherlands; d. June 18, 1922; Amsterdam) Dutch astronomer.

Kapteyn studied at Utrecht University and became professor of astronomy at the University of Groningen in 1878. Kapteyn was a very careful stellar observer and using David Gill's photographs of the southern hemisphere skies, he published in 1904 a catalog of over 450 000 stars within 19 degrees of the south celestial pole. He repeated William Herschel's count of the stars by sampling various parts of the heavens and supported Herschel's view that the Galaxy was lens-shaped with the Sun near the center; but his estimate of its size was different from Herschel's — 55 000 light-years long and 11 000 light-years thick. He pioneered new methods for investigating the distribution of stars in space.

Kapteyn discovered the star, now called *Kapteyn's star*, with the second greatest proper motion — 8.73 seconds annual motion compared to the 10″.3 of Barnard's star. He found this as part of a wider study of the general distribution of the motions of stars in the sky. To his surprise he found, in 1904, that they could be divided into two clear streams: about 3/5 of all stars seem to be heading in one direction and the other 2/5 in the opposite direction. The first stream is directed toward Orion and the second to Scutum, and a line joining them would be parallel to the Milky Way. Kapteyn was unable to explain this phenomena; it was left to his pupil Jan Oort (q.v.) to point out that this is a straightforward consequence of galactic rotation.

KARRER, Paul (b. Apr. 21, 1889; Moscow; d. June 18, 1971; Zurich, Switzerland) Swiss chemist.

Karrer, the son of a dentist, was educated at the University of Zurich where he obtained his PhD. After working in Frankfurt he returned to the University of Zurich in 1918 where he served as professor of chemistry until his retirement in 1959.

Karrer began his research career work-ing on the chemistry of plant pigments. Although he tackled a wide variety of such pigments his most significant result was his determination, by 1930, of the structure of carotene, the yellow pigment found in such vegetables as carrots. By 1931 he had also worked out the structure of vitamin A and synthesized it. The similarity between the two molecules did not escape Karrer's attention and it was later shown that vitamin A is derived from the breakdown of carotene in the liver. Karrer went on to synthesize vitamin B_2 (riboflavin) in 1935 and vitamin E (tocopherol) in 1938.

In 1937 Karrer was awarded, with Nor-man Haworth, the Nobel Chemistry Prize for his work on the "constitution of caro-tenoids, flavins, and vitamins A and B." Karrer was also the author of a much respected textbook, *Lehrbuch der organ-ischen Chemie* (1927; Textbook of Organic Chemistry).

KASTLER, Alfred (b. May 3, 1902; Gebweiler, now Guebwiller in France) French physicist.

Kastler, who was educated at the Ecole Normale Supérieure, originally taught at the University of Bordeaux where he became professor of physics in 1938. He moved to the University of Paris in 1941 where he remained until his retirement in 1972.

Kastler has worked on double-resonance techniques of spectroscopy, using absorption by both optical and radiofrequency radiation to study energy levels in atoms. He also introduced the technique known as 'optical pumping' — a method of exciting atoms to a different energy state. In practical terms Kastler's work led to new frequency standards and new methods for the measurement of weak magnetic fields. Kastler received the 1966 Nobel Physics Prize for his work on double resonance.

KATZ, Bernard (b. Mar. 26, 1911; Leipzig, now in East Germany) German–British neurophysiologist.

Katz received his MD from the University of Leipzig in 1934 and his PhD, under Archibald Hill, from the University of London in 1938. He spent the war in Australia first working with John Eccles and later in the Royal Australian Air Force as a radar operator. Katz returned to London in 1946 to University College and in 1952 became professor of biophysics, a post he retained until his retirement in 1978.

In 1936 Henry Dale demonstrated that peripheral nerves act by releasing the chemical acetylcholine in response to a nerve impulse. To find how this secretion takes place Katz, working in collaboration with the British biophysicist, Paul Fatt, inserted a micropipette at a neuromuscular junction to record the 'end-plate potential' or EPP. He noted a random deflection on the oscilloscope with an amplitude of about 0.5 millivolt even in the absence of all stimulation. At first he assumed such a reading to be interference arising from the machine but the application of curare, an acetycholine antagonist, by abolishing the apparently random EPPs, showed the activity in the nerves is real.

Consequently Katz proposed his quantum hypothesis. He suggested that nerve endings secrete small amounts of acetylcholine in a random manner in specific amounts or quanta. When a nerve is stimulated it does not begin secreting but instead enormously increases the number of quanta of acetycholine released. Katz was able to produce a good deal of evidence for this hypothesis, which he later presented in his important work *Nerve, Muscle and Synapse* (1966).

It was mainly for this work that Katz shared the 1970 Nobel Prize for physiology or medicine with Julius Axelrod and Ulf von Euler.

KEELER, James Edward (b. Sept. 10, 1857; La Salle, Illinois; d. Aug. 12, 1900; San Francisco, California) American astronomer.

In 1881 Keeler graduated from Johns Hopkins University becoming an assistant at the Allegheny Observatory. In 1888 he moved to the Lick Observatory at Mount Hamilton, California, for a short period but returned as director to Allegheny in 1891, being appointed professor of astrophysics in the Western University of Pennsylvania in the same year. He became director of Lick in 1898.

Using spectroscopic methods Keeler made several important discoveries. In 1895 he showed that the rings of Saturn do not rotate uniformly but that the inner border is rotating much faster than the outer. The difference is quite striking, as the innermost edge revolves in about 4 hours while the system's outermost edge needs over 14 hours. This is only possible if the rings are not solid but made from numerous small particles. He also worked on nebulae, photographing and taking the spectra of hundreds. He showed that about 3/4 of them had a spiral structure and demonstrated that their line-of-sight motion showed that they are receding and advancing like the stars. He further studied the spectra of the Orion Nebula and showed that the bright lines in its spectra correspond to the dark lines in the stellar spectra. He was one of the growing band of astronomers who failed to see the supposed canals on Mars despite using a new 36-inch (91-cm) refractor at Allegheny. He died when only 42.

KEENAN, Philip Childs (b. Mar. 31, 1908; Bellevue, Pennsylvania) American astronomer.

Keenan graduated in 1929 from the University of Arizona and obtained his PhD from the University of Chicago in 1932. He worked initially at Chicago's Yerkes Observatory from 1929 until 1942 when he joined the Bureau of Ordnance. With the return of peace Keenan was appointed to the staff of the Perkins Observatory of Ohio State University, becoming professor of astronomy in 1956.

Keenan is best known for his work with William Morgan and Edith Kellman on their *Atlas of Stellar Spectra with an Outline of Spectral Classification* (1943). It was this work that formed the basis for the MKK system of classifying stars by their luminosity in addition to their spectral type.

KEILIN, David (b. Mar. 21, 1887; Moscow; d. Feb. 27, 1963; Cambridge, England) British biologist and entomologist.

Educated at Cambridge University, England, Keilin was professor of biology at Cambridge (1931–52) and also director of the Cambridge Moltena Institute. His most important research was the discovery of the respiratory pigment cytochrome, which, he demonstrated, is present in animal, yeast, and higher plant cells. He also studied the biochemistry of the *Diptera* (true flies), and investigated the respiratory systems and adaptations of certain dipterous larvae and pupae.

KEIR, James (b. Sept. 29, 1735; Edinburgh; d. Oct. 11, 1820; West Bromwich, England) British chemist and industrialist.

Keir was the youngest of 18 children. He came from a prosperous family, being educated at Edinburgh High School and Edinburgh University where he started a lifelong friendship with Erasmus Darwin. He left the university without graduating to join the army and served in the West Indies reaching the rank of captain before resigning in 1768.

Keir settled near Birmingham and became a leading member of the famous Lunar society, an organization founded to promote interest in science and its applications. At this time Keir translated Pierre Macquer's *Dictionary of Chemistry* (1776), which was one of the key volumes whereby chemical knowledge was transmitted to mechanics and engineers. He served as an assistant to Joseph Priestley during his stay in Birmingham. In 1778 he acted as general manager for the firm of Boulton and Watt.

Together with James Watt and Matthew Boulton, Keir started a venture to obtain soda from nonvegetable sources. He tried to extract it from potassium and sodium sulfates, which were waste products of the vitriol industry. He passed these waste products slowly through a sludge of lime, producing an insoluble calcium sulfate and a weak solution of alkali. He then used this in soap production. By 1801 Keir's alkali factory, which he founded in 1780, was paying excise duty on the production of £10000 worth of soap. As a pure producer of alkali the venture was not a success; the future was to lie with the Leblanc process.

KEITH, Sir Arthur (b. Feb. 5, 1866; Old Machan, Scotland; d. Jan. 7, 1955; Downe, England) British anatomist.

Keith, the son of a farmer, was educated at the University of Aberdeen, where he qualified as a doctor in 1888. He served as a medical officer in Siam (now Thailand) from 1889 until 1892, when his interest in the comparative anatomy of the primates was first aroused. On his return to Europe he studied anatomy in Leipzig and London before being appointed (1895) demonstrator in anatomy at the London Hospital. In 1908 Keith moved to the Royal College of Surgeons, where he served as curator of the Hunterian Museum until his retirement in 1933.

On 18 December, 1912, Arthur Woodward and Charles Dawson announced to the Geological Society the discovery at Piltdown in Sussex of a remarkable skull, which apparently combined the mandible of an ape with the cranium of a man. Here at last, it was felt, was solid evidence for the antiquity of man. Although some at the meeting were skeptical of the find, suggesting that the skull and jaw must have come from two different individuals, Keith was not among them. It thus appeared that a man with a cranial capacity of 1500 cc (as estimated by Keith) and with the jaw of an ape had coexisted with the mastodon. Keith, in the first edition of his *Antiquity of Man* (1915), dated Piltdown man to the beginning of the Pliocene, which was then assumed to be about a million years ago. With the change in geological fashion Keith was forced to halve the date of Piltdown man in the second edition of his book (1925).

In 1915 Keith estimated the actual separation of man from the apes to have taken place in the lower Miocene, then considered to be some 2–4 million years ago. This meant that Keith was unable to accommodate the discovery of the famous Taung skull by Raymond Dart in 1924, and consequently he denied that Dart's *Australopithecus* was either man or a link between ape and man, considering it to be a pure ape having affinities with two living apes, the gorilla and the chimpanzee.

Keith lived long enough to witness the exposure of Piltdown man by Kenneth Oakley in 1949, using modern fluorine dating techniques. These showed the fossil to date back only as far as the Pleistocene, while later work (1953) revealed its fraudulent nature by assigning markedly different dates to the skull and jaw. When Oakley made a special journey to the 87-year old Keith to inform him of his results, he commented "I think you are probably right, but it will take me some time to adjust myself to the new view."

KEKULÉ VON STRADONITZ, Friedrich August (b. Sept. 7, 1829; Darmstadt, now in West Germany; d. July 13, 1896; Bonn) German chemist.

As a youth Kekulé showed considerable skill in drawing and was consequently encouraged to be an architect. Although he began as a student of architecture at Giessen he soon switched, despite family opposition, to the study of chemistry, which he continued abroad. He first went to Paris in the period 1851–52 where he studied under Jean Dumas and Charles Gerhardt who influenced him greatly. He worked in Switzerland for a while before taking a post in England in 1854–55 as a laboratory assistant at St. Bartholomew's Hospital, London. While in London he met and was influenced by Alexander Williamson and William Odling. He accepted an unsalaried post at the University of Heidelberg before his appointment to the chair of chemistry at Ghent in 1858. He then moved to the chemistry chair at the University of Bonn in 1867, where he remained for the rest of his life.

Kekulé's main work was done on the structure of the carbon atom and its compounds. It has often been claimed that he had changed his career from the architecture of buildings to the architecture of molecules. Certainly, after Kekulé it was much easier to visualize the form of atoms and their combinations. In 1852 Edward Frankland had pointed out that each kind of atom can combine with only so many other atoms. Thus hydrogen can combine with only one other atom at a time, oxygen could combine with two, nitrogen with three, and carbon with four. Such combining power soon became known as the valency (valence) of an atom. Each atom would be either uni-, bi-, tri-, quadrivalent, or some higher figure.

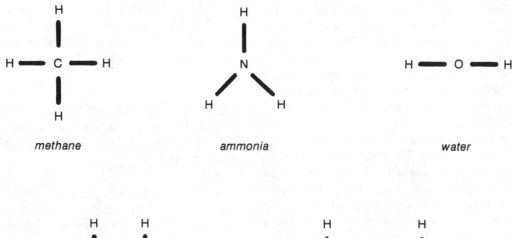

methane ammonia water

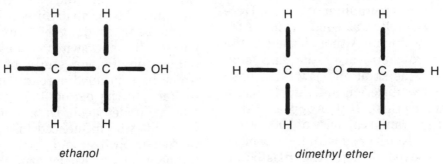

ethanol dimethyl ether

In 1858 both Kekulé and Archibald Couper saw how to use this insight of Frankland to revolutionize organic chemistry. They both assumed that carbon was quadrivalent and that one of the four bonds of the carbon atom could be used to join with another carbon atom. The idea came to him, he later claimed, while traveling on a London bus to Clapham Road. He fell into a reverie, "and lo, the atoms were gamboling before my eyes ... I saw frequently how two smaller atoms united to form a pair; how a larger one embraced two smaller ones; how still larger ones kept hold of three or even four of the smaller ... I saw how the longer ones formed a chain ... (and then) the cry of the conductor 'Clapham Road' awakened me from my dreaming; but I spent part of the night in putting on paper at least sketches of these dream forms." He published his results in 1858 in his paper *The Constitution and the Metamorphoses of Chemical Compounds and the Chemical Nature of Carbon* and in the first volume of his *Lehrbuch der organische Chemie*

(1859; Textbook of Organic Chemistry).

The diagrams of carbon compounds used today come not from Kekulé but from Alexander Crum Brown in 1865. Kekulé's own notation, known as 'Kekulé sausages', in which atoms were represented by a cumbersome system of circles, was soon dropped. The gains from such representations were immediate. It can be seen why two molecules could have the same number of atoms of each element and yet differ in properties. Thus C_2H_6O represents both ethanol and dimethyl ether (see illustration). If the rules of valence are observed these are the only two ways in which two carbon, six hydrogen, and one oxygen atom can be combined and indeed these are the only two compounds of the formula ever observed.

While Kekulé had dramatic success demonstrating how organic compounds could be constructed from carbon chains, one set of compounds, the aromatics, resisted all such treatment. Benzene, discovered by Michael Faraday in 1825, had

Kekulé's original
formula for benzene, with
a ring of alternating
double and single bonds.

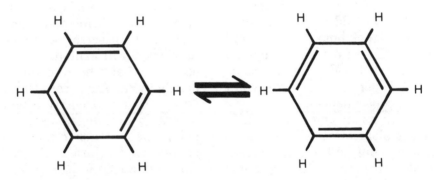

Later he proposed an oscillating structure with two forms in equilibrium with each other. This explained the isomers of benzene compounds.

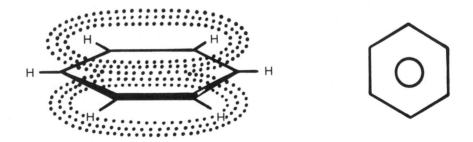

BENZENE Structures

The modern molecular-orbital picture is of a ring with six equal bonds with electrons from double bonds delocalized above and below the rings.

431

the formula C_6H_6, which, on the assumption of a quadrivalent carbon atom, just could not be represented as any kind of chain. The best that could be done with alternating single and double carbon bonds would still violate the valence rules, for at the end of the chain the carbon atoms will both have an unfilled bond. Kekulé once more has left a description of how the solution of the puzzle came to him. In 1890 he recalled that while working on his textbook in 1865, "I dozed off. Again the atoms danced before my eyes. This time the smaller groups remained in the background. My inner eye ... now distinguished bigger forms of manifold configurations. Long rows, more densely joined; everything in motion, contorting and turning like snakes. And behold what was that? One of the snakes took hold of its own tail and whirled derisively before my eyes. I woke up as though I had been struck by lightning; again I spent the rest of the night working out the consequences."

The snake with its tail in its mouth is in fact an ancient alchemical symbol and is named Ouroboros but, to Kekulé, it meant a more prosaic image, that of a ring. For if the two ends of the benzene chain are joined to each other then benzene will have been shown to have a ring structure in which the valence rules have all been observed. Again the rewards in understanding were immediate. It was now obvious why substitution for one of benzene's hydrogen atoms always produced the same compound. The mono-substituted derivative C_6H_5X was completely symmetrical whichever H atom it replaced. Each of the hydrogen atoms were replaced by NH_2 and in each case the same compound, aniline $C_6H_5.NH_2$, was obtained.

Such was the revolution in organic chemistry initiated by Kekulé. Together with new methods introduced by Stanislao Cannizzaro at Karlsruhe in 1860 for the determination of atomic weight, a new age of chemistry was about to dawn in which the conflicts and uncertainties of the first half of the 19th century would be replaced by a unified chemical theory, notation, and practice. After this it comes as something

of a shock to discover that Kekulé had no firm belief in the existence of atoms. Whether they exist he argued in 1867 "has but little significance from a chemical point of view; its discussion belongs rather to metaphysics. In chemistry we have only to decide whether the assumption of atoms is an hypothesis adapted to the explanation of chemical phenomena."

KELLNER, Karl (b. Sept. 1, 1851; Vienna; d. June 7, 1905; Vienna) Austrian chemical engineer.

Kellner worked in Vienna as an engineer. In 1894 he took out a patent on the manufacture of caustic soda from the electrolysis of brine and founded the Konsortium für Electrochemische Industrie at Salzburg for its exploitation. The same discovery had also been made quite independently by the American, Hamilton Castner (q.v.). To avoid costly litigation the two inventors exchanged patents, and plants using the *Castner–Kellner process* were opened at Niagara Falls in 1896 and in England in 1897 at Runcorn in Cheshire.

KELVIN, William Thomson, Baron Kelvin of Largs (b. June 26, 1824; Belfast; d. Dec. 17, 1907; Largs, Scotland) British theoretical and experimental physicist.

Kelvin was an extremely precocious child intellectually and he matriculated at Glasgow University at the astonishingly early age of 10. He went on to Cambridge after which he returned to Glasgow to become professor of natural philosophy. He was to occupy this chair for 53 years. It was in Glasgow that Kelvin organized and ran one of Britain's first adequately equipped physical laboratories. In 1892 in recognition of his contributions to science he was raised to the peerage as Baron Kelvin of Largs. Kelvin was a devout member of the Scottish Free Church.

Kelvin's work on electromagnetism is second only to that of Michael Faraday and James Clerk Maxwell. Together with

Faraday he was responsible for the introduction of the concept of an electromagnetic field. Kelvin was of a much more mathematical turn of mind than Faraday, but it was left to Maxwell to weld the ideas of Faraday and Kelvin together into a powerful, elegant, and succinct mathematical theory. But Maxwell's work would have been greatly hampered without some of the penetrating suggestions made by Kelvin. Particularly important is a fundamental paper of 1847 in which Kelvin drew an analogy between an electrostatic field and an incompressible elastic solid. Kelvin made many other innovations including the introduction of the use of vectors to represent magnetic induction and magnetic force. He also put his knowledge of electromagnetism to use in many practical inventions of which the transatlantic electric telegraph cable and the mirror galvanometer were among the most important.

Kelvin's other great area of work was thermodynamics. He was one of the first to understand and appreciate the importance of James Joule's seminal work in the field. In his 1852 paper on the *Dissipation of Mechanical Energy* Kelvin set out the fundamentally important law of conservation of energy that was to be so important in the physics of the second half of the 19th century. In his work on thermodynamics Kelvin assimilated and developed the work of the great pioneers of the subject, Nicolas Carnot and Joule. He also collaborated with Joule in experimental work. One of the important results of Kelvin's work was his introduction of the concept of *absolute zero* and his recognition of the theoretical importance of the absolute scale of temperature, which is named in his honor. Kelvin was able to calculate the value of absolute zero from theoretical considerations. One of the first formulations of the second law of thermodynamics was given by Kelvin. With Joule (q.v.) he first demonstrated the *Joule–Kelvin effect*. He also made important contributions to the theory of elasticity and some basic contributions to hydrodynamics in which he collaborated with George Stokes.

KENDALL, Edward Calvin (b. Mar. 8, 1886; South Norwalk, Connecticut; d. May 4, 1972; Rochester, Minnesota) American biochemist.

Kendall, a dentist's son, studied chemistry at Columbia University where he obtained his PhD in 1910. After working briefly at St. Luke's Hospital in New York from 1911 to 1914, Kendall moved to the Mayo Foundation in Rochester, Minnesota, where from 1921 to 1951 he served as professor of physiological chemistry.

In 1914 Kendall achieved an early success by isolating the active constituent of the thyroid gland. The importance of hormones in the physiology of the body had become apparent through the work of William Bayliss and Ernest Starling on the pancreas. Kendall was able to demonstrate the presence of a physiologically active compound of the amino acid tyrosine and iodine, which he named thyroxin.

Kendall was led from this to investigate the more complex activity of the adrenal gland. This gland secretes a large number of steroids, many of which Kendall succeeded in isolating. Four compounds, labeled A, B, E, and F, seemed to possess significant physiological activity. They were shown to affect the metabolism of proteins and carbohydrates and in their absence animals seemed to lose the ability to deal with toxic substances. It was therefore hoped that some of these compounds might turn out to be therapeutically useful. After much effort sufficient compound A was obtained but, to Kendall's surprise and disappointment, it was shown to have little effect on Addison's disease, a complaint caused by a deficient secretion from the adrenal cortex. Kendall was more successful with his compound E — later known as cortisone to avoid confusion with vitamin E — when in 1947 a practical method for its production was established. Clinical trials showed it to be effective against rheumatoid arthritis. It was for this work that Kendall shared the 1950 Nobel Prize for physiology or medicine with Tadeus Reichstein and Philip Hench.

KENDREW, Sir John Cowdery (b. Mar. 24, 1917; Oxford, England) British biochemist.

Kendrew graduated in natural science from Cambridge University in 1939, and spent the war years working for the Ministry of Aircraft Production, becoming an honorary wing commander in 1944. In 1946 he joined Max Perutz at Cambridge and, like Perutz, used x-ray diffraction techniques to study the crystalline structure of proteins, particularly that of the muscle protein myoglobin. X-ray diffraction, or crystallography, involves placing a crystal in front of a photographic plate and rotating the crystal in a beam of x-rays. The pattern of dots that is formed on the plate by the x-rays can be analyzed to find the positions of the atoms in the crystal. The technique had been used successfully to show the structures of small molecules but Kendrew's progress with the much larger myoglobin structure was slow, especially since diffraction patterns yield no information on the phases of the directed x-rays. However in 1953 Perutz made a breakthrough by incorporating atoms of heavy elements into the protein crystals. Kendrew modified this new method and applied it successfully in his myoglobin studies, so that four years later he had built up a rough model of the three-dimensional structure of myoglobin. By 1959 he had greatly clarified the structure and could pinpoint most of the atoms.

Kendrew and Perutz received the 1962 Nobel Prize for chemistry for their work on protein structure. Kendrew was knighted in 1974 and is presently director general of the European Molecular Biology Laboratory in Heidelberg.

KENNELLY, Arthur Edwin (b. Dec. 17, 1861; near Bombay, India; d. June 18, 1939; Boston, Massachusetts) British–American electrical engineer.

Kennelly, the son of an Irish-born employee of the East India Company, was educated in Europe. He left school at the age of 14 to become office boy to the London Society of Telegraph Engineers. From 1876 to 1886 he worked for the Eastern Telegraph Company, acquiring an engineering education through practice and independent study. He emigrated to America in 1887 and became an assistant to Thomas Edison and a consulting engineer. In 1894, together with E. J. Houston, he founded his own consulting firm. Kennelly was professor of electrical engineering at Harvard University from 1902 to his retirement in 1930; between 1913 and 1925 he held a second appointment as professor of electrical communication at the Massachusetts Institute of Technology.

Kennelly made many contributions to the theory and practice of electrical engineering. These included the representation of quantities by complex variables, a mathematical treatment that helped in understanding the behavior of electrical circuits. In 1902 he explained the Atlantic transmission of radio waves by suggesting that they were reflected back to Earth by some layer of electrically charged particles in the upper atmosphere (suggested independently by Oliver Heaviside and called the *Kennelly–Heaviside layer*). Kennelly was a great scientific administrator and made contributions to the development of electrical units and standards.

KEPLER, Johannes (b. Dec. 27, 1571; Würtemburg, now in West Germany; d. Nov. 15, 1630; Regensburg, now in West Germany) German astronomer.

Kepler's grandfather had been the local burgomaster but his father seems to have been a humble soldier away on military service for most of Kepler's early youth. His mother was described by Kepler as "quarrelsome, of a bad disposition." She was later to be accused of witchcraft. Originally intended for the Church, he graduated from the University of Tübingen in 1591 and went on to study in the theological faculty. In 1594 he was offered a teaching post in mathematics in the seminary at Gratz in Styria. It was from his teacher, Mästlin, who was one of the earliest scholars fully to comprehend and accept the work of Nicolaus Copernicus, that the young Kepler acquired his early Copernicanism. In addition to his teaching at Gratz and such usual duties as mathematicians were expected to do in those days Kepler published his first book — *Mysterium cosmographicum* (1596). The book expresses very clearly the belief in a mathematical harmony underlying the universe, a harmony he was to spend the rest of his life searching for. In this work he tried to show that the universe was structured on the model of Plato's five regular solids. Although the work verges on the cranky and obsessive it shows that Kepler was already searching for some more general mathematical relationship than could be found in Copernicus.

He married in 1597 shortly before he was forced to leave Gratz when, in 1598, all Lutheran teachers and preachers were ordered to leave the city immediately. Fortunately for Kepler he had an invitation to work with Tycho Brahe who had recently become the Imperial Mathematician in Prague. Tycho was the greatest observational astronomer of the century and he had with him the results of his last 20 years' observations. Kepler joined him in 1600 and although their relationship was not an easy one it was certainly profitable. Tycho assigned him the task of working out the orbit of Mars. Somewhat rashly Kepler boasted he would solve it in a week — it took him eight years of unremitting effort. Not only did Kepler lack the computing assistance now taken for granted but he was also working before the invention of logarithms. It was during this period that he discovered his first two laws, and thus, with Galileo, began to offer an alternative physics to that of Aristotle. The first law asserts that planets describe elliptic orbits with the Sun at one focus while the second law asserts that the line joining the Sun to a planet sweeps out equal areas in equal times. The laws were published in his magnum opus *Astronomia nova* (1610; New Astronomy).

Tycho had died in 1601 leaving Kepler with his post, his observations, and a strong obligation to complete and publish his tables under the patronage of their master, the emperor Rudolph II. This obligation was to prove even more onerous and time consuming than the orbit of Mars. It involved dealing with Tycho's predatory kin, attempting, vainly, to extract money from the emperor to pay for the work, which he ended up financing himself, and trying to find a suitable printer. All this, it must be realized, was done against the background of the Thirty Years War, marauding soldiery, and numerous epidemics. The *Tabulae Rudolphinae* was not completed until 1627 but remained the standard work for the best part of a century.

While serving the emperor in Prague, Kepler had also produced a major work *Optics* (1604), which included a good approximation of Snell's law, improved refraction tables, and discussion of the pinhole camera. In the same year he observed only the second new star visible to the naked eye since antiquity. He showed, as Tycho had done with the new star of 1572, that it exhibited no parallax and must therefore be situated far beyond the solar system. He studied and wrote upon the bright comet of 1607 — later to be called Halley's comet — and those of 1618 in his *Three Tracts on Comets* (1619). His final work in Prague the *Dioptrics* (1611) has been called the first work of geometrical optics.

In 1611 Kepler's wife and son died, civil war broke out in Prague, and Rudolph was forced to abdicate. Kepler moved to Linz in the following year to take up a post as a mathematics teacher and surveyor. Here he stayed for 14 years. He married again in 1613. While in Linz he produced a work that, starting from the simple problem of measuring the volume of his wine cask, moved on to more general problems of mensuration — *Nova stereometria* (1615). One further crisis he had to face was his mother's trial for witchcraft in Würtemburg. The trial dragged on for three years before she was finally freed. His greatest work of this period *Harmonices mundi*

(1619) returns to the search for the underlying mathematical harmony expressed in his first work of 1596. It is here that he stated his third law: the squares of the periods of any two planets are proportional to the cubes of their mean distance from the Sun. After the completion of the Rudolphine tables Kepler took service under a new patron, the Imperial General Wallenstein. He settled at Sagan in Silesia. In return for the horoscopes Wallenstein expected from him Kepler was provided with a press, a generous salary, and the peace to publish his ephemerides and to prepare his work of science fiction — *A Dream, or Astronomy of the Moon* (1634). He left Sagan in 1630, during one of Wallenstein's temporary military setbacks, to see the emperor in Ratisbon hoping for a payment of the 12 000 florins still owed him. He died there of a fever a few days later.

As a scientist Kepler is of immense importance. Copernicus was in many ways a traditional thinker, still passionately committed to circles. Kepler broke away from this mode of thought and in so doing posed questions of planetary motion that it took a Newton to answer.

KERR, John (b. Dec. 17, 1824; Ardrossan, Scotland; d. Aug. 18, 1907; Glasgow, Scotland) British physicist.

Kerr studied at Glasgow University and carried out research work under Lord Kelvin. He taught mathematics at a training college in Glasgow. His most important achievement was the discovery that when glass and other insulators are placed in a strong electric field birefringence is caused (the *Kerr effect*). Kerr also described the behavior of polarized light when reflected from the polished pole of an electromagnet.

KERST, Donald William (b. Nov. 1, 1911; Galena, Illinois) American physicist.

Kerst's name is primarily associated with the development of the betatron, a machine capable of accelerating beta particles (electrons) to speeds approaching that of light. Graduating at the University of Wisconsin in 1937, Kerst went on to be assistant professor at the University of Illinois, becoming full professor in 1943. In 1939 he developed the idea of the cyclotron particle accelerator a stage further. He circulated electrons in a doughnut-shaped vacuum tube, guiding them round the circle in a magnetic field similar to that of a toroidal electrical transformer. The electrons are accelerated, but are kept in their circular orbits by increasing the magnetic field. Kerst was responsible for the building of the largest such machine (the betatron), completed at the University of Illinois in 1950, in which electrons attained energies of up to 310 MeV.

Kerst's work on the betatron, and other nuclear physics work primarily with the Van der Graaf generator, led to his involvement during World War II in the Los Alamos thermonuclear (atom-bomb) project, after which he returned to Illinois. He is now back at the University of Wisconsin, where he has been professor of physics since 1962. In 1945 he was awarded the Comstock Prize of the US National Academy of Sciences.

KETTLEWELL, Henry Bernard Davis (b. Feb. 24, 1907; d. May 1979) British geneticist and lepidopterist.

Kettlewell was educated at Cambridge University and St. Bartholomew's Hospital, London, where he gained his medical qualification in 1933. He practiced in Cranleigh and then worked as an anesthetist in Surrey. After the war he worked in South Africa at the International Locust Control Centre in Cape Town before returning to Britain in 1952 as research fellow in genetics at Oxford, a post he continued to hold until his retirement in 1974.

Kettlewell is best known for his work on the occurrence of melanism — black pigmentation in the epidermis of animals. In

1953 he set out to explain why, in the mid-19th century, certain moth species had a light coloration, which camouflaged them on such backgrounds as light tree trunks where they sat motionless during the day. However by the 1950s, of 760 species of larger moths in Britain 70 had changed their light color and markings for dark or even totally black coloration.

Kettlewell suspected that the success of the melanic form was linked with the industrial revolution and the consequent darkening of the trees by the vast amounts of smoke produced by the 19th-century factories. To test his hypothesis he released large numbers of the dark and light forms of the peppered moth, *Biston betularia*, in the polluted woods around Birmingham and in a distant unpolluted forest. As many of the released moths as possible were recaptured and when the results were analyzed it was found that the light form had a clear advantage over the dark in the unpolluted forest but in the polluted Birmingham woods the result was just the opposite. From this Kettlewell concluded that if the environment of a moth changes so that it is conspicuous by day, then the moth is ruthlessly hunted by predators until it mutates to a form better suited to its new environment. His work was seen as a convincing and dramatic confirmation of the Darwinian hypothesis of natural selection.

KETY, Seymour Solomon (b. Aug. 25, 1915; Philadelphia, Pennsylvania) American neurophysiologist.

Kety was educated at the University of Pennsylvania where he obtained his MD in 1940. He continued working there and was appointed professor of clinical physiology in 1948. In 1951 he also took on the directorship of the National Institutes of Health. Since 1967 he has been professor of psychiatry at Harvard.

Kety's first major success was his development of a treatment for lead poisoning using the lead-citrate complex. He later concentrated on measuring the

blood flow and energy metabolism of the brain. One of the most interesting results arising from this was his demonstration that the brain's energy consumption during sleep is the same as in the conscious state.

Kety later worked mainly on the role of biological mechanisms in mental illness. He pointed out that both schizophrenia and manic depression run in families. This led him to conclude that because genes can only express themselves through biochemical mechanisms, the hereditary nature of mental disorders suggests the involvement of biochemical substrates. However, although he started to examine the blood and urine of schizophrenics as early as 1957 for such biochemical substrates, none have yet been specifically identified.

KHORANA, Har Gobind (b. Jan. 9, 1922; Raipur, now in Pakistan) Indian–American chemist.

Khorana gained his BSc (1943) and MSc (1945) from the University of Punjab and then traveled to Liverpool University to work for his doctorate. On receiving his PhD in 1948, he did two years postdoctoral research in Switzerland before taking up a Nuffield Fellowship at Cambridge University. There he worked with Alexander Todd, who fired his interest in nucleic acid research — the field in which Khorana later made his name.

Shortly after Khorana joined Wisconsin University in 1960 he became interested in unraveling the genetic code. He synthesized each of the 64 nucleotide triplets that make up the code, and for this work received the Nobel Prize for physiology or medicine in 1968, sharing the award with Marshall Nirenberg and Robert Holley.

Khorana's next major achievement came in 1970, when he announced the synthesis of the first artificial gene. The same year he moved to the Massachusetts Institute of Technology, where, by 1976, his team had made a second gene, which (unlike the first) was capable of functioning in a living cell. Such work has far-reaching possibilities, bringing scientists a step nearer to understanding gene action. The future could see artificial genes being used to make valuable proteins (e.g. insulin) and perhaps to cure human hereditary diseases.

KIDD, John (b. Sept. 10, 1775; London; d. Sept. 17, 1851; Oxford, England) British chemist.

Kidd was the son of a merchant captain. He was educated at Oxford University, where he graduated in 1797, spending the next four years at Guy's Hospital in London. In 1803 he became the first Aldrichian Professor of Chemistry at Oxford. He stayed in this chair until 1822, when he became professor of physics.

In 1819 Kidd obtained naphthalene from coal tar. This aromatic hydrocarbon, which is used in mothballs, played an important role in the development of aniline dyes by Sir William Perkin 40 years later. Kidd also published in 1809 *Outlines of Mineralogy*. In 1833 he contributed to the 'Bridgewater Treatises'. This was a series commissioned by the earl of Bridgewater in his will in which eight scientists selected by the Royal Society would demonstrate "the Power, Wisdom, and Goodness of God, as manifested in the creation." Kidd's treatise was on *The Adaptation of External Nature to the Physical Condition of Man*.

KIDDINU (*fl.* 379 BC; Babylonia, now in Iraq) Babylonian astronomer.

Almost nothing is known about Kiddinu, although he was head of the astronomical school in the Babylonian city of Sippar, and some late classical writers such as Pliny refer to him as Kidenas. There are references to some lunar eclipse tables that Kiddinu had prepared and he is credited with a new method of construction of ephemerides (tables of planetary motion), the so-called 'System B'. He is also thought to have discovered the precession of the equinoxes — the slow westward motion of the equinoctial points that is caused by the rotation of the Earth's axis.

KIMURA, Motoo (b. Nov. 13, 1924; Okazaki, Japan) Japanese population geneticist.

Kimura was educated at Kyoto University and the University of Wisconsin where he gained his PhD in 1956. He joined the research staff of the National Institute of Genetics, Mishima, and has served since 1964 as head of the population genetics department.

From 1968 onward Kimura has been developing a cogent alternative to the neo-Darwinian synthesis as it emerged in the 1930s in the works of such scholars as J.B.S. Haldane. He has gathered evidence to show that certain mutations can increase in a population without necessarily having any selective advantage. He examined a number of mutant genes whose effects were not apparent in the phenotype and could only be detected by advanced chemical techniques. He found that adaptively they were neither better nor worse than the genes they replaced, concluding that, at the molecular level, most evolutionary changes are the result of 'random drift' of selectively equivalent mutant genes.

Kimura allows that at the level of the phenotype evolution is basically Darwinian but insists that the laws governing molecular evolution are clearly different. Such views have met with much opposition from Darwinians. They have argued that many of the apparently neutral mutations are, on closer examination, found to be selective; also many cases, such as human hemoglobin, do not seem to show the variants expected from Kimura's theory.

KING, Charles Glen (b. Oct. 22, 1896; Entiat, Washington) American biochemist.

King was educated at Washington State University and the University of Pittsburgh, where he obtained his PhD in 1923 and became professor of chemistry in 1930. He later moved to Columbia University in New York, where he held the chair of chemistry from 1946 until his retirement in 1962.

In 1928 Albert Szent-Györgyi isolated from the adrenal gland a substance that he named 'hexuronic acid'; he had in fact discovered vitamin C. It was left to King in 1932 to complete the work. He isolated from lemon juice and cabbages a substance, identical to Szent-Györgyi's hexuronic acid, that possessed powerful antiscorbutic properties. It was vitamin C, later called ascorbic acid. In the following year King determined its formula $(C_6H_8O_6)$.

KINSEY, Alfred Charles (b. June 23, 1894; Hoboken, New Jersey; d. Aug. 25, 1956, Bloomington, Indiana) American zoologist.

Educated at Bowdoin College and Harvard, Kinsey was professor of zoology (from 1920) and director of the Institute for Sex Research, Indiana University, which he helped found, from 1942 until his death.

Kinsey's researches on human sexual behavior, published as *Sexual Behavior in the Human Male* (1948) and *Sexual Behavior in the Human Female* (1953), have attracted much interest and some controversy. His work demonstrated that there was considerable variation in behavior in all social classes and helped to dispose of certain erroneous ideas, for example with regard to juvenile sexual activity as well as homosexuality. Even though based on many (about 18 500) carefully conducted personal interviews, Kinsey's findings have been criticized for sampling limitations and the general unreliability of personal communication in this sphere of human activity.

KIPPING, Frederic Stanley (b. Aug. 16, 1863; Manchester, England; d. May 1, 1949; Criccieth, Wales) British chemist.

Kipping, a banker's son, was educated at Owens College, the forerunner of Manchester University. After a period as chemist at the Manchester gas works and postgraduate work in Munich, Kipping took up his first academic appointment at Heriot-Watt College in Edinburgh in 1885. From 1890 to 1897 he was chief demonstrator at the City and Guilds College in London and in 1897 was appointed to the chair of chemistry at Nottingham University, where he remained until his retirement in 1936.

Kipping is best known as the author, with William Perkin, Jr., of *Organic Chemistry* (1894). This was one of the first works to be devoted to organic chemistry alone, and was the basic textbook for organic chemists for over fifty years.

One of the burning issues of the day when Kipping was an undergraduate was that of stereoisomerism, which had earlier been demonstrated in carbon and its compounds by Jacobus Van't Hoff. Working with William Pope, Kipping showed that such isomerism was not exclusive to carbon but was detectable in nitrogen and other atoms.

Kipping went on to show the same effect in silicon, discovering between 1905 and 1907 a number of asymmetric silicon compounds. This was the beginning of Kipping's exhaustive study of the chemistry of silicon, on which he published 51 papers.

KIRCHHOFF, Gustav Robert (b. Mar. 12, 1824; Königsberg, now Kaliningrad in the Soviet Union; d. Oct. 17, 1887; Berlin) German physicist.

Kirchhoff studied at Königsberg, graduating in 1847. Three years later he was appointed professor at Breslau. He moved to Heidelberg, where Robert Bunsen was professor of chemistry, in 1854.

Kirchhoff was one of the foremost physicists of the 19th century and is remembered as one of the founders of the science of spectroscopy. He is also known for *Kirchhoff's laws*, formulated in 1845 while he was still a student, which refer to the currents and electromotive forces in electrical networks.

In 1859 he published an explanation of the dark lines in the Sun's spectrum discovered by Josef von Fraunhofer, in which he suggested that they are due to absorption of certain wavelengths by substances in the Sun's atmosphere. He later formulated *Kirchhoff's law of radiation*, which concerns the emission and absorption of radiation by a hot body. It states that the rate of emission of energy by a body is equal to the rate at which the body absorbs energy (both emission and absorption being in a given direction at a given wavelength). Kirchhoff gave a final proof of this in 1861.

In about 1860 Bunsen was analyzing the colors given off by heating chemicals to incandescence, using colored glass to distinguish between similar shades. Kirchhoff joined this research when he suggested that the observation of spectral lines, by dispersing the light with a prism, would be a more precise way of testing the color of the light. Kirchhoff and Bunsen found that each substance emitted light that had its own unique pattern of spectral lines — a discovery that began the spectroscopic method of chemical analysis. In 1860, a few months after publishing these results, they discovered a new metal, which they called cesium and the next year found rubidium. Kirchhoff and Bunsen also constructed improved forms of the spectroscope for such work and Kirchhoff showed that, if a gas emitted certain wavelengths of light then it would absorb those wavelengths from light passing through it.

Kirchhoff was crippled by an accident in mid-life but remained in good spirits and, when his health forced him to stop experimental work in 1875, he was offered the chair of theoretical physics in Berlin. He remained there until his death 12 years later.

KIRKWOOD, Daniel (b. Sept. 27, 1814; Harford County, Maryland; d. June 11, 1895; Riverside, California) American astronomer.

Kirkwood became professor of mathematics at the University of Delaware in 1851, moving to the University of Indiana in 1856. In 1857 he noted that the asteroids (planetoids) are not evenly distributed in between the orbits of Mars and Jupiter but that there are areas in which no — or very few — asteroids orbit. He showed that these gaps in the asteroid belt — since known as *Kirkwood gaps* — occur where the period of revolution of an asteroid would have been an exact simple fraction of the Jovian period. Kirkwood explained that any asteroids in these areas would eventually be forced into other orbits by perturbations caused by Jupiter. Similarly he was able to explain gaps in the rings of Saturn (the Cassini division) as being caused by the satellite Mimas. Kirkwood published his findings in *The Asteroids* (1887).

KIRWAN, Richard (b. Aug. 1, 1733; Galway, now in the Republic of Ireland; d. June 22, 1812; Dublin) Irish chemist and mineralogist.

Kirwan studied in France to become a Jesuit but returned to Ireland after only a year, where he inherited the family estates following his brother's death in a duel in 1755. Kirwan was called to the Irish bar in 1766 but gave up law just two years later to devote himself to science. He was made a fellow of the Royal Society in 1780 and won the Copley medal in 1782 for his work on chemical affinity. In 1787 he settled in Dublin, where he remained until his death. In 1799 he was elected president of the Royal Irish Academy.

Kirwan was at first a staunch supporter of the phlogiston theory and in 1787 he wrote *Essay on Phlogiston*, which was translated into French. He conceded to Antoine Lavoisier's criticism of this and Lavoisier's subsequent evidence of oxygen by giving up his support of the theory in 1791.

Kirwan was also an eminent mineralogist and published, in 1784, his *Elements of Mineralogy*, which has been described as the first systematic work on the subject in English. His *Geological Essays* (1799) brought him into conflict with James Hutton over the chemical composition of rocks. He received news from Karl Scheele of the bleaching properties of chlorine and quickly had it tested and marketed in both Lancashire and Ireland.

KISTIAKOWSKY, George Bogdan (b. Nov. 18, 1900; Kiev, now in the Soviet Union) Russian–American chemist.

Kistiakowsky came from a family of academics. He began his education in Kiev but, after fighting against the Bolsheviks, completed it in Berlin. He moved to America in 1926 working first at Princeton before moving to Harvard where he was appointed professor of chemistry in 1937, a post he retained until his retirement in 1971.

His most important work during the war was as head of the Explosives Division at Los Alamos (1944–45). On being told of the project his initial reaction had been: "Dr. Oppenheimer is mad to think this thing will make a bomb." The basic device, proposed by Seth Neddermeyer, consisted of a thin hollow sphere of uranium that would become critical only when 'squeezed' together. In theory this was achieved by surrounding the subcritical uranium with conventional explosives whose detonation would compress the radioactive material into a critical mass. To work the process must take place in less than a millionth of a second and with great precision and accuracy. Right to the very end there was considerable doubt as to whether Kistiakowsky could solve the technical problems involved.

After the war Kistiakowsky, very much a figure of the scientific establishment, spent much time advising numerous governmental bodies. From 1959 until 1961 he served as special assistant for science and technology to President Eisenhower, later writing an account of this period in *A Scientist at the White House* (1976). More recently he has spoken out about the dangers of nuclear weapons.

KITASATO, Baron Shibasaburo (b. Dec. 20, 1852; Oguni, Japan; d. June 13, 1931; Nakanojo, Japan) Japanese bacteriologist.

After graduating from the medical school of the University of Tokyo in 1883, Kitasato went to Berlin to study under Robert Koch. A close and long-lasting friendship developed between the two men.

While in Berlin Kitasato worked with Emil von Behring and in 1890 they announced the discovery of antitoxins of diphtheria and tetanus. They showed that if nonimmune animals were injected with increasing sublethal doses of tetanus toxin, the animals became resistant to the disease. Their paper laid the basis for all future treatment with antitoxins and founded a new field in science, that of serology. Kitasato returned to Japan and became director of the Institute of Infectious Diseases in 1892. Two years later there was an outbreak of bubonic plague in Hong Kong and he succeeded in isolating the plague bacillus, *Pasteurella pestis*. In 1898 he isolated the microorganism that causes dysentery.

He founded the Kitasato Institute for Medical Research in 1914 and became dean of the medical school, Keio University, Tokyo. In 1924 he was created a baron. In 1908 Koch visited Japan and Kitasato secretly obtained clippings of the visitor's hair and fingernails. When Koch died in May 1910, Kitasato built a small shrine for the relics in front of his laboratory; when Kitasato died, his remains were placed in the same shrine, next to those of his respected master.

KITTEL, Charles (b. July 18, 1916; New York City) American physicist.

Kittel, regarded by many as the leading authority on the physics of the solid state, graduated from Cambridge University,

KJELDAHL

England, with a BA in 1938 and gained his PhD from the University of Wisconsin in 1941. He was an experimental physicist at the Naval Ordnance Laboratories, Washington (1940–42) and an operations analyst with the US Fleet (1943–45). After a short spell as a physics research associate at the Massachusetts Institute of Technology, he worked as a research physicist with the Bell Telephones Laboratories (1947–50). From there he took up an associate professorship at the University of California at Berkeley, becoming full professor of physics in 1951.

During the 1950s Kittel published several important papers on the properties and structure of solids. These were concerned with: antiferroelectric crystals; electron-spin resonance in the study of conduction electrons in metals; the nature of 'holes' in the process of electrical conduction; plasma-resonance effects in semiconductor crystals; ferromagnetic resonance and domain theory; and spin-resonance absorption in antiferromagnetic crystals. He is widely known for his textbook *Introduction to Solid State Physics* (1953), successive editions of which have served generations of physics students.

KJELDAHL, Johan Gustav Christoffer Thorsager (b. Aug. 16, 1849; Jagerpris, Denmark; d. July 18, 1900; Tisvildeleje, Denmark) Danish chemist.

Kjeldahl, the son of a physician, was educated at the Roskilde Gymnasium and the Technical University of Denmark, Copenhagen. After working briefly at the Royal Veterinary and Agricultural University he joined the laboratory set up by the brewer Carl Jacobsen in 1876 to introduce scientific methods into his Carlsberg brewery founded the previous year. Kjeldahl directed the chemistry department of the laboratory from 1876 until his fatal heart attack in 1900.

Kjeldahl is still widely known to chemists for the method named for him, first described in 1883, for the estimation of the nitrogen content of compounds. It was much quicker, more accurate, and capable of being operated on a larger scale than the earlier combustion-tube method dating back to Jean Dumas. It utilized the fact that the nitrogen in a nitrogenous organic compound heated with concentrated sulfuric acid will be converted into ammonium sulfate. The ammonia can then be released by introducing an alkaline solution, and then distilled into a standard acid, its amount being determined by titration.

His name is also remembered with the Kjeldahl flask, the round-bottomed, long-necked flask used by him in the operation of his method.

KLAPROTH, Martin Heinrich (b. Dec. 1, 1743; Wernigerode, now in East Germany; d. Jan. 1, 1817; Berlin) German chemist.

Klaproth was apprenticed as an apothecary. After working in Hannover and Danzig he moved to Berlin where he set up his own business. In 1792 he became lecturer in chemistry at the Berlin Artillery School and in 1810 he became the first professor of chemistry at the University of Berlin.

His main fame as a chemist rests on his discovery of several new elements. In 1789 he discovered zirconium, named from zircon, the mineral from which it was isolated. In the same year he extracted uranium from pitchblende and named it for the newly discovered planet, Uranus. He also rediscovered titanium in 1795, about four years after its original discovery, and discovered chromium in 1798. Klaproth used the Latin *tellus* (earth) in his naming of tellurium (1798), which had been discovered by Muller von Richtenstein in 1782. In 1803 he discovered cerium oxide, named after the newly discovered asteroid, Ceres. He made important improvements to chemical analysis by bringing samples to a constant weight through drying and ignition.

Klaproth's son, Heinrich Julius, became a noted orientalist.

442

KLEIN, (Christian) Felix (b. Nov. 25, 1849; Düsseldorf, now in West Germany; d. Jan. 22, 1925; Göttingen, now in West Germany) German mathematician.

Klein, one of the great formative influences on the development of modern geometry, studied at Bonn, Göttingen, and Berlin. He worked with Sophus Lie — a collaboration that was particularly fruitful for both of them and led to the theory of groups of geometrical transformations. This work was later to play a crucial role in Klein's own ideas on geometry.

Klein took up the chair in mathematics at the University of Erlangen in 1872 and his inaugural lecture was the occasion of his formulation of his famous *Erlangen Programm*, a suggestion of a way in which the study of geometry could be both unified and generalized. Throughout the 19th century, with the work of such mathematicians as Karl Friedrich Gauss, Janós Bolyai, Nikolai Lobachevsky, and Bernhard Riemann, the idea of what a 'geometry' could be had been taken increasingly beyond the conception Euclid had of it and Klein's ideas helped show how these diverse geometries could all be seen as particular cases of one general concept. Klein's central idea was to think of a geometry as the theory of the invariants of a particular group of transformations. His *Erlangen Programm* was justly influential in guiding the further development of the subject. In particular Klein's ideas led to an even closer connection between geometry and algebra.

Klein also worked on projective geometry, which he generalized beyond three dimensions, and on the wider application of group theory, for example, to the rotational symmetries of regular solids. His name is remembered in topology for the *Klein bottle*, a one-sided closed surface, not constructible in three-dimensional Euclidean space. In 1886 Klein took up a chair at Göttingen and was influential in building Göttingen up into a great center for mathematics.

KLINGENSTIERNA, Samuel (b. 1698; Linköping, Sweden; d. Oct. 26, 1765; Stockholm) Swedish mathematician and physicist.

Before embarking on his mathematical and scientific studies Klingenstierna studied law at Uppsala. He was appointed secretary to the Swedish treasury (1720) but also had interests in philosophy and science and was allowed to continue his studies at Uppsala. In 1727 he was awarded a scholarship, which enabled him to travel in Europe. He traveled to Marburg where he studied with the Leibnizian philosopher Christian Wolff and also to Basel to study mathematics with Johann I Bernoulli. Klingenstierna became professor of mathematics at Uppsala and later professor of physics there (1750). His last appointment was the highly prestigious one of tutor to the crown prince (1756–64).

Klingenstierna's most notable scientific work was in the field of optics. He was able to show that some of Newton's views on the refraction of light were incorrect and made practical use of this discovery in producing designs for lenses free from chromatic and spherical aberration.

KOCH, (Heinrich Hermann) Robert (b. Dec. 11, 1843; Klausthal, now in West Germany; d. May 27, 1910; Baden-Baden, now in West Germany) German bacteriologist.

Koch, the son of a mining official, studied medicine at the University of Göttingen where he was a pupil of Jacob Henle. After graduating in 1866 and serving in the Franco-Prussian War, Koch was appointed district medical officer in Wollstein. Here, working alone with only the most modest of resources, Koch began the research that was to make him, with Pasteur, one of the two founders of the new science of bacteriology.

Koch saw more clearly than anyone before what was involved in bacteriological research and achieved his first success with anthrax. Whereas Casimir Davaine had succeeded in transmitting anthrax from one cow to another by the injection of blood, Koch saw that the emerging germ theory required something more specific. It needed to be the germ that was injected rather than a fluid that could only be presumed to contain the organism. He thus spent three years devising techniques to isolate the anthrax bacillus from the blood of infected cattle and then to produce pure cultures of the germ.

By 1876 Koch was ready to publish the life history of the anthrax bacillus. He had found that while the bacillus in its normal state is somewhat sensitive and unable to survive long outside the body of its host, it forms resting spores, which are particularly hardy. Such spores, persisting in deserted ground, are responsible for the apparently spontaneous outbreaks of anthrax in healthy and isolated herds. Koch followed this with work on septicemia, during which he developed techniques for obtaining pure cultures.

With these triumphs behind him Koch at last achieved official recognition, being appointed to the Imperial Health Office in Berlin in 1880. In this office Koch, with the aid of his assistants Friedrich Löffler and Georg Gaffky, began one of the great periods of medical discovery. Much of this was based upon techniques of staining and culture growth developed by Koch in the obscurity of Wollstein. He developed culture media suitable for bacterial growth, proceeding from liquid media to boiled potato, to the still commonly used agar plates. Agar plates together with the new stains derived from aniline dies constituted the heart of Koch's technique.

With them he made, in 1882, his most famous discovery — the bacillus responsible for TB. In the second half of the 19th century TB, responsible for one in seven of all European deaths, was the most feared of all diseases. The difficulties Koch faced were formidable. The bacillus was only about a third of the size of the anthrax bacillus, grew much more slowly, and in general was more difficult too detect. With great patience Koch managed to culture the thin rod-shaped bacilli, which he used to inoculate four guinea pigs. All four developed TB while two uninoculated controls remained uninfected.

The fame won by Koch for this work brought him into open competition with Pasteur, a competition fanned by Franco-German nationalism in the aftermath of the 1870 war. In 1883 both sides met in Egypt to study cholera. The French, under Emile Roux, seem to have mistakenly confused platelets in the blood with the vibrio responsible for cholera. Koch, noting microorganisms in the small intestines of the victims, took them to be the cause of the disease, an assumption confirmed when he observed the same comma-shaped rods in the intestines of Indian victims. At this point Koch was forced to violate his own rules because, although he failed to infect experimental animals with pure strains of the vibrio, he nonetheless declared the organism to be the cause.

In 1885 Koch was appointed professor of hygiene at the University of Berlin and in 1891 became head of the newly formed Institute of Infectious Diseases. The pressure on Koch to 'earn' this latter appointment led him to announce in 1890 the discovery of a substance he claimed could prevent the growth of tubercle bacilli in the body. The new drug, a sterile liquid containing dead tubercle bacilli, which he named tuberculin, was consequently in huge demand. However it had little effect in most cases and probably exacerbated some. It later proved useful however in testing whether patients have experienced tuberculosis infection, by noting their local reaction to an injection of tuberculin.

Koch resigned the directorship of the Institute in 1904 to become one of the first of the emerging breed of international expert. Indulging his passion for travel, Koch spent his last years advising South Africa on rinderpest, India on bubonic plague, Java on malaria, and East Africa on sleeping sickness.

In 1905 Koch was awarded the Nobel Prize for physiology or medicine for "his discoveries in regard to tuberculosis." Perhaps more important than this, or any of his other specific discoveries, was his formulation of the so-called Koch's postulates. To establish that an organism is the cause of a disease we must, Koch declared, first find it in all cases of the disease examined; secondly it must be prepared and maintained in a pure culture and finally it must, though several generations away from the original germ, still be capable of producing the original infection. Such postulates, first formulated fully in 1890, rigorously followed, established clinical bacteriology as a scientific practice.

KOCHER, Emil Theodor (b. Aug. 25, 1841; Bern, Switzerland; d. July 27, 1917; Bern) Swiss surgeon.

Kocher, an engineer's son, graduated in medicine from the University of Bern in 1865. He later studied surgery in Berlin, Paris, and in London under Joseph Lister, and Vienna under Theodor Billroth. Kocher served as professor of clinical surgery at the University of Bern from 1872 until his retirement in 1911 although he continued as head of the University surgical clinic until his death.

Using Lister's antiseptic techniques, Kocher, following the initiative of Billroth, played an important role in developing the operation of thyroidectomy for the treatment of goiter, a not uncommon complaint in Switzerland. By 1914 Kocher was able to report a mortality of only 4.5% from over 2000 operations.

Earlier however, Kocher discovered that while technically successful the operation was responsible for the unnecessary ruin of many lives. In 1883, he found to his horror that something like a third of his patients who had undergone thyroidectomy were suffering from what was politely termed operative myxedema; they had in fact been turned into cretins once the source of the thyroid hormone (thyroxine) had been removed. Kocher showed that such tragedies could be prevented by not removing the whole of the thyroid, for even a small portion possesses sufficient physiological activity to prevent such appalling consequences.

For this work Kocher was awarded the 1909 Nobel Prize for physiology or medicine.

KOHLRAUSCH, Friedrich Wilhelm Georg (b. Oct. 14, 1840; Rinteln, now in West Germany; d. Jan. 17, 1910; Marburg, now in West Germany) German physicist.

Kohlrausch's father, R. H. A. Kohlrausch, was also a famous physicist who served as professor at the University of Erlangen. Friedrich studied at Erlangen and also at Göttingen, where he gained his PhD in 1863. He held a series of professorial appointments at Göttingen, Frankfurt, Darmstadt, Würzburg, Strasbourg, and Berlin and was elected to the Academy of Sciences in Berlin in 1895.

Kohlrausch is remembered for his work on the electrical conductivity of solutions. He was able to measure the electrical resistance of electrolytes (substances that, by transferring ions, conduct electricity in solutions) by introducing an alternating current to prevent polarization of the electrodes. In this way he recorded the conductivity of electrolytes at various solute concentrations and discovered that conductivity increases with increased dilution. This finding led to the formulation of *Kohlrausch's law* of the independent migration of ions.

KOHN, Walter (b. Mar. 7, 1923; Vienna) Austrian–American physicist.

Kohn emigrated to England in 1939 and was interned and sent to Canada in 1940. Here he studied at the University of Toronto and later at Harvard, where he gained his PhD in 1948. After holding a junior appointment at Harvard he moved to the Carnegie Institution in 1950, remaining there until 1960 when he became professor of physics at the University of California, San Diego. Since 1979 Kohn has also served there as director of the Institute of Theoretical Physics.

Kohn has worked mainly in the field of solid-state physics, publishing work on the electronic structure of solids and solid surfaces.

KO HUNG (b. *c.* 283; Kiangsu province, China; d. 343; Kuangtung province, China) Chinese alchemist.

Ko Hung, the son of a provincial governor, served in various official posts until he retired to the mountains to devote himself to his chemical researches. He received an early education in Confucian ethics but became interested in Taoism, with its cult of physical immortality, and attempted to combine the two.

In about 317 he finished his classic work the *Pao-piu-tzu* or the *Book of the Preservation-of-Solidarity Master*, which is divided into two parts. The first part contains Ko Hung's alchemical studies and the search for the elixir of immortality. It includes a recipe for an elixir called gold cinnabar. The gold implied in this recipe was not in fact the natural element but the artificial transmuted gold for which there were numerous obscure recipes. Attempts to produce this gold helped alchemists gain a considerable amount of knowledge of and skill with chemical reactions and equipment. Ko Hung, for example, gives the first account of the process for making tin(IV) sulfide, which was widely used in 'gold' paints. This process was not described in Europe until the 14th century. One unfortunate result of Ko Hung's work was that it led to numerous cases of elixir poisoning as the artificial 'golds' produced by the alchemists tended to be rich in such toxic ingredients as mercury, arsenic, and silver.

The second part of Ko Hung's book concentrates on Confucian ethical principles.

KOLBE, Adolph Wilhelm Hermann (b. Sept. 27, 1818; Göttingen, now in West Germany; d. Nov. 25, 1884, Leipzig, now in East Germany) German chemist.

Kolbe, the son of a clergyman and the eldest of 15 children, studied under Friedrich Wöhler at Göttingen. In 1842 he went to Marburg as Robert Bunsen's assistant and learned his method of gas analysis. In 1845 he went to London to work as Lyon Playfair's assistant on the analysis of mine gases for a commission set up to investigate recent explosions in coal mines. He was professor of chemistry at Marburg from 1851 until he moved to Leipzig to succeed Justus von Liebig in 1865.

Kolbe made a number of advances in organic chemistry. He was the first to synthesize acetic acid from inorganic materials (following Wöhler's synthesis of urea). The *Kolbe method* is a technique for making hydrocarbons by electrolysis of solutions of salts of fatty acids.

He produced a *Textbook of Organic Chemistry* (1854–60), which collected all the methods of preparing organic compounds. He also, in 1854, edited Liebig's and Wöhler's *Dictionary of Chemistry*.

KOLLER, Carl (b. Dec. 3, 1857; Schüttenhoffen, now Susice in Czechoslovakia; d. Mar. 22, 1944; New York City) Austrian-American ophthalmologist.

Koller was educated at the University of Vienna, where he obtained his MD in 1882. After a few years working for the department of ophthalmology as an intern, Koller emigrated to America in 1888 setting up in private practice in New York.

In 1884 Sigmund Freud drew the attention of the world to the drug cocaine. Although he failed to appreciate its true value he did arouse the interest of his colleagues Koller and another ophthalmologist, L. Königstein. While Freud and Königstein spent the summer away from Vienna, Koller performed a number of crucial experiments on animals and himself. He discovered that after bathing his eye in a solution of cocaine he could take a pin and prick the cornea without any awareness of the touch, let alone pain. Without delay Koller published his discovery of local anesthesia on 15 September, 1884.

By the time Freud and Königstein were

ready to begin their own experiments they found that Koller had already gained all the credit. Although all three were later to dispute to whom the real credit for the discovery belonged, it was appropriate that when, in 1885, Freud's father needed an operation for glaucoma the local anesthetic was administered by Koller, assisted by Freud, with the actual surgery performed by Königstein.

KÖLLIKER, Rudolph Albert von (b. July 6, 1817; Zurich, Switzerland; d. Nov. 2, 1905; Würzburg, now in West Germany) Swiss histologist and embryologist.

Kölliker qualified in medicine at Heidelberg in 1842, and later held professorships at Zurich and Würzburg. Celebrated for his microscopic work on tissues, Kölliker provided much evidence to show that cells cannot arise freely, but only from existing cells. He was the first to isolate the cells of smooth muscle (1848), as expounded in *Handbuch der Gewebelehre des Menschen* (1852; Manual of Human Histology): probably the best early text on the subject. He showed that nerve fibers are elongated parts of cells, thus anticipating the neuron theory, and demonstrated the cellular nature of eggs and sperm, showing for example that sperm are formed from the tubular walls of the testis, just as pollen grains are formed from cells of the anthers. Again anticipating modern discoveries, Kölliker believed the cell nucleus carried the key to heredity. His pioneering studies of cellular embryology mark him as one of the founders of the science. His book *Entwicklungsgeschichte des Menschen und der höheren Tiere* (1861; Embryology of Man and Higher Animals) is a classic text in embryology.

KOLMOGOROV, Andrei Nikolaievich (b. Apr. 25, 1903; Tambov, now in the Soviet Union) Soviet mathematician.

Kolmogorov was educated at Moscow State University, graduating in 1925. He became a research associate at the university, later a professor (1931), and in 1933 was appointed director of the Institute of Mathematics there. He has made distinguished contributions to a wide variety of mathematical topics. He is best known for his work on the theoretical foundations of probability, but has also made lasting contributions to such diverse subjects as Fourier analysis, automata theory, and intuitionism.

In 1933 Kolmogorov published his major treatise on probability, translated into English in 1950 as *The Foundations of the Theory of Probability*. This is a landmark in the development of the theory, for in it he presents the first fully axiomatic treatment of the subject. The book also contains the first full realization of the basic and underivable nature of the so-called 'additivity assumption' about probability, first put forward by Jakob 1 Bernoulli. This claims simply that if an event can be realized in any one of an infinite number of mutually exclusive ways, the probability of the event is simply the sum of the probabilities of each of these ways. This assumption is fundamental to the whole measure-theoretic study of probability.

Kolmogorov's interest in Luitzen Brouwer's intuitionism led him to prove that intuitionistic arithmetic, as formalized by Brouwer's disciple Arend Heyting, is consistent if and only if classical arithmetic is. In 1936 Kolmogorov settled a key problem in Fourier analysis when he constructed a function which is (Lebesgue) integrable, but whose Fourier series diverges at every point. In 1939, the same year in which he was elected an academician of the Soviet Academy of Sciences, he published a paper on the extrapolation of time series. This was later taken much further by Norbert Wiener and became known as 'single-series prediction'.

KOPP, Hermann Franz Moritz (b. Oct. 30, 1817; Hanau, now in West Germany; d. Feb. 20, 1892; Heidelberg, now in West Germany) German chemist and historian of chemistry.

Kopp was the son of a physician. He studied chemistry at the University of Heidelberg and obtained his PhD from Marburg. He was professor of chemistry at Giessen (1852–63) before he moved to the chair at Heidelberg.

Kopp is best remembered for his monumental work *Geschichte der Chemie* (1843–47; History of Chemistry), begun in 1841 while he was an unsalaried lecturer at Giessen. As a chemist he was noted for his extensive and precise work in measuring such properties as boiling points, thermal expansion, molecular volume, and specific gravity (relative density) for many elements and compounds.

KÖPPEN, Wladimir Peter (b. Sept. 25, 1846; St. Petersburg, now Leningrad in the Soviet Union; d. June 22, 1940; Graz, Austria) German climatologist.

Köppen was educated at the universities of St. Petersburg, Heidelberg, and Leipzig. Although he began his career in 1872 with the Russian meteorological service he moved to Germany shortly afterward where, in 1875, he was appointed director of the meteorological research department of the German Naval Observatory at Hamburg, a post he retained until the end of World War I when he was succeeded by his son-in-law Alfred Wegener.

Köppen is mainly remembered today for the mathematical system of climatic classification he first formulated in 1900 and subsequently modified several times before 1936. He began by distinguishing between five broad climatic types — tropical rainy, dry, warm temperate, cold forest, and polar — symbolized by the letters A to E respectively. He further defined three patterns of precipitation: a climate with no dry period (f), with a dry summer period (s), and with a dry winter period (w). Four geographical zones were also introduced — steppe (S), desert (W), tundra (T), and perpetual frost (F). With such a technique some 60 climatic types are theoretically possible although Köppen argued that only 11 are in fact realized.

Köppen further modified his scheme by introducing six temperature categories, which enabled him to make fine adjustments to his initial 11 classes. Though by no means the only such classification in existence, Köppen's system is still widely and conveniently used on climatic maps.

In his long career Köppen produced a number of substantial volumes, including a joint work with Wegener, *Die Klimate der geologishen Vorzeit* (1924; The Climate of Geological Prehistory), one of the founding texts of paleoclimatology. He also coedited, with Rudolph Geiger, a five-volume *Handbuch der Klimatologie* (Handbook of Climatology), begun in 1927 and nearing completion on his death in 1940.

KORNBERG, Arthur (b. Mar. 3, 1918; Brooklyn, New York) American biochemist.

In 1937 Kornberg graduated from the City College of New York in biology and chemistry, after which he studied medicine at Rochester University, gaining his MD in 1941. He joined the National Institutes of Health, Bethesda, where from 1942 to 1953 he directed research on enzymes. During this period he helped elucidate the reactions leading to the formation of two important coenzymes, flavin adenine dinucleotide (FAD) and diphosphopyridine nucleotide (DPN; later renamed nicotinamide adenine dinucleotide — NAD).

From 1953 to 1959 Kornberg was professor of microbiology at Washington University. In 1956, while investigating the synthesis of coenzymes, he discovered an enzyme that catalyzes the formation of polynucleotides from nucleoside triphosphates. This enzyme, which he named DNA polymerase, can be used to synthesize short DNA molecules in a test tube, given the appropriate triphosphate bases and a DNA template. For the discovery and isolation of this enzyme, Kornberg was awarded the 1959 Nobel Prize for physiology or medicine, sharing the award with Severo Ochoa, who discovered the enzyme catalyzing the formation of RNA.

Kornberg was chairman of the biochemistry department at Stanford University from 1959 and his work there has contributed to the understanding of the synthesis of phospholipids and many reactions of the tricarboxylic acid, or Krebs cycle.

KOROLEV, Sergei Pavlovich (b. Jan. 14, 1907; Zhitomir, now in the Soviet Union; d. Jan. 14, 1966; Moscow) Soviet rocket engineer.

Both of Korolev's parents were teachers. He was educated at the Kiev Polytechnic and the Moscow Higher Technical School from 1926 to 1929. An early interest in gliders and the writings of Konstantin Tsiolkovsky aroused in Korolev a fascination with the problems of space flight. He helped to found and direct the Gruppa Izucheniya Reaktivnogo Dvizheniya (GIRD) (the Institute for Jet Research) in 1931 in Moscow.

At some later time, for unknown reasons Korolev and most of his colleagues at GIRD were caught up in the Great Terror and imprisoned in the Arctic. He appears to have spent most of the war in one of the many special prison research centers before being released to cooperate with and direct the captured German rocket experts.

The details of Korolev's later work were only released on his death when he was described in his official obituary as responsible for "the manned space ships in which Man made his first flight to the Cosmos." In his lifetime he was referred to simply as the 'chief spacecraft designer'. Nevertheless his successes included the first satellite ever launched on October 4, 1957, the development of the Vostok, Voskhod, and Soyuz manned spacecraft, and the Venus and Mars probes of 1961–62.

KOSSEL, Albrecht (b. Sept. 16, 1853; Rostock, now in East Germany; d. July 5, 1927; Heidelberg, now in West Germany) German biochemist.

Professor of physiology at the universities of Marburg and Heidelberg (1895–1923), Kossel first studied medicine, but turned his attention to biochemistry under the influence of Felix Hoppe-Seyler, whose assistant he was at Strasbourg (1877–81). Kossel was also for a time a colleague of Emil Du Bois-Reymond. Whilst with Hoppe-Seyler, Kossel continued the latter's investigations of the cell substance called nuclein, demonstrating that it contained both protein and nonprotein (nucleic acid) parts. He was further able to show that the nucleic acids, when broken down, produced nitrogen-bearing compounds (purines and pyrimidines) as well as carbohydrates. Kossel also studied the proteins in spermatozoa, being the first to isolate the amino acid histidine. He was awarded the Nobel Prize for physiology or medicine in 1910 for his work on cells and proteins.

KOSTERLITZ, Hans Walter (b. Apr. 27, 1903) German–British psychopharmacologist.

Kosterlitz was educated at the universities of Heidelberg, Freiburg, and Berlin where he obtained his MD in 1929. He remained there as an assistant until 1933 when, with the rise of the Nazis, he sought safety in Britain. He joined the staff of Aberdeen University in 1934 where he later served as professor of pharmacology and chemistry from 1968 until 1973 when he became director of the university's drug addiction research unit.

For many years Kosterlitz had been working on the effects of morphine on mammalian physiology when in 1975, in collaboration with J. Hughes, he made his most dramatic discovery. They were investigating the effect of morphine in inhibiting electrically induced contractions in the guinea-pig intestine and, to their surprise, discovered that the same effect could be produced by extracts of brain tissue. When it turned out that the effect of the extract could be inhibited by naloxone, a morphia antagonist, it seemed likely to them that they had in fact stumbled on the endogenous opiates, discussed earlier by Solomon Snyder, and named by them enkephalins.

They quickly succeeded in isolating two such enkephalins from pig's brains and found them to be almost identical peptides consisting of five amino acids differing at one site only and consequently known as methionine and leucine enkephalins. When it was further shown that they possessed analgesic properties hopes were raised once more of the possibility of developing a nonaddictive yet powerful pain killer. Research is still continuing.

KOUWENHOVEN, William Bennett (b. Jan. 13, 1886; Brooklyn, New York; d. Nov. 10, 1975; Baltimore, Maryland) American electrical engineer.

Kouwenhoven began his career as an instructor in physics at the Brooklyn Polytechnic in 1906. After a brief period as an instructor in electrical engineering at Washington University from 1913 to 1914 he moved to Johns Hopkins University where he later served as professor of electrical engineering from 1930 until his retirement in 1954.

In the 1930s Kouwenhoven introduced the first practical electrical defibrillator for delivering an alternating current discharge to the heart. It was not however until the postwar years that the technique became widely used. The method is used to cure ventricular fibrillation, a heart condition in which the normal rhythmical contractions are modified or cease owing to irregular twitchings of the heart wall.

In 1959 Kouwenhoven also introduced the technique of closed chest cardiac massage, a first-aid method that is used to keep alive people whose hearts have stopped beating or who have stopped breathing. The technique can maintain life for up to an hour.

KOVALEVSKAYA, Sofya Vasilyevna (Sonya Kovalevski) (b. Jan. 15, 1850; Moscow; d. Feb. 10, 1891; Stockholm) Russian mathematician.

Kovalevskaya came from a cultured aristocratic background and studied mathematics privately. In 1869 she went to study at the University of Heidelberg, where her teachers included Gustav Kirchhoff and Hermann von Helmholtz. In 1871 she moved on to the University of Berlin to study with Karl Weierstrass. Since women were not allowed to attend lectures, Kovalevskaya studied privately with Weierstrass and a lifelong friendship developed between them.

In 1874 when she took her doctorate (on partial differential equations) at the University of Göttingen, she had already produced original pieces of research on such varied topics as the constitution of the rings of Saturn and Abelian integrals, and had made important contributions to the theory of differential equations. However, in spite of her obvious outstanding talents and the determined backing of her influential friend Weierstrass, Kovalevskaya was unable to find an academic post anywhere in Europe, so strong was the prejudice against academic women at that time. She was thus compelled to return to Russia and settle down to family life.

However after her husband's death the family's fortunes declined rapidly, and an academic job again became more of a necessity. This time Weierstrass was able to persuade the Swedish mathematician Mittag-Leffler to offer Kovalevskaya a lectureship at Stockholm University. Her initial researches were in analysis, under Weierstrass's influence, and she wrote a memoir *On the Rotation of a Solid Body About a Fixed Point* (1888), which won her the coveted Prix Borodin from the French Academy. Later she won a further prize from the Swedish Academy with another memoir on the same subject. Kovalevskaya had a considerable literary talent in addition to her mathematical gifts, and wrote numerous novels together with some autobiographical sketches.

KOVALEVSKI, Aleksandr Onufrievich (b. Nov. 19, 1840; Shustyanka, near Dvinsk, now Daugavpils in the Soviet Union; d. Nov. 22, 1901; St. Petersburg, now Leningrad in the Soviet Union) Russian zoologist and embryologist.

Kovalevski took a science doctorate at the University of St. Petersburg (now Leningrad State University), where he later taught and became professor (1891–93). He also taught at the universities of Kazan (1868–69), Kiev (1869–74), and Odessa (1874–90) and in 1890 was elected to the Russian Academy of Sciences.

One of Kovalevski's most notable contributions to zoological science and the fuller understanding of evolution lay in his demonstration that all multicellular animals display a common pattern of physiological development. His research into the embryology of primitive chordates such as *Amphioxus* (the lancelet), *Balanoglossus* (the acorn worm), and the sea squirts, particularly his demonstration of the links between them and the craniates, provided the basis for later studies of the evolutionary history of the vertebrates, and led to the Gastraea theory of Haeckel. Kovalevski's most important publications are *Development of Amphioxus lanceolatus* (1865) and *Anatomy and Development of Phoronis* (1887).

KOZYREV, Nikolay Aleksandrovich (b. Sept. 2, 1908; St. Petersburg, now Leningrad in the Soviet Union) Soviet astronomer.

Kozyrev studied at the University of Leningrad where he graduated in 1928. In 1931 he joined the Pulkovo Astronomical Observatory, near Leningrad, and has also worked at the Kharkov and the Crimean astrophysical observatories. From 1936 to 1948 he was imprisoned under the Stalin regime.

Kozyrev's work has included planetary studies and research into stellar atmospheres and stellar structure. In 1958 he reported some remarkable observations of the Moon that demonstrated that it was not completely inert. He was observing the central peak of the Alphonsus crater when "it became strongly washed out and of an unusual reddish hue." The disturbance lasted for at least half an hour and was distinguished from all other reports of strange transient lunar phenomena by being supported with a spectrogram. This revealed a marked increase in temperature together with the release of a cloud of carbon particles. Since Kozyrev's report other transient red spots have been seen and an examination of past records has shown that they were noticed as far back as the 18th century. It is thought that Kozyrev was observing some form of volcanic activity.

KRAFT, Robert Paul (b. June 16, 1927; Seattle, Washington) American astronomer.

Kraft graduated in 1947 from the University of Washington and obtained his PhD in 1955 from the University of California, Berkeley. He held brief appointments at Whittier College, the Mount Wilson and Palomar Observatories, and the Universities of Indiana and Chicago before returning to the Mount Wilson and Palomar Observatories in 1960. In 1967 Kraft moved to Lick Observatory as professor of astronomy.

Kraft has worked mainly in the fields of stellar spectroscopy and galactic structure. He is best known for his work on novae and supernovae. He has proposed that most if not all stars on which novae erupt are small dense white dwarfs that are members of binary systems. This led him to construct a dynamical model of novae based on the passage of material from the larger to the smaller white-dwarf member of the binary.

KRAMER, Paul Jackson (b. May 8, 1904; Brookville, Indiana) American plant physiologist.

Kramer graduated in botany from the University of Miami and obtained his PhD from Ohio State University in 1931. He immediately joined the faculty of Duke University, South Carolina, and spent his entire career there serving as professor of botany from 1945 until his retirement in 1974.

Kramer has worked on problems of the absorption of water by plants, surveying the subject in his *Plant and Soil Water Relationships* (1949). He demonstrated that two different mechanisms are involved in water uptake by roots, depending on whether the plants are transpiring quickly or slowly. He also showed the importance of taking plant water stress into account when making correlations between soil moisture and plant growth. In studies using radioactively labeled elements he found that the region of maximum absorption in roots is not the tip but the area several centimeters behind the tip where the xylem conducting vessels are fully formed. Other researches led Kramer to the conclusion that substantial amounts of minerals enter plant roots passively in the transpiration stream.

Kramer has also worked on the physiology of trees, publishing with Theodore Kozlowski *The Physiology of Woody Plants* (1979), an update of an earlier 1960 joint work.

KRATZER, Nicolas (b. 1486; Munich, now in West Germany; d. 1550; possibly in Oxford, England) German astronomer, horologist, and instrument maker.

Kratzer spent 30 years in England, working for part of that time at the court of Henry VIII, and played an important part in introducing knowledge of scientific instruments and techniques of instrument making to England. He had his portrait painted by Holbein whose famous picture 'The Ambassadors' apparently contains many of Kratzer's instruments.

KRAUS, Charles August (b. Aug. 15, 1875; Knightsville, Indiana; d. June 27, 1967; East Providence, Rhode Island) American chemist.

Brought up on a Kansas farm, Kraus was educated at the University of Kansas, Johns Hopkins University, and the Massachusetts Institute of Technology where he obtained his PhD in 1908. After holding junior appointments at the University of California and MIT Kraus served successively as professor of chemistry at Clark University (1914–24) and at Brown University from 1924 until his retirement in 1946.

A noted experimentalist, Kraus worked on liquid ammonia. He was especially concerned with the solubility of various elements, particularly the alkali metals, in ammonia. He also made an important contribution to industrial chemistry in 1922 when, at the request of the Standard Oil Company of New Jersey, he developed processes for the commercial production of tetraethyl lead. This permitted Thomas Midgley's discovery of its antiknock properties to be fully utilized and thus made possible the high-compression engine.

During World War II Kraus worked on the Manhattan Project (the atom-bomb project) on problems connected with the purification of uranium salts.

KREBS, Sir Hans Adolf (b. Aug. 25, 1900; Hildesheim, now in West Germany) German-British biochemist.

Krebs, the son of an ear, nose, and throat specialist, was educated at the universities of Göttingen, Freiburg, Munich, Berlin, and Hamburg, obtaining his MD in 1925. He taught at the Kaiser Wilhelm Institute, Berlin and the University of Freiburg but in 1933, with the growth of the Nazi movement, decided to leave Germany. Consequently he moved to England, where from 1935 to 1954 he served as professor of biochemistry at Sheffield University; after 1945 he was appointed director of the Medical Rese-

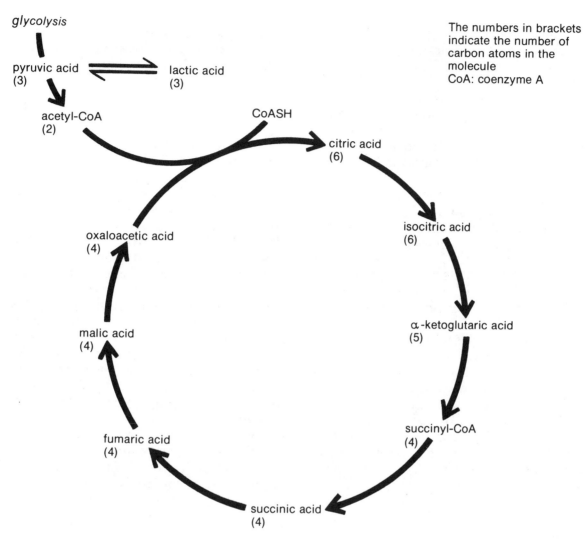

glycolysis

pyruvic acid (3) ⇌ lactic acid (3)

acetyl-CoA (2)

CoASH

citric acid (6)

isocitric acid (6)

α-ketoglutaric acid (5)

succinyl-CoA (4)

succinic acid (4)

fumaric acid (4)

malic acid (4)

oxaloacetic acid (4)

The numbers in brackets indicate the number of carbon atoms in the molecule
CoA: coenzyme A

THE TRICARBOXYLIC ACID CYCLE (Krebs cycle) The purpose of the TCA cycle is to complete the oxidation of glucose begun in glycolysis. In the sequence of reactions from citric acid to oxaloacetic acid, pyruvic acid is oxidized to carbon dioxide and water. During this process considerable amounts of energy are released – 93% of the total energy released in glucose oxidation.

arch Council's Cell Metabolism Unit at Sheffield. In 1954 Krebs moved to Oxford to take the Whitley Chair of Biochemistry, a post he held until his retirement in 1967.

Krebs is best known for his discovery of the *Krebs cycle* (or tricarboxylic acid cycle) in 1937. This is a continuation of the work of Carl and Gerty Cori, who had shown how carbohydrates, such as glycogen, are broken down in the body to lactic acid; Krebs completed the process by working out how the lactic acid is

metabolized to carbon dioxide and water. When he began this work little was known apart from the fact that the process involved the consumption of oxygen, which could be increased, according to Albert Szent-Györgyi, by the four-carbon compounds succinic acid, fumaric acid, malic acid, and oxaloacetic acid. Krebs himself demonstrated in 1937 that the six-carbon citric acid is also involved in the cycle.

By studying the process in pigeon breast muscle Krebs was able to piece together the clues already collected into a coherent scheme. The three-carbon lactic acid is first broken down to a two-carbon molecule unfamiliar to Krebs; it was in fact later identified by Fritz Lipmann as coenzyme A. This then combines with the four-carbon oxaloacetic acid to form the six-carbon citric acid. The citric acid then undergoes a cycle of reactions to be converted to oxaloacetic acid once more. During this cycle two molecules of carbon dioxide are given up and hydrogen atoms are released; the hydrogen is then oxidized in the electron transport chain with the production of energy. Much of the detail of this aspect of the cycle was later filled in by Lipmann, with whom Krebs shared the 1953 Nobel Prize for physiology or medicine.

Krebs fully appreciated the significance of the cycle, pointing out the important fact that it is the common terminal pathway for the chemical breakdown of *all* foodstuffs.

In 1932, with K. Henselheit, Krebs was responsible for the introduction of another cycle. This was the urea cycle, whereby amino acids (the constituents of protein) eliminate their nitrogen in the form of urea, which is excreted in urine. This left the remainder of the amino acid to give up its potential energy and participate in a variety of metabolic pathways.

KROGH, Schack August Steenberg (b. Nov. 15, 1874; Grenaa, Denmark; d. Sept. 13, 1949; Copenhagen) Danish physiologist.

Krogh, the son of a brewer, was educated at the Aarhus gymnasium and the University of Copenhagen, where he obtained his PhD in 1903. He spent his whole career at the university, serving as professor of animal physiology from 1916 until his retirement in 1945.

Krogh first worked on problems of respiration. He argued, against his teacher Christian Bohr, that the absorption of oxygen in the lungs and the elimination of carbon dioxide took place by diffusion alone.

He made precise measurements to show that the oxygen pressure was always higher in the air sacs than in the blood and, consequently, there was no need to assume any kind of nervous control.

It was, however, with his studies of the capillary system that Krogh achieved his most dramatic success. The simplest explanation of its action was to assume it was under the direct hydraulic control of the heart and arteries: the stronger the heart beat, the greater the amount of blood flowing through the capillaries. Krogh had little difficulty in showing the inadequacy of such a scheme by demonstrating that even among a group of capillaries fed by the same arteriole some were so narrow that they almost prevented the passage of red cells while others were quite dilated, allowing the free passage of the blood. Not content with this descriptive account Krogh went on to make a more quantitative demonstration. Working with frogs, which he injected with Indian ink shortly before killing, he showed that in sample areas of resting muscle the number of visible (stained) capillaries was about 5 per square millimeter; in stimulated muscle, however, the number was increased to 190 per sq. mm. From this he concluded that there must be a physiological mechanism to control the action of the capillaries in response to the needs of the body. It was for this work, fully described in *The Anatomy and Physiology of Capillaries* (1922), that Krogh was awarded the 1920 Nobel Prize in physiology or medicine.

KRONECKER, Leopold (b. Dec. 7, 1823; Liegnitz, now Legnica in Poland; d. Dec. 29, 1891; Berlin) German mathematician.

Kronecker studied mathematics at Berlin but he did not become a professional mathematician until relatively late in life. He worked, highly successfully, as a businessman until he had made enough money to abandon commerce and devote himself fully to mathematics. He taught at Berlin from 1861, and, in 1883, was appointed professor. Outside mathematics

Kronecker's interests were wide. He was a highly cultured man who used his wealth to patronize the arts. He also had a deep interest in philosophy and Christian theology, although he was not converted to Christianity until shortly before his death.

Kronecker's mathematical work was almost entirely in the fields of number theory and higher algebra, although he also made some contributions to the theory of elliptic functions. His work on algebraic numbers was inspired by his constructivist outlook, which involved a distrust of nonconstructive proofs in mathematics and a suspicion of the infinite and all kinds of number other than the natural numbers. This attitude led him to rewrite large areas of algebraic number theory in order to avoid reference to such suspect entities as imaginary or irrational numbers. Kronecker's constructivism is summed up in a famous remark he made during an after-dinner speech: "God made the integers, all else is the work of man." His suspicion of nonconstructive methods led Kronecker into fierce controversy with two of the leading mathematicians of his day, Karl Weierstrass and Georg Cantor. His outlook anticipates to a considerable extent the views of the Dutch mathematician L. E. J. Brouwer.

Kronecker was also one of the first to understand thoroughly and use Evariste Galois's work in the theory of equations. The *Kronecker delta function* is named for him.

KUFFLER, Stephen William (b. Aug. 24, 1913; Tap, Hungary) American neurophysiologist.

Kuffler was educated at the University of Vienna where he obtained his MD in 1937. He worked in Sydney, Australia, with John Eccles and Bernard Katz from 1938 to 1945 when he moved to America. There Kuffler worked first at Johns Hopkins from 1947 until 1959 when he became professor of neurophysiology at Harvard.

In 1953 Kuffler reported the results of certain experiments on the ganglion cells of the retina that did much to stimulate the later important work of David Hubel and Torsten Weisel. Electrodes were inserted in a cat's brain and recordings made when a small spot of light, about 0.2 millimeter in diameter, was shone onto the cat's receptive field. He found that in one area the spot of light excites a ganglion cell and produces an 'on' response, but such an 'on' response can be converted to an inhibitory 'off' response by simply shifting the spot by 1 mm or less across the retinal surface. He thus went on to propose that there are only two basic receptive field types in the cat's retina, the 'on' and 'off' center.

Kuffler has also worked on synaptic transmission and, with the American neurophysiologist John Nicholls, has collaborated on the stimulating text, *From Neuron to Brain* (1976).

KUHN, Richard (b. Dec. 3, 1900; Vienna; d. July 31, 1967; Heidelberg, West Germany) Austrian-German chemist.

Kuhn was educated at the universities of Vienna and of Munich, where he obtained his PhD in 1922. He worked at the Federal Institute of Technology in Zurich from 1926 to 1929 when he moved to the University of Heidelberg to serve as professor of chemistry and, from 1950, as professor of biochemistry.

Like Paul Karrer, Kuhn worked mainly on the chemistry of plant pigments and vitamins, repeating many of Karrer's results. In particular Kuhn, independently of Karrer, worked out the structures of vitamins A and B_2, and, in 1938, he also synthesized vitamin B_6.

For his work on carotenoids and vitamins Kuhn was awarded the Nobel Prize for chemistry in 1938, the year following the same award to Karrer. Hitler however objected to the award and Kuhn was forced to wait until the end of the war before he was allowed to receive the prize.

KÜHNE, Wilhelm Friedrich (b. Mar. 28, 1837; Hamburg, now in West Germany; d. June 10, 1900; Heidelberg, now in West Germany) German physiologist.

Willy Kühne, the son of a wealthy merchant, was educated at the University of Göttingen where he obtained his PhD on induced diabetes in frogs in 1856. He studied further in Jena, Berlin, Paris (under Claude Bernard), and Vienna before joining Rudolf Virchow's Berlin institute in 1861. Kühne later held chairs of physiology, first at Amsterdam from 1868 and from 1871 until his retirement in 1899 at Heidelberg.

Kühne worked with Russell Chittenden on problems of digestion, and he isolated trypsin from pancreatic juice. In 1859, working with the sartorius muscle, he demonstrated that nerve fibers can conduct impulses both ways, and also showed that chemical and electrical stimuli can be used to excite muscle fibers directly.

He also, in the late 1870s, coined the term 'rhodopsin' for the substance, also known as visual purple, first discovered in the retinal rods by Franz Boll in 1876. It was soon realized that the pigment was bleached out of the retina by light and resynthesized in the dark. Kühne realized that this could be used to photograph the eye, to take what he termed an 'optogram' by the process of 'optography'. To achieve this he placed a rabbit facing a barred window after having its head covered with cloth to allow the rhodopsin to accumulate. After three minutes it was decapitated and the retina removed and fixed in alum clearly revealing a picture of a barred window.

Later investigations of rhodopsin by such scholars as George Wald revealed much about the mechanism of vision.

KUIPER, Gerard Peter (b. Dec. 7, 1905; Harenkarspel, Netherlands; d. Dec. 24, 1973; Mexico City) Dutch-American astronomer.

Kuiper studied at the University of Leiden where he obtained his BSc in 1927 and his PhD in 1933. He immediately emigrated to America where he took up an appointment at the Lick Observatory in California and then lectured (1935–36) at Harvard. In 1936 he joined the Yerkes Observatory and in 1939 moved to the McDonald Observatory in Texas, both run by the University of Chicago. He served as their director (1947–49, 1957–60) and was also professor of astronomy (1943–60). From 1960 to 1973 he was head of the Lunar and Planetary Laboratory of the University of Arizona.

Kuiper's main research work was on the solar system. He discovered two new satellites: Miranda, the fifth Uranian satellite in 1948 and Nereid, the second Neptunian satellite in 1949. He also investigated planetary atmospheres and succeeded in detecting carbon dioxide in the Martian atmosphere in 1948. Four years earlier he had found evidence of methane in the atmosphere of Saturn's largest satellite, Titan.

In 1950 he produced some intriguing data on Pluto. Based on observations made with the 200-inch (5-m) reflector at the Palomar Observatory he estimated the diameter of Pluto as 0.23 seconds of arc, which was equivalent to about 3600 miles (5800 km) or half the Earth's diameter. But as its mass was supposed to be roughly the same as that of the Earth it implied the unlikely conclusion that Pluto had a density of about ten times that of the Earth. Recent measurements, however, reveal that Pluto's mass is only 0.2% and its diameter roughly a quarter of Earth's. Kuiper also speculated on the origin of the planets and proposed in 1949 his theory that each planet evolved from its own gaseous cloud that was not initially part of the Sun. This is not generally accepted.

With the advent of the space age, Kuiper became closely involved with several space missions, including the Ranger program, 1961–65, in which the first close-up photographs of the Moon were obtained, and the Mariner 10 flight to

Venus and Mercury, which was launched in 1973 shortly before his death.

KUNDT, August Eduard Eberhard Adolph (b. Nov. 18, 1839; Schwerin, now in East Germany; d. May 21, 1894; Israelsdorf, now in West Germany) German physicist.

Kundt studied at Berlin University, where he received his doctorate in 1864. He was made a professor of physics at the Federal Institute of Technology, Zurich, in 1868 and, three years later, obtained a similar post in Strasbourg.

His fame rests largely on his experimental determination of the speed of sound. His apparatus involved a pipe closed at one end and containing a small amount of fine powder. A vibrating disk at the open end was used to set up standing waves in the pipe, causing the dust to settle in regular nodes down the pipe. From the distance between the nodes the speed of sound could be calculated. The apparatus is known as *Kundt's tube*.

In 1888 he was appointed to the chair of physics in Berlin and, with his student, Wilhelm Röntgen, he demonstrated the rotation of the plane of polarization for light traveling through a gas in a magnetic field.

KURCHATOV, Igor Vasilievich (b. Jan. 12, 1903; Sim, now in the Soviet Union; d. Feb. 7, 1960; Moscow) Soviet physicist.

Kurchatov, the son of a surveyor, was educated at the University of the Crimea, from which he graduated in 1923. Shortly afterwards he was appointed to the Leningrad Physico-Technical Institute where, in 1938, he became director of the nuclear physics laboratory. At some time during the war he moved to Moscow to take control of his country's military and industrial atomic research.

Under Kurchatov's direction the Soviet atomic program was remarkably successful. The Soviet Union exploded its first atomic bomb in 1949, its first hydrogen bomb in 1952, and constructed a nuclear power station in 1954.

KURTI, Nicholas (b. May 14, 1908; Budapest) Hungarian–British physicist.

Kurti was educated at the Budapest Gymnasium and the universities of Paris and Berlin. After a brief period teaching at Breslau, he moved to England in 1933 and joined the Clarendon Laboratory at Oxford. He remained there, apart from the war years spent on the development of the UK atomic-energy project, and eventually served as professor of physics from 1967 until his retirement in 1975.

Kurti has been one of the pioneers in work on low-temperature physics. At the Clarendon Laboratory he worked on methods of achieving low temperatures and studying thermal and magnetic properties at these temperatures. In his work he has produced temperatures as low as 10^{-6} K to study the ordering of nuclear spins under such conditions.

KUSCH, Polykarp (b. Jan. 26, 1911; Blankenburg, now in East Germany) American physicist.

Kusch spent all but the first year of his life as a resident of the USA, becoming a naturalized citizen in 1922. His early education was in the Midwest of the United States, and his undergraduate studies were at the Case Institute of Technology, Cleveland, Ohio. Starting in chemistry, he made an early switch to physics, and gained his BS in 1931. He followed this with work as a research assistant at the University of Illinois on problems of optical molecular spectroscopy, gaining his MS there in 1933 and his PhD in 1936. This was followed by a short period at the University of Minnesota researching mass spectroscopy (1936–37). From 1937 to 1972 he has been associated with the physics department of Columbia University, New York City, apart from interruptions in World War II when he was engaged in special research on the military applications of vacuum tubes and microwave generators at Westinghouse Electric Corporation (1941–42) and Bell Telephone Laboratories (1944–46).

At Columbia, Kusch began work under Isidor Rabi on the first radiofrequency spectroscopy experiments using atomic and molecular beams. His research was principally on the fine details of the interactions of the constituent particles of atoms and molecules with each other and with an externally applied magnetic field. In particular, Kusch made very accurate determinations of the magnetic moment (or strength) of the electron as deduced from the hyperfine structure of the energy levels in certain elements, and in 1947 found a discrepancy of about 0.1% between the observed value and that predicted by theory. Although minute, this anomaly was of great significance to theories of the interactions of electrons and electromagnetic radiation (now known as quantum electrodynamics). It was for his precise work in measuring the electron's magnetic moment that he received the 1955 Nobel Prize for physics, sharing it with Willis Lamb, who performed independent but related experiments at Columbia University on the hyperfine structure of the hydrogen atom.

Kusch's career at Columbia University took him to associate professorship (1946), professorship (1949), executive director of the Columbia Radiation Laboratory (1952–60), vice president and dean of the faculty (1969–70), and executive vice president and provost (1970–71). In 1972 he left to become professor of physics, and then Eugene McDermott Professor, at the University of Texas at Dallas.